T0256375

ADVANCED SERVER VIRTUALIZATION

VMware® and Microsoft® Platforms in the Virtual Data Center

Other Auerbach Publications in Software Development, Software Engineering, and Project Management

The Complete Project Management Office Handbook
Gerard M. Hill
0-8493-2173-5

Complex IT Project Management: 16 Steps to Success
Peter Schulte
0-8493-1932-3

Creating Components: Object Oriented, Concurrent, and Distributed Computing in Java
Charles W. Kann
0-8493-1499-2

The Hands-On Project Office: Guaranteeing ROI and On-Time Delivery
Richard M. Kesner
0-8493-1991-9

Interpreting the CMMI®: A Process Improvement Approach
Margaret Kulpa and Kent Johnson
0-8493-1654-5

ISO 9001:2000 for Software and Systems Providers: An Engineering Approach
Robert Bamford and William John Deibler II
0-8493-2063-1

The Laws of Software Process: A New Model for the Production and Management of Software
Phillip G. Armour
0-8493-1489-5

Real Process Improvement Using the CMMI®
Michael West
0-8493-2109-3

Six Sigma Software Development
Christine Tayntor
0-8493-1193-4

Software Architecture Design Patterns in Java
Partha Kuchana
0-8493-2142-5

Software Configuration Management
Jessica Keyes 0-8493-1976-5

Software Engineering for Image Processing
Phillip A. Laplante 0-8493-1376-7

Software Engineering Handbook
Jessica Keyes 0-8493-1479-8

Software Engineering Measurement
John C. Munson 0-8493-1503-4

Software Metrics: A Guide to Planning, Analysis, and Application
C.R. Pandian
0-8493-1661-8

Software Testing: A Craftsman's Approach, Second Edition
Paul C. Jorgensen
0-8493-0809-7

Software Testing and Continuous Quality Improvement, Second Edition
William E. Lewis
0-8493-2524-2

IS Management Handbook, 8th Edition
Carol V. Brown and Heikki Topi, Editors
0-8493-1595-9

Lightweight Enterprise Architectures
Fenix Theuerkorn
0-8493-2114-X

Outsourcing Software Development Offshore: Making It Work
Tandy Gold
0-8493-1943-9

Maximizing ROI on Software Development
Vijay Sikka
0-8493-2312-6

Implementing the IT Balanced Scorecard
Jessica Keyes
0-8493-2621-4

AUERBACH PUBLICATIONS
www.auerbach-publications.com
To Order Call: 1-800-272-7737 • Fax: 1-800-374-3401
E-mail: orders@crcpress.com

ADVANCED SERVER VIRTUALIZATION

VMware® and Microsoft® Platforms in the Virtual Data Center

David Marshall
Wade A. Reynolds
and Dave McCrory

Auerbach Publications
Taylor & Francis Group
Boca Raton   New York

Auerbach Publications is an imprint of the
Taylor & Francis Group, an informa business

Published in 2006 by
Auerbach Publications
Taylor & Francis Group
6000 Broken Sound Parkway NW, Suite 300
Boca Raton, FL 33487-2742

© 2006 by Taylor & Francis Group, LLC
Auerbach is an imprint of Taylor & Francis Group

No claim to original U.S. Government works
1 0 9 8 7 6 5 4 3 2 1

International Standard Book Number-10: 0-8493-3931-6 (Hardcover)
International Standard Book Number-13: 978-0978-0-8493-3931-8 (Hardcover)

Taylor & Francis Group
is the Academic Division of Informa plc.

Visit the Taylor & Francis Web site at
http://www.taylorandfrancis.com

and the Auerbach Publications Web site at
http://www.auerbach-publications.com

About the Authors

David Marshall is currently employed as a Senior Software Engineer for Surgient, Inc., the leading software provider of on-demand applications. He holds a B.S. degree in Finance as well as an Information Technology Certification from the University of New Orleans. He is Microsoft Certified and has attained numerous certifications from CompTia. Marshall has been working with virtualization software for nearly six years. While working for a startup company, ProTier, he became one of the few people in the country to work with server class virtualization products such as VMware ESX Server, Connectix Virtual Server, and Microsoft Virtual Server while each were still in their Alpha stage. Using this knowledge, he was able to help contribute to the writing of ProTier's product manual and training guides. As a Systems Engineer and a Deployment Manager with ProTier, he was able to create and implement complex solutions for a number of Fortune 1000 clients. Continuing to expand his virtualization knowledge to other platforms and other products, Marshall contributes to Surgient's products and its customers. Prior to joining ProTier and Surgient, he enjoyed a long and successful career employed as a Project Manager and Systems Manager for Bank One Louisiana. He can be reached at david.marshall@vmbook.info.

Wade A. Reynolds is currently employed as an Architect in the Professional Services department of Surgient Inc., an Austin, Texas based company that provides leading-edge software solutions that leverage server virtualization technology. He has been designing and implementing enterprise solutions using server virtualization technology for more than four years with VMware ESX Server and Microsoft Virtual Server. Reynolds has a strong background in software development, database design, networked systems engineering, and system integration. He earned MCP certification and worked as the Senior Solutions Developer for SCP Pool Corporation, the world's largest pool supply distributor, where he architected and implemented enterprise-level business applications, databases, and processes, and as a consultant for General Electric, where his server and networking skills were honed. He can be contacted at wade.reynolds@vmbook.info.

Dave McCrory currently works as an expert in Enterprise Data Center Virtualization and Hosting Technologies. McCrory has been granted two U.S. Patents and has five others pending, all based on Data Center Management and Virtualization technologies. He has worked with Microsoft Virtual Server in its Alpha stage as well as with its predecessor, Connectix Virtual Server. While working with these products, he provided these companies with assistance on the original designs. Additionally, he also was the first successful Alpha site for VMware ESX Server. Previously, he had also worked as a consultant for both Sprint and General Electric. McCrory also founded ProTier, a startup company that wrote virtualization management software that was later acquired by Surgient Inc. He has also attained Microsoft Certified Systems Engineer, Master Certified Netware Engineer, and Citrix Certified Administrator certifications. He can be reached at dave.mccrory@vmbook.info.

Contents

Acknowledgments

Without trying to sound too cliché, we realize that this book would not be possible without the help of many people. Although we cannot thank everyone by name, we appreciate all of the hard work, dedication, and energy that everyone has contributed. Virtualization is a subject that all three of us hold in high regard, and we each have a strong belief in the endless possibilities that it can provide to the IT community.

We'd like to begin by thanking all of those who helped contribute to the book. We owe a great deal of thanks to the wonderful team at Auerbach Publications, Taylor and Francis Group. Our editor, John Wyzalek, has been incredibly easy and flexible to work with during the course of this project. Julie Spadaro, our project editor, did a fantastic job overseeing the production of our book. Their guidance along the way has been invaluable. And a special thank you to Lynn Goeller and her team at EvS Communications for their diligent work handling the copyediting, page layout, and proofreading of the book.

Next, we'd like to acknowledge the work of our contributing authors. For his work on chapter 16, we want to thank Robert Oster, Senior Network Engineer and IT Services Manager at Universal Data, Inc. He has years of experience working with virtualization platforms and was one of the founders of ProTier, a pioneering software company in the virtualization application arena. For his work on chapter 25, we would like to thank Richard Cardona, Principal Engineer at Surgient, Inc. His expertise at scripting and programming against the major virtualization platforms was key to the creation of this chapter. Thank you both for lending us your time and creativity.

We also need to offer a special thank you to Surgient, Inc. for allowing us to write this book, for giving us the opportunity to work with virtualization day in and day out, and for allowing us to explore new opportunities.

Family is an important facet in each of our lives. Without our family members, this book would have been impossible to write.

"Writing a book is an exercise in fortitude, and without the constant support of my family, I wouldn't have had the energy to complete this project. My wife, Donna, and my children, Megan and Haley, deserve more than a thank you for their tireless efforts in supporting me through those long months of me being locked away in my office working on the book. It isn't easy giving up the weekends, but they understood. I also need to thank my parents, David and Sandra Marshall, and my sister, Tammy Lapeyrouse, for helping to foster creativity growing up and for pushing me to strive for excellence."

DAVID MARSHALL

"I would like to personally thank my family, Leanna, Elaina, and Madison, for putting up with my difficult schedules while this book was being created and for supporting my efforts. I also want to thank Susan and Don Townsend, Jesse Reynolds, Evan Mersch, Robert James Reynolds, Warren and Hellen Borgeson, Robert "Red" Borgeson and Leta Borgeson, Melanie "Honey Bee" Peoples, Joseph Gebbia, and all of my cousins, for always believing in me. For this I am truly blessed."

WADE REYNOLDS

"I would like to offer a special thanks to the most extraordinary companion and friend anyone could ever have, my wife Sonya, as well as my children Nick, Julia, Travis, and Olivia. In addition, I need to thank my family: my parents Dennis and Lolly, my brother Dan and my sister Morgan. Finally I would like to thank all of my friends, family, and the original ProTier team."

DAVE McCRORY

Part I

Basic Concepts

Chapter 1

Introduction to Server Virtualization

This chapter provides a high-level overview and background of virtualization technology. The most basic concepts are introduced as well as a discussion of the differences between emulation, simulation, and virtualization technologies.

Overview of Virtualization Technology

Virtualization technology is a way of making a physical computer function as if it were two or more computers, each nonphysical or "virtualized" computer is provided with the same basic architecture as that of a generic physical computer. There are several ways to do this, each has its pros and cons. The book will primarily discuss software-based server virtualization, but will touch on other forms including hardware partitioning, emulation, and simulation.

In order to make a physical computer function as more than one computer, its physical hardware characteristics must be recreated through the use of software. This is accomplished by a software layer called abstraction. Abstraction software is used in many software systems, including inside the Windows operating system families. The Windows Hardware Abstraction Layer (HAL) is an excellent example of abstraction. The Windows HAL provides a common way for all drivers and software to talk to the hardware in a common/unified format. This makes the job of writing software and drivers easier because developers don't have to write custom software for each brand or type of computer that they want their code to run on. Abstraction, as it relates to virtualization, is the representation of a set of common hardware devices that are entirely software driven. This is basically software that looks and acts like hardware. Virtualization technology allows the installation of an operating system on hardware that does not really exist.

Virtualization is a concept that allows a computer's resources to be divided or shared by multiple environments simultaneously. These environments can interoperate or be totally unaware of each other. A single environment may or may not be aware that it is running in a virtual environment. Environments are most commonly known as virtual machines (VMs). VMs will almost always house an installation of an operating system (e.g., Linux, Windows, etc.). These operating system installations are commonly known as Guest operating systems. Instructions for a VM are usually passed directly to the physical hardware that allows the environment to operate faster and more efficiently than emulation, although more complex instructions must be trapped and interpreted in order to ensure proper compatibility and abstraction with the physical hardware.

In order to better understand a virtualized computer environment, it is beneficial to compare the basic computer organization of a typical physical computer to that of a computer running a virtualization platform and virtualized environments. The arrangement of a typical computer has a set of hardware devices onto which is installed an operating system (e.g., Linux or Windows) and one or more applications installed into the operating system. Figure 1.1 shows this arrangement.

Inside a computer hosting a virtualization platform, the arrangement may be slightly different because the computer has a set of hardware onto which the operating system (e.g., Linux or Windows) is installed. The operating system has a virtualization platform installed into which one or more virtual machines are created, each acting as a set of separate hardware and capable of having an operating system and applications installed as shown in Figure 1.2.

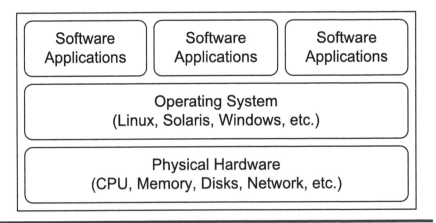

Figure 1.1 Traditional System Architecture.

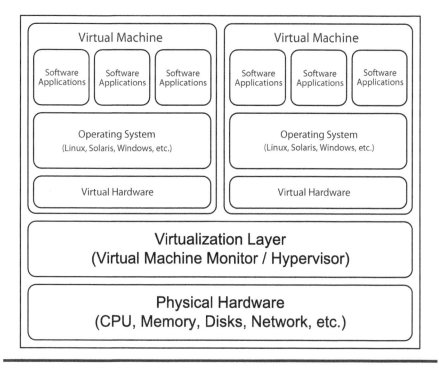

Figure 1.2 Virtualized System Architecture 1.

Another common arrangement of a virtualized computing system is one in which the virtualization platform is installed directly onto the computer's hardware. This form of virtualization provides a platform on which one or more virtual machines can be created, each capable of having a unique operating system and applications installed. This layout is shown in Figure 1.3.

Implementations of server virtualization include:

- **VMware ESX Server**
  This is the fastest performing and most mature server virtualization platform to date. VMware ESX Server runs directly on the physical hardware to maximize efficiency.
- **VMware GSX Server**
  VMware GSX Server is a lightweight server virtualization platform, originally based on VMware's workstation product. VMware GSX Server must be installed into either a Linux or Windows operating system.
- **Microsoft Virtual Server 2005**
  Microsoft Virtual Server 2005 is a server virtualization platform based on technology acquired by Connectix Corporation. Virtual Server 2005 must

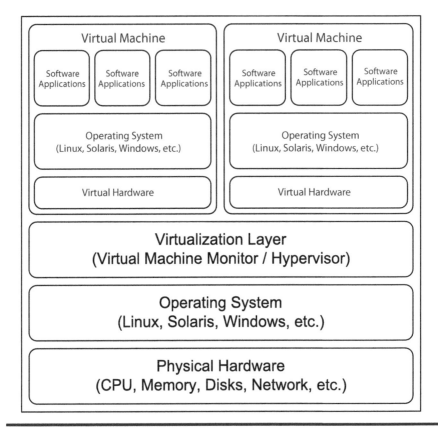

Figure 1.3 Virtualized System Architecture 2.

be installed into a Windows 2003 Server or Windows XP Professional operating system (Microsoft does not support Virtual Server 2005 on Windows XP Professional for production use).

The benefits of using virtualization are numerous and include the following:

- **Portability**
  The ability to have a consistent hardware platform, even if the real hardware beneath is from different manufacturers.
- **Manageability**
  Virtual environments can be managed easily and offer access to the virtual hardware.
- **Efficiency**
  When properly implemented, server virtualization allows the physical hardware to be used more efficiently, allowing higher utilization of the hardware's resources.

When to use server virtualization:

- **Server consolidation**
  Server consolidation allows many physical servers to be virtualized and hosted on as little as a single physical server leveraging virtualization. Most servers today are far underutilized, running between 8 percent and 12 percent utilization.
- **Legacy application support**
  This provides an upgrade path for moving legacy applications and operating systems onto new hardware without incurring issues due to incompatibilities with newer hardware platforms.
- **Multiple operating system support**
  This is beneficial in environments where development and testing of many operating systems is necessary.
- **Software demonstration**
  By using virtualization, demonstrations and beta software can be run in a consistent manner.
- **Development, testing, and debugging**
  Because of the strong isolation between the environment and the virtualization platform, it becomes easy to perform software testing and debugging.
- **Technical training and E-learning**
  In many advanced classes today, several computers are required for each student. By using virtualization, companies can reduce the number of computers required to teach a class and the time it takes to set up the next class.

When server virtualization should not be used:

- **Testing of x86 virtualization**
  Do not test virtualization inside of virtualization. This will cause double time slicing and will not be useable. This limitation only applies to x86 virtualization. IBM's older virtualization was engineered to support this type of usage.
- **Computer games**
  The performance requirements are simply too great to successfully test and play high end games in virtual environments.
- **Specialized hardware and peripherals**
  There is no way today to leverage custom hardware peripherals/cards in a virtualization platform. This is because there is no emulation or representation of these devices in the virtual environment.
- **Performance testing**
  The overhead of virtualization will cause an inaccurate view of performance.

- **Hardware driver debugging**
  Because all virtual machines in each version of virtualization are the same and the hardware is fixed and emulated, there is no way to test or debug hardware drivers on this platform.

History of Virtualization

The history of virtualization technology goes back further than most people might think (see Figure 1.4). In fact the idea of virtualization was first discussed as far back as the late 1950's. The following will attempt to chronicle the significant events that occurred from the early 1960's through today and the impact that each had on x86 server virtualization.

In the early 1960's, IBM introduced Time Sharing which was the original driving force behind virtualization. Today, many people associate time sharing with mainframe computers, but arguably x86 could be headed in this direction under the name On-Demand Computing. In 1964, IBM introduced the IBM System/360, which provided limited virtualization capabilities and was architected by the legendary Gene Amdahl. Later in 1964, the CP-40 was released and gave way to the first mentions of Virtual Machines and Virtual Memory. In 1965, the System/360 Model 67 and TSS (Time Sharing System) were developed. This was followed in 1967 by another release of CP-40 and CMS, which put into production a system supporting 14 VMs each having 256K of Virtual Memory.

A new iteration of the CP-40 called CP-67 Version 1 debuted in 1968. This provided a much needed boost in both performance and stability to CP-40. CP-67 Version 2 in 1969 gave way to a new scheduler and PL/I support and in 1970 CP-67 Version 3 had free storage sub pool support which provided additional performance and the addition of SLT instruction. Finally in 1971, Version 3.1 of CP-67 was released with high speed I/O enhancements.

In 1972, the System/370 Advanced Function was released and had new Address Relocation Hardware and now supported four new operating systems (VM/370, DOS/VS, OS/VS1, and OS/VS2). As VM technology became more popular in the IBM community, the MVMUA (Metropolitan VM User Association) was founded in New York in 1973. The introduction of VM/370 Release 2 in 1974 contained the first iteration of VMA (Virtual Machine Assist) Microcode. Also in 1974, Gerald J. Popek and Robert P. Goldberg created a set of formal requirements for architectures titled "Formal Requirements for Virtualizable Third Generation Architectures."

This led to a quiet period in the virtualization space from 1974 to 1987, when the rise of the Internet gave way to the need for TCP/IP support. In 1987, VM TCP/IP also known as FAL made TCP/IP available to VMs.

The following events directly lead to the current set of available x86 server virtualization technologies and platforms.

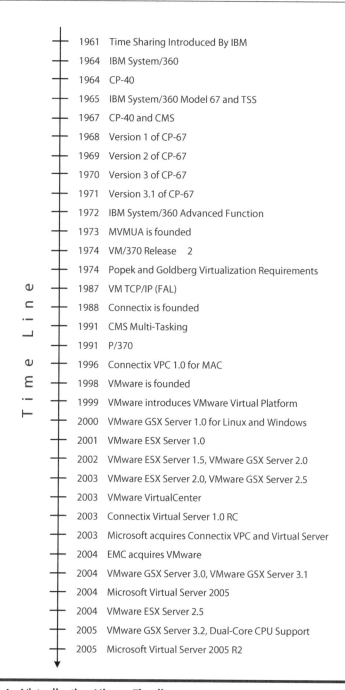

1961   Time Sharing Introduced By IBM

1964   IBM System/360

1964   CP-40

1965   IBM System/360 Model 67 and TSS

1967   CP-40 and CMS

1968   Version 1 of CP-67

1969   Version 2 of CP-67

1970   Version 3 of CP-67

1971   Version 3.1 of CP-67

1972   IBM System/360 Advanced Function

1973   MVMUA is founded

1974   VM/370 Release   2

1974   Popek and Goldberg Virtualization Requirements

1987   VM TCP/IP (FAL)

1988   Connectix is founded

1991   CMS Multi-Tasking

1991   P/370

1996   Connectix VPC 1.0 for MAC

1998   VMware is founded

1999   VMware introduces VMware Virtual Platform

2000   VMware GSX Server 1.0 for Linux and Windows

2001   VMware ESX Server 1.0

2002   VMware ESX Server 1.5, VMware GSX Server 2.0

2003   VMware ESX Server 2.0, VMware GSX Server 2.5

2003   VMware VirtualCenter

2003   Connectix Virtual Server 1.0 RC

2003   Microsoft acquires Connectix VPC and Virtual Server

2004   EMC acquires VMware

2004   VMware GSX Server 3.0, VMware GSX Server 3.1

2004   Microsoft Virtual Server 2005

2004   VMware ESX Server 2.5

2005   VMware GSX Server 3.2, Dual-Core CPU Support

2005   Microsoft Virtual Server 2005 R2

Figure 1.4   Virtualization History Timeline.

In 1988, a small company, Connectix Corporation, was founded and provided solutions for Apple Macintosh (Mac) systems. Connectix became well known for its innovative approach to solving problems that Apple either could not or would not solve. One such example of this was Mode32, a solution to the 24-bit memory addressing problem on the Motorola 68020 and 68030 processors used in early Macs. Another product by Connectix was SpeedDoubler, a product that provided a high-performance emulation bridge from the Motorola 68000 processors to the Power PC-based processors. Following SpeedDoubler was RAM Doubler, which provided a way to double a Mac's memory by compressing and decompressing the contents of RAM on the fly.

Connectix's experience with the Mac would lead them to create a new product named Connectix Virtual PC 1.0 for the Mac. The Virtual PC 1.0 product was quite a feat of programming in that it incorporated a binary translation engine to translate instructions from a virtual Intel x86 processor to a physical Power PC processor used in the Macs. This example of emulation technology would lead Connectix into virtualization technologies.

In 1998, VMware was founded by Diane Greene and husband Dr. Mendel Rosenblum along with two students from Stanford University and a colleague from Berkley. On October of 1998, these founders filed for a patent regarding new virtualization techniques based on research conducted at Stanford University. The patent was awarded on May 28, 2002.

On February 8, 1999, VMware introduced "VMware Virtual Platform" to market. This product is considered by many to be the first commercial x86 virtualization platform, and would later become the VMware Workstation product.

In late 2000, VMware released their first server virtualization platform, VMware GSX Server 1.0. This product was aimed at workgroup class server implementations and installed on top of either a Linux or Windows operating system. The following year, VMware took x86 server virtualization to the next level with the release of VMware ESX Server 1.0, a mainframe class server virtualization platform. Unlike VMware GSX Server, VMware ESX Server installs on bare metal and provides a more stable and high performance computing environment due to its native Hypervisor otherwise known as a Virtual Machine Monitor (VMM) which requires much less overhead. From 2002 to present, VMware has continued to release updated versions of both GSX Server and ESX Server platforms adding new capabilities and enhancing performance.

Connectix built a relationship with Microsoft which was based on the bundling of operating system packs for Connectix's Virtual PC for Mac product. Later, Connectix provided the PocketPC emulation technology embedded in Microsoft's Visual Studio.NET application. Connectix entered the x86 server virtualization arena with their release candidate version of the Connectix Virtual Server product in early 2003. Connectix Virtual Server would not make it to market as a Connectix product however, as Microsoft acquired from Connectix the intellectual property rights for both Virtual PC for Mac and Windows as well as Connectix Virtual Server.

Microsoft's virtualization plan is focused on supporting legacy application rehosting, server consolidation, and automation of software development and test environments. They released their first virtualization product, Microsoft Virtual PC 2004, on December 2, 2003. Microsoft's planned entry into the x86 server virtualization market, Microsoft Virtual Server 2004, was delayed in order to implement heavy security modifications due to the new Microsoft security initiative. The final product, Microsoft Virtual Server 2005, was released in mid 2004 with two versions, Microsoft Virtual Server 2005 Standard Edition (supporting up to four physical processors) and Microsoft Virtual Server 2005 Enterprise Edition (supporting up to 32 physical processors).

VMware was acquired by EMC on January 9, 2004. This appeared to some as a surprise; however the underlying reason was that, like EMC's acquisition of Documentum and Legato, they were aiming for software applications which consume very large quantities of storage space. VMware remains as an independent subsidiary of EMC and is still headed by CEO Diane Greene.

Today, both Intel and AMD have introduced new technologies to provide better support for virtualization. These technologies include multicore processors, Intel's Virtualization Technology (originally known as Vanderpool and Silvervale), and AMD's Pacifica project. Unlike previous x86 processors, Vanderpool, Silvervale, and Pacifica are expected to meet the Popek and Goldberg requirements for virtualization architectures.

Emulation, Simulation, and Virtualization

Emulation is a concept that allows one environment to act or behave as if it were another environment. This could also be described as sophisticated impersonation. An environment is an execution platform, operating system, or hardware architecture. Instructions are interpreted from the executing environment into instructions that the real, underlying environment understands. Emulation is used for running legacy environments, operating system development, and software testing. Emulated environments incur a high performance penalty when compared to virtualized systems due to the overhead of the interpreter.

Common implementations of emulation include:

■ **Bochs**
  Bochs is an open source x86 emulator which emulates the x86 processor, devices, and BIOS.
■ **MAME**
  The Multiple Arcade Machine Emulator allows arcade ROM software to run on Windows. It emulates the arcade hardware for which the games were originally programmed.

- **Virtual PC for Mac**
  Virtual PC for Mac emulates the x86 hardware environment which allows Microsoft Windows operating systems to be installed and run.
- **WINE**
  WINE enables Windows applications to run on Linux, FreeBSD, and Solaris. It emulates portions of the Windows operating system, but the code executes natively on the x86 processor. Ironically, the name WINE is a recursive acronym which stands for "WINE Is Not an Emulator."

Simulation is a concept in which an environment imitates another environment. This imitation simply accepts pre-defined inputs and provides pre-defined responses. This is arguably the easiest or least complex concept to implement. An environment is an execution platform, operating system, or hardware architecture. Simulators are used differently than both emulation and virtualization. They are primarily used in hardware and microchip design and prototyping. By doing this, testing can be done on hardware and microchips yet to be built! This reduces the costs and risks associated with mistakes being made on hardware and chips before they are fabricated.

Common implementations of simulation include:

- **Cadence and Synopsis**
  These companies provide chip design software along with simulators to test viability, performance and other metrics. These are great examples of the capability that simulators provide.
- **Simics**
  The Simics evolved from gsim in 1991. Simics is able to run unmodified operating systems using its simulated processors and devices.
- **SimOS**
  The SimOS project was developed at Stanford University in 1992. It simulated the SPRITE system on SPARC hardware. Other implementations of SimOS supported MIPS-based SGI systems, Digital Alpha Processors and the Power PC.

Summary

The use of emulators and simulators have their places, however virtualization is the only technology that enables revolutionary capabilities in the datacenter. Virtualization provides the benefits necessary to give IT organizations the ability to save costs on hardware and increase the efficiency of server deployments, provisioning, and management. Virtualization also enables physical hardware independence, which gives IT the flexibility and freedom of not being locked in to a single vendor's hardware solution.

The history of virtualization goes back much further than most people realize. Several significant developments occurred in the early 1960s, in the late 1980s, and the early 1990s. These developments lead to the founding of the two pioneering companies in the x86 server virtualization space, VMware, and Connectix. Together these two companies have defined x86 server virtualization and created the market for server consolidation. Both companies have been acquired (VMware by EMC and Connectix by Microsoft) and their technology continues to lead to innovations in the computer industry.

While virtualization solves many of the problems for IT, it is not a universal solution to all problems. There are times in which virtualization is not mature enough of a technology to be applied, such as with applications requiring high processor utilization or heavy multiprocessing capabilities (those consuming the resources of a four-way or greater server) or when the need for high end graphics display is needed (such as doing 3D design work in a CAD/CAM application like Unigraphics). The next chapters will cover the specifics of how and when to implement server virtualization using best practices learned through real experiences, enabling successful server virtualization deployments across all uses.

Chapter 2

Types of Server Virtualization Technologies

There are many different approaches and technologies used to implement virtualized systems. It is important to be aware of these technologies and how they differ from x86 server virtualization. This chapter provides a high-level overview of these approaches, how they are used, and their differentiation.

Virtualization technology comes in several forms. The set of virtualization technologies used in enterprise server systems are collectively referred to as partitioning technologies. Although this book is primarily focused on server virtualization by means of software partitioning, for completeness, the differences between hardware, software, application, resource, and service partitioning are explained as well as other types of virtualization including operating systems and runtime environments.

Physical Partitioning

Physical partitioning refers to the separation of execution environments by literally using physically separate hardware devices or by using physical hardware-based partitioning.

Physical hardware separation (see Figure 2.1) is the easiest and most prolific form of partitioning. It is the practice of using multiple physical servers (or computers), each having a single instance of an operating system, to serve different needs or purposes. A common example of this practice is an organization that has a separate server for each of the following server roles or applications: file sharing, print spooling, domain authentication and authorization, database

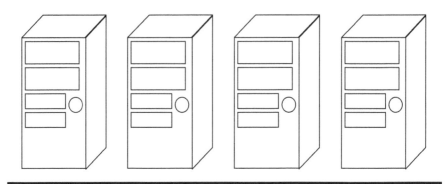

Figure 2.1   Physical Hardware Separation.

server, email server, web server, FTP server, and so on. Physical hardware separation is commonly driven by applications that have mutually exclusive requirements of the hardware devices and/or operating system, applications with high resource utilization, or server stability. Some applications cannot share the same environment as other applications because they were designed to have control of the entire operating system and the server's resources. Other applications have high resource utilization such as processor, memory, intensive disk I/O, storage size limitations, or network adapter bandwidth that often requires a dedicated server. Consider installing Microsoft SQL Server and Microsoft Exchange Server together on a single server. Although it is technically possible, it is likely that each server application will perform poorly as they continuously compete for control of the same system resources.

Applications have also been separated onto dedicated physical servers because of the idea that it is generally more stable to have fewer applications running within the same instance of an operating system, usually because of poor resource management by the operating system (whether true or perceived) or because of poor resource handling or wasteful resource utilization by an application. Another reason that applications are installed on separate hardware is because they were designed and written for different operating systems or different hardware architectures. For example, Microsoft BizTalk Server must be installed onto a Windows operating system-based server with an Intel processor whereas applications written for IBM's OS/400 operating system must be installed on IBM AS/400 server hardware, while applications written for the Microsoft Windows operating system must be installed on IA-32 compatible computer hardware.

Hardware partitioning is a highly-specialized hardware technology that allows the computing resources of a single, physical computer to be divided into multiple partitions (often called hard partitions), each of which can host its own, isolated instance of an operating system. Hardware partitioning has existed for quite some time, originating in high-end mainframe systems from IBM. Today, there are several hardware partitioning technologies available, although each implementation is proprietary and requires very specific server hardware and software to be used. In some implementations, only one or two very specific operating systems are supported. In general, all of the required components of a system featuring hardware partitioning are only available from a single vendor, due to their proprietary nature.

One of the key advantages of hardware partitioning is its very efficient resource sharing and management capabilities. These systems are much more efficient than equivalent software partitioning systems because the resource management between hard partitions is handled using separate hardware components (chips, circuits, memory, storage, etc.). The specialized software (sometimes referred to as microcode) that performs the actual resource management resides in the specialized resource management hardware components as well. As a result, the available performance in each hard partition is maximized and remains unaffected by the resource management system's overhead. This is very different from software partitioning technologies where the partitioning occurs in software that is executed using the same hardware that is being managed and shared. Another advantage, available in some implementations of hardware partitioning, is electrical isolation of each hard partition. Electrical isolation in hardware partitioning systems allows a hardware fault to occur in one hard partition while not affecting any other hard partition in the same system. Systems offering hardware partitioning technologies are usually mid-range to high-end computing systems that are generally very scalable (usually scaling up) and robust.

Hardware partitioning systems have several disadvantages: expensive, proprietary hardware and software, additional costs incurred by the support and maintenance of the proprietary hardware, limited support for various operating systems, limited hardware portability for an existing installed base of hard partitions, and vendor lock-in. Proprietary hardware and software systems almost always have additional costs for installation, training, support, and maintenance due to the lack of expertise of most IT organizations with these types of systems. Often vendors will only allow their services organization to perform the installation and support of these systems. Hardware partitioning systems generally only allow one type of operating system to be installed; of course, each hard partition supports a separate instance of that operating system. There are some systems that are more flexible and support more than one operating system, but it is almost always limited to operating systems provided by the vendor. Aside from limited operating system support, hardware partitioning systems have very limited portability of existing partitions. Generally, these partitions may only be moved to systems comprised of the same vendor's hardware because of the lack of complete hardware abstraction. Investment in proprietary hardware and software systems almost always leads an organization into what is known as vendor lock-in. Vendor lock-in occurs when an organization has made an investment in a single vendor's proprietary technologies and it thus is cost prohibitive for the organization to move to a different technology or vendor. Vendor lock-in affects

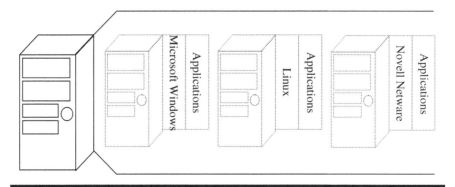

Figure 2.2 Hardware Partitioning.

organizations for long periods of time, usually five or more years at a time. Of course, the vendor reaps the benefit of vendor lock-in because of the expense and difficulty an organization faces when attempting to switch to another vendor. The organization suffers due to cost and inflexibility in changing hardware and software, which makes it difficult to quickly move on to new opportunities.

Hardware partitioning systems (see Figure 2.2) are available from the following vendors (listed with their current technologies):

- HP—nPartition (Hard Partitions)
- IBM—LPAR and DLPAR (Logical Partitioning and Dynamic Logical Partitioning)
- Sun Microsystems—Dynamic System Domains
- Unisys—Dynamic Partitioning

Logical Partitioning

Logical partitioning refers to the separation of execution environments within a computing system using logic implemented through software. There are different ways in which the resources of a computer system may be managed and shared. Logical partitioning includes software partitioning, resource partitioning, and service partitioning technologies.

Software partitioning is a software-based technology that allows the resources of a single, physical computer to be divided into multiple partitions (also called soft partitions or virtual machines), each of which can host its own, isolated instance of an operating system. Software partitioning is generally similar to hardware partitioning in that multiple instances of operating systems may coexist on a single physical server. The major difference between hardware and software partitioning is that in software partitioning, the isolation of each soft partition and the management of the shared resources of the computer are completely handled by a special software layer called a Virtual Machine Monitor (VMM) or Hypervisor. The VMM, as well as each operating system within each soft partition, all consume computing resources from the same set of hardware, thus software partitioning incurs overhead that does not exist in hardware partitioning. The overhead produced by the VMM varies from each implementation of software partitioning systems, but always has an impact on the performance of each soft partition. Depending on how resources are managed by the VMM, it is conceivable that the computing resources consumed by each soft partition could also impact the VMM's performance as well. Software partitioning implementations exist on mid-range to high-end computing systems as well as commodity server and workstation computers. Server virtualization (and the term virtualization) as described in this book refers directly to server-based software partitioning systems, generically referred to as virtualization platforms.

Software partitioning systems are generally implemented in one of two ways. They are either hosted as an application in an existing operating system installed on a physical computer or they are installed natively on a physical computer without an operating system (see Figure 2.3). When software partitioning systems are hosted in an existing operating system, they gain the advantages of leveraging that operating system's resource management capabilities, its hardware compatibility, and application programming interfaces (APIs). This allows the software partitioning system to be smaller and potentially easier to write and support. This configuration also imposes the deficiencies and inefficiencies of the host operating system upon the software partitioning system as well as the additional resource consumption of the host operating system. Hosted software partitioning systems generally have more overhead and less performance than their native counterparts. Current server-based implementations of software partitioning systems include Microsoft Virtual Server and VMware GSX Server for, Windows both of which run in a Windows Server operating system and VMware GSX Server for Linux, which runs in a Linux operating system.

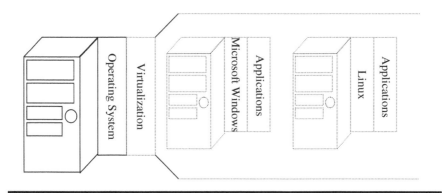

Figure 2.3   Software Partitioning Hosted in an Existing Operating System.

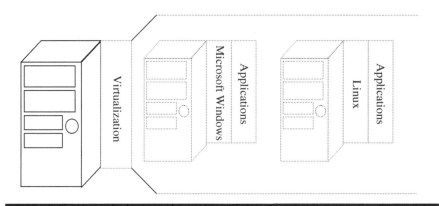

Figure 2.4   Software Partitioning Installed Natively on Hardware.

Software partitioning systems installed natively onto "bare metal" (the physical computer hardware) without an operating system are generally more efficient in their management of the computer's resources (see Figure 2.4). This is because the software partitioning system has full control over those resources. Although this type of implementation is more difficult to write and support, it is not burdened by the overhead of another operating system, generally allowing more performance for each soft partition. VMware ESX Server is currently the most mature implementation of a natively installed software partitioning system for x86-based server architectures.

A big advantage of software partitioning systems available for x86-based computers over hardware partitioning is cost. These systems run on standardized, commodity server hardware, which is much less expensive than the proprietary hardware partitioning systems. Because the hardware is also standardized across the industry, most IT organizations have the necessary skills to properly scope, deploy, configure, and administer the hardware today. This also lessens the implementation and support costs of software partitioning versus hardware partitioning. Software partitioning systems also offer the advantage of hardware portability. Each soft partition (or virtual machine) is fully abstracted from the underlying hardware that allows the partition to be moved to any physical computer that has the software partitioning system installed. An example being two computers having dramatically different hardware, such as a dual-processor, rack-mounted server and a laptop computer each running Microsoft Virtual Server. This is a powerful concept that makes server virtualization platforms very powerful in their capabilities. The benefit is also realized in terms of hardware upgrades because as long as the software partitioning system is supported on newer hardware, each soft partition will run as expected and in most cases it is trivial to move the soft partitions to another physical computer. The issue of vendor lock-in is also avoided in regard to the physical hardware since software partitioning systems for x86-based computer architectures can be installed on many different manufacturer's hardware (again due to industry standardization).

Software partitioning systems use a combination of emulation, simulation, and pass-through in their hardware abstraction methods. Each soft partition "sees" its own set of hardware resources that it may consume. This leads to an interesting question: can a software-partitioning virtualization platform be installed and used within a soft partition? Although this is theoretically possible, it is highly impractical and unusable as a solution. In some cases, depending on the specific virtualization platforms used, the virtualization platform may not even complete the installation process. In other cases, operating systems installed in a soft partition of another soft partition execute too slowly to be used effectively. This is most likely due to the multiplication of overhead within the system. For instance, when using preemptive multi-tasking operating systems for the host platform installed directly on the hardware and for the operating systems installed in each soft partition, the physical effect of time-slicing the physical CPU between all of the processes is multiplied for those processes executing within the first and second-level soft partitions. If more than one soft partition is created in the virtualization platform installed in a soft partition, the effect is worsened because the multiplier increases. It is generally a bad idea to embed entire software partitioning systems within existing soft partitions.

Software partitioning systems are available from the following vendors (listed with their current virtualization products):

- Hewlett-Packard (HP)
  - vPars (Virtual Partitions)
- Microsoft
  - Microsoft Virtual Server Standard Edition
  - Microsoft Virtual Server Enterprise Edition
  - Microsoft Virtual PC
- VMware
  - VMware ESX Server
  - VMware GSX Server
  - VMware Workstation
- Serenity Systems
  - Serenity Virtual Station (SVISTA)

Application partitioning (see Figure 2.5) is a software-based technology that allows the operating system resources on which an application depends to be placed in an alternate container within the operating system without the application's knowledge. These resources are said to be virtualized by the application partitioning system. The isolated application can then be executed in multiple instances simultaneously in the same operating system, by one or more users, without the application instances interfering with one another. Each instance of the application has no knowledge that the other instances exist and the application does not require any modifications to be hosted by the application partitioning system. The primary advantage of an application partitioning system is

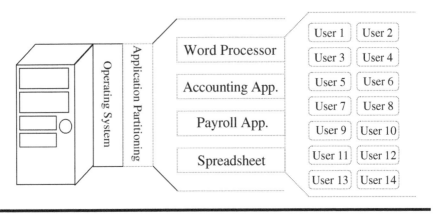

Figure 2.5 Application Partitioning.

that any application, regardless if it was designed to be used by a single user or multiple users, can be centrally managed and made available in a distributed fashion. A single server can execute many instances of the application and each application instance state is written into a separate container. Each container is automatically handled by the application partitioning system. Application partitioning can consolidate a single application from multiple desktop computers and servers onto a single server and the application can be managed much like a single instance of the application. The operating system itself is not completely abstracted from the application, only certain subcomponents such as data storage facilities (file systems), therefore only applications normally run on the operating system being used are allowed to be hosted under the application partitioning system.

Application partitioning systems are available from the following companies (listed with their product name):

- Citrix—Metaframe Presentation Server
- Ensim—VPS
- Softricity—SoftGrid
- SWSoft—Virtuozzo
- Tarantella—Secure Global Desktop

Resource partitioning is a software-based technology that abstracts how certain operating system resources are allocated to application instances or individual processes executing within the operating system (see Figure 2.6). This technology is used to control resource consumption of applications and processes, allowing more granular control than what is provided by the operating system. Resource partitioning systems also allow the resource consumption to be controlled not only at the application or process level, but also by the combination of application or process and user account. Resource partitioning systems enable the

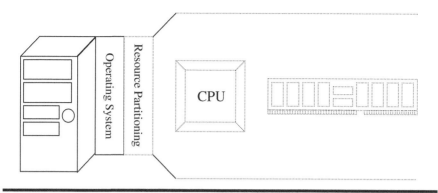

Figure 2.6   Resource Partitioning.

operating system to become Quality-of-Service enabled. Application instances or processes can be given parameters, which allow certain minimum and maximum levels of resource utilization such as CPU, memory, and disk I/O to be effectively controlled and managed. Just as in application partitioning, resource partitioning does not abstract the entire operating system from an application, therefore only applications that would normally run on the operating system being used are allowed to be controlled by the resource partitioning system.

Resource partitioning systems are available from the following companies (listed with their product name):

- Aurema—ARMTech
- Microsoft—Windows System Resource Manager
- HP—Process Resource Manager (PRM)
- Unisys—Application Sentinel for Resource Management

Service partitioning is a software-based technology in which a single application instance provides multiple, isolated instances of a service (see Figure 2.7).

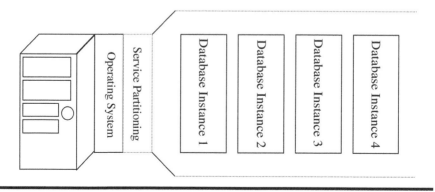

Figure 2.7   Service Partitioning.

Each instance of the service usually appears to consumers of that service to be a dedicated application instance (and often a dedicated server instance). Abstraction between the service application and the operating system is not required. The abstraction occurs on top of the application instance, which allows multiple instances of the application's service to coexist. The level of isolation between service instances can vary greatly between implementations of service partitioning, and in some systems can even be controlled, providing complete isolation at one extreme and no isolation at the other extreme of the isolation configuration settings. Common examples of service partitioning systems include database and web server applications. In a database server application, a single instance of the database server executes within the operating system. The primary service of the database server is to provide database access. Database servers can typically provide multiple databases per server instance. Each database can be configured to appear to a consumer to be the only database on the server, when in reality there may be 20 databases being concurrently accessed by 500 users. Most modern Web server applications allow multiple "virtual" Web sites to be created and hosted simultaneously from a single instance of the application. Each Web site is isolated from the other and, from a Web surfer's point-of-view, each Web site appears as if it is hosted on its own dedicated server, when in reality, there may be 100 Web sites running concurrently from the single Web server application instance.

There are too many examples of service partitioning systems (see Figure 2.7) to list in this book, but a few examples include the following:

- IBM DB2 Universal
- Microsoft Internet Information Services (IIS) WWW Publishing Service
- Microsoft SQL Server
- Oracle Database

Operating Systems and Runtime Environments

Although it is not often described as a type of virtualization technology, operating systems are actually one of the most common types of virtualization technologies. The operating system can be thought of as one virtual machine implemented in software used to abstract the computer's hardware resources. Software applications that reside and execute within an operating system use the operating system's facilities to access hardware instead of directly accessing the hardware, usually though a module called a device driver.

Some programming frameworks include a special runtime environment designed to run on top of the operating system. Software written against the framework runs on top of the operating system as well but also strongly relies on the runtime environment (or virtual machine as they are sometimes called) to perform its tasks. This type of virtualization does not provide a complete execution environment and relies on an operating system and its resources to do its job. Examples include the Microsoft .NET Framework and Sun's Java among many others.

Summary

In general, virtualization technology is available in many forms to meet different sets of requirements. Some of the virtualization technologies described here can be used effectively together such as operating systems and software partitioning or software partitioning and resource partitioning while others should never be used together as in the case of using a software partitioning system within a soft partition of an existing software partitioning system. Throughout the rest of the book, the term virtualization platform will be used to refer to software partitioning systems run on top of Intel x86 hardware and designed to be used as server systems, including products available from Microsoft (Virtual Server) and VMware (ESX Server and GSX Server).

Chapter 3

Server Virtualization Concepts

Servers are made up of multiple layers of hardware and software. Together, these layers create what we know as the system. Typical server hardware components include the following: processor; memory storage devices such as hard drives, floppy drives and CD/DVD drives; network adapters; peripheral connectors such as USB, serial and parallel ports, and video adapters. The software layer of the system is made up of the operating system, the applications and the device drivers that control the hardware components. The device drivers that are installed on the operating system normally create a one-to-one relationship between the hardware and the operating system controlling it. Virtualization allows us to overcome the exclusive device ownership of these hardware components, which causes the physical server to be constrained into running a single operating system instance at a time.

How a typical x86 physical server operates is probably already well understood. By using that knowledge, along with the following concepts, further insight will be gained into how virtualization operates and how it differs from the physical server world.

Host Servers, Virtual Machines, and Guest Operating Systems

The fundamental concept is the virtualization layer. Throughout the book, the term virtualization layer, also generically referred to as virtualization, will refer to a generic implementation of a software partitioning system designed for x86 server hardware. The virtualization layer consists of the software components used to create the abstraction between the physical hardware and virtual environments. When referring to a specific implementation of a virtualization layer, such as Microsoft Virtual Server or VMware ESX Server, the term virtualization platform is commonly used. A virtualization platform refers to a very specific implementation of a virtualization layer. Although most virtualization layer concepts are common among most virtualization platforms, there are differences between the available virtualization platforms. Depending on the virtualization platform, the virtualization layer software may be installed directly on the server hardware or it may be installed into an existing operating system residing on the server hardware. In each case, the virtualization layer's main component is the Virtual Machine Monitor (VMM), sometimes referred to as the Hypervisor. The VMM's primary task is abstracting the real computer resources and providing the virtual environments in which operating systems may be installed. These environments are usually referred to as virtual machines.

A virtual machine is a single, isolated execution environment that is created through software by the virtualization layer, which appears to be almost exactly like a physical x86 computer. A virtual machine, also referred to as a VM or virtual server, represents a single virtual computer. A compatible operating system and applications may be installed into a virtual machine. Although the VMM creates and manages the virtual machines, virtual machines also require resources of a physical host server in order to run. These resources are allocated through the VMM and the virtual machine and by default do not have any knowledge of the existence of the host server or the virtualization layer. It simply "sees" the virtual hardware exposed by the VMM as if it were real hardware. Some of the virtual hardware is emulated or simulated by the virtualization layer and some of it actually maps to real hardware, exposed through the VMM in a very controlled manner.

The host server is probably the most familiar component. The host server is the physical, bare metal, x86 server computer on which the virtualization layer resides. Throughout the book, it may be referred to as the host server, the physical server, the physical host server, or simply as the host. If the host server has an operating system installed, the operating system is referred to as the host operating system or host OS. The host server is referred to as a "host" because it hosts the virtualization layer and one or more guest servers or virtual machines.

A guest server is another term for a virtual machine. It is a term that is used to easily differentiate a physical server, also called a host server, from a virtual server, also called a guest server. Guest servers have an operating system installed that is compatible with the virtual hardware and often with the host server. This operating system does not have to be the same operating system installed on the host server (i.e., if the host server has an operating system). An instance of an operating system that resides in a guest server is referred to as the guest operating system or guest OS. Guest servers are isolated from each other and, by default, have no knowledge of the virtualization layer or other guest servers. This isolation is referred to as Host/Guest isolation.

The term guest server is often used interchangeably with the term virtual machine. The term guest operating system or guest OS always refers to an instance of an operating system installed in a guest server (or virtual machine).

To better define the virtualization layer, virtualization platform, virtual machine, host server, and guest OS concepts, the following example uses real products within a real-world scenario. A host server may be a Dell, IBM, or HP physical server that has Microsoft Windows Server 2003 Standard Edition installed as its operating system. Within this operating system, Microsoft Virtual Server 2005 is installed. Microsoft Virtual Server (MSVS) runs as a server application within the Windows Server 2003 operating system and it is the virtualization platform providing the virtualization layer that abstracts the Windows Server 2003 resources and manages the virtual machines. There are 3 virtual machines (or guest servers) hosted on this host server labeled as Server-A, Server-B, and Server-C. Server-A has Microsoft Windows 2000 Server installed as its guest OS. Server-B has Red Hat Linux installed as its guest OS. Server-C has Novell Netware installed as its guest OS. Each of the guest servers are booted and run independently of one another. If needed, they could communicate with each other or even the host server using normal TCP/IP networking communications.

Virtual Hardware Overview

Virtual hardware is made up of a set of virtual devices or virtual device interfaces that are exposed to a virtual machine. Some of these devices or device interfaces are automatically provided by the virtualization layer and cannot be configured. Other virtual hardware devices can be completely controlled and configured as needed within the virtualization layer. The most common virtual hardware devices will be discussed in detail; however, to get a more in-depth understanding of what each of these virtual devices are and how they function, they will also be contrasted against their physical counterparts.

Processor

The processor is the most significant piece of hardware in a computer. Also referred to as the central processing unit (CPU), the processor is often thought of as the brains of a computer. Its primary function is to perform complex calculations on data. In conventional x86 servers, there are often one, two, or four processors, with high-end servers having eight or more. Traditionally, operating systems are responsible for sending instructions to the physical processor(s) to perform requested commands.

Most server virtualization platforms support uniprocessor virtual machines, that is, virtual machines with a single virtual processor. However, the virtual processor is not a fully emulated processor. Completely emulating the processor would cause a severe performance bottleneck. Instead, the virtualization plat-form generally traps instructions issued by virtual machines and either passes the instruction through to the physical processor or emulates the instruction by issuing one or more different instructions to the physical processor and return-ing the expected result to the virtual processor. Depending on the virtualization platform and its configuration, it is possible for instructions from a single virtual processor to be executed sequentially across one or more physical processors in the host server. This is not in any way multiprocessing, as the instructions are not executed in parallel, but it can be performed in order to optimize the processor resource scheduler in the VMM and to help increase virtual machine performance. Virtualization platforms often allow a configuration setting per virtual machine called CPU affinity that defines which physical processors in the host server may be used to execute instructions issued by a virtual machine. In some cases, it may prove beneficial to restrict one or more low-priority virtual machines to a single processor using the CPU affinity setting while other virtual machines are allowed to utilize all processors in the host server.

Dual processor symmetric multiprocessing (SMP) support within virtual ma-chines is also supported by some virtualization platforms. In the future, four-way processor support will also be available for virtual machines. Today, Intel offers high-end processors that make available a feature known as HyperThreading (HT). HT technology can optimize instructions sent to a processor so that the processor's subsystems can, in some cases, simultaneously execute more than one instruction during the same clock cycle. HT is not the same as dual processors, but can give a significant performance increase. Some virtualization platforms can also take advantage of HT technology if it is available in the processors used in the host servers. Other virtualization platforms do not support HT and HT must explicitly be turned off in the host server's BIOS in order for the virtualiza-tion platform to work correctly.

Besides CPU affinity controls, most virtualization platforms also allow fine-grained settings of the processing resources available to each virtual machine. Usually, the minimum and maximum percentage of the host server's total pro-cessing resources can be configured. This is useful when one virtual machine requires a better guarantee of processing resources on the host server. Another processor resource management setting that is commonly available is the relative resource allotment. This feature is designed to give fine-grained priorities to the VMM's processor scheduler.

Memory

Computers typically use random access memory (RAM) as the temporary, high-speed storage location of data that is currently being used by the processor(s). Memory is many thousand times faster than disk access, so programs and data are loaded one time from disk into memory before being used by the processors.

Just as their physical counterparts, virtual machines require memory as well. As of this writing, 3.6GB of memory is the maximum amount of memory that can be assigned to a single virtual machine in most virtualization platforms. This limitation exists because 32-bit x86 architecture systems support a maximum memory size per process of 4GB and the virtualization platform consumes some of that memory as overhead. Currently, there is no virtual physical address extensions feature (or virtual PAE) designed to overcome this limitation on 32-bit systems.

The virtual memory allocated to a virtual machine usually maps directly to physical memory of the host server. The term virtual memory in this context should not be confused with virtual memory as in a paging or swap file as used by many operating systems to extend the amount of physical memory available by using hard disk storage as additional memory. The virtualization platform's VMM manages the memory addresses allocated to a virtual machine. In some cases, some of the virtual machine's memory will map to physical memory of the host server and some may actually map to either the host server's paging or swap file memory or to the virtualization platform's swap file, if supported. Any paged memory must be swapped back into physical memory before it can be used by the virtual processor, just as in a physical computer. This is handled by either the virtualization platform or the host operating system.

In most cases, there is a one-to-one ratio between each unit of memory assigned to a virtual machine as it maps to the host server's physical memory. For example, if a host server has three virtual machines and VM A is configured with 256MB of memory, VM B is configured with 256MB of memory and VM C is configured with 512MB of memory, a total of 1GB (1024MB) of memory is mapped between the virtual machines and the host server's physical memory. The host server would typically need at least 1GB of memory to support the virtual machines plus enough memory to support the host operating system, the virtualization platform and any other applications that may be installed on the host server.

Some virtualization platforms support over commitment or oversubscription of memory resources. This allows the virtualization platform to allocate more memory to the virtual machines than there is physical memory in the host server. This is possible because the virtualization platform will use a swap file on the hard disk to store data that is unneeded at any given point in time so that currently needed data is available in real physical memory. When that data is no longer needed, it will be swapped out to disk as other data is loaded into memory.

In order to make efficient usage of memory resources, some virtualization platforms can consolidate redundant memory. For example, if a host server has three virtual machines all of which have the same guest operating system installed, it is highly likely that the same modules will be loaded by each virtual machine into memory. Instead of allowing the same programs and data to be loaded into memory multiple times, the virtualization platform consolidates common memory artifacts so that they exist only once in physical memory. This reduces the amount of physical memory used and allows more over commitment and less paging to occur.

Hard Disk Drives

Hard disk drives are the most commonly used hardware components to provide long-term, nonvolatile data storage. Unlike a computer's memory, its hard disk drives, or disks, are able to persist data for long periods of time, even when the computer is powered off. Modern hard disk drives provide massive amounts of storage that is very inexpensive relative to the cost of memory chips. The most significant difference between hard disk drives and memory for data storage is that hard disk drives are typically the slowest device in the data access chain, usually thousands of times slower than memory. Data is often first read from a hard disk drive and placed into the computer's memory before it can be used by the processor. When data is changed in memory, it often must be written back to the hard disk drives for permanent storage.

There are two common types of hard disk interfaces, IDE and SCSI. These interfaces support the disk drives that are directly connected to a physical computer. They differ from each other in physical aspects such as the types of physical connectors, cables, and electrical signals, as well as in software including the protocol used to transfer data between the hard disk drive and the computer to which it is connected.

Depending on the virtualization platform, virtual machines may also contain both IDE and SCSI interfaces and disk drives. As in the physical world, IDE and SCSI drives exhibit certain characteristics and follow certain standards at the virtualized layer.

When dealing with desktop computers, the most popular hard disk of choice is the Integrated Device Electronics (IDE) interface-based hard disk. It is important to note, the term IDE used here is a generic term to describe all variants of the IDE (EIDE, ATA, PATA, UDMA) and Serial ATA interface-based drives. Most physical motherboards have support for one or two IDE controllers. Each IDE controller has two channels, each of which supports up to two devices (that is, four devices per IDE controller). These drives are then further designated as master (primary) and slave (secondary) devices on each IDE channel.

The hard disk interface of choice for servers is the Small Computer Systems Interface (SCSI, pronounced "skuzzy"). Like IDE, we are going to use the term SCSI as a generic term to describe all the various SCSI protocols and interface variants that exist. SCSI is a much more advanced interface than its IDE competitor. Typical SCSI controllers support one, two, or four channels. A single SCSI channel is typically capable of supporting up to eight devices (one of which is the host controller).

Virtual machines make use of virtual hard disk drives to satisfy its long-term data storage requirements. A virtual hard disk drive appears much like a physical hard disk drive to the guest operating system installed in a virtual machine. The typical virtual hard disk drive actually stores its data within one or more files residing on the host server. The files contain the stored image of an entire hard disk drive and appears as a single hard disk drive to the guest operating system. The virtual hard disk drive is typically created by the virtualization platform, usually through its management interface, and at the point of creation, its interface (IDE or SCSI) and the disks size must be specified. The newly created virtual hard disk drive is initially empty and unformatted, just as if it were a new physical hard disk drive. An interesting aspect of virtual hard disk drives is that the interface of the hard disk drive is completely independent of the physical hardware used by the host server, which means that if host server only supported IDE hard disk drives, it is possible to create SCSI virtual hard disk drives as long as the virtualization platform supports SCSI virtual hard disk drives. The reverse is also true. A host server that only supports SCSI hard disk drives may have IDE virtual hard disk drives depending on IDE support from virtualization platform. Virtualization platforms usually support at least one of the two hard disk drive interfaces and some support both IDE and SCSI virtual hard disk drives. Virtual hard disk drives exhibit certain characteristics and follow certain standards of the interface used just as in physical servers. In a virtual machine, there are obviously no physical interconnects, cables, or terminators, but the software interfaces are the same as in physical hard disk drives. The IDE channel schemes or SCSI IDs and the protocols they use work the same way as they do in physical servers.

Virtual machines typically have at least one virtual hard disk drive on which the guest operating system is installed and from which the virtual machines boots. Virtual machines may have more than one virtual hard disk drive, if necessary. The limit of the number of virtual hard disk drives that may be attached to a virtual machine is dependent upon the virtualization platform and it does often vary between the different platforms and different versions of the same platform. Because the virtual hard disk drive operates much like a physical hard disk drive, it too can be partitioned into one or more logical volumes and can be formatted to use different file systems, as required.

Virtual hard disk drives are portable. They may be created independently of any virtual machine on a given host server. They can be copied or moved between host servers. They can be attached to any virtual machine as needed, but typically a single copy of a virtual hard disk drive may only be used with a single virtual machine at a given point in time. The portability of virtual hard disk drives is enhanced by the fact that the guest operating system typically only requires one driver type for all virtual hard disk drives that may be attached to it, unlike its physical counterpart where different drives may be needed from different manufacturers or BIOS updates may be needed to support hard disk drives of larger sizes.

When a virtual hard disk drive is attached to a virtual machine, it is actually attached to a compatible virtual hard disk controller of the specified virtual machine. Depending on the virtualization platform, virtual machines may contain one or more virtual hard disk drive controllers of the same or differing interfaces. A virtual hard disk drive that is attached to a virtual machine is mapped by the VMM to the physical files residing on the host server. I/O requests from the virtual machine to which it is attached are handled by the VMM and the physical files on the host server are updated as necessary.

Virtual hard disk drives also support additional features and functionality that are not normally possible with physical hard disk drives. Different virtual hard disk drive types exist. A virtual hard disk drive can exist only as one of these types: a fixed disk, a dynamic disk, a differencing disk, or a raw disk. Additionally, virtual hard disk drives can be configured to have a redo or undo log file that alters the persistence behavior of the drive. These virtual hard disk drive features are available on most, but not all, virtualization platforms. The implementations of these features vary slightly between different virtualization platforms, but the most common aspects are detailed below.

A fixed disk is a virtual hard disk drive that most closely resembles a physical hard disk drive. The fixed disk is represented by a fixed-extent file residing on the host server. When created, the file is sized immediately to its maximum size, consuming an equal amount of storage from the host server. Like all virtual hard disk drives, the fixed disk is empty upon creation. For example, when a 10GB fixed virtual hard disk drive is created, a static 10GB file is created on the host server. This file represents the fixed disk and will contain all of its data. The file on the host server will always remain 10GB in size. It will not change, even when data is written to the fixed disk or when data is deleted from the fixed disk. Fixed disks will typically provide better performance than dynamic disks because there is no overhead due to file growth (see Figure 3.1).

A dynamic disk is a virtual hard disk drive that begins as a sparse file, consuming only the amount of storage from the host server that is needed, and grows as new data is written to the virtual hard disk drive. When created, the maximum size of the disk is specified, but the file representing the disk is sized only to the size needed to store its data at that point in time. The dynamic disk cannot grow in excess of its maximum size. For example, when a 10GB dynamic

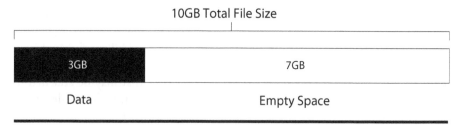

Figure 3.1   Fixed Disk File.

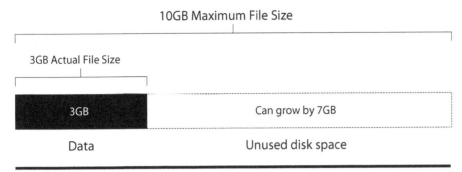

Figure 3.2   Dynamic Disk File.

virtual hard disk drive is created, the maximum size of 10GB is stored within the dynamic disks' internal data structures. The file on the host server representing the dynamic disk at first may only be a few kilobytes in size. Once the process of installing a guest operating system begins, the dynamic disk will grow as new data is written to fill the disk. When files are deleted from a dynamic disk, the file on the host server representing the dynamic disk will not change (it will not shrink). Instead, the deleted sectors are marked and are reused as necessary (see Figure 3.2).

A differencing disk is a special type of dynamic virtual hard disk drive that is dependent on a parent disk. Differencing disks share a parent/child relationship with another virtual hard disk drive in which the differencing disk is the child. The combination of the differencing disk and its parent virtual hard disk drive create a single virtual hard disk drive as it appears to the virtual machine to which the differencing disk is attached. Once a differencing disk is linked to a parent disk, the parent virtual hard disk drive becomes read-only. Any changes made thereafter are saved into the differencing disk, which grows as needed. The parent of the differencing disk, however, controls the maximum disk size overall. When a read on the disk occurs, the most recent changes are always returned. First the read occurs in the parent disk and then in the differencing disk, returning the most current data from the differencing disk, if it exists in the differencing disk. If the parent disk of a differencing disk is ever altered in any way, the differencing disk will become invalid, as its relationship to the parent disk depends upon the state of the parent disk at the time they are linked. Differencing disks are covered in detail later in the book (see Figure 3.3).

A raw disk is the mounting of either an entire physical hard disk drive or a logical volume on a physical hard disk drive to a virtual machine. Raw disks are useful in special circumstances where a virtual machine may need to access data that already exists on a physical disk or when high disk performance is required. Raw disks are not virtual hard disk drives, but appear as any other virtual hard disk drive to the virtual machine to which it mounted.

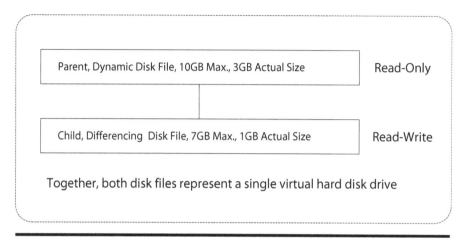

Figure 3.3 Differencing Disk Files.

By default, all virtual hard disk drives are persistent. That is, changes made to the virtual hard disk drive occur immediately and are permanent, much like those made on a physical hard disk drive. Most virtualization platforms have a feature to modify the persistence mode of a virtual hard disk drive. A redo or undo disk (also called a redo log file) is a special disk that is created when a virtual hard disk drive's persistence mode is changed (see Figure 3.4). The undo disk is similar to a dynamic disk. It is linked to its parent disk when it is created, the parent disk becomes read-only, and all changes are written to the undo disk (see Figure 3.5). A virtual machine must be powered off to enable any of its virtual hard disk drives to have their persistence mode changed. Once changed, the virtual machine is powered on and booted normally. At the point of powering on

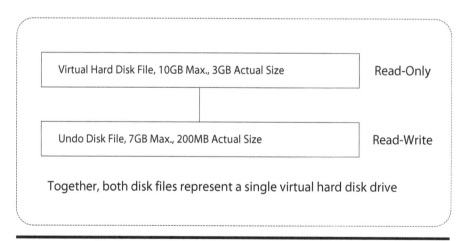

Figure 3.4 Undo Disk Files.

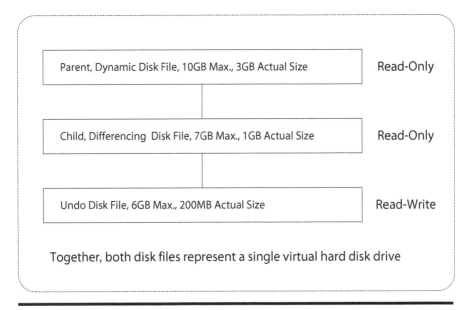

Figure 3.5 Differencing and Undo Disk Files.

the virtual machine, any virtual hard disk drive attached to the virtual machine that is in undo mode and does not already have an undo disk file on the host server has a new, empty undo disk file created. Undo disks are temporary disks that allow users to decide later how the data should be handled. Undo disks may be discarded (deleted), in which case all changes made to the virtual machine when the undo disk was created are permanently lost and the virtual hard disk drive will revert to its previous, unmodified state of the parent disk. Undo disks can be left alone, in which case all changes to the virtual hard disk drive continue to be written to the undo disk and it will continue to grow.

Undo disks can also be committed into their parent virtual hard disk drive. Committing an undo disk is the process of merging the changes written into the undo disk into the parent disk permanently. Once an undo disk is committed, the undo disk is discarded as it is useless from this point onward because its parent disk has been modified.

Floppy Disk Drives

Computers are slowly moving away from the use of floppy disk drives; however, they still refuse to completely disappear in either the physical or virtual world. The floppy disk drive has remained relatively standard and unchanged for many years. A virtual floppy disk drive can read and write to a physical floppy diskette that is inserted into the host server's floppy disk drive. By mapping the host server's floppy disk drive to the virtual machine, the guest operating system can interact with the host floppy disk drive as if it were physically attached to the virtual machine. One important distinction between the physical and the virtual floppy disk drive is that a virtual floppy disk can be mapped to a floppy disk image file located on the host server. A floppy disk image file (also known as a floppy image) can be created by most virtualization management utilities or by using third-party tools. By mounting or attaching a virtual floppy image to a virtual machine rather than to the physical drive, huge performance increases in both read and write speed will be realized. This performance increase is due to the information being read from a file residing on a hard disk drive instead of from a physical floppy disk drive with very slow access, read and write times. Virtual floppy disk drives are needed in some cases to assist the installation of some guest operating systems.

CD/DVD-ROM Drives

The CD/DVD drive has taken the place of the floppy drive as the preferred storage of choice. CD and DVD discs have become the standard medium for distribution of large quantities of data. The average CD can hold between 650 and 700MB while a standard DVD can hold 4.7GB. Compared to the 1.44MB that the floppy disk provides, it is easy to see why the CD/DVD has replaced the floppy disk. CD/DVD media, like most things in the computer industry, follow certain standards and guidelines. These standards, known as the ISO 9660, were published by the International Organization for Standardization. The ISO 9660 standard defines a file system for CD-ROM and DVD-ROM media. Its aim is to provide compatibility and support between different computer operating systems such as Microsoft Windows, Microsoft DOS, the MacOS, UNIX, and the various flavors of Linux, so data may easily be shared and exchanged between them.

It is common to transfer the contents of a CD-ROM electronically as a file disk image. A disk image of an ISO 9660 file system normally has a file extension of .iso. For this reason, these images are referred to as "ISO images." An ISO image, therefore, is a file that represents a complete copy of a specific computer file system, most commonly the CD medium. While there are tools out there that allow modifications to an ISO file, the ISO 9660 is specified to be read-only. An ISO file that contains an image of an ISO 9660 file system can be manipulated in a number of different ways. The file can be written (burned is the common term) back onto CD-R(W) media or mounted as a device with the Linux loop back file system or a Windows third-party tool. A common use of ISO images is to create distribution discs of software such as operating systems and large applications to be transmitted over the Internet. Additionally, backing up CD media to ISO files and executing them from a mount point can save wear and tear on the media and keep the CD-ROM from being accidentally scratched and destroyed. Finally, ISO files have become a major data distribution method in both, emulation and virtualization.

Even virtualized machines need access to and the ability to share large quantities of data. CD-ROM discs are the media of choice when it comes to moving data between virtual machines or when operating systems or applications need to be installed on a virtual machine. Like the virtual floppy drive, a virtual CD/DVD drive can read physical media that is inserted into the host server. By mapping the host server's CD/DVD drive to the virtual machine, the guest operating system will interact with the host drive, as if the media were physically inserted into the VM. Also like the virtual floppy drive, there is an important distinction to be made between the virtual and the physical CD/DVD drive. A virtual CD/DVD drive can be mapped to a physical file located on the host's file system. This file, as explained above, has been defined as an ISO image. By mounting to a virtual ISO image rather than a physical drive, a huge performance boost in reading the disc is achieved. At the physical level, file reads from a hard disk are much faster than file reads from a CD-ROM.

Network Adapters

There are some distinctions between the host network adapter and the guest network adapter. Depending on configuration, these virtual network adapters can be isolated into a separate private network that only communicates with other virtual network adapters in that private network. They can be isolated by themselves so that no communication occurs with other machines. Or they can be joined to a network in which they only communicate with the host machine. Another option is for several machines to be part of a private network that also allows them to talk to the host. Virtual network adapters can also talk directly through the host network adapter as if they were a separate network interface on the host's network. And finally, it is possible for the virtual network adapter to communicate through the host network adapter as if it were the host adapter (through a process called NAT).

Serial Ports

A serial port is a port, or an interface, on a computer system where information is transmitted in or out one bit at a time. Throughout the computer system's history, most serial ports conformed to the RS-232 or RS-422 standards. Using a simple cable and this general purpose interface, the serial port can be used to connect almost any type of device. Through the serial port, the computer can be connected to devices such as terminals, modems, keyboards, mice and printers. Originally specified as a 25 pin D-type connector, most of these pins were unused since data was only being transmitted one bit at a time. Therefore, these devices were replaced with parallel port devices, and later, USB and Firewire devices.

Traditionally, the PC's serial port default hardware configuration of the first four ports is configured according to the following table in Figure 3.6. Within

Port Name	Interrupt	Starting I/O Port	Ending I/O Port
COM 1	IRQ 4	0x3f8	0x3ff
COM 2	IRQ 3	0x2f8	0x2ff
COM 3	IRQ 4	0x3e8	0x3ef
COM 4	IRQ 3	0x2e8	0x2ef

Figure 3.6 Typical Serial Port Configuration.

the Linux operating system, the serial port devices follow the naming convention of /dev/ttySn, where n is a numerical value starting with 0. For example, the first serial port device would be identified as /dev/ttyS0 and the fourth device would be identified as /dev/ttyS4.

Because the four ports share IRQs, some operating systems may have a problem with devices attached and trying to use the same IRQ. When an IRQ conflict occurs, one or more devices will either stop working all together, or intermittent problems with the devices may happen.

Within virtualization, a virtual machine may be configured to have a virtualized serial port. There are a number of uses for the serial port within a virtual machine. The serial port can be mapped to the host server's serial port, and then make use of the host's physically attached device(s). A virtual machine could therefore use a modem that is attached to its host. Additionally, a virtual serial port can be redirected to send its output to a file on the host server. This is useful when trying to capture the data that an application running in a virtual machine may send to the serial port. It may also be used to send smaller sized files from the virtual machine to its host server when networking isn't available. And finally, the virtual serial port can be mapped to a named pipe. This is especially useful for debugging purposes. For example, a kernel debugging program can be running in a virtual machine connected via the virtual serial port to debug kernel code.

Parallel Ports

A parallel port is a port, or an interface, on a computer system where data is transmitted in or out eight bits at a time. The data is transmitted in parallel, across more than one wire at a time. Contrary to the serial port, the parallel port is able to transmit one bit of data across multiple wires, rather than a across a single cable. The parallel port was specified as a 25 pin connector (DB-25). It

Port Name	Interrupt	Starting I/O Port	Ending I/O Port
LPT 1	IRQ 7	0x378	0x37f
LPT 2	IRQ 5	0x278	0x27f

Figure 3.7   Typical Parallel Port Configuration.

was originally named the Centronics port after the company that designed it. Originally designed to connect devices that needed relatively high bandwidth, the interface was ideal for connecting PCs to printer devices. As needs grew, a newer type of parallel port was designed, the enhanced parallel port (EPP) and the extended capabilities port (ECP). Both supported the same connectors as the original Centronics port. With these new ports came greater speeds. Support for bidirectional communication and a transfer rate of ten times the speed of the Centronics port, gave way to the creation and rise of new devices such as parallel port data drives.

Traditionally, the PC's parallel port default hardware configuration of the first two ports is configured according to the following table in Figure 3.7. Within the Linux operating system, the parallel port devices follow the naming convention of /dev/lp0 and /dev/parport.

Within virtualization, a virtual machine may be configured to have a virtualized parallel port. Like the serial port, the virtual parallel port can be mapped to the host's parallel port. The virtual machine can then make use of the host's attached devices. While not every physical device will work within the virtual machine, many do. The obvious choice of using a parallel port in a virtual machine is to allow the virtual machine to send output to a physical printer. Other uses may include mapping the parallel port to make use of a data drive or an application security dongle.

USB Ports

A relative newcomer to the computer port scene is the universal serial bus (USB). The USB design consists of a single host controller and multiple devices connected in a tree like formation using special hub devices. At least one hub, the root hub, always exists. The root hub is attached directly to the host controller. The hardware that contains the host controller and the root hub is called the Host Controller Device (HCD). The HCD is defined by the hardware manufacturer. Found in many of today's computer systems is the Intel specifications, the Universal Host Controller Interface (UHCI) and the Extended Host Controller Interface (EHCI). Devices that attach to the bus can either be custom devices or class devices. A custom device requires a custom driver to accompany it in order for the device to be used. On the other hand, a class device follows the same behavior and interface descriptors, so that the same device driver may be used for devices that are members of the same class.

One advantage to using USB over serial or parallel ports is that a single USB port can be used to connect up to 127 peripheral devices. Common uses of the USB port are connecting devices such as mice, keyboards, printers, scanners, removable hard drives, and networking components. Unlike a SCSI bus, devices on a USB chain do not require a terminator. Another advantage of using USB, certain devices that require a low power draw can receive their power from the bus, thereby reducing the need for extra power sources. USB was originally designed for ease of use. By allowing devices to chain from a single host, the need to add multiple expansion cards to the computer's bus was removed. Additionally, USB added improved plug and play ability as well as the capability of hot swapping devices without the need for a reboot of the system. Because of these types of features, USB is quickly becoming the standard of choice for peripheral manufacturers of devices such as printers and scanners.

Like the virtualized serial port and parallel port, the virtual machine can map to the USB port on the host server. By doing so, the virtual machine can make use of most of the devices attached to the USB port of the host server, as long as the guest operating system also supports USB. While the popularity of USB is on the rise, not all x86 server virtualization platforms support it. Currently, VMware ESX Server and Microsoft Virtual Server do not support the mapping of USB ports. This could change as the demand for this functionality increases. In the mean time, however, the VMware's GSX Server product does support USB. It currently emulates a two port USB 1.1 UHCI controller and therefore maps to the host server's USB controller.

Some alternatives have been explored to make use of USB devices in these nonsupported x86 server virtualization platforms. A relatively new product has appeared on the market that allows a USB device to be connected to a network via a hub. These network USB hubs allow the device to operate over IP technology making it easy to connect USB devices anywhere on the LAN. Typically, software drivers are loaded in the guest operating system, making the USB ports appear to be locally attached with the same Plug-and-Play user experience as a traditional USB port.

Keyboard and Mouse

The keyboard is the device that allows the entering of data into a computer. Over the years, the keyboard has been modified and updated, however it has remained fairly standard in its layout. The English language keyboard has followed the QWERTY key scheme. This standard layout of letters, numbers, and punctuation gets its name from the first six letter keys of the top row: QWERTY.

Originally created in the 1800s for mechanical typewriters, the layout of keys of the QWERTY keyboard was designed specifically to slow down the typist, so as not to jam the keys. As previously stated, the keyboard has gone through relatively minor changes: the original PC keyboard having 84 keys, the AT keyboard also with 84 keys, and the enhanced keyboard with 101 keys. The keyboard has acquired several special keys through the years. Some of the additional keys were created to improve productivity for office applications, while others were added to enhance the performance of the operating system.

A mouse is a pointing device for computers that is typically fitted with one or more buttons that have different functions depending on the operating system or application running. The mouse's 2D motion is then translated into the movement of the cursor or pointer on a display screen. The device derived its name through its appearance. Early mice had a mouse like shape and a cord that resembled a tail. Additionally, the movement of the device and the pointer on the display screen seemed to scurry around much like a mouse. Originally invented in 1963 by Douglas Englebart at the Stanford Research Center and later perfected by Xerox in the 1970s, the mouse would later become indispensable for computer users. With the addition of graphical user interface (GUI) operating systems and graphical applications such as CAD and painting programs, terms like point and click and drag and drop became common. The mouse helped the computer to become easier to use and operate. Mice can connect to their host computer in one of several ways. They typically use a thin electrical cord to connect such as the serial, PS/2 or USB port. Today, mice also use wireless communication to transmit data, such as infrared, RF, and Bluetooth.

Typically, x86 server virtualization software will support and operate as a standard PS/2 keyboard and PS/2 mouse. In general, the keyboard and mouse work the same in a virtual machine as it does for the host machine. However, some keyboard shortcut commands do not work the same in a virtual machine as it does within the host. For example, when pressing CTRL+ALT+DELETE on the keyboard, the shortcut keyboard command interacts with the host machine and the host operating system, not the virtual machine or the guest operating system. Another keyboard shortcut is typically available to perform the same keyboard shortcut, or sometimes a mouse menu driven command is available to perform the same action. Any time a virtual machine accesses an I/O device, there is a performance hit from a world switch between the VMM and the host. This is important to note for devices with high sustained throughput and low latency. However, for a keyboard and mouse, this is not a major concern since they both have very short duration and low processing overhead events.

Keyboard and mouse handling may cause some confusion. When having multiple windows open (host operating system and/or multiple guest operating system windows), it may cause some alarm as to where the mouse pointer is focused. Typically, by clicking inside of the guest operating system window, the mouse and keyboard then become bound to the virtual machine. This is called "mouse capture" or "mouse grab." The mouse and keyboard are then focused inside of the guest operating system. Both keyboard and mouse control within a virtual machine can be enhanced to perform much closer to that of the host machine by installing a set of drivers related to the virtualization software being used. These drivers will be discussed later under each virtualization platform.

Summary

The server virtualization concepts presented in this chapter are the key foundation to understanding the various server virtualization platforms and how to take advantage of them. The flexibility provided by virtualization offers many advantages over its physical counterparts. The ability to simultaneously run different types of operating systems on a single server provides a method of using the server's hardware to full utilization. The ability to chain and manipulate virtual hard disk files provides portability that cannot be found with other technologies. These capabilities are the main reason that virtualization is showing such explosive growth throughout the IT community.

The fact that the virtual processor uses pass-through techniques to the physical process and that the memory allocated to virtual machines mostly maps to physical memory gives server virtualization acceptable performance to be used in production environments. It is the same reason why server virtualization does not support guest operating systems outside of what is supported by the underlying physical hardware.

Part II

Planning

Chapter 4

Business Cases for Server Virtualization

The first step in planning to deploy server virtualization technologies is to understand how it can be applied to business objectives. This chapter describes the key areas of information technology to which server virtualization can be effectively applied and how it relates to common business goals. It also shows how common short-term and long-term problems can be addressed using server virtualization technology and where it should not be used.

Solving Business Problems

Aside from the pure novelty of running more than one operating system on a single computer at the same time, server virtualization technology was designed to be used to help solve business problems. Virtualization can be used in a very straight-forward manner much like physical servers and when used in this way can help reduce physical server hardware costs by consolidating multiple servers onto a single server. This usage is commonly referred to as server consolidation. Virtualization provides new features that are either unavailable or unobtainable on physical server hardware. One of the most profound benefits of virtualization is the abstraction between virtual machines and the physical hardware, thereby making virtual machines portable. In this way, virtualization simplifies and enhances legacy server and application support, while providing new opportunities in disaster recovery and high-availability scenarios. Because virtual machines are much easier to deploy than physical servers and because the software nature of virtualization technology lends itself well to automation of provisioning, on-demand and adaptive computing are more easily realized.

Server Consolidation

Many organizations today have several servers, each performing a dedicated task. These servers include file servers, print servers, e-mail servers, Web servers, database servers, and other application servers. It is not uncommon to have applications that require or strongly recommend a dedicated server, usually because the software does not particularly coexist well with other applications installed within the same operating system. In these situations, organizations will purchase small dedicated servers to host these applications, many of which have a low rate of utilization because the application only has a small amount of users or because it may only be used infrequently, such as once a month. The problem with this scenario is that the organization must incur a capital expenditure of $6,000 or more and that the processor, memory, and disk storage of the new dedicated server are highly underutilized and essentially wasted. Over time, the data center may support many small, highly underutilized servers hosting dedicated applications, also incurring the data center hosting costs (ping, power, and pipe) for each server.

Server virtualization can help organizations save money in the datacenter through server consolidation. Many, if not all, of the organization's highly underutilized application servers may be moved from physical hardware into virtual machines. Applications requiring a dedicated server still meet that requirement because a virtual machine is a dedicated server with its own, fully isolated virtual hardware and operating system. Many of these virtual machines may be hosted on a single physical server by means of the virtualization platform. As new dedicated application servers are needed, instead of purchasing new physical servers, virtual machines may be created on existing virtualization host servers. The density of virtual machines, which may be hosted on a single virtualization host server, depends on several factors including the number of processors, the amount of memory, and disk storage space on the physical host server, the virtualization platform (installed on the host server), and the amount of resources consumed by the virtual machines. It is not uncommon to have 10:1 or higher server consolidation ratios for highly underutilized servers.

Legacy Server and Application Support

A common pain point of many information technology organizations is that, over time, legacy hardware and software must be maintained. The term legacy commonly refers to either outdated and possibly unsupported computing systems or systems comprised of components of a previous version. Replacing legacy systems with new systems is always a challenge, both technically and in business terms. Legacy systems exist because of many reasons. These may include a very high cost to completely replace the system due to a large investment in capital expenditure, training, and customization of the system. Legacy systems may also be sensitive, mission critical resources that cannot easily be replaced. Sometimes legacy systems must be maintained because they cannot be replaced because it was purchased from a third-party company no longer in business or from one that no longer supports the system, or possibly because of a lack of expertise in the system's internals. In some cases, it costs less to maintain legacy systems than it does to replace them, but over time legacy systems typically become more unusable because they often are not able to scale up because of costs or technology limitations.

For example, an organization may have invested in a custom software application designed to run under the Microsoft Windows NT 3.51 Server operating system many years ago. The application in this example was written in such a way that it will not work with any other version of the Windows operating system. The application is becoming a productivity bottleneck because its utilization has grown over the years while running on the same hardware. The organization wishes to upgrade the server hardware on which the application and operating system are installed upon, but cannot because the newer hardware available today does not have the appropriate support for the older operating system. There are no available chipset and storage drivers that will work with the older operating system while allowing it to use top-of-the-line processors, memory, and disks to solve the legacy application's ability to scale up. Additionally, because the application was custom-written, there are no newer versions of the application available and the costs to switch to a different application that provides like functionality is cost prohibitive.

Server virtualization can solve legacy server and application support issues. Migrating the legacy servers to virtual machines inherently abstracts the physical hardware from the legacy software, including the operating system and the applications, allowing the legacy hardware to be discarded or reused elsewhere as needed. Because the legacy software now uses virtualized hardware, it can be moved to any host server as necessary, making the legacy server portable. Aside from its newly gained portability, the legacy server migrated to a virtual machine can be hosted on and use any hardware that is supported by the virtualization platform and the host server.

Continuing the previous example, the organization decides to migrate the legacy server to a virtual machine. They choose a virtualization platform that allows them to host the migrated server on modern, high-end server equipment, which addresses the bottleneck issues while adding the portability necessary to move the server to better hardware in the future, if the need arises.

Additional savings in terms of hosting can be realized by migrating legacy servers to virtual servers in order to decommission older, inefficient hardware and by increasing overall server utilization.

Disaster Recovery

Disaster recovery is a term used to describe the strategy and processes used by an information technology organization to ensure that in the event of a disaster that damages or destroys the organization's computing infrastructure, a minimal recovery of the computing infrastructure and data can be accomplished in a reasonable amount of time to provide business continuance. Disaster recovery strategies are almost always an afterthought in most organizations, probably because it is like paying for insurance. When an event occurs, however, it is the disaster recovery strategy that can save a company from going out of business, thus providing business continuance. Although disaster recovery strategies encompass a wide range of considerations, one of the most common activities is data backup.

Backing up the data of an organization is critically important to help not only with disaster recovery, but also to help to recover from day to day mistakes, such as when a user inadvertently deletes an important document, or to help protect data lost from a malicious intruder. There are many theories and methods of performing data backup. Most commonly, only an application's data is backed up instead of the application itself or the operating system. This is typically done to save space within the backup system (and to reduce the cost of the backup system) because the application's code and the operating system itself changes rarely. It is also traditionally more difficult to restore an operating system and applications from backups versus reinstalling them and then applying data afterwards. Because of these methods, the restoration of systems becomes a much harder, longer task. Although complete system restoration is rare (hopefully), the amount of time it takes to restore systems is critical to business continuance.

Virtualization technology can help improve disaster recovery strategies in many ways. Since virtual machines, their guest operating systems, all installed applications, and data reside within one or more files on the host server, it is simple to backup an entire virtual machine. To backup the virtual machine, make a copy of the virtual machine's configuration files and its virtual disk files. Backing up entire virtual machines usually does require more backup storage space because of the size of the virtual disk files, but the benefits are worthwhile. In the event of a disaster, the entire virtual machine can be restored in the time it takes to recopy the virtual machine's configuration and disk files. Installation and configuration of neither operating systems nor applications is necessary. In the same amount of time it takes to rebuild a single standard Windows server, configure it, apply patches and updates, install applications, and restore data, many virtual machines can be restored, possibly 10, 20, 30, or more.

Another aspect of using virtualization in regards to disaster recovery is that when a disaster occurs and a recovery must take place, the proper hardware components must be obtained on which to recover the systems. Traditionally, older hardware is stored offsite to be used for recovery and only the core, mission critical servers can be restored because of hardware limitations. Any secondary systems cannot be restored until more hardware is acquired. Using virtualization, a few physical servers able to support the virtualization platform being used are required for recovery. The most critical virtual machines can easily be restored onto any of the virtualization platform-compliant hardware and shortly after that, other secondary systems may also be restored onto the same servers utilizing the unused hardware resources (much like server consolidation).

Virtualization can also help aid in disaster recovery even if not all of an organization's servers are virtualized. For instance, high-performance, highly utilized file and mail servers may not be virtualized in production. Other servers within the organization are consolidated using server virtualization. As part of the organization's disaster recovery strategy, there are virtual machines already created but not used that replicate the functionality of the file and mail servers. When the time comes to recover these servers, the virtual versions provide very quick service restoration times and will usually be adequate until the proper hardware can be acquired.

High Availability

Although disaster recovery strategies address business continuance in the event of a catastrophic disaster, they do not address the needs of fault tolerance and system robustness. High-availability strategies provide business continuance through the use of fault-tolerant systems, usually by implementing redundant system components such as RAID storage systems or clustered servers. Most highly available systems must be available more than 99 percent of the time, meaning that the systems must be able to recover from a number of different component failures. One of the most common methods of providing a highly available system is through the use of clustered servers. In a server cluster, there are at least two servers that have the same applications and configuration and share access to the same data. When the active server in the cluster experiences a fault (such as a failed network adapter or hard drive failure), one of the other servers in the cluster take over and become the active server in order to provide nonstop services. One of the issues associated with server clusters is the additional cost of server hardware that is mostly unused while it is waiting for a failure to occur.

Server virtualization can provide an inexpensive method of implementing server clusters by using virtual machines in a cluster. Virtual machines can be clustered with other virtual machines or other physical servers. Using virtual machines in server clusters works well with server consolidation. While the primary server in the cluster is active, the secondary server, a virtual machine, will usually consume very few resources, allowing it to be placed on a host server along with other servers. If the primary server in a server cluster is also a virtual machine, it should be placed on a separate physical host server in order to maximize the cluster's uptime.

Adaptive Computing

Another area where server virtualization provides business value is in adaptive computing. Adaptive computing consists of server systems that have the ability to autonomously reconfigure themselves to address changing requirements. Adaptive computing is also referred to as autonomous computing, grid computing, on-demand computing, or utility computing. On-demand computing as referred to in this book is different from adaptive computing.

Server virtualization can work well with adaptive computing initiatives because of the ease of virtual machine provisioning. For example, consider a bank of Web application servers in a load balanced cluster. The Web application utilization rises and the overall performance of the application decreases. The system then allocates resources on a virtualization host server on which it creates two additional virtual machines using the same Web application server image. Once the two virtual machines have been created they are booted up and added dynamically to the existing cluster. The two additional servers help spread the application's workload over more computing resources, thus increasing the overall application performance. When the application's utilization falls off, the two additional servers are no longer needed and they are powered off and deleted.

This type of adaptive computing can be applied to many applications that share a common set of virtualization host server resources on which to dynamically create virtual machines. In addition to dynamically responding to needs, adaptive computing systems can have capacity scheduled in order to help optimize computing resource utilization. For instance, during the week an application may have five virtual machines on which to perform its work, but over the weekend, three of the virtual machines may be scheduled to be reconfigured to work with a different application to help with back-end processing.

Adaptive computing scenarios can be achieved with physical hardware, including traditional server and blade servers, but typically at an increased cost and increased level of complexity as compared to using server virtualization.

On-Demand Computing

Virtualization technology easily facilitates on-demand computing systems that can quickly allocate one or more servers to a group of users for a short time and reclaim and reuse those resources once the users' time has expired or if they have released the resources. This type of system is commonly used to provide virtual labs used by system administrators and developers for testing software configurations. It is also used to provide virtual training labs within a learning management system, whether it is a physical class or an e-learning system accessed over the Internet.

Once again, the ease of provisioning virtual machines supports on-demand systems very well, but it is the virtual machine's ability to discard changes made to their virtual hard disk drives, resetting them to a pristine state, where the most value is gained. Building these types of systems without using virtualization is very difficult and expensive.

Limitations of Server Virtualization

Virtualization technology opens the data center to new possibilities that may provide cost savings and new types of functionality, but virtualization does have its limits. Not every server or application is well suited to be run in a virtual machine. Some applications are highly performance-sensitive, such as databases, data warehousing applications, business intelligence, reporting, and many others. These applications usually require multiple processors and massive amounts of memory. At the present time, server virtualization platforms support virtual machines with either a single processor or at most dual processors and up to 3.6GB of memory. In the near future, these limitations will likely be overcome, although for performance-sensitive applications, it may still not be enough to justify running them as virtual machines. This is because virtual machines are not only sharing resources with other virtual machines on the same host server, but because the virtualization platform itself incurs a small amount of overhead that can negatively impact performance-sensitive applications.

Virtualization technology does not support graphics-intensive applications very well at this time. Graphics-intensive applications and games usually require the use of high-performance video cards. In the virtual machine, the video card is a virtual device implemented in software and at this time does not support advanced graphics acceleration features. Even if the virtual video card device did have support for advanced graphics acceleration, it would invariably place more overhead on the system's physical processors.

Much like the problems with graphics-intensive applications, applications requiring specialized hardware cannot be used within a virtual machine. Specialized hardware refers to any nonstandard hardware device, commonly PCI cards. At the present time, virtualization platforms are generally closed systems and new types of virtual hardware cannot be created by third-parties. In the future, this limitation may be overcome, at which time third-parties may have the ability to write their own virtual hardware devices in order to connect specialized physical hardware devices to virtual machines.

Summary

Server virtualization can be used in many ways to help solve business problems. Server consolidation can reduce data center costs while enabling the virtualized servers to be backed up in an easier manner helping with disaster recovery. The lifetime of legacy servers and applications can be significantly extended and the performance increased by moving them to virtual machines. Disaster recovery strategies can be enhanced through the use of server virtualization, which can dramatically reduce the time and complexity required to restore vital systems in the event of a catastrophic event, improving the chances of business continuance. Server virtualization can also help reduce the costs involved in creating highly-available systems, also aiding in business continuance through increased fault tolerance. In addition to cost reduction, server virtualization opens up new opportunities by providing the capabilities to easily create adaptive and on-demand computing systems increasing an organization's productivity. Server virtualization is not the answer to all business problems, however, and some systems do not lend themselves well to be run within virtual machines, including performance-sensitive applications, graphics-intensive applications, and applications requiring specialized hardware. It is important to take these limits into consideration when planning for server consolidation projects, legacy server and application support, disaster recovery, and high availability solutions. All in all, virtualization can save the organization thousands to millions of dollars through more efficient and effective use of hardware.

Chapter 5

Other Uses of Server Virtualization

This chapter provides soup-to-nuts server virtualization usage scenarios, which build upon the ideas presented in the previous chapter. Practical use cases are presented to show how server virtualization solves problems more easily than traditional approaches. These pain points or problems facing organizations cross over into their IT departments. By utilizing virtualization, these departments can learn to solve these problems in a more efficient manner, saving on both time and cost, and allowing their departments to succeed in areas that would previously cause them productivity problems without answers. These departments are made up of the following groups:

- Software Development and QA/Testing
- Technical Support and Help Desk
- Software Training and E-Learning Systems

Software Development and QA/Testing

Let's face it; software manufacturing is not getting any easier. On the contrary, it is becoming more and more difficult to get a quality software product to market. As the number of operating system choices (along with their hot fixes, patches, and service packs) continue to increase, the development and testing effort to ensure the application performs as expected on each platform becomes exhausting. In addition, today's applications may also need to support multiple browser versions, various databases, and have strong interoperability with other applications. The problems compound as software manufacturers are faced with obstacles such as a decreasing budget, the demand for a shorter product life cycle, and the need to deliver the products to market quickly. Unfortunately in today's world of software, it is sometimes more important to be the first to market rather than the best. However, time to market and quality of product do not have to be mutually exclusive. In fact, by accepting virtualization as a tool, it can help address the department budget problem, accelerate the development cycle, and improve product quality and productivity.

Reduce Budget

From a business standpoint, software manufacturers face the challenge of delivering their product to market at a competitive price. One way to do so is by controlling the budget costs associated with the development and testing organization. Building out a development and QA lab is both expensive and time consuming. Consider the costs associated with a single server: the price of the server itself, rack space, disk space, network gear, cabling, power consumption, cooling, and maintenance costs to name but a few. With a virtualization solution in place, software manufacturers can streamline their resources and not only lower hardware costs but also significantly reduce operation costs.

- Hardware expenditures are immediately reduced by 50 to 80 percent.
- The cost for multiple desktop machines for each developer goes away.
- The need for additional data center or lab space is either delayed or eliminated.
- Power consumption and cooling costs go down.
- Cabling costs and complexity are decreased.
- Hardware maintenance and associated management costs from IT are minimized.

Virtualization can help reduce hardware expenditures in a number of ways. First and foremost, future purchases of server and desktop equipment can be minimized. Because virtualization allows a single machine to be sliced into a number of virtual machines, less hardware needs to be purchased going forward. For example, while a developer may currently have three or four desktop computers at his desk, this can easily be replaced with a single machine running multiple virtual machines. Likewise, a server in a test lab that is currently running one instance of an operating system can be further consolidated into multiple virtual machines. Depending on the horse power of the physical server and the requirements of the applications, it is not uncommon to get anywhere from a 4 or 12:1 server consolidation ratio. Server consolidation in the test lab alone could save a company millions of dollars on hardware expenditures.

Additionally, existing physical equipment found in a development and testing lab is more than likely being underutilized. In a production environment, server equipment is generally running at between 5 and 20 percent utilization. However, in a development and test environment, this is considered idle and wasted server capacity. Virtualization pushes a host server to between 60 and 80 percent utilization, which translates to a successful and properly used test server. The aggregate is that there is a significant reduction in dedicated hardware equipment and an increase in utilization.

Finally, server consolidation and an increase in server utilization bring about a natural reduction in the number of physical servers needed in a development and QA lab. Not only does it lower a company's hardware costs, but it also helps to reduce operational costs. The lab can now be scaled out in a smoother and more cost effective manner. With less physical equipment comes the additional cost savings of less floor space needed, reduced power consumption, less air conditioning required for cooling and even cabling costs and complexity are reduced. And on top of it all, maintenance and management costs are also minimized. A decline in server count yields a significant savings for the IT department. They no longer need to order and rack as much equipment and they do not need as many maintenance or support contracts, due to the reduction in equipment needs. This also allows IT staff to have more time to be responsive to other types of requests made by the development and testing organization.

Accelerating Development and Testing Cycle

While cutting costs is important, if it takes four years to develop and test a software product, then chances are that boat has already sailed. Software manufacturers are trying to create a product that meets a need in the marketplace. However, with the rate at which the industry changes, the window to meet that need gets more and more narrow. It is for this reason that software manufacturers are searching for solutions to accelerate the development and testing cycles of their products.

One such method is found at the core of virtualization: the ability to slice one physical computer into many individual computers. Without this feature, developers must keep multiple computers at their desk in order to properly platform test and unit test their code. Or even worse, if a developer wanted to test their code against two different operating systems and only had one physical machine, they would have to test one operating system all the way through, rebuild the machine, and then test it again all the way through against the second operating system. With virtualization, a developer can greatly increase the development cycle by utilizing multiple virtual images on the same physical computer. There is no longer a need to have a cluttered work area with various computer builds or spend the time reimaging, rebuilding, and retesting against the same machine.

To help accelerate the testing cycle, virtualization provides another key component commonly called the undoable disk. Undoable disks make testing in a clean and reproducible test environment almost trivial. In the past, a QA team would either have to put their faith in the uninstaller program to completely remove all remnants of the application and leave it in a clean state, provide multiple physical machines for parallel testing and spend a lot of valuable testing time rebuilding or reimaging machines. Now, a tester can easily step through a test scenario and at any stage simply power the virtual machine off, discard the changes made and resume from a previous state by leveraging the undoable disk feature that virtualization provides. If a new build or patch is available, the tester simply needs to update the virtual machine, power it off to commit the changes, and then power the virtual machine back on to resume testing. This is an enormous advantage over traditional physical computer solutions.

Part of accelerating the product cycle can include virtualization's ability to help with isolated sandbox testing. Virtualization can provide a "network in a box," in other words, it can provide virtual machines with isolated virtual network environments. Developers and testers can now create real-world networking environments without messy cables and without waiting for IT help and approval. Sandbox testing can now easily be accomplished without the fear of compromising the production network environment. Another advantage to using the virtual network, developers and testers can quickly obtain IP addresses without having to bother the network administrator. And best of all, no additional hardware is needed to quickly test between different operating system environments. Therefore, a virtual machine running Windows XP and Internet Explorer as its Web browser can communicate with a Linux virtual machine running an Apache Web server, all internally to the host server without ever going out onto the physical network.

And finally, most development and testing organizations are all too familiar with lab inefficiency and obscene server provisioning time. It happens all the time, a developer or tester needs a piece of hardware to test part of the product and they have to go through a time consuming process to justify the need. After contacting IT, there is a procurement process involved that includes equipment setup time. When all is said and done, it takes anywhere from five to eight weeks to justify, order and receive, build and rack the server, and then install the software. When done properly with virtualization, this process can take as little as five minutes. Imagine the acceleration of a production cycle when employees can gain control of needed resources within minutes rather than waiting weeks.

Improve Product Quality and Productivity

In addition to accelerating the development and testing cycle, virtualization can dramatically improve the quality of an application as well as greatly increase the productivity of both the development and test groups. With software applications, the name of the game is getting the application to market as quickly as possible. However, sacrificing product quality to be first is not the answer. The market is littered with applications that "made it first." But with disregard for product quality, those companies ostracized their customers and ended up losing the race anyway. Virtualization may not be the Holy Grail, but it does provide certain features to help boost product quality and productivity.

Virtual machine portability allows the development team and the test team to work together more efficiently. Now, when the QA group identifies a bug within the product, it can easily be reproduced by the developer. Instead of the developer trying to reproduce the bug on a dissimilar system setup, they can simply use the QA virtual machine exhibiting the problem. Once QA identifies the bug, the virtual machine can be powered down and the virtual disk files can be copied to the developer's machine. Once the virtual machine is powered back on, the developer can not only quickly see the bug reproduced but then also have a machine to validate any code corrections that are made to resolve the bug.

Most virtualization platforms provide an API for software developers to be able to automate routine events. Testing organizations can then leverage these APIs to help with automated testing. Using custom and third-party application testing tools, scripts can be run to control and manipulate virtual machines via APIs in ways that may are not possible on physical servers. This helps test teams to automate software testing against a high volume of machines and a large number of configurations.

Finally, virtualization provides a platform for software manufacturers to create a standardized development and testing environment. The difficult process of configuring hardware and installing software every time a new environment is needed can finally be eliminated. By performing the setup once for each environment type, a library of template images is created (see Figure 5.1). These

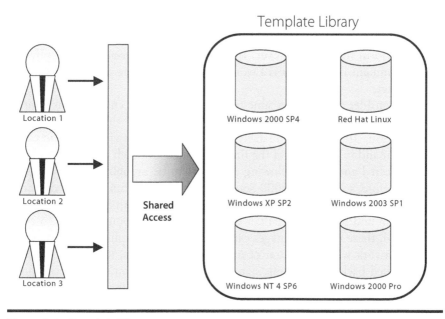

Figure 5.1 Template Library.

virtual machine template images ensure a consistent environment is created no matter who sets it up. It also greatly enhances the quality of a product and the productivity of an organization because developers can now spend more time writing and testing code and less time building and rebuilding environments. The consistency and speed at which these template environments are built also greatly enhance project quality in the QA department. Test groups can now provide more rigorous testing, testing more diverse environments in less time than before. Template images can be created with different operating systems, various browsers and multiple languages. As quickly as template images can be rolled out, the QA department can instantly create an entire test bank for regression testing. With more time spent testing the product and less time building the environments, the quality of the product becomes that much greater.

Take the following scenario as an example: A testing organization is tasked with testing a multi-tier Web application. The application requires a database back-end, either Microsoft SQL Server or Oracle Database. The Web application can be installed on Windows 2000 Server, Windows 2003 Server, or Red Hat Enterprise Linux. The Web application also requires either IIS or Apache be installed. And finally, the Web application officially supports either Microsoft IE 5.5, 6.0, or Mozilla Firefox 1.0. The testing matrix in this example can become daunting when using physical equipment. Imagine needing a physical server for every possible combination.

At first, it may not seem to be that cumbersome. However, when you start adding up the number of service packs and hot fixes alone for each operating system, database, and browser, the list grows exponentially. Then, when an individual tester runs through one test iteration and either hits a road block or makes it through to the end, what happens next? They need to clean off the system by uninstalling, reimaging, or rebuilding the server so they can perform the next test or perform the same test over. The time it takes between tests in a physical lab environment is so long, it is a wonder that any software product ever makes it to market.

Now consider running the same tests against a virtual environment leveraging a library of template images and the toolset found within the virtualization platform. This same test matrix can be accomplished with a fraction of the equipment and in a fraction of the time. A template of each environment build can be created and stored, allowing templates to be brought on and offline at will. Therefore, a Windows 2000 Server virtual machine can be created, a copy of the virtual hard disk file can be saved, then updated with Service Pack 1, and saved again and so on, rather than starting from a barebones state each time. In the end, these template images can be rolled out and plugged together in a virtual network within a matter of minutes. If a test fails, the virtual machine can be rolled back to a previous state and the test can continue just as soon as the machine is powered back on. With this scenario, months of test time can be saved and the product can be released to market much more quickly and with a higher degree of quality.

While virtualization does solve many of the problems facing software development and testing organizations, it does not fit well when performing performance testing or testing software that interacts with proprietary hardware devices. With virtualization, the resources that are being consumed on the physical machine make true performance testing of an application next to impossible. The virtual machine is sharing its hardware resources with other virtual machines running, the host operating system as well as the virtualization application itself. While the resources are being mapped out and distributed to the virtual machines, there is a performance hit being taken, which will cause an inaccurate view for performance testing of an application. It is therefore suggested that for this type of testing, a dedicated physical server or group of physical servers be used. The only exception to this rule, being if the application is planned to be run inside of a virtual machine as the production environment.

When the software being tested must interact with nonstandard hardware devices, such as PCI cards, it must be tested on physical hardware. At the present time, virtualization platforms are limited in the way physical hardware of the host server is mapped as virtual hardware to virtual machines. The available virtualization platforms are currently closed systems in regards to third-party virtual hardware devices. This limitation could be overcome in the future if the manufacturers of the virtualization platforms decide to open their systems to allow third-party virtual hardware devices. This would allow third parties to write their own virtual hardware to map proprietary hardware devices into a virtual machine. Some hardware devices may be mapped into a virtual machine through the use of parallel, serial, or USB ports, such as security dongles or keys.

Technical Support and Help Desk

There is a buzz today that is focused on a company's call center or technical support department. Companies are making the claim that they are committed to customer satisfaction and customer service; however, they are faced with increased customer expectations while at the same time faced with a decrease in annual budget. This dilemma usually causes confusion and frustration for those people answering the customer's calls, namely the support team. By giving the support team the proper tools to do their job, their frustration level goes down and their productivity goes up, this supports better customer service and a happier support team.

The current trend for most company's support shops is cost reduction, increased efficiencies and effectiveness, and making the most of their current investments. To that end, server virtualization is going to become a huge key factor for running a highly successful technical support shop. By utilizing server virtualization, a technical support team can reduce the amount of time spent per call, narrow down the complex problems faster to improve response time, and decrease the overall support costs to the company. By adding server virtualization to the list of tools available to supporting customer problems, the complex problems that may have taken days or weeks to identify and resolve may now be able to be answered within a fraction of the time. In addition to saving response time, server virtualization can also help with budget problems.

From a budget standpoint, it is nearly impossible for a technical support group to have enough equipment to match every possible problem/situational matrix. This matrix can be broken down into various types of hardware and software configurations. On the hardware matrix, does the computer have SCSI or IDE drives? Does the computer have a CD-ROM or multiple CD-ROM drives? On the software matrix, what operating system is running on the computer? What service packs or hot fixes are currently installed? What version of the application is running? What other applications are running on the computer? In order to reduce hardware and lab maintenance costs, companies currently combat this problem in a number of ways. For example, a company may provide its support staff with multiple machines, each allowing them to multi boot to various operating systems. Unfortunately, this takes time in both the initial setup and the rebooting involved during calls. It also does not come close to fulfilling the potentially large matrix involved. It is also possible that the hardware available is not suitable for part of the matrix. Perhaps the hardware of the computer does not allow Microsoft Windows NT or Red Hat Linux to install. Others may choose to have an even smaller subset of computer equipment available, but have a library of multiple images available, such as Symantec Ghost images. Again, both initial setup and imaging can take a very long time. Once a support call comes into the call center and the technical support specialist determines the caller's setup, it may take hours to reconfigure a machine with the proper image and software before troubleshooting can even begin. Finally, another choice some shops are forced to take is by working through the problem by memory and experience. The technical support specialist may try to walk the caller through different application or operating system screens purely by memory, also known as flying by the seat of your pants. Server virtualization solves many of these problems.

Obviously, if a company could staff an on-site technical support specialist at each customer's location, the efficiency and effectiveness of technical support would be through the roof, unfortunately, so would the cost. By utilizing server virtualization, a technical support group can also increase their efficiency and effectiveness, as well as keep the costs down. To combat the overwhelming matrix, server virtualization can minimize the amount of computer hardware and lab resources needed to cover most of the possible hardware and software combinations. Within a virtual machine, it is relatively easy to quickly modify certain hardware configurations. A technical support specialist could quickly change the amount of ram, the disk drive type, the CD-ROM configuration, or even whether or not the virtual machine has a serial port. On the software configuration side of the matrix, a call center can house a library of configurations on a local file server. These software configurations can then be used to quickly replicate a caller's computing environment. For example, when a call comes in, the technical support specialist can find out what hardware configuration is being used, what operating system is running, what service pack, patch level, or build version is being used, what application version is installed, etc. A virtual machine image with a matching configuration can then be copied over to the host server and powered on, or if the image already exists on the host server, it can be started from a saved state. This would allow the technical support specialist to start troubleshooting and diagnosing the problem for the caller within minutes of answering the phone. All of this could be accomplished with just one physical server per technical support specialist or one physical server shared across a team.

It is also possible for a call center to get a near replica of a customer's server for troubleshooting purposes. As server virtualization makes its way across the IT industry, it will become more and more commonplace for customers to install their applications within a virtual machine. If the machine in question is a virtual machine, the caller can either shutdown the machine in question or use a backup copy of that machine's disk file and send a copy to the call center for troubleshooting. If the machine cannot be down for a long period of time, it can be suspended or put into a saved state. Once in this state, it can be quickly copied and resumed or restored. If the customer is not using virtualization, one of many methods of physical to virtual (P2V) conversions can be used to make a virtual machine from the problem physical server. This is undoubtedly one of the better ways to troubleshoot a customer's machine without having to be there locally and also having the ability to make changes without affecting a production machine.

Virtualization also allows the technical support specialist to always start with a clean operating system environment. It is important to know when troubleshooting a problem that the starting point is clean, in good working order, and has not been touched by anyone else inside or outside of the team. As stated briefly in chapter 3, these clean starting points can be used over and over again by using a virtualization process known as undo disks. If during the troubleshooting process a machine crashes or blue screens, the technical support specialist can simply discard the changes made during troubleshooting and resume troubleshooting from the original clean starting point within minutes. The difference between discarding the changes in a virtual machine and reinstalling or reimaging a physical server could be the difference between helping the customer and helping the customer choose a new vendor.

In addition to configuration changes, server virtualization will also help a call center with easy network isolation during troubleshooting. This is important for a number of reasons. First and foremost, network security. While troubleshooting a problem, it is highly reasonable to assume that network connectivity will be needed. Think for a moment, if the server in question does not have any anti-virus software or if the patch level is not up to date, what would this do to the call center's network? Within minutes of the machine being powered on, the entire network could become compromised. Once again, by using virtualization and its virtual network cards and virtual network, the machine can be safely powered on and isolated from the production network and still maintain network connectivity between multiple virtual machine environments or the outside world. If the virtual machine crashes or causes a problem, only the virtual machine and those virtual machines connected to it in the isolated network are affected. The physical host server and the other virtual machines on that host server are spared, as is the production network.

Finally, virtualization creates another tool for the technical support specialist. While troubleshooting a product for a customer, if the technical support specialist discovers the problem is a bug within the company's software, they would usually just log the bug within some bug tracking software for the development team or the QA team. Now, along with the text description of the bug, the technical support specialist can attach a copy of the customer's virtual machine that exhibits the defect. This helps the development group to quickly see the defect and create a hot fix or a patch to resolve the problem. Again, the time to resolve the problem for the customer is greatly diminished.

Software Training and E-Learning Systems

As applications and training environments become more complicated, it is becoming commonplace for instructors to spend more of their time setting up the classroom rather than actually teaching the course. The alternative is forcing the instructor to come in on weekends to setup, deploy, and properly test the classroom environment, or to hire a separate position to fill this gap. By making use of server virtualization, a training organization will learn to configure and deploy a variety of training scenarios quickly and efficiently, in a repeatable fashion. Gone are the days of simple simulation; today, students require hands-on learning, and instructors will learn how to provide it through server virtualization and classroom cloning.

Whether a corporate training center, university, technical vocational institution, or an in-house training group, server virtualization can be used as a tool to help make the training more efficient and effective, easier on the instructor as well as more profitable for the organization. Within all of these various software training organizations, the same types of problems are being faced and they are eating away at company resources. Trainers are confronted with the following problems on a regular basis and each can be solved through the use of server virtualization:

- Updating labs and course scenarios
- Dealing with variations in student machines inside of single classrooms
- Installing and reinstalling operating systems and software applications
- Recreating machines with imaging software
- Reconfiguring hardware
- Modifying networking layout
- Resetting a problem machine back to a specific state
- Troubleshooting software and hardware problems

Benefits of Virtualization

Server virtualization is not the answer for all problems currently facing training organizations; however, it does provide a solution path for most of the common problems that software trainers battle daily. The benefits that server virtualization brings to the software training and E-learning space are enormous, both in time and cost savings.

Software training organizations are constantly looking for ways to improve the student experience in their classrooms and to increase the quality of instruction by their staff. Through server virtualization, students can have hands-on experience and the freedom to explore both the system and the software without fear of crashing the operating system or corrupting the application. With this freedom, students are allowed to learn from their mistakes without reprisal, thereby learning from doing, rather than just following along a step by step manual. If a student accidentally crashes the server, the instructor can simply roll the system back to a previous state, rather than interrupting the class schedule. This freedom is also extended into the instructor's ability to easily teach across multiple operating systems. If an application can be installed across multiple operating systems, the instructor and students can switch from one operating system to another quickly and easily to see how the same application operates in a different environment. Prior to virtualization, this could only be accomplished quickly by using multiple computers per student or by dual booting the machines.

A major expense to a training organization is the delivery cost and the time to rebuild a classroom environment. Instructors can now quickly restore student workstations to a clean state for the next class by using virtualization's undoable disks. Rather than manually rebuilding or reimaging the machine, an instructor can simply choose to discard the changes to the machine made by the student during the course of the class. Instead of taking possibly an hour or two to restore the entire classroom of machines, it would now take seconds. Another method of reducing delivery costs is by having the organization create a library of standardized classroom images on a file server, each of which can be quickly rolled out to multiple machines in the class. Complex courseware can be easily setup in a fraction of the time. The instructor merely copies the necessary classroom images from the file server to the host machines, and then registers those virtual machines within the virtualization software. Therefore, the setup time for a complex multi-server course is greatly diminished and the instructor can focus on teaching rather than deploying.

In addition to reducing the delivery time, the hardware investment required to teach all of the various software training courses is also greatly reduced. For instance, in the previous example, a complex course may require multiple computers per student to properly learn an application. Rather than having to purchase more than one high-end desktop machine with all of the bells and whistles per student, a single server with virtualization could accommodate the entire environment and handle more than one student. This allows training organizations to maximize the use of their existing hardware.

Another benefit is the ability to reduce the level of difficulty required in setting up the classroom. As stated above, some courses are complex in nature due to the shear volume of machines needed in an environment for each student. For example, a course may require an environment to have an application server, a database server, and a mail server. By using a library of images as previously stated, the course can be setup very quickly and easily. Using server virtualization, there is very little difference between setting up a single server course or a complex multi-server course. Another level of complexity is due to the networking of the machines in the classroom. The need for IT to help with router and switch configuration has also been reduced. Once the initial physical network is created, the instructor can easily create virtual networks and modify network connectivity through the virtualization software. There is no need for an instructor or an IT worker to modify the switch or pull cables.

As stated earlier in this chapter, virtualization can greatly diminish the amount of time that the software delivery cycle takes. By speeding up development and increasing the reliability of the QA process, the gap between software delivery cycle and training is greatly diminished. Training can begin almost immediately after the release of a new or upgraded software application.

Finally, virtualization helps increase revenue and profitability for the software training organization. With faster setup times and less setup delays, training centers can offer and schedule more classes. Also, by making better use of their hardware and facilities, more students can be added per class. As an example, Figure 5.2 explains how virtualization can affect a training organization's profitability.

The benefits of server virtualization to a training organization are quite staggering, however the student equally benefits. By allowing the student to have a hands-on experience and freely experiment with the system, the reinforcement is that much greater. Companies have begun to shy away from hands on training

Training Scenario	Setup Time per Class (Hours)	Number of Classes per Week	Setup Time per Week	Setup Time per Year (assumes 50 weeks)
Long	8	1	8	400
Mid	2	4	8	400
Short	0.25	8	2	100
		Total Time Spent per Year in Hours		900
		Estimated Instructor Cost per Hour		$15
		Cost to Training Center for Yearly Setup Time		**$13,500**

Training Scenario	Setup Time per Year (assumes 50 weeks)	Number of Classes Lost in Setup Time per Year	Number of Students in a Class	Total Students Lost per Year
Long	400	10	10	100
Mid	400	40	14	560
Short	100	20	18	360

Training Scenario	Total Students Lost per Year	Charge per Student	Revenue Lost
Long	100	$1,700	$170,000
Mid	560	$700	$392,000
Short	360	$200	$72,000
	Cost to Training Center of Lost Student/Class Revenue		**$634,000**

Total Savings	$647,500

Key

Scenarios	Length
Long	1 Week
Mid	2 Days
Short	1/2 Day

Definitions

Setup Time	The time spent configuring an environment for a class
Lost Student/Class	The lost opportunity due to setup time
Total Savings	The gross savings if virtualization were implemented to solve the setup issues.

Figure 5.2 Virtualization Creates ROI for Training.

due to the continuing rise of its cost; however, by utilizing server virtualization, they can now efficiently and cost-effectively offer this type of training solution to everyone.

Summary

Whether the organization is responsible for software development and QA, technical support or training, server virtualization can provide the solution to many of the problems that are currently being faced. When planned properly, server virtualization can help to reduce costs, increase efficiency and effectiveness, and make the most of a company's current investments. These things are easily accomplished with just a few key features found within server virtualization. Undo disks are a quick and easy way to roll a system back to a previous state within seconds allowing the end-user to always start over with a fresh system. Through the use of disk image cloning, entire networks can be created within a very short period of time, with very little hands-on interaction needed. By virtualizing the hardware and the hard drive, virtual machines are encapsulated and therefore portable, easily being moved from one type of physical server to another. And finally, server equipment can now be fully utilized and house multiple machines of various operating systems for more than one individual. In the future, other interesting ways of using server virtualization will continue to drive down costs and increase productivity.

Chapter 6

Planning for Deployment

It is essential to have a well-developed deployment plan in place to success-fully build a production system using server virtualization technology. Before a server virtualization project should be implemented, a solid understanding of the project is required. This understanding is realized by learning the issues and considerations specific to server virtualization, defining the use case, obtaining the specific requirements, and planning the deployment. By taking the time to properly plan and document the project, the implementation will have a much higher degree of success and less risk. This chapter covers many server virtual-ization considerations that affect the design and implementation of new server virtualization systems. It is important to be aware of the many issues regarding hardware compatibility, software licensing, capacity, scalability, and many other factors that affect decisions about hardware, software, and outside services.

Selecting a Server Virtualization Platform

When deciding upon which server virtualization platform to use for a specific project or will be deployed in the data center, it is important to understand the many factors that may influence the decision. Not all server virtualization plat-forms are created equal. Like most operating systems or software, it is generally a good idea to evaluate the different server virtualization platforms in house before making a decision. Reading reviews and talking with those experienced with one or more server virtualization platforms may be one of the most common start-ing points in the decision making process. But testing the software in house is one of the best, more objective methods. This discussion will focus on the three major server virtualization platforms available today: Microsoft Virtual Server (MSVS), VMware GSX Server, and VMware ESX Server.

Below is a list of considerations to keep in mind when evaluating server virtualization platforms.

- **Hardware Compatibility**
  When considering server virtualization, it is important to understand that not all x86 server virtualization platforms will work with all x86 server hardware. Generally, MSVS and GSX Server will work with nearly any hardware that is supported by the host server's operating system, which can be Windows for MSVS and GSX Server or Linux for GSX Server. ESX Server does not have a host operating system as it has its own microkernel and is installed directly on the server hardware. In order for ESX Server to work on a particular set of server hardware, it must have ESX Server drivers available for each piece of hardware, which is much more limited than the available hardware device drivers available to Linux and Windows. In particular, ESX Server does not support ATA hard disk drives and only supports a limited set of SCSI, RAID, and SAN host adapters. It is important to know if existing hardware will work with the various server virtualization platforms and if upgrades or additional components can be added to make noncompliant existing hardware useful. If existing hardware cannot be used, it is important to ensure that all components of new servers are compatible with the chosen platform.

- **Host Operating System Support**
  When MSVS or GSX Server is being considered, it is important to know exactly what host operating system will be used to support the server virtualization platform. It is not just a simple matter of choosing Linux or Windows, but of knowing which version, edition, and revisions may be required to be successful. When considering GSX Server for Linux, it is important to know which Linux distributions and kernel versions are compatible for use as a host operating system.

  ESX Server eliminates the need to select and install a host operating system because it supplies its own microkernel that is installed directly on the host server hardware. Even though at first glance it appears that ESX Server is installed on top of a Linux operating system, it is not. This confusion usually results from the fact that ESX Server provides a facility known as the Service Console to which users may connect using command-line interface clients such as telnet or ssh in order to perform advanced administrative tasks. The ESX Server Service Console is actually a special virtual machine running a Linux operating system that has special hooks into the ESX Server operating environment.

- **Guest Operating System Support**
  Although most server virtualization platforms can run most 32-bit, IA-32 (or x86) and some 64-bit, x64 operating systems in a virtual machine, the server virtualization platform vendors do not support every possible guest

operating system. In some cases, such as MSVS, only a subset of the platform vendor's Windows operating system is officially supported. It is very prudent to not use unsupported configurations in a production environment to eliminate risk, even when the given configuration may work most of the time. Before a server virtualization platform decision can be made, it should be evaluated from the standpoint of supported guest operating systems. This topic is discussed in more detail later in the chapter.

■ **Application Support**
Depending on the use case of the server virtualization system being deployed, the application support topic may or may not be a large issue. When virtual machines are planned on being used in a production environment, it is wise to find out if the intended production applications will be supported for production use by the server virtualization platform vendor or the vendor of the application. Some server virtualization platform vendors may not fully support certain enterprise-class applications hosted with their server virtualization platform in a production environment. It is very important to try to reduce the amount of risk and to know exactly what support options are available when the need arises, especially for production systems. This topic is discussed in more detail later in the chapter.

■ **Capacity**
Server virtualization platforms also differ in the capacities they support. Capacity metrics including the number of supported processors, the minimum and maximum amount of memory, the maximum size of virtual hard disks, and the maximum number of supported virtual machines will affect the overall VM density of the system.

■ **Scalability**
Server virtualization systems are able to scale out very well. By adding more host servers, the overall virtual machine capacity is increased. But in terms of cost savings, it may be beneficial to scale each host server up rather than out. Will adding more processors and memory to an existing host server increase the number of supported virtual machines? Does the server virtualization platform (along with its host operating system, if applicable) and host server hardware allow more physical resources to be added at a later date? If so, what will the availability of the needed components be when needed? Asking these questions will help to properly assess sizing and scalability requirements.

■ **Features**
The various features that are supported by the different server virtualization platforms can also affect the decision making process. At the current time, MSVS does not support Intel's HyperThreading feature and only supports virtual machines with a single processor while ESX Server supports both processors with HyperThreading enabled as well as the optional Virtual

SMP™ add-on component that allows virtual machines to have two virtual processors. Although HyperThreading is not supported in MSVS, MSVS will run with HyperThreading enabled, but undesirable side effects and performance issues may occur. HyperThreading can also adversely affect GSX Server as well; therefore it is recommended that HyperThreading be disabled for GSX Server host servers. ESX Server supports only fixed, virtual SCSI hard disks, while MSVS and GSX Server support both fixed and dynamically expanding virtual hard disks using either IDE or SCSI interfaces. ESX Server also supports the over-commitment of memory as well as memory consolidation. Both of these features can greatly increase the amount of active virtual machines on each host server (also referred to as the VM density).

- **Stability**
  The stability and robustness of the server virtualization platform can also play a large role in the decision making process, especially for mission critical production systems. The level of maturity in each server virtualization platform should be considered as well as the release history and the product's overall longevity. These factors may give some insight to each platform's level of stability.

- **Maintenance and Uptime**
  Another factor to consider is how the platform is maintained in regard to product updates such as security patches and product fixes. It is not uncommon for server virtualization platforms hosted on top of an existing operating system such as MSVS and GSX Server to require critical updates on a regular basis. If the updates to the virtualization platform or to the host operating system require a reboot, then downtime must be factored for all virtual machines that reside upon that host server. Most updates on Linux host operating systems or ESX Server do not require a reboot for updates to be installed and applied. This factor is usually critically important to production systems.

- **Performance**
  The performance of the server virtualization platforms is a very difficult metric to use to make a decision upon. Published reviews and benchmarks may be biased or may not even apply to the specific use case of the solution planning to be implemented. When performance is a key factor in the decision making process, it is usually best to create a test environment in which to compare and contrast the various server virtualization platforms relative to the use case. Although this is much more expensive in terms of costs and time, it may be the only method of obtaining reliable information worthy of using to make a decision.

- **Ease of Use**
  Another aspect to be aware of when comparing server virtualization platforms is the ease of use. Some platforms are very easy to learn and use, typi-

cally MSVS and GSX Server because they are hosted on an already familiar host operating system such as Windows or Linux. That is not to say that ESX Server is not easy to learn and use, but many advanced features of ESX Server, such as backing up virtual machines, are managed through its Linux-based Service Console. This requires command-line interface Linux knowledge and skills that may not be present in an all Windows environment or organization. It is practical to know what skill sets are currently available and how they match up to the server virtualization platforms being considered. Sometimes it is beneficial to bring in experienced virtualization consultants to help design and deploy an organization's first server virtualization project, shifting some of the liability away from the organization onto the consultants, while still attempting to administer the solution using internal skills for the long term.

- **Manageability**
  The available methods of configuring and managing the server virtualization hosts should also be taken into consideration when considering virtualization platforms. GSX Server and MSVS require a host operating system, such as Linux or Windows. That host operating system can be used to run the management tools provided by the virtualization platform to manage itself. This can easily be taken for granted as it is not the case when considering ESX Server. ESX Server requires another computer with TCP/IP connectivity to the ESX Server equipped with a Web browser and either a telnet or ssh client terminal in order to configure and manage the host. Additionally, the native virtual machine remote control software available with ESX Server, VMRC, must also be installed on a remote computer. It is essential that the administrators of an ESX Server system have a workstation with proper connectivity to the ESX Server host servers in addition to the servers themselves. The level of server virtualization platform support of third-party management tools, such as backup and monitoring applications, being considered can also play a role in which platform will be chosen.

- **Support**
  The levels of available support from the server virtualization platform vendor may also be considered when comparing virtualization platforms. Terms of support agreements vary and some vendors may actually offer a limited amount of support and offer extended support facilities at an extra cost. Knowing what levels of support are available and understanding the terms of that support is especially important when the use case is for a production environment.

- **Training**
  The availability of quality training is another consideration. If an organization does not possess the proper skill sets to deploy or manage a server virtualization system, it may need to have its employees trained. The

availability, quality, and costs involved in obtaining proper training on the various server virtualization platforms could have a significant impact on the overall decision. The source of the training is also an important consideration, especially when also considering the use case of the overall solution. For some use cases, vendor training may be perfectly adequate, but for some use cases, such as on-demand computing and high availability, more specialized expertise may be required. Additionally, bringing in outside consultants to help design and implement the solution will boost the success rate of the project while reducing some the risk. Combining the consultant's work with hands-on training of the organization's staff may prove to be a more valuable approach when compared to traditional training efforts.

- **Cost**
  Finally, most decisions almost always come down to the bottom line, the cost. The available server virtualization platforms differ greatly in cost. Some such as MSVS and GSX Server also incur the cost for an additional operating system license used by the host server. The use case of the server virtualization platform can also affect costs. Companies that host virtual machines for their clients may have different licensing terms than companies using server virtualization for server consolidation and disaster recovery purposes. It may also be necessary to factor in the cost of upgrades to the server virtualization platform and to obtain the history of major version releases in order to gauge how often an upgrade may be necessary and whether upgrades will incur additional costs. Server virtualization can also cause cost increases for other software application licenses, such as management agents and clients presently used throughout an existing data center. The following list contains some common types of software for which additional licenses may need to be purchased for host servers and virtual machines:
  a. Antivirus Clients
  b. Backup Agents
  c. Management Agents (such as SMS)
  d. Monitoring Agents (such as MOM, NetIQ, Tivoli)

This covers the most common factors to be considered when choosing a server virtualization platform. However, depending on the use case and the environment in which the server virtualization platform will be used, other factors may apply.

Hardware

Selecting the hardware necessary for a server virtualization deployment may seem easy at first. But, after digging into the details, it soon becomes evident that there are many factors at work.

The difficulty lies in balancing the cost, capabilities, and compatibility, referred to as the 3 C's. Cost and required capabilities should be referenced in the Use Case and Requirements documents. Compatibility is often a derivative of the selected server virtualization platform. Before attempting to select the server hardware, it is important to know exactly what server virtualization platform will be used and what host operating system will be used, if applicable. It becomes easy to take the server architecture into the wrong direction by losing focus on any one of the 3 C's.

For example, host servers with a single processor, 1GB of memory, and 100GB of hard disk storage space could be purchased for less then US$5,000.00. This solution would not be very useful as it could probably support no more than two or three virtual machines, although it is very inexpensive. On the other hand, host servers with sixteen processors, 64GB of memory, and 1TB of hard disk storage may support forty or more virtual machines at a cost of more than US$500,000.

For the reasons illustrated above, it makes sense to try and balance out cost versus capability needs in regards to server hardware. In most scenarios, two-way (dual processors) or four-way (quad processors) servers with at least 4GB of memory will probably be good choices from both cost and performance. This may change dramatically in the near future due to processor advancements such as multi-core processors and hardware-level virtualization support built into the processor.

Intel and AMD have plans to release dual-core and multi-core processors that have more than one processor die on a single wafer, or chip. It is estimated that in dual-core processors, performance will be increased over traditional single core processors by an additional 80 percent. Later mutli-core designs with four or more cores per chip will likely see larger performance increases, especially as more software becomes optimized for these highly-parallel processing designs. Aside from multi-core processors, Intel's VT (once code-named Vanderpool) and AMD's code-named Pacifica technologies will provide additional hardware-level support for virtualization technologies into the processor. Although availability of the specifications of these technologies is limited at this time, it is expected that future processors will be virtualization aware, offloading some of the work that is done completely in software today, while at the same time making virtualization easier to implement on these processors, bringing them closer to the Popek and Goldberg virtualization requirements. These technologies will offer enhanced virtualization support that should not only enhance performance in virtualized systems, but should offer more robust architectures that could ultimately blur the line between computing on physical hardware versus virtual machines.

It is equally important to select server hardware that is compatible with the selected server virtualization platform and host operating system. This is usually less of an issue when the host operating system is Microsoft Windows because of the large availability of hardware drivers for the Windows operating system. When considering GSX Server for Linux or ESX Server, careful attention must be exercised to ensure that all hardware components are compatible and device drivers are available for the chosen platform. This includes chipset drivers, disk controller drivers, network adapters, SAN host bus adapters, and so forth. When considering ESX Server, it is wise to fully read the VMware ESX Server Installation Guide before selecting server hardware and if a SAN will be used in conjunction with server virtualization, the VMware ESX Server SAN Configuration Guide should also be consulted. Hardware device drivers for VMware ESX Server are only available from VMware, not from the hardware manufacturers.

Common pitfalls to be aware of are the hardware limitations of the host operating system. For example, if it is planned to use MSVS hosted on top of Microsoft Windows Server 2003 Standard Edition, it is useless to purchase server hardware with more than four processors or more than 8GB of memory because that version and edition of the Windows operating system does not support more than four processors and 8GB of memory. If 16GB of memory were needed in the previous example, Microsoft Windows Server 2003 Enterprise Edition is the better choice as it supports up to eight processors and up to 32GB of memory. It is easy to focus solely on the features and capacities of the server virtualization platform and forget to check the available capacities of the host operating system.

When selecting server hardware components for server virtualization hosts, it is important to know that a minimum of two network adapters is usually required. One network adapter is bound to the host server operating system and the other is bound to one or more virtual machines. Virtual machines can share a single network adapter, but it is generally a bad idea to share the network adapter used by the host server with the virtual machines. Depending on the speed of the network adapters selected and the number of virtual machines that will be placed on a single host, it may be necessary to have more than one network card reserved for virtual machines. If any one virtual machine has any network bandwidth-intensive applications installed, it may be necessary to reserve one network adapter just for that virtual machine. It is not uncommon for host servers to have three or more network adapter cards installed, even two or three dual or quad port Ethernet server adapters. When using Ethernet server adapters with more than one port, each port usually acts as a separate network adapter and therefore the host can use one port while the other ports may be used for virtual machines. Another network adapter consideration is using load-balancing, fault-tolerant network adapters and binding more than one network adapter or port together in a team to increase bandwidth and fault-tolerance. In this case, a minimum of two ports would be required for each teamed network adapter. It is possible to use teamed network adapters for the host or the virtual machines. Teamed network adapters require explicit support from both the physical network adapter cards being used and the drivers installed into the host operating system.

Host Server Usage

It is highly recommended that the role of host servers in a server virtualization solution be completely dedicated to server virtualization. This is implicitly chosen for ESX Server deployments, but it may not be obvious to new users of MSVS or GSX Server. It may be tempting to try to purpose a Windows or Linux-based virtualization host server as a dual or multi-role server, handling file sharing, print serving, a Web application, or a database server alongside server virtualization. Doing this will ultimately cause more server resources to be consumed by the host server operating systems and its applications, which will severely limit the number of active virtual machines as well as decrease their performance. Virtualization host servers should be dedicated to the role of hosting virtual machines. It may be advantageous to place the necessary services on a server running in a virtual machine on the host server, depending on the application or services resource or performance needs. Host servers should have their configuration minimally optimized by removing unneeded software packages and operating system components, disabling unneeded services, and by turning off unneeded operating system features, including enhanced graphical display features.

Software Licenses

Understanding the pitfalls of software licensing on your server virtualization deployment is very important and can be one of the most complex aspects of a deployment. The rise of mainstream virtualization technology, such as x86 server virtualization, is causing confusion today regarding operating system and software licensing. Virtualization technology is causing a major paradigm shift in software licensing schemes, for better or worse. Most software vendors have not yet attempted to adjust their licensing schemes to account for their software running inside of virtual machines. Some vendors are not even aware of how server virtualization might impact their current licensing schemes, not accounting for the architectural and philosophical changes that are brought about by virtualization technology.

Because of this lack of visibility into virtualization, there are some interpretations that must be made in order to stay in compliance with software licenses. It is highly recommended to contact the software company and to request an exception or written interpretation as to how their licensing scheme is affected or not affected by the fact that their software will be running inside virtual machines. However, this may not always be practical. When it is not practical, there are some simple things that can be done to attempt to stay in compliance in most situations.

Below is a list of several common licensing scenarios and how to adapt them to virtualization.

- **Instance-based licensing**
  Instance-based licensing is the most common type of software licensing scheme. Each time the software is installed, it requires a license. The consumer will purchase a fixed number of licenses (or seats) and the software may legally be installed on the same number of computers, whether physical or virtual. This is one of the easiest to manage licensing schemes and it works the same way on virtual machines as it does with physical computers. These licenses are usually worded in such a way that little to no interpretation is necessary when considering virtualization.
- **Computer-based licensing**
  Computer-based licensing allows software to be installed more than once on a single computer, possibly even limitless instances, but only requires one license per computer. In some cases, it may be interpreted that some computer-based licensing schemes may allow the software to be installed an unlimited amount of times within multiple virtual machines on a given host and only have to acquire one license per host server. Care must be taken, and it is highly advisable to either contact the manufacturer for clarification or to treat each virtual machine as a separate computer in regards to the terms of the license to ensure that licensing compliance is properly met.
- **Processor-based licensing**
  Processor-based licensing schemes incur a cost for each processor or a different cost based upon the number of processors installed in the computer. Depending upon the exact verbiage of the license agreement, the license may only apply to the number of physical processors installed in the computer or only to the number of processors available to the virtual machine. The licensing costs could also apply once per physical server or virtual server depending on how the license is written. This scenario is one of the most confusing of all licensing schemes as it could work in favor of the vendor or the consumer depending on the interpretation of the license. For example, a license may be written such that the software may be installed as many times as needed on the same computer and the consumer must pay an amount based upon the number of processors installed in the computer. If this license were applied to a host server that has two processors and hosts twelve uniprocessor virtual machines, it may be interpreted by the consumer that it is legal to install the software into all twelve virtual machines and only pay once for the two processors installed in the

host server. However, this may have not been the intention of the software vendor. The software vendor may argue that the consumer must pay for twelve single processor licenses instead of one two-processor license. In another similar situation, it may have been perfectly legal to pay for a single two-processor license and install the software on as many virtual machines as can be hosted upon that host server. But in some cases, even though it is legal and approved by the vendor, it may not be possible depending upon the software vendor's licensing protection system, such as a Web-based activation system that only allows the software to be activated one time or a physical dongle device that acts as a key to unlock the software and may prevent the software from being installed in a virtual machine all together. In this situation, the only recourse is to contact the software vendor for help in resolving the licensing issue. The recommended and easiest method to use to stay in compliance with processor-based licensing is to purchase a processor license for each virtual processor used by each virtual machine Although this may seem expensive or aggressive in terms of licensing, it will almost always guarantee licensing compliance with the software vendor.

- **Fixed user-based licensing**
  Some software is licensed by an amount of fixed or named users that will access the software. In this licensing scheme, one license is purchased for each exact user of the software, regardless of whether they are all using the software at the same time or not. This licensing scheme works the same way in virtual machines as it does on physical computers. For example, consider a scenario having five virtual machines with the software installed and each virtual machine is licensed for five specific user accounts. Even if all five user accounts represent the same five users across all virtual machines, a total of twenty-five licenses are required.

- **Concurrent user-based licensing**
  In the concurrent user-based licensing scheme, software licenses are required for the total number of simultaneous users connecting to or using the software. This licensing scheme is much more flexible than the fixed user-based licensing scheme. Concurrent user-based licensing works the same way in virtualization as it does on physical computers. One aspect of this type of licensing that tends to vary among software vendors, is how the license controls the number of installed instances. Some software vendors may allow the software to be installed only once and may also require a separate instance-based license in addition to user licenses while other vendors may allow the software to be installed many times as long as the total concurrent user limit is not exceeded. For example, a server operating system may require an instance license to be installed once, either on a physical computer or a virtual

machine. It may then also require a license for each user that connects to the server in order to consume its services. If it is decided that this server is mission critical and must be clustered to increase its availability, an additional instance license would be required to install the server operating system on another computer, whether physical or virtual. In another example, a Web-based application is installed on a corporate intranet. The software is licensed for 20 concurrent users. No license was needed to install the software, but no more than 20 users will be allowed to connect to and use the application at any given point in time. If the company decides that the application was mission critical and wants to put the application in a load-balanced cluster to increase the application's availability, no additional licenses are required for the additional installation of the application. In the third and final example of concurrent user-based licensing, a company may have purchased 100 concurrent user licenses for a useful text editor. The license allows the software to be installed many times without any additional licenses. Many people in the company use the text editor, but only for short, specific tasks. Some users may not use it every day. It is also decided that this tool should be placed on every server in order to facilitate easier server administration. There are 20 physical servers and 40 virtual servers. The software may be installed more than 100 times, but as long as no more than 100 copies are being used concurrently, the company is in compliance.

- **Device connection-based licensing**
  In device connection-based licensing schemes, a license is required for every device that connects to the software. This is usually found in enterprise server applications. The term device usually refers to any user, computer, or other device or account that connects to the software. The verbiage on most device connection-based licenses will almost always be either vague enough or complete enough to include virtual machines or virtual devices. Device connection license schemes should be treated the same way under virtualization as is would be on physical computers, whether virtual machines act in the client or server role in relation to the software.

The list above is a sample of the most common licensing schemes. It does not attempt to cover every scheme in existence because there are simply too many variations and they often change frequently. It is a good idea to read and understand the licensing scheme for each piece of software that will be installed into virtual machines. It is also advisable to audit the software licenses on a quarterly or semi-annually basis to check for changes in the licensing schemes. As virtualization technologies continue to develop and grow, many software vendors will become aware of the issues around licensing and virtualization and will adjust accordingly. A good rule of thumb to remember is that treating virtual machines as equals to physical computers in regards to software licensing usually avoids any issues.

Supported Versus Unsupported Guest Operating Systems

The issue of running guest operating systems not officially supported by the server virtualization platform vendor sparks a lot of controversy. It is important to understand the implications of using software such as server virtualization in unsupported configurations, especially when considering doing this in a production system. Depending on an organization's level of comfort with the officially unsupported guest operating system and the virtualization platform and depending on the use case of the server virtualization implementation, it may be well justified by the organization to absorb the amount risk associated in using an unsupported configuration. Figure 6.1 shows a matrix of currently supported guest operating systems by virtualization platform.

Currently, GSX Server has official support for the widest range of guest operating systems, followed by ESX Server, followed by MSVS. What does having official support for a guest operating system from the virtualization platform vendor really mean? It does not necessarily mean that an unsupported guest operating system will not install and run properly in a virtual machine. There are many unsupported IA-32 (or x86) guest operating systems that will run as expected within the available server virtualization platforms. Primarily, it means that the virtualization platform vendor will not be able to provide assistance in the advent of a malfunction, bug, or other issue that could arise. The vendor will not assume responsibility or risk in these cases and will generally not spend time attempting to support such configurations, even if it is truly caused by a fault in their software. It costs a large amount of money to provide product support, and the vendors cannot support every possible configuration, just as a hardware provider cannot support every conceivable operating system and configuration for their systems. Second, the guest enhancement software provided by the virtualization platform vendor (MSVS has Virtual Server Additions and ESX Server and GSX Server have VMware Tools) is likely not available for unsupported operating systems. The existing Linux versions of these add-in software tools may not work properly in other Linux distributions or versions. The guest enhancement software usually consists of a set of optimized device drivers designed to help the guest operating system perform better with the specific set of virtual hardware exposed by the virtual machine as well as a background service that manages such things as communications with the host server, VM heartbeats, and time synchronization, among other features.

In general, unsupported guest operating systems will run slower than a supported operating system with the guest enhancement software installed. There will usually be performance and usability issues when attempting to access virtual machines that have an unsupported guest operating system installed using the virtualization platform's native remote control technology, such as Virtual Machine Remote Control in MSVS and the VMware Remote Console in ESX Server and GSX Server. This is primarily due to the lack of optimized keyboard,

	Guest Operating System					
Virtualization Platform	Microsoft DOS (MS-DOS)	Microsoft Windows 3.1	Microsoft Windows for Workgroups 3.11	Microsoft Windows 95	Microsoft Windows 98	Microsoft Windows Millennium Edition
Microsoft Virtual Server R2						
VMware ESX Server 2.5.2						
VMware GSX Server 3.2.1	Y	Y	Y	Y	Y	Y

	Guest Operating System					
Virtualization Platform	Microsoft Windows NT 4.0 Server SP6a	Microsoft Windows 2000	Microsoft Windows XP	Microsoft Wndows Server 2003 RTM, SP1	Microsoft Wndows Server 2003 R2	Microsoft Wndows Vista Beta
Microsoft Virtual Server R2	Y	Y	Y	Y	Y	
VMware ESX Server 2.5.2	Y	Y	Y	Y		
VMware GSX Server 3.2.1	Y	Y	Y	Y		Y

	Guest Operating System					
Virtualization Platform	Red Hat Linux 6.2, 7.0, 7.1	Red Hat Linux 7.2, 7.3, 8, 9	Red Hat Enterprise Linux 2.1, 3.0	Red Hat Enterprise Linux 4.0	SUSE Linux Enterprise Server 7	SUSE Linux Enterprise Server 8, 9
Microsoft Virtual Server R2						
VMware ESX Server 2.5.2		Y	Y			Y
VMware GSX Server 3.2.1	Y	Y	Y	Y	Y	Y

	Guest Operating System					
Virtualization Platform	SUSE Linux 7.3, 8.0, 8.1	SUSE Linux 8.2, 9.0, 9.1, 9.2	SUSE Linux 9.3	Mandrake Linux 8.0, 8.1, 8.2	Mandrake Linux 9.0, 9.1, 9.2	Mandrake Linux 10.0, 10.1
Microsoft Virtual Server R2						
VMware ESX Server 2.5.2		Y	Y			
VMware GSX Server 3.2.1	Y	Y		Y	Y	Y

	Guest Operating System					
Virtualization Platform	FreeBSD 4.9, 5.0, 5.2	FreeBSD 4.10	Novell NetWare 4.2 Server	Novell NetWare 5.1, 6.0, 6.5 Server	Solaris x86 9, 10	Turbolinux 7, ES 8, WS 8
Microsoft Virtual Server R2						
VMware ESX Server 2.5.2		Y		Y		
VMware GSX Server 3.2.1	Y		Y	Y	Y	Y

Figure 6.1 Supported Guest Operating Systems by Server Virtualization Platform.

mouse, and video drivers in the guest operating system usually supplied by the guest enhancement software package. In this case it is usually very difficult or nearly impossible to effectively control the mouse pointer and often a single keystroke may be repeated several times within the virtual machine. If the overall performance of the virtual machine is acceptable, unsupported guest operating systems may be used successfully. There are other methods that may be used to access the virtual machine such as network-connected telnet, ssh, and remote control applications such as VNC.

Using unsupported guest operating systems imparts risk onto the organization. Depending on the use case for server virtualization, the risk may be minimal or nonexistent. For example, if the organization is conducting research and development activities in regards to server virtualization itself, this may actually be necessary. In some software development and test environments, it may be safe to use unsupported guest operating systems.

The lack of support for many potential guest operating systems may also create new opportunities for software vendors. It may be beneficial for third-party companies to produce and market their own versions of the guest enhancement software for unsupported guest operating systems on server virtualization platforms. Of course, this would only truly be beneficial to production environments if the third-party software vendor also fully supported the guest operating system using their tools along with the virtualization platform and their software package as a unit. This may be a burden that keeps it from becoming a reality. On the other hand, there are already some open source initiatives in which optimized drivers have been built for some unsupported guest operating systems, such as Sun Solaris x86 on VMware. Open source solutions never imply any guaranteed support, but often have less risk than using an unsupported configuration alone. The open source software communities are often quick to offer a helping hand when needed.

Support from Software Vendors

Virtualization is a technology that has been around for quite some time, yet it is really just now becoming mainstream. Because of this, many people in the information technology industry, including many software vendors, are not virtualization savvy. Support issues can arise from mixing virtualization with software applications from vendors that have little or no virtualization experience. Some software vendors will not support their products if their products are installed and used in virtual machines. The basic argument that these vendors will use is that there are too many unknown variables in the way that the virtualization technology affects the guest operating system and other software applications installed within a virtual machine. Of course, it may not be stated in such terms, but that is by far the most common argument. To the vendors, the virtual machine is an unknown, black box into which they have no visibility; therefore they often do not wish to support it. These issues will usually come to light when a legitimate support call is made to the vendor and the vendor's support analysis discovers the use of virtualization or when a vendor sends out a consultant to implement their software and the consultant discovers that they will be installing software into a virtual machine. When a legitimate support issue arises, it most often has nothing to do with the virtualization technology. Even so, many vendors will not be so easily convinced. They may completely refuse to support the software or they may be reasonable and will want the issue to be reproduced using physical hardware. With some vendors, it will be easy to negotiate a reasonable resolution when working with virtualization and with others there may be no compromise. When placing legitimate support calls to a software vendor, it may be beneficial not to volunteer the fact that their software is running within a virtual machine. Only if the vendor queries as to what server equipment their software is being used on is it recommended to let them know that it is installed within a virtual machine. At that time, it is also recommended to give them information regarding the virtualization platform, version, and possibly even the specification of the physical server hardware. Sometimes, a more reasonable vendor may even get the virtualization platform vendor's support organization involved to help them solve the issue.

As server virtualization continues to grow as a mainstream technology that is present in most data centers, more and more software vendors will also catch on and begin supporting their products within virtual machines. This may actually become a necessity as the software vendors' competition may use their support of virtualization as marketing leverage. The outcome is a positive and natural evolution of the industry, which will further catapult virtualization technology's growth.

Unexpected Server Growth

A common side effect that often takes place in server virtualization systems is unexpected server growth. Server growth is the unexpected addition of unplanned virtual machines. In some ways, this can be thought of as virtual server sprawl. It primarily occurs after a server virtualization system has been deployed in the data center and the need arises to position new servers. Server virtualization makes it very easy to deploy new servers in a very short amount of time. This is not necessarily bad unless it negatively impacts the existing virtual machines. Depending on the use case for the initial server virtualization deployment, it could be a very bad situation, such as creating normal enterprise application server virtual machines on a server virtualization system that was built for on-demand computing. In this situation, the application server virtual machines are essentially diminishing the overall capacity of the on-demand server system. Unexpected server growth not only impacts the production system, but can also increase operating system and software licensing costs.

Unexpected server growth also occurs out of the natural need for a development and test server virtualization environment. Architects, developers, system administrators, and system engineers will always have a need for a disconnected, nonproduction server virtualization system in which they can design, develop, and test new methods of using the virtualization platform features, new server and network layouts, test new operating systems and software, construct virtual machine base images, and perform other nonproduction tasks and experiments without disturbing or impacting the production environment. The size and scope of the nonproduction server virtualization environment that is needed can vary greatly depending on its planed usage, but as a base line, the host servers should generally be the exact same configuration of the production host servers in order to provide an minimally adequate nonproduction test system deployed alongside the production system. Additionally, the development and test server virtualization environment should be separated from the production network either physically or by a firewall and it should have a dedicated switch to provide the interconnects between host servers.

Another cause of unexpected server growth to be aware of is the creation of utility virtual machines. Unlike development or test virtual machines, a utility virtual machine may be created purposefully on production systems. Sometimes they are temporary and sometimes it is useful to have one or more permanent utility virtual machines handy for administration purposes. Utility virtual machines are often used to temporarily mount disks from other virtual machines in order to perform some task such as expanding or shrinking logical partitions on the virtual hard disk. Even though the usage of utility virtual machines is usually limited and they can often be powered off most of the time, they do consume resources while in use and possibly operating system and software licenses as well.

The following guidelines can help combat unexpected server growth in production systems:

- Include an adequate development and test server virtualization environment in the deployment plans if there is not an existing facility.
- Ensure that everyone that has direct access to the server virtualization host servers fully understands and adheres to the use case.
- If there is a need for more than one use case for server virtualization technologies, plan for each use case accordingly.
- Plan for about 20 percent more capacity than what is initially required to handle immediate growth.

Virtual Machine Density

The number of virtual machines residing on a single host server is referred to as virtual machine density, or VM density. When a high VM density is achieved, overall costs are generally lowered by sharing and better utilizing the host server's resources. Many factors must be considered to properly estimate VM density.

- The operating system and virtualization platform installed on each host server
- The number of processors in each host server
- The amount of available memory in each host server
- The amount of available disk storage space on each host server
- The guest operating system and applications installed on each virtual machine
- The number of virtual processors configured for each virtual machine
- The amount of memory allocated to each virtual machine
- The size of all virtual hard disks of each virtual machine
- The amount of idle processor consumption of each virtual machine
- The expected utilization of each virtual machine
- The acceptable performance of each virtual machine
- The expected usage of each virtual machine

The operating system and virtualization platform installed on each host server defines the overall environment in which the virtual machines will reside. Together, they set the initial boundaries of the environment by their supported capabilities and features. For example, if each host server will have Microsoft Windows Server 2003 Standard Edition as its operating system and Microsoft Virtual Server 2005 Standard Edition as the virtualization platform, the number of physical processors is limited to four, the maximum amount of physical memory is limited to 8GB, the maximum number of virtual processors is limited to one per virtual machine, the maximum amount of memory per virtual machine is 3.6GB, and no more than sixty-four virtual machines may be created on each host. Furthermore, if each virtual machine is expected to have 1GB of memory, a maximum of seven virtual machines per host is possible because the host operating system consumes some of the 8GB of maximum memory. In this example, 8GB is the maximum amount of memory because that is the maximum amount of memory supported by the version and edition of the Windows operating system being used. It is very important to be aware of these types of limitations early in the planning process.

The number of processors installed in each host server defines the maximum amount of processing power and parallelism capabilities. Some server virtualization platforms also restrict the maximum number of virtual machines per physical processor installed in the host server. A general rule of thumb is that the more physical processors installed, more virtual machines can be created. In reality, this is only true to a certain point, especially when considering very generic virtual machines with low utilization and low performance metrics. It is also recommended to have a minimum of two processors in each host server in order to achieve good overall system performance.

The amount of available memory in each host server is one of the most important considerations of VM density. Memory in server virtualization is one of the most scare resources in the entire system. It is less sharable than processors and disk space. Larger memory footprints of each virtual machine lower the VM density of a host server. When planning server virtualization solutions, it is a good idea to obtain as much physical memory as can be afforded, with a minimum recommended amount of memory being 4GB. With less than 4GB of memory on the host servers, it is difficult to achieve good VM densities to help lower overall costs. It is also important to consider the amount of memory that will be consumed by the operating system, virtualization platform, and any other applications running on the same host server.

The amount of available disk storage space on each host server is another consideration of VM density. There must be enough disk storage to account for the operating system, paging or swap files, the virtualization platform binaries, and any other applications that will be installed on each host server. Additionally, there must be enough storage space left over to accommodate each virtual machine's configuration files and virtual hard disk files. Depending on how the virtual machines will be used, storage space to cover redo/undo disk files or suspended virtual machine state files may also need consideration. The features of the virtualization platform also play a key role in determining host disk storage space. For instance, Microsoft Virtual Server supports dynamic virtual hard disks that only consume the amount of host disk space as is needed up to a predefined maximum size while VMware ESX Server only supports fixed virtual hard disks that consume the same amount of host disk space as the size of the virtual disk. When implementing server virtualization systems that rely on the use of redo/undo disks, a good estimation of each redo/undo disk is very important to ensure that the host does not run out of disk space. If the system is using a SAN, each LUN must be sized appropriately based on the considerations mentioned above.

The guest operating system and applications installed on each virtual machine must be considered as it must have enough virtual resources present to properly support it. Typically, a well-tuned Linux operating system will require less memory and disk resources than most Windows operating systems. Knowing exactly what operating systems, editions, versions, service pack levels, and what applications will be installed in each virtual machine can help gauge the amount of memory and disk space required.

The number of virtual processors configured for each virtual machine may also need consideration. Most server virtualization platforms available only support virtual machines with one processor, but VMware ESX Server along with VMware Virtual SMP add-on can allow virtual machines with up to two processors when hosted on a physical server with two or more physical processors. In this case, virtual machines with more performance needs can be configured with two processors and others with just one. It is usually beneficial to spread out dual processor virtual machines across many host servers as often as possible to help maximize their performance. By placing many dual processor virtual machines on a single host with two processors, for example, will likely cause a processor resource bottleneck on the physical server that will in turn impact the performance of the virtual machines on that host.

The amount of memory allocated to each virtual machine will impact VM density in conjunction with the amount of memory available on each host server. Generally, each virtual machine should only be configured with just enough memory to perform its intended task. Performance considerations may alter the amount of memory needed, depending on the applications installed in the virtual machine.

The size of all virtual hard disks of each virtual machine must be considered in conjunction with the amount of available hard disk storage space on the host server. A good balance between having enough disk space in the virtual machine to accommodate log file growth and application data storage and having a surplus of disk space is the ideal goal, especially when using fixed virtual hard disks. Although virtual hard disks can be expanded or shrunk as needed, it is not a trivial process and can cause downtime for the virtual machine, so this feature should not be relied upon in lieu of good storage requirements estimation practices.

The amount of idle processor consumption of each virtual machine is a consideration unique to virtualization. Even when a booted virtual machine is idle, it may consume some processor resources, even if only 1–2 percent of the virtual processor. When this is combined with the processor overhead of the virtualization platform and multiplied by a number of virtual machines, a considerable amount of the host server's available processors may be consumed. This is especially evident in host servers with a very high VM density of more than 10:1. The guest operating systems of the virtual machines may in some cases be tweaked to cut down the amount of idle processor cycles being consumed, but some tweaks may remove useful features, such as ACPI compliance.

The expected utilization of each virtual machine is one of the more important factors when considering VM density. A high number of virtual machines each having a fairly low rate of utilization (20 percent or less) will be good candidates for being placed on the same host server in order to achieve high VM density. It is also a good idea to spread out virtual machines with heavier utilization across as many host servers as possible and combine these with low utilization virtual machines in order to achieve better VM densities and general performance.

Availability Considerations

Availability refers to the reliability of the system usually measured as the percentage of time the system provides the expected services. Availability is often referred to as uptime. A highly available system is one that runs without interruption, 24 hours a day, 7 days a week. Highly available systems use fault-tolerant components that can withstand the failure of a subcomponent to keep the system operational and assure data integrity. When planning server virtualization systems, availability consideration should be given to the host system and the virtual machines. Systems with high-availability requirements usually incur more planning and more cost and are more complex.

Most physical server hardware is fairly fault tolerant. They usually include features such as redundant power supplies, hot-swappable fans and expansion cards, RAID storage, and teamed network adapters configured for load-balancing and fault-tolerance. High-end servers even include redundant memory modules and processor voltage regulator modules. Although these almost standard features greatly improve the fault-tolerance of the server, they do not provide a complete high-availability solution.

Although server virtualization technology can be used to enable high-availability solutions, other use cases may require that some or all virtual machines need to be highly available. Virtual machines are only as fault-tolerant as the host server and the virtualization platform on which they reside. To achieve higher levels of availability, server clustering is usually required. Just as physical servers may be clustered to provide high availability, so too can virtual machines be clustered. Virtual machines, participating as nodes in a single server cluster, should reside on separate host servers from one another to improve fault-tolerance and the overall availability. Different server virtualization platforms have differing levels of support for virtual server clusters, especially when regarding the shared storage of the clustered server, or quorum. When considering the need for highly available virtual machines, the costs of the additional capacity must be factored in as well as the complexities and additional requirements imposed by the more specialized needs of server clusters, such as additional networking requirements for private cluster networks over which the nodes in a cluster monitor each other, the quorum, and the fault-tolerance features of the physical host servers. The guest operating systems used in clustered configurations may also need to support server clustering, which may also require additional licenses or an upgraded version of the operating system.

High-availability server virtualization, including server clustering, is an advanced configuration that will introduce more complexities in the overall solution. It is important to properly gauge the organization's on-hand skill sets and know when additional training or outside consulting is needed. Bringing in outside experts early in the planning stages will usually help avoid major issues later in the project.

Data and System Backup Considerations

Adding new systems into existing data centers will always have an impact on existing data center management systems and the data backup systems are no exception. Server virtualization tends to greatly amplify this impact by potentially adding another level of complexity and larger than usual demand on existing data backup systems and strategies. In some cases, server virtualization systems may not easily fit into existing data and system backup processes. The traditional concerns are the costs imposed by possibly needing additional backup system agents to install on the host server or the virtual machines, the storage capacity of the backup system, the backup time capacity of the backup system, and costs incurred by the need for additional persistent media and offsite storage. Besides the traditional backup issues, server virtualization will impose two dimensions of back up: backing up the host server and backing up the virtual machines residing on that host.

System backup for virtualization host servers is usually much like system backup for traditional physical servers, especially when dealing with server virtualization platforms requiring a host operating system. In addition to the core operating system, the virtual machine configuration and log files should be backed up. The virtual machines should always be backed up as well, but there are several different strategies regarding virtual machine backup that can have a huge impact on storage capacity, costs, and time. ESX Server can more of a challenge when considering host server backup. Many existing backup agents are not compatible with ESX Server and its special VMFS file system, although new solutions are beginning to appear. In many cases, system administrators create custom backup scripts using shell scripting or Perl scripts that are scheduled using cron within the ESX Server Service Console.

When considering virtual machine back up, there are two major methodologies that are commonly used. One method is to back up each virtual machine's virtual hard disk files that reside of the host server on a scheduled basis, such as daily or weekly. These files tend to be large, multi-gigabyte files. Virtual machine disk file sizes commonly range from 2GB to over 100GB. It is very expensive to back up every virtual machine daily not only because of the massive amount of storage capacity that is needed, but because, in many cases, the virtual machines must be powered off in order to back them up. This is not totally true for every virtualization platform and every configuration, but it is the most reliable way to back up a virtual machine's disk files. In some configurations and virtualization platforms, such as ESX Server, it is possible to back up a live virtual machine. Because the file sizes are large, the backups can take a long time to complete, especially if the network bandwidth between the host server and the backup storage devices is slow. Using a high-performance SAN can solve this problem, but it is very expensive in terms of hardware, software, and services costs. Backing up each virtual machine's disk files provides a best-case scenario when the virtual machines must be restored. Depending of the level of importance of the virtual machines, the costs and time it takes to back up entire virtual machines daily or weekly may be well worth it after experiencing a system failure causing the backed up virtual machines to be restored. It is also important to note that highly available virtual machines that are clustered make it easier to back up each virtual machine in the cluster because the services provided by the cluster will continue to run while the other nodes are backing up. When considering a daily virtual machine backup plan, it is also important to ensure that all of the virtual machines can be backed up with the allotted time. It is possible in some situations, based upon the size and quantity of virtual machines, that it will take more than a twenty-four-hour period to back up every virtual machine.

Another method that is used to back up virtual machines is to create one initial back up of the virtual machine's disk files and then back up the virtual machine using the same methods for typical servers. In this scenario, the operating system and data residing within the virtual machine are usually backed up daily using the same mechanisms that are used for physical servers. This method provides a good balance between the cost of backups and the ease of restoration. If the virtual machine ever needs to be restored, the virtual machine's disk files are restored to the host server first, which quickly establishes the base virtual machine and then operating system and data backups can be applied within the virtual machine using normal data restoration techniques.

Disaster Recovery Considerations

Much like the considerations regarding data and system backup, the overall disaster recovery strategies that are in place must be considered in terms of the impact the will be caused when implementing a server virtualization system. Although server virtualization use cases can actually benefit disaster recovery plans, existing disaster recovery strategies will almost never consider the use or requirements of server virtualization. Two of the most important elements to consider when the use case of server virtualization is *not* disaster recovery are the costs of additional standby equipment able to support the restoration of virtual machines in the case of a disaster and the required skill sets and knowledge to be able to perform system restorations.

Even when disaster recovery is not the use case for a server virtualization implementation, it may be very beneficial to consider using server virtualization as part of the overall disaster recovery strategy aside from restoring virtualized systems. In fact, it is possible to have created virtual machines that are the equivalents of the core physical servers, using the same operating systems and applications. These virtual machines can be backed up and stored in an offline state. They are not used on a daily basis. They would, however, be used to quickly restore several core services in the event of a disaster by restoring the virtual machines and then by applying the backed up data from the normal, physical servers to the virtual machine equivalents until the proper hardware can be acquired or rebuilt as necessary. Although the virtual machines would likely run at a lesser performance level, they would work in a temporary situation to help ensure business continuance.

Monitoring Considerations

Most established data centers will often have a centralized server monitoring system in place to keep track of the health and status of servers and applications. Once server virtualization becomes a part of the data center, it will likely affect the existing server monitoring system. The server monitoring system will probably be able to monitor the host servers without any problems. At this time, many server monitoring solutions do not have any capabilities for monitoring virtual machines within the context of the virtualization platform. They may be able to monitor virtual machines in a more limited method by installing the monitoring agents into each virtual machine, but the monitoring system would not know the virtual machines apart from the physical servers. Some monitoring systems are just starting to produce add-ins that understand and support monitoring on some virtualization platforms. As time goes on and virtualization technology continues to grow inside the data center, better monitoring solutions will become available for virtualization.

Another way server virtualization may affect existing server monitoring systems is by the increased cost of monitoring the host servers and all of the virtual machines. Most monitoring systems are licensed by the capacity of servers they monitor. Once server virtualization is introduced into the data center, the number of servers that need to be monitored will tend to grow quickly, which will likely increase server monitoring costs in terms of requiring more licenses. It is a good idea to be aware of this issue and to plan ahead for the costs of additional server monitoring.

Network Considerations

New server virtualization implementations will have an impact on those existing networks to which the host servers and virtual machines are connected. Host servers have a higher potential than traditional physical servers to have more Ethernet adapters, most of which service the virtual machines on that host. This in turn directly impacts the number of available switch ports that will be needed. Additional switches may be needed and the costs involved in acquiring and installing new switches must be factored into the project.

Some organizations create segmented networks using VLANs, which are usually configured at the switch. It is important to note that if the host servers or one or more virtual machines must be connected to different VLANs, a network adapter in each host must be dedicated for each VLAN-specific connection. One of the most common configurations is to use a host server to run several virtual machines on the server network and one virtual machine is a public Web server connected to the DMZ, not the normal server network. This virtual machine must be bound to a dedicated network adapter in the host server that is physically connected into the DMZ switch or VLAN. Other virtual machines on the same host that also require DMZ connections could share the same network adapter, if needed.

When planning a deployment, it is a good practice to create logical diagrams that show each virtual machine within their host servers. Each network connection should be drawn in the diagram originating from either a virtual machine or a host server, through the physical network adapter, and ending at the network to which it should be connected. This exercise is effective in determining the number of network adapters needed for each host server as well as the number and configuration of each virtual network, also referred to as virtual switches. Figure 6.2 shows a simple example host server network diagram.

In the Figure 6.2 diagram, there are three separate networks, the Server Network, the DMZ, and Cluster Network 1. These networks are represented logically in the diagram, but may represent physically separate networks or ports in a managed network switch, members of different VLANs, network segments isolated logically (another form of virtualization). Network Adapter 0 is dedicated to the host server and is connected to the Server Network. Network Adapter 1 is shared by virtual machines. It is also connected to the Server Network and, internally on Host 1, and bound to Virtual Switch 0. Virtual Machines 1, 2, 3, and 8 all share Network Adapter 1 through Virtual Switch 0. Virtual Machines 4 and 6 require public Internet access because they are possibly Web servers. They share Network Adapter 2 through Virtual Switch 1. Network Adapter 2 is connected to the DMZ network. Virtual Machine 8 is dual-homed, meaning that it has two virtual network adapters connected to two different networks. One of Virtual Machine 8's virtual network adapters is connected to Virtual Switch 0. This is bound to Network Adapter 1, which is connected to the Server Network. Virtual Machine 8's other virtual network adapter is connected to Virtual Switch 2, which is bound to Network Adapter 3. Network Adapter 3 is connected to a private network, Cluster Network 1, used to carry heartbeat packets between Virtual Machine 8 and another computer with which it is clustered. Virtual Machines 7, 9, and 10 are connected to Virtual Switch 3. Because Virtual Switch

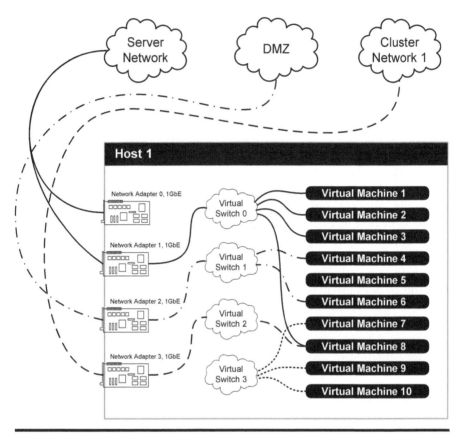

Figure 6.2 Host Server Network Diagram.

3 is not bound to a network adapter in the host, Virtual Machines 7, 9, and 10 have to connectivity external to Host 1. In fact, they can only communicate with each other via the private virtual network created by Virtual Switch 3. Virtual Machine 5 is not connected to a virtual switch and is therefore not networked to any other computer. Virtual Machines 1, 2, and 3 can also communicate with each other without having to send packets out through the network adapter because they share a virtual switch. The same is true of Virtual Machines 4 and 6.

Performance Considerations

Performance can be very difficult to estimate or measure in advance when planning a new server virtualization deployment. It is always better to make conservative performance estimates, especially if performance is a sensitive issue. To properly size for performance, real-world testing and benchmarking must be performed. Real-world testing and benchmarking refers to creating a test environment that is identical to that of the planned production environment with the exception of the scale. The hardware and software must be installed and configured exactly as in a production system in order to obtain useful performance metrics. It is highly recommended that evaluation equipment be acquired, even for short evaluation-only terms, such as 30 days, so that in-house testing and benchmarking can be completed. For some organizations, this may not be possible. Obtaining third-party white papers with similar benchmarking using similar equipment and server virtualization platforms may be the only option for some organizations on which to base their planning. In this case, many assumptions are being made that could invariably be wrong; therefore there is much higher risk in using this option of gauging the performance of the use case.

Ensuring adequate performance is often important because if the applications running on the server virtualization systems do not perform well, the consumers of those applications may deem the deployment or the technology a failure, even when the systems are executing as planned. If applications are planned to be migrated from an existing physical server environment to a server virtualization environment, performance testing is imperative in order to ensure that the final production configuration of the virtualized system meets or exceeds the existing expected performance levels.

Below are several common bottlenecks to look at if the application being tested is not performing as expected.

Processor

The processor is one of the most common performance bottlenecks in server virtualization and requires a great deal of attention. Processor cycles are a precious commodity due to their finite compute power. Server virtualization platforms usually offer tools which can help manage processor resource usage across virtual machines, such as limiting a virtual machine's processor usage or giving another virtual machine a minimum guaranteed amount of processor resources.

The virtual machine layout across host servers in conjunction with the use case plays a major role in how processor usage is affected, which in turn affects performance. For instance, consider a training scenario where there are five host servers each hosting ten virtual machines. Each virtual machine uses an identical image, so they are all exactly the same. This setup will allow 50 users to be trained concurrently, each having a single virtual machined assigned. Through the course of the training, the students are all performing the same tasks at the same time. This can severely impact processor performance, since the processor load will likely be very high on each host because each virtual machine is asking for the same amount of processor resources simultaneously. The exact type of applications being used within the virtual machines will also play a role in the amount of processor resources being used, but the use case amplifies the effect. The solution to bad performance in this scenario may be to reduce the

VM density, which will increase the number of hosts needed. The optimum VM density must be determined through testing. It may be five or even as few as three virtual machines per host.

Another example is needed to show how use case plays a role in processor performance. In this scenario, the use case is simply an enterprise server consolidation project implemented to reduce costs due to server sprawl. There are five host servers with an average of ten virtual machines on each host. Each virtual machine is different from one another. They have different memory sizes, disk sizes, different guest operating system and software applications. The usage of each virtual machine also varies greatly, but most are highly underutilized servers. Because each virtual machine will be placing a small average load on each host, the processors are not severely loaded, which in turn will translate into better performance for each virtual machine in contrast to the previous training scenario.

Memory

Memory-based performance bottlenecks can occur for different reasons. One of the most common causes of memory-based bottlenecks is a virtual machine that does not have enough memory allocated. This typically causes the virtual machine to have a very high amount of page faults, swapping data between memory and the swap file. This is usually solved by adding memory to the virtual machine. Sometimes memory cannot be added to a virtual machine because it has already used the maximum amount of memory assignable by the server virtualization platform, currently 3.6GB. If a virtual machine's performance is severely impacted by memory constraints and it is using the maximum amount of memory assignable to a virtual machine, that server is most likely not a good candidate for server virtualization. To correct the issue, the server's software components could either be distributed among several virtual machines or the server may not be a good candidate for server virtualization.

Memory performance issues can also be caused by faulty memory modules. It is recommended to run server diagnostics routines on each new server for at least 24 hours prior to use in order to fully test the hardware for faults.

Disk I/O

Disk I/O bottlenecks are caused by the fact there are only a limited number of I/O operations that can occur on a disk subsystem within a given period of time. When several virtual machines' virtual hard disk files are hosted on the same disk subsystem of the host server and they are placing a heavy load on their virtual disks, overall I/O performance will degrade system wide. Virtual machines with consistently high I/O volumes should either be placed on a host with low volume I/O virtual machines or fewer virtual machines. Another option is to place high-volume virtual machines' virtual hard disk files onto their own dedicated disk on the host server, which also has a dedicated disk controller channel to the physical disk controller. If a virtual machine's I/O demands are too great, it may be placed on a host with very few or no other virtual machines. In some cases, extremely high I/O demands may deem that a particular application is not a good candidate for server virtualization, but this is very rare. Additionally, disk I/O resource controls may be available in the server virtualization platform. In this case, it may necessary to allocate more disk I/O resources to a single virtual machine using the platform's resource controls.

Network

Network performance issues usually arise in server virtualization because many virtual machines typically share a single network adapter. This is especially true when using a Fast Ethernet (10/100) network. Most modern server network adapters today use Gigabit Ethernet (10/100/1000). Gigabit Ethernet is preferred when planning server virtualization systems, but the network adapter, cabling, and switches must all support Gigabit Ethernet in order to take advantage of the increased bandwidth. Although Gigabit Ethernet provides a large amount of bandwidth, there are times when too many virtual machines are sharing a single network adapter which may cause a networking bottleneck. It is recommended to dedicate an entire network adapter to virtual machines running network bandwidth-intensive applications and to share a separate network adapter for other virtual machines on the same host server that have medium to low network bandwidth utilization. Even though most servers have at least two Gigabit Ethernet adapter ports, it is recommended to have at least three to four Gigabit Ethernet adapter ports available on each host server. This is fairly easy to accommodate as two or four port server network adapters are readily available which only consume one PCI slot in the server. Depending on the use case, it is not uncommon to have six or eight Gigabit Ethernet adapter ports on a host server. For each network adapter port on each server that will be used, a corresponding switch port must also be available.

Performance is a large concern for most server virtualization efforts. Poor performance may cause some to erroneously place blame on virtualization technology, even though the issues may be quite solvable. It is also important to realize that acceptable performance is relative to the use case. In a high-volume production system, database servers require the highest performance and placing these types of applications and services into a virtual machine in this type of use case may be a bad idea. That same database may perform poorly within a uniprocessor virtual machine, but it may be good enough when performing quality assurance testing on that database during development. In this use case, the high performance is traded for the flexibilities and features that server virtualization can provide to reduce time and costs.

Security Considerations

Security is a very important consideration in the deployment plan. Aside from the additional costs that could be incurred from the needs for additional security software licenses such as antivirus client licenses for each host server and virtual machine, there are other considerations that could affect the overall architecture of the system.

The exposure of any host servers or virtual machines to the Internet is one of the most primary security concerns. It is highly recommended that host servers and virtualization platform management software are not placed on an Internet-facing connection. Host servers should always be placed behind a firewall on an internal network and should never be placed in a DMZ or directly connected to the Internet. The reason for the recommendation is that if a host server is compromised, all of the virtual machines on that are host can easily be compromised or at the very least powered off and deleted. There are techniques that can be used to harden the host server's operating system, and this should be done, but even using a security-optimized, hardened system is no substitute for good perimeter security and access control architectures and practices. If host servers should need to be managed remotely, a reliable VPN connection should be used.

When a virtual machine is required to be available via the Internet, some special considerations must be recognized. A virtual machine can be safely placed on the Internet in conjunction with other good best practices such as using a DMZ segment in the network design to separate the internal network from devices in the DMZ and to protect devices in the DMZ from the Internet with a firewall. In addition, the physical connection to the DMZ network segment (either a physically separate switch or a special port in a managed switch then bound to the DMZ VLAN) must exist from the network adapter. For virtual machines, this means that at least one physical network adapter in the hosts server should be dedicated to the DMZ switch connection (see Figure 6.3). Only virtual machines that require a DMZ connection should be connected to virtual switches on the host server that are bound to the DMZ network adapter.

A question that is often asked is, "Can a virtual machine be used to compromise its host server?" Although no known compromises exist today which could be used to attack a host server from within a virtual machine, it is conceivable that it could be accomplished through the virtualization platform's communication mechanisms between host server and virtual machines used by the platform's guest operating system enhancement tools (Virtual Server Additions for MSVS and VMware Tools for ESX Server and GSX Server). It is for this reason that administrators should plan to check regularly (weekly, if possible) for new security updates for the host server operating system and the virtualization platform.

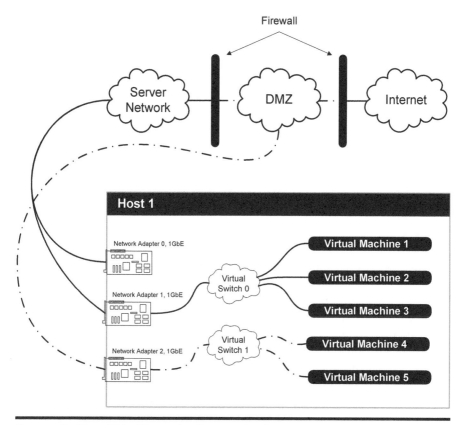

Figure 6.3   Virtual Machine-to-DMZ Network Diagram.

If a virtual machine is compromised, for instance, because of an unpatched guest operating system being placed directly on the Internet, it can affect the host server and virtual machines. In this case, the compromised virtual machine can be used to launch attacks elsewhere on the network to which it is attached as well as the Internet, if outbound Internet access exists. Depending on the virtual machine's resource configuration within the host server, the attacker could cause the virtual machine to execute attacks causing the CPU and memory utilization of the virtual machine to spike for extended periods of time, thereby eating up valuable resources from the host server that may be needed by other virtual machines. The result would be a performance issue realized on the host server and other virtual machines on that host server. It is essential to never connect any computers directly to the Internet (except in very special circumstances), and to never connect an unpatched virtual machine to any live network. New virtual machines can be connected to a virtual switch within the virtualization platform that is not bound to any outbound network adapters in the host server. This allows the virtual machine to have a valid network stack installed and configured, but disconnected from a real network, making the virtual machine safe from network attacks while security updates can be applied by an administrator or system engineer through the virtual machine's console.

It is also very important to realize that anyone able access to a host server can affect the virtual machines on that host server. They may not have access to log into those virtual machines, but if they can make changes to the host operating system, such as modifying files, accessing the virtualization platform management tools, or even having the ability to restart or shut the host server down, they will affect the virtual machines externally.

Use Case

The use case is the critical first step in building a solid foundation for a successful server virtualization solution deployment. It defines how and why a particular technology and solution, in this case server virtualization, will be used. Most projects do not follow a formal process for creating a use case and this can cause many problems throughout the deployment. Creating the Use Case Document ensures alignment of stake holders in the project, business and technical, which ensures that a common goal and vision is understood and agreed upon by all. It can also be used to show key business stakeholders that a problem exists and to propose the intended solution. The Use Case Document also serves as the foundation of the Requirements Document, which is explained later.

The Use Case Document should identify the specific business and technical stakeholders, describe in detail the problem being addressed, the proposed solution to the problem, and other details of the proposed solution such as impacts, costs, and returns.

Use Case Document Outline

1. **Document the stakeholders**
   a. Identify the End Users
      The end users are business stakeholders which must interface with or are impacted by the proposed solution. End users can also be affected by the problems and may have the best insight on the issues which need to be addressed.
   b. Identify the Project Owner
      The project owner is the primary business stakeholder which has the overall authority to approve the project and its costs. The project owner usually sets the high-level goals and timelines.
   c. Identify the Project Manager
      The project manager is the primary business stakeholder which manages the day-to-day implementation of the project from a business

standpoint, collecting requirements, ensuring that timelines are kept on track, that milestones are met, and that costs are kept within budget. The project manager usually reports to the project owner and directly interfaces with the system architect, lead system engineer, and the implementation team.

    d. Identify the System Architect

      The system architect is the primary technical stakeholder charged with the overall design of the solution. The system architect must make major technical decisions, such as what hardware, software, and outside services will be used and how the overall solution will be constructed.

    e. Identify the Lead System Engineer

      The lead system engineer is the primary technical stakeholder charged with the overall technical leadership and decision making during the implementation. The lead system engineer is usually responsible for ordering the hardware, software, and services, and delegating tasks to the rest of the implementation team. In some cases, the same person can fill the system architect and lead system engineer roles.

    f. Identify the Implementation Team

      The implementation team consists of technical stakeholders responsible for carrying out the implementation. The lead system engineer is almost always also a member of the implementation team. The implementation team carries out all technical tasks related to the completion of the project, including installing hardware, software, and directing outside services.

2. **Document the problem addressed in detail**
   a. Describe the current situation
   b. Identify the cause of the problem
   c. Describe the current systems and technologies in place which are associated with the problem or the solution
   d. Describe the current processes in place which are associated with the problem or the solution

3. **Document the proposed solution**
   a. Describe the solution—this is the goal and vision
   b. Describe the changes the solution will impart to existing systems and processes

4. **Document the details of the solution**
   a. Describe the impact on existing systems and processes the solution will impart
   b. Describe all items that need to be purchased including hardware, software licenses, and services
   c. Describe the risks
   d. Describe the costs
   e. Describe the Return On Investment (ROI)

When creating the Use Case Document, it is important to involve all of the stakeholders. Interviewing the stakeholders is a good method of gathering the initial information for the document and to get an understanding of each stake holder's perceptions regarding the project. It is also very important to understand the problem driving the project from both the business and technical point-of-views to ensure that the proposed solution is able to meet the requirements and work within the constraints of both. Addressing the problem with a proposed solution will ultimately cause changes to be made to existing systems and processes. Below is a sample list of interview questions which will help gather important information which will be used to build the Use Case Document.

- What is driving the necessity of the changes?
- What is the desired outcome of the changes?
- What is the expected life expectancy of the proposed solution?
- What existing systems will be impacted by the changes?
  - Administration and Management
  - Data and System Backup
  - Disaster Recovery
  - Intranet
  - Monitoring
  - Networking
  - Security
  - Storage
- What existing processes or job functions will be impacted by the changes?
  - Business
  - Development
  - Education/Training
  - Helpdesk/Support Staff
  - System Administration
  - Testing/QA
- What business or technical problems might be anticipated with the changes?
- What business constraints may impact the proposed solution?
  - Budget
  - Time
  - Human Resources
- What technical constraints may impact the proposed solution?
  - Hardware limitations
  - Limited data center floor space
  - Network infrastructure limitations
  - Operating system restrictions
  - Inadequate skill sets and knowledge

Once the Use Case Document has been created, it can be used as a tool to obtain approval for the project or mark the start the project. The primary stakeholders should have a meeting to focus on communicating the goal and overall vision. The project manager, system architect, and lead system engineer can then proceed to create the Requirements Document.

Requirements

All successful projects are generally governed by a set of rules used to define what exact needs must be fulfilled, the constraints of the project, and the success criteria. These rules are the project's requirements. The Requirements Document sets the overall scope of the project in terms of budget and time at a high level. It details the needs of the project and the success criteria, a set of rules which determine if the project was successful after its completion.

Once a project officially begins, the Requirements Document should be created. The Project Manager is usually responsible for the creation of the Requirements Document, although it is not uncommon for the System Architect and Lead System Engineer roles to have direct input into the document. The Use case Document contains all of the initial information needed to start building the Requirements Document. It is also a good idea to include the Use Case Document into the Requirements Document. The Requirements Document must provide detailed information regarding the problem and the solution being implemented. It does not contain information about how to implement the exact solution, however. It will serve as an input to the Deployment Plan Document.

Deployment Plan

The deployment plan, also referred to as the project plan, is used to manage the flow of the project, maintaining the project schedule and milestones. Based upon the Requirements Document, the Deployment Plan Document is used to track the project through completion. The deployment plan should also include all of the major and detailed steps of the project including the ordering of equipment, installing and configuring the equipment and host server operating systems and virtualization platform software, building of virtual machine images, and conduction all other aspects of the deployment. The deployment plan should also include detailed networking and server layout diagrams.

Summary

During the planning stages of a server virtualization deployment, a large amount of information must be gathered. In addition, there are a number of server virtualization-specific considerations to be aware of. It is important for the implementers and those who manage them to be aware of the technical considerations and how they affect the choices which are made. The information presented in this chapter can be leveraged into making a server virtualization deployment a success.

Chapter 7

Server Virtualization Platform Differences

At the current time, there are two major vendors of IA-32 (or x86) server virtualization platforms, Microsoft and VMware. This chapter attempts to explain the differences between Microsoft Virtual Server 2005, VMware GSX Server, and VMware ESX Server. It continues with a discussion on why one platform would be used over another through the use of real-world use cases (see Figure 7.1). And finally, a high-level virtual machine specification matrix is provided for a quick comparison of the three platforms.

 Each subsection will have either a product or company name in (parenthesis) that indicates which company or product is the strongest or best fit for this specific topic or use.

Software Maturity (VMware)

Where VMware stands out is in their product maturity. They are considered to have released the first commercially available x86 virtualization platform to market back in February of 1999. So, they have been at this for quite some time. VMware GSX Server is a third-generation product with 1.0 having been released near the end of 2000. VMware GSX Server is currently at version 3.2.1. VMware ESX Server has been shipping for well over four years now and is currently at version 2.5.2. VMware products have not only been time tested; the company also claims to have well over two million registered users and an installation base in over 5,000 corporations. On the other hand, Microsoft's Virtual Server 2005 product is a 1.0 release that was released around October of 2004.

Comparing Real World Use Cases		
Microsoft Virtual Server 2005 R2	**VMware GSX Server 3.2**	**VMware ESX Server 2.5**
Automation of development and test environments	Departmental server consolidation	Production server consolidation
Department and branch office server consolidation	Software development and test lab automation	Cost effective disaster recovery (DR)
Legacy application re-hosting	Legacy application migration	Cost effective high availability (HA)
	Cost effective disaster recovery (DR)	Guaranteed service level agreements
	Cost effective high availability (HA)	

Figure 7.1

While that may not seem like a very long time, it is important to remember that Microsoft purchased the product from Connectix, which had a release candidate of the product in early 2003. Microsoft's current version, Microsoft Virtual Server 2005 R2, was released to manufacturing on November 15, 2005. Within a short time frame, Microsoft has quickly gained acceptance and adoption of its virtualization products.

Host and Guest Operating System Support (VMware GSX Server)

VMware GSX Server by far has the largest matrix of supported host and guest operating systems. ESX Server is its own host operating system as it installs on bare metal. Its guest operating system support is also impressive, supporting a number of Microsoft and Linux derivatives. Microsoft Virtual Server 2005 on the other hand, only supports a small set of Microsoft operating systems for the host, and a small set of guest operating systems made up of entirely Microsoft operating systems. Microsoft Virtual Server 2005 R2 adds support for several 64-bit Microsoft x64 guest operating systems as well as support for Microsoft Windows Server 2003 SP1 (all editions) and Microsoft Windows Server 2003 R2 (all editions), in 32-bit and 64-bit (x64) versions as host and guest operating systems. Although Microsoft in April 2005 announced future plans to support additional third-party guest operating systems on Microsoft Virtual Server 2005 R2, the exact details of the specific guest operating systems that may be supported and the terms of support have not yet been released. At the time of this writing, Microsoft Virtual Server 2005 R2 only supports Microsoft guest operating systems.

Training and Certification (VMware)

Currently, VMware offers courses with extensive hands-on labs, case studies, and course materials designed to be used as on the job reference tools. Courses such as GSX Server System Management and Virtual Infrastructure with ESX Server and VirtualCenter provide a solid classroom environment, which is required to become a VMware Certified Professional. Currently, Microsoft does not offer a certified curriculum or certification track for Virtual Server.

Management and User Interface (VMware GSX Server)

All three platforms offer a Web-based management interface to manage a single virtualization host at a time. In addition to the Web application, VMware GSX Server also offers the VMware Virtual Machine Console, which is a client-based application. And for an additional sum of money, both companies offer other products that can help manage a larger virtualization environment. In 2003, VMware launched a brand new product to help manage and provision an entire server virtualization farm, VMware VirtualCenter. It manages a server farm made up of both GSX Server and ESX Server hosts and virtual machines. Not to be outdone, Microsoft introduced a management pack add-on to its Microsoft Operations Manager (MOM) solution to help manage and monitor Virtual Server environments.

Ease of Creating Virtual Machines
(VMware GSX Server)

When using virtualization, one of the key components and often-used features is going to be creating virtual machines. And while all platform management interfaces have an option to do it, some are much better and more user friendly than others. Microsoft Virtual Server's new virtual machine configuration process can be a little confusing at first because there is no easy work flow to follow. But after the first two or three virtual machines are created, its lack of hand holding through the process becomes a distant memory and quickly becomes second nature. VMware ESX Server does a somewhat better job of stepping through the process; however, it is VMware GSX Server's new virtual machine Wizard that leads the pack. It can even make creating the first virtual machine seem simple. To quickly create a virtual machine, it offers a typical path that takes care of most of the environmental settings with default responses. To gain more control over the creation process, a custom path is offered where more options and settings are made available.

Hardware Support
(Microsoft Virtual Server and VMware GSX Server)

Virtual Server and GSX Server provide the best hardware support of the three platforms. Both products can install on top of almost any x86 server hardware. ESX Server on the other hand has a huge downfall when it comes to the physical hardware that it supports. To deliver such high performance, the ESX Server architecture accesses devices directly through device drivers on the ESX Server machine rather than through a host operating system such as with GSX Server or Virtual Server. The price paid for the improved performance is the limiting factor of supporting only a specific set of devices and certain qualified server families/models. Specific hardware must be present to install and use the product.

Technical Support (Microsoft Virtual Server)

With the rapid increase in use of virtualization products throughout the industry, the question of technical support has come up on more than one occasion. With the introduction of virtualization, there are now multiple levels of technical support required. Support is still needed for the hardware, host operating system, and now support is needed for the virtualization platform software, and the virtualized guest operating system.

The host operating system support for VMware GSX Server or Microsoft Virtual Server depends on the platform. Microsoft Virtual Server only installs on top of a Microsoft operating system. Therefore, the support is no different than the support received from Microsoft on a normal server installation of the operating system. GSX Server offers a choice, it can either be installed on top of a Microsoft operating system (again, providing the same level of support as on a normal server installation) or a Linux operating system. The Linux operating system would be covered under the same level of support agreement as if there was no virtualization software installed and it was running some other type of application. ESX Server, on the other hand, provides its own highly efficient hypervisor/kernel as the host operating system. It then makes use of a service console originally based on a modified Red Hat Linux operating system. The ESX Server operating system is supported by VMware technical support and is covered under the service agreement purchased with the product.

Unlike the host operating systems, the support provided for the guest operating systems can vary. Specifically, the support provided to a Microsoft guest

Solutions Supported in a Virtualization Infrustructure			
Solution	MSVS	GSX Server	ESX Server
Legacy application migration	**	*	*
Software development and test lab automation	**	**	*
Department and branch office server consolidation	**	**	*
Production server consolidation	*	*	**
Guaranteed service level agreements	*	*	**
Cost effective disaster recovery (DR)	*	*	**
Cost effective high availability (HA)	*	*	**

* = Good Fit

** = Best Fit

Figure 7.2

operating system can vary from one virtualization platform to the next. Microsoft will fully support a Microsoft operating system that is installed inside of a Microsoft Virtual Server virtual machine based on the support agreement purchased with the operating system software. On the other hand, support of a Microsoft operating system in a VMware virtual machine will vary depending on how the products were purchased. If a hardware vendor (such as Dell, IBM, or HP) resells or packages a VMware product with a Microsoft operating system, the hardware vendor will typically provide support for both the VMware software and the Microsoft operating system. If a VMware product is purchased directly from VMware or one of their authorized resellers, VMware or the reseller will provide support on the VMware product based on the support agreement purchased. However, in each of these instances, Microsoft will provide a different level of support for a Microsoft guest operating system that is running inside of a VMware virtual machine. If a Microsoft Premier-level support agreement was purchased with the operating system software, Microsoft will provide "commercially reasonable efforts" to support its software. Once such efforts are exhausted, Microsoft support specialists may request the problem be reproduced on a physical machine to continue with the investigation. Likewise, if a Microsoft Premier-level agreement was not purchased with the operating system, a Microsoft support specialist may request the problem be reproduced on a physical machine before any investigation begins.

Performance (VMware ESX Server)

Without going into benchmark tests, the overall performance of the three products can be summed up succinctly: VMware ESX Server overall has the best performance. This is due to a number of reasons. Perhaps the biggest boost in performance is due to the fact that ESX Server runs within its own kernel, which means there is very little overhead from the host operating system allowing its performance to be near that of a physical server. Because of ESX Server's CPU affinity and granular resource control over CPU, memory, network, and disk I/O, the other platforms are unable to surpass the scalability that ESX Server offers. By being able to over allocate its memory, ESX Server is able to run a greater number of virtual machines at the same time. And by allowing virtual machine I/O to pass directly through to the host devices, performance is greatly exceeded over hosted virtualization that inserts the overhead of an intervening Windows or Linux host operating system. Unlike the other two products, ESX Server also supports virtual Symmetric Multi-Processing (SMP) on the guest operating system. On the negative side, GSX Server and Virtual Server are both in contention for processor and memory resources with the host operating system. This further separates them from ESX Server as far as performance is concerned. Although Virtual Server does offer better virtual machine control through CPU resource allocation, the control is nowhere near as sophisticated as what ESX Server offers.

Price (Microsoft Virtual Server)

All three virtualization platforms have their pros and cons. But let's face it, when it comes right down to it, sometimes the biggest factor in a company's decision making process is "how much is the solution going to cost." Each product can be purchased from a number of different resellers, vendors, or in some cases even directly from the manufacturer. To try and compare the cost of these products as fairly as possible, the prices were found from a single reseller. The most inexpensive platform was Microsoft Virtual Server. The reseller offers a single server 4CPU license copy for $476.28. Coming in next was VMware GSX Server. The same reseller offers a single server 2CPU license copy for $1,299.28. And finally, the most expensive (although highest performing) product was VMware ESX Server. The reseller offers a single server 2CPU license copy for $4,109.46.

This is by no means the only packages offered from these manufacturers nor is this reseller the only one in the market. These prices are offered as a quick and easy way to compare what a single reseller is charging. Not to be confused, Microsoft Virtual Server also offers a 32CPU version, while VMware GSX Server offers an unlimited CPU version, and ESX Server offers numerous CPU count packages. Although pricing can fluctuate and vary from one reseller to the next, the general idea is that Microsoft Virtual Server is the most inexpensive, followed by VMware GSX Server, and then VMware ESX Server.

In late 2005, Microsoft announced new licensing and pricing for Microsoft Virtual Server 2005 R2. At the time of this writing, the server license for Microsoft Virtual Server R2 Standard Edition is $99.00 US and for Enterprise Edition it is $199.00 US. Microsoft Virtual Server 2005 R2 also requires a host server operating system license for one of the following Microsoft operating systems:

- Windows Server 2003 Standard Edition or later
- Windows Server 2003 Enterprise Edition or later
- Windows Server 2003 Datacenter Edition or later
- Windows Small Business Server 2003 Standard Edition or later
- Windows Small Business Server 2003 Premium Edition or later
- Windows XP Professional (for non-production use only)
- Windows Server 2003 x64 Standard Edition or later
- Windows Server 2003 x64 Enterprise Edition or later
- Windows Server 2003 x64 Datacenter Edition or later
- Windows XP Professional x64 (for non-production use only)

Detailed information regarding Microsoft Virtual Server 2005 R2 licensing and pricing can be found at http://www.microsoft.com/windowsserversystem/virtual-server/howtobuy/default.mspx.

Usage Scenarios

Each of these three products is designed for running enterprise server operating systems and applications. Some of the primary real-world usage scenarios for a server-class virtualization product are:

- **Software Development and Test Lab Automation**
  Server virtualization is ideal for situations that require frequent server reconfiguration as is required with software development and testing. By providing automated configuration, integration, and management of virtual machines, a software development and test group can become more productive and offer better test coverage throughout the software life cycle. Both, Microsoft and VMware, provide an adequate feature set to accomplish this use case. By making use of Virtual Server's Undo disk, GSX Server's Snapshot, or ESX Server's REDO disk modes, a virtual machine can quickly be rolled back to a pristine state prior to the problem event. Virtual Server's differencing disks can easily help to create a variety of configurations from a single base disk, which can be extremely useful for things such as a large testing matrix or software patch testing.
- **Legacy Application Migration and Rehosting**
  Many companies are still running applications that require older operating systems such as Microsoft Windows NT Server 4.0. Upgrading the application can either be too costly, or is not even offered as an option. There are two other problems associated with these legacy applications.

First, support for Windows NT Server 4.0 as an operating system is coming to an end. Second, the servers running these applications are also aging and probably nearing end of life with the hardware vendor. Migrating these applications to newer equipment may prove difficult, as drivers for the new equipment may not be readily available from the vendor for an outdated operating system. Even if drivers were available, it probably would not be cost effective to run an older operating system and application on a powerful new server. The server would be way underutilized for the amount of money invested. Migrating these applications to virtual machines enables efficient use of modern hardware resources. All three virtualization platforms can successfully support a legacy application and operating system inside of a virtual machine. However, if the legacy operating system is Microsoft Windows NT Server 4.0, Microsoft Virtual Server may be the better platform choice simply because of potentially better technical support. If the legacy application is running on a Linux operating system, either VMware platform will probably be better suited to rehost the application.

- **Department and Branch Server Consolidation**
  Many departments and branch offices have servers that are being underutilized. Another problem is the number of servers being managed because of the applications that are installed. They either need different operating systems, different versions of the same operating system, or they cannot be installed on a server with any other application (needs application isolation). These are all excellent examples of servers and applications that can be consolidated into virtual machines that run on far fewer physical servers. While all three platforms can perform this function, it may come down to a cost decision. Depending on the size of the department or branch and the number of applications and servers needing to be consolidated, VMware ESX Server may get priced out of the running. If the size is relatively small, and cost is a major factor in the decision making process, the scalability of ESX Server may not be needed, and therefore Virtual Server or GSX Server would be the better fit.

- **Production Data Center Consolidation**
  As in the previous topic, consolidating servers in a production data center can be a very important use case. The cost of doing business in a data center can become highly overwhelming when paying for ping, power, and pipe in a hosted facility. If the data center is internally supported, there are even more costs associated with the number of physical servers and rack space such as cooling, real estate costs, and general management. In both cases, fewer physical servers generally translate into less overhead and expenses. Server consolidation in a production data center differs slightly from a department or branch consolidation. The need for scalability, sta-

bility, and performance will almost always outweigh the cost in any well run facility. In this scenario, nothing surpasses VMware ESX Server.

- **Cost-effective Disaster Recovery (DR)**
  Disaster recovery is an integral element of a business continuity strategy. Implementing a virtualization solution can help realize capital cost savings, improvements in time to recovery, as well as reliability of recovery. Rather than using a costly 1-to-1 mapping of production servers to DR servers, virtualization makes it possible for many production servers to be recovered on as few as one DR server. Virtualization does more than just reduce the number of servers needed in a disaster recovery site; it also provides a hardware agnostic platform that offers the flexibility of being able to restore systems without identical or near-identical hardware. Any of the three platforms can easily provide a disaster recovery solution for a company. There are limiting factors in the decision, such as the size of the implementation and the types of applications that are being recovered, as well as the amount of time the DR facility will be online once activated. If the disaster recovery period has a relatively short-lived window, either Virtual Server or GSX Server should be able to handle the task quite well. Unfortunately, predicting the length of time that a DR facility will have to remain online is about as easy as predicting when a disaster will strike. Therefore, it is more important to look at the amount of servers that will need to be serviced and the amount of resources that are needed by the applications. VMware ESX Server provides a more robust platform, and by making use of its resource allocation abilities along with its virtual SMP, it is able to provide more peace of mind that the failover will be able to provide the necessary processing power needed to meet the expectations of most applications for a longer period of time.

- **Cost-effective High Availability (HA)**
  A cost-effective high-availability solution has similar results to that of a cost-effective disaster recovery solution. Maximizing server uptime has become increasingly more important and critical to the productivity and satisfaction of a company's customers or employees. What used to be sold as a premium, HA is more and more becoming an entitlement, something that end users have just come to expect. Using virtualization, network load balancing, standby, replication, and clustering of machines has become cost-effective and a lot easier to implement. All three platforms have the ability to provide each of these functions; however, combining the virtualization platform with third-party tools or add-on packages creates a more effective HA solution. One of the biggest problems with Virtual Server and GSX Server for Windows is uptime. Since both platforms have a Windows Server operating system underneath, the host server and all virtual machines will need to be taken down on a fairly regular basis for update and patch management.

GSX Server for Linux does not have this problem; however, it is not as robust and does not perform as well as ESX Server.

■ **Guaranteed Service Level Agreements**
When consolidating virtual machines onto a single hardware platform, the virtual machines will probably require different server workloads based on the different applications that they are running. One application may be more CPU intensive while another application may require more memory. In this scenario, ESX Server provides the best guaranteed service level agreements by making use of its resource controls for virtual machine CPU, memory, disk I/O, and network I/O. ESX Server uses a proportional-share based policy to guarantee service levels. Resources can be divided into a number of shares where each virtual machine is then given a proportionate amount of the shares for each of these resources. Neither of the other two platforms has this level of granularity of resource control, and therefore cannot match the guaranteed service level agreement of ESX Server.

Virtual Machine Specifications

Each virtual machine created with one of the server virtualization products provides a platform that includes the devices listed in Figure 7.3. Each of these devices can be seen by the virtual machine's guest operating system.

Summary

The two major vendors of x86 server virtualization are Microsoft and VMware. VMware has been shipping server virtualization software for over four years. They provide two packages: GSX Server and ESX Server. Microsoft, on the other hand, has only been shipping its product, Virtual Server 2005, since October of 2004, although the product had been under development for quite some time by a company that Microsoft acquired the Intellectual Property from, Connectix. All three of these products are powerful virtualization platforms. However, as with any software tool, knowing what problem the solution is attempting to solve helps determine which package should be purchased. All three products can perform similar functions, but a company will be most satisfied with it once they have selected the right package for the job.

Virtual Machine Specifications			
	ESX	**GSX**	**MSVS**
Virtual Processor	Dependent on system processor -Intel Pentium II or later. Provides one or two virtual processors per virtual machine. systems.	Same processor as that of the host (but no extended 64-bit support). Single processor per virtual machine on SMP	Virtualizes a physical CPU on x86-based systems. Single processor per virtual machine on SMP systems.
Virtual Chip Set	Intel 440BX-based motherboard with NS338 SIO chip and 2093AA IOAPIC	Intel 440BX-based motherboard with NS338 SIO chip and 82093AA IOAPIC	Intel 440BX-based motherboard with PIIX4
Virtual BIOS	PhoenixBIOS 4.0 Release 6 with VESA BIOS	PhoenixBIOS 4.0 Release 6 with VESA BIOS	AMI BIOS
Virtual Memory	Supports up to 3.6GB of memory per virtual machine	Supports up to 3.6GB of memory per virtual machine	Use up to 64GB of host RAM and supports up to 3.6GB per virtual machine
Virtual Graphics	VGA and SVGA support	VGA and SVGA support	Emulates S3 Trio64 with 4MB of VRAM for VESA 2.0 - VGA and SVGA
Virtual IDE Drives	Emulates up to 4 IDE DVD/CD-ROM drives.	Emulates up to 4 IDE hard disks or DVD/CD-ROM drives. Virtual hard drives can provide up to 128GB of storage per IDE channel.	Emulates up to 4 IDE hard disks or DVD/CD-ROM drives. Virtual hard drives can provide up to 128GB of storage per IDE channel.
Virtual SCSI Devices	Supports up to 4 virtual SCSI adapters per virtual machine with up to 15 devices per adapter. Support up to 9TB per virtual disk.	Supports up to 60 devices on up to 4 virtual SCSI controllers. SCSI virtual disks can support up to 256GB of storage. Supports Generic SCSI devices such as scanners, CD-ROM, and tape drives.	Supports up to 4 virtual SCSI controllers per virtual machine, controlling up to 7 virtual hard disks per virtual machine for a total of 56TB of maximum storage. SCSI virtual disks can support up to 2TB of storage.
Virtual SCSI Adapter	Emulates a Mylex BusLogic BT-958 compatible host bus adapter, or a LSI Logic Ultra160 LSI53C10xx SCSI controller	Emulates a Mylex BusLogic BT958 compatible host bus adapter, or a LSI Logic Ultra160 LSI53C10xx SCSI controller	Emulates a multi-port Adaptec 7870 SCSI controller

Figure 7.3

Virtual Machine Specifications			
	ESX	GSX	MSVS
Virtual PCI Slots	5 virtual PCI slots per virtual machine	Six virtual PCI slots per virtual machine	Chipset supports six, but Microsoft does not define.
Virtual Floppy Drives	Supports up to two 1.44MB floppy drives per virtual machine	Supports up to two 1.44MB floppy drives per virtual machine	Supports up to two 1.44MB floppy drives per virtual machine
Virtual Serial Ports	Up to 2 serial ports per virtual machine	Up to 4 serial ports per virtual machine	Up to 2 serial ports per virtual machine
Virtual Parallel Ports	Supports 1 LPT Port per virtual machine	Supports up to 3 bidirectional LPT ports per virtual machine	Supports 1 LPT Port per virtual machine
Virtual USB Ports	None	Supports a two-port USB 1.1 UHCI controller	None
Virtual Keyboard	104-key Windows 95/98 enhanced	104-key Windows 95/98 enhanced	104-key Windows compatible keyboard with PS/2 interface
Virtual Input Device	Supports PS/2 mouse	PS/2 mouse and serial tablet support	Microsoft Intellimouse with PS/2 interface
Virtual Ethernet Card	Up to 4 virtual Ethernet adapters per virtual machine.	Up to 4 virtual Ethernet adapters per virtual machine.	Emulates a DEC 21140 10/100MB multi-port Ethernet card. Supports up to 4 independent network connections.
Virtual Networking	Supports 32 virtual Ethernet switches	Supports 9 virtual Ethernet switches	An unlimited number of virtual switches
Virtual Sound Adapter	Does not currently include an emulated sound card	Supports sound output and input. Creative Labs Sound Blaster AudioPCI emulation.	Does not currently include an emulated sound card

Figure 7.3 Continued.

Part III

Implementing Microsoft Virtual Server

Chapter 8

The Microsoft Virtual Server Platform

An in-depth introduction and product background to the Microsoft Virtual Server 2005 platform is provided in this chapter along with platform-specific deployment planning requirements. Product-specific features are introduced here as well as the two editions of the platform, Microsoft Virtual Server 2005 Standard Edition and Enterprise Edition.

Product Background

Microsoft Virtual Server 2005 was released in September of 2004. Microsoft Virtual Server 2005 was a direct result of the acquisition of intellectual property from Connectix Corporation's Virtual Server product, which was never actually released. Connectix Virtual Server was in a release candidate state in early 2003 when it was acquired by Microsoft. The reason for the delayed release (over a year) had more to do with the implementation of security and security audits of the product following Microsoft's Secure Computing Initiative than it did with new functionality.

The Virtual Server code base was and still is based upon the code developed to power the Virtual PC product, which was also acquired by Microsoft at the same time as the Virtual Server Intellectual Property. Virtual PC provided a refined base virtual hardware platform in which to build a server class virtual hardware layer. Because Virtual Server was developed from Virtual PC's code base, Virtual Server's virtual hard disk files are compatible with Virtual PC's virtual hard disk files. The Virtual Server's virtual machine hardware layer is also very similar to that of Virtual PC's. There are exceptions to this and it should be noted that Virtual Server does not have support for some Virtual PC hardware such as a virtual sound card.

With the release of Virtual Server 2005 R2, Microsoft added the long awaited support of 64-bit host processors (supporting both AMD64 and Intel IA-32e/EM64T) running 64-bit host operating systems. Sixty-four-bit support is significant in that it will allow Virtual Server to operate on hardware platforms that support greater memory support, higher performance, and will have greater longevity.

Microsoft Virtual Server is installed on a physical server that is running a 32-bit version of Microsoft Windows Server 2003 (Standard, Enterprise, or Datacenter Edition), Microsoft Windows Small Business Server 2003 (Standard, or Premium Edition), or Microsoft Windows XP Professional (for non-production use only). When installing Microsoft Virtual Server 2005 R2, the choice of operating system on the physical server is expanded to include Microsoft's 64-bit operating systems such as Microsoft Windows Server 2003 (x64 Standard, Enterprise, or Datacenter Edition) or Microsoft Windows XP Professional x64 (for nonproduction use only). Virtual machines are configured within Virtual Server in nearly an identical fashion to that of a physical server. An operating system, known as a guest operating system, is then installed on the virtual machine. Virtual Server's list of currently supported guest operating systems is limited to a number of Microsoft operating systems. Virtual machines can have server class versions of Microsoft Windows installed within them that include Windows NT Server 4.0 with Service Pack 6a, Windows 2000 (Server and Advanced Server), Windows Small Business Server 2003 (Standard or Premium Edition), or Windows Server 2003 (Standard, Enterprise or Web Edition). Virtual Server 2005 R2 also adds support for Windows XP SP2. Although no other operating systems are currently officially supported as guest operating systems, Microsoft announced in April 2005 future plans to support additional third-party operating systems, including certain Linux distributions, on Virtual Server 2005 R2. The exact details of the specific guest operating systems that will be supported and the method of support for these platforms have not yet been revealed.

Virtual Server handles the task of virtualizing the real physical hardware and providing a virtual platform for each virtual machine. Individual virtual machines have their own set of independent virtual hardware. Virtual hardware under Virtual Server includes a virtual motherboard with an Intel 440BX chipset (this is a Pentium II-based chipset operating on a 100MHz bus clock) and a PIIX4 (PCI ISA Interface Xelerator), a virtual PCI controller. The virtual motherboard also comes with an 8259 APIC and an American Megatrends (AMI) BIOS. Based on the available host memory, a virtual machine can support up to 3.6GB of RAM. Each virtual machine also has a virtual video card that emulates the S3 Trio64 graphics adapter with 4MB of video memory. Each virtual machine supports up to 4 IDE devices and up to 4 virtual SCSI controllers based on the Adaptec 7870 chipset, supporting up to 28 virtual SCSI hard disks and providing support for over 56TB of storage. One virtual floppy disk drive, two virtual serial ports, and one virtual parallel port are also supported by the virtual hardware. In addition, the virtual hardware emulates a multiport DEC 21140 10/100TX 100MB Ethernet network adapter with one to four network connections. Virtual Server also attaches each virtual machine's individual virtual Ethernet card to a virtual switch. This virtual switch can then either be attached as a connection directly to other virtual machines, through the host as if it were a physical network adapter, or with the installation of the Microsoft Loopback adapter under the host operating system to the host operating system itself. The virtual Ethernet switches allow for greater flexibility and security.

Virtual Server's management is done through a Web-based interface backed by Microsoft's Internet Information Services (IIS). Virtual Server's management interface is simple to use and allows for the configuration and control of virtual machines and Virtual Server itself. Management interface control includes creating, monitoring, stopping, starting, restarting, and suspending virtual machines. The management interface also has an ActiveX Control that provides console-based access to its virtual machines. The Virtual Machine Remote Console (VMRC) connects through Virtual Server to the virtual keyboard, video, and mouse (KVM) of the virtual hardware. KVM access provides total control over the virtual machine and the guest operating system installed on it.

Today's Virtual Server product provides an excellent platform, however, Microsoft has plans to deprecate the product over the next few years by integrating the technology and its capabilities as core components and feature sets to one of their next major releases of Windows Server (possibly into Longhorn). Until then, the performance and capabilities of Virtual Server should continue to improve and provide a more robust and powerful platform for use in all aspects of IT and the Datacenter.

Product Editions

Microsoft Virtual Server presently comes in two editions:

- Microsoft Virtual Server 2005, Standard Edition (SE)
- Microsoft Virtual Server 2005, Enterprise Edition (EE)

The specifications for Virtual Server 2005 SE and EE are listed in Figure 8.1

More often than not, Standard Edition will be adequate for normal usage scenarios. It is important to realize that in most cases, the cost of hardware systems exceeding 4-way processors become prohibitively expensive, unless there is a specific need. Being that all versions of Microsoft Virtual Server are currently limited to providing virtual machines with a maximum of one CPU's worth of resources, there are few advantages to leveraging higher level Symmetric Multi-Processing (SMP) systems.

Microsoft Virtual Server 2005 R2 Enterprise Edition and Standard Edition System Requirements	
Number of Processors	Standard Edition supports 1 to 4 processors. Enterprise Edition supprts as many processors as is supported by the host operating system.
Processor Speed	Minimum 550MHz, 1.0GHz or higher is recommended
Processor Types	AMD Athlon, AMD Athlon 64, AMD Athlon 64 X2, AMD Duron, AMD Opteron (single and dual core), AMD Sempron, Intel Celeron, Intel Pentium III, Intel Pentium 4, Intel Xeon
Memory	Minimum 256MB, not including memory needed for each virtual machine. The maximum memory supported is equal to the memory supported by the host operating system.
Hard Disk Storage	Minimum 2GB, not including host hard disk storage needed for each virtual machine. The maximum hard disk storage supported is equal to the memory supported by the host operating system.
Video	Super VGA or higher resolution (800 x 600 or higher)
Host Operating Systems	**32-bit Host Operating Systems:** Microsoft Windows Server 2003 Standard, Enterprise, Datacenter Editions Microsoft Windows Server 2003 R2 Standard, Enterprise, Datacenter Editions Microsoft Windows Small Business Server 2003 Standard, Premium Editions (or later) Microsoft Windows XP Professional (not for production use) **64-bit Host Operating Systems:** Microsoft Windows Server 2003 x64 Standard, Enterprise, Datacenter Editions Microsoft Windows Server 2003 R2 x64 Standard, Enterprise, Datacenter Editions Microsoft Windows XP Professional x64 (not for production use)

Figure 8.1   Virtual Server 2005 Specifications.

The only difference between Microsoft Virtual Server 2005 Standard Edition and Microsoft Virtual Server 2005 Enterprise Edition is the number of processors supported. Microsoft Virtual Server 2005 Standard Edition supports up to four physical processors, whereas Microsoft Virtual Server 2005 Enterprise Edition supports up to thirty-two physical processors.

 If the host server supports Hyper-Threading (HT) Technology, this will not count against the Standard Edition support of four processors, as this number is based on physical processors and it will also not count against the Enterprise Edition for the same reason.

Hardware Requirements

Processor

Based on a minimal set of requirements, Microsoft recommends a CPU speed of 1.0 GHz or higher. So what exactly do they mean by "higher"? In chapter 7, it was recommended that the processor decision is based upon using and running Microsoft Virtual Server on a diverse number of hardware platforms with many different types of workloads running inside of the virtual machines. An easy rule of thumb to follow is the faster and more CPUs, the better the performance. This must however be balanced with the additional costs associated with the increase in speed and number of processors.

Memory

Memory requirements for host operating systems as prescribed by Microsoft do not take into account the memory required by any of the virtual machines. This is an important concept to understand as the lack of adequate memory will limit the number of virtual machines that can be run concurrently (if any can be run at all). Each guest operating system will consume the amount of memory allocated to it while the virtual machine is powered on, plus an additional 32MB of memory for the host operating system to manage, monitor, and control it. In addition, there must be enough memory available for the host operating system, which for Windows Server 2003 is a minimum of 512MB, to run effectively. Each instance of Windows Server 2003 running inside of a virtual machine will also require 512MB of memory to run effectively.

In addition to the above memory requirements, Virtual Server itself will consume memory for controlling the context switching and other virtualization capabilities it provides. It is recommended that an additional 512MB to 1GB of memory be allocated in addition to the 512MB for the host operating system, specifically for Virtual Server.

Disk

Disk space and performance are as critical as processor and memory in its direct impact on guest virtual machine performance. The Microsoft recommendation of 2GB of available hard disk space does not take into account the disk space requirements of the virtual machines. As discussed in chapter 7, the proper way to size and evaluate hard disk subsystems is to provide adequate performance under varying loads.

Bear in mind that when virtual machines are launched, they will consume additional physical hard disk space beyond just that of their virtual hard disk file. With the release of Virtual Server 2005 R2, a blank saved state file (.VSV) is created when the virtual machine is launched. This file is the size of the memory being used by the running virtual machine. So, if you have a virtual machine that has 512MB of memory reserved for it, an extra 512MB file will be created on the host's physical disk. This will consume disk space that may not have been accounted for in your initial planning. Prior to the release of R2, this file would only be created when someone attempted to save state the virtual machine. With a pre-created saved state file in place during the launch of a virtual machine, Microsoft could better guarantee that the user would be able to save the state of a virtual machine rather than find out when it is too late that the host server does not have enough disk space to accommodate the action.

Network

Microsoft host operating systems do not require permanent network connectivity, however to perform any useful functions there should be one or more network cards present to deliver proper server class functionality. The specific details and options of the recommended configurations are provided in chapter 7.

Display

The minimum required graphics display card must provide at least 800×600 resolution and 256 colors. Although this is not recommended, as it will be nearly impossible to administer the physical host server at such a low resolution and color depth. For the best performance, a graphics display card providing at least 1024×768 resolution and 16.7 million colors should be used. This will also allow for easy administration of virtual machines from their physical host if necessary.

Software Requirements

Host Operating System

Virtual Server 2005 supports Windows Server 2003 Standard, Enterprise, and Data Center Editions. The differences and reasons as to why one would be chosen over the other are fairly straightforward. Windows Server 2003 Standard offers support for up to four physical processors and 4GB of memory, Windows Server 2003 Enterprise supports up to eight physical processors and 32GB of memory, and Windows Server 2003 Data Center supports up to thirty-two physical processors and 64GB of memory. There are only a few instances when it would make sense to run Virtual Server on anything beyond Windows Server 2003 Enterprise Edition due to the high cost of hardware and software for a Data Center Edition class of machine.

Virtual Server Administration Interface

Virtual Server's administration is done through a Web-based interface that requires Microsoft Internet Information Services (IIS) version 6.0. Only Microsoft Internet Explorer is supported as a browsing interface into the administration site and for full functionality, ActiveX Controls must be enabled.

Virtual Server Scripting

Microsoft has included a COM API scripting interface for automating the control and management of virtual machines. The COM API will be fully explored in chapter 25.

Summary

Microsoft Virtual Server 2005 is a new platform that is maturing rapidly. There are several capabilities that are lacking when compared to some of the more mature virtualization platforms, however the licensing costs easily make up for this short coming. Because Virtual Server leverages the Microsoft Windows Server 2003 family of operating systems as its platform, it gains the ability to support the broadest number of hardware platforms of any virtualization platform (matching that of VMware's GSX server for Windows, which leverages the Windows operating systems as well). Support for guest operating systems is currently limited to Microsoft only-based platforms, but with the introduction of Virtual Server 2005 R2 the support will ultimately expand to include Linux and other non-Microsoft-based operating systems. Licensing is simply based on the number of processors that are going to be used, either a maximum of four or thirty-two. Hardware and software requirements are simply any server that runs and can support Microsoft Windows Server 2003 Standard Edition or greater. It is recommended that the server being used be upgraded if it was not originally ordered with specifications for the specific purpose of providing virtualization services.

Chapter 9

Installing Microsoft Virtual Server

Although Microsoft provides a straight-forward installation Wizard for Microsoft Virtual Server 2005 R2, this chapter covers the entire installation process, including system requirements and host server preparation. The Microsoft Virtual Server 2005 R2 installer is less complex than other common Microsoft application installers, such as Microsoft Office 2003 or Microsoft SQL Server 2005, and provides a consistent, Wizard-based approach that will be comfortable to those whom have already worked with other Microsoft products on a Microsoft Windows operating system. All options and aspects of the installation are covered in this chapter, allowing the reader to understand each option along with the ramifications of that option before doing an actual install. The installation of the Standard Edition is identical to the installation of the Enterprise Edition. This chapter may also be used as a reference during the planning of the installation to ensure a repeatable and stable platform where the desired capabilities are consistently delivered.

Virtual Server 2005 R2 Requirements

Before installing Microsoft Virtual Server R2, it is important to make sure that your server and operating system meet all of the requirements. If a previous version (such as a beta or evaluation copy) is installed, it should be completely removed before installing a newer version. Before uninstalling a previous version of Microsoft Virtual Server, the Virtual Server service should first be stopped and then the Add/Remove Program Files under Control Panel can be used to select the previous version of Microsoft Virtual Server and uninstalled by clicking the Remove button. This will uninstall the previous version of Microsoft Virtual Server.

When installing Virtual Server, the local administrator or a local user's account with administrative privileges must be used. Virtual Server should only be installed for production use on a Windows Server 2003-based operating system, however it will install on a Windows XP Professional with SP2 host operating system for non-production use.

Preparing the Host Server

Preparing the server is the first in a critical series of steps ensuring that the system will be stable and provide adequate performance.

- Ensure the server is properly cabled with the necessary power cables. Dual power supplies connected to separate power leads is preferred.
- Connect any KVM type solution to the host server for remote management.
- Connect all Ethernet ports that will be used (unused ports can also be connected if desired).
- Upgrade to Gigabit Ethernet, if possible.
- Team multiple network adapters for best performance.
- Download and install the latest BIOS and then configure its settings appropriately.
- Download and upgrade any firmware that needs to be updated.
- Configure the RAID controller.
    1. Configure the RAID controller for optimized write operations.
    2. A multi-channel controller card should be configured with one channel configured as a mirrored pair for the operating system and the other channel configured as RAID 5 with four or more drives in the RAID set if possible for the virtual machines.
    3. The default stripe size is acceptable.
    4. Assign physical hard drives.
    5. Create logical volumes.
- Delete all existing partitions including any server manufacturer's support partition.
- Format using a high-performance file system such as NTFS.
- Install and configure the host operating system.

Preparing the Host Operating System

The host operating system is the next critical step in building the proper platform for Virtual Server. The detailed steps involved in installing the host operating system will not be covered in this book. It is assumed that a basic level of understanding and experience with installing a Windows operating system already exists. The proper configuration is covered below, including all required options and steps.

- Microsoft Internet Information Server (IIS) 5.1 or 6 World Wide Web Services must be installed and the services must be started and operating without errors.
- Ensure that the Physical Address Edition (/PAE) option is set in the boot. ini file if greater than 4GB of memory is being used.
- Confirm the correct amount of memory is being reported by the host operating system.
- Ensure that the paging file is of adequate size.
- Stop any unnecessary services.
- Install only the necessary packages and applications rather than loading down the host operating system. It should only serve as the virtualization platform.
- Disable all protocols and services on any network adapters that will be used exclusively by virtual machines, including TCP/IP. After the installation, ensure that Virtual Machine Network Services is enabled on these network adapters.
- Defragment the host operating system's hard disk.
- Clear all event logs in Event Viewer.
- Set the system's advanced performance settings for the processor to be optimized for background services.
- Set any antivirus software to skip scanning of virtualization configuration files, virtual hard disk image files, floppy image files, and CD/DVD-ROM ISO image files. Additionally, real-time scanning should be disabled entirely and scanning should be scheduled for nightly scans instead.

Installing Microsoft Virtual Server 2005 R2

Microsoft Virtual Server 2005 R2 uses a Microsoft Windows Installer-based installation Wizard much like other current Microsoft applications. The installation Wizard is straight-forward and is very consistent with other Microsoft application installation Wizards. This section provides step-by-step installation instructions together with screenshots that clearly show each available option. In this example, Microsoft Virtual Server 2005 R2 Enterprise Edition will be installed on a host server running Microsoft Windows Server 2003 R2 Enterprise Edition.

The installation media for Microsoft Virtual Server 2005 R2 is a single executable setup file. This setup file should be copied onto the host server and then executed. Once the setup file has been started, the installation process will begin.

No other applications should be running when installing Microsoft Virtual Server 2005 R2.

The installer will load and present the initial setup Wizard screen as shown in Figure 9.1. There are three options available: Install Microsoft Virtual Server 2005 R2, View Release Notes, and Exit. To continue the installation, the button labeled Install Microsoft Virtual Server 2005 R2 must be clicked.

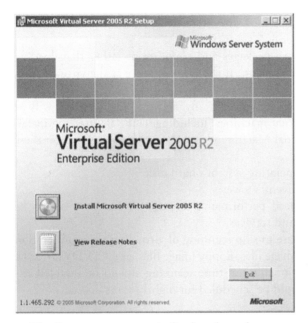

Figure 9.1 Microsoft Virtual Server 2005 R2 Setup Menu.

The license agreement is displayed on the next screen (see Figure 9.2) of the Wizard. It must be read and accepted before the installation process can continue. The option labeled, "I accept the terms in the license agreement," must be

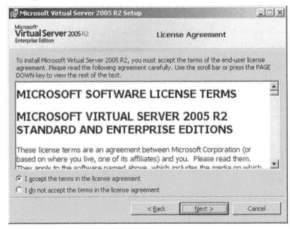

Figure 9.2 License Agreement.

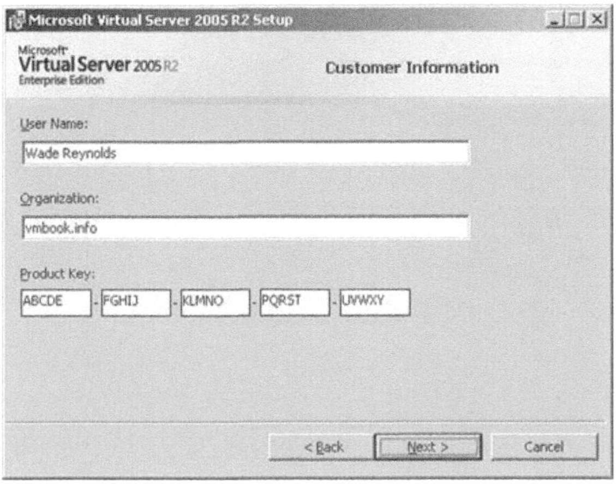

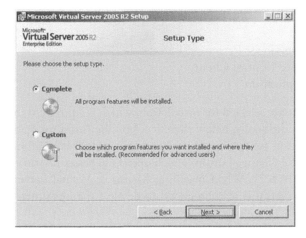

Figure 9.3   Customer Information.

selected before the Next button is enabled. Once the license agreement has been accepted, the Next button is clicked.

The Customer Information screen has three input fields that must be filled out as shown in Figure 9.3. The User Name field requires the name of the licensed owner of the software and the Organization field is used to optionally input an organization name of the user. The Product Key field requires the entry of a valid Microsoft Virtual Server 2005 R2 serial number. Once these fields are filled out properly, the Next button must be clicked to continue the installation.

The Setup Type screen is displayed next and it provides a decision point for the installation. Either the Complete or the Custom option must be selected. The Complete option installs all options and reduces the number of installation Wizard screens presented (see Figure 9.4). It is also the default option. The Custom setup type allows exact features to be installed as required (see Figure 9.5). If the Custom option is selected, extra Wizard screens will be presented in order for the Custom installation features to be selected or deselected as required. After a setup type is selected, the Next button is clicked to proceed.

Figure 9.4   Setup Type, Complete Installation.

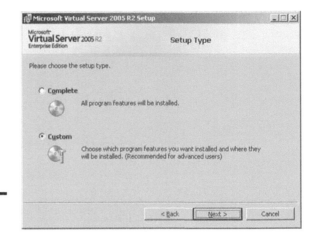

Figure 9.5 Setup Type, Custom Installation.

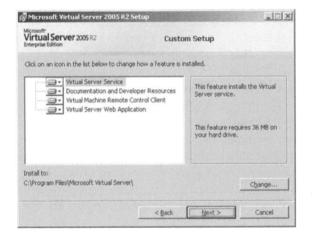

Figure 9.6 Custom Setup, Default Options.

If the Custom setup type was selected the Custom Setup screen is displayed as shown in Figure 9.6. The Custom Setup screen displays the four available features that may be installed:

- Virtual Server Service
- Documentation and Developer Resources
- Virtual Machine Remote Control Client
- Virtual Server Web Application

By default, all four options are selected for installation, which is equivalent to the Complete setup type. Additionally, below the select box the Install to field displays the installation location for the feature currently selected. This location can be changed by clicking the Change button, which opens the Select Destination Folder screen (see Figure 9.7). When installing Microsoft Virtual Server 2005 R2 on a production server, it is recommended to deselect the Documen-

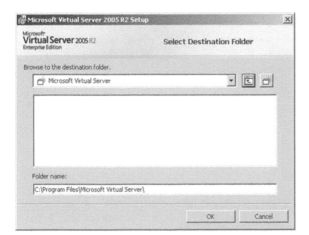

Figure 9.7   Select Destination Folder.

Figure 9.8   Custom Setup, Recommended Production Options.

tation and Developer Resources feature as shown in Figure 9.8. This follows a general best practice of not installing documentation, code samples, and SDK information onto production servers. These features should only be installed onto non-production developer and test servers. After all Custom installation options have been selected, the Next button on the Custom Setup screen is clicked to continue the installation.

The next set of installer screens are displayed for if either the Complete or Custom setup type was used. There are two screens named Configure Components. The first Configure Components screen allows the configuration of the TCP port that will be configured for the Virtual Server Administration Website as shown in Figure 9.9. By default, the value is port 1024. In this example, the default value is used. Additionally, this screen also has an option to select the user account context under which the Administration Website will reside. The default option (used in this example) is to run the Administration Website as the authenticated user. The other available option is to run the Administration

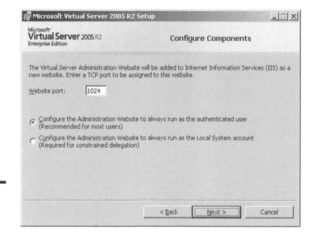

Figure 9.9 Configure Components, Windows Server 2003 Host.

Website as the Local System account. The default option (run as authenticated user) will provide ease of use when accessing the Administration Website because the user will not have to interactively authenticate.

 When installing Virtual Server on a host server running Microsoft Windows XP Professional SP2, the first Configure Components screen is different than what is displayed on a Windows Server system as shown in Figure 9.10. Because of the limits placed on the version of IIS used on Windows XP (version 5.1, only one Web site, limited user connectivity), the port selection defaults to that of the local IIS Web site and cannot be changed. This is because Windows XP's version of IIS only allows one Web site and Virtual Server will install under a new virtual directory/Web application under the default Web site. Additionally, the account options are removed

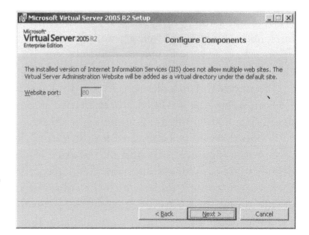

Figure 9.10 Configure Components, Windows XP professional SP2 Host.

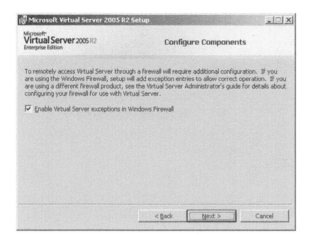

Figure 9.11 Configure Components, Windows Firewall Option.

from this screen as well and Virtual Server will run under the account configured for the default Web site.

The next Configure Components screen allows Virtual Server exception rules to be enabled or disabled in Windows Firewall as shown in Figure 9.11. The default options are to enable the exceptions in Windows Firewall. In this example, the default option is used. The Next button continues to the next installer screen.

The Ready to Install screen (see Figure 9.12) is shown next. This is the last chance to use the Back button to return to previous installation option screens to make option changes or to use the Cancel button to exit the installer before any changes have been made to the host server. The Install button should be clicked to proceed to install the product.

Once the installation begins, the status screen is displayed and it will begin to create the installation script as shown in Figure 9.13. Once the installation script

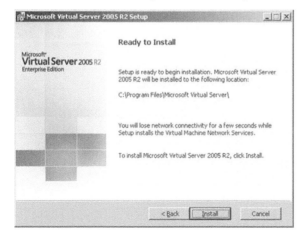

Figure 9.12 Ready to Install.

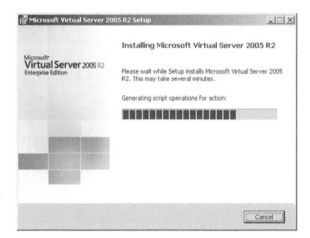

Figure 9.13 Installing, Generating Script.

has been generated, it will be executed and the installer will begin to modify the host server, installing the proper bits where necessary. During the installation process, the status bar is used to monitor the status of the installation (see Figure 9.14). This installation generally only takes a few minutes. After the installer has completed the installation actions, the Setup Complete screen is displayed as shown in Figure 9.15. The Finish button is used to exit the installer.

After the installation is complete, an Internet Explorer browser window is automatically opened by the installer and will navigate to the Installation Summary screen as shown in Figure 9.16. After reviewing the Installation Summary Web page, it is safe to close the browser window. The Installation Summary Web page can be viewed later as a shortcut to it is installed under the Microsoft Virtual Server program group.

A new program group labeled Microsoft Virtual Server is installed and is accessible from the Windows Start menu under the All Programs menu item as shown in Figure 9.17. This program group contains the following shortcuts:

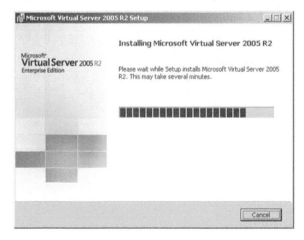

Figure 9.14 Installation Progress.

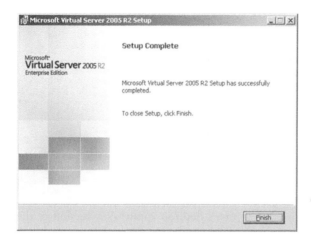

Figure 9.15   Setup Complete.

Installation Summary

Installation Folder
Microsoft® Virtual Server 2005 R2 has been successfully installed to the following location:
C:\Program Files\Microsoft Virtual Server

Administration Website
The Virtual Server Administration Website, which you can use to configure and manage Virtual Server, has been added to Internet Information Services (IIS). You can open this website from the Start menu. To do this, click **Start**, point to **All Programs**, point to **Microsoft Virtual Server**, and then click **Virtual Server Administration Website**. You can also use the following URL to open the Administration Website:

http://vmbookhost:1024/VirtualServer/VSWebApp.exe?view=1

Access Control
Access to the Administration Website and the Virtual Server COM interfaces is restricted to the Local Administrators group. You can change this setting from the Administration Website. To do this, click **Server Properties**, click **Virtual Server security**, and then change the permissions. For detailed instructions, see the Virtual Server documentation.

Documentation
To get help for a particular element of the Administration Website, click the help button. In addition, an Administrator's Guide for configuring and managing Virtual Server and a Programmer's Guide for using the Virtual Server COM interfaces is located in the following folder:

C:\Program Files\Microsoft Virtual Server\Documentation

You can also open the documentation from the **Microsoft Virtual Server** menu in the Start menu.

Figure 9.16   Installation Summary Web Page.

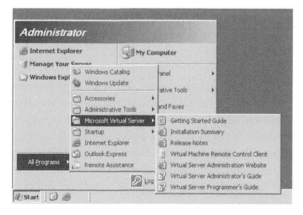

Figure 9.17   Microsoft Virtual Server Program Group.

- Getting Started Guide
- Installation Summary
- Release Notes
- Virtual Machine Remote Control Client
- Virtual Server Administration Website
- Virtual Server Administrator's Guide
- Virtual Server Programmer's Guide

The Microsoft Virtual Server program group contains two shortcuts to actual programs. The Virtual Machine Remote Control (VMRC) Client is an executable application that allows remote console connections to Microsoft Virtual Server virtual machines running on the local server or remote servers running Microsoft Virtual Server. This is a Windows desktop application version of the VMRC ActiveX control that is used from within the Virtual Server Administration Website. The shortcut labeled Virtual Server Administration Website launches Internet Explorer to connect to the locally hosted (in IIS) Virtual Server Administration Website. This Web application is used to configure and manage Microsoft Virtual Server and its virtual machines. It can also connect to and manage remote servers running Microsoft Virtual Server.

The remaining shortcuts are all documentation shortcuts. The Installation Summary is an HTML document, the same Installation Summary document that was displayed at the end of the installation process. The Release Notes shortcut also opens an HTML document displaying the product's last minute release note documentation.

The Getting Started Guide is a Word or Wordpad document that has useful information used to get Microsoft Virtual Server up and running quickly. The Virtual Server Administrator's Guide is the official Microsoft online documentation (in Microsoft HTML Help format) for installing and managing Microsoft Virtual Server and all of its various features. The Virtual Server Programmer's Guide is the official Microsoft online documentation (in Microsoft HTML Help format), which is a mini SDK for programming applications that automate and interact with Microsoft Virtual Server.

Summary

Microsoft Virtual Server 2005 R2 likely has the easiest, most straight-forward setup process of all of the leading server virtualization platforms to date. It is consistent with all current Microsoft application installers and is very intuitive. The default setup options can easily be used without worry of leaving security holes open in the system, although it is recommended that the documentation and developer resources not be installed onto production servers as a best practice. After the product has been installed, it does not require a reboot and may be configured and used immediately.

Chapter 10

Configuring Microsoft Virtual Server

Once installed, Microsoft Virtual Server 2005 is ready for configuration. This chapter covers the proper configuration of Microsoft Virtual Server 2005 R2, including security, management, and tools that supply an easy to use and highly productive interface. It is critical that Microsoft Virtual Server 2005 be properly configured to garner all of the capabilities that are built into Virtual Server. Managing virtual machines and the host server can be a labor intensive process if Virtual Server is not configured properly to maximize productivity. It is important to learn how to properly use the management interface as mistakes can harm both host server and virtual machine performance, or can quite possibly render a virtual machine unusable.

Tools

Microsoft Virtual Server 2005 has a myriad of tools and options available for configuring and manipulating the behavior of Virtual Server. Each of these tools and options will be examined in detail as each step in the configuration process is explained.

Virtual Server Administration Website

Microsoft Virtual Server 2005 is controlled through the Virtual Server Administration Website, here as known as the Administration Website. The Administration Website is the only user accessible interface into Virtual Server. The only other way to interact with Virtual Server is to use the COM API driven scripting interface, which is covered in chapter 25.

To begin the configuration of Virtual Server, the Administration Website must be launched. The Administration Website can be launched by selecting Start > All Programs > Microsoft Virtual Server > Virtual Server Administration Website. The default web browser will launch and open the management Website.

The Virtual Server Administration Website requires Microsoft Internet Explorer 5.5 or later for full functionality.

Upon launching the Administration Website, the management interface provides the current status of any previously configured virtual machines. As this example is a first time installation and configuration, there should be no configured virtual machines present. The page should be pretty sparse in details at the moment. On the left hand side of the page exists a column with several headings and sub-sections. Each of these subsections is created based on the type of tasks that can be performed under its heading. This chapter focuses on the subsection located at the bottom of the column with the heading titled Virtual Server (see Figure 10.1). The Virtual Server group provides the interface into the configuration settings and behavior of the core virtualization platform as well as the behavior of the Administration Website.

Server Properties

The first option under the Virtual Server heading is Server Properties. Upon selecting Server Properties, the following page of information is presented (see Figure 10.2).

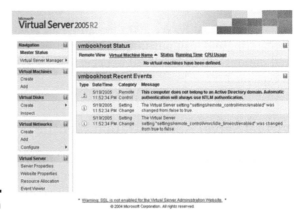

Figure 10.1   Administration Website.

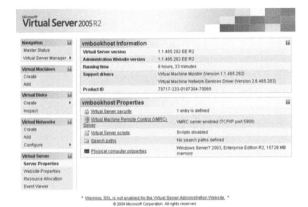

Figure 10.2   Server Properties.

The Server Properties page supplies information regarding the Virtual Server virtualization platform itself. Information on this page includes:

- Virtual Server version—The version of the virtualization control services that enforce the rules set by configuring settings in the Virtual Server Administration Website tool. Provides an administrator user with a quick glance method of identifying the version, build, and service pack level of Virtual Server.
- Administration Website version—Provides the version of the Server Properties Web page currently being viewed. Also provides an administrator user with the ability to check for a version mismatch or incompatibility between the Administration Website and the virtualization control services.
- Running time—Shows the amount of time in days, hours, and minutes that the virtualization services have been running on the physical host server, since the last reboot of the system or the last restart of the Virtual Server service.
- Support drivers—Lists the two drivers installed on the host operating system by Virtual Server that provide essential support functions. They provide the virtualization and coordination of the primary components of the host server and supply the interfaces for the virtual machines.

The support drivers mentioned above consist of the Virtual Machine Monitor and the Virtual Machine Network Services Driver. The Virtual Machine Monitor provides and enforces memory allocation and CPU resource allocation of the host system to the virtual machines. It is responsible for the basic creation and management of virtual machines. The Virtual Machine Network Services Driver allows the virtual network services provided by Virtual Server to interface with the host network cards and is therefore responsible for providing network connectivity for virtual machines.

Figure 10.3 Virtual Server Security Properties.

The submenu under Server Properties titled Virtual Server security is explored next.

Virtual Server Security Properties

The Virtual Server Security Properties page (see Figure 10.3) supplies a basic interface into the security settings of Virtual Server. Security governance includes permissions that apply to Virtual Server and to virtual machines and virtual network configuration files. It is important to realize that the options supplied by the Virtual Server Security Properties page are limited to control over virtual machines that Virtual Server is hosting. If a more granular control is required (such as control over specific virtual networks or virtual hard disks), it is recommended that Access Control Lists (ACLs) on the specific files and folders be used. ACLs are directory and file level permissions that can be set via the Microsoft Management Console (MMC).

The options available under the Security Properties page are:

- Remove—Deletes the selected rule from the list. It is important to realize that once a rule is removed, it is completely gone from the system and will have to be recreated if that rule is required in the future.
- User or group—Specifies what user name or group the permission entry being created should apply to.
- Type—Allow or Deny, decides what security philosophy should be used for this user account or group. Allow grants specific access (based on the permission selections below it). Deny prevents specific access (also based on the permission selections below it).
- Permissions—These are the specific access types that can be controlled:
  - Full—Selecting this check box will automatically select all of the other permissions for this entry.

- Modify—Selecting this check box alters the permission to add virtual machines and virtual networks to Virtual Server. It also alters permission to make changes to Virtual Server Search Paths and Script Settings, as well as the VMRC Server Properties.
- View—Selecting this check box alters the permission to read Virtual Server configuration information as well as configuration information for virtual machines (assuming the user has the proper file system permissions). It also controls the ability to read Virtual Server event logs and controls whether or not the user or group can use the VMRC to manage virtual machines for which they have the appropriate permissions.
- Remove—Selecting this check box alters the permission to remove a virtual machine or virtual network configuration from the system.
- Change permissions—Selecting this check box provides a method of altering access and settings on the Virtual Server Security Properties page. Essentially, if a user is granted this permission, they can grant themselves or anyone else full access to any virtual machine.
- Control—Selecting this check box alters the permission to access the Component Object Model (COM) API. It allows the user or group member to manage Virtual Server using either the COM interface or the Administration Website. Without this permission, a user or group member will not have any administrative control over Virtual Server.
- Special Permissions—This check box provides notification if there are special permissions in place for the Virtual Server folder. It does not provide a method for altering these permissions.
- Add entry—Allows additional rules to be created.
- OK—Returns to the Server Properties page.

 It is a good practice to keep the number of rules to a minimum, as the risk of security holes increases along with the complexity and difficulty in management as the number of rules increases.

Securing Virtual Server and IIS

Securing Virtual Server and IIS are critical components in ensuring that the Virtual Server host and guest machines will not be compromised. In order to maintain a high level of security, while still providing all of the needed administrative functionality, a series of best practices should be followed. Below is a listing of best practices and information regarding the proper securing of Virtual Server and IIS.

Configuring Security Permissions on Files and Folders via ACLs

Security can be applied granularly on virtual machines, virtual networks, and virtual hard disk files. By using the tables below, settings can easily be applied to lock down access to any of these resources (see Figure 10.4 and Figure 10.5).

The following is a list of security best practices for Virtual Server:

- The Administration Website uses a Common Gateway Interface (CGI) application for data transfer—VSWebApp.exe. This application controls a single instance of Virtual Server and enables authenticated administration and remote access. In order to use the Virtual Server Administration Website, user accounts must have Execute permissions to the folder containing the Virtual Server Web Application, VSWebApp.exe. To secure the Web application, modify the permissions on the folder located by default at C:\Program Files\Microsoft Virtual Server\WebSite\VirtualServer. Execute permission should only be given to a select group of users.
- Secure the individual configuration files and resource files associated with the Virtual Server components, such as the virtual machine configuration (.vmc) files, the virtual network configuration (.vnc) files, and the virtual hard disk (.vhd) files. Permissions should only be given to the appropriate groups or users that need access to these components. By default, the administrator group should have permissions to these files.

 By using the NTFS file system access permissions, the primary components that make up a virtual machine can be restricted and secured to allow access to only those user accounts or groups that need permission. Because Virtual Server does not provide direct access to security controls for these components, securing the virtual machine configuration (.vmc) files, and the virtual hard disk (.vhd) files all rely on the NTFS file system. For ease of management, it is recommended that these files be contained in a single folder representing the virtual machine. Other files associated with the virtual machine, such as undo disks and saved state files will be automatically created in the same folder that contains the virtual machine configuration file. To provide ease of administration and security configuration, it is recommended that the folder structure containing these virtual machine files be configured to something more appropriate than the default Shared Virtual Machine folder in C:\Documents and Settings\All Users\Documents.

- Virtual Server should be operating behind a firewall for proper security, and should only open port 1024 (the default port) to allow access to the Virtual Server Administration Website. SSL should also be enabled if at all possible to provide a more secure administration experience.

	Virtual Machines	Virtual Networks	Virtual Hard Disks	Virtual Floppy/ISO
Extension	.vmc	.vnc	.vhd .vud .vdd	.flp .iso
Read Permissions	View security settings on this file	View security settings on this file	View security settings on this file	View security settings on this file
Change Permissions	Alter security settings on this file	Alter security settings on this file	Alter security settings on this file	Alter security settings on this file
Read Data	View configuration information and view VMRC	View configuration information	Read information from hard disk	Read information from media
Write Data	Alter configuration information	Alter configuration information	Write information to hard disk (Read Required)	Write to media (.flp only)
Execute File	Change power state and control with VMRC	Ability to use/connect	Ability to use	Ability to use
Delete	Delete the configuration	Delete the configuration	Delete the hard disk	Delete the media

Figure 10.4   File Security.

Folder Name	Virtual Machine Helper	
Path	C:\Documents and Settings\All Users\Application Data\Microsoft\Virtual Machine Helper	
Default Users & Permissions	Administrator	FC
	Creator Owner	FC
	SYSTEM	R&E, CF/WD, CF/AD
	Network Service	R&E, CF/WD, CF/AD

Folder Name	Virtual Server Webapp	
Path	C:\Documents and Settings\All Users\Application Data\Microsoft\Virtual Server Webapp	
Default Users & Permissions	Administrators	FC
	Everyone	R&E
	Power Users	All except FC
	SYSTEM	FC
	Users	R&E

Folder Name	Virtual Networks	
Path	C:\Documents and Settings\All Users\Application Data\Microsoft\Shared Virtual Networks	
Default Users & Permissions	Administrators	FC
	CREATOR OWNER	FC
	NETWORK SERVICE	R&E, CF/WD, CF/AD
	SYSTEM	R&E, CF/WD, CF/AD

Folder Name	Virtual Machines	
Path	C:\Documents and Settings\All Users\Application Data\Microsoft\Shared Virtual Machines	
Default Users & Permissions	Administrators	FC
	CREATOR OWNER	FC
	NETWORK SERVICE	R&E, CF/WD, CF/AD
	SYSTEM	R&E, CF/WD, CF/AD

Folder Name	Shared Virtual Machine Folders	
Path	C:\Documents and Settings\All Users\Shared Documents\Shared Virtual Machines	
Default Users & Permissions	Administrators	FC
	CREATOR OWNER	FC
	NETWORKS SERVICE	R&E, CF/WD, CF/AD
	SYSTEM	R&E

Folder Name	Shared Virtual Network Files	
Path	C:\Documents and Settings\All Users]Shared Documents\Shared Virtual Networks	
Default Users & Permissions	Administrators	FC
	CREATOR OWNER	FC
	NETWORKS SERVICE	R&E, CF/WD, CF/AD
	SYSTEM	R&E, CF/WD, CF/AD

Permissions Key	FC - Full Control	R&E - Read and Execute
	CF/WD - Create Files/Write Data	CF/AD - Create Folder/Append Data

Figure 10.5   Folder Security.

- If the Virtual Machine Remote Control (VMRC) client and server are going to be used, port 5900 (the default port) must be opened for the base VMRC server and ports 137 and 138, the Transmission Control Protocol (TCP) and User Datagram Protocol (UDP) ports, must be opened for the Kerberos V5 ticket-granting authority.
- If Active Directory integration is being used, all proper user security must be checked and enforced against both the physical host server and all virtual machines.

 It is strongly recommended to implement Secure Socket Layer (SSL) security for the Administration Website and the VMRC connections, especially when using Basic authentication since passwords are transmitted in plaintext.

The following is a list of security best practices for IIS when used with Virtual Server:

- Do not host other Web sites on the Virtual Server host machine. Web sites should be hosted on nonvirtualization platform physical servers or within virtual machines.
- With the exception of the Virtual Server Web Application and components, all other Web, FTP, and SMTP services listed in the IIS Manager should be removed.
- IP address restrictions can be used to limit access to the management interface.
  1. In IIS Manager, in the Websites directory, right click the management interface Website and then select Properties.
  2. Click the Directory Security tab.
  3. Click Edit in the IP address and domain name restrictions section.
  4. Click either Granted access or Denied access. When selecting Denied access, access to all computers and domains are denied. When selecting Granted access, access to all computers and domains are granted, except to those specifically denied access.
  5. Click Add and then select either Single computer or Group of computers.
  6. Enter either the IP address or the Network ID and Subnet mask and then click OK.

Antivirus Software

A Windows guest operating system exposed to the outside world needs virus protection as much as any physical server does. It does not matter if antivirus software is installed on the host server. A virtual machine needs its own copy of antivirus installed. Unlike a physical server, there are a few things to consider when configuring an antivirus solution in a Windows guest operating system.

- Be sure to account for the extra overhead that an antivirus solution provides when creating a virtual machine configuration file. During the planning process, make sure enough disk space is available for virus definition downloads and enough memory and processor is available to run the software and the virus scanning.
- If there are a number of running virtual machines on the host server, be sure to stagger the virus scanning schedule. If all of the virtual machines on the host server start their virus scans at the same time, the host server performance may become starved for resources.
- If the antivirus software provides real-time scanning, monitor the processor utilization to make sure the process is not running higher than normal. In some cases, real-time virus scanning on the guest operating system may spike to a percentage of utilization beyond what is acceptable. If this is the case, modifying the real-time scan to only scan files that have been modified as opposed to all files should bring processor utilization back to a normal and acceptable amount.

Operating System and Application Security Patches

It is important to keep the guest operating system and all applications up to date with any security patches or service packs. Operating systems and applications installed on a virtual machine suffer from the same security concerns and problems as those faced in a physical server. If an application such as a Web server (IIS or Apache) becomes exploited, it should be patched immediately. However, if a guest operating system comes out with a new update, it is not always a good idea to quickly update the virtual machine. A new service pack in the guest operating system may cause problems for the host platform. Case in point, the Windows Server 2003 Service Pack 1 was not officially supported as a guest operating system until Virtual Server 2005 R2 was released. While that does not mean that the service pack would definitely not function correctly in the virtual machine, it does mean that it was not officially supported. And as such, Microsoft support would not be able to help troubleshoot any problems that may arise.

 It is important to note that there is in fact a performance issue with running Windows Server 2003 Service Pack 1 in a virtual machine prior to the release of the new virtual machine additions that are supplied with Microsoft Virtual Server 2005 R2.

Virtual Machine Remote Control Server

The Virtual Machine Remote Control (VMRC) Server Properties page provides access to the configuration and settings for connection to virtual machines (see Figure 10.6). Each of these settings and what they do are reviewed in detail below.

The following is a list of the settings, subsettings and their functionality.

- VMRC server
  - Enable—Determines if remote control services are going to be available on the host server. This option is enabled by default. When unchecked, virtual machines cannot be managed by using the VMRC.
  - TCP/IP address—The TCP/IP address to use for VMRC sessions. The addresses of configured network adapters appear in the drop-down list.
  - TCP/IP port—Tells the VMRC server which port to use for VMRC sessions. The default setting is port 5900; however any port number in the full range (from 1 to 65,535) can be selected. To allow access to the VMRC from outside of the firewall, the appropriate ports must be opened. It is recommended that the port number be changed from the default for security reasons.
  - Default screen resolution—The resolution at which the VMRC client receives from the server if the VMRC client is using its default settings. This setting is a global setting. To change the setting for a specific virtual machine, the display resolution should be adjusted in the guest operating system. The default setting is 800×600, and it is recommended that the default setting be used unless there is a specific need to change the

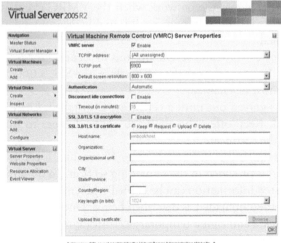

Figure 10.6 VMRC Server Properties.

setting. It is important to understand that the higher the resolution selected, the slower the refresh rate that the VMRC client will be capable of. The slow refresh is due to the amount of image information that has to be transferred from the VMRC server to the client. Hence, the higher the resolution, the higher the data and bandwidth needed to support it.

- Authentication—The authentication method to use for the VMRC client.
  - Automatic—Correctly selects either NTLM or Kerberos where appropriate (the default setting).
  - NTLM—Provides access via any authorized local Windows account.
  - Kerberos—Provides access via Active Directory-based authentication. For Kerberos authentication to work, the client computer must be joined to a Microsoft Windows Server 2003 or a Microsoft Windows 2000 domain.
- Disconnect idle connections—Provides a method of terminating VMRC client connections that are inactive for a predetermined period of time specified in the Timeout field. Disconnecting idle connections is an important security measure that is turned off by default.
  - Enable—Selecting this checkbox will activate this feature.
  - Timeout—Default value is 15 minutes. This value determines the time (in minutes) before an idle VMRC connection is disconnected. The recommended time should be as aggressive as possible, without making it too difficult to work. A good starting point would be between 5 and 10 minutes. The maximum value allowed is 1,440 minutes (which translates to a 24 hour period).
- SSL 3.0/TLS 1.0 encryption—To enable the encryption setting, the checkbox must be selected and then the certificate information listed under SSL 3.0/TLS 1.0 certificate must be supplied. Enabling this feature will encrypt the data that is transferred across the network when the VMRC client is used. This setting is disabled by default; however it is highly recommended that the setting be enabled.
- SSL 3.0/TLS 1.0 certificate—Provides several options in securing the host server with a certificate. To access the certificate interface, the SSL 3.0/TLS 1.0 encryption setting must be enabled.
  - Keep—This option is grayed out until a certificate is installed. Once a certificate is installed, Keep offers the ability to apply changes to this page without losing the certificate.
  - Request—Creates a request for a TLS certificate. The request is created when the information is provided in the remaining section. To obtain a certificate, the requested information can be copied and sent to a certification authority and then uploaded as described below. Until that time, Virtual Server will create and sign a temporary certificate to use until a valid certificate is received.

- Upload—Provides a mechanism for uploading a certificate once it has been obtained from a certificate authority.
- Delete—Used when a certificate is being removed from the host system. Delete is most commonly used if a newly created certificate is being generated and an old certificate is already in place.
- Host name—The name of the computer that is running the Virtual Server service.
- Organization—The name of the company or organization.
- Organization Unit—This field is optional. Used to identify the name of the organizational unit within the company that is making the request.
- City—The city where the organization is located.
- State/Province—The state or providence in which the organization is located.
- Country/Region—The country or region where the organization is located.
- Key length (in bits) —The length, in bits, of the public key on the certificate. There are few (if any) who have been able to break a key operating at 512 bits, however a key length greater than 512 can be chosen.
- Upload this certificate—The location to specify an SSL 3.0/TLS 1.0 certificate to use with VMRC. The certificate must be located on the computer running the Virtual Server service. The full path to the certificate can be entered manually or the Browse button can be used to locate it.

Virtual Server Scripts

The Virtual Server Scripts page provides automated responses to events occurring on the host system. These events may be driven by activities on the host system itself or virtual machines interacting with the host system. The Virtual Server Scripts page provides a brief view into what can be done by interfacing with the COM API. The Virtual Server Scripts page (see Figure 10.7) is described in detail below.

The first section is the Virtual Server Script Settings. This section has two options:

- Enable scripts attached to this server—The setting is disabled by default. Enabling this option allows for the execution of scripts on the host server which can have serious security implications. Poorly written or malicious scripts can cause havoc on the host server. On the other hand, when done correctly, scripts can offer ease of management through the use of automation.
- Enable scripts attached to virtual machines running on this server—This setting is also disabled by default. It allows for the execution of scripts that

Figure 10.7 Virtual Server Script Settings.

interact with virtual machines running on the host server. The same pros and cons can apply here. The pros allow better manageability by automating many common tasks, including automated shut downs, starts, resets, etc. And again, the cons are that malicious or poorly written scripts may cause the virtual machines to fail unexpectedly.

The second section is the Virtual Server Attached Scripts where a particular script can be specified to run when a Virtual Server event occurs, or where a previously specified script can be removed. These are all event driven scripts, meaning they are executed when a specific event occurs. It is important to note that entries cannot be made into these fields until at least one of the enable script options in Virtual Server Script Settings has been enabled.

Each of the options below is self explanatory:

- Command-line action when Virtual Server starts
- Command-line action when Virtual Server stops
- Command-line action when any virtual machine is turned on
- Command-line action when any virtual machine is restored
- Command-line action when any virtual machine is turned off (saved)
- Command-line action when any virtual machine is turned off (not saved)
- Command-line action when any virtual machine is turned off within the guest environment
- Command-line action when any virtual machine is reset
- Command-line action when no heartbeat is detected for any virtual machine

- Command-line action when any virtual machine experiences a guest processor error
- Command-line action when any virtual machine receives a warning due to low disk space on the physical computer
- Command-line action when any virtual machine receives an error due to low disk space on the physical computer

 In addition to command-line actions, Virtual Server can also execute scripts that are specified for a Virtual Server event. As an example, a script named PowerOn.vbs can be executed by using CScript, the command-line version of Windows Script Host. To execute the PowerOn.vbs script, the following syntax should be used: cscript PowerOn.vbs.

Virtual Server Search Paths

The Virtual Server Search Paths page (see Figure 10.8) is not a required configuration page; however, it can make Virtual Server management much simpler in a number of ways.

- **Default virtual machine configuration folder**
  This field specifies the folder or location where virtual machine configuration (.vmc) files and virtual hard disks (.vhd) are stored. It is recommended that the default location for configuration files be changed before the first virtual machine is created. The location should be standardized across all virtualization platform installs. Any virtual hard disk files that are created while creating a virtual machine through Virtual Server's interface will be

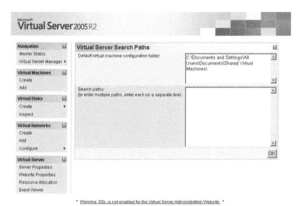

Figure 10.8 Virtual Server Search Paths.

stored in this same location. And since virtual hard disk files are usually very large in size, it is recommended that the virtual machine configuration folder be created on a very high capacity storage volume or that the disk files be separated from the configuration file.

■ **Search paths (to enter multiple paths, enter each on a separate line)**
Search paths provide a way for the Virtual Server Administration Website to populate list boxes used to specify the location of files such as virtual machine configuration (.vmc) files, virtual hard disk (.vhd) files, virtual floppy disk (.vfd) files, and ISO image (.iso) files. Search paths must be entered with fully qualified path names. They can be local paths (such as driver letter:\folder\subfolder) or network paths using Universal Naming Convention (UNC) path names (such as \\full computer name\folder\ subfolder or \\IP address\folder\subfolder). However, search paths going across a network share offer additional failure points as well as an increase in security risks. It is recommended that a standard directory structure be created for media such as ISO images and virtual floppy disks. The standard directory structure can then be added to the search path allowing the files to be automatically made available to all users with the proper access controls in place.

Physical Computer Properties

The Physical Computer Properties page (see Figure 10.9) provides information about the physical computer on which Microsoft Virtual Server 2005 is running, along with what resources Virtual Server thinks it can leverage. Each of the four areas covered will be described and explained below.

The Physical Computer Properties page is broken up into four areas: Processors, Memory, Network connections, and Operating system.

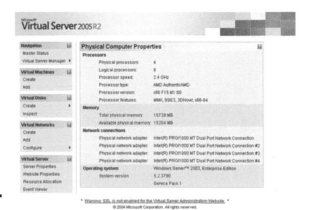

Figure 10.9 Physical Computer Properties.

- Processors—Covers all of the pertinent information needed to determine how much processing power is available to Virtual Server.
  - Physical processors—Lists the number of physical processors that Windows has identified on the host server.
  - Logical processors—Provides the number of logical processors that Windows has identified on the host server. Logical processors distinguish themselves from physical processor by representing the number of physical processors plus any HyperThreading Technology available. This means that if HyperThreading is turned on and the host server had two processors previously displayed, it would now show four processors, even though no physical processors were added.
  - Processor speed—The speed of the host server's physical processor in either MHz or GHz.
  - Processor type—Identifies the class of processor found on the host server.
  - Processor version—Provides the Instruction Set, Family, Stepping, and Model information about the processor.
  - Processor features—Identifies the features provided by the host server's processor such as MMX, SSE3, and 3DNow.
- Memory—Encompasses the memory parameters that provide resources to Virtual Server. The following two elements make up the memory section.
  - Total physical memory—Represents the total physical memory of the host system, as reported to it by the Windows host operating system.
  - Available physical memory—Shows the remaining physical memory that is available to Virtual Server for virtual machines. This number is also reported by the Windows host operating system. It is calculated by subtracting all of the applications and processes that are currently running on the system and consuming memory. It is important to realize that virtual machines cannot be allocated more memory than is represented as available under Available physical memory.
- Network connections—Shows the physical network adapters that are being reported as installed in the Windows host operating system. These are the adapters that can be selected to provide connectivity to the virtual machines.
  - Physical network adapter—Entries under network connections are different from machine to machine, depending on the number of network cards and the number of network ports. Each entry represents a network port as it is represented to the Windows host operating system.
- Operating system—Represents the version of the host operating system that is running, along with specific details.
  - System version—Provides the name of the host operating system, as well as its version, build number, and Service Pack level.

Administration Website Properties

The Administration Website Properties page (see Figure 10.10) is where the parameters of the Virtual Server Administration Website are controlled. These parameters can be altered to provide only the specific data that an administrator needs to see.

The Administration Website Properties page is composed of five sections. Each section contains a group of custom parameters that affect the administration experience of Microsoft Virtual Server 2005. The page also provides an option to change the auto refresh rate of the Administration Website. It provides the frequency (measured in seconds) at which the Administration Website is automatically refreshed. Setting a value less than 60 may impact performance as there is a slight drain on system resources as the requested data (both graphical and numeric) is retrieved, rendered, and displayed. To completely disable the automatic refresh, a value of 0 can be entered. However, in so doing, the browser will need to be manually refreshed to see any changes made, including any changes in the state of a virtual machine.

The first section is titled Master status view and is the default landing page when an administrator first logs into the Administration Website. The Master status view provides a consolidated view into the status of the Virtual Server host.

- Number of virtual machines per page—Controls the number of virtual machines to display on one page of the Master Status page.

Figure 10.10 Administration Website Properties.

- View columns—This entry has four check boxes that can be selected to control the display of the virtual machine attributes, such as the Remote View icon (the screen thumbnail), Status, Running Time, and CPU Usage.
  - Remote View—Remote View provides a screen thumbnail picture of what is happening inside of the virtual machine's console window at a given point in time. The remote view is a valuable tool to quickly scan the console status of large numbers of virtual machines.
  - Status—Displays the current virtual machine status and shows the latest event or power state that the machine has experienced.
  - Running Time—Provides the time that a virtual machine has been continuously operating on the host.
  - CPU Usage—Depicts the utilization of the virtual machine on a single processor, not the overall usage against all CPUs on the host.

Recent Events Properties

The second section, titled Recent events properties, controls the display of events that Microsoft Virtual Server 2005 has sent or registered with the Windows Event System. The Recent Events can be a useful tool in troubleshooting problems with Virtual Server.

- Display recent events on master status page—Allows the display of the most recent events occurring in the Virtual Server Event Log to appear on the Status page.
- Show error events—A filter setting to determine if error events should be displayed on the Master Status page under the recent events section (located at the bottom of the page).
- Show warning events—A filter setting to determine if warning events should be displayed on the Master Status page under the recent events section (located at the bottom of the page).
- Show information events—A filter setting to determine if informational events should be displayed on the Master Status page under the recent events section (located at the bottom of the page).
- Number of recent events to display—Controls the number of recent events that will be shown at the bottom of the Master Status page. The default setting is 5 and is usually enough for a quick status of what is occurring on the machine or to catch a mistake that may have just happened.

Event Viewer Properties

The third section is titled Event viewer properties. It refers to the Event Viewer page and only offers a single configuration change.

- Number of events displayed per page—Controls the number of events that are displayed on the Event Viewer page for Virtual Server, with 20 being the default.

The fourth section is titled Virtual Machine Remote Control properties and also offers only a single configuration change.

- Use reduced colors (improves performance)—As stated in the description, this check box option will reduce the number of displayed colors on the Virtual Machine Remote Control (VMRC) display in order to provide better performance (especially over low bandwidth connections). This is a global setting that affects the VMRC display for all virtual machines.

Virtual Server Manager Search Paths

The fifth and final section is titled Virtual Server Manager search paths, which provides the ability to enter multiple Virtual Server hosts for ease of administering several hosts from a single Virtual Server Administration Website. This setting is not commonly used as it could pose a potential security risk.

- Virtual Server Manager search paths—A text box in which each server that is going to be controlled is entered on a separate line. The full computer name or IP address of the server running the instance of Virtual Server to be managed must be entered. In addition, a change to either the configuration of the domain controller's constrained delegation or a change to IIS authentication (for both the current VirtualServer Web site as well as all of the managed host server's VirtualServer Web sites) from Integrated Windows authentication to Basic authentication. Thus, the potential security risk.

Resource Allocation

The CPU Resource Allocation page (see Figure 10.11) provides an administrator with the ability to control the CPU resources provided to each virtual machine and the importance of that virtual machine regarding CPU resource consumption. This flexibility allows administrators to divide up CPU resources to different virtual machines or to dedicate a single CPU to a single virtual machine. It is important to note that the specific CPU that will be given to a virtual machine (called CPU affinity) is decided by Virtual Server and cannot be set by the administrator. To more easily view this information, the columns on the page can be sorted by clicking on any of the column headings.

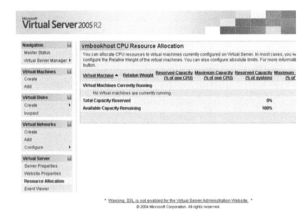

Figure 10.11 CPU Resource Allocation.

- Virtual Machine—Identifies the virtual machine that is affected by the settings that follow it on that row. By moving the cursor over the virtual machine name, a context menu is displayed which provides the ability to edit the machine's configuration, change its power state, or to remove the virtual machine from the console entirely. Additional context items that are offered based on the state of the virtual machine include:
  - Restore from Saved State
  - Discard Saved State
  - Merge Undo Disks
  - Discard Undo Disks
- Relative Weight—This setting controls the priority in which a virtual machine is given CPU resources. The number can range from 1 to 10,000 and is set to 100 by default so that their resource requirements are equal, and none is given preference over the other. The greater the number, the greater the priority. A virtual machine with a higher relative weight is dynamically allocated additional resources as needed from other virtual machines that have a lower relative weight.
- Reserved Capacity (% of one CPU)—Reserved Capacity is the guaranteed amount of a single CPU that a virtual machine is given. It is more specific than relative weight in that it guarantees the resources. Think of it as the minimum.
- Maximum Capacity (% of one CPU)—The highest percentage of the total resources of a single CPU that can be consumed by a virtual machine at any given time. Think of it as the maximum.
- Reserved Capacity (% of system)—Simply displays the percentage of total system CPU capacity reserved for the virtual machine. This provides a view into what resources are being reserved against overall system capacity.

- Maximum Capacity (% of system)—Shows the maximum system CPU capacity that can be consumed by a virtual machine at a given time. It also provides a view into what overall system resources would remain if the virtual machine were to hit its maximum capacity.
- CPU Usage—Displays the CPU utilization for the virtual machine over the previous minute in a graphical representation. This gives a quick insight into what is happening across the system on a per virtual machine basis.
- Total Capacity Reserved—The total CPU capacity of the system that is reserved by virtual machines that are currently powered on. If the system has multiple CPUs, the Figure represents the available percentage of all CPUs combined.
- Available Capacity Remaining—The total CPU capacity of the system that is currently available (not reserved) for use by virtual machines. If the system has multiple CPUs, the Figure represents the available percentage of all CPUs combined.

Event Viewer

The final grouping under Virtual Server is the Event Viewer grouping (see Figure 10.12). Event Viewer is incredibly valuable when determining if there are any problems with Virtual Server and if so, what the causes may be.

On the Event Viewer page there are four columns:

- Type—Offers a graphical representation of different levels of event information.
  - Information—Status changes or updates from the system
  - Warnings—Unexpected conditions or state changes that occur

Figure 10.12   Event Viewer.

- • Errors—System disruptions, exceptions, or problems that the system is encountering.
- ▪ Date/Time—Gives the specific date and time in which the event occurred, which is useful for analyzing trends or looking for the original occurrence of a problem.
- ▪ Category
  - • Setting Change—Represents a change in Virtual Server or a virtual machine's settings.
  - • Virtual Machine—Shows events that occur between the host and virtual machine, such as a power down.
  - • Remote Control—Displays events related to users connecting to and disconnecting to remote consoles of virtual machines.
- ▪ Message—Provides details into the event such as cause of the event, the path of the file being affected by the event, or notifies that something has been changed in the system.

There are three heading selections that can be made in the Event Viewer page. Each of these allows rapid navigation through the vast number of events. The first two are sorting selections, "Newer events" (which as it sounds brings the newer events to the top of the visible list) and "Older events" (which brings the oldest events to the top of the visible list). These two selections save time in navigating long lists of Event Viewer messages, especially if the event that is being searched for is in the beginning or at the end of the list. The third and final selection that can be made is labeled "Change filter". The Change filter selection allows for narrowing down the scope of displayed events into a more specific grouping. The available groupings are:

- ▪ All events—Displays all of the virtual machine events in the system (the default setting).
- ▪ Virtual Server events—Lists only Virtual Server system events.
- ▪ Virtual Disk Operation events—Lists only virtual disk events, such as creations and merges.
- ▪ Preference Change events—Displays when a change has been made.
- ▪ Remote Control events—Occurs when the remote control receives connection changes, including idle disconnects and users authenticating to virtual machine remote control sessions.
- ▪ Virtual Machine events—Events driven by virtual machine state changes and errors.

Summary

Microsoft Virtual Server 2005's configuration and management choices using the Administration Website are powerful, yet simple to use. Being able to properly secure Virtual Server to ensure reliable and uncompromised access to all hosted virtual machines is critical. In addition to security, resource management controls must be placed on virtual machines to ensure that a single virtual machine does not consume all of the system resources away from other virtual machines. This is accomplished by using CPU resource allocation. Finally, viewing events provides key insights into what may be causing performance, application, or stability problems by showing what is happening between the interactions of the host operating system, the virtualization layer, and the virtual machines themselves. By using all of the tools provided by the Administration Website, Virtual Server can be used trouble free and to its fullest potential.

Chapter 11

Creating a Microsoft Virtual Server Virtual Machine

Creating a virtual machine is an essential part of using Microsoft Virtual Server 2005. Building upon the previous two chapters, this chapter provides the next step in properly deploying Virtual Server by walking through the creation of a basic virtual machine and installing its guest operating system. The installation of the guest operating system is not covered in full detail, but instead focuses on the primary configuration steps and the configuration of the guest operating system to support being installed in a virtual machine. Virtual machine configuration files and settings are also discussed in detail.

Preparation

The first thing to do when preparing for the creation of a virtual machine and the installation of its guest operating system is to determine the purpose of the virtual machine. The virtual machine's purpose must be decided to have proper planning. Virtual machines can be created with the intent of using them as a web server, database server, application server, test server, or for some other general purpose. Proper planning allows for creating or leveraging template images, cloning, copying, and management of virtual machines. Below are sample questions that will assist in the preparation and planning, although chapters 6 and 24 go into much further detail to assist in this process.

- Which operating system is needed?
- What applications need to be installed?
- How much memory does this configuration require to operate smoothly?
- How much disk space is needed?
- What type of networking, if any, is required?
- What other resources or devices are needed in this configuration?
- Is there a dependency on another server or group of servers?

Once the planning and purpose has been decided upon, it is important to gather all of the software and hardware needed to create the virtual machine. A physical server with the proper hardware and enough resources to support both Virtual Server and the planned virtual machines is required. The operating system software and installation media (physical media and/or ISO images), application software, drivers (floppy disks, media or images), virtual machine templates or other virtual machines that are dependencies, as well as any license keys, must all be collected to begin a trouble free creation process.

There are also many optimizations that can be made to the host server and inside of the guest operating system either during the operating system installation or postinstallation.

- Screen savers should be disabled on the host server before the guest operating system is installed.
- Screen savers on the guest operating system may be too CPU intensive for the host server.
- Verify the operating system media or image is not an OEM copy that requires installation on specific hardware. If so, when the initialization process begins, the virtual hardware will not match the expected vendor hardware and the installation will fail.
- As with physical servers, a separate operating system or application license is usually required for each virtual machine in which it is installed. Audit all software and operating system licenses to ensure that proper compliance is maintained.
- A guest operating system's hibernation feature is not supported and should not be used; instead, it should be disabled in favor of using the save state feature found in Virtual Server.

 If processor utilization is the only problem that must be temporarily resolved, the pause feature can be used in lieu of the save state feature. The pause feature is much faster than the save state feature. The pause feature is susceptible to having a power off event causing data corruption, whereas the save state feature does not have this problem. This problem exists due to the fact that the pause function does not dump the memory contents of the virtual machine to disk, whereas the save state feature does dump the contents of memory to a disk file. By having the contents of memory on disk, if a power off or power loss event occurs on the host or guest, the system still has an intact memory map.

- Microsoft's Activation policy can cause havoc when creating a template image or when making configuration changes to a virtual machine. Certain configuration changes may require reactivating the guest operating system. Under normal circumstances, if three or more hardware components change, the activation Wizard becomes active again and requires reactivation. It is therefore best to either create the virtual machine in its final form with little or no changes made after the fact to the hardware or to use volume license key-based media, where activation is not required.
- Migrating virtual machines from one host to the next when a different type of processor is used may cause issues. For example, some operating systems become sensitive to a move from an AMD-based processor to an Intel-based processor. Other situations may also arise by moving from one class of processor to another, such as from a Pentium II-based processor to a Xeon-based processor.
- Antivirus software running real-time or active-based virus scanning can have major impacts on performance of both host and guest operating systems.
- An inadequately sized host page file may also cause performance problems for the system.

Once all the media and information has been gathered, creating and provisioning virtual machines becomes a far easier and less error prone exercise.

Creating a Virtual Machine

To create a new virtual machine, follow these steps:

1. The Master Status page of the Microsoft Virtual Server Administration Website contains a set of menus on the left side of the page. The Create menu item under the Virtual Machines menu is used to begin the process of creating a new virtual machine, as shown in Figure 11.1.

Figure 11.1   Selecting the Create link from the Master Status page.

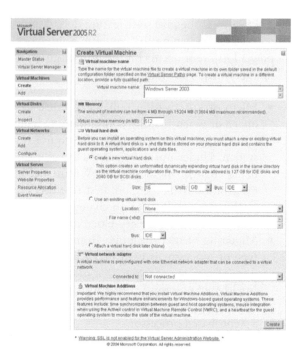

Figure 11.2 The Create Virtual Machine page.

2. The Create Virtual Machine page is displayed as shown in Figure 11.2. This page is used to configure the minimum required information necessary to create a new virtual machine.

   a. The new virtual machine being created requires a name. In this example, the virtual machine is named "Windows Server 2003".

   b. The default value for the memory setting is 128MB, which may be acceptable for very small, lightweight virtual machines, but typical virtual machines, especially those used as servers, require more than 128MB of memory, such as 512MB, 1GB, or more.

 Virtual Server has a limit of 3.6GB of memory per virtual machine. This is a limitation of the virtual hardware on Virtual Server. To provide more than 3.6GB of memory, Virtual Server's virtual hardware would have to support virtual Physical Address Extensions (PAE).

   c. A new virtual machine requires a virtual hard disk drive device. The options available include the ability to create a new, empty virtual hard disk drive, use an existing virtual hard disk drive, or to attach a virtual hard disk drive later. The new virtual machine is not very useful without a virtual hard disk drive; therefore this example will create a new virtual hard disk drive, taking the default options for size (16GB) and interface (IDE). Although a new 16GB virtual hard disk seems excessive in size, the disk that is created is a dynamic disk, which means it only consumes the amount of physical hard disk space that it requires and will grow over time as needed but it will not exceed 16GB. The IDE interface was selected because it provides a simple, straight-forward initial setup. The other option is to use a virtual SCSI interface but it requires extra steps during the installation of the guest operating system in most cases, requiring the Virtual Server SCSI Shunt Driver to be installed from the included SCSI Shunt Driver virtual floppy disk image usually located at C:\Program Files\Microsoft Virtual Server\Virtual Machine Additions\SCSI Shunt Driver.vfd. The new virtual hard disk drive will be created in the default location, C:\Documents and Settings\All Users\Documents\Shared Virtual Machines\<VmName>\<VmName>.vhd where <VmName> is the name chosen for the new virtual machine.

    d. The new virtual machine is created with a single virtual network adapter that can optionally be connected to an external or internal virtual network. For this example, the Not Connected option will be used (the default value). Not Connected specified that the virtual network adapter is not connected to a network, similar to a physical, wired network adapter that does not have a network cable attached.

3. Once all of the optional have been configured on the Create Virtual Machine page, the Create button located in the bottom right corner of the page is then used to create the virtual machine.

4. Virtual Server will create the new virtual machine and afterwards, the Status and Configuration page for the new virtual machine will be displayed as shown in Figure 11.3. The virtual machine's Status and Configuration page can also be navigated to from the Master Status page by placing the mouse over the virtual machine's name and clicking the Edit Configuration menu item from the popup menu that is displayed.

5. From the "Windows Server 2003" Status page is a section labeled "Windows Server 2003" Configuration that displays the virtual machine's various configuration settings and virtual hardware devices. From this section, the CD/DVD device configuration link is used to modify the CD/DVD device configuration for the virtual machine as shown in Figure 11.3.

6. In order to install a guest operating system into the new virtual machine, the virtual machine must have access to installation media, commonly a bootable CD/DVD-ROM media mounted from a mapped physical device on the host server or an ISO image of a CD-ROM or DVD-ROM mounted as a virtual CD/DVD-ROM device. Figure 11.4 shows the CD/DVD Drive Properties page. In this example, an existing ISO image of the Microsoft Windows Server 2003 Standard Edition installation media

Figure 11.3 The new virtual machine's Status page.

is mounted to the default virtual CD/DVD-ROM drive on IDE1:0. If bootable installation media is not used, a separate boot floppy disk will be needed to boot and run the guest operating system installer. Most modern operating systems are available today on bootable CD/DVD-ROM media or directly as a bootable ISO image. Once the CD/DVD drive is configured, the OK button is used to save the changes. The "Windows Server

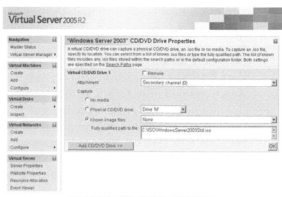

Figure 11.4 The CD/DVD Drive Properties page.

Figure 11.5 Powering on a virtual machine from the Master Status page.

2003" Status and Configuration page is displayed again now showing the changes made to the CD/DVD drive in the Configuration section.

7. In order to begin the process of installing the guest operating system in the virtual machine, the virtual machine will need to power on and boot from the ISO image mounted in the previous step. The virtual machine can be powered on from either the Status and Configuration page or from the Master Status page. In this example, the virtual machine will be powered on from the Master Status page by floating the mouse pointer over the name of the virtual machine to display a popup menu and then selecting the Turn On menu item as shown in Figure 11.5. Once the Turn On option is clicked, the virtual machine will be powered on and will start to boot any attached bootable media in the boot order defined in the virtual machine's BIOS.

8. The virtual machine's console output can be viewed and manipulated interactively by using a tool named Virtual Machine Remote Console, or VMRC. VMRC is a subcomponent of Microsoft Virtual Server that allows access to the console of virtual machines (keyboard, video, and mouse access). From within the Virtual Server Administration Website, VMRC is implemented as an ActiveX component hosted inside of a Web page. After the virtual machine has been powered on, its icon displayed either on the Master Status page or the Status and Configuration page will change, displaying a mini-screen shot of the current state of the virtual machine. If the icon is clicked, the VMRC tool is launched and its will attempt to connect to the virtual machine. Figure 11.6 shows the VMRC connection to the virtual machine named "Windows Server 2003" as it performs the POST (Power On Self Test) process before the BIOS attempt to boot an operating system.

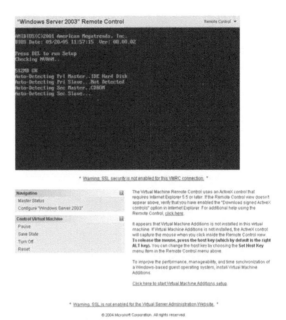

Figure 11.6   VMRC displaying a virtual machine that is performing POST.

 By default, Microsoft Virtual Server's VMRC server is disabled as shown in Figure 11.7. Before VMRC can be used, the VMRC server must be enabled on the Virtual Machine Remote Console (VMRC) Server Properties page. Navigate to this page by clicking the Server Properties menu item under the Virtual Server menu on the left side of the Master Status page, and then by clicking the link labeled Virtual Machine Remote Control (VMRC) Server.

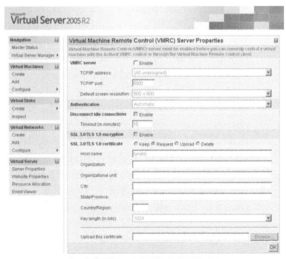

Figure 11.7   The VMRC server is disabled by default.

The first time that a virtual machine is accessed using VMRC from the Virtual Server Administration Website, the VMRC ActiveX control will need to be installed. The Web browser, usually Internet Explorer, will prompt you to install the ActiveX control. The Web browser may not attempt to automatically install the VMRC ActiveX control if the machine that is accessing the Virtual Server Administration Website is running one of the following operating systems.

■ Microsoft Windows XP Home or Professional with Service Pack 2 or later
■ Microsoft Windows Server 2003 (Any Edition) with Service Pack 1 or later
■ Microsoft Windows Server 2003 R2 (Any Edition) or later

The version of Internet Explorer installed in these operating systems blocks ActiveX controls by default. If the Control-Key is pressed and held before clicking a link that leads to the VMRC page, the ActiveX security block feature will be bypassed. Otherwise, the VMRC ActiveX control will have to be allowed to be installed by clicking on the Internet Explorer notification bar and taking the appropriate action. Once the VMRC ActiveX control has been successfully installed, the virtual machine's console screen will be displayed.

 Depending on the security setting of the host operating system and that of Virtual Server, you may be prompted to authenticate when accessing virtual machines using VMRC.

Using VMRC

To use the VMRC interface from the Virtual Server Administration Website, the mouse must be positioned over the console area of the VMRC window and the left mouse button must be clicked in order to give focus into the virtual machine's console. Once this is done, the mouse and keyboard are "stuck" inside the console window; therefore all actions are applied to the virtual machine. To remove focus from the virtual machine's console and return control back to the computer running the Web browser, the right ALT-key must be used. Once pressed, the right ALT-key will transfer focus away from the virtual machine's console in VMRC and back to the computer running the Web browser. The mouse position of the virtual machine's mouse will remain at the point it was when the right ALT-key was pressed when the virtual machine does not have Virtual Machine Additions installed. The operation of the mouse inside the virtual machine before Virtual Machine Additions are installed may be choppy or unusable in some cases. When this occurs, the keyboard must be used to perform the installation tasks. Once the guest operating system is installed and Virtual Machine Additions are installed, the mouse behavior will return to normal and will be more integrated with the VMRC console window.

Installing a Guest Operating System

After a virtual machine has been created, a guest operating system is usually installed. Installing a guest operating system in a virtual machine is nearly the same as installing an operating system on a physical computer. The guest operating system being installed is not aware that it is being installed inside of a virtual machine rather than a physical computer. The resources that are assigned to the virtual machine, including processors, memory, disks, and network adapters will be detected and installed just as they would be on a physical computer.

MICROSOFT WINDOWS SERVER INSTALLATION

The example used above to create a new virtual machine will be continued in this section. The virtual machine in the example is named "Windows Server 2003," therefore the guest operating system that will be installed is Microsoft Windows Server 2003 Standard Edition. This is a very common guest operating system that is used on the Microsoft Virtual Server 2005 R2 virtualization platform.

The virtual machine that was created has the Microsoft Windows Server 2003 Standard Edition installation media, an ISO image, mounted to the default virtual CD/DVD-ROM drive. The virtual machine was then powered on, which will cause the BIOS to perform POST and then it will attempt to boot an operating system using the default boot order specified in the virtual machine's BIOS. The default boot order is Removable Media (floppy drive), hard disk, and CD/DVD drive. Because there is no floppy media mounted to the virtual machine and because the virtual hard drive is empty, the BIOS will attempt to boot from the virtual CD/DVD-ROM media that is mounted. The Microsoft Windows Server 2003 installation media is bootable.

First, the BIOS performs POST as shown in Figure 11.6. Depending on the amount of time it takes between the actual moment that the virtual machine was powered on and when the virtual machine's console window is displayed in VMRC after activating the remote control from either the Master Status page or the virtual machine's Status and Configuration page, the POST sequence may have already completed and the virtual machine may have already started to boot the guest operating system. The POST process occurs very quickly and once the remote control is activated, the system may force an interactive authentication with the VMRC ActiveX control. Once the virtual machine has booted, the initial setup screen for the Windows Server 2003 installer is displayed as shown in Figure 11.8.

The ENTER-key should be pressed to begin a clean installation of Microsoft Windows Server 2003 Standard Edition on the new virtual machine. The End User License Agreement must be accepted by pressing the F8-key on the following screen. On the partitioning screen, the default option should be selected, which is to use the unpartitioned space available on the virtual hard disk drive. The next screen will displays the available formatting options. The partition should be formatted using the NTFS file system. The quick format option is

Figure 11.8 The Windows Server 2003 setup screen.

not recommended. Once the installer begins the formatting process, the screen shown in Figure 11.9 is displayed. The format operation usually takes much less time on the dynamic virtual hard disk than it would on an equivalent physical

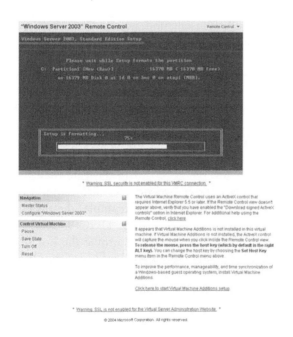

Figure 11.9 Formatting the partition using NTFS.

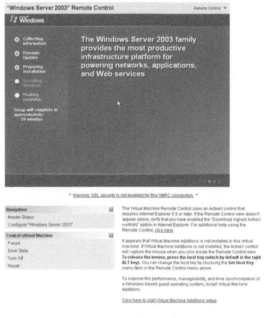

Figure 11.10   The Windows Server 2003 GUI Installer.

hard disk. After the formatting process has completed, the installer will copy files from the installation media to the virtual hard disk drive. Once completed, it will reboot and enter the next phase of the installation, which will use a graphics user interface (GUI) instead of the character-mode user interface that is used initially as shown in Figure 11.10.

After the main file copying and device detection portion of the GUI installer has completed, it will display several dialog windows in which configuration information must be supplied, including the keyboard and mouse setup, date and time setup, the license key, host name, domain/workgroup name, Administrator password, and the initial networking configuration as shown in Figure 11.11. Use the keyboard and mouse to navigate and supply the required information. If the mouse is not working properly, use the keyboard to navigate by using the TAB-key, SHIFT-TAB-key combination to move focus to the Next buttons and the SPACEBAR-key to press the buttons. For this example, the default networking configuration options are used (Typical Settings, DHCP). Once all of the information has been supplied, the installer will continue the installation process by finalizing the installation using the supplied information. Once completed, the installer will reboot the system. Once the reboot is complete, the normal Windows Logon screen will be displayed in the virtual machine's console window as shown in Figure 11.12.

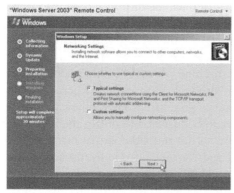

Figure 11.11   GUI Installer network configuration screen.

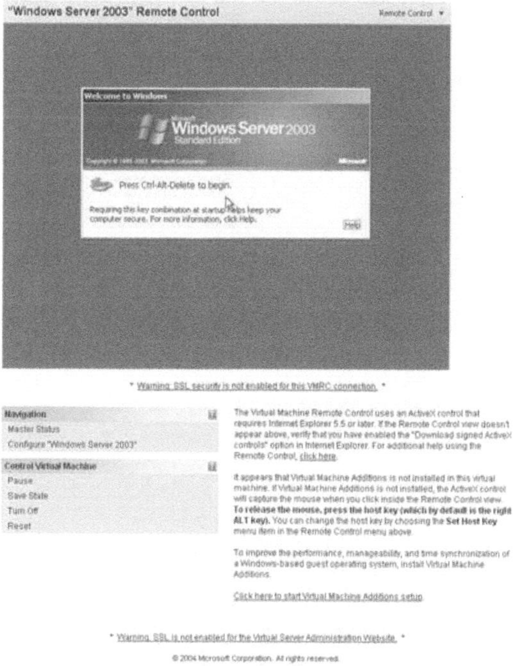

Figure 11.12   The Windows Server 2003 logon screen.

After logging on to Windows, the desktop will be displayed with the taskbar at the bottom of the screen. It is very important to install the Virtual Machine Additions into the virtual machine's guest operating system at this point. Virtual Machine Additions is a package of drivers and tools created to enhance the usability and performance of the virtual machine. Virtual Machine Additions are specific to the guest operating system, although most current Microsoft Windows operating systems will use the same version. Just as a new physical computer will require specific hardware drivers to be installed to obtain the maximum functionality and performance possible, so too must the virtual machine have Virtual Machine Additions installed. The drivers included in the package equate to the physical hardware drivers that would be installed on a physical computer, but instead apply to the virtual hardware exposed to the virtual machine by the Microsoft Virtual Server virtualization platform. Virtual Machine Additions will also greatly improve the operation of the keyboard and mouse as used through the VMRC utility.

The virtual machine's console window should be exited by pressing the right-ALT-key (also called the host key). Below the VMRC console window is a block of text describing the VMRC ActiveX control as well as Virtual Machine Additions. Below that text is a link labeled "Click here to start Virtual Machine Additions setup" as shown in Figure 11.13. Clicking this link will begin the installation of Virtual Machine Additions within the virtual machine. This link

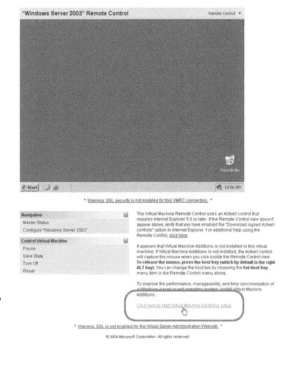

Figure 11.13   Virtual Machine Additions setup link.

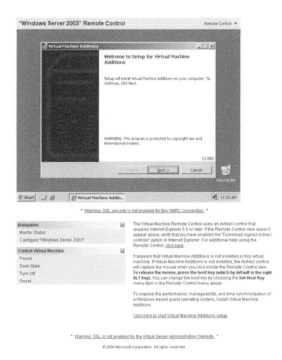

Figure 11.14 Virtual Machine Additions installer welcome screen.

should only be used after the virtual machine has been fully booted and an interactive session has been started. Once the link is clicked, the Virtual Machine Additions installer will be visible in the virtual machine's console window, as shown in Figure 11.14.

Once focus is returned to the virtual machine, the Next button in the Virtual Machine Additions installer Wizard should be selected in order to begin the installation process. The installation process will complete automatically. Once completed, the Virtual Machine Additions Setup Complete screen will be displayed in the installer Wizard as shown in Figure 11.15. The Finish button should then be clicked to gracefully exit the installer. The system will require a reboot (see Figure 11.16) in order for the drivers installed with the Virtual Machine Additions to load properly. The virtual machine should be rebooted immediately.

Upon a reboot of the system and after logging on, the system will detect the new virtual video card driver and will offer to automatically adjust the screen resolution and color depth (see Figure 11.17). After approving the changes made to the Windows environment, the system is now ready to have patches and updates installed. For Windows operating systems with a network connection, it is highly recommended to use the Windows Update service (or a local Microsoft Software Update Services Server). All critical security patches and updates should be installed immediately.

Figure 11.15 Virtual Machine Additions Setup Complete.

Figure 11.16 Virtual Machine Additions reboot prompt.

Figure 11.17   Display Settings optimization prompt.

Under the virtual machine's console window are two menus, the Navigation menu and the Control Virtual Machine menu. The Control Virtual Machine menu has the following options available:

- Pause
- Save State
- Turn Off
- Reset

This is a standard set of options that apply to all virtual machines regardless of the current state of the virtual machine. After a virtual machine has Virtual Machine Additions installed and is fully booted, a new option will be added to the menu (pending a browser refresh) labeled Shut Down Guest OS as shown in Figure 11.18. Where did the Shut Down Guest OS option come from? This option appears if Virtual Server detects that the virtual machine has Virtual Machine Additions installed. The option saves time when a graceful shutdown of a virtual machine is required by eliminating the need to change focus to the virtual machine, possibly logging into the virtual machine, and then going through the various steps needed to shut down the guest operating system. Instead, the entire process can be handled by the Virtual Machine Additions. This completes the installation of Windows Server 2003.

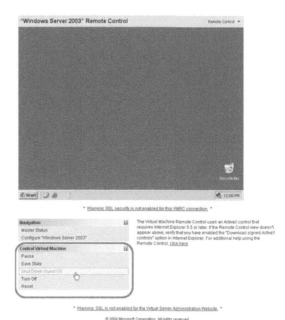

**Figure 11.18   Shut Down
Guest OS menu item.**

Red Hat Linux 9 Installation

Although Microsoft Virtual Server 2005 R2 does not currently support non-Microsoft operating systems at the time of this writing, Microsoft did announce in April of 2005 that support for select third-party operating systems may be added in the future, possibly as an add-on. Because there is no official support for non-Microsoft guest operating systems in Virtual Server, Virtual Machine Additions do not exist for unsupported operating system.

Red Hat Linux 9 is an unsupported guest operating system that will install and run under Virtual Server. Because there are no compatible Virtual Machine Additions available for this operating system, its graphic user interface support lacks good performance, but is functional. Red Hat Linux 9 is a fairly compatible and well-known Linux distribution and therefore it is a good candidate for an unsupported guest operating system installation. Please note that it is not generally recommended to use unsupported guest operating systems in production environments.

Before Red Hat Linux 9 can be installed into a virtual machine, a new virtual machine must be created first. The virtual machine was created by following the example presented earlier in this chapter in the Creating a Virtual Machine section. Instead of naming the new virtual machine "Windows Server 2003" the name "RedHatLinux9" was used. Instead of mounting the installation media for Microsoft Windows Server 2003, the bootable ISO image for CD 1 of the Red hat Linux 9 installation media was mounted to the virtual CD/DVD drive.

After the installation media has been mounted, the virtual machine can be powered on and booted from the CD/DVD drive. The installation media has a boot loader that presents the installation boot menu as shown in Figure 11.19. This example uses the graphical mode installer; therefore the ENTER-key is pressed. Next, the installer displays a prompt for the installation media test process (see Figure 11.20). The Skip option should be selected to save time. The graphical mode installer will then boot.

After the graphic mode installer has started, the welcome screen will be displayed as shown in Figure 11.21. The Next button is then clicked to continue the installation. After several basic installation option screens such as keyboard and mouse configuration options, the "Installation Type" screen will be displayed as shown in Figure 11.22. The "Server" option is used in this example, as this is the most likely candidate for installing Red Hat Linux in a virtual server environment. The Next button is clicked to continue the installation. The disk partitioning setup follows and the default option, "Automatically partition," is chosen for simplicity as shown in Figure 11.23. The remaining installation screens are then completed by supplying the necessary information and taking the default options where necessary until the "About to Install" screen is displayed as shown in Figure 11.24. This is the last chance to return to previous installation screens to make selection changes. After the Next button is clicked, the installation will begin transferring the install image to the virtual hard disk as

Figure 11.19 The Red Hat Linux 9 Installer Boot Menu.

Figure 11.20   Red Hat Linux 9 CD media test option.

Figure 11.21   Red Hat Linux 9 graphic mode installer welcome screen.

Figure 11.22 Red Hat Linux 9 Installation Type.

shown in Figure 11.25. During the installation process, the progress (see Figure 11.26) bar is displayed for each package that is installed as well as for the overall process.

During the installation process and depending on the optional packages that were selected to be installed, the installer may prompt for additional installation media CDs. The Red Hat Linux 9 installation media for x86 consists of 3 CD-ROM ISO images. Under the virtual machine console window is a menu labeled Navigation under which there is a menu item named Configure "Red-HatLinux9" as shown in Figure 11.27. After clicking the Configure "RedHat-Linux9" menu item, the "RedHatLinux9" Status and Configuration screen is displayed (see Figure 11.28) in the Virtual Server Administration Website. From this screen, the CD/DVD link under the Configuration section is used to access the media attached to the virtual CD/DVD drive. Because the virtual machine is currently running, the virtual hardware cannot be changed, but the media in the virtual CD/DVD drive can be changed. This is equivalent to ejecting the CD-ROM media in a physical CD-ROM drive and changing it with another CD-ROM. Figure 11.29 shows the CD/DVD Drive Properties page for the "RedHatLinux9" virtual machine. From this page, the path to the ISO image installation media should be changed to the proper ISO image representing the

**Figure 11.23　Red Hat
Linux 9 Disk Partition Setup.**

**Figure 11.24　Red Hat
Linux 9 About to Install.**

Figure 11.25   Red Hat Linux 9
Transferring Install Image.

Figure 11.26   Red Hat
Linux 9 Installation
Progress.

Figure 11.27   Red Hat Linux 9 Prompt for additional installation media.

Figure 11.28   Status and Configuration page for the "RedHatLinux9" virtual machine.

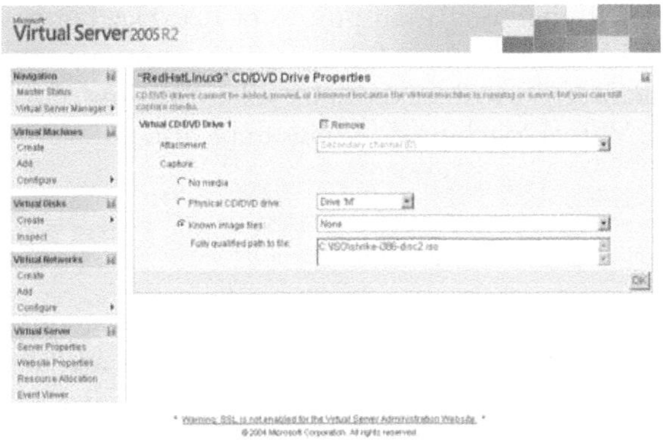

Figure 11.29 Changing the installation media in the virtual CD/DVD drive.

CD that the installer is requesting and then the OK button is clicked to save the changes. Clicking on the icon of the virtual machine from either the Master Status page or from the Status and Configuration page will navigate back to the VRMC page for the virtual machine, allowing the continuation of the installation process.

After the completion of the file copying process, the "Congratulations" screen is displayed (see Figure 11.30) marking the end of the Red Hat Linux 9 installation. The Exit button is then clicked and the virtual machine will reboot. Once

Figure 11.30 Red Hat Linux 9 Installation Complete.

the virtual machine has rebooted, the installation process of Red Hat Linux 9 is finished. Once again, because Red Hat Linux 9 is currently an unsupported guest operating system of Microsoft Virtual Server 2005 R2 at the time of this writing, there are no available Virtual Machine Additions to be installed.

Summary

Creating a virtual machine is a simple task that can be accomplished in minutes. It is important to gain a broad understanding of each option that is available while creating a virtual machine as well as understanding their direct impact on both the host server and the virtual machine itself. By following common installation procedures, most supported and non-supported guest operating systems can be installed with minimal effort. After completing an installation of a guest operating system, Virtual Machine Additions should be installed (if available) as they provide usability and performance gains to the guest operating system as well as providing usability enhancements inside the VMRC window.

Chapter 12

Microsoft Virtual Server Advanced Topics

A comprehensive look at the Microsoft Virtual Server platform is provided in this chapter. It covers platform-specific implementation of common and advanced virtualization platform features such as an in-depth discussion of the technical details of virtual machines, hard drives, networking, and resource management. This chapter provides the additional knowledge to successfully build and manage a Virtual Server deployment and implementation.

Virtual Machine Additions

An important part of Virtual Server is the use of Virtual Machine Additions. Virtual Machine Additions provides a similar set of capabilities to that of VMware Tools. Virtual Machine Additions is a collection of device drivers, services, and registry changes installed onto the guest operating system. The Virtual Machine Additions provide better interaction and integrations with the host operating system. Through these integrations, a significant boost in guest operating system performance is achieved as well as better usability. Virtual Machine Additions must be installed after the guest operating system has been installed; however the installation process is almost entirely automated.

Virtual Machine Additions do not consume much disk space on the guest operating system. As a requirement, the guest operating system must be compatible with Virtual Machine Additions and access to a virtual CD-ROM drive must be provided through the virtual machine configuration. Virtual Machine Additions come in the form of an ISO image that, when mounted, executes the installation program. If auto-run has been disabled, the ISO can be browsed to using My Computer and the Additions can be installed by executing the setup.exe file.

 Virtual Machine Additions can also be installed from the command line. To do this, change to the location of the virtual CD-ROM and enter the following command:

```
setup.exe  -s  -v"/qn  [Reboot=ReallySuppress]"
```

The -s parameter hides the user interface entirely. The -v parameter passes parameters directly to the installation program (msiexec.exe). The /qn parameter hides the user interface. The [Reboot=Really Suppress] stops the guest operating system from restarting after the Virtual Machine Additions installation is complete. It is important to note that the -s parameter is independent of the -v parameter and vice versa. However, the /qn and [Reboot=ReallySuppress] require the -v parameter. The /qn parameter can be run without [Reboot=ReallySuppress] and vice versa.

 As of this writing, Virtual Server does not offer Virtual Machine Additions support for non-Microsoft guest operating systems. It was hoped that with the release of Microsoft Virtual Server 2005 R2, Microsoft would add Additions for third-party operating systems. Unfortunately, this did not happen. In April of 2005, Microsoft made an announcement stating they plan on providing support for third-party operating systems, including Linux distributions, some time in the future.

With the release of Microsoft Virtual Server 2005 R2, the product currently supports Virtual Machine Additions for the Microsoft Windows Server 2003 family of operating systems, Microsoft Windows 2000 Server family of operating systems, and Microsoft Windows NT 4.0 Service Pack 6a. In addition, Microsoft provides Virtual Machine Additions and support for Microsoft Windows XP SP2.

 Think of a virtual machine as you would a physical computer. If you install an operating system on a physical computer, chances are the computer will operate fairly well with most devices functioning with an out of the box generic driver installed by the operating system. However, if you want the latest 3-D graphics card to perform with all of its benefits and functionality, you will probably want to install an optimized or the latest release of the driver for the video card. Think of Virtual Machine Additions as the collection of the latest and most optimized drivers available.

Installing the Virtual Machine Additions will install virtualization aware services along with the device drivers. The drivers and services work in conjunction with each other to provide better device support and integration into the guest operating system. Many additional features become available simply by installing Virtual Machine Additions. Each feature is addressed below.

Time Synchronization

Time Synchronization will be very inaccurate without the installation of Virtual Machine Additions. The inaccuracy of the virtual machine hardware providing a proper timer is due to the resource sharing that is provided by Virtual Server and the complexities caused by emulating so much virtual hardware. Virtual Machine Additions provides a method of synchronizing with the host's time, making it far more accurate than without.

 There are two interesting changes to the time synchronization feature in Microsoft Virtual Server 2005. First, Microsoft Virtual Server 2005 does not support different time zones between the host and guest operating systems using the time synchronization feature. This is fixed in Microsoft Virtual Server 2005 R2. The module has been modified to be more accurate. Second, Microsoft Virtual Server 2005 R2 makes the time inside of the virtual machine much more reliable, even when Virtual Machine Additions is not installed.

 The host time synchronization feature of Virtual Machine Additions can lead to unpredictable and unwanted results if the host operating system and guest operating system are in different domains. Therefore, if the host and guest operating systems are in different domains, the time synchronization feature should be disabled. In addition, if a virtual machine is configured as a domain controller, the time synchronization feature should be disabled and the guest operating system should instead use an external source for time synchronization.

Customized Video Card

Virtual Machine Additions automatically installs an optimized video driver that is specific to the guest operating system. Video optimization is accomplished through a specialized S3 Trio64 video driver developed with virtualization integration in mind. The video card adapter provides 4MB of VRAM as well as other performance enhancements such as VESA 2.0 compliance, 2D graphics accelerator and hardware cursor, and support for DirectX. It also provides the guest operating system with better color depth and higher screen resolutions.

Integrated Mouse

Once Virtual Machine Additions is installed inside of the guest operating system, the integrated mouse functionality will be automatically enabled. This allows for better mouse tracking performance inside of the virtual machine when it is being controlled with the Virtual Machine Remote Control ActiveX component (built into the Virtual Server Web-based administration interface) and the full Virtual Machine Remote Control client. The integrated mouse also provides seamless movement between the host operating system windows and any virtual machine window. This makes the remote administration and control aspects of virtual machines and Virtual Server far easier and more productive.

 There are some operating systems such as Microsoft Windows NT4 that do not come with all of the necessary drivers to get even basic virtual hardware support. An example would be the virtual network adapter driver. This driver can only be obtained by using the Virtual Machine Additions.

Passing Information from the Host to the Guest Operating System

A capability that is gained, but not often exploited within Virtual Server, is being able to pass information from the host operating system into the guest operating system. This is useful for a variety of reasons including: customizations upon startup of a virtual machine and sending out update information into virtual machines while they are running. To pass information from the host operating system, there are a few requirements that must be met:

1. The virtual machine must be powered on and the guest operating system must be booted.
2. Microsoft Virtual Machine Additions must be installed inside of the guest operating system.

3. The information to be passed must be done so by interfacing with Virtual Server's COM API.

Below is a description of the COM API interface used to accomplish this.

This is the COM API that passes the information into the guest operating system:

vm.GuestOS.SetParameter({The Keyname is passed as an argument here}, {The Value to be placed in the Keyname is passed here})

This is the registry location within the guest operating system where the information passed from the COM API on the host operating system will be inserted:

```
HKLM\SOFTWARE\Microsoft\Virtual Machine\Guest\
                  Parameters
```

Virtual Machines

Deleting a Virtual Machine

When a virtual machine must be deleted, there is more involved than simply going to the Virtual Server Administration Website and selecting Remove. Doing so will only remove the virtual machine from Virtual Server; it will not delete the virtual machine files. The virtual hard disk files and several configuration files will still remain on the system. If the location of where these files are stored is known, then the deletion process becomes straight forward. Once the virtual machine is removed from Virtual Server, the virtual machine can be deleted by going to the location of its files (configuration, networking, and hard disk files) and simply deleting them from the system. Since this is all that actually comprises a virtual machine, deleting these files is the equivalent of deleting the virtual machine itself. When following the best practices, these files should all be located in a single folder that encompasses the virtual machine component files. And therefore, it should be as simple as deleting the virtual machine's folder.

The default locations of the files that make up a virtual machine are listed below:

*   `C:\Documents and Settings\All Users\Application Data\Microsoft\Virtual Server\Virtual Machines`— This folder contains shortcuts to virtual machine files. If a shortcut exists here, it is registered inside of the Administration Website and with Virtual Server.
*   `C:\Documents and Settings\All Users\Application Data\Microsoft\Virtual Server\Virtual Networks`—

This folder contains shortcuts to virtual network definition files. If a shortcut exists here, it is registered inside of the Administration Website and with Virtual Server.

- `C:\Documents and Settings\All Users\Shared Documents\Shared Virtual Machines\`—This folder contains subfolders that represent virtual machines. Each folder contains all of the files that comprise the virtual machine including: Configuration, State, Virtual Hard Disk, and Virtual Floppy.
- `C:\Documents and Settings\All Users\Shared Documents\Shared Virtual Networks`—This folder contains configuration files for all of the virtual networks created in Virtual Server.

Save State and Restoring a Virtual Machine

There are several features in Virtual Server that can be used to temporarily free up resources on the physical host. The Save State function allows a virtual machine to be "frozen" in time for either a short or incredibly long period of time. One of the differences between a save state and a shut down is that a saved state provides the ability to quickly resume right where the virtual machine was left off. This is accomplished by stopping all I/O operations on the virtual machine simultaneously, and then taking the contents of the virtual machine's memory and system state and copying it to a file on the host server's hard disk. This is the "freezing" process. The restore process can then be thought of as the "thawing" process of the virtual machine. The thawing process actually entails copying the memory contents from the file where it was stored when the virtual machine was put into a saved state back into the virtual memory space. Once this has been completed, Virtual Server restores the I/O to the virtual machine and the virtual machine and guest operating system are unaware that they were ever in this saved state.

Discard Saved State

The Discard Saved State option allows the virtual machine to have its memory and system state deleted. This will allow the system to be in the equivalent state of a powered off machine. Discarding Saved State provides a simple way to change a machine's state from Saved to Powered Off.

The file extension for the memory contents of a virtual machine saved state file is .vsv. The saved state file is by default stored in the same directory as the virtual machine's configuration file. An important factor to take into consideration is that when a virtual machine is put into a saved state and the contents of memory are dumped into a file, the size of the saved state file can be considerably large. If a virtual machine has 2GB of memory allocated to it, a 2GB file will be created when the system is put into a saved state.

 Microsoft Virtual Server 2005 R2 handles the saved state in a slightly different way than its predecessor. In the previous release, Virtual Server created a saved state (.vsv) file when the Saved State feature was activated. With the introduction of Microsoft Virtual Server 2005 R2, Virtual Server now reserves sufficient space on the physical disk to save the state of each running virtual machine. It does this by creating an empty saved state (.vsv) file that is equal in size to the amount of memory currently allocated to the virtual machine plus a 20 MB buffer. For example, if 256MB of memory is allocated to a virtual machine, Virtual Server will create an empty saved state file that is 276MB in size. If the virtual machine is powered off, the saved state file is deleted. If the save state feature is activated, the empty file is simply overwritten with a populated .vsv file. Microsoft made this change to ensure that the user does not run out of physical disk space before trying to save state a virtual machine. With a precreated saved state file, Virtual Server is better able to guarantee that any running virtual machine should have enough disk space to be able to save state. If there is insufficient disk space to create the .vsv file, the virtual machine will not start. In order to power on the virtual machine, additional space on the physical disk must be made available.

Virtual Hard Disk Controllers

There are two types of virtual hard disk controllers for use in Virtual Server. The first type is IDE, which provides a uniform layer of compatibility across all guest operating systems. IDE provides reasonable throughput while offering up to four virtual hard disk interfaces, each supporting a virtual hard disk of up to 128GB. Only one IDE controller is supported inside a virtual machine.

The second type of controller is a SCSI controller. The SCSI controller is based on a multi-port Adaptec 7870 chipset and provides a higher level of throughput than the IDE controller while offering up to seven virtual hard disk interfaces, each supporting a virtual hard disk of up to 2TB. Up to four SCSI controllers are supported inside of a single virtual machine offering a total of up to 56TB of storage. The limitation is that some guest operating systems do not support the Adaptec 7870-based controller or require special drivers in order to provide support.

Virtual Hard Disks

Disk Types: Virtual and Physical

The most frequently used disk type in a Virtual Server environment is the dynamically expanding virtual hard disk. However, Virtual Server provides several other different disk types that can be used. These other disk types include: Fixed Size, Differencing, and Linked. Each of these disk types has a unique set of properties and can be leveraged to accomplish a wide variety of tasks. Each of these disk types will be explored further, along with how to enable them, find out what their functions are, and why they might be used.

Dynamic Disks

A dynamically expanding virtual hard disk is (as previously explained) one in which the size of the virtual hard disk (.vhd) file will grow as needed over time. The file grows as data is written to it. The limit to the size to which it can grow is equivalent to the size of the hard drive it is emulating. If a 16GB virtual hard disk (the default) is chosen, it will start off as a 32KB file, however it begins to grow in size as it is used, potentially growing all the way to a maximum of 16GB in file size. Described below is each of the options available when creating a dynamically expanding virtual hard disk under the Virtual Server Administration Website.

Selecting the Dynamically Expanding Virtual Hard Disk type will bring up the page with the same name in its title. The Dynamically Expanding Virtual Hard Disk page provides four options:

1. Location—The path or directory in which the virtual hard disk file will be located. The default location for virtual machine hard disk files is `C:\Documents and Settings\All Users\Documents\ Shared Virtual Machines\`. The actual files are then located in a subdirectory that is named after the virtual machine. If the folder does not appear in the drop down list, the fully qualified path to the folder must be typed in the following step.
2. Virtual hard disk file name—The name given to the hard disk file. The name should be unique and independently identify the machine that it belongs to or the function that it serves. It is important to realize that this name can be changed, simply by renaming the disk file and then reflecting that name change in the virtual machine's configuration. It is not necessary to include a file name extension.
3. Size—The size entered is the maximum size that the dynamically expanding virtual hard disk can reach. The size should be selected by choosing the correct size that corresponds to the units selected in the drop down list located in the next entry field. For example, if the units are going to

be selected as GB, then the size would be entered as 4 for a 4GB disk. On the other hand, if the units are going to be selected as MB, then the same disk would have a size entered as 4096.

4. Units—The dropdown list is used to complete the size of the virtual disk from the previous step. This entry provides an option to use different types of units for the selection of virtual hard disk sizes, either MB (for Megabytes) or GB (for Gigabytes).

Fixed Disks

A fixed size virtual hard disk is static in size contrary to the dynamically expanding virtual hard disk. A fixed size virtual hard disk has its maximum file size determined when the file is created. For example, when a fixed size virtual hard disk of 4GB is created, Virtual Server creates a 4GB file on the host server. When the file is created, it starts out at its maximum file size (in this case, 4GB) and even as data is added to the disk file, it remains at its maximum file size (i.e., 4GB).

The size of a fixed disk does not change because all of the storage space is reserved and pre-allocated at the time of creation. A fixed disk more closely resembles the way a physical disk operates. The preallocated space is filled as needed as data is written to the disk. Because a fixed disk is written to in this manner, it is more likely to be contiguous than a dynamically expanding hard disk. Since its writes are more contiguous, there is less fragmentation, and therefore it provides better performance. There is also a slight performance gain because a fixed disk does not have the overhead of a dynamically expanding disk. The price of the performance gain is paid in the amount of disk space consumed on the host server. The larger the size of a fixed disk, the more immediate is the disk consumption on the host server. The pain is equally noticed when trying to back up, copy, or move a fixed disk from one storage area to the next. Because the disk is preallocated, the fixed size disk loses some of its portability due to its large file size.

Selecting the Fixed Size Virtual Hard Disk type will bring up the page with the same name in its title. The Fixed Size Virtual Hard Disk page provides four options:

1. Location—The path or directory in which the virtual hard disk file will be located. The default location for virtual machine hard disk files is `C:\Documents and Settings\All Users\Documents\ Shared Virtual Machines\`. The actual files are then located in a subdirectory that is named after the virtual machine. If the folder does not appear in the drop down list, the fully qualified path to the folder must be typed in the following step.

2. Virtual hard disk file name—The name given to the hard disk file. The name should be unique and independently identify the machine that it belongs to or the function that it serves. It is important to realize that this name can be changed, simply by renaming the disk file and then reflecting that name change in the virtual machine's configuration. It is not necessary to include a file name extension.

3. Size—The size entered is the size that the fixed disk will be. The size should be selected by choosing the correct size that corresponds to the units selected in the drop down list located in the next entry field. For example, if the units are going to be selected as GB, then the size would be entered as 4 for a 4GB disk. On the other hand, if the units are going to be selected as MB, then the same disk would have a size entered as 4096.

4. Units—The dropdown list is used to complete the size of the virtual disk from the previous step. This entry provides an option to use different types of units for the selection of virtual hard disk sizes, either MB (for Megabytes) or GB (for Gigabytes).

Differencing Disks

Differencing disks are derived from a parent-child relationship between virtual hard disk files. The differencing disk is the child and the associated virtual hard disk is considered the parent. The child disk stores a record of all the changes made as well as the writes that were intended for the parent disk, and it provides the method to save the changes without actually altering the parent disk. The parent hard disk provides the original content and when in a relationship, the child disk depends on the parent disk not changing. The child disk is mapped as an overlay file to the parent disk. Because of this, if the parent disk changes, then all of its children will be rendered useless as the parent file that they each depend on will no longer be a valid binary reference (see Figure 12.1).

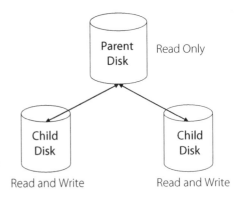

Figure 12.1 Parent Child Relationships.

The following are settings and explanations that can be chosen from inside of the Virtual Server Administration Website to create a differencing disk:

1. Location—The path or directory in which the virtual hard disk file will be located. The default location for virtual machine hard disk files is `C:\Documents and Settings\All Users\Documents\ Shared Virtual Machines\`. The actual files are then located in a subdirectory that is named after the virtual machine. If the folder does not appear in the drop down list, the fully qualified path to the folder must be typed in the following step.

2. Virtual hard disk file name—The name given to the hard disk file. The name should be unique and independently identify the machine that it belongs to or the function that it serves. Since it is a differencing disk, it is recommended that the name include a designation indicating that it is a differencing disk, and referencing that it has a parent disk by possibly utilizing the parent's name, a differencing disk designation, or a unique identifier. It is important to realize that the name can be changed, simply by renaming the disk file name and reflecting this change in the virtual machine's configuration.

3. Known virtual hard disks—Represents the current virtual hard disk files that are in the virtual hard disk search path or that are currently being used by virtual machines. This is useful when a differencing disk is being created that is based on a disk that has already been registered or used previously. It also provides a convenience factor in not requiring a fully qualified path to the location of the virtual hard disk. If defaults are always used, then this will always be fully populated. However, the reverse is true as well: if the defaults are not used, then the virtual hard disks will not be populated.

If there are a limited number of alternative locations in which virtual hard disks are going to be stored, the Virtual Server Administration Website has a link under Server Properties, where additional search paths can be entered. By adding the alternative locations to the search paths, all of your virtual hard disk files will be automatically populated, just as if they were in the default directory.

4. Fully qualified path to parent virtual hard disk—Something that was previously alluded to is the fact that multiple differencing disks can reference the same parent. For example, if a parent virtual hard disk was a base install of Windows Server 2003, it could have several children that are quite different. The first child disk could be an installation of Microsoft SQL Server 2000, the second child disk could be an installation of Microsoft

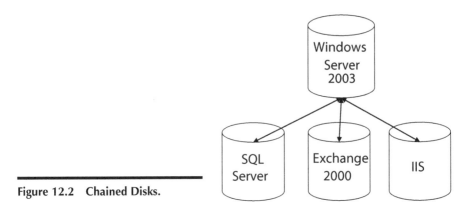

Figure 12.2   Chained Disks.

Exchange Server 2003, and the third child disk could be an IIS Web server. All of the children can start from the same parent, but be incredibly divergent in their content.

Children can also act as parents. An example of this concept would be if the SQL server were to have two differencing disks attached to it. The first disk could be an install of the latest service pack available while the second disk could be an install of an earlier released service pack. Each of these disks rely on the SQL server as its parent, however the SQL server depends on the Windows Server 2003 image to be its parent. These are called Chained Differencing Disks or Disk Chains. Figure 12.2 explains a Chained Disk with a graphical representation.

 Always set a parent disk file as read-only under the NTFS file system as this will ensure that a parent disk is never altered. If a parent disk is changed, all of its children disks are rendered useless and any data written to them is effectively lost. Another recommended practice is to store a second copy of a parent disk on the local disk or have a backup copy stored somewhere else on the network.

Chained Differencing Disks or Disk Chains

Disk Chains are an incredibly flexible tool, allowing for many different configurations and scenarios. As mentioned above, differencing disks can be both parents and children at the same time. The chaining effect allows different software stacks to be installed on the same base virtual machine, simply by creating separate differencing disks. Disk chains must be used with caution however, because if one of the above links is altered and there is no backup copy, all of the other links (or children) become invalid. Operations on parent disks should

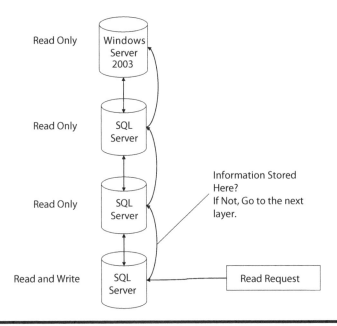

Figure 12.3   Chained Disk Performance.

only be done through another differencing disk that was created for that specific purpose.

There is a small penalty paid in the fact that differencing disks must traverse through the child and the parent to do disk reads. The last child in a differencing disk chain will always be the disk that receives all disk writes. However, all disks in the chain will receive reads, including the last child. So in essence, the longer the chain, the worse the disk performance will be. Also, the more fragmented the parent disks are, the worse performance will be. A detailed explanation of the read/write scenario and the performance problems associated with disk chaining is contained in Figure 12.3.

Linked Virtual Hard Disks

A linked virtual hard disk is a virtual hard disk that points to a physical disk drive for the purpose of converting a physical disk to a virtual disk. Linked virtual hard disks are logical mapping pointers to the physical sectors on a physical disk. Linked virtual hard disks also provide the highest level of performance of all disk types, due to the fact that they are physical disks and therefore all read and write requests occur against a physical drive and not a file on a file system in a drive array or on a physical disk. By having a dedicated I/O path, it provides far more bandwidth than the shared I/O path that is normally used by virtual hard disks.

Linked virtual hard disks actually have their I/O pass through the pointer file; however, this pointer file is static and provides virtually no latency effect on overall performance of I/O on the virtual machine.

Linked virtual hard disks have a great deal of flexibility and can be used to quickly access data as a secondary disk on a virtual machine or as a method of using a peripheral device such as a USB external hard disk drive or a USB flash drive directly inside a virtual machine. There are also many other possibilities available for using a linked virtual hard disk. It is also important to note that disk writes are to the physical disk and they are not reversible. There is no support for differencing disks tied to linked virtual hard disks, neither is there any support for undo disks.

Creating a linked virtual hard disk type will bring up the page with the same name in its title. The Linked Virtual Hard Disk page provides three options:

1. Location—The location for the pointer file that will direct Virtual Server's I/O requests through and down into the actual physical disk that is connected.
2. Virtual hard disk file name—The name of the pointer file to be used by Virtual Server for the I/O redirection.
3. Physical computer drive—Select the physical hard disk that will be linked through the pointer file. It is imperative that the correct drive is linked, because as mentioned above, if any disk writes occur to the physical drive, they are irreversible.

Creating a Virtual Hard Disk

To create a virtual hard disk, go to the Master Status page of the Virtual Server Administration Website, and on the left hand side of the page locate the box titled Virtual Disks. Under the selection, choose the Create link. Upon moving the mouse over the Create link, a side menu will be displayed. Select the disk type to be created where choices include: Dynamically Expanding Virtual Hard Disk, Fixed Size Virtual Hard Disk, Differencing Virtual Hard Disk, Linked Virtual Hard Disk, and Virtual Floppy Disk. Once the settings have been entered, click the Create button.

Virtual Floppy Disks

Virtual floppy disks provide a simple method of placing a floppy drive image into a virtual machine. A virtual floppy disk can easily be created with Virtual Server. To add files into a virtual floppy disk, either mount the disk to a virtual machine or use one of the free tools available on the internet to add and remove files. Virtual floppy disks are especially useful for adding SCSI drivers or network drivers to virtual machines during an operating system installation. They also offer an easy way of transferring data from one virtual machine to another without having to connect them both to the same network. The down side is that virtual floppy disks are very limited in the amount of data that can be stored on them; however, this is the same limitation that their physical counterparts have been subject to.

To create a virtual floppy disk using the Virtual Server Administration Website, enter the following information after clicking on Create and then selecting Virtual Floppy Disk.

1. Location—The path or directory in which the virtual floppy disk file will be located. Because there is no default location for a floppy disk, either a folder must be selected from the drop down list or it must be manually entered as a fully qualified path name along with a floppy disk file name in the next step.
2. Virtual floppy disk file name—The name given to the virtual floppy disk's associated file.

 It is always a good idea to give a very descriptive name to a floppy disk image file as it makes them easier to distinguish and identify amongst a large group of disk files. A good way of deciding on a name is to think of what would be written on the label if this were a physical floppy disk. It is also a good idea to locate the floppy disk image files in a shared directory somewhere on the network that is easily accessible by all host servers. This reduces floppy disk image file clutter on host servers, and it also creates economies of scale by only having to create the image file once and only using up storage for that image file in one location.

Virtual Hard Disk Modes

Undo Disks

Undo (.vud) disks are very similar to differencing disks. Undo disks provide a method to either save or reject changes that are made inside of a virtual machine. As each change is made (software installed or uninstalled, files copied or deleted, users added or removed) to the virtual machine, the changes are written to a separate file. This allows isolation of changes to a virtual machine. When the virtual machine is shut down, Virtual Server offers the options to keep, commit, or discard the changes. Keep simply retains the undo disk and therefore the changes that were made to the virtual machine for the next time when the virtual machine is powered on. Any additional writes to the disk are then added and accumulated to the same undo disk. Commit actually applies or merges the changes that were made into the parent disk of the virtual machine. Since all of the changes and writes that had been accumulating within the undo disk are now merged into the parent disk, the undo disk is no longer needed and discarded. When the virtual machine is next powered on, a new undo disk is created and any and all changes and writes will start to accumulate within the new undo disk. Discard simply deletes the undo disk along with all of the changes that had been made to the virtual machine. These options are explained in more detail below.

The main difference between an undo disk and a differencing disk is that the undo disks apply to all virtual hard disks attached to a virtual machine while a differencing disk applies to only one virtual hard disk.

Undo disks are the children of a parent virtual hard disk. The parent virtual hard disk can be any type of virtual hard disk except another undo disk. This makes it possible to have a chained differencing disk that can then have an undo disk attached to it. Undo disks are very useful for providing an automated control against a virtual machine. The reason that it is referred to as "against a virtual machine" is that undo disks are stored with the virtual machine configuration (.vmc) file. Pairing the undo disks with the configuration file makes it easier to copy and move the undo disks without becoming confused as to which virtual hard disk belongs to which undo disk.

Undo disks can become fragmented on the hard disk, just like any other file on the host. It is recommended that undo disks not be used for extended periods of time under high utilization. This causes problems due to the ever increasing size of the undo disk files and the decrease in performance as the undo disks become more and more fragmented.

Undo disks provide several options when a virtual machine is being shut down or after it has already been shut down.

1. Commit—Commit will merge all of the changes since the undo disk was created into the parent virtual hard disk. Committing will avoid the problem of the undo disk becoming too large or fragmented; however, it permanently and irrevocably merges the changes into the parent disk. The only way to revert the parent disk to its previous state is to have a copy of the parent disk in another location. Once a commit has completed, the virtual machine will create a new undo disk when it is powered on again, assuming that undo disks remain enabled.

2. Discard—Discard will permanently delete the undo disk. Discard will eliminate all the perceived changes that were made. If undo disks are still enabled, a new undo disk will be created when the virtual machine is powered on again.
3. Keep—Keep will allow the undo disk to remain in its state unchanged. Keep is the equivalent to a "NOOP" or "do nothing" disk.

 Unlike other virtualization platforms, Microsoft Virtual Server 2005 R2 only offers undo disks and no other disk modes. The reason that there are no other disk modes needed is due to the unique ability of Virtual Server to support chained differencing disks.

Inspecting Disks

Inspecting a virtual hard disk will provide information about the virtual hard disk. Inspection also provides the capabilities listed below including: Merging Disks, Converting Disks, and Compacting Disks.

To begin inspecting a virtual hard disk, go to the Virtual Disks section on the Virtual Server Administration Website and click on Inspect. Choose either Known virtual hard disks or Fully qualified path to file. Once this choice has been made and the virtual hard disk identified, click Inspect. The following information is revealed about the hard disk.

- Virtual disk type—Identifies the type of virtual hard disk that the virtual hard disk was configured as. It can either be fixed, dynamically expanding, differencing, or linked.
- Fully qualified path to file—Provides the location of the virtual hard disk (.vhd) file.
- Maximum virtual hard disk size—Shows the maximum size of the virtual disk that was defined during creation.
- Current virtual hard disk size—Shows the current size of the virtual hard disk. This number can change for a dynamically expanding disk, but remains static for a fixed disk.
- Host drive identifier—Shows the physical disk to which the linked virtual hard disk is attached.

After the system has inspected the disk, a select group of operations can be performed on the virtual hard disk. These operations vary from one disk to another based on the type of disk that was inspected.

Merging Virtual Hard Disks

Merging disks allows a child disk to be combined with a parent disk as either an update to the parent or as a new separate and unique disk. To merge a disk, select the Merge with Parent or Merge with New option. After selecting the merge method, if Merge with New was chosen, the Merged Virtual Hard Disk type must be chosen along with the name and location of the new disk file.

 Be careful when merging a disk with a parent. If the parent is set to read-only under NTFS, it must be set back to read/write permissions. If the parent has any other child disks, upon beginning the merge process with the parent (assuming that New was not the option chosen) any children besides the current child being operated on will no longer be able to operate, due to the parent no longer being unmodified.

Converting Disk Types

Converting Fixed to Dynamic

Converting a fixed disk to a dynamic disk is usually done when a fixed disk is consuming too much disk space. The conversion process actually creates a second virtual hard disk and then copies the contents from the original to the newly created disk. The newly created dynamic disk is smaller than the fixed disk. The caveat is that if the fixed disk is full, then the dynamic disk will be expanded with data to the same size as the fixed disk and there will be no space savings. Another method of making sure that the new dynamic disk is the smallest size possible is to use the Virtual Disk Precompactor utility and then compact the dynamic disk to make it the smallest size possible. The compacting section later on in this chapter describes the recommended steps to make a dynamic disk the smallest size possible.

Converting Dynamic to Fixed

Converting a dynamic disk to a fixed disk is commonly used to optimize performance of a virtual machine. The performance increase is very slight, but may be critical in some instances of high utilization. The penalty for doing this is the fixed disk will consume the entire amount of space that the dynamic disk may have grown to. This will make the disk file more difficult to move and copy due to the increased file size.

It is important to understand, for a brief period of time, both a dynamic and a fixed disk version will exist on the host system. Before doing this or other types of conversions, adequate disk space must be available or the results could be disastrous.

Converting Linked to Dynamic

Converting a linked disk to a dynamic disk is used to move data from a physical hard disk into a virtual hard disk. This can be useful for several reasons including moving a data drive from a physical implementation over to a newly built virtual machine that will be taking over the same function or if a machine needs to be converted from physical to virtual.

First, the problems of doing linked disk conversions must be addressed. If a linked disk is mounted as a drive with a drive letter on the host operating system, it cannot be used as a linked disk. A linked disk cannot be the host operating system boot disk. Any disk that is mounted with a drive letter and has files that are in use cannot be used or read properly. A linked disk cannot be used from a mapped network drive. Changes to linked disks are changes to the actual physical hard disk, so be forewarned that these changes are permanent.

Second, when attempting to convert a disk that is bootable, but has been added as a secondary disk on a host server, the disk will mount. The conversion can be done, however the problem remains that due to the differences in the underlying hardware between the physical machine and the virtual machine, the results of attempting to startup the new virtual hard disk after the conversion is likely to fail. The only way to avoid this problem is to use a tool, such as the one provided by Microsoft called SysPrep. SysPrep removes all of these drivers and dependencies from the original physical machine and allows windows to do a partial reinstall of the drivers and specific configuration variables to facilitate a clean and properly configured operating system. Sysprep is discussed in detail in the Template Guest Operating System Image Concepts section of chapter 24.

Converting Linked to Fixed

The same caveats and problems that exist for converting a linked disk to a dynamic disk exist for converting from a linked disk to a fixed disk. The only exception is that a fixed disk will be the same size as the original linked disk—there absolutely *must* be enough free disk space in the location where the fixed disk is to be stored.

Compacting Dynamic Disks

Compacting a dynamic disk provides a method of reducing a dynamic disk that has grown larger than desired. The compacting process eliminates all of the excess space in a virtual hard disk. This is done by examining the virtual hard disk and finding the end of the data being stored on the disk and making the file shrink to the end of the data. It is recommended that the Virtual Disk Precompactor utility be used to prepare the disk for compacting.

 If Microsoft Virtual Server 2005 R2 is not available, the Virtual Disk Precompactor utility that comes with Virtual PC 2004 Service Pack 1 will operate in the same fashion as the Virtual Disk Precompactor released with Microsoft Virtual Server 2005 R2. This method is supported by Microsoft.

Virtual Disk Precompactor

The Virtual Disk Precompactor, which comes with Microsoft Virtual Server 2005 R2 and Virtual PC 2004 Service Pack 1, is a utility that should be run before running the Disk Compactor process. The Virtual Disk Precompactor writes a series of zeros (called zeroing out) to all of the empty space inside of the dynamic disk. This ensures that when the Disk Compactor is run that it will eliminate all of the empty space inside of the dynamic disk thereby making it smaller in size. Before running the Virtual Disk Precompactor, it is recommended that the inside of the virtual hard disk be cleaned of any unnecessary files and that the virtual hard disk be defragmented. When defragmenting the virtual hard disk, if the Microsoft defragment tool is used, it may be beneficial to run the tool multiple times to ensure full and complete defragmentation. Third-party tools such as Executive Software's Diskeeper and Raxco's Perfect Disk do an excellent job of defragmentation in a few simple passes and in some cases even in a single pass. If time savings is very important in this process than looking at a third-party tool may be very beneficial.

Once these steps have been followed, run the Virtual Disk Precompactor utility and then use the Compact Virtual Hard Disk function of Virtual Server. Following this process will provide the absolute smallest size dynamic disk that can be obtained.

Virtual Networking

Virtual networking is often a confusing term when it comes to virtualization. Virtual networks along with virtual hard disks are two of the greatest strengths that virtualization offers. Virtual networking provides the ability to create and manipulate networking hardware inside of a host server by doing it virtually using software and drivers. There is a central component to Microsoft's implementation of virtual networking. It is the critical piece to their Virtual Networking model—the Virtual Switch.

Virtual Switches

Under Microsoft Virtual Server 2005 R2 there are several networks that are automatically created during the installation process. These networks are actually virtual switches that are connected to a physical network adapter. It is important to understand however, that a virtual switch does not have to be connected to a physical network adapter; this will be discussed later in this section.

Virtual switching and network configuration is accomplished through a protocol filter driver that is listed in each physical network adapter's protocol stack on the host as Virtual Machine Network Services. Effectively, this provides a method for a virtual switch to interface with the host server's physical network adapter. Additional networks can also be created and pointed through the filter driver to a specific network adapter and multiple networks/virtual switches can be attached or share the same physical network adapter. It is important to note that when a virtual switch is connected to a physical network adapter, any virtual machines attached to the virtual switch will be unable to communicate with the host. This is a security feature designed into Virtual Server (see Figure 12.4).

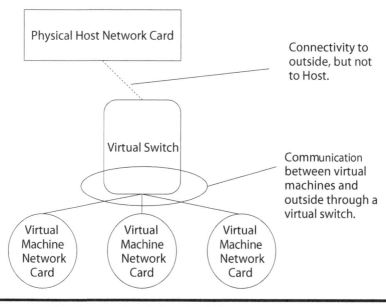

Figure 12.4   Virtual Network and Virtual Switch.

The inability to communicate from the virtual machine to the host across the virtual network switch was implemented as a security measure to prevent users or malicious code inside of a virtual machine from being able to attack or impact the operating condition of the host server.

Network Adapter

A single virtual network adapter is automatically installed as part of the virtual machine hardware by default when a virtual machine is configured under Virtual Server. This behavior makes sense because nearly all virtual machines will need to communicate with another resource on a network. There is a limit to the number of virtual network adapters that can be configured inside of a single virtual machine, and that limit is four. Under most circumstances, a single virtual network adapter is adequate.

Virtual Machines Communicating with the Host

It is possible to setup communications between the physical host server and its virtual machines. This can be accomplished by using the Microsoft Loopback adapter. The installation of the Microsoft Loopback adapter is quite straight forward. Go to the Control Panel and select Add Hardware. Next, select the option to manually add hardware, and pick Network adapters. When prompted for the manufacturer, select Microsoft. In the Network Adapter box, click Microsoft Loopback Adapter and then click Next followed by Finish. Once the Microsoft Loopback adapter has been added, create a new virtual network and attach it to the Loopback adapter. The Loopback adapter should then be given an IP address. Now any virtual machines that are attached to the newly created network can be given an IP address on the same subnet as the host server's Loopback adapter, allowing the virtual machine and the host server to communicate with each other.

After the Loopback adapter is installed, its TCP/IP properties should be manually configured. If the TCP/IP properties are configured to use DHCP, the adapter will eventually use an automatic IP address (169.254.x.x) because the adapter is not actually connected to any physical media and therefore it cannot reach a DHCP server.

Virtual Machines Communicating with Each Other Privately

Private virtual machine to virtual machine networks can be created to provide a very efficient and secure network between virtual machines. A private virtual machine network is effectively attaching virtual machines to a dedicated virtual switch with no outside connectivity. There is no limit to the number of virtual machines that can be attached to a virtual switch, provided that they reside on the same physical host. This provides a great deal of flexibility when doing testing and troubleshooting of multi-tiered applications. To create a private network, simply create a new network under virtual server and do not attach it to any physical network or Loopback interfaces.

DHCP Server

Another facet of a virtual network is the Dynamic Host Configuration Protocol (DHCP) server that is built into Microsoft Virtual Server 2005 R2. The DHCP server can be activated going to the Virtual Networks link in the Virtual Server Administration Website, then clicking on the virtual network to be configured located under the Configure link. To configure the virtual DHCP server, click the DHCP server link. Click the Enabled check box and enter in the desired DHCP server settings. Once all the settings have been entered, click the OK button located in the lower right hand corner.

 The virtual DHCP server will only give addresses to virtual network cards on the virtual network. This behavior is intentional by design. If a DHCP server is required to give out addresses to both physical and virtual machines, then it must be a normal DHCP server that is installed in either a virtual machine or on a physical machine located on the physical network.

DHCP Server Settings

Configuring the virtual DHCP server is easier in Virtual Server than almost any other DHCP serving application around. The following is an explanation of the available settings used to properly configure the virtual DHCP server.

- Network address denotes the base IP address range of addresses managed by this DHCP server.
- Network mask is the subnet class that will be used by the DHCP server.
- Starting IP address begins the range of IP addresses that the DHCP server will distribute to client virtual machines.
- Ending IP address ends the range of IP addresses that the DHCP server will distribute to client virtual machines.
- Virtual DHCP server address is the IP address of this virtual DHCP server.
- Default gateway address will populate the default gateway on each client machine that receives an IP address from the DHCP server. It is the IP address of a local IP router (gateway) that forwards traffic beyond this virtual network.

- DNS servers will populate the DNS information inside of each client machine so that they can resolve a domain host name query.
- WINS servers will populate the WINS information inside of each client machine.
- IP address lease time will determine when a client virtual machine must request a new lease. The minimum value allowed is 60 seconds.
- Lease renewal time indicates when a client virtual machine should attempt to renew its lease from the original DHCP server before it expires. The minimum value allowed is 30 seconds.
- Lease rebinding time decides how long before the client virtual machine should request a lease renewal from any DHCP server on the network instead of just the original DHCP server that issued the lease. The minimum value allowed is 45 seconds.

Dynamic MAC Addresses

Dynamic MAC addresses are useful for quick testing or when there will be a small number of virtual machines used throughout the entire network. The reason that dynamic MAC addresses are not desirable for large scale deployments is due to the possibility of multiple virtual machines ending up with the same assigned dynamic MAC address. When this occurs, network problems start happening mysteriously throughout the network or some virtual machines begin to behave erratically without any reason. The solution is to avoid using dynamic MAC addresses all together by utilizing static MAC addresses.

Static MAC Addresses

Static MAC addresses can ensure that there are never duplicate MAC addresses on the network. It is recommended that a standard be created to allow the creation and uniqueness of static MAC addresses throughout the network. Creating a table or spreadsheet to track static MAC address information is a good way to start out; however if virtual machines are being tied into a physical network, the best way to ensure proper enforcement is to use DHCP on the physical network for IP address assignments. By using DHCP and tying the distribution of IP addresses to MAC addresses, it is ensured that there will not be any duplicate MAC addresses or IP addresses. This is because most DHCP server software will not allow a duplicate MAC address or IP address to be entered into the assignment table.

 A simple way to enhance network security and control over IP addresses is by preventing other IP addresses from being distributed by the DHCP server except to those that have registered MAC addresses within the assignment table.

Some virtualization platforms support virtual Network Address Translation (NAT). Microsoft Virtual Server 2005 R2 does not have a function that supports any internal NAT of any kind. However, NAT via a network device on the physical network is supported.

Creating a virtual network is simple using the Virtual Server Administration Website. Once logged in, select the section Virtual Networks and choose the Create link. After clicking the Create link, the New Virtual Network Properties page is opened.

Creating a Virtual Network or Virtual Switch

The first step is to choose a descriptive name for the virtual network, then decide whether it will be connected to one of the host server's physical adapters, the Microsoft Loopback adapter (if it has been installed), or not bound to an adapter at all (this will create a virtual machine to virtual machine only network). Next, choose if there are any virtual machines listed that should be attached to the virtual network being created. If there are any further notes about the virtual network, they can be supplied in the notes field. Finally, click the OK button located in the lower right corner of the page.

After clicking the OK button, the Virtual Network Properties page of the new virtual network that has been created is now displayed. This is also the location where the DHCP configuration option can be selected.

Adding or Removing a Virtual Network Adapter

To add or remove a virtual network adapter from a virtual machine under Microsoft Virtual Server 2005 R2, go to the Status page for the specific virtual machine that will have the virtual network adapter either added or removed. At the Status page, scroll down to the section labeled Network adapters and click on the link. The Network Adapter Properties page is now displayed. This page allows for the removal and addition of virtual network adapters. To add a virtual network adapter, click on the button labeled Add Network Adapter and to remove a virtual network adapter, click on the Remove check box above the network adapter information of the network adapter to be removed, and then click the OK button.

Creating a Dynamic or Static MAC Address

There is another property on the Network Adapter Properties page that offers some additional flexibility—the Dynamic or Static MAC address option. To configure a dynamic MAC address, click on the radio button next to the word Dynamic. Dynamic is the default setting for all virtual network adapters in the system. If a static MAC address is desired, click on the Static radio button and type in the desired MAC address. It is important that the MAC address is entered in the exact format as the sample MAC address displayed by default. If this is not done correctly, the configuration will cause an error to occur and prompt with the correct format to use. The dynamic MAC address format is six groupings of two hexadecimal numbers separated by dashes, i.e., 32-FF-A3-67-4B-DE.

 When switching from a dynamic MAC address to a static MAC address, make sure to actually click the radio button next to static. All too often it is assumed that when entering the MAC address in the static text field, the software should be intelligent enough to automatically select the static radio button. Unfortunately, this is not the case. If you type in a static MAC address but forget to switch the radio button and then click OK, the virtual machine configuration file will not be updated with the new MAC address and it will continue to use a dynamically assigned MAC address.

Resource Management

Resource management inside of Virtual Server 2005 is limited when compared to VMware ESX Server; however the control over CPU resources is superior to that of VMware GSX server. Microsoft employs a system of granular control over the CPU resources consumed and reserved for virtual machines. Resource management of CPUs is done through the Virtual Server Administration Website, under the section titled Virtual Server and the link titled Resource Allocation. This section provides three variables per virtual machine managed by the system, they are:

1. Relative Weight
2. Reserved Capacity
3. Maximum Capacity

For a detailed look into what each of these do and how they effect virtual machines, please see chapter 10. It should be noted that to optimize the system, all virtual machines should be given specific resource settings and there should always be some capacity left for the host operating system.

Performance Optimization

This section describes several recommended hardware, software, and configuration optimizations that can be applied to Microsoft Virtual Server 2005 R2 in order to enable optimum virtual machine performance. Although the recommendations presented here do not have to be used for virtual machines to function, they should be used when deploying virtual machines in a production environment.

File System

Microsoft Virtual Server 2005 R2 requires the NTFS file system on the host; this is due to Virtual Server's reliance on the file system level security for all of the security aspects of Virtual Server.

Memory

Microsoft Virtual Server 2005 R2 should be given as much memory as possible. This holds true for the host operating system that the platform is operating on, in addition to being able to provide the virtual machines with as much memory as possible. It is important to realize that with each virtual machine that is added, there is an additional amount of memory used not only by the allocation of reserved memory for the virtual machine, but for management overhead of the Virtual Server application to manage that virtual machine.

The actual amount of each virtual machine's memory usage can be calculated by taking the amount of memory allocated to the virtual machine in Virtual Server and adding an additional 32MB. As an example, if there is a virtual machine with 1024MB of memory allocated inside Virtual Server, then the total memory usage by that virtual machine will be 1024MB for the virtual machine and 32MB for Virtual Server's management overhead, totaling 1056MB of memory. Likewise, if there were ten virtual machines, each assigned 1024MB of memory, then the total memory usage by virtual machines on that host server would be 10,560MB of memory. 10,240MB of memory directly allocated to the virtual machine configuration, and another 320MB of memory allocated to Virtual Server management overhead.

Processor

Another important performance optimization is to provide Virtual Server with as much CPU compute power as possible. This can be achieved by adding processors, breaking up virtual machines into a balance of high utilization virtual machines along with low utilization machines onto the same server and never combining too many high utilization virtual machines on the same physical host server. CPU cycles are a precious commodity on physical servers running virtualization and must be carefully monitored to ensure peak performance. Virtual Server itself should be given at least 15 percent of one of the CPUs on the host server strictly for management and operating overhead.

Disk I/O

Virtual machine hard disk image files should reside on a physical disk drive on the host server that is separate from the physical disk drive on which the host server's operating system and applications reside. A physical disk drive or storage array that is dedicated to virtual machine hard disk image storage will provide increased performance. High performance disks, such as 10K RPM or 15K RPM Ultra320 SCSI disks, should be used when possible for the highest levels of disk I/O performance.

A common disk configuration for physical host servers using local storage is to configure a pair of 10K RPM Ultra320 SCSI disks on a single channel connected to a high-performance RAID controller and configured into a RAID 1 array of mirrored disks on which the host server's operating system and application are installed (system disk). A separate set of three or more 15K RPM Ultra320 SCSI disks are then configured into a RAID-5 striped parity array and connected to the RAID controller on a separate channel than that of the system disk. The virtual machine hard disk image files (and any undo disk files) are configured to reside on the RAID-5 array.

 A Storage Area Network (SAN) based solution is a great way of increasing disk I/O performance while keeping storage management to a minimum. The downside of a SAN is its cost; a SAN is more costly in terms of capital expenditure relative to local server storage. Other storage alternatives may prove to be more cost effective; however, the scalability will more than likely not be able to compete with that of a SAN.

Antivirus

If the host server has antivirus applications or clients installed, they should be configured to run daily scans only. Real-time antivirus or spyware protection will severely impact the host server's performance. Additionally, virtual machine configuration files, virtual hard disk image files, undo disk files, floppy image files, and ISO image files should be excluded fro the antivirus or spyware scans to reduce performance bottlenecks.

Defragmenting Files

The host server should generally not use the file defragmentation utility that is provided with Windows operating systems in order to perform background file defragmenting. Although it is a good idea to have files arranged in contiguous blocks on the hard disks, a robust, no intrusive solution should be used. The Microsoft-provided defragmentation utility can consume a large amount of available disk I/O or processor resources that can adversely affect the operating of virtual machine hosted on the server. There are good third-party utilities available that are optimized for production server environments that offer a good balance between the resource needs of the server and the background defragmentation utility.

Host Server Usage

The physical host server on which Microsoft Virtual Server 2005 R2 is installed should be dedicated to hosting virtual machines as a virtualization platform server. It should not share its resources with other applications or processes. It is not recommended to run Microsoft Virtual Server 2005 R2 and other applications including but not limited to a Windows domain controller, a file server, a print server, Microsoft Exchange Server, Microsoft SQL Server, Microsoft ISA Server, MOM, Microsoft SMS, IIS Web servers or application servers outside of the Virtual Server Administration Website, FTP or NNTP services, other Web or application servers such as Apache, Tomcat, WebLogic, WebSphere, or other database servers such as MySQL, Oracle, Sybase, and others. The virtual machines generally require memory and processor resources that are in direct conflict with other applications running on the host server. In addition to dedicating the host server to the virtualization platform, all unneeded services should be uninstalled or stopped and disabled.

Performance Counters

When at least one virtual machine is running, the Virtual Machine's performance object is available under the Performance Logs and Alerts under Microsoft Windows Server 2003 host operating system. The Virtual Machine's performance object exposes two memory-oriented counters, Allocated MB and Allocated Pages. The Allocated MB counter displays the amount of memory currently allocated to each virtual machine in units of megabytes (MB). The Allocated Pages counter displays the number of memory pages currently allocated to each virtual machine. Each virtual machine instance can be monitored individually or all instances can be monitored collectively.

Virtual Machine Configuration

Virtual machine creation should be done by creating fixed disks operating against the Adaptec 7870 Virtual SCSI Controller. Fixed disks remove the overhead of dynamically expanding disks as needed, but the trade-off is that the disks consume their maximum storage capacity on the host server's file system. Virtual machines should not have any unnecessary media attached, nor should they have more virtual networks attached than is necessary.

Virtual machines should (if at all possible) always have Virtual Machine Additions installed and the version of Virtual Machine Additions should always match the version of Microsoft Virtual Server that is running on the host server. Not only do Virtual Machine Additions provide performance enhancements to the guest operating system, but they also provide optimizations in the interface between the virtual machine and VMM layer.

Virtual Server Management

A small increase in performance can be gained on a Microsoft Virtual Server host by reducing the application overhead on the host operating system. When installing Microsoft Virtual Server, the custom installation option can be used to install only the Virtual Server Service while deselecting the Documentation and Developer Resources, Virtual Machine Remote Control Client, and Virtual Server Web Application. Additionally, if this minimal configuration is used, the host server will not require IIS to be installed. This removes the management components from the Virtual Server host. The host must then be managed remotely by installing just the Virtual Server Web Application and Virtual Server Remote Control Client on another computer and directing those applications to the Virtual Server host.

Host Clustering

Microsoft Virtual Server 2005 R2 supports a new feature known as host clustering. This feature improves the availability of virtual machines running under Microsoft Virtual Server 2005 R2 and provides additional benefits, such as facilitating a no-downtime maintenance window for hardware or software updates to the host server. Host Clustering improves the availability of virtual machines by monitoring the state of the Microsoft Virtual Server 2005 R2 host server nodes in a cluster and providing failover from one node to another during a node failure. The failover ensures that all of the virtual machines that were running on the failed node are quickly brought back up on another node in the cluster. It is important to understand that Host Clustering does not cluster the virtual machines, instead it clusters the host servers providing the Microsoft Virtual Server 2005 R2 virtualization platform itself, eliminating the platform or a single host server from becoming a single-point of failure.

Host Clustering Requirements

Each node in a Host Cluster must meet the default installation requirements of Microsoft Virtual Server 2005 R2 at a minimum. Additionally, Microsoft states that each node in the cluster must have identical hardware components including processor make, model, and version. Each host server used as a node in the cluster must meet all of the requirements of cluster computers listed in the Windows Server Catalog (previously known as the Hardware Compatibility List).

Microsoft Virtual Server 2005 R2 Host Clustering leverages the Microsoft Clustering services that are available by default in Microsoft Windows Server 2003. For each node in the cluster, the following host operating systems can be used to support Host Clustering.

- Microsoft Windows Server 2003 with SP1 Enterprise Edition, 32-bit
- Microsoft Windows Server 2003 with SP1 Datacenter Edition, 32-bit
- Microsoft Windows Server 2003 R2 Enterprise Edition, 32-bit
- Microsoft Windows Server 2003 R2 Datacenter Edition, 32-bit
- Microsoft Windows Server 2003 x64 with SP1 Enterprise Edition, 64-bit
- Microsoft Windows Server 2003 x64 with SP1 Datacenter Edition, 64-bit
- Microsoft Windows Server 2003 x64 R2 Enterprise Edition, 64-bit
- Microsoft Windows Server 2003 x64 R2 Datacenter Edition, 64-bit

Each node must have at least two network adapters installed. One network adapter in each node must be dedicated to the private cluster network. If the cluster is using iSCSI storage, this requirement is in addition to the network adapter requirements of the iSCSI solution. The network adapters used in the private cluster network cannot be a part of a teamed network adapter solution.

The cluster requires shared storage to which each node in the cluster is connected. The shared storage device must be a qualified device listed in the Windows Server Catalog. The shared storage device may be a SCSI attached solution, an iSCSI solution, or a Fibre Channel SAN solution. Each node in the cluster will require connectivity to the shared storage device, which may also require additional hardware such as network adapter or host bus adapters (HBAs). The shared storage device must be configured with a minimum of two volumes. One volume is used as the quorum for the cluster. The other volume is used to store the files for the virtual machines running in the Host Cluster. If a single volume is used to store the files for all virtual machines hosted in the cluster, all virtual machine must failover as a single unit. If each virtual machine has its own volume configured on the shared storage device, the virtual machines can failover as separate units.

Virtual machines that are hosted within a Host Cluster must have Virtual Machine Additions installed and it must be the version of Virtual Machine Additions that ships with Microsoft Virtual Server 2005 R2.

The Microsoft-provided Havm.vbs script must be copied to each node of the cluster. The Havm.vbs (high availability virtual machine) script is configured as a Generic Script resource in the cluster. It provides consistent functionality to ensure that virtual machines hosted in the cluster failover correctly and also restart virtual machines that stop running.

Requirements for iSCSI and Host Clustering

If iSCSI storage will be used with the Host Clustering solution, an additional network adapter or iSCSI HBA will be required for each node in the cluster in addition to the network adapter requirements listed in the previous section. One network adapter in each node of the cluster must be dedicated to the iSCSI storage network. Additionally, the Microsoft iSCSI initiator 2.0 or higher must be used. At a minimum, the Microsoft iSCSI Initiator service must be installed, even when using iSCSI HBAs. Gigabit network adapters or HBAs should be used for the iSCSI connectivity at a minimum.

Additional Resources for Host Clustering

Microsoft offers a great document, *Virtual Server Host Clustering Step-by-Step Guide for Virtual Server 2005 R2.* It describes in great detail an entire Host Clustering implementation along with the Havm.vbs script. Although the document does not ship with the Microsoft Virtual Server 2005 R2 product, the document can be downloaded in Microsoft Word format from Microsoft's Web site. The URL is provided below and is also available on the book's Web site, http://www.vmbook.info/links.

Microsoft Virtual Server Home Page
    http://go.microsoft.com/fwlink/?LinkId=28331
Virtual Server Host Clustering Step-by-Step Guide for Virtual Server 2005 R2
    http://go.microsoft.com/fwlink/?LinkId=55644
Windows Server Catalog
    http://go.microsoft.com/fwlink/?LinkId=4303

iSCSI Support

Microsoft Virtual Server 2005 R2 supports remote storage using the iSCSI protocol when used with Microsoft Windows Server 2003 and the Microsoft iSCSI Initiator. iSCSI provides the opportunity to create a centralized, remote storage system that is much easier to deploy and manage than its Fibre Channel counterpart, as well as generally being more cost effective. Aside from the benefits of a centralized remote storage system, iSCSI also meets the storage needs required by Host Clustering and virtual-to-virtual clustering across physical host server boundaries (also called guest clustering).

iSCSI Requirements

iSCSI requires an additional network adapter or iSCSI host bus adapter (HBA) to be installed in the host server that is dedicated to the iSCSI storage network.

This is referred to as the storage adapter. If the storage adapter is a network adapter (as opposed to an iSCSI HBA, a multifunction offload device), it is highly recommended that a gigabit adapter or better is used. The storage adapter is always completely dedicated to the remote storage network and cannot be used for normal client-server network communication. The host server should have at least two other network adapters aside from the storage adapter to handle client-server network traffic for the host server itself and another to be dedicated for virtual machine network traffic.

The Microsoft iSCSI Initiator 2.0 or later must be used. If the storage adapter is an iSCSI HBA, just the Microsoft iSCSI Initiator service must be installed.

iSCSI is designed to be connected to an Ethernet storage network. It is possible to connect Fibre Channel sourced LUNs to an iSCSI storage adapter, but this requires additional iSCSI-to-Fibre Channel bridge hardware and software that is outside the scope of this book.

Additional iSCSI Resources

For more in-depth technical details of iSCSI and the configuration of iSCSI with Microsoft Virtual 2005 R2, Microsoft has published a Word document titled Using iSCSI with Virtual Server 2005 R2. It discusses the usage and configuration of iSCSI for guest and host clustering as well as providing a good technical foundation for the technology in terms of Virtual Server. Other technologies are also discussed including the Microsoft iSCSI Initiator and Microsoft iSNS (Internet Storage Name Service). The URL is provided below and can also be found on this volume's Web site, http://vmbook.info/links.

Using iSCSI with Virtual Server 2005 R2
   http://go.microsoft.com/fwlink/?LinkId=55646
Microsoft iSCSI Software Initiator 2.0
   http://go.microsoft.com/fwlink/?linkid=44352
Microsoft iSNS Server
   http://go.microsoft.com/fwlink/?LinkID=55830
Microsoft Storage Technologies – iSCSI
   http://go.microsoft.com/fwlink/?linkid=50522

Unattended Installation

Microsoft Virtual Server 2005 R2 supports the ability to be installed from a command-line interface. Using the features of the command-line interface installation, an unattended installation of Microsoft Virtual Server can be achieved. The Microsoft Virtual Server 2005 R2 installer ships as a Setup.exe file. Packaged inside the Setup.exe file is an MSI installer file (a .msi file). The command-line installation is performed using the .msi file, but its parameters can also be passed to the Setup.exe file as well. If desired, the .msi installer file can be extracted from the Setup.exe file and used directly. Throughout this section, the Setup.exe installer file will be assumed to be named Setup.exe in the file system.

Extracting the MSI File

The process of extracting the .msi installer file from the Setup.exe file is simple. From a Windows command-prompt, execute the following command:

```
Setup.exe /c /t C:\Temp
```

The command assumes that the Microsoft Virtual Server 2005 R2 installer file, Setup.exe, resides in the current directory. It extracts the .msi installer file into the C:\Temp directory. The drive letter and path to the destination directory may be changed as necessary. The result is that a file named "Virtual Server 2005 Install.msi" is extracted from the Setup.exe file and is placed into the destination directory, C:\Temp. After the execution of the command in this example, a new file, C:\Temp\ Virtual Server 2005 Install.msi, now exists. This is the .msi file that is referred to throughout the Unattended Installation section of this chapter.

Command-Line Installation Approaches

To perform an unattended installation of Microsoft Virtual Server 2005 R2, the command-line installation is used. There are two methods that can be used to install from the command-line. The primary method is to use the well-documented MSI approach with the .msi that is extracted from the Setup.exe file (see Extracting the MSI File above). The second approach is to perform the command-line installation using the Setup.exe file directly, passing it the options that are used with the first approach. Since the two methods do not really differ in their core implementations, the .msi file approach will be described in detail and can be applied to the second approach.

Windows installer Details

The primary method of installing Microsoft Virtual Server 2005 R2 from the command line uses Windows Installer technologies along with the .msi file that is extracted from the Microsoft Virtual Server 2005 R2 Setup.exe file. The .msi file is a Windows Installer package. Windows Installer is used to install the product from the command-line using the executable Windows Installer file named msiexec.exe. The basic command used to perform an unattended installation is:

```
msiexec.exe /i "Virtual Server 2005 Install.msi"
            PIDKEY=<PIDKEY> /qn
```

The /i switch tells msiexec.exe to install the package specified by the string, "Virtual Server 2005 Install.msi," which is the file name of the .msi file that is extracted from the Setup.exe file. The PIDKEY=<PIDKEY> argument tells msiexec.exe that the product key number to use for the installation is <PID-KEY>. The token, <PIDKEY>, should be replaced with the actual product key for Microsoft Virtual Server 2005 R2. The /qn switch is used to tell msiexec.exe to use no user interface. The installer will run fully unattended without prompting for any user input.

There are several other options that can be used with msiexec.exe to customize the installation from the command-line.

- SERVICESSTARTUPMANUAL=<value>
  If <value> is set to 1, the Virtual Server service startup value will be set to manual. The default value is 0 for a service startup value of automatic.
- WEBSITEDEFAULTPORT=<value>
  Specifies the TCP port number to be used for the Administration Website.
- INSTALLDIR=<value>
  Specifies the directory under which the product will be installed. The default location is the "Program Files" directory.

For more details and additional installation options, please refer to the Virtual Server Administrator's Guide that is installed with the product.

To perform an installation from command-line without having to extract the .msi file, the following command can be used:

```
Setup.exe /v" PIDKEY=<PIDKEY> /qn"
```

The string specified in the double-quotes following the /v switch in the command above is passed to the encapsulated .msi file.

 When specifying the value of <PIDKEY> using your valid product key, you must remove the dashes from the string. Product keys for Microsoft Virtual Server 2005 R2 use the format, AAAAA-BBBBB-CCCCC-DDDDD-EEEEE. The value passed into either version of the command-line installer must not have the minus characters, such as AAAAABBBBBCCCCCDDDDDEE EEE. Otherwise, the installation will fail.

The results for an unattended installation can be obtained from the Windows Application Event Log using the Event Viewer MMC snap-in usually found under the Administrative Tools program group. The Source column in Event Viewer will be listed as MsiInstaller. If the installation succeeds, the event type will be information and the description will contain text such as, "Product:

Microsoft Virtual Server 2005 R2 — Installation completed successfully." If the installation fails, the event type will be error and the description will contain text about the reason for the failure such as, "Product: Microsoft Virtual Server 2005 R2 — The Product Key is invalid."

The command for an unattended installation can be placed inside a batch file to simply reuse. Additionally, the .msi installer package can be customized into a Windows Installer transforms package (a .mst file) that can be used to encapsulate common options within the installation package. For more information, search the Microsoft Web site at http://msdn.microsoft.com for Merges and Transforms subset of the Windows Installer section of the Microsoft Platform SDK.

Upgrading to R2

Microsoft Virtual Server 2005 has an in-place upgrade path from the original Microsoft Virtual Server 2005 RTM release to the current Microsoft Virtual Server 2005 R2 release. An in-place upgrade can only be performed on full product versions of Microsoft Virtual Server 2005. Beta, release candidate, and trial versions are not supported for in-place upgrades. In order to upgrade from a beta, release candidate, or trial version, the existing product must be uninstalled and the new version can then be installed afterwards. In-place upgrades do not require the existing product to be uninstalled; however the upgrade process does differ slightly from the usual installation procedures.

Before attempting to perform and in-place upgrade or an uninstall/reinstall upgrade, it is important to first shut down, power off, and back up all virtual machines, including all virtual machines in a suspended state, before attempting to upgrade the host server. Aside from just the virtual machine disk image files, all other MSVS files should be backed up as well, including the Virtual Server configuration file, all virtual machine configuration files, all virtual network configuration files, and any undo disk files. The default locations that should be backed up are listed below.

- <AllUsers>\Application Data\Microsoft\Virtual Server\Options.xml
- <AllUsers>\Application Data\Microsoft\Virtual Server\Virtual Machines*
- <AllUsers>\Application Data\Microsoft\Virtual Server\Virtual Networks*
- <AllUsers>\Application Data\Microsoft\Virtual Server Webapp*
- <AllUsers>\Documents\Shared Virtual Machines*
- <AllUsers>\Documents\Shared Virtual Networks*

The token, <AllUsers> used in the list above represents the path to the special folder for documents and setting for all users. By default, this path is C:\Documents and Settings\All Users, although it may vary from system to system.

Virtual machine files including virtual machine configuration files, hard disk image files, and undo disk files may also be located in other directories depending on each system's configuration. These files also need to be backed up before upgrading the host server.

The Virtual Server service and the Virtual Machine Helper service must be stopped before upgrading the host server. This can be done from command-line using the NET STOP command or from the services.msc MMC snap-in usually located under Administrative Tools in the Windows Start menu.

Before upgrading the host server, it is recommended to perform a Windows update on the host server, updating the service pack level and installing any critical security updates.

Once the host server is ready to be upgraded in-place, the normal installation process for installing Microsoft Virtual Server 2005 R2 on a single computer is used to perform the upgrade. This process is discussed in chapter 9.

After the in-place upgrade installation process has been completed on the host server, Virtual Machine Additions must be reinstalled into the guest operating system of each virtual machine. Once all virtual machines have been upgraded, the in-place upgrade is complete.

Summary

Microsoft Virtual Server 2005 R2 has many important advanced features and considerations regarding configuration, management, and performance optimizations. By understanding these advanced topics, better performance and stability for both host and guest operating systems can be achieved. Proper configuration must include Virtual Machine Additions, as it provides critical performance enhancements. Selecting the proper virtual hard disk controller, disk type, and disk mode are very important if proper manageability and acceptable disk I/O are going to be realized. Virtual hard disk type conversions can be incredibly useful when trying to manage large numbers of virtual machines on hosts that have limited amounts of hard disk space. Virtual networks and switches provide powerful configuration options when deciding how virtual machines should communicate with each other, the host server, and the external network. Microsoft Virtual Server 2005 R2 supports administrator-friendly unattended installations that can ease the deployment of host servers. The host clustering features allow Microsoft Virtual Server 2005 R2 to run highly available production systems without the need for a large investment in third-party, proprietary failover solutions. Coupled with Microsoft Windows Server 2003 R2, Microsoft Virtual Server 2005 R2 provides a very stable virtualization platform on which to host enterprise-class virtual servers.

Part IV

Implementing VMware ESX Server

Chapter 13

The VMware ESX Server Platform

VMware ESX Server is undoubtedly the most widely deployed and most stable server virtualization platform. Designed for production use, enterprise-class server virtualization, VMware ESX Server provides a feature rich virtualization platform while having the smallest possible overhead due to its hypervisor design. This chapter covers the platform's background, deployment planning requirements, and overviews platform-specific features.

Product Background

VMware's ESX Server was released in March of 2001. The release followed VMware GSX Server and VMware Workstation. VMware GSX Server was developed to be a workgroup class solution, providing simple administration on a familiar host platform; however performance was lost due to the host platform overhead. During early prerelease versions of VMware ESX Server, it was necessary to install a copy of Red Hat Linux first, then after completing the install, the kernel would have to be replaced with a custom kernel written by VMware.

ESX Server is a hypervisor-based virtualization platform. A hypervisor provides the most efficient use of resources in a virtualization platform because it does not reply upon a host operating system and can minimize the resource overhead. VMware's decision to build an incredibly lightweight bare metal operating system was a simple one. VMware wanted to create an enterprise class virtualization platform and realized early on that to be successful, performance and granularity of resource control would be critical components. In May of 2002, VMware released ESX Server 1.5 providing support for uniprocessor virtual machines, tight SAN integration, and advanced resource controls. In July of 2003 VMware announced ESX Server 2.0, which provided support for up to two processors with the VMware Virtual SMP add-on product. Virtual SMP is supported only by ESX Server 2.x and above. In the second half of 2005, VMware will likely introduce four-way Virtual SMP support. Multiprocessing support is critical for enterprises wanting to use virtual machines on high utilization production class systems.

ESX Server hosts virtual machines running a broad range of operating systems. To achieve such wide support, ESX Server emulates a generic virtual hardware platform. Each virtual machine leverages its own virtual hardware consisting of a single or dual-processor system with an Intel 440BX motherboard including an NS338 SIO (Serial Input Output) chip and five virtual PCI slots. A Phoenix Bios 4.0 Release 6 acts as the BIOS for the system. Depending on the host server's capacity, up to 3.6 GB of memory can be given to a single virtual machine. Each virtual machine also has a virtual SVGA graphics card, up to four virtual SCSI controllers supporting fifteen devices per controller, up to two virtual 1.44 MB floppy drives, up to four virtual CD/DVD-ROM drives, two serial ports, one parallel port, and up to four virtual network adapters. The total number of virtual SCSI controllers and network adapters together cannot exceed five devices because each virtual machine is limited to five virtual PCI slots. As discussed later in the chapter, there are specific restrictions as to which physical hardware devices are supported by ESX Server.

A primarily remote management paradigm is used by ESX Server. There is a minimal console provided for manipulation of disk files, installing server packages and updates, and manipulating specific settings. The remote management interface provides the ability to create, monitor, stop, start, reboot and suspend virtual machines. It also provides integration for the VMware Remote Console (VMRC) application, allowing direct virtual machine console access. Both the remote management interface and the VMRC application are run from a workstation (client) desktop. This provides an easy to use system for controlling and accessing virtual machines during the administration process. Both the Web interface and the VMRC support the use secure connections via SSL. In addition to the remote management and VMRC interfaces, VMware also provides a scripting API to automate ESX Server management tasks.

Today VMware has the most powerful and mature platform available in the enterprise virtualization space. This was accomplished by focusing on performance and function above all else. With each release of ESX Server, more and more enterprises are making the decision to move to virtualization in their production environments. VMware is steadily gaining traction in the mission critical and production enterprise data center space by providing a low-overhead, high-performance solution.

Platform Specifics

At the core of ESX Server is a series of modules that provide capabilities to regulate CPU affinity, memory allocation and oversubscription, network bandwidth throttling, and I/O bandwidth control. These modules along with the capabilities offered with VMFS make up the ESX Server base platform.

Virtual Machine File System (VMFS)

VMFS is a file system created by VMware as a solution to large file support and performance issues that haunted existing Linux-based file systems. The VMFS file system addresses control, security, and management issues associated with virtual machine hard disk files. VMFS allows virtual hard disk files to be created contiguously by ESX Server, which enhances access speeds from disk to virtualization platform. Some native Linux commands do not work with the VMFS file system. VMware provides alternative commands that are compatible with the VMFS file system and may be used from the Service Console. For example, VMware provides the vdf command as a VMFS-compatible alternative to the df command. VMFS is the premier virtual hard disk file system available.

Differences between VMFS-1 and VMFS-2

VMFS-1 was introduced in the original release of ESX Server 1.0 Server, new with the introduction of ESX Server 2.0 and above is the VMFS-2 file system. The differences between the two are shown in Figure 13.1.

Hardware Requirements

ESX Server's biggest weakness is the limited amount of hardware components that it supports. This is because VMware uses a closed driver model, therefore VMware must provide all of the necessary hardware driver support in the ESX Server product. There are no vendor-supplied, ESX Server-specific drivers available. This makes the requirements that must be met for ESX Server to work cor-

	VMFS-1	VMFS-2
Volumes Supported	128	128
Maximum Volume Size	2TB	2TB
Number of Extents	1	32
Multi-Server Access to Volume	Clustering Only	Any
Raw Disk Mapping	No	Yes

Figure 13.1   Comparison of VMFS-1 and VMFS-2 File Systems.

rectly far more stringent than that of VMware GSX Server or Microsoft Virtual Server both of which run on any supported Linux or Windows hardware. The advantage to this limited hardware set is the hardware resource control capabilities and the performance gains. Below are descriptions of each of the system components and the specific requirements that must be met.

Processor

CPU requirements for ESX Server are not incredibly high, however to actually take advantage of any real consolidation or performance benefits, a far higher set of CPU requirements must be met. The minimum requirements for ESX Server 2.5 are dual Pentium III 700MHz or better CPUs or dual AMD Opteron or better CPUs. This is for a single CPU-based virtual machine solution for an SMP-based dual CPU-based virtual machine solution dual Pentium III 900MHz or better CPUs are required or dual AMD Opteron or better CPUs. The real-world requirements are much greater, however. To benefit from all of the capabilities of ESX Server, CPUs should be Pentium 4 Xeon 2.8 GHz or better dual CPUs or the AMD Opteron equivalent. Obviously the more CPU compute power that can be leverage, the greater the benefits realized from ESX Server. ESX Server will support up to 16 way systems out of the box.

Memory

ESX Server-based virtual machines and for that matter all virtual machines will benefit from as much memory as possible. It is important to realize that the ESX Server kernel itself consumes a minimal amount of memory for itself as well as additionally memory for each virtual machine that it is providing resources to. In addition, each virtual machine consumes memory. Memory in ESX Server can be over-subscribed, unlike other virtualization platforms. This allows more memory to be allocated to virtual machines than is actually available on the hardware. Over-subscription of memory provides great advantages as long as a mix of low utilization virtual machines is combined with a few heavy workload virtual machines. The idea behind memory over-subscription is to utilize the normally wasted memory by the low utilization virtual machines and reclaim it back to the system until needed. In the event that all of the virtual machines memory requirements consume greater than the system can provide, extra memory is supplied by swapping to disk. Swapping to disk does create a significant performance impact to all virtual machines that do not have dedicated memory.

The base memory requirement of ESX Server is 512MB, although this is incredibly inadequate when it comes to using ESX Server for any real purposes. A minimum configuration would have 2GB to 4GB of memory. An average system configuration would have 8GB to 16GB of memory and a highly utilized system would have 16GB to 64GB of memory. This should give enough memory to both the virtual machines and the vmnix kernel to provide optimal performance.

Disk

Disk I/O is one of the most significant bottlenecks that can impact virtual machine performance. It is also the most limited in upgradeability. Disk I/O is the aggregate of all of the VMs on the server and therefore if many virtual machines are disk intensive, there are a very limited number of things that can be done. Due to this, it is important that a high performance RAID controller or Fiber Channel HBA be used. The greater the cache and the number of drives, the better performance should be. Disk latency, access time, bandwidth, and interface bandwidth should all carefully examined and chosen.

The minimum requirements are a RAID controller or HBA listed on the ESX Server disk controller compatibility list, located on VMware's website. To provide better performance, it is recommended that the operating system, swap file, and VMFS partition(s) all be tied to separate controllers and disk arrays. This will provide the maximum performance for ESX Server itself and the virtual machines it is hosting. The maximum number of controllers supported is 16 and each VMFS-2-based partition can hold up to 64TB.

Network

ESX Server supports most major Ethernet network cards including; Intel PRO/100 and 1000 series network cards, 3Com 9xx network cards, and the Broadcom NetXtreme 570x Gigabit series of network cards. There is a need for at least two network interfaces on ESX Server. This is due to the Service Console's requirement of a dedicated network adapter. More than one network interface can be used for virtual machine networking. In fact, if there are only a few virtual machines and the network bandwidth demands are high enough; it can be beneficial to dedicate a network interface to each virtual machine. Another alternative is to dedicate only a few network interfaces to specific virtual machines and then use a single remaining shared interface for the remaining virtual machines that need network connectivity.

 ESX Server 2.5 Server requires at least two network interfaces, which can be on a single network card, embedded network card, or across two separate network cards. Some earlier versions of ESX Server supported a single network interface that leveraged a shared mode between the Service Console and the VMKernel. This proved to be very troublesome solution and posed both security and performance problem, and is not a recommended configuration.

Display

Because ESX Server is built to be administered and used remotely, the local display requirements are minimal and do not need to be upgraded. The minimal requirements for an ESX Server display adapter is a 256 color (VGA) based card. A standard 65536 colors (SVGA) or better card is preferred.

Software Requirements

ESX Server software requirements are only for the client-based control utilities. This is because of the ESX Server hypervisor model that requires it to run on the bare metal host and not on top of another operating system. The client control-based management utilities allow for the administration of the server and the hosted virtual machines on the server.

VMware Management Interface

The following browsers are supported by the VMware Management Interface for ESX Server; Internet Explorer 5.5 and higher 6.0 should be used if at all possible, Netscape Navigator 7.0 or higher, Mozilla 1.x, Firefox 1.x will also work, however it will not be officially supported until ESX Server 3.0. The VMware Management Interface supports the previously listed Web browsers on both the Linux and Windows platforms.

VMware Remote Console

The VMware Remote Console (VMRC) provides direct console access to virtual machines. VMRC is a standalone application that is directly launched from the VMware Management Interface or in interactive mode from a Windows or Linux desktop. VMRC requirements are common Linux and Windows client operating systems.

Scripting/API

VMware ESX Server provides a built-in Perl Scripting base. In addition there is an API available in the VMware's Virtual Center product that allows management of both ESX Server and GSX Server. These interfaces allow a great deal of flexibility, customization, and automation of management functions in ESX Server.

Summary

VMware ESX Server is the premier enterprise virtualization platform. For more than four years, the product has evolved to become the most powerful, stable, and scalable commercial server virtualization platform on the market today. ESX Server's performance is the best of all of the commercial virtualization products available. Guest operating system support is incredibly broad; the only shortcoming is the limited host server hardware supported. This limitation sounds worse than it truly is, as most current servers by most major vendors are in fact supported. VMware's licensing mechanism for ESX Server is based on the number of physical processors located in the host server. As with any virtualization solution, more hardware resources equals more usefulness. ESX Server provides strict control over all of the critical system resources. This granular control combined with native SAN support provides a solution to a wide range of problems in the enterprise today. VMware ESX Server is the only proven solution to use in mission critical enterprise data center environments.

Chapter 14

Installing VMware ESX Server

The basic installation of VMware ESX Server 2.5.2 is covered in this chapter. Details such as the physical server's BIOS settings, a discussion on hardware drivers for ESX Server, and the ESX Server installation on a bare-metal server with screenshots are presented. This chapter will give insight and will set expectations for those system engineers that have never before installed VMware ESX Server.

VMware ESX Server 2.5.2 Requirements

VMware ESX Server has the most restrictive server requirements when compared to Microsoft Virtual Server and VMware GSX Server. Because of the highly optimized nature of ESX Server, it is natural to have a more stringent set of requirements. The requirements are very important and very different from the other virtualization platforms and care must be taken to review this section very carefully before making large-scale or costly decisions regarding system components, such as physical server hardware.

Basic Server Hardware Requirements:

- At least two physical processors, Intel Pentium III Xeon 700MHz and higher or AMD Opteron processors in 32-bit mode
- At least 900MHz and higher processors are required when using Virtual SMP
- 512MB memory minimum, but 4GB recommended as the minimum
- At least two Ethernet network adapters

- At least one SCSI controller, SCSI RAID controller, or Fibre Channel adapter
- At least one SCSI disk, SCSI RAID logical disk, or Fibre Channel LUN with at least 4GB of available space, but two disks are recommended, one for the ESX Server operating system and one for the VMFS volumes
- A CD/DVD-ROM drive that is bootable

In addition to the basic server hardware requirements listed above, not all server hardware makes and models are supported. Because VMware ESX Server does not run on top of a host operating system such as Linux or Windows, it requires ESX Server-specific hardware drivers. These drivers are currently only available from VMware and most are distributed with ESX Server. VMware produces up-to-date compatibility guides that provide very granular hardware compatibility information for servers, SCSI controllers, RAID controllers, Fibre Channel HBAs, SAN devices, and network adapters. The three most important compatibility guides are listed below.

- **Systems Compatibility**
  The Systems Compatibility guide provides information on the qualified guest operating systems, server hardware, and systems management applications for ESX Server. When using this guide in determining which servers will be used for new ESX Server implementation, the I/O Compatibility guide should also be consulted to ensure that the proper SCSI, RAID, and network adapter components installed in the selected servers are compatible with ESX Server.
- **I/O Compatibility**
  The I/O Compatibility guide provides information on the qualified SCSI and RAID controllers as well as supported network adapters for ESX Server. This information is critical when designing the server configuration that will be used in a new ESX Server implementation. The information in this guide should be used along with the server information provided in the Systems Compatibility guide.
- **SAN Compatibility**
  The SAN Compatibility guide provides information on the qualified SAN components including storage arrays and host bus adapters (HBAs) for use with ESX Server. In addition to the supported makes and models of supported SAN equipment, the guide also provides information regarding the compatible uses of certain features when SAN technology is used in an ESX Server system, including clustering, multipathing, and booting from SAN support.

The VMware compatibility guides are available on VMware's Web site using the following URL: http://www.vmware.com/support/resources/esx_resources.html.

Aside from the server hardware requirements, at least one workstation computer is required to perform the final configuration and management of the ESX Server upon completion of the basic installation procedures. The workstation computer requires network connectivity and a Web browser, such as Microsoft Internet Explorer, which is used to access ESX Server's Web-based Management User Interface (MUI).

Preparing the Host Server

The host server requires minimal preparation before ESX Server can be installed. The basic preparation includes ensuring that the server is set up and installed in its proper location, such as a server rack in the data center, and that it is cabled properly and has power. All server components should be installed at or before this stage, including processors, memory, SCSI controllers, RAID controllers, Fibre Channel HBAs, SCSI disks, network adapters, and any external storage devices, such as SCSI-attached storage. All network adapters should be cabled and patched into the proper switch ports. External storage devices should be properly cabled to the server, have all of its disks installed, and should be powered on. Fibre Channel HBAs should be properly cabled to the proper switches.

Once the server hardware is fully set up it should be powered on and have the following items configured:

- Update the server's firmware
- Configure the server's BIOS
  - Configure the CD/DVD-ROM device as a bootable device
  - Enable/Disable HyperThreading, if necessary
- Configure the SCSI BIOS for all SCSI controllers
- Configure the RAID arrays and logical drives for all RAID controllers
- Configure the BIOS for Fibre Channel HBAs, if necessary

At this point, the server is ready to have VMware ESX Server installed.

Preparing the Host Operating System

Because VMware ESX Server is a Hypervisor-style of virtualization platform, it does not install or run within an existing operating system. Instead, VMware ESX Server provides its own optimized kernel and is installed directly onto physical server hardware, often referred to as a bare-metal installation. There is no host operating system to be configured with VMware ESX Server. Once the server hardware has been properly configured, the installation process can begin.

Preparing to Install VMware ESX Server

Before starting the VMware ESX Server installation process, the following items and information should be readily available:

- The VMware ESX Server installation CD-ROM media
- A valid license key for VMware ESX Server
- A valid license key for VMware Virtual SMP (only required if Virtual SMP is to be enabled and used)
- The host name of the new ESX Server
- The TCP/IP configuration information for the new ESX Server's Service Console
  - IP Address
  - Subnet Mask
  - Gateway
  - DNS Server IP Address(es)
  - Fully qualified domain name of the server (optional)

VMware ESX Server supports several different installation options. Two installation modes may be used: the graphical installation mode and the text mode installer. The graphics installation mode uses a graphic user interface and the keyboard and mouse to perform the installation. This installation mode is supported by most up-to-date server hardware. The text mode installer is a down-level install that uses a character-based display during the installation. The text mode installer is primarily used if the server hardware does not have a graphics chipset that is compatible with ESX Server's installer. The choice of the installer mode does not affect the end-product of the installation, only the installer.

The ESX Server installer also supports several installation options that affect the installer and may also affect the type of installation that is performed. The boot options are listed below:

- **noapic**
  The noapic boot option disables the Advanced Programmable Interrupt Controller (APIC) during the installation.
- **text**
  he text boot option forces the use of the text mode installer.
- **driver disk**
  The driver disk boot option causes the installer to prompt the user for a driver disk at the appropriate point during the installation. This option is used if the server hardware requires additional drivers obtained separately from VMware.
- **bootfromsan**
  The bootfromsan boot option is used when installing the ESX Server on a Storage Area Network (SAN). This option uses the graphical installer.

- **bootfromsan-text**

  The bootfromsan-text boot option is used when installing the ESX Server on a Storage Area Network (SAN) and uses text mode installer.

Installing VMware ESX Server 2.5.2

This section walks through a standard, graphical mode installation of VMware ESX Server 2.5.2.

1. Power on the server and insert the VMware ESX Server CD-ROM installation media into the CD/DVD-ROM drive during the server's POST sequence. If prompted to press any key to boot from CD-ROM, press any key. The server will boot from the CD-ROM and the installation process will begin.
2. Installation boot options are shown in Figure 14.1. Choose the default installation options by pressing the Enter key. The installer will begin booting and the screen shown in Figure 14.2 will be displayed.

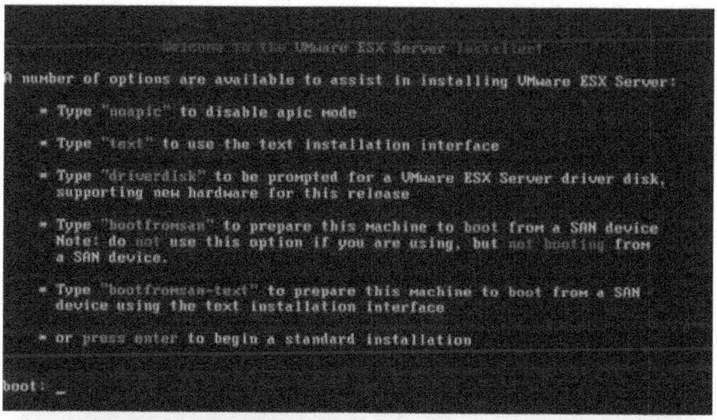

Figure 14.1 Installation Boot Options.

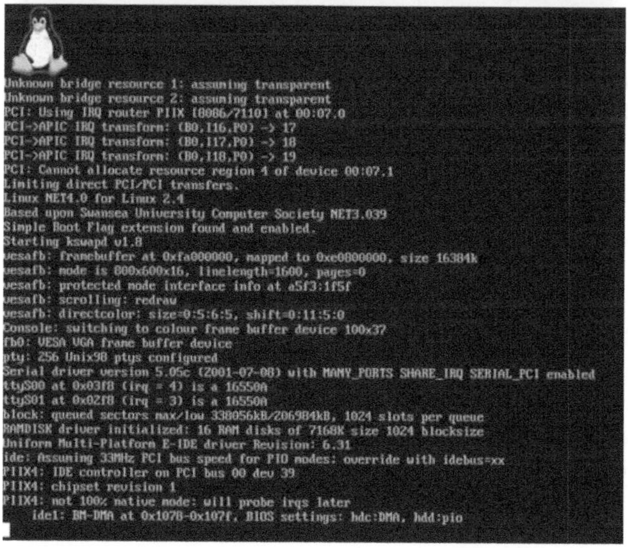

Figure 14.2 Console Output During Boot.

**Figure 14.3 VMware ESX
Server Installer Splash
Screen.**

Once the installer boot process is complete, the VMware ESX Server installer splash screen will be displayed as shown in Figure 14.3.

3. Welcome
    The Welcome screen is now displayed (see Figure 14.4). At this point, the installation information gathering process is about to begin. Click the Next button to proceed.

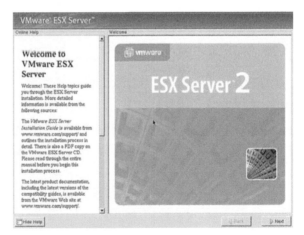

**Figure 14.4 VMware ESX
Server Installer Welcome
Screen.**

4. Installation Type
    On the Installation Type screen (see Figure 14.5), select the Install option and then select the Custom option under the main Install option selection. Click the Next button to proceed.
5. Keyboard Configuration
    On the Keyboard Configuration screen (see Figure 14.6), select the proper keyboard type in the Model field. In the Layout field, select the proper keyboard key layout type. In the Dead Keys field, select the Enable Dead Keys option. Click the Next button to proceed.

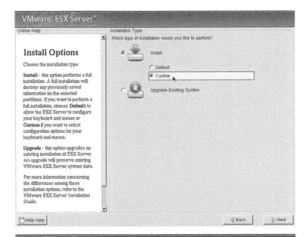

Figure 14.5 Select Installation Type.

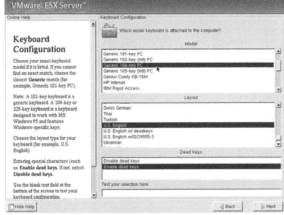

Figure 14.6 Keyboard Configuration Options.

6. Mouse Configuration

   On the Mouse Configuration screen (see Figure 14.7), select the proper mouse type. If the mouse being used is a two-button mouse, check the Emulate 3 Buttons checkbox. Click the Next button to proceed.

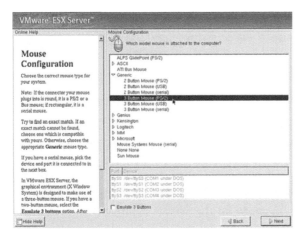

Figure 14.7 Mouse Configuration Options.

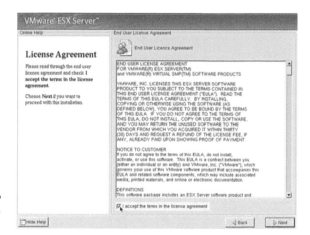

Figure 14.8   License Agreement.

7. End User License Agreement
    On the End User License Agreement screen (see Figure 14.8), read the end user license agreement and then, upon agreement, check the field labeled "I accept" the terms in the license agreement. Click the Next button to proceed.

8. VMware ESX Serial Numbers
    Enter a valid VMware ESX Server license key into the VMware ESX Server field (see Figure 14.9). Optionally, if VMware Virtual SMP is planned to be enabled and used, enter a valid license key for Virtual SMP into the VMware Virtual SMP for ESX Server field. Click the Next button to proceed.

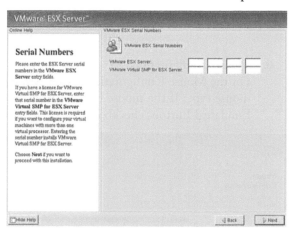

Figure 14.9   Serial Numbers.

9. Device Allocation
    On the device allocation screen (see Figure 14.10), several options may exist depending upon the specific hardware configuration. The Reserved Memory field should be set to a proper value depending on the number of virtual machines that will be hosted on the ESX Server. It is usually better to select more reserved memory for the Service Console than is planned.

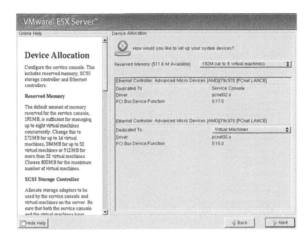

Figure 14.10   Device Allocation for the Service Console.

The first network adapter discovered is allocated to the Service Console by default and cannot be used by virtual machines. In the Dedicated To field for all remaining network adapters, select either the Service Console or Virtual Machines. In most installations, this value should be set to Virtual Machines. If one or more storage devices are discovered, their Dedicated To field should also be set to either the Service Console or Virtual Machines. If the storage device is dedicated to the Service Console, its storage cannot be used to hold VMFS volumes or virtual machines. If the storage device will contain virtual machine virtual disk files, select Virtual Machines and then select the Share with Service Console option. This will allow the storage to be used to contain VMFS volumes and virtual machines and will be accessible from the Service Console for administration purposes. Click the Next button to proceed.

10. Partition Table Popup

     For each drive attached to the system that is not partitioned, a warning popup will be displayed (see Figure 14.11). Click the Yes button to initialize the drive and proceed to the disk partitioning step.

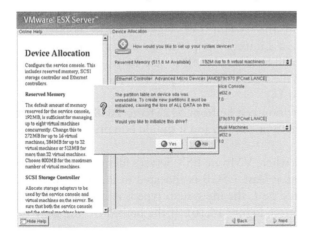

Figure 14.11   Partition Table Warning Popup.

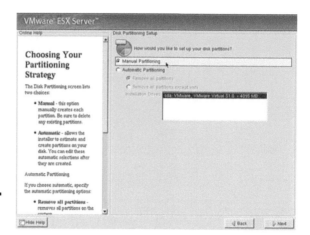

Figure 14.12 Disk Partition Strategy Options.

11. Disk Partitioning Setup
    Select the manual Partitioning option (see Figure 14.12) and then click the Next button to proceed.

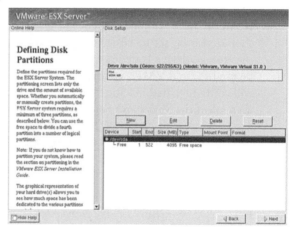

Figure 14.13 Partitioning the Disk.

12. Disk Setup
    For the first drive in the system (see Figure 14.13), configure a Linux boot partition, a Linux swap partition, and a root partition. The boot partition should be about 50MB in size, have a mount point of /boot, and use the ext3 file system. The boot partition should be a primary partition (see Figure 14.14).

    The Linux swap partition can be from 512MB to 2048MB in size. It should have a file system type of swap and it should be a primary partition (see Figure 14.15).

    The root partition is where VMware ESX Server's files will be installed. It is recommended that at least 1.5GB is allocated to the root partition. The mount point should be /, the file system type is ext3, and it should be a primary partition (see Figure 14.16). If the boot drive will only be

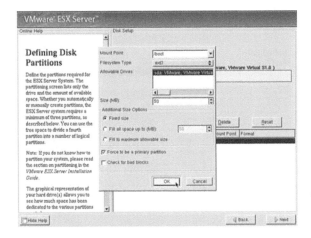

Figure 14.14 Boot Partition Options.

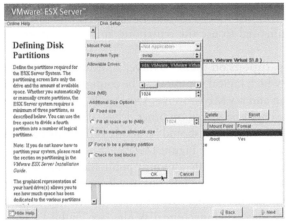

Figure 14.15 Swap Partition Options.

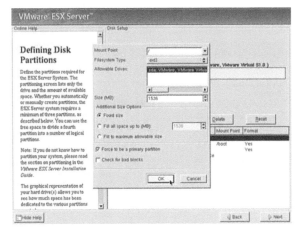

Figure 14.16 Root Partition Options.

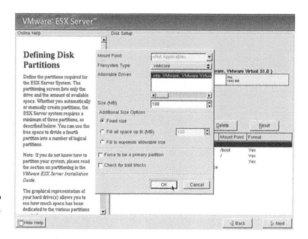

Figure 14.17 VMware Core Dump Partition Options.

used to contain the system files and no virtual machine disk files, the root partition could be configured to use the remaining amount of space on the disk.

To configure more partitions on the boot drive, an extended partition must be created under which logical volumes can be configured to contain the core dump partition and a VMFS volume. Optionally, the core dump and the VMFS volume could be placed on other drives, if available.

The VMware core dump partition should be about 100MB in size and has a file system type of vmkcore (see Figure 14.17).

The VMFS volume does not require a mount point and has a file system type of vmfs2. The size can vary widely, but usually consumes the rest of the available space of the drive on which it is placed in order to give maximum storage space for virtual machine disk files (see Figure 14.18).

After all disk partitions have been configured, click the Next button to proceed.

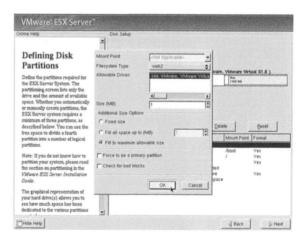

Figure 14.18 VMFS-2 Partition Options.

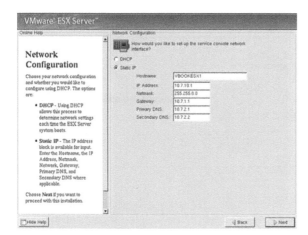

Figure 14.19 Service Console Network Configuration Options.

13. Network Configuration

    Select the Static IP option and then configure the TCP/IP configuration properties for the Service Console (see Figure 14.19). The IP address configuration of the Service Console's network adapter is considered to be the IP address info for the physical server.

14. Time Zone Selection

    Set the time zone of the ESX Server either by using the Location tab and selecting the proper location either from the graphical view or by selecting the city in the list at the bottom (see Figure 14.20). Optionally, the time zone can be set by using the UTC Offset tab and selecting the proper UTC offset value for the server's time zone (see Figure 14.21).

    Once the time zone has been selected, click the Next button to proceed.

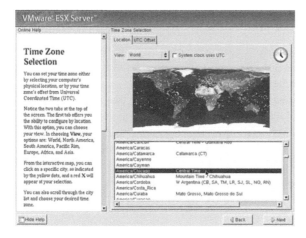

Figure 14.20 Time Zone Configuration by Location.

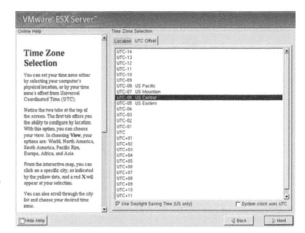

Figure 14.21 Time Zone Configuration by UTC Offset.

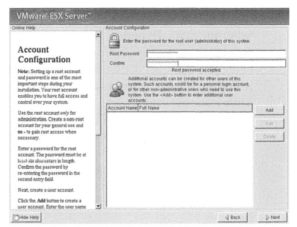

Figure 14.22 Root Account Configuration.

15. Account Configuration

Enter the password for the ESX Server's root account into the Root Password and Confirm fields (see Figure 14.22). Once the root password has been accepted, additional user accounts may be created if necessary. Click the Add button to add new users.

Enter the new user's account name into the User Name field. Optionally, enter the user's full name into the Full Name field (see Figure 14.23). Enter the new user's password into the Password and Confirm fields. Click the OK button to accept the new user account. Add additional user accounts as necessary (see Figure 14.24).

Once all of the initial accounts have been created, click the Next button to proceed.

16. About to Install

The About to Install screen (see Figure 14.25) is the last step before the actual file copying and configuration occurs. This is the last chance to use

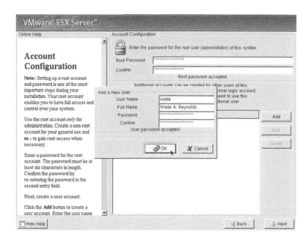

Figure 14.23 Adding a New User.

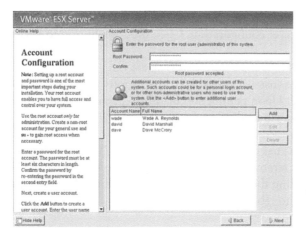

Figure 14.24 Additional User Accounts.

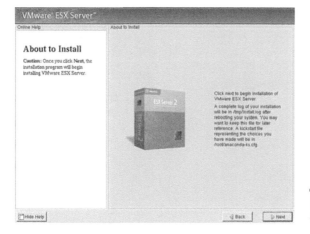

Figure 14.25 Installation Confirmation.

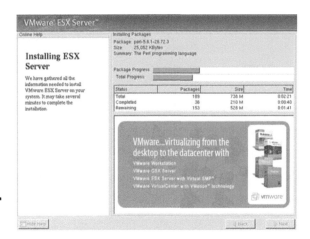

Figure 14.26   Installation Status

the Back button to return to previous screens to make adjustments or changes to the ESX Server configuration. Click the Next button to begin the installation.

17. Installing Packages

During the part of the installation process, the various packages are installed and configured. Upon completion of this step, the final screen of the installation process will be displayed (see Figure 14.26).

18. Congratulations

The installation process has completed (see Figure 14.27). Follow the on-screen instructions by removing any floppy diskette media and any CD-ROM media used during the installation process. Click the Next button or press the Enter key to reboot the server.

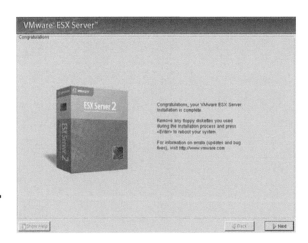

Figure 14.27   Installation Complete.

Summary

VMware ESX Server is generally installed using the methods described above. The text mode installer configures the same data using a character-based user interface instead of a VGA graphical user interface. Many of the configuration options can be changed after the installation with the exception of the boot-fromsan option. If this option is not selected, ESX Server must be installed on local disks and if it is selected, it must be installed on a LUN of a SAN. The installation process can generally be completed in less than 30 minutes when the proper preparation has been made. After an ESX Server has been installed it must be configured. To configure an ESX Server and create virtual machines, knowledge of the various management tools must be acquired. The next chapter covers the configuration and management of VMware ESX Server followed by a step-by-step creation of a virtual machine.

Chapter 15

Configuring VMware ESX Server

Once a base ESX Server has been installed, it is necessary to complete the installation by setting up the basic server configuration. This chapter discusses the tools and processes of performing the final configuration of the ESX Server installed in the previous chapter. Also covered are optional configuration settings including security and performance settings.

Management Interface

The primary management tool for ESX Server is the Web-based application named the VMware Management Interface. The Management Interface uses a Web-based graphical user interface to present the various monitoring and management capabilities of a single VMware ESX Server (see Figure 15.1).

The Management Interface, also referred to as the MUI (a legacy term), provides facilities for the following management tasks:

- Virtual Machines
  - Add, Edit, Delete, View
    - Create Virtual Machine
    - Edit Virtual Machine Properties
    - Edit Virtual Machine Hardware
      - Add Device
      - Remove Device
      - Connect Device
      - Disconnect Device
      - Configure Device

Figure 15.1 The VMware ESX Server Management Interface Status Monitor.

- Delete Virtual Machine
- Register Virtual Machine
- Unregister Virtual Machine
- Monitor current state
  - CPU usage of system
  - Memory usage of the system
    - Total memory allocated
    - Memory allocated but not used
    - Memory allocated and used
    - Shared memory
    - Swap file usage
    - Memory usage by system and by virtual machines
  - Power State of each virtual machine
  - VMware Tools State of each virtual machine
  - Heartbeat of each virtual machine
  - CPU usage of each virtual machine
  - Memory usage of each virtual machine
  - Disk I/O usage of each virtual machine
  - Network Bandwidth usage of each virtual machine
- Control virtual machines
  - Power On
  - Power Off
  - Reset
  - Suspend
  - Resume
  - Shut Down
  - Restart
  - Storage
    - Add, Edit, Delete, View VMFS Volumes
    - Manage SAN Adapters and LUNs

- VMFS Swap Files
  - Add, Edit, Delete, View
- Virtual Networks
  - Add, Edit, Delete, View
  - Bind to physical adapters
  - Create port groups (Bind network adapters)
- Service Console
  - CPU resource settings
  - Disk I/O resource settings
- ESX Server System Settings
  - Boot profile
  - Device allocation
  - Licensing
  - Security profile
  - Reserved system memory
  - SNMP Configuration
  - User management
  - Virtual machine startup and shut down policies
  - Advanced system settings

The Management Interface is accessed from a workstation computer separately from the ESX Server using a Web browser such as Firefox or Internet Explorer. The user simply opens a Web browser and navigates to the ESX Server's address, either its DNS-resolvable hostname or its raw IP address (the IP address of the Service Console). By default, the Management Interface uses SSL to secure the entire session's communications. The SSL certificate that is used is generated during the installation of ESX Server and is not a third-party certificate provided by a secure certificate vendor. This does not lessen the security provided, but the issuer will likely not be recognized by the Web browser and therefore it will cause a security alert in the Web browser upon navigating to the Management Interface. The options are to accept the certificate and continue with the session or to install the certificate in the Web browser so that each new session with the particular ESX Server does not always begin with a certificate warning. Once the certificate issue has been resolved, the user may log into the Management Interface using the proper ESX Server credentials set up previously during installation. The root account may also be used to log in to the Management Interface.

After a new ESX Server installation, the user logs into the Management Interface, they are presented with a popup window containing the initial configuration Wizard that walks the user through the minimum required configuration tasks. During this process, the ESX Server will have to be rebooted. If the Wizard window is left open during the reboot, it will continue once the ESX Server has finished rebooting. If the Wizard window is closed during the reboot, the ESX Server cannot be configured using the Wizard and the remaining tasks will have

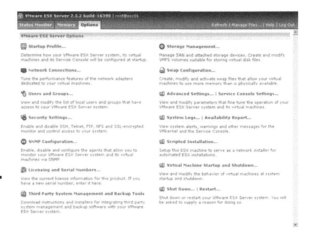

Figure 15.2 The VMware ESX Server Management Interface Options Tab.

to be performed using the configuration sections provided on the Options tab of the main Management Interface screen. All of the same options that exist in the configuration wizard reside on this tab (see Figure 15.2). The configuration Wizard forces a reboot after the Startup Profile section is configured, therefore the remaining areas requiring configuration are (in order):

- Storage Management
- Network Configuration
- Swap Configuration
- Security Settings
- Users and Groups

Once these areas have been configured initially, the ESX Server is ready for use. The Status Monitor tab (Figure 15.3) should not have any warning messages or virtual machines at this time.

Figure 15.3 Initial, Empty Status Monitor Tab.

Virtual Machine Remote Console (VMRC)

VMware ESX Server provides the VMware Remote Console application for Windows and Linux. VMware Remote Console is commonly referred to as VMRC. The VMRC application provides remote control access to a virtual machine's console. It basically emulates a physical keyboard, mouse, and monitor that would normally be plugged into a physical server. VMRC can be connected to a virtual machine when the virtual machine is in any state. The remote connection that VMRC creates does not directly connect to the virtual machine. It actually connects to the ESX Server Service Console. Therefore, virtual machines that do not have virtual network adapters can be accessed as well as virtual machines that do have network adapters. This is useful if there is a network outage that only affects a virtual machine because the virtual machine can still be accessed using VMRC, even though the virtual machine does not have any network access. This will work as long as there is not a network outage that affects the ESX Server's network.

When connecting to a virtual machine that is powered off or suspended, the console cannot be displayed. Instead, the virtual machine's name and configuration and power state is displayed Figure 15.4).

When connecting to a virtual machine that is powered on, the current view of the virtual machine's console is displayed. This is interesting because if the VMRC application is opened a few seconds after the virtual machine is powered on (such as from the Management Interface), it is likely that the virtual machine will be in POST (Power On Self Test) and the BIOS POST screens will be displayed, just like a physical server. VMRC is useful to access the BIOS of a virtual machine. Pressing F2 during the beginning of POST will enter the BIOS configuration utility (see Figure 15.5).

VMRC is used to connect to and control virtual machines. Because it is a remote application, its communication is secured but it does require authentication and authorization. The same permissions that control a user's access to

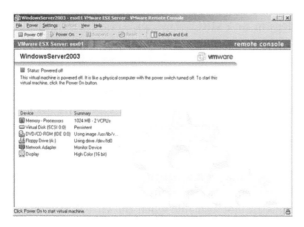

Figure 15.4 VMRC Connected to a Virtual Machine that is Powered Off.

Figure 15.5   VMRC During a Virtual Machine's POST.

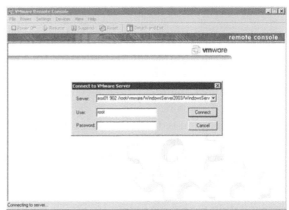

Figure 15.6   VMRC Log-in.

a virtual machine (file permissions on the virtual machine's configuration file) control a user's access to the virtual machine through VMRC. Before a remote session can begin, the user must log in (see Figure 15.6).

Once a user successfully logs in to VMRC, they can access the virtual machine. VMRC can control the virtual machine's power state, just as in the Management Interface. Access to the power controls, including Power off, Power On, Suspend, and Reset, are provided in the Power application menu as well as in the toolbar. Soft power options are also available through the Power menu including Shut Down Guest Operating System and Restart Guest Operating System. Of course, just as with the Management Interface, the Shut Down and Restart Guest Operating System functions require that the virtual machines have VMware Tools installed and running.

VMRC also provides limited access to edit a virtual machine's configuration remotely through a graphical user interface accessed through the VMRC Settings application menu. Most options are not available when the virtual machine is powered on, and when the virtual machine is powered off, only a limited subset of the virtual machine's entire configuration is remotely editable through the provided interface. The Settings menu also provides an option named Connected Users that displays all of the users currently connected to the virtual machine though VMRC, the Management Interface, and the Perl API. More than one user at a time can remotely use VMRC to connect to the same virtual machine. This provides a simple shadowing feature. Each user will have interactive access to the virtual machine, so if the effort is not coordinated, chaos will likely reign. This feature can be very useful to demonstrate to or train an individual using a virtual machine.

 If you are connected to a virtual machine through VMRC and you notice the mouse moving by itself or other actions such as typing that you are not performing, it is likely that another user is connected to the same virtual machine using VMRC. Click the Settings application menu in VMRC and then click the Connected Users menu item to display the connected users in order to confirm and identify the other user.

The Devices application menu item displays the virtual machine's removable devices and their current state. This includes floppy drives, CD/DVD-ROM drives, and network adapters. Using the options under the Display menu, devices can be connected or disconnected on-the-fly. This is useful to disconnect a network adapter to quickly simulate a network outage in the virtual machine.

Service Console

VMware ESX Server hosts a special virtual machine used to manage the ESX system. This special virtual machine is named the Service Console and is sometimes referred to as the Console operating system or Console OS. The Service Console is a specially modified version of the Linux operating system (i.e., the Red Hat Linux 7.2 distribution) that runs as a virtual machine that is not obvious or apparent. This virtual machine is created automatically and is not managed along with virtual machines created by users. The Service Console has special "hooks" into the part of the VMware ESX Server operating system to manage virtual machines, the VMKernel. Upon configuring a new ESX Server installation, the first physical network adapter discovered in the server, eth0, is always reserved for use by the Service Console by default. This allows network access to the Service Console using either telnet or ssh (preferred) and also allows access to the VMware ESX Server Web-based Management Interface (Management Interface), served by an instance of the Apache Web server and hosted within the Service Console. All configured VMFS volumes are always mounted to the

Service Console during boot up of ESX Server under the /vmfs directory. This allows command-line access to the VMFS volumes and the virtual disk files (and redo log files) contained within.

The Service Console presents a Linux command-line interface. It can be accessed at the physical console or remotely using tools such as telnet or ssh. Once a session with the Service Console has been started and root-level access has been acquired, the system can be managed as needed. Normal Linux commands are used for most file system operations with a few exceptions. File permissions work as they do in a Linux environment.

In ESX Server the vdf command replaces the Linux df command, which is used to display the amount of free space on each mounted file system. The df command does not display free space for any mounted VMFS volumes, so the vdf command should be used instead. The command, vdf -h, displays the results in human-readable format.

Boot Profiles and LILO

ESX Server uses LILO configured in the Service Console to manage the initial boot up process. LILO, the Linux Loader, is a common boot loader used in Linux operating systems. In ESX Server, there are usually three boot profiles configured labeled linux, linux-up, and esx. The linux and linux-up boot profiles allow ESX Server to start with only the Service Console enabled and not the VMKernel. In this mode, maintenance can be performed against the VMKernel and the rest of the system as required, but virtual machines cannot be used. The linux-up boot profile is essentially the same as the linux boot profile but boots in uniprocessor mode. The linux or linux-up boot profiles are generally used during patch installations and upgrades of ESX Server. The esx boot profile is the primary boot profile used by ESX Server. This boot profile starts ESX Server with the Service Console and the VMKernel enabled. In this mode, normal management can be performed as well as the use of virtual machines.

The LILO boot loader stores its configuration in the /etc/lilo.conf file. To change the default boot profile, the line containing default=<label> can be modified where <label> is the label of the desired default boot profile obtained under the appropriate boot profile definition defined by the image=<config> sections in the same file. Anytime /etc/lilo.conf is edited, the lilo command must be issued immediately after the changes have been saved to apply them to the boot loader.

How to Access and Log in to the Service Console at the Physical Server

The Service Console can be accessed at the physical server's console by pressing the Alt-F2 key combination. Pressing Alt-F1 at the physical console returns the user back to the ESX Server welcome screen, but will not automatically log the user out of the Service Console session. The user should always log out of the Service Console session before returning to the welcome screen by using the exit command. If additional terminals are needed at the physical console, Alt-F2, Alt-F3, Alt-F4, and Alt-F5 each provide access to a separate Service Console session. Each session is separate from one another; therefore, logging out of one session does not log the user out of other sessions.

How to Access and Log in to the Service Console Remotely

The Service Console can also be accessed remotely using either Telnet or secure shell (ssh), which is preferred. Before using Telnet, the security settings of the ESX Server may have to be set to Medium or lower using the Web-based Management Interface. When logging into the Service Console, the root account can only be used directly at the log-in prompt when the user is either at the physical console or is using ssh. When using Telnet, the root account cannot log in directly. An alternate user account must be used and then the su - command can then be issued to assume root-level access.

Basic Linux Commands

The Service Console is used to perform advanced administration tasks on the ESX Server. The Service Console is a Linux operating system that runs at run-level 3, full multi-user mode with a character-based display or command-line interface. To manage the ESX Server, there are several special ESX commands that can be used to perform various functions, but these commands are not very useful without a basic set of standard Linux commands. Although it is recommended that readers of this book have a fundamental set of Linux command-line skills and Bash shell knowledge, a few basic commands are documented here with practical, not textbook complete, descriptions and example usages.

- cat
  The cat command is used to concatenate files and to display the concatenated files' output. If only one file is specified, its contents are displayed. The cat command is useful to quickly display small text files such as configuration, log, and script files. The cat command is not very good for displaying large files, especially large log files. See the tail command for additional information on large files. Examples:
  - Display the contents of the configuration file for the Ethernet 0 network adapter.
    ```
    # cat /etc/sysconfig/network-scripts/ifcfg-
    eth0
    ```

- Display the concatenated contents of myfile1 and myfile2, both of which reside in the current directory.

  ```
  # cat myfile1 myfile2
  ```

- cd

  The cd command changes the current directory to the specified directory. Examples:
  - Change the current directory to the root of the directory tree.

    ```
    # cd /
    ```

  - Change the current directory to the parent directory, located up one level in the directory tree.

    ```
    # cd ..
    ```

  - Change the current directory to the parent directory of the current directory's parent directory, located up two levels in the directory tree.

    ```
    # cd ../..
    ```

  - Change the current directory to the /etc directory.

    ```
    # cd /etc
    ```

  - Change the current directory to the /etc/sysconfig/network-scripts directory.

    ```
    # cd /etc/sysconfig/network-scripts
    ```

  - Change the current directory to the /vmfs directory.

    ```
    # cd /vmfs
    ```

- chmod

  The chmod command is used to modify access permission for a file or directory. The permissions can be specified in symbolic mode or octal mode. Examples:
  - Remove read, write, and execute permissions for all users for the file named myfile located in the /tmp directory using symbolic mode.

    ```
    # chmod a-rwx /tmp/myfile
    ```

  - Remove read, write, and execute permissions for all users for the file named myfile located in the /tmp directory using octal mode.

    ```
    # chmod 000 /tmp/myfile
    ```

  - Grant the owner of the file named myfile located in the /tmp directory read, write, and execute permissions using symbolic mode.

    ```
    # chmod u+rwx /tmp/myfile
    ```

  - Grant the owner of the file named myfile located in the /tmp directory read, write, and execute permissions (7) using octal mode.

    ```
    # chmod 700 /tmp/myfile
    ```

  - Grant users in the file's group of the file named myfile located in the /tmp directory read and write permissions using symbolic mode.

    ```
    # chmod g+rwx /tmp/myfile
    ```

- Grant users in the file's group of the file named myfile located in the /tmp directory read and write permissions (6) using octal mode. Grant the owner of the file read, write, and execute permissions (7).

   ```
   # chmod 760 /tmp/myfile
   ```

- chown
  The chown command changes the owner of a file directory. Examples:
  - Change the owner of the file named myfile located in the /tmp directory to the user johndoe.

     ```
     # chown johndoe /tmp/myfile
     ```

  - Change the owner of the file named myfile located in the /tmp directory to the root account.

     ```
     # chown root /tmp/myfile
     ```

- cp
  The cp command copies the specified file to the specified location. If a new filename is specified along with the new location, the new copy of the file will use the specified file name. Example:
  - Copy the file named myfile located in the /tmp directory into the /home directory. The path to the copied file is /home/myfile.

     ```
     # cp /tmp/myfile /home
     ```

  - Copy the file named myfile located in the /tmp directory into the /home directory naming the copy to MyFile.txt. The path to the copied file is /home/MyFile.txt.

     ```
     # cp /tmp/myfile /home/MyFile.txt
     ```

- date
  Display or set the current system date and time. The system clock is independent of the hardware clock. Example:
  - Display the system clock's current date and time.

     ```
     # date
     ```

- df
  The df command displays disk usage information for all mounted file systems and partitions. When used in the ESX Server Service Console, only the standard Linux file systems and partitions are displayed. The mounted VMFS are not displayed. ESX Server provides a specialized version of the df command that includes the disk usage data for the VMFS volumes named vdf. See the vdf command in the ESX Server Commands section. Examples:
  - Display the disk usage information for non-VMFS volumes.

     ```
     # df
     ```

  - Display the disk usage information for non-VMFS volumes in human-readable format.

     ```
     # df -h
     ```

- hostname
  Displays the hostname of the ESX Server. Example:
  - Display the ESX Server's hostname.
    ```
    # hostname
    ```
- hwclock
  Display or set the hardware clock's date and time. The hardware clock is independent of the system clock. Example:
  - Display the hardware clock's current date and time.
    ```
    # hwclock
    ```
- info
  The info command opens the info documents that contains online documentation for Linux. Once the info documents are opened, the arrow keys can be used to position the cursor under a dictionary item and when the Enter key is pressed, the info document for that item will be displayed. When reading an info document, the header line at the top of the screen usually contains links such as Next, Previous, and Up. To navigate the links in the header, the key corresponding to the link name should be pressed. For example, to return to the main menu, press the u key to navigate Up until the main menu is reached. The q key will quit the info document reader when pressed and return the user to the command line.
- kill
  The kill command forces a running process to terminate. The kill command must have the process identifier (pid) of the process to be killed specified as an argument to the command. The ps command can be used to obtain the pid of a running process. Example:
  - For the process with a pid of 1344 to stop running.
    ```
    # kill 1344
    ```
- ll
  The ll command is actually an alias for the ls command with the -l switch (the same as issuing the ls -l command). See ls for more information.
- ls
  The ls command lists the contents of a directory. If no directory is specified, the current directory is listed. The -l switch displays the directory's contents using the long list format, showing more details such as directory and file permissions, the owner and group, and the size of the file in addition to the name. Use the -h switch to display file sizes in human-readable format instead of the raw bytes (e.g., KB, MB, GB, etc.). Examples:
  - List the contents of the current directory.
    ```
    # ls
    ```
  - List the contents of the current directory using the long list format.
    ```
    # ls -l
    ```

- List the contents of the current directory using the long list format and displaying file sizes in human-readable form.

  ```
  # ls -lh
  ```

- List the contents of the current directory using the long list format, without displaying group membership, and displaying file sizes in human-readable form.

  ```
  # ls -lGh
  ```

- List the contents of the /etc/sysconfig/network-scripts directory.

  ```
  # ls /etc/sysconfig/network-scripts
  ```

- List the contents of the /etc/sysconfig/network-scripts directory using the long list format and displaying file sizes in human-readable form.

  ```
  # ls -lh /etc/sysconfig/network-scripts
  ```

- List all files with a file name that ends with .REDO located in the /vmfs/vmhba0:1:0:1 VMFS volume in long list format in human readable form.

  ```
  # ls -lh /vmfs/vmhba0:1:0:1/*.REDO
  ```

■ man

The man command displays the online manual pages for the specified command. This is the online help for many Linux commands. When viewing a man page, the up and down arrow keys are used to scroll through the text. The q key is used to quit viewing the man page and return to the command prompt. Examples:

- Display the online manual pages for the chmod command.

  ```
  # man chmod
  ```

- Display the online manual pages for the ls command.

  ```
  # man ls
  ```

- Display the online manual pages for the man command.

  ```
  # man man
  ```

- Display the online manual pages for the vi text editor program.

  ```
  # man vi
  ```

■ mkdir

The mkdir command creates the specified directory. Example:

- Create a new directory named test in the /home directory.

  ```
  # mkdir /home/test
  ```

■ mv

The mv command moves or renames a file or directory. If a new destination directory is supplied to the command, the file or directory is moved. If the location is the same, but a new file or directory name is supplied, the file or directory is renamed. Examples:

- Move the test directory located in the /home directory into the /tmp directory.

  ```
  # mv /home/test /tmp
  ```

- Rename the directory named test located in the /tmp directory to test-dir.

  ```
  # mv /tmp/test /tmp/testdir
  ```

- Move the directory named testdir located in the /tmp directory into the /home directory.

  ```
  # mv /tmp/testdir /home
  ```

- Rename the directory named testdir located in the /home directory to test.

  ```
  # mv /home/testdir /home/test
  ```

■ nano

Nano is a text editor that is useful for Linux beginners. It is much more intuitive than vi and uses an on-screen menu help system that displays available options in a menu at the bottom of the editor's screen. Nano can be used to create and edit any text file including configuration files, scripts, and programs.

■ passwd

The passwd command is used to set (or change) a user's password. If the command is issued without specifying a username, it will change the password of the active account issuing the command. Once the command is issued, the active user will be prompted to enter and confirm the new password. If the new password is entered correctly and confirmed, the user's password will be changed. Example:

- Change the password of the active user.

  ```
  # passwd
  ```

- Change the password for the user named johndoe.

  ```
  # passwd johndoe
  ```

■ ps

The ps command displays information about the running processes in a Linux system. When used inside the ESX Server Service Console, it lists the processes running inside the Service Console only. It cannot display information about processes running in the VMKernel. The ps command is useful in determining if a program or script is currently running or to obtain the process identifier (pid) of a process. The ps command supports a multitude of switches, which alters the amount of information displayed. The list of processes can also be piped into the grep command to filter the list displayed by specifying a useful regular expression to the grep command. Examples:

- Display a full listing of all processes running in the Service Console.

  ```
  # ps -ef
  ```

- Display a full listing of all processes running in the Service Console piped into a grep command, which filters the lines displayed to only those that contain cp in order to see all of the currently running copy processes using the cp command.

  ```
  # ps -ef | grep cp
  ```
- Display a full listing of all processes running in the Service Console piped into a grep command, which filters the lines displayed to only those processes that are running under the /usr/bin/perl program (shows running Perl scripts).

  ```
  # ps -ef | grep /usr/bin/perl
  ```
- Display a full listing of all processes running in the Service Console piped into a grep command, which filters the lines displayed to only vmware-serverd processes.

  ```
  # ps -ef | grep vmware-serverd
  ```

■ rm

The rm command removes the specified file. Use rm with the -f switch to force the delete without prompting for confirmation. Examples:
- Delete the file named myfile located in the /tmp directory.

  ```
  # rm /tmp/myfile
  ```
- Delete the file named myfile located in the /tmp directory and do not prompt for confirmation (forced delete).

  ```
  # rm -f /tmp/myfile
  ```

■ rmdir

The rmdir command removes the specified directory. The directory must be empty of subdirectories and files. Example:
- Remove the directory named test located in the /home directory.

  ```
  # rmdir /home/test
  ```

■ tail

The tail command displays the last ten lines of the specified file. The number of lines displayed can be modified if necessary. This command is good for viewing the latest entries in large log files. Examples:
- Display the last ten lines of the /var/logs/messages log file.

  ```
  # tail /var/log/messages
  ```
- Display the last 20 lines of the /var/logs/messages log file.

  ```
  # tail -n 20 /var/log/messages
  ```

■ top

The top command displays a real-time view of the current processor activity and the top processes consuming CPU resources. The q key is used to quit and return to the command line. When used in the ESX Server Service Console, the top command displays information limited only to the Service Console virtual machine, not the overall ESX Server or VMKernel.

See the esxtop command under the ESX Server Command section. Example:

• Display the top processes.

```
# top
```

- vi

  Vi is a common Linux/Unix text editor. It is used to create and edit files such as configuration files, scripts, and programs. Documenting the usage of vi is out of scope for this book, but there are many online resources that fully document the use of this text editor. Vi can be intimidating or frustrating at first since it is not a very intuitive program, but it is a very powerful and useful text editor. Example:

  • Open the vi text editor and edit the file named myfile located in the /tmp directory. If the file does not exist and changes are saved, the file will be created.

    ```
    # vi /tmp/myfile
    ```

ESX Server Commands

To manage the specific facilities of ESX Server through the Service Console, commands specific to VMware ESX Server only must be emplpyed. These commands include: esxtop, vdf, vmkfstools, and vmware-cmd, all of which are discussed in detail below.

- esxtop

  The esxtop command is an ESX Server-specific version of the Linux top command. It provides resource usage data in real-time for the physical server running ESX Server including the processors, memory, and network adapters. Additionally, it provides details on the VMKernel processes or worlds. When esxtop is active, press the f key to enter the field selection page. This page allows the user to select the fields displayed on the main esxtop display. While on the field selection page, press the key associated to the letter next to each field to toggle the field's selection state. Selected fields have an asterisk character to the left of the field. To return the main esxtop display, press the ESC key. Press the q key to quit esxtop and return to a command prompt. Example:

  • Display resource usage data on the physical server and the VMKernel.

    ```
    # esxtop
    ```

- vdf

  The vdf command is an ESX Server-specific version of the Linux df command, which displays disk usage and free space for all mounted file systems. The vdf command displays the same information as df but also includes all mounted VMFS volumes. Examples:

- Display file system disk usage and free space.

    ```
    # vdf
    ```

- Display file system disk usage and free space in human-readable format.

    ```
    # vdf -h
    ```

■ vmkfstools

The vmkfstools command provides many options used to perform management tasks on VMFS volumes, virtual disk files, and REDO log files stored in VMFS volumes. Although many of the tasks vmkfstools can perform are also available through the Web-based Management Interface, there are some tasks and options only available through the vmkfstools command directly. Only the Service Console's root account can use the vmkfstools command. The vmkfstools command has two available syntaxes:

- Syntax 1 is used when specifying a SCSI device

    ```
    # vmkfstools <command> <options>
    <device>[:<file>]
    ```

    The <command> token specifies the command to be performed either in short or long form. The <options> token specifies any optional parameters that may be specified or required by the command. The <device> token specifies the SCSI device or VMFS volume using the vmhba mount point or VMFS volume label (symbolic link or alias). If a file is required as a target of the command, the <file> token represents the filename of a file stored in the specified <device>.

- Syntax 2 is used when specifying the path to a VMFS volume or file

    ```
    # vmkfstools <command> <options> <path>
    ```

    The <command> token specifies the command to be performed either in short or long form. The value of the <command> token is case-sensitive. The <options> token specifies any optional parameters that may be specified or required by the command. The <path> token specifies an absolute path to either a directory or file under the /vmfs directory. The path can target either a VMFS volume or a file contained in a VMFS volume. The VMFS volume may be specified using either its vmhba mount point or its VMFS volume label (symbolic link or alias).

    The vmkfstools command supports the following commands:

- -b --blocksize #[gGmMkK]

    The block size command is used only with the vmkfstools create VMFS command (-c) as an option. The block size specified must be a power of 2 and must be at least 1MB in size. The default block size is 1MB. The size is expressed as an integer followed by the size specifier g or G for gigabytes, m or M for megabytes, or k or K for kilobytes.

- -c --createfile #[gGmMkK]

    The create file command is used to create a new virtual disk file in the specified VMFS volume. The size of the file must be specified.

The size is expressed as an integer followed by the size specifier g or G for gigabytes, m or M for megabytes, or k or K for kilobytes. Examples:

■ Create a new 5 megabyte virtual disk file named mynewdisk.vmdk in the VMFS volume located on vmhba01:0:1 using the short command specifier and Syntax 1.

```
# vmkfstools -c 5M vmhba0:1:0:1:mynewdisk.
vmdk
```

■ Create a new 10 gigabyte virtual disk file named mynewdisk.vmdk in the VMFS volume located on the device with a VMFS label of lun1 using the long command specifier and Syntax 2.

```
# vmkfstools --createfile 10G /vmfs/lun1/ten-
gigdisk.vmdk
```

• -C --createfs [vmfs1|vmfs2]

The create VMFS command is used to create a new VMFS volume on an existing disk partition. The command requires the version of the VMFS volume that is to be created, either vmfs1 for a VMFS-1 volume or vmfs2 for a VMFS-2 volume. It is recommended that VMFS-2 volumes are created instead of VMFS-1 volumes. Optionally, the block size command or the numfiles command may be used in conjunction with the create VMFS command. Vmkfstools Syntax 1 must be used with the create VMFS command because the vmhba device cannot be mounted to the /vmfs directory before it exists. Examples:

■ Create a new VMFS-2 volume on vmhba0:1:0:1 using the short command specifier and Syntax 1.

```
# vmkfstools -C vmfs2 vmhba0:1:0:1
```

■ Create a new VMFS-2 volume on vmhba0:1:0:1 using the long command specifier and Syntax 1.

```
# vmkfstools --createfs vmfs2 vmhba0:1:0:1
```

■ Create a new VMFS-2 volume on vmhba0:1:0:1 setting the block size to 2MB using the long command specifier for the create VMFS command and the short command specifier for the block size command.

```
# vmkfstools --createfs vmfs2 -b 2M vm-
hba0:1:0:1
```

■ Create a new VMFS-2 volume on vmhba0:1:0:1 setting the maximum number of files to 1024 using the long command specifier for the create VMFS command and the short command specifier for the numfiles command.

```
# vmkfstools --createfs vmfs2 -n 1024 vm-
hba0:1:0:1
```

- Create a new VMFS-2 volume on vmhba0:1:0:1 setting the maximum number of files to 64 using the long command specifier for the create VMFS command and the numfiles command.

  ```
  # vmkfstools --createfs vmfs2 --numfiles 64
  vmhba0:1:0:1
  ```

- Create a new VMFS-2 volume on vmhba0:1:0:1 setting the block size to 2MB and the maximum number of files to 4096. The vmkfstools command is using the short command specifier for the create VMFS command, the block size command, and the numfiles command.

  ```
  # vmkfstools -C vmfs2 -b 4M -n 4096 vm-
  hba0:1:0:1
  ```

- -e --exportfile dstFile

  The export file command is used to export the contents of a virtual disk file to another device or physical server. Exported virtual disk files do not contain the empty disk space and are therefore usually much smaller than the original disk file. If a virtual disk file is exported and it has a REDO log, the contents of the REDO log are not included in the exported disk file. If a REDO log file is exported, the contents of the REDO log file's parent disk file and the REDO log file are written to the exported disk as if they had been merged by the commit command (see the vmkfstools -m, --commit command). Disk files that have been exported can be restored to the same or another ESX Server by using the vmkfstools import command. The export file command is also used to export virtual disk files to use in VMware GSX Server or VMware Workstation virtualization platforms. The dstFile parameter of the export file command is the path to the destination file of the export. The exported file can reside on the same or another VMFS volume or an ext2, ext3, or NFS file system. Examples:

  - Export the virtual disk file named rh9.vmdk. The file resides in the VMFS volume located on vmhba0:1:0:1 to a file named rh9_exp. vmdk located in the /tmp directory of the Service Console using the short command specifier and Syntax 1.

    ```
    # vmkfstools -e /tmp/rh9_exp.vmdk vmh-
    ba0:1:0:1:rh9.vmdk
    ```

  - Export the virtual disk file named rh9.vmdk. The file resides in the VMFS volume located on vmhba0:1:0:1 to a file named rh9_exp. vmdk located in the /tmp directory of the Service Console using the long command specifier and Syntax 2.

    ```
    # vmkfstools --exportfile /tmp/rh9_exp.vmdk
    /vmfs/vmhba0:1:0:1/rh9.vmdk
    ```

- -F --config [public|shared|writable]

  The config command sets the access mode of the specified VMFS volume. The valid modes are public, shared, and writable. ESX Server is used to also support the private access mode, which is now deprecated. Existing VMFS volumes now in private mode should be changed to public mode. The default access mode is public. Public mode allows multiple physical ESX Servers to access the VMFS volume. Public VMFS-2 volumes allow concurrent access to the volume using file locking mechanisms to ensure consistency. Public VMFS-1 volumes do not support concurrent access by multiple servers and must reside on a shared storage system. Shared mode allows multiple virtual machines across multiple physical ESX Servers to access the same virtual disk file concurrently. Shared mode is only supported on VMFS-2 volumes. In contrast, public mode only allows concurrent access to the VMFS volume, not individual disk files. Shared mode is typically configured on VMFS volumes used for failover clustering (Active-Passive). Writable mode is used when changes to the file system metadata are required and multiple physical ESX Servers are using the VMFS volume. When virtual machines are active, this metadata becomes read-only and it becomes impossible to create, remove, or change the size of disk files. When it is necessary to make changes, the VMFS volume must first be set to writable mode. Before writable mode can bet set, all virtual machines accessing the VMFS volume must be either powered off or suspended. Examples:

  - Change the access mode of the VMFS volume located on vmhba0:1:0:1 to shared using the short command specifier and Syntax 1.

    ```
    # vmkfstools -F shared vmhba0:1:0:1
    ```

  - Change the access mode of the VMFS volume located on vmhba0:1:0:1 to shared using the long command specifier and Syntax 2.

    ```
    # vmkfstools --config writable /vmfs/vm-
    hba0:1:0:1
    ```

- -g --geometry

  The geometry command is used to display the disk geometry of a virtual disk file. The geometry output is displayed in the C/H/S format where C is the number of cylinders, H is the number of heads, and S is the number of sectors. This information is useful when disk geometry must be explicitly defined in a virtual machine's configuration file after the disk is imported from either VMware GSX Server or VMware Workstation virtualization platforms. Examples:

  - Display the disk geometry of the virtual disk named rh9.vmdk resides in the VMFS volume located on vmhba0:1:0:1 using the short command specifier and Syntax 1.

```
# vmkfstools -g vmhba0:1:0:1:rh9.vmdk
```

- Display the disk geometry of the virtual disk named rh9.vmdk located in the VMFS volume located on vmhba0:1:0:1 using the long command specifier and Syntax 2.

```
# vmkfstools --geometry /vmfs/vmhba0:1:0:1/
rh9.vmdk
```

- -h --human-readable
The human-readable command is only used with the vmkfstools list (-l) command as an option. File sizes are displayed in an easy-to-read format instead of raw bytes.
- -i --importfile srcFile
The import file command is used to import a virtual disk file that has been previously exported from the same or another ESX Server or a virtual disk file from the VMware GSX Server or VMware Workstation virtualization platforms. The srcFile parameter specified the path to the virtual disk file that is to be imported. This file may reside on the same or another VMFS volume, an ext2, ext3, or an NFS file system. The destination of the import is the specified VMFS volume of the import file command. The destination VMFS volume must have enough free space to contain the maximum disk size of the virtual disk file being imported as the file will be expanded to its maximum size during the import process. Examples:
  - Import the virtual disk file named rh9_exp.vmdk residing in the / tmp directory of the Service Console to a virtual disk file named rh9.vmdk located in the VMFS volume located on vmhba0:1:0:1 using the short command specifier and Syntax 1.

```
# vmkfstools -i /tmp/rh9_exp.vmdk vmh-
ba0:1:0:1:rh9.vmdk
```

  - Import the virtual disk file named rh9_exp.vmdk residing in the / tmp directory of the Service Console to a virtual disk file named rh9.vmdk located in the VMFS volume located on vmhba0:1:0:1 using the long command specifier and Syntax 2.

```
# vmkfstools -importfile /tmp/rh9_exp.vmdk
/vmfs/vmhba0:1:0:1/rh9.vmdk
```

- -k --createswapfile #[gGmMkK]
The create swap file command is used to create a new swap file or resize an existing swap file. The size of the swap file must be specified. The size is expressed as an integer followed by the size specifier g or G for gigabytes, m or M for megabytes, or k or K for kilobytes. Only user accounts with root permissions can create or resize a swap file. When resizing an existing swap file, it must first be deactivated by using the vmkfstools deactivate swap file command (-y). After creating a new swap file or after resizing an existing swap file, the swap file should

be activated using the vmkfstools activate swap file command (-w). Examples:

- Create a new swap file or resize an existing swap file named SwapFile. vswp specifying a size of 8 gigabytes. The file resides in the VMFS volume located on vmhba0:1:0:1 using the short command specifier and Syntax 1.

  ```
  # vmkfstools -k 8G vmhba0:1:0:1:SwapFile.
  vswp
  ```

- Create a new swap file or resize an existing swap file named SwapFile. vswp specifying a size of 16 gigabytes. The file resides in the VMFS volume located on vmhba0:1:0:1 using the long command specifier and Syntax 2.

  ```
  # vmkfstools --createswapfile 16G /vmfs/
  vmhba0:1:0:1/SwapFile.vswp
  ```

- -l --list
  The list command is used to display a detailed listing on the contents of the specified VMFS volume. Optionally, the human-readable and verbose mapping commands can be specified to modify the output of the list command. Examples:

  - Display the contents of the VMFS volume located on vmhba0:1:0:1 using the short command specifier and Syntax 1.

    ```
    # vmkfstools -l vmhba:0:1:0:1
    ```

  - Display the contents of the VMFS volume located on vmhba0:1:0:1 in human-readable format and displaying the verbose mappings option using the short command specifier and Syntax 2.

    ```
    # vmkfstools -l -h -M /vmfs/vmhba:0:1:0:1
    ```

  - Display the contents of the VMFS volume located on vmhba0:1:0:1 in human-readable format and displaying the verbose mappings option using the long command specifier and Syntax 1.

    ```
    # vmkfstools --list --human-readable --ver-
    bosemappings vmhba:0:1:0:1
    ```

- -L --lock [reserve|release|reset|lunreset]
  The lock command manages the locking reservations of raw disks and LUNs. Using this command can disrupt the operations of other servers, especially when using a SAN. The reserve parameter is used to reserve, or gain exclusive access to, the raw disk or LUN containing the specified VMFS volume. The server on which the reserve command was issued can access the disk normally, but other servers will receive a SCSI reservation error upon attempting to access the disk.

The release parameter is used to release the reservation made by using the reserve parameter above. The reset parameter is used to issue a SCSI reset to the specified disk. This will release reservations held by another server. The lunreset parameter is used to perform a reset against a specific LUN instead of an entire disk. Examples:

- Reserve the disk containing the VMFS volume located on vmhba0:1:0:1 using the short command specifier and Syntax 1.

  ```
  # vmkfstools -L reserve vmhba0:1:0:1
  ```

- Release the disk containing the VMFS volume located on vmhba0:1:0:1 using the long command specifier and Syntax 2.

  ```
  # vmkfstools --lock release vmhba0:1:0:1
  ```

- Reset the disk containing the VMFS volume located on vmhba0:1:0:1 using the long command specifier and Syntax 2.

  ```
  # vmkfstools --lock reset /vmfs/vmhba0:1:0:1
  ```

- -m --commit

  The commit command is used to permanently merge the contents of a REDO log file into its parent virtual disk file. Examples:

  - Merge the contents of the REDO log file named myvm.vmdk.REDO located in vmhba:0:1:0:1 into its parent disk file named myvm.vmdk using the short command specifier and Syntax 1.

    ```
    # vmkfstools -m vmhba0:1:0:1:myvm.vmdk.REDO
    ```

  - Merge the contents of the REDO log file named myvm.vmdk.REDO located in vmhba:0:1:0:1 into its parent disk file named myvm.vmdk using the long command specifier and Syntax 2.

    ```
    # vmkfstools --commit /vmfs/vmhba0:1:0:1/
    myvm.vmdk.REDO
    ```

- -M --verbosemappings

  The verbose mappings command is only used with the vmkfstools list (-l) command as an option. When specified with the list command, it displays the vmhba name, which corresponds to each raw disk mapping, if any exist. No extra information is displayed if no raw disk mappings exist.

- -n --numfiles #

  The numfiles command is only used with the vmkfstools create VMFS (-C) command or the vmkfstools extend VMFS command (-Z) as an option. By default, VMFS volumes are created with a maximum number of 256 files. Upon the creation of a VMFS volume, the maximum number of files can be specified. This is useful when a system is planned to have many small disk files, REDO log files, and suspend files within a VMFS volume that exceeds 256. Conversely, it may be useful to lower the number of maximum files to ensure that only a specific number of files are ever used, such as 32 or 64.

- -P --querypartitions

  The query partitions command is used to display the attributes of the specified VMFS volume or raw device mapping. Examples:
  - Display the attributes of the VMFS volume located on vmhba0:1:0:1 using the short command specifier and Syntax 1.

    ```
    # vmkfstools -P vmhba0:1:0:1
    ```
  - Display the attributes of the raw device with a mapping file named my_raw_device.vmdk located on vmhba0:1:0:1 using the long command specifier and Syntax 1.

    ```
    # vmkfstools --querypartitions vmhba0:1:0:1:
    my_raw_device.vmdk
    ```

- -r --maprawdisk raw-SCSIDevice

  The map raw disk command maps a raw disk or LUN to a raw device mapping file located on a VMFS-2 volume. The raw-SCSIDevice parameter specifies the device or LUN that will be mapped. Examples:
  - Map the device, vmhba2:0:0:1, to a raw device mapping file named my_raw_device.vmdk residing on the VMFS volume located on vmhba0:1:0:1 using the short command specifier and Syntax 1.

    ```
    # vmkfstools -r vmhba2:0:0:1 vmhba0:1:0:1:
    my_raw_device.vmdk
    ```
  - Map the device, vmhba2:0:0:1, to a raw device mapping file named my_raw_device.vmdk residing on the VMFS volume located on vmhba0:1:0:1 using the long command specifier and Syntax 2.

    ```
    # vmkfstools --maprawdisk vmhba2:0:0:1 /
    vmfs/vmhba0:1:0:1/my_raw_device.vmdk
    ```

- -R --recover

  The recover command is used to unlock a VMFS volume used by multiple physical ESX Servers when other vmkfstools report that the volume is locked and, in reality, no other servers are using the volume. No other server can be using the VMFS volume when this command is issued. Examples:
  - Recover the VMFS volume located on vmhba0:1:0:1 using the short command specifier and Syntax 1.

    ```
    # vmkfstools -r vmhba0:1:0:1
    ```
  - Recover the VMFS volume located on vmhba0:1:0:1 using the long command specifier and Syntax 2.

    ```
    # vmkfstools --recover /vmfs/vmhba0:1:0:1
    ```

- -s --scan

  The scan command is used to scan the specified vmhba for new devices and LUNs. This command is only intended for use with Fibre Channel adapters, and the cos-rescan.sh script is recommended to be used over this command. After the scan has completed, use the ls /vmfs command to see the new LUNs. Examples:

- Scan the adapter, vmhba0, for new LUNs using the short command specifier and Syntax 1.

  ```
  # vmkfstools -s vmhba0
  ```

- Scan the adapter, vmhba0, for new LUNs using the long command specifier and Syntax 1.

  ```
  # vmkfstools --scan vmhba0
  ```

- -S --setfsname fsName

  The set VMFS name command is used to create a label for the specified VMFS volume. The label is actually a symbolic link (or alias) residing in the /vmfs directory of the Service Console. The VMFS volume label can be used in place of the vmhba name. Examples:

  - Set the label, lun1, on the VMFS volume located on vmhba0:1:0:1 using the short command specifier and Syntax 1.

    ```
    # vmkfstools -S lun1 vmhba0:1:0:1
    ```

  - Set the label, lun1, on the VMFS volume located on vmhba0:1:0:1 using the long command specifier and Syntax 2.

    ```
    # vmkfstools --setfsname lun1 /vmfs/vm-
    hba0:1:0:1
    ```

- -T --tovmfs2

  The tovmfs2 command is used to convert a VMFS-1 volume to a VMFS-2 volume. The conversion is a one-way process and cannot be reversed. It is advised to back up all data on the VMFS-1 volume before attempting to convert the volume to a VMFS-2 volume. If the VMFS-1 volume has an active swap file, the swap file must be deactivated before attempting to convert the volume. The swap file can be reactivated normally after the conversion is complete. If the VMFS-1 volume is set to private access mode, it will automatically be changed to public access mode because private access mode has been deprecated in VMFS-2. Before attempting the conversion, all virtual machines residing on the VMFS-1 volume must be powered off. Examples:

  - Convert the VMFS-1 volume located on vmhba0:1:0:1 to a VMFS-2 volume using the short command specifier and Syntax 1.

    ```
    # vmkfstools -T vmhba0:1:0:1
    ```

  - Convert the VMFS-1 volume located on vmhba0:1:0:1 to a VMFS-2 volume using the long command specifier and Syntax 1.

    ```
    # vmkfstools --tovmfs2 vmhba0:1:0:1
    ```

- -w --activateswapfile

  The activate swap file command is used to activate an existing swap file. A swap file must be activated before virtual machines can be used. To use this command, users must have root permissions. Examples:

- Activate the swap file named SwapFile.vswp residing in the VMFS volume located on vmhba0:1:0:1 using the short command specifier and Syntax 1.

  ```
  # vmkfstools -w vmhba0:1:0:1:SwapFile.vswp
  ```

- Activate the swap file named SwapFile.vswp residing in the VMFS volume located on vmhba0:1:0:1 using the long command specifier and Syntax 2.

  ```
  # vmkfstools --activateswapfile /vmfs/vm-
  hba0:1:0:1/SwapFile.vswp
  ```

- -X --extendfile #[gGmMkK]

  The extend file command is used to extend or shrink an existing virtual disk file. The total size of the virtual disk file is specified. The size is expressed as an integer followed by the size specifier g or G for gigabytes, m or M for megabytes, or k or K for kilobytes. If the total size of the file specified is greater than the actual disk file, the disk file will be extended, otherwise the disk file will shrink in size. There must be enough free space in the VMFS volume in which the disk file resides to accommodate the new file size. Using the command to shrink disk files is dangerous and care must be taken to ensure that data loss does not occur. Examples:

  - Extend the existing 10GB disk file named rh9.vmdk residing in the VMFS volume located on vmhba0:1:0:1 to 15GB using the short command specifier and Syntax 1.

    ```
    # vmkfstools -X 15G vmhba0:1:0:1:rh9.vmdk
    ```

  - Extend the existing 10GB disk file named rh9.vmdk residing in the VMFS volume located on vmhba0:1:0:1 to 15GB using the long command specifier and Syntax 2.

    ```
    # vmkfstools --extendfile 15G /vmfs/vmh-
    ba0:1:0:1/rh9.vmdk
    ```

  - Shrink the existing 10GB disk file named rh9.vmdk residing in the VMFS volume located on vmhba0:1:0:1 to 8GB using the short command specifier and Syntax 1.

    ```
    # vmkfstools -X 8G vmhba0:1:0:1:rh9.vmdk
    ```

- -y --deactivateswapfile fileID

  The deactivate swap file command is used to deactivate a swap file. Before the swap file can be deactivated, all virtual machines must be powered off or suspended. When deactivating a swap file, the swap file is specified by its file identifier (fileID). The fileID can be obtained by reading the contents of the virtual proc file, /proc/vmware/swap/stats. Examples:

- Deactivate the swap file with a fileID of 0 using the short command specifier.

    ```
    # vmkfstools -y 0
    ```

- Deactivate the swap file with a fileID of 0 using the long command specifier.

    ```
    # vmkfstools --deactivateswapfile 0
    ```

- -z --nozero

  The nozero command is used only with the vmkfstools create file command (-c) as an option. It is used to disable a security feature in a virtual disk used to prevent the virtual machine from reading uninitialized sectors of the virtual disk. The nozero command option should only be used for shared virtual disks used in clustering.

- -Z --extendfs extension-SCSIDevice

  The extend VMFS command is used to extend an existing VMFS-2 volume across another physical disk partition residing on the same or another physical disk. Each partition across which a VMFS-2 volume resides is called an extent. A VMFS-2 volume may span up to 32 extents. The new extent being added to the existing VMFS-2 volume is specified by the extension-SCSIDevice parameter. All data on the partition specified by extension-SCSIDevice will be permanently lost. By default, each time a VMFS-2 volume is extended, an additional 64 files is added to the existing number of maximum files. This number can be specified by including the numfiles command option (-n). Examples:

  - Extend the VMFS volume located on vmhba0:1:0:1 onto the partition specified by vmhba2:0:0:1 adding the default 64 additional maximum number of files using the short command specifier and Syntax 1.

      ```
      # vmkfstools -Z vmhba2:0:0:1 vmhba0:1:0:1
      ```

  - Extend the VMFS volume located on vmhba0:1:0:1 onto the partition specified by vmhba2:0:0:1 adding the default 64 additional maximum number of files using the long command specifier and Syntax 2.

      ```
      # vmkfstools --extendfs vmhba2:0:0:1 /vmfs/
      vmhba0:1:0:1
      ```

  - Extend the VMFS volume located on vmhba0:1:0:1 onto the partition specified by vmhba2:0:0:1 adding an additional 1024 maximum number of files using the short command specifier and Syntax 1.

      ```
      # vmkfstools -Z -n 1024 vmhba2:0:0:1 vm-
      hba0:1:0:1
      ```

- vmware-cmd

  The vmware-cmd command is used to perform various operations with virtual machines. It uses two different command syntaxes: server operations and virtual machine operations.

In the following list of operations supported by the vmware-cmd utility, the token, <vm-config>, is used to represent the absolute path to the configuration file of the virtual machine to which the operation is applied.

Server Operations Supported by vmware-cmd

- List virtual machines on the local server

  ```
  # vmware-cmd -l
  ```
- Register a virtual machine

  ```
  # vmware-cmd -s register <vm-config>
  ```
- Unregister a virtual machine

  ```
  # vmware-cmd -s unregister <vm-config>)
  ```

Virtual Machine Operations Supported by vmware-cmd

- addredo

  Add a redo log to a running virtual machine's disk. Once the redo log is added, all changes are written into the new redo log file. The redo log file is stored in the same VMFS volume as the parent disk specified by <disk-name>. The disk can be in append, persistent, or undoable mode. If the disk already has a redo log file, a second-level redo log file is added (a .REDO.REDO log). Disks in nonpersistent mode or that already have a second-level redo log file cannot have a redo log file added. The redo log file added by the addredo command is automatically committed when the virtual machine is powered off unless the changes were committed previously.

  ```
  # vmware-cmd <vm-config> addredo <disk-name>
  ```
- answer

  Prompt a user to answer the question for the virtual machine waiting for input. This usually occurs when a virtual machine's disks are in undoable mode and the virtual machine has been shut down and powered off.

  ```
  # vmware-cmd <vm-config> answer
  ```
- commit

  Merge changes written into a running virtual machine's disk's redo log file. The <disk-name> token specifies the name of the virtual disk to be committed. The <level> token specifies which redo log to commit. Valid values for <level> are 0 or 1, where 0 is most commonly used, and 1 is used only when there is a second-level redo log file and the first-level redo log file should be committed. The <freeze> token specifies if the virtual machine should be temporarily "frozen" during the commit process. Valid values for the <freeze> token are 0 or 1, where 0 specifies that the virtual machine should not be frozen and 1 specifies that the virtual machine must be frozen during the commit. If the value of <level> is 0, the virtual machine is frozen and the value of the <freeze> token is ignored. The <wait> token specifies if the command returns immediately or if it blocks during the commit process. Valid value for the <wait> token are 0 or 1, where 0 specifies that the command should not wait and returns immediately and 1 specifies that the command should wait and blocks until the commit has completed.

```
# vmware-cmd <vm-config> commit <disk-name>
<level> <freeze> <wait>
```

- connectdevice
  Connect a device to a virtual machine. This only applies to connectable devices including the virtual floppy drive, virtual CD/DVD-ROM drives, and virtual Ethernet adapters. The virtual CPU, memory, virtual SCSI controllers, or virtual hard disks cannot be connected or disconnected. The <device-name> token is the name of the device to connect, such as floppy0, ide0:1, or ethernet0.

```
# vmware-cmd <vm-config> connectdevice
<device-name>
```

- disconnectdevice
  Disconnect a device from a virtual machine. This only applies to connectable devices, including the virtual floppy drive, virtual CD/DVD-ROM drives, and virtual Ethernet adapters. The virtual CPU, memory, virtual SCSI controllers, or virtual hard disks cannot be connected or disconnected. The <device-name> token is the name of the device to disconnect, such as floppy0, ide0:1, or ethernet0.

```
# vmware-cmd <vm-config> disconnectdevice
<device-name>
```

- getcapabilities
  Obtain the permissions of a virtual machine for the current user. An integer value is retuned as a bit field comprised of the following values:
  - 1 - execute
  - 2 - write
  - 4 - read

  Therefore, a result of 4 specifies read permissions only, a value of 6 specifies read and write permissions, and a value of 7 specifies read, write, and execute permissions.

```
# vmware-cmd <vm-config> getcapabilities
```

- getconfig
  Obtain the value of a keyword/value pair stored in a virtual machine's configuration file. The virtual machine configuration file is comprised of a set of keyword/value pairs, one per line. The keyword represents a single property of the virtual machine, such as a device setting, and is separated from the value by an equal character (=).

  ```
  # vmware-cmd <vm-config> getconfig <keyword>
  ```

- getconfigfile
  Obtain the configuration file name for a running virtual machine.

  ```
  # vmware-cmd <vm-config> getconfigfile
  ```

- getguestinfo
  Obtain the value of a GuestInfo variable for a virtual machine. GuestInfo variables are custom keyword/value pairs that are accessible from inside the virtual machine through facilities in VMware Tools. All GuestInfo variables are user-defined. The first time the setguestinfo operation is used, the specified GuestInfo variable, identified by its <keyword>, is created. If an existing GuestInfo variable is set again, its value is updated. GuestInfo variables can only be created and set for running virtual machines. The GuestInfo variables are not persisted and are discarded when the virtual machine is powered off.

  ```
  # vmware-cmd <vm-config> getguestinfo
  <keyword>
  ```

- getheartbeat
  Obtain the current heartbeat count value for a running virtual machine. The virtual machine must have VMware Tools installed in order to produce a heartbeat. The count is updated once per second and starts from zero. If a virtual machine stops sending heartbeat signals to ESX Server, the number will stop incrementing.

  ```
  # vmware-cmd <vm-config> getheartbeat
  ```

- getid
  Obtain the unique world identifier for a running virtual machine.

  ```
  # vmware-cmd <vm-config> getid
  ```

- getpid
  Obtain the process identifier for a running virtual machine.

  ```
  # vmware-cmd <vm-config> getpid
  ```

- getproductinfo
  Obtain the value of a product information keyword for a virtual machine. Although the values are global to the ESX Server, a valid path to a virtual machine configuration file is required for the operation to work properly. Valid values for the <keyword> token are:
  - product —Returns the product name, esx.

- platform—Returns the platform name, vmnix.
- build—Returns the build number of ESX Server.
- majorversion—Returns the major portion of the version number of ESX Server.
- minorversion—Returns the minor portion of the version number of ESX Server.
- revision—Returns the revision portion of the version number of ESX Server.

```
# vmware-cmd <vm-config> getproductinfo
<keyword>
```

- getremoteconnection
  Obtain the total number of remote connections to a virtual machine. Remote connections include connections from the Management Interface, VMRC, or the scripting API.

```
# vmware-cmd <vm-config> getremoteconnections
```

- getresource
  Obtain the value of a resource variable for a virtual machine specified by the <resource-variable> token. See the Resource Variables section for a list of valid resource variables.

```
# vmware-cmd <vm-config> getresource
<resource-variable>
```

- getstate
  Obtain the power state of a virtual machine.

```
# vmware-cmd <vm-config> getstate
```

- gettoolslastactive
  Obtain the time in seconds since the last heartbeat signal was received from a running virtual machine.

```
# vmware-cmd <vm-config> gettoolslastactive
```

- getuptime
  Obtain the uptime of the guest operating system of a running virtual machine.

```
# vmware-cmd <vm-config> getuptime
```

- reset
  Reset a virtual machine. Restarts or resets the virtual machine. The default <power-op> is soft if a <power-op> is not specified.

```
# vmware-cmd <vm-config> reset <power-op>
```

- setconfig
  Set the value of a keyword/value pair stored in a virtual machine's configuration file. The virtual machine configuration file is comprised of a set of keyword/value pairs, one per line. The keyword represents a single

property of the virtual machine, such as a device setting, and is separated from the value by an equal character (=). The values set by this command only affect running virtual machines and the changes are not saved into the virtual machine's configuration file.

```
# vmware-cmd <vm-config> setconfig <keyword>
<value>
```

- setguestinfo
  Set a GuestInfo variable for a virtual machine. GuestInfo variables are custom keyword/value pairs that are accessible from inside the virtual machine through facilities in VMware Tools. All GuestInfo variables are user-defined. The first time the setguestinfo operation is used, the specified GuestInfo variable, identified by its <keyword>, is created. If an existing GuestInfo variable is set again, its value is updated. GuestInfo variables can only be created and set for running virtual machines. The GuestInfo variables are not persisted and are discarded when the virtual machine is powered off.

```
# vmware-cmd <vm-config> setguestinfo
<keyword> <value>
```

- setresource
  Set the value of a resource variable for a virtual machine. The <resource-variable> token specifies which resource variable should be set and the <value> token represents the new value of the resource variable. See the Resource Variables section for a list of valid resource variables.

```
# vmware-cmd <vm-config> setresource
<resource-variable> <value>
```

- start
  Start a virtual machine. If the virtual machine is powered off, it will be powered on. If the virtual machine is suspended, it will be resumed.

```
# vmware-cmd <vm-config> start <power-op>
```

- stop
  Stop a virtual machine. Shuts down and then powers off the virtual machine. The default <power-op> is soft if a <power-op> is not specified.

```
# vmware-cmd <vm-config> stop <power-op>
```

- suspend
  Suspend a virtual machine. The virtual machine must be powered on. The default <power-op> is soft if a <power-op> is not specified.

```
# vmware-cmd <vm-config> suspend <power-op>
```

Power Operation Values

- hard
  Hard power operations forces the power state change immediately and without condition. When powering off or resetting a virtual machine, this is akin to pressing the main power button or the reset button of a physical computer.
- soft
  Soft power operations always attempt to gracefully handle the guest operating system before attempting to apply the power state change. The virtual machine on which a soft power operation is being performed must have VMware Tools installed and running. When powering off a virtual machine, the shut down event script in VMware Tools is first executed and then the guest operating system is shut down gracefully. When resetting a virtual machine, its guest operating system is instead restarted gracefully. When suspending a virtual machine, the defined suspend scripts within the virtual machine (see VMware Tools) are first executed. When powering on a virtual machine, the power on event script in VMware Tools is executed when VMware Tools becomes available. When resuming a virtual machine that was previously suspended, the resume event script in VMware Tools is executed when VMware Tools becomes available.
- trysoft
  The trysoft power operation always attempts to perform a soft power operation first and if the soft power operation fails, a hard power operation is then used.

Resource Variables for Virtual Machines

- cpu.affinity
  A comma-delimited list of CPU numbers on which the virtual machine can be executed. This resource variable is read and write capable.
- cpu.emin, cpu.<vcpu>.emin
  The effective minimum percentage of CPU allocation for a virtual machine. By default, cpu.emin reports the value for virtual CPU0 only. The alternate form can be used where <vcpu> is the zero-based number of the virtual CPU for which the value will be reported. This resource variable is read-only.
- cpu.extrasec, cpu.<vcpu>.extrasec
  The amount of cumulative processor time consumed by the virtual processor above the effective minimum CPU allocation defined by the cpu.emin resource variable. The value is expressed as a floating-point number which is the amount of time in milliseconds. By default, cpu.extrasec reports the

value for virtual CPU0 only. The alternate form can be used where <vcpu> is the zero-based number of the virtual CPU for which the value will be reported. This resource variable is read-only.

- cpu.htSharing
  Defines the policy regarding the sharing of HyperThreading processor resources by a virtual machine. Valid values for this resource variable are:
  - any
    The virtual machine's virtual CPU may share HyperThreaded processor resources at any time with any other virtual CPUs from the same or other virtual machines.
  - internal
    The virtual machine's virtual CPU may share HyperThreaded processor resources at any time with any other virtual CPUs from the same virtual machine only. This only applies to ESX Servers with VMware Virtual SMP installed and to virtual machines with more than one virtual processor.
  - none
    The virtual machine's virtual CPU may never share HyperThreaded processor resources at any time with any other virtual CPUs from the same or other virtual machines.
    The default value is any. This resource variable is read and write capable.

- cpu.max
  The maximum percentage of CPU allocation for the virtual machine's virtual processors. The valid range of value is from zero to (100 * number_of_virtual_processors). A virtual machine with two virtual processors has a valid potential range from 0 to 200. This resource variable is read and write capable.

- cpu.min
  The minimum percentage of CPU allocation guaranteed for the virtual machine. This resource variable is read and write capable.

- cpu.number
  The number of processors assigned to the virtual machine. This resource variable is read-only.

- cpu.shares
  The number of CPU resources shares assigned to the virtual machine. This resource variable is read and write capable.

- cpu.syssec, cpu.<vcpu>.syssec
  The amount of CPU time consumed by the VMKernel for the virtual machine performing system operations such as disk or network I/O. This is a subset of the time reported by the cpu.usedsec resource variable. The value is expressed as a floating point number and represents the number of milliseconds of CPU time used. By default, cpu.syssec reports the value

for virtual CPU0 only. The alternate form can be used where <vcpu> is the zero-based number of the virtual CPU for which the value will be reported. This resource variable is read-only.

- cpu.uptime, cpu.<vcpu>.uptime
  The number of seconds since the virtual machine was powered on. By default, cpu.uptime reports the value for virtual CPU0 only. The alternate form can be used where <vcpu> is the zero-based number of the virtual CPU for which the value will be reported. This resource variable is read-only.
- cpu.usedsec, cpu.<vcpu>.usedsec
  The total amount of CPU time used by a virtual machine. By default, cpu.usedsec reports the value for virtual CPU0 only. The alternate form can be used where <vcpu> is the zero-based number of the virtual CPU for which the value will be reported. This resource variable is read-only.
- cpu.waitsec, cpu.<vcpu>.waitsec
  The total amount of idle or blocked CPU time for the virtual machine. By default, cpu.waitsec reports the value for virtual CPU0 only. The alternate form can be used where <vcpu> is the zero-based number of the virtual CPU for which the value will be reported. This resource variable is read-only.
- disk.HTL
  Returns a space-delimited set of Host Target LUNs (HTL). This resource variable is read-only.
- disk.<HTL>.busResets
  The total number of bus resets invoked by commands originating from the virtual machine on the specified Host Target LUN (<HTL>). This resource variable is read-only.
- disk.<HTL>.cmds
  The total number of commands issued by the virtual machine to the specified Host Target LUN (<HTL>). This resource variable is read-only.
- disk.<HTL>.cmdsAborted
  The total number of commands issued by the virtual machine to the specified Host Target LUN (<HTL>) that were aborted. This resource variable is read-only.
- disk.<HTL>.KBread
  The total number of kilobytes read from the specified Host Target LUN (<HTL>) by the virtual machine. This resource variable is read-only.
- disk.<HTL>.KBwritten
  The total number of kilobytes written to the specified Host Target LUN (<HTL>) by the virtual machine. This resource variable is read-only.
- disk.<HTL>.reads
  The total number of reads on the specified Host Target LUN (<HTL>) by the virtual machine. This resource variable is read-only.

- disk.<HTL>.shares
  The total number of shares allocated to the virtual machine on the specified Host Target LUN (<HTL>). This resource variable is read and write capable.
- disk.<HTL>.writes
  The total number of writes on the specified Host Target LUN (<HTL>) by the virtual machine. This resource variable is read-only.
- mem.active
  The amount of actively used memory by a virtual machine. The value represents the memory in kilobytes. This resource variable is read-only.
- mem.affinity
  The NUMA node memory affinity of a virtual machine. This resource variable is read and write capable.
- mem.cpt-tgt
  The number of kilobytes of memory that the virtual machine reads into physical memory from its suspend file if the virtual machine is swapping from a suspended state file. Otherwise, a value of zero is retuned. This resource variable is read-only.
- mem.cptread
  The number of kilobytes of the virtual machine's suspend file that has been read into physical memory. A virtual machine's suspended state file may act as a special swap file for the VMKernel when the virtual machine is resumed and system memory is low. This resource variable is read-only.
- mem.max
  The absolute maximum amount of memory that the virtual machine can use expressed in megabytes. This resource variable is read and write capable.
- mem.mctltgt
  The size of the vmmemctl balloon driver in the guest operating system of the virtual machine in kilobytes. This resource variable is read-only.
- mem.memctl
  The number of kilobytes of memory reclaimed after the vmmemctl runs for a virtual machine. This resource variable is read-only.
- mem.min
  The absolute minimum amount of memory that the virtual machine will have allocated expressed in megabytes. This resource variable is read and write capable.
- mem.overhd
  The number of kilobytes of memory overhead of a virtual machine. This resource variable is read-only.
- mem.ovhdmax
  The maximum number of kilobytes of memory overhead of a virtual machine. This resource variable is read-only.

- mem.shared
  The number of kilobytes of memory that is transparently shared (or consolidated) for a virtual machine with other virtual machines running on the same ESX Server. This resource variable is read-only.
- mem.shares
  The number of memory resource shares assigned to the virtual machine. This resource variable is read and write capable.
- mem.size
  The actual number of kilobytes of memory consumed by a virtual machine. This resource variable is read-only.
- mem.sizetgt
  The targeted memory size of a virtual machine expressed in kilobytes. This resource variable is read-only.
- mem.swapin
  The total number of kilobytes of data swapped into memory since the virtual machine was powered on. This resource variable is read-only.
- mem.swapout
  The total number of kilobytes of data swapped from memory onto disk since the virtual machine was powered on. This resource variable is read-only.
- mem.swapped
  The total number of kilobytes of data swapped into and out of the VMFS volume's swap file since the virtual machine was powered on. This resource variable is read-only.
- mem.swaptgt
  The targeted number of kilobytes of memory to swap to the VMFS volume's swap file for a virtual machine. This resource variable is read-only.
- net.adapters
  Returns a space-delimited set of MAC addresses that correspond to each virtual network adapter installed in the virtual machine. This resource variable is read-only.
- net.<mac>.totKBRx
  The total number of kilobytes of data received by the virtual network adapter identified by its MAC address, specified by <mac>, including both local and remote network traffic. This resource variable is read-only.
- net.<mac>.totKBTx
  The total number of kilobytes of data transmitted by the virtual network adapter identified by its MAC address, specified by <mac>, including both local and remote network traffic. This resource variable is read-only
- net.<mac>.totPktsRx
  The total number of packets of data received by the virtual network adapter identified by its MAC address, specified by <mac>, including both local and remote network traffic. This resource variable is read-only.

- net.<mac>.totPktsTx
  The total number of packets of data transmitted by the virtual network adapter identified by its MAC address, specified by <mac>, including both local and remote network traffic. This resource variable is read-only.
- pid
  Returns the VMKernel process identifier for the virtual machine. This resource variable is read-only.
- uptime
  Returns the uptime of the virtual machine expressed in seconds. This resource variable is read-only.
- worldid
  Returns the unique world identifier for the virtual machine. This resource variable is read-only.

How to Edit a Virtual Machine's Configuration File in the Service Console

The Service Console is useful for making detailed configuration changes to the system or virtual machines. Sometimes it is necessary or useful to edit a virtual machine's configuration file manually. This can be accomplished in the Service Console using a text editor such as nano or vi. A virtual machine's configuration file is a text file made up of several keyword/value pairs. One keyword/value pair is placed on each line. Lines beginning with the # character are comments and are ignored. Empty lines or lines containing only white space characters are also ignored. The order in which the keyword/value pairs appear does not affect the operation or use of the configuration file. On a single line containing a keyword/value pair, the keyword is the first entry on the line followed by an equals character (=) followed by the value. The value usually appears within a set of quotation marks, but this is not absolutely required, although if quotation marks are not used and the value contains special characters including a space, the value will have to be properly escaped. The keywords describe the various properties of the virtual machine or a property of one of the virtual machine's virtual hardware devices. Virtual hardware devices usually require several lines in the configuration file to fully describe. Keywords may consist of a single word but many are multiple words delimited by a period character (.). This is especially true of virtual hardware devices, where the first part of the keyword is the virtual device name followed by a period followed by a property of that device.

Virtual hardware devices may be completely removed from a virtual machine by removing all entries from the configuration file that represents the particular device. Likewise, a new virtual hardware device can be added by simply adding all of the necessary configuration file keyword/value pairs that represent the device along with a proper set of values. Of course, when adding or removing devices from a virtual machine, the virtual machine must first be powered off.

ESX Server caches a virtual machine's configuration file in memory after it has been powered on at least once. After editing a virtual machine's configuration file, the changes may not take effect immediately because ESX Server caches the virtual machine's configuration and has not reloaded the updated file. A simple method used to force ESX Server to reload the configuration file is to open the virtual machine from the Management Interface with VMRC before powering on the virtual machine. ESX Server will either automatically reload the configuration file or it will prompt the user to reload the configuration file. Once the configuration file has been reloaded, the changes will take effect and the virtual machine may be powered on. Unregistering and reregistering a virtual machine will cause its configuration file to be reloaded as well as rebooting the ESX Server itself, which is a drastic measure (the physical ESX Server should rarely be rebooted once ESX Server is installed and configured).

The Proc File System (procfs)

The ESX Server Service Console, like other Linux systems, implements the process file system, or procfs. It is a virtual, in-memory file system designed to allow programs to access kernel data using normal file I/O mechanisms. Procfs is located at /proc. Because procfs is virtual, the files do not exist. ESX Server extends the Linux procfs to include a multitude of ESX Server data from the Service Console and from the VMKernel. All ESX Server procfs data is located at /proc/vmware. The real-time in-memory configuration values and statistics are located within the vmware directory under /procfs. The majority of the available data is read-only. Some of the ESX Server procfs virtual files can have values updated, although in many cases, nearly all settings are better handled through the Management Interface. System monitoring and management agents can use the extended procfs to obtain much of the required data about the running state of the ESX Server and its virtual machines.

The list below outlines the VMware ESX Server procfs virtual files sorted by their parent directory.

- /proc/vmware/:
  - chipset
  - cpuinfo
  - debug
  - interrupts
  - intr-tracker
  - log
  - mem
  - pci
  - procstats
  - rpcStats
- stats
- thermmon
- timers
- uptime
- version
- vmkstor
- watchpoints
- /proc/vmware/buddy:
  - kvmap
  - kvmap-verbose
  - memmap-0-hi

- memmap-0-hi-verbose
- memmap-0-lo
- memmap-0-lo-verbose
- xmap
- xmap-verbose
- /proc/vmware/config/Cpu:
  - BoundLagQuanta
  - CellMigratePeriod
  - ConsoleMinCpu
  - ConsoleOSWarpPeriod
  - CreditAgePeriod
  - IdlePackageRebalancePeriod
  - MachineClearThreshold
  - MigratePenalty
  - MigratePeriod
  - PreemptPenalty
  - Quantum
  - RunnerMovePeriod
  - SharesPerVcpuHigh
  - SharesPerVcpuLow
  - SharesPerVcpuNormal
  - SkewSampleThreshold
  - SkewSampleUsec
- /proc/vmware/config/Disk:
  - DelayOnBusy
  - MaskLUNs
  - MaxLUN
  - MaxResetLatency
  - MaxVCNotReadyTime
  - PathEvalTime
  - ResetLatency
  - ResetMaxRetries
  - ResetOnFailover
  - ResetOverdueLogPeriod
  - ResetPeriod
  - ResetThreadExpires
  - ResetThreadMax
  - ResetThreadMin
  - RetryUnitAttention
  - SANDevicesWithAPFailover
  - SchedNumReqOutstanding
  - SchedQControlSeqReqs
  - SchedQControlVMSwitches
- SchedQuantum
- SectorMaxDiff
- SharesHigh
- SharesLow
- SharesNormal
- SupportSparseLUN
- UseDeviceReset
- UseLunReset
- UseReportLUN
- /proc/vmware/config/File-System:
  - LockRetries
  - RemoteFSEnabled
- /proc/vmware/config/Irq:
  - BestVcpuRouting
  - IRQMaxLoadPct
  - IRQRebalancePeriod
  - RoutingPolicy
- /proc/vmware/config/Mem:
  - AdmitHeapMin
  - AllocHighThreshold
  - BalancePeriod
  - CtlMaxBSD
  - CtlMaxLInux
  - CtlMaxNT4
  - CtlMaxNT5
  - CtlMaxPercent
  - IdleTax
  - MinFreePct
  - SamplePeriod
  - ShareCOSBufSize
  - ShareScanTotal
  - ShareScanVM
  - SharesPerMBHigh
  - SharesPerMBLow
  - SharesPerMBNormal
  - SwapAbortTimeoutMs
  - SwapFileOnSAN
  - SwapIORetry
  - SwapShared
- /proc/vmware/config/Migrate:
  - AllocZeroPgs
  - Enabled

- MemChksum
- MinReservation
- NetTimeout
- PageInProgress
- PageInTimeout
- PreCopyLeftMB
- PreCopyMinProgressMB
- SwapExistingVMs
- SwapIncomingPgs
- TSMaster
- /proc/vmware/config/Misc:
  - BlueScreenTimeout
  - ConsoleShareXfer
  - CosCorefile
  - DebugMemEnable
  - EnableHighDMA
  - KVMapGuardUncached
  - LogToFile
  - LogToSerial
  - LogWldPrefix
  - MemAdmitMapEntriesMin
  - MemMapEntriesLow
  - MinimalPanic
  - ProcVerbose
  - PsodOnCosPanic
  - SerialBaudRate
  - SerialPort
  - TimerHardPeriod
  - TimerMinGuestPeriod
  - VmkperfPerWorld
- /proc/vmware/config/Net:
  - ClusterHaltCheck
  - CopiesBeforeRemap
  - DisableWatchdog
  - MaxMallocPackets
  - MaxPrivateSKBs
  - MaxRecvPackets
  - NotifySwitch
  - PktsDeferXmitIntIfKeeping
  - PktsPerXmitInterrupt
  - ProcVerbose
  - RXClusterCPUSamplePeriod
  - RXClusterDelayOff

- RXClusterDelayOn
- RXClusterDelayTDec
- RXClusterDelayTInc
- RXClusterTMaxFreq
- RXClusterTMigrateDelay
- RXClusterTMigrateThresh
- RXClusterTMinFreq
- RXClusterThreshOff
- RXClusterThreshOn
- RXClusterTimerCPU
- RecvClusterDynAdjRate
- RecvClusterDynQueueMax
- RecvClusterOffCount
- RecvClusterOnCount
- RecvClusterQueueMax
- RecvClusterTimeoutCount
- RecvClusterTimeoutMS
- RecvCopyLength
- SwitchFailoverBeacon-EtherType
- SwitchFailoverBeaconInterval
- SwitchFailoverThreshold
- TCPIPLog
- TcpSegmentationOffload
- VlanTrunking
- XmitClusterOffCount
- XmitClusterOnCount
- XmitClusterQueueMax
- XmitClusterTimeoutCount
- XmitClusterTimeoutMS
- XmitInterruptIfStopped
- XmitInterruptTimeout
- XmitMinWinZeroCopyLen
- ZeroSpeedLinkDown
- /proc/vmware/config/Numa:
  - AutoMemAffinity
  - Debug
  - MigImbalanceThreshold
  - PageMig
  - Rebalance
  - RebalancePeriod
- /proc/vmware/config/Scsi:
  - ConflictRetries

- LogAborts
- LogMultiPath
- PassthroughLocking
- /proc/vmware/filters:
  - status
  - xmit
  - xmitpop
  - xmitpush
- /proc/vmware/filters/xmit:
  - There are no available transmit filters available at this time.
- /proc/vmware/images/ <module>:
  - id
  - loadmap
- /proc/vmware/loglevels:
  - APIC
  - Action
  - Alloc
  - BH
  - Bluescreen
  - Bond
  - Buddy
  - Chipset
  - Compress
  - Cow
  - CpuMetrics
  - CpuSched
  - DVGA
  - Dump
  - EventHisto
  - FS
  - FS1
  - FS2
  - FSS
  - Helper
  - Histogram
  - Host
  - IDT
  - IOAPIC
  - IRQ
  - IT
  - Im
  - Init
  - KVMap
  - Kseg
  - LinBlock
  - LinChar
  - LinNet
  - LinPCI
  - LinProc
  - LinSCSI
  - LinStress
  - LinStubs
  - Log
  - MCE
  - Mem
  - MemMap
  - MemSched
  - Migrate
  - MigrateLog
  - MigrateNet
  - MigrateQueue
  - Mod
  - NF
  - NMI
  - NUMA
  - NUMASched
  - Net
  - NetDiscover
  - NetTOE
  - PCI
  - PIC
  - PShare
  - Parse
  - Partition
  - Post
  - Proc
  - RPC
  - RTC
  - SCSI
  - SMP
  - SP
  - Serial
  - Swap

- TLB
- Tcpip
- TcpipLoader
- Tcpip_Support
- ThermMon
- TimeStamp
- Timer
- Tso
- User
- Util
- VMKAsyncIO
- VMKUC
- Vlan
- VmkStats
- VmkStress
- VmkSysInfo
- VmkTag
- Vmkperf
- Watchpoint
- World
- XMap
- /proc/vmware/net:
  - stats
- /proc/vmware/net/<net-device>:
  - <mac>
  - config
  - stats
- /proc/vmware/pshare:
  - overhead
  - status
- /proc/vmware/sched:
  - cpu
  - cpu-load
  - cpu-run-times
  - cpu-state-counts
  - cpu-state-times
  - cpu-verbose
  - events
  - idle
  - mem
  - mem-verbose
  - ncpus
  - reservations
- /proc/vmware/scsi/<vmhba>:
  - <device:target>
  - <lun:partition>
  - stats
- /proc/vmware/swap:
  - stats
- /proc/vmware/vm/<vm-id>:
  - cpu
  - disk
  - mem
  - names
  - net
  - swap
  - userRPC
- /proc/vmware/vm/<vm-id>/cpu:
  - affinity
  - debug
  - max
  - min
  - run-times
  - shares
  - state-counts
  - state-times
  - status
  - wait-stats
- /proc/vmware/vm/<vm-id>/ disk:
  - <HTL>
- /proc/vmware/vm/<vm-id>/ mem:
  - affinity
  - min
  - numa
  - pshare
  - remap
  - shares
  - status
- /proc/vmware/vm/<vm-id>/net:
  - <mac>
- /proc/vmware/vmkperf:
  - enable
- /proc/vmware/vmkperf/enable:
  - 64k_alias

- branch
- branch_mispred
- branch_nottaken
- branch_nottaken_mispred
- branch_nottaken_pred
- branch_pred
- branch_taken
- branch_taken_mispred
- branch_taken_pred
- cycles
- dtlb_page_walk
- instr_retired

- itlb_miss
- itlb_page_walk
- l1miss
- l2miss
- l2readhit
- l2readmiss
- machine_clear_any
- machine_clear_order
- machine_clear_ot
- machine_clear_selfmod
- tcache_miss

Procfs can be monitored in real-time by management and monitoring agents to provide alerts when certain thresholds are reached in the various files, especially, status-type files. The procfs interface is yet another advanced capability of ESX Server that differentiates itself from other virtualization platforms.

Summary

VMware ESX Server provides several management methods and tools used to perform configuration and monitoring of the system and virtual machines. Although most of the management tasks must be performed remotely from a workstation that is separate from the physical server, the Web-based Management Interface is very accessible, secure, and easy to use. The VMRC application is also available for both Windows and Linux platforms and is very similar in use to other VMware virtualization platforms in its presentation and use. Advanced system administrators will likely appreciate the management capabilities of the Linux-based Service Console. From the Service Console, low-level management tasks can be performed and it is the home of external management, monitoring, and system backup agents. From within the Service Console, management tasks can be automated using common bash shell scripts or Perl scripts. ESX Server offers some of the most flexible configuration and management options of all of the server virtualization platforms available.

Chapter 16

Creating a VMware ESX Server Virtual Machine

The basic guidelines of creating virtual machines in VMware ESX Server do not differ much from those of VMware GSX Server or even Microsoft's Virtual Server. However, management of virtual machines is where this Enterprise version of VMware's technology really shines. The overhead used by the Linux-based host operating system (also known as a Hypervisor) is far less that its GSX Server predecessor. Keep in mind that ESX Server can host up to 80 virtual machines at a time and requires a minimum of two processors. Here are the details of creating a virtual machine under VMware ESX Server 2.5.2.

Preparation

Always keep in mind which guest operating system will be installed before creating a virtual machine. The basic requirements for all systems may vary by a great deal. Beyond just the basic requirements of the guest operating system, applications come heavily into play. Database or mail servers, for example, will require many more resources than a basic Windows Domain Controller for example. The following is a minimal list of requirements that should be determined prior to creating a virtual machine:

- Amount of required memory
- Amount of required disk space
- Networking card assignment
- Required media such as CD-ROMs, or floppy disks
- Proper Disk Mode to be used

VMware ESX Server supports four types of disk modes. Depending on the role of the virtual machine, one of the following disk modes may be better suited for the task than the others.

- **Persistent**
  Persistent mode writes all changes immediately to the disk. Once changes are made, they cannot be reverted back to a previous state. This is the same behavior as a physical disk in a physical server.
- **Nonpersistent**
  Nonpersistent mode discards any changes made to the disk once the virtual machine is rebooted or powered off.
- **Undoable**
  Undoable mode forces the user to decide what action to take with the changes written to the disk upon reboot or power off of the virtual machine. Disks can be discarded, kept, or committed depending on requirements.
- **Append**
  Append mode writes changes into a redo log to the disk image. All changes are kept separate from the primary disk file. This allows a user to revert back to a previously known state or to commit changes as necessary. No actions are taken upon reboot or power off of the virtual machine.

More in information regarding ESX Server's disk modes can be found in chapter 17 in the Virtual Disk Modes section.

Make sure that all software and license information needed for installation has been obtained and is available. Verify that all necessary drivers, especially SCSI drivers have been collected. Finally, keep in mind these tips before beginning the virtual machine creation:

- Screen savers on the guest operating system can often be too CPU intensive for the host server.
- Verify the guest operating system media or image is not an OEM copy that requires installation on specific hardware. If so, when the initialization process begins, the virtual hardware will not match the expected vendor hardware and the installation will fail.
- As with physical servers, a separate guest operating system or application license is usually required for each virtual machine in which it is installed. Verify all software and operating system licenses to ensure that proper compliance is maintained.
- Guest operating systems cannot use their hibernation feature, it is not supported and should not be used; instead, it should be disabled in favor of using the virtual machine suspend feature.
- Remember, Microsoft's activation policy can cause havoc when creating a template image or when making configuration changes to a virtual machine. Certain configuration changes may require reactivating the guest operating system. Under normal circumstances if three or more hardware

components change, the activation Wizard becomes active again and requires reactivation. It is therefore best to either create the virtual machine in its final form with little or no changes made after the fact to the hardware or to use volume license key-based media that does not require an activation key. Microsoft operating systems that currently require activation include Microsoft Windows XP and Microsoft Windows Server 2003.

Creating a Virtual Machine with Microsoft Windows Server 2003 Guest OS

The easiest method of creating a new virtual machine in ESX Server is to use the Add Virtual Machine Wizard, which is available through the Web-based ESX Server Management User Interface (MUI). Be sure to disable any popup blocker software before continuing.

1. Open the MUI by opening a Web browser, such as Microsoft Internet Explorer, and navigating to https://<hostname>. The <hostname> token above is either the DNS-resolvable host name of the ESX Server or the IP address of the ESX Server. A security alert dialog box may popup containing a warning regarding the validity of server's security certificate (see Figure 16.1). If this occurs, accept the certificate.

    The log-in screen will be displayed (see Figure 16.2).

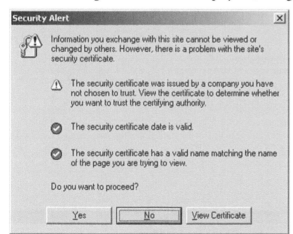

Figure 16.1   Security Alert popup dialog when accessing the MUI.

Figure 16.2 (below) VMware ESX Server Management User Interface (MUI) Log-in Screen.

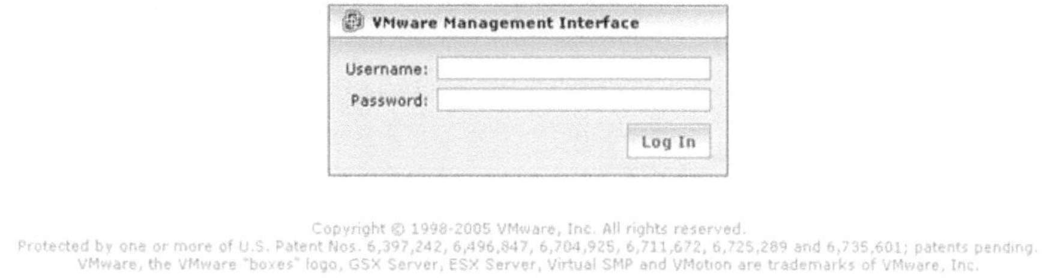

Figure 16.3 Logging in to the MUI.

2. Log in to the MUI using an account with the appropriate permissions, such as the root account (see Figure 16.3).

3. Once logged in, the Status Monitor screen is displayed. Click the Add Virtual Machine button located at the lower-right side of the screen (see Figure 16.4).

   The Add Virtual Machine Wizard will start in a new popup window (see Figure 16.5).

4. From the Guest Operating System drop-down box, select the option labeled Microsoft Windows Server 2003, Standard Edition (see Figure 16.6).

   The Display Name and Location fields' values will change after a guest operating system selection has been made (see Figure 16.7).

Figure 16.4 Status Monitor.

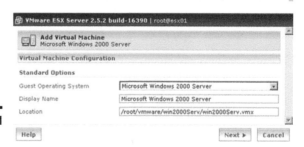

Figure 16.5 Add Virtual Machine Wizard.

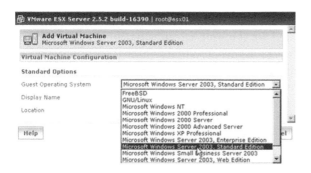

Figure 16.6 Selecting a guest operating system.

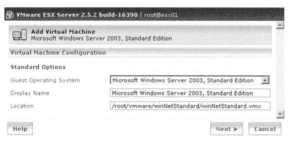

Figure 16.7 Display Name and Location field values will change.

Figure 16.8 Giving the new virtual machine a name and location.

Enter a new display name that is appropriate for the virtual machine being created (see Figure 16.8). Be sure to enter a name that allows it to be easily distinguished from others that have been created or that are planned to be created. Verify that the location and name of the new virtual machine's configuration file is unique to all other virtual machines on the ESX Server. If there is already a virtual machine with the same guest operating system, the filename will have to be modified to make it unique.

A good best practice to follow when naming new virtual machines and deciding their path and configuration file name is to keep the names the same. Each virtual machine must have its configuration file reside in a dedicated directory. The directory and file name used for the configuration should be in all lower case and contain no spaces. This is not a hard requirement, but it will keep your implementation consistent and simplify administration of the system.

For example, if a new virtual machine was given the name, Intranet Web Server, and was created by the root account, its configuration file name and path would be /root/vmware/intranet_web_server/intranet_web_server.vmx. Continuing this theme, the virtual machine's virtual hard disk file name should be intranet_web_server.vmdk.

When this is completed, proceed by clicking the Next button.

5. The next step is used to configure the processors and memory of the virtual machine. If the ESX Server does not have a valid VirtualSMP license configured, the new virtual machine will be limited to a single virtual processor. Otherwise, either one or two processors must be selected under the Processors section.

   In the Memory field, enter the virtual machine's maximum amount of memory in megabytes (see Figure 16.9). This value cannot exceed 3600MB (3.5GB) per virtual machine as this is the maximum amount of memory support for any virtual machine.

Figure 16.9 Configuring processors and memory.

If the virtual machine will have Citrix Metaframe or Presentation Server installed into the guest operating system, check the Citrix Terminal Services checkbox.

To proceed, click the Next button. The virtual machine will now be created. This may take a minute or two. While the virtual machine is being created, the screen shown in Figure 16.10 will be displayed:

Figure 16.10 The new virtual machine is being created.

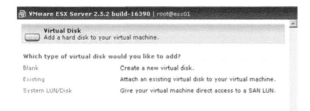

Figure 16.11 Choosing the type of virtual hard disk.

6. Once the virtual machine has been created, a virtual hard disk must be added. The type of virtual hard disk must be selected at this point (see Figure 16.11). If the ESX Server was not installed with SAN options, the System LUN/Disk option will be disabled and unavailable. If there is an existing virtual hard disk that should be attached to the new virtual machine, the Existing options should be selected. Otherwise, a new, blank virtual hard disk should be created by clicking the Blank option.

7. The virtual hard disk must be configured.
   • If the Blank option was selected in step 6, the following screen shown in Figure 13.12 will be displayed:
     If there is more than one VMFS volume mounted in the ESX Server, a drop-down selection box will appear in the Image File Location field. Otherwise, the name of the only VMFS volume mount point will be displayed as text in this field. The name of the new virtual disk file must be entered into the Image File Name field. It is a good idea to keep this file name the same as the virtual machine's name. The Capacity field must contain the size of the new virtual hard disk in megabytes. In the Virtual SCSI Node field, select the SCSI ID of the new virtual hard disk. It is usually best if the first disk has an ID of 0:0. Under the Disk Mode section, select the proper disk mode of the virtual hard disk. This option can be changed later. It is usually best to place the new virtual

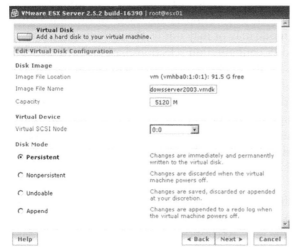

Figure 16.12 Configuring a new, blank virtual hard disk.

Figure 16.13 Configuring an existing virtual hard disk.

hard disk in Persistent mode initially during the installation of the guest operating system.

• If the Existing option was selected in step 6, the following screen shown in Figure 16.13 will be displayed.

If there is more than one VMFS volume mounted in the ESX Server, a drop-down selection box will appear in the Image File Location field. Otherwise, the name of the only VMFS volume mount point will be displayed as text in this field. The Image File Name field will contain a list of existing virtual hard disk image files that reside in the selected Image File Location. Upon selecting an existing virtual disk image file, its size will be displayed read-only in the Capacity field. In the Virtual SCSI Node field, select the SCSI ID of the new virtual hard disk. It is usually best if the first disk has an ID of 0:0. Under the Disk Mode section, select the proper disk mode of the virtual hard disk. This option can be changed later. Depending on the usage of the new virtual machine, Persistent mode may or may not be the desired disk mode.

Once the virtual disk configuration selections have been made, click the Next button to save the configuration. The following screen shown in Figure 16.14 will be displayed.

8. After a few moments, the Add Virtual Machine Wizard window will close and be replaced by another popup window, the Virtual Machine Configuration window. The Virtual Machine Configuration window will start with the Hardware tab selected, displaying the complete set of virtual hardware installed and configured for the new virtual machine (see Figure 16.15).

Clicking the Close link in the upper right-hand corner of the window will close the Virtual Machine Configuration window. At this point, the Status Monitor tab of the main MUI window will have refreshed its data, displaying the newly created virtual machine (see Figure 16.16).

Figure 16.14 Saving the virtual hard disk configuration.

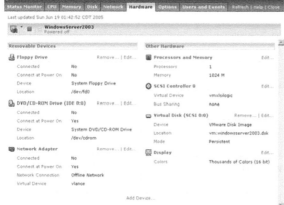

Figure 16.15 Virtual Machine Configuration Window, Hardware Tab.

Figure 16.16 ESX Server MUI with one virtual machine.

The virtual machine has been created and the process is complete.

Installing a Guest Operating System

Installing a guest operating system onto a virtual machine's virtual hard disk drive is once again the same as installing an operating system on a physical computer. Remember that the guest operating system being installed is not aware that it is being installed inside of a virtual machine and not on physical hardware. The resources that are assigned to the virtual machine, such as memory, disk, controller, CPU, and network will be detected and installed just as they would be on a physical computer.

Although the basic procedure is much the same throughout many virtual server platforms, ESX version 2.5.2 only supports the following operating systems:

- Microsoft Windows NT 4.0
- Microsoft Windows 2000
- Microsoft Windows XP
- Microsoft Windows Server 2003
- FreeBSD 4.10
- Novell NetWare 5.1 & 6.5 Server
- Red Hat Linux 7.2 - 9.0
- Red Hat Linux Advanced Server 2.1
- Red Hat Enterprise Linux 2.1 & 3.0
- SuSE Linux 8.2 - 9.2
- SuSE Linux Enterprise Server 8 & 9

Installing Windows Server 2003 in a Virtual Machine

The supported operating systems mentioned above interact with the x86-compatible virtual hardware represented in the virtualization layer presented by ESX. Therefore, only 32-bit, x86-compatible operating systems are supported for installation. Microsoft Windows Server 2003 Standard Edition will be used as one example for installing a guest operating system on a virtual machine.

Please note, with VMware ESX Server, either CD-ROM installation media must be placed into the host server's physical CD-ROM drive or an ISO file may be created from the installation media and mounted as a virtual CD-ROM device in the new virtual machine. Unlike VMware GSX Server, a remote workstation CD-ROM device cannot be attached to a virtual machine.

Basic installation of the guest operating system will be performed much like a physical machine; however, the Remote Console will be used to power on and power off the virtual machine. Click Power-on with the CD in the drive and begin the install. Notice the BIOS screen does not differ from what would be seen on a physical machine.

Follow these remaining steps to begin installation:

1. As long as the boot order in the BIOS has not been changed, the virtual machine will boot from the CD-ROM media and the Windows installation begins. If CD-ROM is not listed before the hard disk, update the BIOS boot order to allow the virtual machine to boot off the CD-ROM media first.

2. If the virtual disk drive was created as a SCSI disk, a driver may need to be added to the operating system installation. Windows will prompt for any third-party SCSI or RAID drivers that need to be installed. If SCSI was chosen, a driver dependency exists based on the SCSI adapter type (BusLogic or LSI Logic) and the guest operating system chosen. If the operating system does not have a built-in driver for the adapter, a floppy disk or floppy image containing the driver must be created. When prompted, click F6 and attach the floppy media to the virtual machine. When prompted for drivers, click S to specify a driver and then press <ENTER> once the floppy media is mounted. The driver will then be installed during the SCSI and RAID driver installation section of the operating system.

3. For this example, the virtual machine was created with a SCSI virtual disk and an LSI Logic SCSI adapter. Microsoft Windows Server 2003 contains a built-in driver for the LSI Logic controller, and therefore, does not need a third-party driver diskette.

4. If the vlance network adapter was enabled, an AMD PC/NET Family Ethernet Adapter would be detected and set up automatically. Since the operating system does not have a built-in driver for this network card, the device will not be configured until VMware Tools are installed and the vmxnet driver is added to the system.

5. Follow the installation steps according to the instructions on the screen just as if the operating system were being installed on a physical server.

 When the Windows installation finishes and reboots, to log in to the system, VMware remaps the Ctrl + Alt + Delete key combination to Ctrl + Alt + Insert. The key combination can also be passed to the virtual machine by using the menu system in VMRC, selecting Power > Send Ctrl-Alt-Del.

After the guest operating system installation is completed, VMware Tools should immediately be installed. To learn more about VMware Tools, see chapter 17.

VMware Tools for a Windows Installation

VMware Tools supports all Microsoft Windows guest operating systems. The detailed steps for installing VMware Tools vary from one version of Microsoft Windows to the next. The installation procedures listed below will follow along

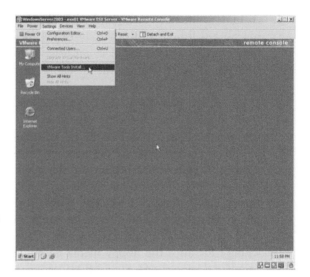

Figure 16.17 Starting the installation of VMware Tools for Windows.

with the previous example of a Microsoft Windows Server 2003 Standard Edition guest operating system. To install VMware Tools, follow these steps:

1. After the virtual machine is powered on, connect to the virtual machine using VMRC and log in to the virtual machine as an administrator.

2. Once the guest operating system has completely booted, click Settings > Install VMware Tools (see Figure 16.17).

   The system prompts with a warning message stating the guest operating system must be running to continue. Since the virtual machine is powered on and an administrator account is logged in, click Install to continue (see Figure 16.18).

Figure 16.18 VMware Tools installation warning message.

3. If autorun is not enabled in the guest operating system, the VMware Tools installer must be launched manually. Click Start > Run and enter D:\setup\setup.exe (where D: is the drive letter of the first virtual CD-ROM drive). The installation Wizard launches the application and the VMware Tools welcome page appears (see Figure 16.19).

Figure 16.19   VMware Tools installation Wizard splash screen.

Figure 16.20   VMware Tools installation Wizard welcome screen.

Once the VMware Tools installation Wizard has finished initializing, the welcome screen is displayed (see Figure 16.20).

Click Next to begin the installation of VMware Tools.

 A physical CD-ROM drive or physical media is not needed to install VMware Tools. The tools are supplied by VMware and are located on an ISO image that is copied to the host server during the ESX Server installation. When VMware Tools are installed, the ISO image is automatically mounted to the virtual machine. Once the tools installation is complete, the ISO image will unmount itself from the virtual CD-ROM drive, which then returns to its previous state.

4. The Setup Type dialog box appears and offers three installation choices: Typical, Complete, and Custom (see Figure 16.21).

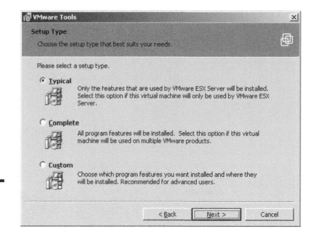

Figure 16.21 VMware Tools setup type selection screen.

- Typical—A typical installation only installs the features that are used by VMware ESX Server. Unless the virtual machine image is going to be shared with a Workstation environment, the typical installation method is an appropriate choice.
- Complete—A complete installation installs all program features. The complete installation should be selected if the virtual machine is going to be shared with a Workstation environment. The install adds features that are supported in other platforms, but not ESX Server.
- Custom—A custom installation gives control over which individual features are installed and where they are installed. The installer can always be run again at a later time to add or remove individual features.

    In this example, select the Typical installation and click Next to continue.

5. The Wizard is now ready to begin installation (see Figure 16.22). This is the last opportunity to make any changes to the VMware Tools installa-

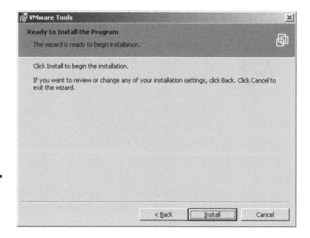

Figure 16.22 VMware Tools ready to install confirmation screen.

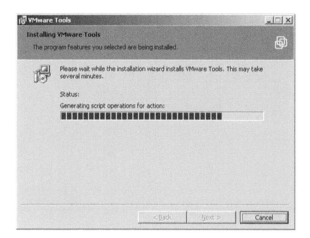

Figure 16.23   Installing VMware Tools.

tion. To make changes, click Back until the dialog screen appears where changes are needed.

If no changes are necessary, click Install to begin the installation.

6. The installer begins copying files (see Figure 16.23).

When the installer begins to install the virtual drivers, one or more Digital Signature Not Found dialog boxes may appear. The virtual drivers are safe to install, and the installer can be safely allowed to continue.

7. After the installer finishes installing the drivers, a second dialog box appears warning hardware acceleration may not be enabled in the virtual machine (see Figure 16.24). To increase mouse and video performance, hardware acceleration should be enabled.

Click Yes. The installer will open a Notepad window with instructions as well as the Display Properties window (see Figure 16.25). The Notepad window can be closed.

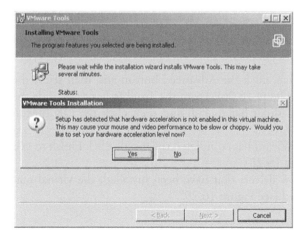

Figure 16.24   VMware Tools hardware acceleration warning.

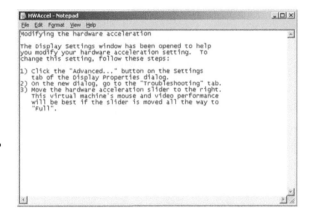

Figure 16.25 Notepad window with hardware acceleration setting instructions.

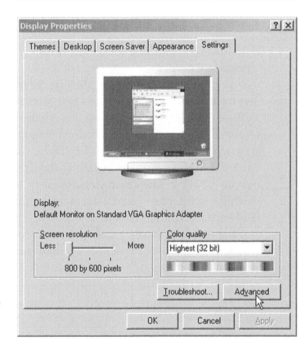

Figure 16.26 Display Properties dialog box.

From the Settings tab, click the Advanced button and then select the Troubleshoot tab (see Figure 16.26). From the Troubleshoot tab, slide the Hardware acceleration slider bar to Full and then click the OK button (see Figure 16.27).

8. Once the installation Wizard has completed the install, click Finish to exit the Wizard. (see Figure 16.28)

To initialize any new drivers that have been installed, the virtual machine must be rebooted (see Figure 16.29).

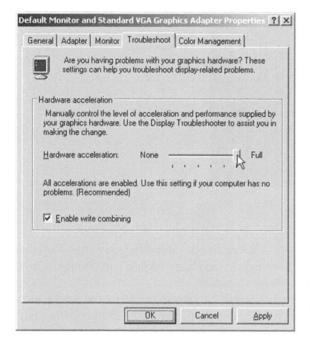

Figure 16.27   Setting the hardware acceleration properties.

Figure 16.28   VMware Tools installation Wizard completed.

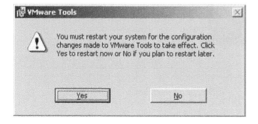

Figure 16.29   VMware Tools prompt to reboot.

Figure 16.30 VMware Tools After Installation dialog box.

Before rebooting the virtual machine at this point, you may see another dialog box titled After Installation (see Figure 16.30), containing the message, After installation, please click Next.

In this case, ignore the prompt to reboot the virtual machine for a moment and click the Next button on the After Installation dialog box. The dialog box will issue a warning message (see Figure 16.31). Click the Finish button.

Reboot the virtual machine either by clicking the Yes button on the VMware Tools dialog box prompting for the reboot of the virtual machine (see Figure 16.29) or by manually restarting the virtual machine using the normal means. After the virtual machine has been rebooted, the installation of VMware Tools has been completed.

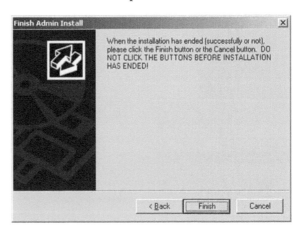

Figure 16.31 VMware Tools Finish Admin Install.

The installation of VMware Tools in a virtual machine is a one time event. After the installation, the enhanced drivers and features that were added will be used by the guest operating system just like any other driver updates performed on a physical server. VMware Tools should be installed in every individual virtual machine as well as any template images that may be created. It is possible for new, updated versions of VMware Tools to get released. If that happens, the tools can be removed, added, or upgraded like many other Windows applications.

Installing a Linux Guest Operating System

As noted in the Windows installation above, the installation media must first be loaded into the machine. Once the media has been inserted, the virtual machine can be powered on to begin the install.

We will demonstrate an installation of Red Hat Linux 9.0.

1. Once the Red Hat Linux 9.0 media is mounted, power on the virtual machine by clicking the Power On button.
2. As long as the boot order in the BIOS has not been changed, the virtual machine will boot from the CD-ROM media and the Red Hat installation begins. If CD-ROM is not listed before hard disk, update the BIOS boot order to allow the virtual machine to boot off the CD-ROM media.

   Red Hat Linux 9.0 needs to be installed using the text mode installer. Choose the text mode installer by typing linux text and then press <ENTER>.
3. Follow the installation steps according to the instructions on the screen just as if the operating system were being installed on a physical server. To ensure a successful installation, follow the choices outlined in the following steps.
4. Choose the language that should be used during the installation process. Then choose the model of keyboard that is attached to the host server. In this example, the English language was selected and US was chosen as the keyboard selection.
5. The next screen is the Mouse Selection screen. The two best selections here are Generic - 3 Button Mouse (PS/2) (select Emulate 3 Buttons for three button mouse support in the virtual machine) or Generic Wheel Mouse (PS/2) (if a wheel mouse is connected). In this example, a generic wheel mouse is selected.
6. For Installation Type, choose either Workstation or Server. This is a high-level detail as to what types of software will be installed on the virtual machine. A more fine grained packaging selection comes later in the install. For this example, Server is selected.

7. A warning message may appear stating the partition table is unreadable, as in Figure 16.5. It simply means that the virtual hard drive needs to be partitioned and formatted before the installation can take place. Select Yes to initialize and erase all the data on the virtual hard drive. It does not affect the physical hard disk on the host server.

8. If the virtual machine was configured with a network configuration, LAN settings can be configured in the Network Configuration screen. Either bootp/dhcp can be selected to allow DHCP to automatically assign TCP/IP settings or the networking settings can be manually entered.

9. In the Video Card Configuration screen, select the Skip X Configuration option.

   After the guest operating system installation is completed, VMware Tools should immediately be installed.

VMware Tools for a Linux Installation

VMware Tools supports many different flavors of the Linux guest operating system. The detailed steps for installing VMware Tools can vary from one version or flavor of Linux to the next. The installation procedures listed below will follow along with the example of a Red Hat Linux 9.0 guest operating system. To install VMware Tools, follow these steps:

1. After the virtual machine is powered on, log in to the virtual machine as root.

2. Once the guest operating system has settled down, click VM > Install VMware Tools. The system prompts with a warning message stating the guest operating system must be running to continue. Since the virtual machine is powered on and the root account is logged in, click Install to continue.

 VMware Tools for a Linux guest operating system must be executed while the system is running in text mode. VMware Tools cannot be installed from a terminal in a GUI X session. If the virtual machine boots to an X server automatically, it can be switched to a text workspace by using the default keys - CTRL+ALT+SPACEBAR, release the SPACEBAR and press the function key (e.g., F2) for a new workspace.

3. As root, mount the VMware Tools ISO image, uncompress the installer while in the /tmp directory and then unmount the ISO image. In keeping with the example, the following steps are performed on a Red Hat Linux

9.0 installation, the commands should be modified to follow the conventions used for other Linux flavors:

```
mount /cdrom
cd /tmp
tar zxf /mnt/vmware-linux-tools.tar.gz
umount /mnt
```

 A physical CD-ROM drive or physical media is not needed to install VMware Tools. The tools are supplied by VMware and are located on an ISO image, which gets copied to the host server during the ESX Server installation.

4.   The VMware Tools installer is uncompressed to the vmware-tools-distrib folder. Change to that folder and run the installer.

```
cd vmware-tools-distrib
./vmware-install.pl
```

5.   The installer then prompts about default directories. In this example, accept the default directories by responding Yes to each question.
6.   Once the final directory is accepted, the VMware Tools configuration program should be executed. The system may ask about running the configuration program /usr/bin/vmware-config-tools.pl. It may prompt: Do you want this program to invoke the command for you now? If so, select Yes to allow the configuration program to execute. Otherwise, run the configuration program manually by entering:

```
./vmware-config-tools.pl
```

7.   To change the virtual machine's display resolution, select the number that corresponds to the desired resolution.
8.   The configuration is complete. Log out of the root account.
9.   Start X window to launch the graphical environment.
10. In a terminal session, launch the VMware Toolbox by executing the following command:

```
vmware-toolbox &
```

 The installation of VMware Tools in a virtual machine is a one time event. After the installation, the enhanced drivers and features that were added will be used by the guest operating system just like any other driver updates performed on a physical server. VMware Tools should be installed in every individual virtual machine as well as any template images that may be created. It is possible for new, updated versions of VMware Tools to be released. If that happens, the tools can be removed and added like many other Linux applications. To remove VMware Tools from the Linux guest operating system, log in as root and execute the following command:

```
./vmware-uninstall-tools.pl.
```

Summary

The most important part of the planning process is virtual machine creation. Knowledge of the virtual machine's role(s) and requirements before the creation of the virtual machine is very important. Many virtual machines and their installed operating systems can be reused and duplicated easily if the proper planning is put into place.

Remember that even though these virtual machines act and look very much like physical servers, there are certain caveats, and more importantly, features that virtual machines bring to the table. To take full advantage of these features, proper planning must take place.

Chapter 17

VMware ESX Server Advanced Topics

Continuing the study into the VMware ESX Server platform, this chapter provides platform-specific coverage of virtualization features including VMware Tools, virtual machines, hard drives, virtual networking, resource management and optimization techniques.

 VMware ESX Server can be used with disk storage that is local to each physical host server or with remote storage area networks (SAN). VMware ESX Server has many unique capabilities and features that exist only when connected and used primarily with a SAN. The subject of VMware ESX Server used with SAN technology comprises enough material for a complete book by itself and therefore will not be covered in depth in this book. For completeness, SAN-only-based features may be mentioned throughout this chapter where applicable, although no in-depth coverage will be provided. The most common configurations and uses of VMware ESX Server using local server storage are covered in depth.

VMware Tools

VMware ESX Server provides an optional set of virtualization platform extensions to its virtual machines in a package known as VMware Tools. VMware Tools contains a set of optimized, guest operating system-specific drivers and services designed to enhance the performance of virtual machines and add integrated features. Although virtual machines can be used without VMware Tools, it is highly recommended to install VMware Tools into supported guest operating systems to optimize not only overall performance of the virtual machine, but the usability and ultimately, the manageability of the virtual machine. VMware Tools is bundled with VMware ESX Server, but the package is not automatically installed into guest operating systems. It is recommended to install VMware Tools after the completion of the guest operating system installation in a virtual machine.

VMware Tools is platform-specific on three fronts. Each virtualization platform offered by VMware including VMware Workstation, VMware ESX Server, and VMware GSX Server has its own version of VMware Tools. Although each VMware platform-specific version of VMware Tools is very similar, they are not 100 percent compatible or interchangeable. This is the first front of differentiation. Aside from the different VMware platform-specific versions of VMware Tools, the second front of differentiation is that each version of VMware Tools within a given platform, such as VMware ESX Server differs from each other in supported features. The version of VMware Tools that ships with VMware ESX Server 1.5.2 for instance, is different from the version of VMware Tool that ships with VMware ESX Server 2.5.2. The third front of differentiation of VMware Tools is that VMware Tools is also specific to the guest operating system, supporting FreeBSD, Linux, Microsoft Windows, or Novell NetWare.

VMware Tools provides a set of optimized drivers that are specific to the virtual hardware presented to the virtual machines by ESX Server and also specific to the guest operating system. These drivers (and kernel modules) not only increase the overall performance of the virtual machine, but also enhance the stability of the virtual machine as well as provide a better user experience when working with the virtual machine using remote control technology, such as the VMware Remote Console application. The drivers provided by VMware Tools are akin to the drivers provided by the manufacturers of physical hardware, such as motherboard chipset drivers, video card drivers, keyboard drivers, and mouse drivers. VMware Tools allows the guest operating system to take full advantage of the resources and performance offered by ESX Server.

VMware Tools also provides a set of system services in addition to the optimized drivers in a component referred to as the VMware Tools service or the guest service. These services provide such features including a "heartbeat" signal, time synchronization, and automated scripts. The services provided by VMware Tools are only available if VMware Tools is installed and the VMware Tools service is running. These services are covered in more detail later in this chapter.

VMware ESX Server provides installation media for VMware Tools in the form of platform-specific ISO images. These ISO images are located in the /usr/lib/vmware/isoimages directory of ESX Server. The current version of ESX Server ships with four VMware Tools ISO images: freebsd.iso, linux.iso, windows.iso, and netware.iso. These ISO images can be mounted to a virtual machine as virtual CD/DVD-ROM media and accessed inside the virtual machine's guest operating system through the virtual CD/DVD-ROM drive.

When working with a virtual machine that has a Microsoft Windows-based guest operating system and when using VMware Remote Console (VMRC), the presence of VMware Tools will be discovered by the VMRC application once the virtual machine is fully booted. If it does not detect VMware Tools, VMRC will display a message at the bottom of its application window in the status bar area to inform the user that VMware Tools is not running. The exact message text is "VMware Tools is not running. Click on this text to install." The user can initiate the installation of VMware Tools inside the virtual machine's guest operating system by either clicking the VMware Tools message in the status bar of the VMRC application window or by clicking the Settings menu at the top of the VMRC application window and then by selecting the "VMware Tools Install…" option. Once one of the two methods has been invoked, the installation of VMware Tools will begin inside the guest operating system like magic. Behind the scenes, the media in the virtual machine's virtual CD/DVD-ROM device is temporarily changed to the VMware Tools ISO image for Microsoft Windows-based operating systems (/usr/lib/vmware/isoimages/windows.iso) and the installation program is automatically executed.

VMware Tools: Time Synchronization

The VMware Tools service provides the ability to synchronize the date and time of guest operating systems' clocks with the current system date and time of the ESX host server. When time synchronization between the virtual machine and the host server is enabled in VMware Tools, the date and time value in the virtual machine's guest operating system is updated once every second. Time synchronization is important when virtual machines are resumed after being suspended or after having their redo logs committed as well as for time-sensitive software that may be installed within the virtual machine. It is generally recommended to only use one method of time synchronization within a virtual machine. It is usually better to have the virtual machine synchronize its time with the ESX host server using the VMware Tools service time synchronization feature unless the virtual machine is acting as a domain controller, in which case the virtual machine should have the VMware Tools time synchronization feature disabled and use another means of time synchronization such as an NTP client. If one or more virtual machines on an ESX host server are using the VMware Tools time synchronization feature, the ESX host server's Service Console should have its system clock synchronized externally by using a scheduled NTP client or by some other means. The system clock in the ESX Server Service Console tends to drift over time and should always be synchronized to ensure not only that its hosted virtual machines are properly synchronized, but also to ensure valid timestamps in log file entries. When time synchronization is used, the VMware Tools service must run under an account that has administrative or root privileges. Under Windows-based operating systems, the Local System account is used by default and satisfies this requirement. In Linux-based operating systems, the toolbox should run under the root account.

VMware Tools: Heartbeat Service

The VMware Tools service automatically sends a heartbeat signal to the ESX host server so that ESX Server can determine if the guest operating system inside a virtual machine is running. Virtual machines that do not have VMware Tools installed or those that may have the VMware Tool service disabled will not transmit the heartbeat to the ESX host server.

The Web-based VMware Management Interface for an ESX host server displays each virtual machine's heartbeat status as a small, vertical bar graph. The graph displays the average percentage of heartbeats received from a guest operating system's VMware Tools service in the previous minute. This value is used as a quick method of determining the overall health of a virtual machine. A virtual machine that has a heavy load placed upon it may not send 100 percent of the expected heartbeat signals, even under normal operating conditions. The bar graph has three color states when receiving heartbeats: red, yellow, and green. Red is displayed when a very low number of heartbeats have been received relative to the number of heartbeats expected. Only one of the three bars will be displayed when the graph is red. This occurs when a virtual machine has just been started and the expected number of heartbeats is unknown or when a virtual machine sends a very low number of heartbeats, which could be a sign of trouble. Yellow is displayed when the number of heartbeats is below normal, but not yet critical. Only two of the three bars in the graph are displayed when the graph is yellow. Green is displayed when the expected number of heartbeats is received. All three of the bars in the graph as displayed when the graph is green. The graph will be disabled and will be shown in a grayed-out color when heartbeats cannot be received. This occurs when the virtual machine is powered off, has just been powered on but the VMware Tools service has not yet been started, the VMware Tools service is not running (such as when it is manually stopped or disabled), or when the virtual machine does not have VMware Tools installed.

VMware Tools: Clipboard Integration

When accessing a virtual machine through the VMware Remote Console application (VMRC), clipboard integration is enabled if the virtual machine has VMware Tools installed. This allows data to be exchanged between the virtual machine and the computer running VMRC using the clipboard's cut, copy, and paste operations. When exchanging data between a virtual machine and a computer both running a Windows-based guest operating system, the normal Windows clipboard functions are available between the two computers across the VMRC boundary. When exchanging clipboard data with a virtual machine running a Linux-based operating system, the Linux-based operating system must be running X-Windows as clipboard integration does not work with Linux-based operating systems running in command-line mode.

 Sometimes the clipboard integration feature fails to function when the keyboard and mouse are automatically captured or released when crossing the VMRC application window boundary. When exchanging data from the remote computer into the virtual machine using the clipboard, click the VRMC application's Power menu and then select the Grab Input (Ctrl + G) menu item to explicitly have the virtual machine grab the keyboard and mouse input as well as transfer the contents of the remote computer's clipboard to the clipboard of the virtual machine. When exchanging data from the virtual machine to the remote computer using the clipboard, explicitly release the mouse capture from the virtual machine by pressing Ctrl + Alt. This will also transfer the contents of the virtual machine's clipboard to the clipboard of the remote computer. If the clipboard is still not transferred between the computers, ensure that the virtual machine has an up-to-date version of VMware Tools installed and that the VMware Tools service is running.

VMware Tools: Obtaining Data from the ESX Host Server

It is possible for a virtual machine hosted on an ESX host server to obtain a custom, preset string value from the ESX host server. A string value can be specified in a virtual machine's configuration file (the config file, usually ending with the .vmx file extension), through the use of VMware Tools inside the virtual machine's guest operating system and a scripting language, such as a Windows batch file, Perl, or the Linux bash shell, this value can be queried. First, the value must be placed into the virtual machine config file. A new keyword named machine.id must be added to a new line in the config and its value must be set to any relevant string value, such as a meaningful unique identifier, an IP address, or some other value. Once the virtual machine is booted, a special command can be used inside the virtual machine's guest operating system to obtain the value.

For example, the config file for a virtual machine named WindowsServer2003, which is running the Microsoft Windows Server 2003 Standard Edition operating system, if created by the root account may be found in the default location:

```
/root/vmware/WindowsServer2003/ WindowsServer2003.
vmx
```

It is modified by adding the following line:

```
machine.id = "Jupiter 172.16.100.12"
```

The value of machine.id in this example is the host name of the virtual machine followed by a single space character followed by the IP address of the virtual machine. A script running inside the virtual machine's guest operating system can run a script to execute the following command-line to obtain the value:

```
VMwareService --cmd machine.id.get
```

If the virtual machine was running a Linux-based operating system such as Red Hat Linux 9, it would execute the following command-line to obtain the value:

```
/etc/vmware/vmware-guestd --cmd 'machine.id.get'
```

The custom script could use the commands above to obtain the value and use the value to change the host name and IP address of the virtual machine.

If the machine.id data exchanging feature is never needed, it is recommended to disable the feature. This can be done by modifying the config file for each virtual machine to include the following line:

```
isolation.tols.machine.id.get.disable = TRUE
```

This can and should be done for enhanced security purposes if the feature is not being used.

VMware Tools: Automated Scripts

VMware Tools allows the ability for custom scripts to be executed when certain events take place in the virtual machine's guest operating system. These events include power on, shut down, suspend, and resume. In order for custom scripts to be executed automatically upon these events, the VMware Tools service must be running in the virtual machine's guest operating system. The custom scripts can be enabled or disabled as needed.

A set of default custom scripts are automatically installed along with VMware Tools and they are also enabled by default. In a Windows-based guest operating system, these scripts do nothing upon power on and shut down, but if the virtual machine is using DHCP, the custom suspend script releases the IP address and the custom resume script renews the IP address.

Custom scripts for Windows must be Windows batch files. For Linux-based guest operating systems, they can be any executable file, such as a bash shell script or a Perl script. Each custom script is bound to one of the four power-state change events. More information regarding the setup of these custom scripts is detailed below in the VMware Tools Control Panel Interface and VMware Tools Toolbox Interface sections.

For the custom scripts to be executed successfully, the version of VMware Tools installed into the virtual machine's guest operating system must be of the current version supported by the version of VMware ESX Server on which the virtual machine is hosted. It cannot be an older version or a version of VMware Tools from another VMware platform, such as VMware GSX Server or VMware Workstation. Also, the VMware Tools service must be running in order to receive power state change event notification from ESX Server. Custom scripts are not supported for FreeBSD guest operating systems.

 It is recommended that instead of modifying the default custom scripts that you create new custom scripts outside of the VMware Tools installation directory. Anytime VMware Tools is reinstalled or updated to a new version, the default custom scripts are overwritten, causing any changes to them to be discarded. After reinstalling or upgrading VMware Tools in a guest operating system that is using custom scripts, you should always ensure that VMware Tools is still pointing to your custom scripts and not the default scripts.

Additionally, virtual machines running Linux-based operating systems may also specify a custom script that is executed when the virtual machine is powered off or reset. This can be configured by modifying the following file in the Linux-based guest operating system:

```
/etc/vmware/dualconf.vm
```

The following command overrides the default command to be executed when the virtual machine is powered off:

```
/etc/vmware/vmware-guestd --halt-command <command>
```

The following command overrides the default command to be executed when the virtual machine is reset:

```
/etc/vmware/vmware-guestd --reboot-command
<command>
```

The <command> token represents the command to be executed when the power off or reset event occurs.

VMware Tools: Optimized Mouse

When using VMRC to access the desktop of a virtual machine with VMware Tools installed, full mouse integration is enabled. This allows the mouse to move freely between the remote computer and the remotely controlled virtual machine, automatically performing the mouse capture inside the VMRC window and automatically releasing the mouse when leaving the VMRC window boundaries. For virtual machines that do not have VMware Tools installed, automatic mouse capture and release (also called mouse grabbing and ungrabbing or input grabbing) does not occur automatically. In this case, the user must explicitly click into the VMRC window over a portion of the window displaying the virtual machine's desktop in order to perform a mouse capture or use the VMRC application's Power menu and then selecting the Grab Input (Ctrl + G) option. Without VMware Tools, the user must explicitly press the Ctrl + Alt key combination to release mouse capture from the virtual machine.

VMware Tools: Optimized Display

When VMware Tools is installed, the VMware SVGA II display adapter is installed. This allows for higher graphics resolutions and color-depths to be supported in the virtual machine's desktop, especially when using the VMRC application to access the virtual machine. The display performance of the virtual machine is also greatly enhanced.

 In Windows-based guest operating systems, better mouse-tracking performance can be gained by modifying the hardware acceleration of the virtual display adapter, which is at its lowest supported setting by default.

1. Click the Start button on the Windows taskbar.
2. Open the Control Panel.
3. Open the Display applet in the Control Panel.
4. Click on the Settings tab in the Display Properties dialog box.
5. Click on the Advanced button near the bottom of the Display Properties dialog box.
6. Click the Troubleshooting tab.
7. Slide the hardware acceleration slider control to its maximum value (right-most position).
8. Click the OK button.
9. Click the OK button.

VMware Tools: Optimized Network Adapter

By default, ESX Server virtual machines are created with a single vlance network adapter. The vlance virtual network adapter is a low-performance, high-compatibility network adapter that will work with most guest operating systems. It emulates an AMD PC/Net 32 NIC and its drivers are more widely supported. If the virtual machine is configured to use the vmxnet virtual network adapter, it must have VMware Tools installed because the vmxnet network adapter requires specialized drivers (supplied by VMware through VMware Tools) in order to provide enhanced performance. Generally, the performance gains provided by the vmxnet network adapter are only realized when using gigabit Ethernet adapters in the physical ESX host server. The vmxnet virtual network adapter is detected by the guest operating system as a VMware PCI Ethernet Adapter.

 If you plan on using the vmxnet virtual network adapter in your Windows-based guest operating systems, it is advisable to ensure that the virtual network adapter is set to vmxnet in ESX before you ever power on your virtual machine. An issue arises when a Windows-based virtual machine initially uses a vlance virtual network adapter and then is shut down, powered off, and has its network adapter changed to vmxnet. When this occurs, Windows detects the vmxnet network adapter as a completely new network adapter and thinks that the original network adapter is disconnected. The original vlance network adapter is hidden from view in Device Manager but still exists and still retains its network settings, including its TCP/IP stack configuration (IP address, subnet mask, gateway, DNS servers, WINS servers, etc.). The vlance network adapter has become what is referred to as a "Ghost NIC." The network connection name in Windows for the ghost NIC is most likely "Local Area Connection" and the name for the network connection of the current vmxnet network adapter is probably "Local Area Connection 2." Although this may not seem like a problem, when the current vmxnet network adapter is configured with the same TCP/IP configuration as the original vlance network adapter, Windows will issue a warning because it thinks that the vlance network adapter may be connected at some future time (and it will probably never be used again) and it contains the same exact TCP/IP information, mainly the IP address. This is called a local IP address conflict.

When this situation occurs, the best method of cleaning everything up is to open the Windows Device Manager, click on the View menu at the top of the window, and select the Show Hidden Devices option. On the right-hand panel, expand the Network Adapters node in the tree view and uninstall the vlance and the vmxnet network adapters from the system. Then reboot the virtual machine gracefully and allow Windows detect the vmxnet virtual network adapter.

The best method of changing virtual network adapter is to first uninstall the vlance network adapter, shut down the virtual machine, change the network adapter type to vmxnet in ESX, and power on the virtual machine. Using these steps will avoid the ghost NIC issue altogether.

VMware Tools: Windows Service

When VMware Tools is installed into Windows-based guest operating systems, a Windows service named VMware Tools Service is installed. This service provides the VMware Tools services described in this chapter. The service points to the VMwareService.exe file installed into the VMware Tools installation directory. By default, it runs under the Local System account, is enabled, and is set to start automatically.

VMware Tools: Windows Control Panel and Tray Icon

When VMware Tools is installed into Windows-based guest operating systems, a Windows Control Panel applet named VMware Tools is installed. It is displayed inside the Windows Control Panel. Another program, VMwareTray.exe is also installed. This places a VMware Tools icon in the Windows system tray (also called the notification area) that is located on the Windows taskbar near the system clock display. Either the VMware Tools Control Panel icon or the VMware Tools tar icon can be used to open the VMware Tools Properties interface. The VMware Tools Properties interface is used to configure VMware Tools in a virtual machine. Once opened, there are several tabs in the VMware Tools Properties interface window, all of which are described in detail below.

VMware Tools: Windows Properties Interface: Options Tab

The Options tab contains two settings in the Miscellaneous Options section in the form of checkboxes (see Figure 17.1). The first checkbox, "Time synchronization between the virtual machine and the console operating system,"

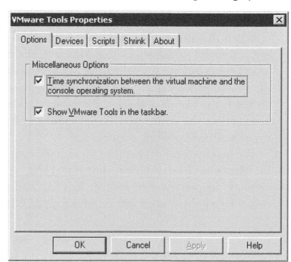

Figure 17.1 VMware Tools Options Tab (Windows).

enables time synchronization when checked and disables time synchronization when unchecked. The second checkbox, "Show VMware Tools in the taskbar," displays the VMware Tools icon in the system tray area of the Windows taskbar when checked and removes this icon from the system tray when unchecked. To open the VMware Tools Properties interface when VMware Tools icon is not displayed in the system tray area of the Windows taskbar, open the VMware Tools applet in the Windows Control Panel.

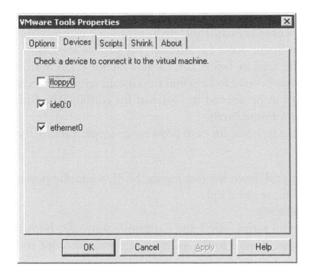

Figure 17.2   VMware Tools Devices Tab (Windows).

VMware Tools: Windows Properties Interface: Devices Tab

The Devices tab displays a list of virtual devices that can be connected and disconnected on-the-fly (see Figure 17.2). These devices are referred to as removable devices and include such virtual devices as the floppy drive, CD/DVD-ROM drives, and network adapters. Only the specific removable devices that appear in a virtual machine's configuration file prior to the virtual machine being powered on may be displayed in this list. Each device listed is associated with a checkbox that appears to the left of each device's label. When a device's checkbox is checked, the device is connected to the virtual machine and may be used. When a device's checkbox is unchecked, the device is disconnected and may not be used by the virtual machine. Alternately, these same settings can be accessed through the VMRC application's Devices menu.

Some removable devices may be mapped to a physical device on the ESX host server such as the floppy drive or a CD/DVD-ROM drive. You may receive an error message when attempting to connect and use a removable device because it may be in use by another virtual machine or the ESX host server itself (the Service Console).

VMware Tools: Windows Properties Interface: Scripts Tab

The Scripts tab configures the set of custom scripts executed in response to one of the four system power state change events: Suspend, Resume, Shut Down Guest, and Power On Guest. The four power states are listed in the drop-down list box labeled Script Event. For each script event listed in the Script Event field, the rest of the properties on the Scripts tab may be configured independently. These settings include enabling or disabling the script by checking or unchecking the Use Script checkbox respectively, setting the default script or a custom script by either selecting the mutually exclusive Default Script or Custom Script radio buttons. If the Custom Script option is selected, the path to the custom script may be specified in the textbox below the Custom Script radio button control. The Browse button may be used to help find the custom script. The Edit button allows a custom script to be opened in Notepad for editing. The Run Now button executes the script immediately.

Changes to the scripting can be made for each power state by performing the following steps:

1. From the Script Event pull down list (see Figure 17.3), select the power state with which to associate the script.
2. Perform one of the following:
   a. To change to a custom script, select the Custom Script radio button and then click Browse. Browse to the location of the saved script and select it.
   b. To modify or customize a script, select either the Custom Script or Default Script radio button and point to the script to be modified. Click the Edit button to open the script into the default editor so that changes can be made to the script.

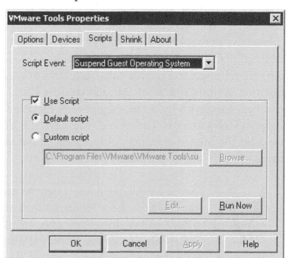

Figure 17.3   VMware Tools Scripts Tab (Windows).

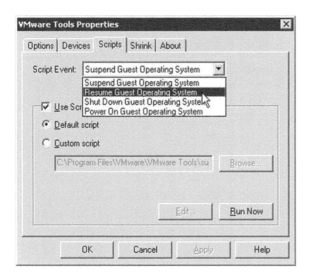

Figure 17.4   VMware Tools Scripts Tab Script Events (Windows).

    c. To test and verify the script, click the Run Now button once the script has been identified.

    d. To disable the script from running, select the Script Event and then uncheck the Use Script check box.

3.   Click Apply to save the settings (see Figure 17.4).

Before making any changes to the scripts, please read the Automated Scripts section above.

VMware Tools: Windows Properties Interface: Shrink Tab

In VMware ESX Server, all virtual hard disk files are fixed and do not grow and therefore cannot shrink as they can in VMware GSX Server. The Shrink tab (see Figure 17.5) in VMware Tools installed in a virtual machine hosted on an ESX host server provides the ability to perform the shrinking preparation inside the virtual machine's guest operating system. This is only useful in ESX Server when the virtual machine will be exported into GSX Server format. If the shrink preparation is performed prior to the export, the exported GSX Server disk files will consume the minimum amount of disk space required in the ESX host server's file system. In order to perform the shrink preparation, the hard disk(s) must be in persistent mode. VMware Tools will not allow the shrink preparation to take place on any disks that are not in persistent mode or are physical disks (see Figure 17.6).

Figure 17.5   VMware Tools Shrink Tab (Windows).

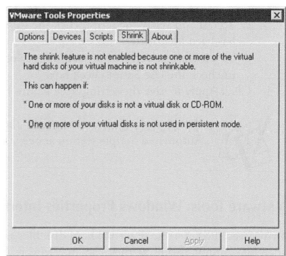

Figure 17.6   VMware Tools Shrink Tab Warning Message (Windows).

VMware Tools: Windows Properties Interface: About Tab

The About tab (see Figure 17.7) provides detailed information about the version of VMware Tools installed (the build number) as well as VMware's copyright and patent information. At the bottom of the tab is a line that indicates whether or not the VMware Tools Service is running. A handy button is also provided that will launch the default Web browser and navigate to VMware's Web site. The build number and the VMware Tools Service state information can be obtained from this screen very easily during troubleshooting.

Figure 17.7 VMware Tools About Tab (Windows).

VMware Tools: Linux Toolbox Interface

When VMware Tools is installed into Linux-based guest operating systems, several driver and program modules are installed. When running in an X-Windows environment, the graphical toolbox utility can be used to manage the VMware Tools options. The command, vmware-toolbox &, starts the VMware Tools Linux toolbox interface. The interface has four tabs that contain the options described below.

VMware Tools: Linux Toolbox Interface: Devices Tab

Much like the Windows version of VMware Tools, the Devices tab displays a list of virtual devices that can be connected and disconnected on-the-fly (see Figure 17.8) These devices are referred to as removable devices and include such virtual devices as the floppy drive, CD/DVD-ROM drives, and network adapters. Only the removable devices that appear in a virtual machine's configuration file prior to the virtual machine being powered are displayed in this list and must have a device present value of TRUE. Each device listed is associated with a tickbox that appears to the left of each device's label. When a device's tickbox is depressed, the device is connected to the virtual machine and may be used. When a device's checkbox is not depressed, the device is disconnected and may not be used by the virtual machine. Removable devices can also be accessed through the VMRC application's Devices menu.

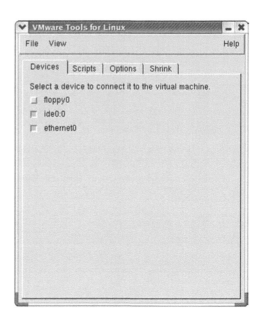

Figure 17.8   VMware Tools Options Tab (Linux).

VMware Tools: Linux Toolbox Interface: Scripts Tab

The Scripts tab (see Figure 17.9) displays a list of scripts executed during various virtual machine power events, such as suspend, resume, shut down, and power on. Each script has a tickbox to the left of its label. A depressed tickbox enables a script, while a tickbox that is not depressed disables the script.

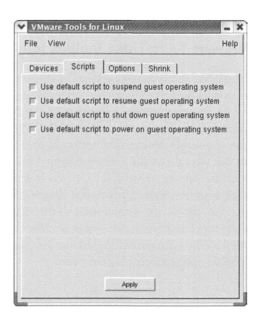

Figure 17.9   VMware Tools Devices Tab (Linux).

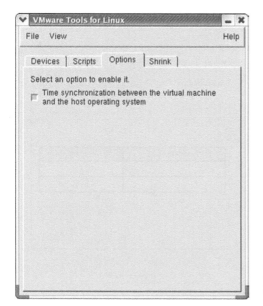

Figure 17.10 VMware Tools Scripts Tab (Linux).

VMware Tools: Linux Toolbox Interface: Options Tab

The Options tab (see Figure 17.10) contains a single tickbox for the time synchronization feature. The feature can be enabled or disabled by ticking or unticking the tickbox next to the setting's label. See the section on VMware Tools time synchronization above for more information about this feature.

VMware Tools: Linux Toolbox Interface: Shrink Tab

In VMware ESX Server, all virtual hard disk files are fixed, do not grow and, therefore, cannot shrink as they can in VMware GSX Server. The Shrink tab in VMware Tools (see Figure 17.11), which is installed in a virtual machine hosted on an ESX host server, provides the ability to perform the shrinking preparation inside the virtual machine's guest operating system. This is only useful in ESX Server when the virtual machine will be exported into GSX Server format. If the shrink preparation is performed prior to the export, the exported GSX Server disk files will consume the minimum amount of disk space required in the ESX host server's file system. In order to perform the shrink preparation, the hard disk(s) must be in persistent mode (see Figure 17.12). VMware Tools will not allow the shrink preparation to take place on any disks not in persistent mode or are physical disks.

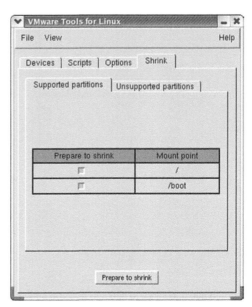

Figure 17.11 VMware Tools Shrink Tab (Linux).

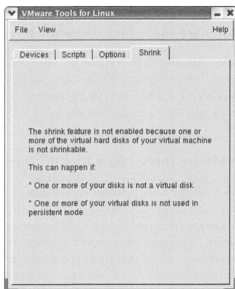

Figure 17.12 VMware Tools Shrink Tab (Linux).

Virtual Machines

Registering and Unregistering Virtual Machines

A virtual machine consists of at least a configuration file and a virtual disk file. Virtual machines can be moved from one ESX host server to another by moving these files. But the existence of these files alone is not enough to be able to manage and use the virtual machines in ESX Server. Virtual machines must be registered on an ESX Server before they can be started. Likewise, virtual machines should be unregistered from an ESX Server before being moved to another server. When a virtual machine is created using the Web-based MUI, it is automatically registered on that ESX Server. VMware ESX Server maintains a list of registered virtual machines in the file, /etc/vmware/vm-list, accessible through the Service Console. Instead of editing this file directly, however, ESX Server provides commands for registering and unregistering virtual machines.

To register a virtual machine, the following command is used:

```
# vmware-cmd -s register <CONFIG_FILE_PATH>/
<CONFIG_FILE_NAME>
```

<CONFIG_FILE_PATH> is the absolute path of the directory containing the configuration file.
<CONFIG_FILE_NAME> is the filename of the configuration file.

For example, to register a virtual machine named win2003std with its configuration file in the default location, the following command may be used:

```
# vmware-cmd -s register /root/vmware/win2003std/
win2003std.vmx
```

To unregister a virtual machine, the following command is used:

```
# vmware-cmd -s unregister <CONFIG_FILE_PATH>/
<CONFIG_FILE_NAME>
```

<CONFIG_FILE_PATH> is the absolute path of the directory containing the configuration file.
<CONFIG_FILE_NAME> is the filename of the configuration file.

Using the same example from above, to unregister a virtual machine named win2003std with its configuration file in the default location, the following command may be used:

```
# vmware-cmd -s unregister /root/vmware/win-
2003std/win2003std.vmx
```

Before unregistering a virtual machine, it must be powered off. Virtual machine configuration files usually have the file extension .vmx but are not restricted from using another file extension. Older versions of VMware ESX Server used .cfg as the extension of a configuration file and this will still work with the current version of ESX Server.

Suspending and Resuming Virtual Machines

VMware ESX Server supports a feature whereby a running virtual machine to be suspended and then later resumed, picking back up from the point where it was suspended without rebooting. This is very similar to a laptop computer using a hibernation feature. When a running virtual machine is suspended, its current state, that is, its RAM is written to disk in a special file using a .vmss extension. This saved state file resides in the same VMFS volume as the virtual machine's disk file. Once a virtual machine has been suspended, it is similar to being powered off in that it is no longer consuming CPU or RAM resources. At a later date, the virtual machine can be resumed. Resuming a virtual machine reverts the process of suspending the virtual machine. It is powered on and its state is read from the .vmss file and the virtual machine picks up from the point where it was suspended. Suspend and resume are useful for quickly provisioning virtual machines such as a stand-by server, or in a testing environment to pause testing at a certain point and resume it later. There must be enough storage space available in the VMFS volume where the virtual machine's disk file resides to contain the amount of RAM allocated to the virtual machine before a suspend can take place. For example, if a virtual machine is configured with 1GB RAM, there must be at least 1GB of free space in the VMFS volume to contain the .vmss file, which will be slightly larger than 1GB. Virtual machine saved state files (.vmss files) can be stored in an alternate location if desired by editing the virtual machine through the Web-based MUI and selecting an alternate storage path.

Virtual machines can be suspended or resumed by using either the Web-based MUI or through the VMRC application. Once a virtual machine is suspended, the virtual machine should not be edited or changed in any way. Its configuration file should not be modified. Virtual machines that have been modified while suspended may not resume correctly and may become corrupt.

Repeatable Resume

VMware ESX Server also supports another version of suspend and resume named repeatable resume. Repeatable resume allows a virtual machine to be permanently locked into the suspended state at the time the virtual machine is suspended. Every time the virtual machine is resumed thereafter, it will always resume from the state created at the point of the original suspend operation. To enable repeatable resume for a virtual machine, use the Service Console to edit the virtual machine's configuration file and add the following line:

```
resume.repeatable = "TRUE"
```

Once the virtual machine's configuration file has been modified and saved, the virtual machine will create a permanent .vmss file upon its next suspend operation. Thereafter, all resume operations will revert the virtual machine at the original suspended state.

VMFS

VMware ESX Server uses a special file system to store the virtual disk files of virtual machines. This file system is named VMFS or Virtual Machine File System. It is a flat file system meaning that is does not have directories. Instead, all files are stored directly in the root of the file system. The virtual hard disk files of virtual machines must reside in a VMFS volume in order to run on ESX Server. VMFS offers a very lightweight, high-performance file system that does not impede the I/O operations for virtual hard disks. VMFS is an optimized file system for virtual machine hard disks.

There are currently two versions of the VMFS file system, VMFS-1 and VMFS-2. VMFS-1 file systems were available in the 1.x versions of VMware ESX Server. VMFS-2 file systems are preferred over VMFS-1 file systems and are available in the 2.0 and later versions of VMware ESX Server. VMFS-2 file systems can span multiple disk partitions and can be expanded over new disk partitions at a later time after the initial creation of the file system. VMFS-1 file systems can be upgraded to VMFS-2 file systems using the vmkfstools –T command.

Although VMFS file systems support very large file sizes, they impose a limit on the total number of files that can be stored in the file system. By default, this value is 256 files. This value can only be modified during the creation of the VMFS-2 file system using the vmkfstools -C command with the optional -n switch or when extending the file system over additional disk partitions using the vmkfstools -Z command with the optional -n switch. When extending VMFS-2 file systems over new disk partitions, if the optional -n switch is not used, an additional 64 files is automatically added to the current number of files limit. The total number of files value can exceed 256 files. This is an important limit to be aware of when designing systems that may have an excessive amount of disk files, redo log files, or suspended state files that will reside in the VMFS volume. Although VMFS volumes can store files of other types such as executable script files and ISO images, it is recommended that only virtual hard disk files, redo log files, suspended state files, and VM swap files reside in VMFS volumes.

Hard Disk Drives

VMware ESX Server virtual machines store their data within one or more hard disk drives in much the same manner of physical computers. In most cases, each virtual machine must have at least one bootable hard disk drive attached containing the core software components of the virtual machine's guest operating system. It is possible, however, to alternatively boot from an attached floppy diskette drive (either a physical floppy diskette drive or a virtual floppy diskette drive that uses a mounted floppy diskette image file), an attached CD/DVD-ROM drive (again, either a physical CD/DVD-ROM drive or a virtual CD/DVD-ROM drive that uses a mounted ISO-9660 image file), or from the network using PXE. The most common configuration is a virtual machine that has a single, bootable hard disk drive containing the guest operating system as well as other software applications and data.

Virtual machines hosted on the VMware ESX Server virtualization platform have several hard disk drive types available. These hard disk drives include virtual SCSI hard disk drives, physical SCSI hard disk drives, and raw LUNs residing on SANs. VMware ESX Server does not include support for virtual IDE hard disk drives like VMware GSX Server or Microsoft Virtual Server. VMware ESX Server does support up to four virtual IDE CD/DVD-ROM drives, however. When an ESX host server is using local storage, that is, storage that resides in or is directly attached to the physical ESX Server, virtual SCSI hard disk drives or physical hard disk drives (also referred to as raw disks) are available options. When an ESX host server utilizes the remote storage of a SAN, virtual SCSI hard disk drives and raw LUNs are available options. Depending upon the exact configuration of the physical host server, it is possible for a single virtual machine hosted within VMware ESX Server to have multiple hard disk drives attached of different types, however this is very unusual.

Raw Device Mappings

Hard disk drives attached to a virtual machine may be physical SCSI hard disk drives that reside in or are attached to the physical ESX host server. Although a single physical SCSI hard disk drive may be attached to a virtual machine, the raw drive does not necessarily have to be a single physical disk. It can also be a logical drive, such as those created by RAID arrays as long as the logical volume exports a valid SCSI serial number. When a physical SCSI hard disk drive is attached to a virtual machine, the virtual machine typically owns the entire disk and its storage capacity is completely allocated to the virtual machine. If the ESX hosts server is attached to a SAN, a raw LUN in the SAN can be attached as a hard disk drive to a virtual machine just like a physical SCSI hard disk drive. For simplicity, physical SCSI hard disk drives and raw LUNs will be referred to as raw devices herein. In previous versions of ESX Server, a raw device that was attached to a virtual machine was called a raw disk because the virtual machine had low-level, direct access to the physical disk drive (raw access). This is not necessarily the case with VMware ESX Server 2.5 and beyond. Instead, raw devices can be attached to a virtual machine using raw device mappings. When a raw device is attached to a virtual machine using raw device mappings, a mapping file that appears as a normal virtual disk file is created in the specified VMFS volume. The virtual machine attaches this mapping file as a SCSI hard disk in order to attach the raw device. All I/O is redirected to and from the raw device. The mapping file only contains metadata used to create the connection between the raw device and the virtual machine. Raw devices can be connected using one of two compatibility mode: physical and virtual. Physical compatibility mode allows direct access to the raw device in much the same way as in versions of VMware ESX Server prior to version 2.5. Virtual compatibility mode allows the attached raw device to act in many ways like a virtual disk. In virtual mode, distributed file system features can be applied to the raw device such as locking and permissions. Raw devices attached in virtual compatibility mode can also have a redo log file just like a virtual disk (see the Virtual Hard Disks section below for details).

Raw devices are useful when high-performance I/O or a large storage capacity within a virtual machine is needed. For example, a virtual machine that runs a database server may use a virtual SCSI hard disk drive as its boot drive, containing the virtual machine's guest operating system and software applications. It may then have a second drive attached, a raw device, which is mapped to a physical, high-speed SCSI drive. The raw device contains the data housed by the database server that runs in the virtual machine.

Raw devices are also recommended to be used as the shared storage and quorum disks in a server cluster, either virtual-to-virtual or virtual-to-physical. Physical hard disk drives are uncommonly used because they effectively negate the benefits of a flexible and shared storage system. They are typically used for specialty applications only, including virtual-to-virtual clustering and virtual-to-physical clustering. The loss of storage flexibility when using raw devices as compared to using virtual SCSI hard disk drives also increases the overall cost of the VMware ESX Server implementation. Raw devices cannot have redo logs when configured in the physical compatibility mode and can only work with physical or logical devices that export a valid SCSI serial number. Because of this limitation, raw device mappings may not work with many block-level storage and RAID devices.

For more information regarding raw device mapping in VMware ESX Server, see the VMware white paper, ESX Server raw Device Mapping available at the following URL.

http://www.vmware.com/pdf/esx25_rawdevicemapping.pdf.

Virtual SCSI Hard Disk Drives

The most common hard disk drive type used in VMware ESX Server virtual machines are virtual SCSI hard disk drives, simply referred to as virtual disks. Virtual disks are the most flexible hard disk drive type available to a virtual machine. Virtual disks in ESX Server appear to be SCSI hard disk drives to virtual machines. Each virtual disk is represented by a file residing on the host server.

This file also referred to as a disk file or an image file contains all of the contents of a virtual machine, including the guest operating system, software applications, data, and free space. Virtual machines must have at least one bootable hard disk drive and it is usually a virtual disk. Just like a physical servers, a virtual machine may have more than one hard disk attached, and therefore may have more than one virtual disk. Virtual disks in VMware ESX Server are always fixed in size. They consume the same amount of disk storage as the virtual disks maximum storage capacity. A 10GB virtual disk consumes 10GB of storage on the ESX host server even when it is completely empty. VMware ESX Server does not use sparse or dynamically expanding disks. Because of this, the trade-off has been made for fast I/O speed over more efficient disk storage methods. VMware ESX Server has no overhead in continuously expanding disks such as in VMware GSX Server or Microsoft Virtual Server. The size of the virtual disk's image file on the host server is the maximum size of the virtual disk. Virtual disks must have partitions created and file systems installed just as a physical disk drive would. Therefore, the usable storage space within the disk depends upon its partition structure. In VMware ESX Server, virtual disks must reside in a special file system named VMFS (Virtual Machine File System) when they are attached to a virtual machine. VMFS is a special file system unique to VMware ESX Server and provides a simplified and optimized file system on top of which the virtual disks reside. Virtual machines will not run if their virtual disks do not reside in a VMFS file system.

Virtual disks have many advantages over physical disks as listed below.

- Virtual disks can share a common storage area on each ESX host server.
- Virtual disks are very portable.
- Virtual disks enable simplified backup and restore operations.
- Virtual disks are easily cloned.
- Virtual disks can have their maximum size expanded or contracted.
- Virtual disks support distributed file system locking and permissions.
- Virtual disks may have redo logs.

Because they are actually files on the ESX host server, they can reside in a centralized storage location on each host server. Multiple virtual disks can reside in this storage location, sharing the overall storage capacity available in the VMFS file system. Because virtual disks are represented by an image file, they are portable. Virtual disks can easily be moved between ESX hosts servers using normal file copying methods. Virtual disk image files can also be copied onto backup servers very easily, which use the advantage of portability to gain huge advancements in terms of backup and restore capabilities. Virtual disk image files can be backed up and restored using simple file copying methods. Because of portability, virtual disk image files can be cloned very easily as well. Although cloning a virtual machine is a much more involved process than just simply copying image files, the fact that the virtual disk image files can be copied between systems eliminates the need of specialized disk cloning software in order to perform the fundamental step of transferring the disk's data during the cloning process. Physical disks have a fixed maximum size in terms of storage capacity. When a virtual disk is created on an ESX Server, its maximum size must be specified. Although the new virtual disk is a fixed disk with a set maximum storage capacity, it can have its size changed at a later date to either expand or contract (shrink) the virtual disk. There are caveats to consider before changing a virtual disk's size, but this feature adds flexibility above and beyond traditional physical servers. Because virtual disks are actually files that reside on the ESX hosts server, they can easily have distributed file system features applied to them including locking and permissions. VMware ESX Server exploits these features quite effectively, using them to implement features such as freezing a running virtual machine and dynamically adding a redo log supporting online backups of an entire virtual machine. File permissions are also used to effectively determine which users can access a virtual machine through the VMware ESX Server interfaces, including the Service Console, the Web-based MUI, and VMRC. Virtual disks may be configured to have redo logs. Redo logs are special disk files that reside in the same VMFS volume as the virtual disk image file on the ESX host server. All changes to the virtual disk are written to the redo log instead of the actual virtual disk file. The original virtual disk file effectively becomes read-only and the sum of the two files, the virtual disk image file and its redo log file together, becomes a single disk. The advantage of the redo log file is that the changes that are written to that file can either be discarded or can be merged back into the original virtual disk image file in a process referred to as committing. When a virtual disk's redo log file is discarded (deleted), it is basically reset back to the state it was in before the redo log file was created. This feature can be used to reset a virtual machine back to a known state after performing testing of a new software package, for example.

VMware ESX Server supports two types of virtual SCSI controller devices, the BusLogic SCSI controller and the LSI Logic SCSI controller. By default, new virtual machines are created using the Bus Logic SCSI controller except for those using Microsoft Windows Server 2003 guest operating system, which defaults to the LSI Logic SCSI controller. Most guest operating systems include a SCSI controller driver that is compatible with the BusLogic SCSI controller. The SCSI controller type used can be changed by editing the virtual machine's hardware, but doing so without loading a compatible driver into the guest operating system first may render the virtual machine unbootable. If the BusLogic SCSI controller must be used with Microsoft Windows XP or Microsoft Windows Server 2003 operating systems, the driver may be needed on a floppy diskette drive during the installation of the guest operating system. The BusLogic driver for Windows may be downloaded from VMware's Web site (http://www.vmware.com/download/downloadscsi.html) in a floppy disk image format that can be mounted to the virtual machine's floppy drive before booting into the Windows operating system installer.

It is also possible to change a virtual machine from using one SCSI controller type to another. The process is a bit more involved than just editing the virtual machine's hardware and changing the virtual SCSI controller type. Doing only this will likely render the virtual machine unbootable because it will not have the proper SCSI controller driver installed. The steps of a simple technique used to accomplish this task are listed below.

1. Shut down and power off the virtual machine.
2. From the Service Console, edit the virtual machine's configuration file in order to add a second SCSI controller of the other type.
3. Add another virtual disk to the virtual machine connected to the new SCSI controller.
4. Boot the virtual machine.
5. Install the drivers for the new SCSI controller.
6. Reboot the virtual machine.
7. Ensure that the new SCSI controller is working.
8. Shut down and power off the virtual machine.
9. From the Service Console, edit the virtual machine's configuration file, changing the original SCSI controller to the new type and remove the second SCSI controller.
10. Boot the virtual machine.
11. Verify that the virtual machine has booted and is working normally.

Virtual Disk Modes

Virtual disks in ESX Server have four different modes of operation listed below.

- Persistent
- Nonpersistent
- Undoable
- Append

These virtual disk modes affect how a virtual disk and its redo log file work. These modes can be applied to virtual disks as well as raw devices which are mapped using the virtual compatibility mode. The four available disk modes are mutually exclusive meaning that a virtual disk can only be in one mode at a time. The mode of a virtual disk only applies to a single virtual disk, not to the entire virtual machine; therefore, a virtual machine with multiple virtual disks can have each virtual disk in a different mode. The mode of a virtual disk can be edited using ESX Server's Web-based MUI. The virtual machine must be powered off before the mode of any attached disks can be changed. Redo log files are automatically created by VMware ESX Server when a virtual machine is powered on and has disks in a mode that uses redo log files (any mode except persistent mode). If the redo log file for a virtual disk already exists at power on, it is used and all new data that is written to the virtual disk is appended into the existing redo log file. If the redo log file does not exist, a new, blank redo log file is created. Redo log files reside in the same VMFS volume as their parent disk file and have the same name as their parent disk file with the additional file extension, .REDO, appended to the file's name. For example, the redo log file for a disk named win2003std.vmdk would be win2003std.vmdk.REDO. The .REDO extension is always capitalized and this does mater since the file system is case-sensitive.

Disks in persistent mode do not have redo log files and act much like a normal hard disk drive in that changes made to the disk are applied immediately. Changes cannot be discarded or undone outside of guest operating system features. This is the most common disk mode.

Disks in nonpersistent mode have a redo log file created automatically when the virtual machine is powered on and the redo log file is automatically discarded when the virtual machine is powered off, discarding all changes written to the virtual disk, resetting it back to its original state.

Disks in undoable mode behave exactly like disks in nonpersistent mode except that changes are not automatically discarded upon power off. Instead, the user is prompted to make a decision upon power off of the virtual machine as to whether the changes should be discarded or saved. Until a decision is made, the redo log file remains on the host server.

Disks in append mode store changes in a redo log file until the redo log file either deleted or until it is committed. Virtual machines with disks in append mode can safely be shut down, powered off, and restarted without fear of losing any changes. Append mode is the most common of the modes to use a redo log file. It is a good choice when performing testing or when installing new software or configurations because the virtual machine can be rebooted without discarding any of the changes in the redo logs and the redo logs can be easily discarded after testing in order to reset the test virtual machine back to its original state or to undo all changes made when installing new software or testing new configurations on other virtual machines if the operations did not work as expected. On the other hand, if the new software or test configurations work as desired, the redo logs can be committed into the virtual disk image file, becoming a permanent part of the disk.

To either discard or commit changes stored in a redo log file, the virtual machine must first be powered off. If the changes are to be discarded, a hard power off of the virtual machine can be performed without gracefully shutting down the virtual machine. This will not damage the guest operating system since the changes will be discarded and the virtual machine will be automatically reset to its original good state. To discard changes, simple use the Service Console to delete the redo log file of the virtual disk by issuing the following command:

```
# rm /vmfs/<VMHBA>/<DISK_FILENAME>.REDO
```

<VMHBA> is the vmhba LUN of the VMFS volume that contains the virtual disk files.

<DISK_FILENAME> is the filename of the virtual disk image file.

For example, if the virtual disk image file is named win2003std.vmdk and it is contained in a VMFS volume with a LUN of vmhba0:0:0:6, the absolute path to the redo log file would be: /vmfs/vmhba0:0:0:6/win2003std.vmdk. The command to remove the redo log file would be:

```
# rm /vmfs/vmhba0:0:0:6/win2003std.vmdk.REDO
```

Optionally, the rm -f command can also be used. The -f switch forces the deletion of the file without first prompting the user. The -f switch should be used with care.

To commit changes from a redo log file into the original virtual disk image file, use the Service Console and issue the following command:

```
# vmkfstools -m <VMHBA>:<DISK_FILENAME>.REDO
```

<VMHBA> is the vmhba LUN of the VMFS volume that contains the virtual disk files.

<DISK_FILENAME> is the filename of the virtual disk image file.

Using the same example from above, if the virtual disk image file is named win2003std.vmdk and it is contained in a VMFS volume with a LUN of vmhba0:0:0:6, the absolute path to the redo log file would be: /vmfs/vmhba0:0:0:6/win2003std.vmdk. The command to commit the redo log file would be:

```
# vmkfstools -m vmhba0:0:0:6:win2003std.vmdk.REDO
```

The vmkfstools command with the -m switch (commit command) will always prompt the user before actually starting the commit process. When the commit process is complete, the redo log file will be gone and all changes will have been merged into the original virtual disk image file.

Virtual disks can be expanded if more storage space is needed within the virtual disk. Of course, there must be at least enough storage capacity available in the VMFS volume that contains the virtual disk to be expanded. The act of expanding virtual disks is simple and does not impose very much risk as in shrinking virtual disks. Once the virtual disk is expanded, the virtual disk image file will have been expanded in size to reflect the new size of the virtual disk. The additional free space created in the virtual disk will be available, but will not likely be usable until the partitions within the virtual disk are expanded as well. This requires additional steps that take place within the guest operating system of the virtual machine after the virtual disk has been expanded in ESX Server. The command to expand a virtual disk is:

```
# vmkfstools -X <SIZE> <VMHBA>:<DISK_FILENAME>
```

<SIZE> is the new, full size of the disk followed by either M for megabytes or G for gigabytes.

<VMHBA> is the vmhba LUN of the VMFS volume that contains the virtual disk files.

<DISK_FILENAME> is the filename of the virtual disk image file to be expanded.

For example, if the virtual disk named win2003std.vmdk, currently 10GB in size needs to be expanded to 15GB, the following command would be used:

```
# vmkfstools -X 15G vmhba0:0:0:6:win2003std.vmdk
```

The virtual disk image file, win2003std.vmdk, would now be 15GB in size and would contain an extra 5GB of free space. Inside the guest operating system, a tool such as Microsoft's diskpart.exe or a third-party tool such as Acronis Partition Expert would have to be used to expand the partitions contained within the virtual disk in order to use the additional 5GB of free space in the virtual machine. In a Linux virtual machine, the fdisk command can be used to expand the partition into the free space.

Virtual disks can also be reduced in size, if necessary. Shrinking a virtual disk can only reduce the amount of free space within the disk. The virtual disk cannot be reduced in size more than the amount of free space because it would corrupt the disk. Shrinking virtual disks is really intended to be performed on disks that have an excessive amount of free space, such as a virtual disk which is 40GB in size and is only using 5GB of space can safely shrink to 10GB. The shrink process is similar to the virtual disk expansion process. However, some required prerequisite steps must be performed before the virtual disk can have the shrink command executed. The shrink process uses the following steps.

1. Boot the virtual machine.
2. Within the guest operating system, defragment the file system and compact the data on the disk.
3. Zero-out the free space in the disk using a third-party tool such as Eraser from within the virtual machine.
4. Resize the partitions contained within the virtual disk using a partition editing tool, shrinking the partition size and increasing the amount of free space within the virtual disk.
5. Gracefully shut down and power off the virtual machine.
6. Execute the shrink command from the Service Console.

The primary step is to compact the data within the virtual disk so that it is not spread out across the virtual disk image file. Once the files have been defragmented and compacted, the free space within the file system contained within the virtual disk needs to be zeroed-out. When files are deleted, the data contained within the deleted files usually remains intact on the disk. This file system uses special markers to know that the deleted files can be overwritten with new data as needed. In order to successfully shrink a virtual disk, that free space must be first overwritten with zero characters, or ASCII 0, null. The ESX Server virtual disk file format recognizes blocks of zeroed-out data as free space. Once the virtual disk has had its free space zeroed-out, its partitions must be resized, making them smaller. After the partitions have been resized, the exact amount of zeroed-out free space can be truncated from the virtual disk file. The virtual machine must be shut down and powered off before the shrink command can be executed. The shrink command is actually the same command used to expand a virtual disk, except that the desired size of the disk is smaller than the current size of the virtual disk image file. The command to shrink a virtual disk is:

```
# vmkfstools -X <SIZE> <VMHBA>:<DISK_FILENAME>
```

<SIZE> is the new, full size of the disk followed by either M for megabytes or G for gigabytes.

<VMHBA> is the vmhba LUN of the VMFS volume that contains the virtual disk files.

<DISK_FILENAME> is the filename of the virtual disk image file to be reduced in size.

For example, if the virtual disk named win2003std.vmdk that is currently 40GB in size needs to be reduced in size to 10GB, the following command would be used:

```
# vmkfstools -X 10G vmhba0:0:0:6:win2003std.vmdk
```

Of course, the main partition within the virtual disk would have been reduced in size by the same amount, removing 30GB of usable space. The calculations used to reduce the partition size must be exactly the same as those used to reduce the disk size through the vmkfstools command. Otherwise the partition could extend past the end of the disk, which will cause extensive SCSI errors in VMware ESX Server. If the partition ends at the same location as the end of the virtual disk or if the partition is smaller than the virtual disk, no errors will occur and the virtual machine should operate normally.

 When expanding or shrinking virtual hard disk images in ESX Server, you will have to edit the size of one of the partitions within the disk. When editing the partition, always ensure that the virtual hard disk image is attached to the virtual machine through which the partition edits will be performed in persistent mode so that the edits to the partition are applied immediately. It is always recommended to first make a backup of the virtual disk file before performing any of the expand or shrink operations upon the disk.

Some operating systems, such as Microsoft Windows, will not allow you to resize the system (or boot) partitions of the virtual machine. Additionally, you may not want to taint the image by installing third-party tools, such as the Eraser utility or one of many partition editing applications. To solve both of these issues, create a virtual machine that it used for utility purposes (a utility virtual machine). Install all of the necessary tools needed to operate on another virtual machine's hard disk drive into the utility virtual machine. Once you have built the utility virtual machine, shut it down, power it off, and then add the disk image that you want to edit as a secondary hard drive to the utility virtual machine. Again, ensure that the disk is attached in persistent mode. Boot the utility virtual machine and perform the required operations on the secondary hard disk drive, which may include defragmentation, zeroing out of the deleted data files, and/or resizing of one or more partitions within the virtual disk. When you are done, shut down and power off the utility virtual machine and remove the secondary hard disk drive. Be sure to keep your utility virtual machine handy for future expand or shrink operations. This technique keeps the tools separate from the image you want to expand or shrink without having to add them directly to the image.

Networking

VMware ESX Sever supports Ethernet network connectivity both to the Service Console and to virtual machines.By default, all networking components discussed are Ethernet-compatible networking components. A minimum of two physical network adapters is required in each physical host to enable networking for both the Service Console and for virtual machines. Up to sixteen physical network adapters are supported per ESX Server. Server network adapters that have two or more ports per adapter are each counted as a separate network adapter, therefore a physical server running ESX Server that has two embedded Ethernet ports plus one PCI dual server network adapter with two Ethernet ports, the ESX Server has four physical network adapters and could support up to twelve additional network adapters.

A minimum of two network adapters per ESX Server is required because the first network adapter discovered during the installation of ESX Server is allocated and dedicated to the Service Console by default. This network adapter is not shared with virtual machines by default and that is the recommended configuration. All physical network adapters detected beyond the first can either be allocated to the Service Console or to virtual machines. Therefore, an ESX Server with two physical network adapters will have the first network adapter allocated to the Service Console and will have the second network adapter allocated to virtual machines. In this scenario, all virtual machines networked externally from the ESX Server will have their traffic routed through the second network adapter, effectively sharing a single network adapter. Although this scenario describes a common minimal networking situation, many other networking configuration are possible that are much more advanced and can deliver features such as fault tolerance, multi-homing, and network isolation to the Service Console and virtual machines.

Networking Components

In VMware ESX Server, several components participate in the networking landscape. These components include:

- Physical network adapters allocated to the Service Console
- Physical network adapters allocated to virtual machines
- Physical network adapter teams
- Virtual network adapters
- Virtual switches
- Virtual networks

Physical Network Adapters in the Service Console

There is an important separation to be aware of between the physical network adapters that are allocated, or reserved, for the Service Console and those that are allocated to the VMKernel for use by virtual machines. By default, physical network adapters reside in one of these two namespaces and are completely isolated from one another. The Service Console cannot access the physical network adapters allocated to the VMKernel and virtual machines cannot access the physical network adapters allocated to the Service Console. This is a default configuration and may be changed, if needed.

Physical network adapters allocated to the Service Console are often referred to as Service Console NICs. The term, NIC, means network interface controller and is synonymous with the term, network adapter, a device used to connect a computer to a network, an Ethernet network in this case. Service Console NICs are used to communicate with the Service Console only. By default, the first physical network adapter discovered during installation is assigned to the Service Console. The Service Console requires a minimum of one physical network adapter in order to fully manage and use ESX Server including the MUI and VMRC.

Physical Network Adapters Allocated to Virtual Machines

The physical network adapters allocated to the VMKernel for use by virtual machines are referred to as either outbound adapters or, more commonly, as vmnics. The term, vmnic, is usually used all in lowercase and generically refers to any one of the physical network adapters allocated to the VMKernel. Specific vmnics are assigned a name based upon an incremental, zero-based numbering system using the format, vmnic<id>, where <id> is the number assigned to the specific vmnic. The first vmnic discovered is named vmnic0. The second vmnic discovered is named vmnic1, and so on. In the Web-based MUI, vmnics are often referred to as outbound adapters. The term, outbound adapter, refers generically to any of the physical network adapters allocated to the VMKernel, the vmnics. Specific outbound adapters are assigned a name based on the same numbering system as the vmnics (outbound adapters and vmnics are the same thing) and use the format, Outbound Adapter <id>, where <id> is the number assigned to the specific outbound adapter. Outbound Adapter 0 is the same physical network adapter as vmnic0, Outbound Adapter 1 is the same physical network adapter as vmnic1, and so on.

Currently, ESX Server supports the following physical network adapter hardware acceleration features:

- Checksum calculation
- TCP segmentation offloading
- VLAN tag processing

ESX Server can take advantage of the hardware acceleration features of physical network adapters allocated to the VMKernel only if the specific features are implemented in the physical network adapter card.

Physical network adapters allocated to the VMKernel can be configured using the MUI. Clicking on the Network Options link on the Options tab of the main window of the MUI will open the Network Connections window. From the Network Connections window, clicking on the Physical Adapters tab will display the list of physical network adapters allocated to the VMKernel and their current state. From this window, it can be determined if the link to each physical network adapter is up or down by looking at the Actual Speed, Duplex field. If the value is Not Connected, the physical network adapter does not currently have a link, meaning that there is no connectivity between the physical network adapter and a network. The Model and Location fields can be used to help map which Ethernet ports in the physical server are associated with which vmnics (or outbound adapters) in the system. The Configured Speed, Duplex field is used to match the physical network adapter's supported speed and duplex to that of the switch to which it is connected. By default, this value is set to Autonegotiate. This means that the physical network adapter and the switch to which it is connected will attempt to automatically determine and configure the optimum settings. This feature does not work well with all network switches. As a best practice, the Configured Speed, Duplex field should be set to the maximum supported value of both the physical network adapter and network switch to which it is connected. Additionally, the port on the network switch to which the physical network adapter is connected should be configured to the same, static speed and duplex settings in the switch. Setting a static value for speed and duplex at both the physical network adapter in ESX Server and at the network switch ensures trouble-free networking communications.

Physical Network Adapter Teams

ESX Server supports network adapter teaming that can provide load balancing and fault tolerance features to virtual machines without requiring special support by the guest operating systems of the virtual machines. Physical network adapters allocated to the VMKernel may optionally be configured to participate in network adapter teaming. Physical network adapters allocated to the Service Console cannot be configured in a team. Network adapter teaming is only supports for physical network adapters used by virtual machines in the current version of VMware ESX Server. ESX Server supports from two to ten physical network adapters per team. Each team forms a new logical network device called a bond. The term bond generically refers to a set of physical network adapters aggregated together into a team. Specific bonds are assigned a name which is based upon an incremental, zero-based numbering system using the format, bond<id>, where <id> is the number assigned to the specific bond. The first bond is named bond0, the second bond is named bond1, the third bond is named bond2, and so on. ESX Server can apply supported physical network adapter hardware acceleration features on if the supported features are common to all physical network adapters participating in a bond. This can affect the performance of a bond and physical network adapters should be carefully chosen when configuring network adapter teaming.

The primary benefits of network adapter teaming is that a team, or bond, performs load balancing on outgoing network traffic, provides an aggregated link that supports IEEE 820.3ad static link aggregation, and provides fault tolerance. If one of the network adapters in a bond becomes disconnected or fails, network traffic is automatically diverted away from that network adapter to the other network adapters in the bond. Because the link is aggregated, there is more potential bandwidth available in a bond versus a single network adapter. These benefits are immediately available to all virtual machines connected to the bond. The virtual machines do not require any special configuration nor does the guest operating system require any special drivers. The network adapter teaming benefits are provided transparently to the virtual machines and the configuration is controlled completely through the Service Console. Network adapter teaming works with both vlance and vmxnet virtual network adapters in virtual machines. Once a physical network adapter is configured as a member of a bond, it can no longer be used as a standalone network adapter. Instead, the bond device created should be used. For example, an ESX Server may have three vmnics available to virtual machines, vmnic0, vmnic1, and vmnic2. In this scenario, all three vmnics are physically connected to the same switch on the same physical network (same VLAN, if VLANS are considered). It is decided that all three network adapters will be configured as a team. A new bond is created that aggregates vmnic0, vmnic1, and vmnic 3. This bond is named bond0. The virtual switch that was previously bound to vmnic0 is changed to bind to bond0 instead. All virtual machines on the ESX Server are reconfigured to connect to the virtual switch that is bound to bond0. The other virtual switches that were bound to vnmic1 and vmnic2 are deleted. All virtual machines now benefit from network adapter teaming. In the data center, an engineer accidentally unplugs the network cable connecting vmnic1 to the switch. No loss of communication occurs because network traffic is routed to vmnic0 and vmnic2 during the outage on vmnic1. The engineer replaces the unplugged network cable and the link resorts back to vmnic1 and the network adapter team can now continue load balancing outgoing network traffic over vmnic1 again. If the network adapters had not been configured in a team, the virtual machines previously connected to the virtual switch bound to vmnic1 would have experienced a loss of connectivity during the outage of vmnic1. Those virtual machines did not experience an outage and had no knowledge that there was a loss of connectivity of a physical network adapter. It should also be noted that the configuration change from individual vmnics to using a network adapter team did not require any configuration changes or downtime of the virtual machines or their guest operating systems.

Virtual Network Adapters

Network adapters installed in virtual machines are referred to as virtual network adapters. Each virtual machine may have from zero to four virtual network adapters.

 In ESX Server, each virtual machine can have up to four virtual network adapters but you must be aware that each virtual network adapter uses one of the five total virtual PCI slots in the virtual machine. Each virtual SCSI controller installed in a virtual machine also requires one virtual PCI slot. Therefore, if there are four virtual network adapters installed in a virtual machine, there can only be one virtual SCSI controller installed in the same virtual machine.

ESX Server supports two different types of virtual network adapters, vlance and vmxnet. The vlance virtual network adapter emulates an AMD PCnet network adapter. It does not usually require any additional drivers in the virtual machine's guest operating system and is therefore highly compatible with many operating systems. Because the vlance network adapter is more of a generic network adapter, it is not optimized for high-performance networking and it will consume more CPU cycles from the guest operating system versus the vmxnet network adapter. Although the vlance network adapter appears as a 10/100 Ethernet adapter within the guest operating system, it is not strictly bound to this limit and data will transfer at the highest rate supported by the physical network adapter or the virtual network connected to the vlance network adapter.

The vmxnet virtual network adapter is an optimized, high-performance virtual network adapter that appears as a VMware PCI Network Adapter within a virtual machine's guest operating system. The vmxnet virtual network adapter is not as compatible as the vlance virtual network adapter. It requires a specialized driver within the guest operating system in order to work properly. The vmxnet driver is installed into the guest operating system when VMware Tools is installed. The higher performance is realized when virtual machines are connected to a gigabit Ethernet physical network adapter (1000Mbps) and use the vmxnet virtual network adapter. The vmxnet virtual network adapter is only supported in guest operating systems that are supported by VMware Tools.

Virtual Switches

Much like in physical networking, a network adapter is usually connected to a switch; a virtual network adapter is connected to a virtual switch. Virtual network adapters do not connect directly to physical network adapters (vmnics or bonds). They either do not have a connection, similar to a network adapter that is unplugged, or they are connected to a virtual switch.

In ESX Server, a virtual switch is a virtual device used to model a physical Ethernet network switch. Virtual switches reside in the ESX Server and are separate components from virtual machines. Virtual switches are identified by a name assigned to the virtual switch by the administrator when the virtual switch is created. Each virtual switch has 32 virtual switch ports, which means that each virtual switch can have up to 32 virtual network adapters connected. Virtual switches provide network connectivity between virtual machines and physical networks or they provide network connectivity internally between virtual machines only.

Virtual switches can be bound to physical network adapters (vmnics) or physical network adapter teams (bonds). A virtual switch bound to at least one vmnic or bond has a bridged connection to that vmnic or bond and all virtual network adapters connected to the virtual switch have access to the physical network connected through the vmnic or bond. This configuration provides physical network access to virtual machines.

Virtual switches not bound to a vmnic or bond are instead bound to a virtual device referred to as a vmnet. A vmnet is virtual device that represents a virtual network that does not have access to any external networks and can only route traffic internally between the virtual network adapters connected to the virtual switch to which it is bound. This configuration provides the ability to create private, isolated virtual networks that reside on a single ESX Server. The term, vmnet, generically refers to one of the vmnet virtual devices within an ESX Server. Specific vmnets are assigned a name based upon an incremental, zero-based numbering system using the format, vmnet_<id>, where <id> is the number assigned to the specific vmnet. The first vmnet created is named vmnet_0, the second vmnet created is named vmnet_1, and so on.

Virtual Networks

Virtual switches implicitly create a logical component referred to as a virtual network. The term, virtual network, in this context is separate and distinct from a vmnet device. A virtual network is a LAN created by all of the virtual network adapters connected to a virtual switch. Virtual networks may or may not have a binding to a physical network. Virtual networks are often identified by the name of the virtual switch used to facilitates the virtual network. It is common to use the terms, virtual switch and virtual network, interchangeably, although it is important to note that a virtual switch is a virtual device that is managed by ESX Server and that a virtual network is a conceptual entity.

The diagram show in Figure 17.13 depicts the networking components of VMware ESX Server.

ESX Server Networking Components Example

Figure 17.13 shows a physical server with six physical Ethernet network adapters installed. These are likely three dual-port Ethernet network adapters, but do not necessarily have to be. VMware ESX Server is installed on top of bare metal, that is, directly on the physical server. ESX Server always has a special virtual machine that is used to manage itself, the Service Console. The Service Console is directly bound to the first physical network adapter discovered during the ESX Server installation process. This network adapter appears as eth0 inside of the Service Console. This network adapter is completely isolated from virtual machines and can only be used by the Service Console, by default. The remaining five physical network adapters are bound to the VMKernel and can be used by virtual machines. They are abstracted internally as vmnic0, vmnic1, vmnic2, vmnic3, and vmnic4. A network adapter team has been configured and is named bond0. The network adapter team, bond0, is made up of 3 physical network adapters in this scenario: vmnic2, vmnic3, and vmnic4. The ESX Server has four virtual switches configured. Virtual Switch 0 is bound to vmnic0. Virtual Switch 1 is bound to vmnic1. Virtual Switch 2 is bound to bond0 , means that vmnic2, vmnic3, and vmnic4 are all bound to the virtual switch. Virtual Switch 3 is not bound to a physical network adapter; therefore it is bound to the internal vmnet_0 device, creating a virtual network that will route traffic internally

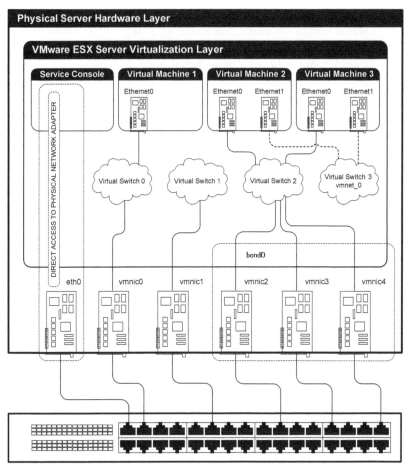

Figure 17.13   VMware ESX Server Networking Components.

between virtual network adapters connected to that virtual switch. There are three virtual machines configured on this ESX Server. Virtual Machine 1 has one virtual network adapter that is connected to Virtual Switch 0. Network traffic from Virtual Machine 1 will be routed through Virtual Switch 0 and on through vmnic0, if necessary. Note that Virtual Switch 1 does not have a virtual network adapter connected. No traffic will be present on Virtual Switch 1 and therefore no traffic will be present on vmnic1, the physical network adapter to which Virtual Switch 1 is bound. Virtual Machine 2 has two virtual network adapters installed. The first virtual network adapter, Ethernet0, is connected to Virtual Switch 2 and the second virtual network adapter, Ethernet1, is connected to Virtual Switch 3. Virtual Machine 3 has an identical network configuration as

Virtual Machine 2. These two virtual machines must be important because they both have their external network connections bound to Virtual Switch 2. Virtual Switch 2 is bound to bond0, which aggregates three physical network adapters. Bond0 could lose up to two physical network adapters without affecting the connectivity to Virtual Machine 2 and Virtual Machine 3. The second virtual network adapter in Virtual Machine 2 and Virtual Machine 3 are connected to Virtual Switch 3, which is a private network because Virtual Switch 3 is not bound to any physical network adapters in the server. Virtual Machine 2 and Virtual Machine 3 can communicate with each other over this link. It is possible that these two virtual machines are clustered and need a private network link in order to monitor each other. This diagram shows a fairly complex networking scenario that is possible with ESX Server, although even more complex configurations are possible.

MAC Addresses

Virtual network adapters can have one or more IP addresses assigned to them. This is completely configured and controlled by the virtual machine's guest operating system. Virtual network adapters must also have a MAC address just as if it were a physical network adapter. Physical network adapters have a globally unique MAC address permanently assigned to each card. Because virtual network adapters are created in software, their MAC addresses cannot be permanently assigned as in a physical network adapter. Instead, the MAC address is a configurable value assigned to each virtual network adapter either dynamically by ESX Server or statically by an administrator. Dynamic MAC addresses are automatically generated by ESX Server and static MAC addresses must be configured explicitly by an administrator for each virtual network adapter that requires a static MAC address. The value of a virtual network adapter's MAC address is stored within the virtual machine's configuration file. If a virtual machine has not been explicitly configured to use a static MAC address for a virtual network adapter, it will have a dynamically generated MAC address assigned to the virtual network adapter. There are three keyword/value pairs in the virtual machine's configuration file that specify the dynamically generated MAC address. They are as follows:

```
Ethernet<id>.addressType = "generated"

Ethernet<id>.generatedAddress = "00:0c:29:1e:
aa:94"

Ethernet<id>.generatedAddressOffset = "0"
```

The <id> token represents the id of the specific virtual network adapter. For virtual machines that have only one virtual network adapter, <id> usually equals 0 (Ethernet0). If a virtual machine has more than one virtual network adapter, the <id> of each virtual network adapter is incremented by 1. A virtual machine configured with two virtual network adapters will have a set of entries for Ethernet0 and another set of entries for Ethernet1 in its configuration file.

The Ethernet<id>.addressType keyword/value pair defines the type of MAC address that is assigned to the virtual network adapter. This keyword/value pair is used for dynamically generated MAC addresses and for static MAC addresses. If a dynamically generated MAC address is being used, the value is "generated." If a static MAC address is being used, the value is "static."

The Ethernet<id>.generatedAddress keyword/value pair contains the actual MAC address that has been dynamically generated and assigned to the virtual machine. This keyword/value is created automatically upon powering on the virtual machine when then Ethernet<id>.addressType keyword has a value of "generated." In ESX Server, dynamically generated MAC addresses always use 00:0C:29 as the first three bytes of the MAC address value. This is one of two Organizationally Unique Identifiers (OUI) assigned to VMware for use with virtual MAC addresses. VMware's other OUI, 00:50:56, is used for static MAC addresses.

The Ethernet<id>.generatedAddressOffset keyword/value pair is also required when using dynamically generated MAC addresses and its value is usually zero. This keyword/value is created automatically upon powering on the virtual machine when then Ethernet<id>.addressType keyword has a value of "generated." This value is the offset used against the virtual machine's UUID (Universally Unique Identifier) when generating MAC addresses.

ESX Server uses an algorithm for generating dynamic MAC addresses that attempts to create MAC address value unique not only within a single ESX Server, but also across ESX Servers. Each virtual machine has a keyword/value pair in its configuration file named uuid.location. This keyword/value pair contains the virtual machine's UUID, which is a 128-bit (16-byte) numeric value that is universally unique within its given context. This means that no other virtual machines will have the same UUID, even across multiple ESX Servers around the world. UUID (also referred to as GUID for Globally Unique Identifiers) generation is very common in many computing scenarios where an object should have a unique name across all space and time. In ESX Server, each virtual machine's UUID is based in part by the absolute path to the virtual machine's configuration file and by the ESX Server's SMBIOS UUID. If a conflict occurs when generating a dynamic MAC address on a single ESX Server, the Ethernet<id>.generatedAddressOffset value is incremented and the algorithm is generates a new MAC address. This iterative process repeats until a unique MAC address is generated. In almost all cases, the unique MAC address is generated on the first attempt. It is important to note that ESX Server cannot check for conflicting MAC addresses across multiple ESX Servers.

Instead of relying on ESX Server to create unique MAC addresses, it is possible to configure static MAC addresses for each virtual network adapter. Static MAC addresses must be explicitly configured by an administrator to be used.

Static MAC addresses in ESX Server must use the VMware OUI, 00:50:56 as the first 3 bytes of the static MAC address value. This is in stark contrast to Microsoft Virtual Server, which allows any MAC address value to be used without restrictions. Furthermore, ESX Server limits the range of allowable values for the fourth byte of static MAC addresses to the range 00 to 3F. Static MAC addresses must be within the following range: 00:50:56:00:00:00 to 00:50:56:3F:FF:FF.

To configure a virtual network adapter to use a static MAC address, the virtual machine's configuration file must be edited as follows.

- Remove the following keyword/value pairs:

    ```
    Ethernet<id>.generatedAddress
    Ethernet<id>.generatedAddressOffset
    ```

- Edit the following keyword/value pair:

    ```
    From:

    Ethernet<id>.addressType = "generated"
    To:
    Ethernet<id>.addressType = "static"
    ```

- Add the following keyword/value pair:

    ```
    Ethernet<id>.address = "<mac>"
    ```

In the listing above, <id> is the Ethernet adapter number of the virtual network adapter being configured with a static MAC address and <mac> is the value of the static MAC address using the format: OO:UU:II:XX:YY:ZZ where OO:UU: II represents the static MAC address OUI for VMware ESX Server, 00:50:56, and XX:YY:ZZ represents the unique MAC address value from 00:00:00 to 3F: FF:FF.

To configure a virtual network adapter to use a dynamically generated MAC address instead of a static MAC address, the virtual machine's configuration file must be edited as follows.

- Remove the following keyword/value pairs:

    ```
    Ethernet<id>.address
    ```

- Edit the following keyword/value pair:

    ```
    From:
    Ethernet<id>.addressType = "static"
    To:
    Ethernet<id>.addressType = "generated" )
    ```

The next time the virtual machine is powered on, the necessary keyword/value pairs that support a dynamically generated MAC address will automatically be added to the virtual machine's configuration file as well as the new, dynamically generated MAC address value.

In ESX Server, MAC address values are colon-delimited unlike Microsoft Virtual Server where MAC address values are hyphen-delimited. As a best practice, the values of MAC addresses should be in all upper case. Another best practice is to configure static MAC addresses for all virtual network adapters in all virtual machines and make the necessary configuration updates before the first time that the virtual machine is powered on. This reduces the chances of configuring the TCP/IP properties of a virtual machine with a dynamic MAC address and then later changing it to a static MAC address and confusing the network switch by ARPing the same IP address with two different MAC addresses.

It is extremely important that MAC addresses within a network are unique. It is a best practice to use a static, unique MAC address for every virtual network adapter across all physical servers, ESX Servers, and virtual machines in an entire data center. Even though MAC addresses realistically only need to be unique within an Ethernet collision domain, the isolation of some physical network switch's VLAN implementations can be suspect. Also, within ESX Server, although virtual switches do provide network isolation, if two isolated virtual switches have virtual network adapters connected which have the same MAC address, strange effects have been experienced even though the two conflicting MAC addresses could never "see" each other. Keeping all MAC addresses of all virtual network adapters 100 percent unique is a good method of eliminating potential and seemingly obscure network problems.

To determine the MAC address of a virtual network adapter within a virtual machine in the Service Console, open the virtual machine's configuration file with an editor such as emacs, vi, or nano in order to manually search for the MAC address value or use the cat command piped into a grep command such as:

```
# cat <config_file_path> | grep [Ee]thernet
[0-9].address
```

or

```
# cat <config_file_path> | grep [Ee]thernet
[0-9].generatedAddress
```

The <config_file_path> token is the path to the virtual machine's configuration file. The first command will output only lines for virtual network adapters containing a static MAC address and the second command will output only lines for virtual network adapters containing a dynamically generated MAC address for the specified virtual machine.

To determine the MAC address of the physical network adapter bound to the Service Console, use the ifconfig command and obtain the value from the ifconfig command's output for eth0, field HWaddr, or simply use the following command:

```
# ifconfig | grep eth0
```

The output from the command above should look similar to the following:

```
eth0 Link encap:Ethernet HWaddr 00:1C:03:B1:14:ED
```

The value following the string token, HWaddr, is the MAC address value of eth0.

The MAC address value of all physical network adapters allocated to the VM-Kernel for use by virtual machines cannot be easily determined because they are never used. The physical server does not have a valid TCP/IP stack bound to any of the vmnic network adapters, therefore their burned-in MAC addresses are never broadcast to the network. Virtual machines connected to virtual switches that are bound to the vmnic network adapters have a TCP/IP stack bound to the virtual network adapter bridged to the physical network adapter. The vmnics act like a bridge device in this context, connecting the external network to the virtual networks within an ESX Server. The MAC addresses of the virtual network adapters are broadcast to the network and for those virtual network adapters bound to external networks, their MAC addresses are broadcast to the physical networks to which they are bridged.

Promiscuous Mode

By default, virtual switches in ESX Server are not allowed to operate in promiscuous mode. This is done for security purposes, reducing the effectiveness of using packet sniffer and network analyzer applications from within a virtual machine. In some cases, there may be a legitimate need to enable promiscuous mode for a virtual switch. This should be done with care. Promiscuous mode can be enabled on virtual switches that are bound to a physical network adapter or a vmnet device. When promiscuous mode is enabled for a virtual switch bound to a physical network adapter, all virtual machines connected to the virtual switch have the potential of reading all packets sent across that network, from other virtual machines as well as any physical machines and other network devices. When promiscuous mode is enabled on a virtual switch not bound to a physical network adapter (one that is instead bound to a vmnet device), all virtual machines connected to the virtual switch have the potential of reading all packets sent across that network, that is, only from other virtual machine connected to the same virtual switch. There is no method of permanently enabling promiscuous mode for a virtual switch. To enable promiscuous mode for a virtual switch, a value is poked into a special virtual file in the /proc file system. This means that the value takes effect in memory only and is not persisted. Upon the next reboot of the ESX Server, the value will revert to its default value, which is to not enable promiscuous mode. Because the necessary virtual file in the /proc file system only exists when a virtual switch is connected to either a physical network adapter or a virtual network adapter, promiscuous mode can only be enabled on virtual switches not bound to a physical network adapter when a powered-on virtual machine has a virtual network adapter connected to the virtual switch. If a virtual switch not bound to physical network adapter has no live connections from virtual machines, the necessary /proc file does not exist and therefore the value cannot be modified. Virtual switches that do have a physical network adapter bound to it can have its promiscuous mode enabled or disabled at any time. Therefore, one method of persisting a virtual switch to have promiscuous mode enabled is to add the command that enables promiscuous mode to the /etc/rc.local boot script in the Service Console.

To determine if promiscuous mode is enabled or disabled, enter the following command in the Service Console using an account with root-level access:

```
# cat /proc/vmware/net/<device>/config | grep
PromiscuousAllowed
```

The <device> token represents the name of the network device being queried, either a vmnic, a vmnet, or a bond. For example, to query vmnic0 for its current promiscuous mode state:

```
# cat /proc/vmware/net/vmnic0/config | grep
PromiscuousAllowed

PromiscuousAllowed No
```

The output from this example displays that promiscuous mode is not enabled for vmnic0.

To change the promiscuous mode enabled state for a network device, use the following command:

```
# echo "PromiscuousAllowed <value>" > /proc/
vmware/net/<device>/config
```

The <value> token must be no to disable promiscuous mode or yes to enable promiscuous mode for the specified <device>. The <device> token represents the name of the network device being queried, either a vmnic, a vmnet, or a bond.

In the following example, vmnic0 is queried to determine if promiscuous mode is enabled. Next, a command is issued to enable promiscuous mode for vmnic0. Finally, the command of the original query is executed again to determine if the promiscuous mode state has been changed for vmnic0.

```
# cat /proc/vmware/net/vmnic0/config | grep
PromiscuousAllowed

PromiscuousAllowed No

# echo "PromiscuousAllowed yes" > /proc/vmware/
net/vmnic0/config
```

```
# cat /proc/vmware/net/vmnic0/config | grep
PromiscuousAllowed

PromiscuousAllowed Yes
```

If a vmnic or bond should have promiscuous mode enabled at all times, the command to enable promiscuous mode for the particular device can be added at the end of the/etc/rc.local boot script. This file can easily be edited using emacs, vi, or nano.

VLAN Tagging (Port Groups)

Virtual switches in ESX Server support the use of VLANs, Virtual Local Area Networks. This feature is also referred to as Port Groups in ESX Server. In the networking community, VLANs are very common as they provide a method of abstracting and isolating network segments from each other. VLAN technology is usually implemented in managed network switches. It is no surprise to discover that in ESX Server, VLANs are implemented as a feature of virtual switches. The term Port Groups is used synonymously with VLAN Tagging. In this context, the term port refers to a virtual Ethernet port in a virtual switch and is not to be confused with the term port as it is used in TCP/IP. VLAN Tagging allows groups of ports in a switch to be bound together to form a virtual local area network, or VLAN. The groups of switch ports defined with the same VLAN ID act as if they were on a dedicated switch and do not see traffic from other VLANs. The VLAN Tagging feature in ESX Server allows connections to virtual switches to belong to a VLAN, which can participate in VLANs external to the ESX Server environment in the physical network. By default, the VLAN Tagging feature is enabled in the VMKernel, but is not used until one or more Port Groups have been configured.

Resource Management

ESX Sever provides very rich facilities for resource management of virtual machines, including the Service Console. There are several techniques used to control and shape the amount of resources allocated to virtual machines. These techniques include:

- Shares
- CPU affinity
- Min/Max percentages
- Min/Max amounts
- Network traffic shaping

The resource management techniques listed above may be used independently or in combination to achieve the desired amount of performance from virtual machines. Most virtual machines should not require resource tweaking. The resource management features of ESX Server are designed to be applied to specific virtual machines that have a high sensitivity to performance.

The primary method used to control how much of a particular resource is given to a virtual machine at a particular point in time is the use of shares. The shares system applies to CPU, memory, and disk resources. By default, all virtual machines are created with an equal number of shares for CPU, memory, and disk. The default number of shares allocated per resource per virtual machine is 1000. Using this default setting, all virtual machines receive the same amount of resources. The default value of 1000 is considered to be the normal amount of shares. The shares system of resource allocation is proportional; therefore if the normal amount of shares is 1000, assigning 2000 shares of a particular resource for a virtual machine allocates double the amount of that resource for that virtual machine relative to the other virtual machines that have the normal amount of shares (1000). For example, consider an ESX Server with three virtual machines: Vm1, Vm2, and Vm3. Vm1 has 2000 CPU shares, Vm2 has 1000 CPU shares, and Vm3 has 500 CPU shares. Vm1 will receive twice the amount of CPU cycles then Vm2 and four times as many CPU cycles as Vm3. VM3 will receive half as many CPU cycles as Vm2. The same amount of CPU cycle would be allocated to the virtual machines if the shares allocated were set to the following values: Vm1 has 200 CPU shares, Vm2 has 100 CPU shares, and Vm3 has 50 CPU shares. This is due to the proportional or relative nature of the shares resource allocation system.

Most ESX Servers run on multiprocessor hardware system such as dual processor or quad processor servers. It is possible to assign virtual machines to run on specific processors. This feature is called CPU affinity. By default, virtual machines' instructions are load balanced across all processors in the server. ESX Server's scheduler determines which processors will execute particular instructions for virtual machines. Using the CPU affinity feature, it is possible to configure a virtual machine to run only on specific processors in the system. Using CPU affinity greatly reduces ESX Server's flexibility in the scheduler to provide optimum performance for all virtual machines.

Another technique used to control resource allocation to virtual machines is Min/Max percentages. ESX Server uses Min/Max percentages with CPU resources. In this scheme, virtual machines can be configured to receive a minimum and a maximum amount of CPU cycle by the overall percentage of CPU cycles available. This is often used to guarantee that a virtual machine receives a guaranteed minimum number of CPU cycles in order to avoid CPU starvation issues. Additionally, a virtual machine can be configured with a maximum of less than 100 percent to limit the amount of CPU cycles allocated to the virtual machine. This is often configured on very low priority virtual machines to avoid having those virtual machines consume too many CPU cycles. The Min/Max percentages can be used independently or together on specific virtual machines as needed. By default, virtual machines are created with a minimum CPU percentage of 0 percent and a maximum CPU percentage of 100 percent.

ESX Server uses the Min/Max amounts technique in addition to shares to control memory allocation for virtual machines. Virtual machines are always configured with an amount of memory. This value is the virtual machine's maximum amount of memory. Memory is allocated to virtual machines as they require it, based upon their shares, and the state of the virtual machine. Memory can be reclaimed and reallocated dynamically by ESX Server when a virtual machine is idle or frees up a block of previously allocated memory. Some virtual machines may require a minimum amount of memory to be always present. Virtual machines can have a minimum amount of memory allocated to them. Upon powering on the virtual machine, ESX Server will allocate the minimum amount of memory to the virtual machine. By default, virtual machines have a minimum memory value of zero. The more memory that is allocated as minimum memory to virtual machines reduces the effectiveness of ESX Server's memory management features.

ESX Server uses only the proportional shares technique to manage disk resources. Disk resources are measured in terms of disk bandwidth for each physical disk or LUN, each represented by a vmhba. The disk bandwidth is calculated in consumption units in which each SCSI command equals on consumption unit and the size of the data to be transferred is converted into a proportional number of additional consumption units. Additionally, each virtual machine may, by default, issue up to eight SCSI commands before being preempted by another virtual machine requesting disk access.

Network bandwidth resources are managed in a much different manner than other resources. Instead of using the proportional shares or Min/Max methods, network bandwidth is controlled by a pluggable network packet filter module. ESX Server ships and supports only one filter module at this time named nfshaper. This module implements a transmit filter that performs network traffic shaping on outgoing traffic. The nfshaper module can be attached and configured for each virtual machine. The traffic shaping feature implemented by the nfshaper module can be used to limit the average bandwidth, peak bandwidth, and the maximum burst size measured in bits per second (bps).

Performance Optimization

Here are some best practices that can be used to gain optimum performance for virtual machines hosted on an ESX Server:

- Ensure that the proper guest operating system type is configured for each virtual machine, Ensure that VMware Tools is properly installed and is up to date in each virtual machine. Before placing a virtual machine running Windows into production, defragment all virtual hard drives attached to the virtual machine. Configure virtual machines that run time-dependant services to have a minimum amount of CPU allocation to prevent CPU starvation. Disable or remove virtual hardware devices that are not needed or used by the guest operating system in each virtual machine. Stop and disable any unneeded services or daemons. Disable and software and operating system features that are not needed in the guest operating systems in each virtual machine. In Windows guest operating systems, disable screen savers, desktop backgrounds, and whiz-bang effects such as fading or sliding menus. In Linux guest operating systems, disable the X server if possible.

■ Allocate an exact amount of memory to each virtual machine. Another technique used to improve performance of virtual machines in ESX Server is to configure the maximum amount of memory for each virtual machine as the minimum amount of memory. This will effectively counteract the benefits of memory overloading in ESX Server and care must be taken to not allocate more memory than is physically available in the system (total amount of system RAM – 1GB is a good rule of thumb). This technique causes ESX Server to allocate an exact amount of physical RAM for each virtual machine upon powering on the virtual machine. The allocation process occurs slowly until the maximum amount of Ram has been allocated. This improves overall system performance because the VMKernel does not have to dynamically resize the amount of memory for virtual machines. Ensure that the Service Console is configured with enough memory. It is important to ensure that the Service Console has enough memory allocated relative to the number of virtual machines running concurrently and the number and types of system management and backup agents. Mware recommends 192MB for systems hosting up to 8 virtual machines, 272MB for up to 16 virtual machines, 384MB for up to 32 virtual machines, and 512MB for more than 32 virtual machines. This recommendation does not consider the amount and type of system management and backup agents that may be installed and running in the Service Console. As a best practice, configure an amount of memory for the Service Console that is at least one step higher than the recommended amount of memory for the amount of virtual machine that will be hosted. If the system will have more than 50 virtual machines registered, it is recommended to configure the maximum amount of memory for the Service Console, 800MB. Close all unused VMRC application windows as soon as possible. Each VMRC application window consumes CPU resources in the Service Console while it is connected. It is highly recommended to only open VMRC windows as needed and close them as soon as possible. Do not leave idle VMRC windows open for long period of time. Do not run CPU-intensive applications within the Service Console. Although the Service Console is designed to run system management and backup agents, it is not designed for heavy processing loads. The Service Console is a virtual machine itself which runs on CPU0. Although its CPU resources can be modified to enhance the Service Console's performance, it is recommended to keep programs with heavy processing loads out of the Service Console. Reduce the density of virtual machines running on each ESX Server. If there are many virtual machines running on one ESX Server that are consuming and severely competing for CPU, memory, or disk resources, consider reducing the density of virtual machines on the ESX Server by moving some of the virtual machine to another ESX Server. Although ESX Server is highly optimized and can run many virtual machines concurrently, it is still possible to stress one or more resources by having heavy processing virtual machines.

Summary

VMware ESX Server contains an amazing amount of features that can be used to create advanced virtualized systems in the data center. This chapter covered the most important advanced features that allow administrators and system engineers to quickly become familiar with ESX Server so that effective solutions can be quickly developed. By far, this chapter is not a definitive study into every advanced feature and capability of ESX Server because that amount of knowledge could easily fill many volumes. More detailed technical information on VMware ESX Server is available at http://www.vmware.com/vmtn/resources/esx_resources.html. This site contains links to documentation, white papers, and technical briefs regarding the current release of ESX Server. VMware ESX Server is continuously being advanced and many new advanced features are likely to be supported in the next major product release from VMware (ESX Server 3.0).

Part V

Implementing VMware GSX Server

Chapter 18

The VMware GSX Server Platform

VMware GSX Server is a widely distributed server virtualization platform, used mostly in smaller workgroup-sized server implementations. Available for both the Linux and Microsoft Windows platforms, this chapter will introduce the platform by detailing the history and background of the product as well as discussing the hardware and software requirements for both editions of the product.

Product Background

In 1999, VMware launched the release of their first product now known as VMware Workstation. This was considered by many to be the first commercially available virtualization platform on the x86-based architecture. In the years following its release, VMware has continued to mature their product line based around their patented virtual machine technology. Near the end of 2000, VMware significantly added to their product line by announcing VMware GSX Server 1.0. Through the years, VMware has upgraded and updated the GSX Server product to create a powerful, stable, and scalable server virtualization platform. As an added bonus, GSX Server also provides a direct upgrade path to VMware ESX Server, VMware's most powerful and scalable server virtualization product and is itself an upgrade path for VMware Workstation users. In April of 2004, VMware announced their 64-bit roadmap for virtualization. With the release of GSX Server 3.1, VMware completed the first milestone for their support of 64-bit computing. It was the first x86 server virtualization product to be released that added support for 64-bit host operating systems, which means there are 64-bit drivers present that allow installation of the product on x86 64-bit platforms. Unfortunately, VMware officially only supports 32-bit guest operating systems within a virtual machine running on a 64-bit host server. This does, however, make it possible to upgrade to 64-bit host operating systems and continue to run existing 32-bit operating systems in virtual machines. With the introduction of support for 64 bit guest operating systems within the VMware Workstation 5.5 release, it is only a matter of time before GSX Server adds official support as well.

VMware GSX Server is enterprise-class virtual infrastructure software designed to run on the x86-based server architecture. GSX Server transforms physical servers into a pool of as many as 64 virtual machines. The product runs as an application on a host operating system to provide a secure, uniform platform to easily deploy, manage, and remotely control multiple servers running as virtual machines. Guest operating systems and applications are isolated within multiple virtual machines residing on a single host server. This means that completely independent installations of Microsoft Windows, Linux, or Novell server operating systems and their applications can run side by side on a single x86 server, and at the same time, save on hardware and management costs. Since VMware GSX Server gives the VM direct access to the host server's resources (such as processor, memory, and disk), virtual machines deliver near-native performance. System resources are then allocated out to any virtual machine based on need to deliver maximum capacity utilization.

GSX Server is installed on a physical server that is running either Microsoft Windows or a Linux server operating system. Then, virtual machines are configured within the software much like a physical server would be. An operating system, known as a guest operating system, would then be installed on the virtual machine. These servers can be loaded with various guest operating systems including standard Microsoft Windows and Linux operating systems. VMware GSX Server handles the task of abstracting the real hardware and providing a virtual system platform for each virtual machine. Therefore, each virtual machine has its own virtual hardware, including a single processor system with an Intel 440BX motherboard complete with a Phoenix BIOS (version 4.0, release 6.0). Depending on the host server's capacity, up to 3.6GB of memory can be allocated to a virtual machine. Each virtual machine can also receive a SVGA graphics card, up to four IDE devices, up to 21 SCSI devices across three virtual SCSI controllers, up to two 1.44 MB floppy drives, up to four serial ports, two parallel ports and two 1.1 USB ports, as many as four virtual Ethernet cards and a virtual keyboard and mouse. Almost any physical device supported by the host operating system can be made available to a virtual machine as long as GSX Server supports it; GSX Server has the broadest device support among all other virtual machine software. Another advantage to using GSX Server is the ability to either bridge virtual LAN interfaces directly to the physical network adapter or to create up to nine virtual Ethernet switches. Creating virtual

Ethernet switches allows for better network isolation and faster communication between virtual machines.

An included suite of management tools makes configuring and managing virtual machines an easy task. For local management and configuration, VMware GSX Server provides the VMware GSX Server Management Console that runs on top of the host server. The local console allows creating, monitoring, stopping, starting, rebooting, and suspending virtual machines. It also allows the virtual machine to be viewed in full screen mode, which makes the virtual machine faster because it has exclusive access to the VM. One of the strengths of GSX Server is that it also allows for remote management. VMware provides either a Web-based management interface (connecting at http://<hostname>:8222) or the VMware Remote Console interface that can be installed on a user's desktop, giving the user the ability to view the virtual machine's display at another computer and controlling it across the network. Both the Web interface and the remote console support secure connections via SSL. In addition to the remote management interfaces, VMware also provides a VmCOM scripting API and a VmPerl Scripting API to automate the GSX Server management tasks.

Over the years, virtualization has continued to mature and therefore gain acceptance within the IT community. With the improvements that VMware has made to the GSX Server product, VMware has been able to earn a place in the software testing and development space within many organizations because of the speed and ease with which an environment can be created, discarded, and recreated. By utilizing these same techniques, VMware was also able to expand into software training and software demonstrations. Additionally, the improvements made to the product have dispelled any fears of using it to implement departmental server consolidation for both new and legacy applications.

Product Versions

VMware GSX Server is currently offered in two versions, based on the host operating system:

- VMware GSX Server for Windows—The host operating system this version installs on must be one of the supported Microsoft Windows operating systems discussed below.
- VMware GSX Server for Linux—The host operating system this version installs on must be one of the supported flavors of the Linux operating system discussed below.

Each product is independent of the other. If both host operating systems are needed, then both versions of VMware GSX Server must be purchased. While both products can be found on the same installation CD-ROM, each product has its own serial number and one cannot be used to install the other.

In addition to versioning the product by host operating system, VMware also further breaks the product down by versioning against the number of processors found within the host server. VMware sells these products, the Windows version and the Linux version, with the following CPU restrictions:

- GSX Server 2-CPU license: for smaller servers running either a single processor or a dual processor configuration
- GSX Server Unlimited CPU license: supports larger servers with up to 32 CPUs

 If the host server supports HyperThreading or contains a dual core (or multi-core) processor, it will not affect the CPU licensing. Therefore, while a host server containing two physical processors that support HyperThreading may appear to the host operating system as a quad processor server, VMware is only concerned with the number of physical processors per socket when determining licensing packages.

 VMware GSX Server has the broadest hardware compatibility and support for the largest array of guest operating systems of any x86 server virtualization platforms on the market (see Figure 18.1).

Hardware Requirements

Processor

VMware GSX Server supports as many as 64 virtual machines running concurrently on a single host server with as many as 32 processors. VMware recommends that no more than four virtual machines should be run concurrently per physical processor. Ultimately, that number should be determined by the resource needs of the guest operating systems and their applications. If the guest operating system has a small footprint when it comes to resources needed, such as a small Linux machine, then more virtual machines could be executed against the processor. If on the other hand, the virtual machine contains a CPU intensive application, such as a Microsoft SQL database, then fewer virtual machines can be executed against the processor. Chapter 7 gives additional details on how to properly size the deployment on a host server. However, based on the minimum recommendations of VMware, GSX Server does not require a lot of processing power. The processor must be a minimum of an Intel Pentium II processor running at a speed of 733 MHz or faster. While this may be the minimum recommendation, it is certainly nowhere near optimal, and as is true with most applications, the faster the processor the better.

VMware GSX Supported Guest Operating Systems	
Guest Operating System	**CPU Architecture**
Microsoft Windows Code Named Longhorn (Experimental Support Only)	32-bit
Windows Server 2003 Enterprise Edition (RTM and SP1)	32-bit
Windows Server 2003 Small Business Server (RTM and SP1)	32-bit
Windows Server 2003 Standard Edition (RTM and SP1)	32-bit
Windows Server 2003 Web Edition (RTM and SP1)	32-bit
Windows XP Professional (RTM, SP1, and SP2)	32-bit
Windows XP Home Edition (RTM, SP1, and SP2)	32-bit
Windows 2000 Professional (RTM, SP1, SP2, SP3, SP4, and SP4 Checked)	32-bit
Windows 2000 Server (RTM, SP1, SP2, SP3, SP4, and SP4 Checked)	32-bit
Windows 2000 Advanced Server (RTM, SP1, SP2, SP3, SP4, and SP4 Checked)	32-bit
Windows NT 4.0 Server with Service Pack 6a	32-bit
Windows NT Workstation 4.0 with Service Pack 6a	32-bit
Windows NT 4.0 Server Terminal Server Edition with Service Pack 6a	32-bit
Windows ME (Millennium Edition)	32-bit
Windows 98 SE	32-bit
Windows 98 (Including Latest Customer Service Packs)	32-bit
Windows 95 (Including Service Pack 1 and All OSR Releases)	32-bit
Windows for Workgroups 3.11	16-bit
Windows 3.1	16-bit
MS-DOS 6.22	16-bit

Figure 18.1a   GSX Server Supported Guest Operating Systems.

GSX Server is compatible with standard 32-bit IA-32 processors and also processors that implement IA-32 64-bit extensions such as AMD's Opteron and Athlon 64 processors and the Intel Xeon EM64T processor when used with supported 32-bit host operating systems. VMware GSX Server 3.2 does not currently support the Intel Itanium processor.

Memory

When considering memory requirements for the host server, it is important to keep in mind that enough memory is needed to run the Microsoft Windows or Linux host operating system, along with enough memory for each virtual machine's guest operating system and the applications running on both the host server and the virtual machines. This concept is important to understand, because the lack of adequate memory will limit the number of virtual machines that can run concurrently or for that matter can be run at all. Also keep in mind,

VMware GSX Supported Guest Operating Systems	
Guest Operating System	**CPU Architecture**
Mandrake Linux 8.0, 8.1, 8.2, 9.0, 9.1, 9.2, 10.0, 10.1	32-bit
Red Hat Enterprise Linux (AS, ES, WS) 2.1, 2.1 Update 6, 3.0, 3.0 Update 4, 4.0	32-bit
Red Hat Enterprise Linux (AS, ES, WS) 3.0	32-bit
Red Hat Enterprise Linux (AS, ES, WS) 3.0 Update 2	32-bit
Red Hat Linux 6.2, 7.0, 7.1, 7.2, 7.3, 8.0, 9.0	32-bit
SuSE Linux Enterprise Server 7 (Including Patch 2)	32-bit
SuSE Linux Enterprise Server 8 (Including Patch 3)	32-bit
SuSE LINUX Enterprise Server 9 Service Pack 1	32-bit
SuSE Linux 7.3, 8.0, 8.1, 8.2, 9.0, 9.1, 9.2, 9.3 (Experimental Support Only)	32-bit
Turbolinux Server 7.0, 8.0	32-bit
Turbolinux Workstation 8.0	32-bit
Novell NetWare 4.2 Support Pack 9	32-bit
Novell NetWare 5.1 Support Pack 6	32-bit
Novell NetWare 6.0 Support Pack 3	32-bit
Novell NetWare 6.5 Support Pack 1	32-bit
Sun Solaris x86 Platform Edition 9 (Experimental Support Only)	32-bit
Sun Solaris x86 Platform Edition 10 Beta (Experimental Support Only)	32-bit
FreeBSD 4.0-4.6.2, 4.8, 4.9, 5.0, 5.2	32-bit

Figure 10.1b   GSX Server Supported Guest Operating Systems.

a guest operating system on a virtual machine will require the same amount of memory that it does on a physical server. Therefore, if a Windows Server 2003 operating system normally takes a minimum of 512MB of memory to run effectively, then the virtual machine will require the same amount of memory.

VMware's recommended minimum amount of memory is 512MB. However, in reality, this is probably just enough memory for a Windows host server with the GSX Server software installed and almost no memory left over for a virtual machine to use. An insufficient amount of memory available to a virtual machine will starve the performance, just like a physical server. The more memory installed inside of the host server, the better. Keep in mind, however, the maximum supported amount of memory for a host server is 64GB for Windows and Linux hosts that support large memory or PAE mode, 4GB for non-PAE mode Windows hosts and 2GB for Linux hosts with kernels in the 2.2.x series.

Disk

The disk space needed for a normal installation of the GSX Server product varies between the Windows version and the Linux version. The Windows version requires 130MB of free disk space to install server, the management interface, the virtual machine console installation, and both scripting packages, VmPerl and VmCOM. The Linux version only requires 20MB of free disk space, but does not install the VmCOM scripting package because it only works with Windows. VMware also recommends the Linux version should have free disk space in the /tmp folder equivalent to 1.5 times the amount of memory found on the host server. Finally, VMware recommends at least 1GB of disk space allocated for each virtual machine created. For a Linux virtual machine, this may be appropriate; however, a Microsoft Windows server installation will greatly surpass this amount. Chapter 7 provides further details on the proper way to size and evaluate hard disk subsystems.

 One thing to keep in mind, the suspend VM function will require additional free disk space. If this feature is used, it will take up approximately the same amount of free disk space as the amount of memory found on the virtual machine. Therefore, a virtual machine with 1GB of memory will consume approximately 1GB of disk space when the suspend feature is activated.

Network

GSX Server will support any Ethernet controller card that the host operating system supports.

While host operating systems do not require permanent network connectivity, from a practicality stand point, one or more network cards should be present to have true server class functionality. Specific details and options for recommended configurations are provided in chapter 7 and GSX Server networking interfaces are discussed in detail in chapter 22.

Display

Obviously, a graphics adapter for the host server will be needed and VMware recommends a 16-bit color or better display adapter. In Windows, the color palette should be set to 65536 colors or true color to allow for the best performance. However, it is possible to get by with anything greater than a 256 color (8-bit) display adapter. Unfortunately, while this may work, it probably will not function up to expectations. One final additional requirement for Linux host servers is an X server that meets the X11R6 specification, such as XFree86, and a video adapter supported by the host server to run virtual machines in full screen mode. If an X server is not installed, then one must be installed. VMware recommends XFree86 version 3.3.4 or higher, with XFree86 version 4.0 being the preferred choice.

Software Requirements

Host Operating System

GSX Server provides a wide range of choices for host operating system requirements (see Figure 18.2). When installing the VMware GSX Server for Windows product, there are two sets of choices, 64-bit hosts and 32-bit hosts. To take advantage of a 64-bit host server, VMware offers support for the Microsoft Windows Server 2003 x64 Edition operating system. Additionally, 32-bit servers may also choose between Microsoft Windows Server 2003 (Web, Standard, and Enterprise including SP1) and Microsoft Windows 2000 Server or Advanced Server with either service pack 3 or 4 installed. When installing the VMware GSX Server for Linux product, there are many more choices available. Most of the major Linux distributions that have been released recently are supported. Specifically, for 64-bit host servers, SUSE LINUX Enterprise Server 8 or one of the three Red Hat Enterprise Linux 3.0 versions: AS, ES or WS. GSX Server 3.2 adds experimental support for Red Hat Enterprise Linux 4, Red Hat Enterprise Linux 3 Update 4, SUSE LINUX Enterprise Server 9 Service Pack 1 and SUSE LINUX 9.2 and 9.3. For 32-bit servers, it is important to check the most recent list on the VMware support site.

Linux versions not listed may work. However, VMware will not support it and the trouble of trying to tweak and troubleshoot it may not be worth the effort. It is therefore best to stick with a supported operating system.

VMware Management Interface

The Windows version of the product has two specific requirements for the management interface to function correctly. First, Microsoft Internet Information Server (IIS) version 5.0 or 6.0 must be installed. Second, one of the following browsers must be used to view and interact with the management interface: Microsoft Internet Explorer 5.5 or 6.0, Netscape Navigator 7.0, Firefox 1.x, or Mozilla 1.x. Similar requirements must be met for the Linux version. The inetd process must be configured and active to allow connections and it also has browser requirements, either Netscape Navigator 7.0, Firefox 1.x, or Mozilla 1.x must be used. Other Web browser software may work, and VMware is constantly updating the product's requirements.

GSX Server Scripting

One of the key features of GSX Server is the ability to automate and script custom management and control functionality. In order to use the VmPerl API, both the Windows and Linux versions require the installation of Perl 5.005x or higher.

VMware GSX Supported Host Operating Systems	
Host Operating System	**CPU Architecture**
Microsoft Windows Server 2003 Enterprise Edition	32-bit
Microsoft Windows Server 2003 Standard Edition	32-bit
Microsoft Windows Server 2003 Web Edition	32-bit
Microsoft Windows Server 2003 Service Pack 1	32-bit
Microsoft Windows 2000 Advanced Server, Service Pack 3 and Service Pack 4	32-bit
Microsoft Windows 2000 Server, Service Pack 3 and Service Pack 4	32-bit
Microsoft Windows Server 2003 x64 Editions	64-bit
Mandrake Linux 9.2, stock 2.4.22-10mdk kernel	32-bit
Mandrake Linux 9.0, stock 2.4.19-16mdk, update 2.4.19-32mdk kernels	32-bit
Mandrake Linux 8.2, stock 2.4.18-6mdk kernel	32-bit
Red Hat Enterprise Linux 3.0 AS, stock 2.4.21-4, update 2.4.21-9, 2.4.21-9.0.1, 2.4.21-15 kernels	32-bit
Red Hat Enterprise Linux 3.0 ES, stock 2.4.21-4, update 2.4.21-9, 2.4.21-9.0.1, 2.4.21-15 kernels	32-bit
Red Hat Enterprise Linux 3.0 WS, stock 2.4.21-4, update 2.4.21-9, 2.4.21-9.0.1, 2.4.21-15 kernels	32-bit
Red Hat Enterprise Linux AS 2.1, stock 2.4.9-3, 2.4.9-e.24summit, update 2.4.9-e.38, 2.4.9-e.40 kernels	32-bit
Red Hat Enterprise Linux ES 2.1, update 2.4.9-16, 2.4.9-e.24summit, 2.4.9-e.38, 2.4.9-e.40 kernels	32-bit
Red Hat Enterprise Linux WS 2.1, update 2.4.9-16, 2.4.9-e.38, 2.4.9-e.40 kernels	32-bit
Red Hat Linux 9.0, update 2.4.20-8, 2.4.20.9, 2.4.20-13, 2.4.20-18, 2.4.20-28, 2.4.20-30.9, 2.4.20-31.9 kernels	32-bit
Red Hat Linux 8.0, stock 2.4.18-14, update 2.4.18-17, 2.4.18-18, 2.4.18-19, 2.4.18-27, 2.4.20-13, 2.4.20-18 kernels	32-bit
Red Hat Linux 7.3, stock 2.4.18-3, update 2.4.9-6, 2.4.9-34, 2.4.18-5, 2.4.18-10, 2.4.18-17, 2.4.18-18, 2.4.1819, 2.4.18-27, 2.4.20-13, 2.4.20-18 kernels	32-bit
Red Hat Linux 7.2, stock 2.4.7-10, update 2.4.9-6, 2.4.9-7, 2.4.9-13, 2.4.9-21, 2.4.9-31, 2.4.9-34, 2.4.18-17, 2.4.18-18, 2.4.18-19, 2.4.18-27, 2.4.20-13, 2.4.20-18 kernels	32-bit
Red Hat Linux 7.1, stock 2.4.2-2, update 2.4.3-12, 2.4.9-6, 2.4.9-34, 2.4.18-17, 2.4.18-18, 2.4.18-19, 2.4.1827, 2.4.20-13, 2.4.20-18 kernels	32-bit

Figure 18.2a   GSX Server Supported Host Operating Systems.

VMware GSX Supported Host Operating Systems	
Host Operating System	**CPU Architecture**
SuSE Linux Enterprise Server 8, stock 2.4.19, update 2.4.21-138, 2.4.21-143, 2.4.21-215 and patch 3 kernels	32-bit
SuSE Linux Enterprise Server 7, stock 2.4.7 and patch 2, update 2.4.18 kernels	32-bit
SUSE LINUX 9.1, stock 2.6.4-52 kernel	32-bit
SUSE LINUX 9.0, stock 2.4.21-99, update 2.4.21-166 kernels	32-bit
SuSE Linux 8.2, stock 2.4.20 kernel	32-bit
SuSE Linux 8.1, update 2.4.19. update 2.4.19-175 kernels	32-bit
SuSE Linux 8.0, stock 2.4.18 kernel	32-bit
SuSE Linux 7.3, stock 2.4.10, update 2.4.18 kernels	32-bit
Turbolinux Server 8.0, stock 2.4.18-1, update 2.4.18-17 kernels	32-bit
Turbolinux Workstation 8.0, stock 2.4.18-1, update 2.4.18-17 kernels	32-bit
Turbolinux Server 7.0, stock 2.4.5-3, update 2.4.18-17 kernels	32-bit
Mandrake Linux 10.0 and 10.1	32-bit
Red Hat Enterprise Linux 4	32-bit
Red Hat Enterprise Linux 3 Update 4	32-bit
Red Hat Enterprise Linux 2.1 Update 6	32-bit
SUSE LINUX Enterprise Server 9 Service Pack 1	32-bit
SUSE LINUX 9.3 (Experimental Support Only)	32-bit
SUSE LINUX 9.2	32-bit
Red Hat Enterprise Linux 3.0 AS — update 2.4.21-15 kernel	64-bit
Red Hat Enterprise Linux 3.0 ES — update 2.4.21-15 kernel	64-bit
Red Hat Enterprise Linux 3.0 WS — update 2.4.21-15 kernel	64-bit
SuSE Linux Enterprise Server 8 — stock 2.4.19, update 2.4.21-138 and patch 3 kernels	64-bit

Figure 18.2b   GSX Server Supported Host Operating Systems.

Additional Software Components

Other Linux host operating system requirements include:

- Linux kernel 2.2.14-5.0 is specifically not supported.
- Standard Linux server installation is required with glibc version 2.1 or higher and libXpm.so.
- The inetd process must be configured and active for VMware Virtual Machine Console and VMware Management Interface connections.

- Version 2.1.36 of the SCSI Generic driver (sg.o) is required to use generic SCSI devices in virtual machines.
- X Server is required to run the VMware Virtual Machine Console.

Summary

VMware GSX Server is a well established server virtualization platform. Since its inception, the product has undergone a number of updates and upgrades to become one of the most powerful, stable and scalable server virtualization platforms. It offers broad compatibility and support to both the host operating system and the guest operating system. It is one of the few platforms on the market that will install on either Linux or Windows and the number of supported guest operating systems, to say the least, is impressive. No other platform comes close to the wide range of operating system support that even includes 64-bit operating systems. VMware's licensing mechanism for GSX Server is based on the host operating system as well as the number of physical processors located in the host server. It not only has a simple to follow licensing methodology, but the hardware and software requirements are also easily met. For such a robust application, the VMware minimal requirements should certainly be found in most servers that are in use today. However, like most applications, the minimal requirements found here probably look good on paper, but in reality, more is better and more resources should be dedicated to properly handle a virtualized environment.

Chapter 19

Chapter 19

Installing VMware GSX Server

Installing VMware GSX Server on either a Windows or Linux server should be no more complicated than installing many other types of applications on either operating system. This chapter will cover the requirements of the product as well as information on the installation and basic configuration of the physical host server and the host operating system. It will then walk through a step-by-step installation of GSX Server. Because the Windows and Linux platforms are so significantly different in their installation process, the chapter will be divided into two sections: the first section will cover GSX Server for Windows followed by information on GSX Server for Linux.

GSX Server for Windows Requirements

Before executing the master installer, there are a few important things to keep in mind. GSX Server will not install on a host server that already has a version of VMware Workstation or VMware ACE installed. If either is already installed, it must be removed or uninstalled from the host server before installation of GSX Server can begin. Additionally, multiple versions of GSX Server cannot be installed on the same host server. If a previous version or build of the product already exists on the host server, then the upgrading GSX Server section in chapter 23 should be followed, otherwise, the previous installation should be uninstalled before continuing. Finally, if another version of the VMware Virtual Machine Console application is installed, it too must be removed before installing GSX Server. This not only includes any previous version of the GSX Server console but also includes any console installation from another platform such as VMware ESX Server.

In order to install GSX Server, either the local Administrator user or a local user with administrative privileges must be logged on. The product should not be installed by a Windows Server 2003 domain account, nor should it be installed on a Windows 2000 Server Active Directory domain controller. These account restrictions are only for installation of the product. Once installed, the product can be initiated and run by a user with normal user privileges.

Preparing the Host Server

Preparing the host server is the first in a critical series of steps ensuring that the system will be stable and provide adequate performance. Because a virtualization host server will by its very nature be placed under a heavier load than a normal server, it is important to properly tune the server for the most optimal performance possible. There are many articles and white papers on the Internet that speak on the subject of performance tuning a server. This section will attempt to provide a number of options that may be beneficial. Because all operating systems and servers are not identical, these options should be tested before using them in a production environment. Assuming the server has had its internal hardware components installed and the server has been racked:

- Ensure the server is properly cabled with the necessary power cables. Dual power supplies connected to separate power leads is preferred.
- Connect any KVM type solution to the host server for remote management.
- Connect all Ethernet ports that will be used (unused ports can also be connected if desired).
- Upgrade to Gigabit Ethernet, if possible.
- Team multiple network adapters for best performance.
- Download and install the latest BIOS and then configure its settings appropriately.
- Download and upgrade any firmware that needs to be updated.
- Configure the RAID controller.
  1. Configure the RAID controller for optimized write operations.
  2. A multi-channel controller card should be configured with one channel configured as a mirrored pair for the operating system and the other channel configured as RAID 5 with four or more drives in the RAID set if possible for the virtual machines.
  3. The default stripe size is acceptable.
  4. Assign physical hard drives.
  5. Create logical volumes.
- Delete all existing partitions including any server manufacturer's support partition.
- Format using a high-performance file system such as NTFS.
- Install and configure the host operating system.

Preparing the Host Operating System

The host operating system is the next critical step in building the proper platform for GSX Server. The detailed steps involved with installing the host operating system will not be covered in this book. It is assumed that a basic level of understanding and experience with installing the server operating system already exists. The proper configuration along with all required steps is covered below.

- Microsoft Internet Information Server (IIS) 5 or 6 must be installed and the services must be started and operating without errors.
- Ensure that the Physical Address Extension (PAE) option is set in the boot. ini file if greater than 4GB of memory is being used.
- Confirm the correct amount of memory is being reported by the host operating system.
- Ensure that the paging file is of adequate size.
- Stop any unnecessary services.
- Install only the necessary packages and applications rather than loading down the host operating system. It should only serve as the virtualization platform.
- If a software firewall is installed on the host operating system, ensure ports 902, 8222, and 8333 are open to allow a connection to the management interface or to the console.
- Update the Windows host server with the latest updates and patches.
- Disable all protocols and services except "VMware Bridge Protocol" on Ethernet ports that will be used exclusively by virtual machines.
- Defragment the host operating system's hard disks.
- Clear all event logs in the event viewer.
- Set the system's advanced performance settings for the processor to be optimized for background services.
- Set any antivirus software to skip scanning the virtualization install path, virtualization program files, configuration files or virtual hard disk, floppy and CD-ROM image files. It may also be a good idea to turn off real-time virus scanning or only scan modified files. Another option is to allow for a nightly scan or configure it to perform a full scan on the weekend.

Installing VMware GSX Server for Windows

The VMware GSX Server for Windows master installer is very similar to most Windows application installations. This section will include step-by-step instructions with screenshots that clearly depict what installation choices are available and being chosen, specific descriptions of each screenshot and the reasons why each choice is being made as well as what other choices are available and what they do.

As a best practice, no other applications should be running during the installation of the product. It is also important to note, GSX Server must be installed on a local drive and not across a network share.

There are two ways to start the GSX Server installation, either by CD-ROM or a downloaded file. If installing from the CD-ROM, click the Windows start button and select Run. Enter Z:\Windows\VMware-gsx-server-installer-<xxxx>.exe, where Z: is the drive letter for the CD-ROM drive and <xxxx> is the series of numbers representing the version and build number of the product.

If installing from a downloaded file, click the Windows start button and select Run. Browse to the location where the downloaded file was saved. As above, the file should be named VMware-gsx-server-installer-<xxxx>.exe, where <xxxx> is the series of numbers representing the version and build number of the product.

 The latest distribution of the product should be downloaded from VMware's Web site at http://www.vmware.com in the download section. Be prepared to log in with your customer account and password before being allowed to download the binaries. If you have not already done so, you should create a customer account and register your product's serial number. Registering your serial number and creating a customer account will also help in the future when needing VMware technical support.

When the installation file is executed, the master installer screen will launch (see Figure 19.1).

There are only two choices at this point, to continue the installation by clicking Next, or to cancel and exit the installation by clicking Cancel. Click Next to continue.

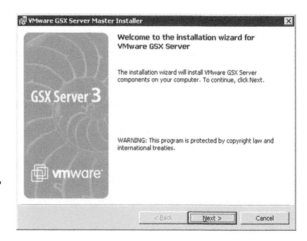

Figure 19.1 VMware GSX Server Master Installer Welcome Screen.

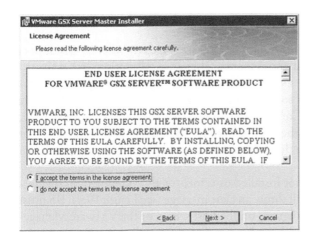

Figure 19.2 VMware GSX Server Master Installer EULA Screen.

The end user license agreement (EULA) page is displayed (see Figure 19.2). The license agreement contained here should be read very carefully. Choosing the radio button labeled "I accept the terms in the license agreement" is a legally binding agreement. If the radio button labeled "I do not accept the terms in the license agreement" is chosen, then the installation will be cancelled and GSX Server will not be installed.

 It is important to also realize that throughout the installation, if the Back button is shown and active, it can be selected to return to the previous screen where a change to a selection may be made. If the option is grayed out, it is no longer possible to return to the previous screen.

If the EULA is found acceptable, click the radio button to agree to the terms and then click Next.

The Setup Type installation page (see Figure 19.3) offers two choices, each of which will be explored in detail.

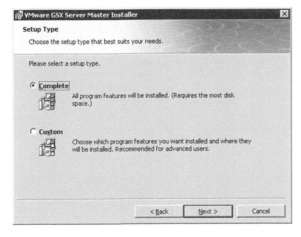

Figure 19.3 VMware GSX Server Master Installer Set-up Type Complete Screen.

Complete Installation

The first choice is Complete. The complete choice is exactly what it sounds like, a complete installation of all components. Therefore, all options are activated and installed. The complete installation will set up the following components on the host server: the server software, the VMware Management Interface, the VMware Virtual Machine Console, the VmCOM API and the VmPerl API. The complete installation is the default installation method and is sufficient for most basic installs. To choose this installation method, select Complete and then click Next.

If Microsoft IIS is either not installed or is incorrectly configured on the host server, the Master Installer will throw an alert message (see Figure 19.4). IIS must be installed and properly configured on the host server, or the VMware Management Interface component will not be installed. To install the component, the

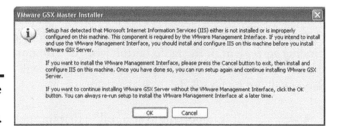

Figure 19.4 VMware GSX Server Master Installer—IIS Missing.

installation must be cancelled by clicking the Cancel button, and then IIS must be installed and properly configured on the host server. Once complete, the installation process can be executed again. Or to continue the installation without the Management Interface, click the OK button. The Management Interface can always be installed at a later time by rerunning setup.

The Destination Folder screen (see Figure 19.5) allows the installation of the GSX Server components to be installed into a directory other than the default

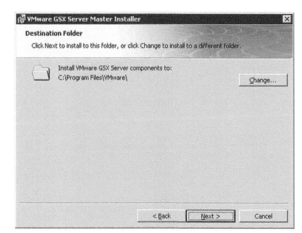

Figure 19.5 VMware GSX Server Master Installer Destination Folder Screen.

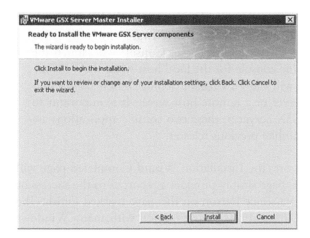

Figure 19.6   VMware GSX Server Master Installer Ready to Begin Installation Screen.

C:\Program Files\VMware. Clicking the Change button allows the default path to be changed either by manually typing in the new path or by browsing to the new path using the mouse. Unless an installation standard must be followed, it is highly recommended that the default path not be changed as this option could affect other software programs that assume the default installation directory. Clicking the OK button accepts the installation path and returns to the previous Destination Folder screen. Clicking the Next button brings up the Ready to Install the VMware GSX Server components screen (see Figure 19.6).

This is the last screen of a complete installation before the actual install takes place. To make any final changes, the Back button is available. To continue the installation, click the Install button to begin copying files to the host server.

If the Master Installer detects that the host server has the CD-ROM autorun feature enabled, the screen shown in see Figure 19.7 will prompt for input during the installation.

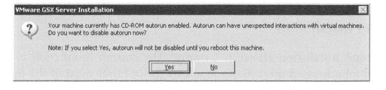

Figure 19.7   VMware GSX Server Master Installer Disable CD-ROM Autorun Screen.

Disabling Autorun will help prevent undesirable interactions between the host server and the virtual machines. If the autorun feature is left enabled, a CD-ROM intended for a guest operating system may start on the host operating system, or a CD-ROM may start simultaneously on both the host server and the virtual machine(s). It is recommended to allow the installer to disable this feature.

Two program shortcuts are then created on the desktop: VMware GSX Server Console and the VMware Virtual Machine Console. The VMware GSX Server Console will launch the virtual machine console for the local host while the VMware Virtual Machine Console will allow a virtual machine console connection to either the local host server or a remote host server. It is important to note that, starting with GSX Server 3, these two console applications are identical in functionality unlike previous releases.

Assuming there are no errors, the Installation Wizard Completed page will appear (see Figure 19.8). This page simply provides a report as to the success or failure of the install. There is a single button on this page marked Finish. The finish button concludes the installation. As is common with many Windows applications, after clicking Finish, it is best to reboot the host server to complete the installation process.

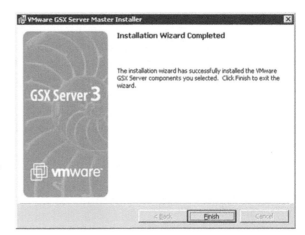

Figure 19.8 VMware GSX Server Master Installer—Installation Complete Screen.

Custom Installation

The second installation choice is Custom. The custom installation is recommended for advanced users. Custom allows control over most of the basic features and functions being installed. It can also provide the same installation options as that of the complete installation by simply making sure that all options are selected. The installer can always be run again at a later date to install any components that were not installed the first time. To choose this installation method, select Custom and then click Next.

The Custom Setup page allows the manipulation of different component features to be installed (see Figure 19.10). It is important to note that the component options are not mutually exclusive. In other words, several different combinations of these options are available. Clicking the arrow to the left of the component will select and deselect the option for installation.

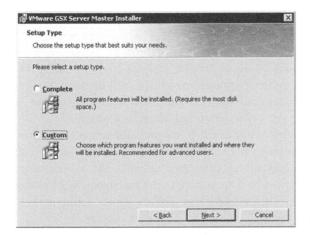

Figure 19.9 VMware GSX Server Master Installer Setup Type Custom Screen.

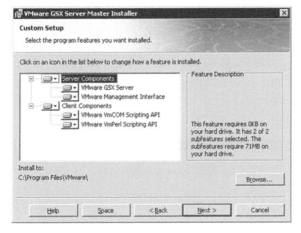

Figure 19.10 VMware GSX Server Master Installer—Custom Feature Description Screen.

The first option is Server Components. It has two subfeatures that can be selected for installation: VMware GSX Server and VMware Management Interface. The VMware GSX Server component provides the core functionality of GSX Server; and without it, it is not possible to create and configure virtual machines or use the system as a host server platform for virtualization. This component must be installed if the server is going to be a virtualization host server. Additionally, the option installs on the host server a local version of the VMware Virtual Machine Console, which is used to view and control virtual machines. This option is not really a necessary component for the host server, but it is installed by default with the core component. The tool allows for keyboard, video and mouse (KVM) control of the virtual machines. However, this component can and should be installed by itself on a client machine to remotely access and control the virtual machines on the host server. Doing so is ideal for both security purposes and to reduce the performance impact of using the tool directly on the physical host server. This tool will be discussed in more detail in chapter 20.

The VMware Management Interface component provides the mechanism for an administrator to have a high-level view of the GSX Server host. It is a Web-based tool for managing the host server and the virtual machines that reside on it. This tool will also be discussed in more detail in chapter 20. For security reasons, it might make sense in some environments to not install the management interface or Microsoft IIS. Most configuration setup and management can be performed remotely by using the VMware Virtual Machine Console.

The second option is Client Components. It has two subfeatures that can be selected for installation: VMware VmCOM Scripting API and VMware VmPerl Scripting API. These packages install a scripting tool, either COM or Perl, which can then be used to create scripts to help automate the management of virtual machines and the host server. The packages also include sample scripts to help get started. Scripting will be covered in more detail within chapter 25.

There are two other options on this page worthy of mention: Space and Browse. Clicking on the Space button will bring up another screen, Disk Space Requirements.

The screen (see Figure 19.11) shows the disk space required for the installation with the selected features, along with the current disk size of each available drive, its free space available, and the remaining amount of space after installation. It provides information that can help determine the best location to install the application.

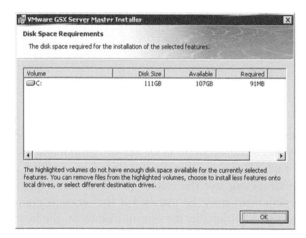

Figure 19.11 VMware GSX Server Master Installer—Disk Space Requirements Screen.

Clicking on Browse opens the Change Current Destination Folder screen (see Figure 19.12). It allows the installation path to be changed to a directory other than the default of C:\Program Files\VMware. The screen allows either the new path to be manually entered by typing the new path or by using the mouse and navigating via the drop-down window. Unless an installation standard must be followed, it is highly recommended that the default path not be changed as this option could affect other software programs that assume the default installation

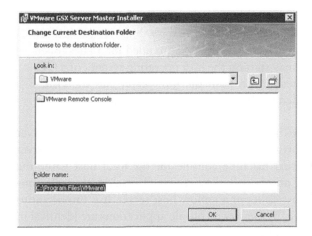

Figure 19.12 VMware GSX Server Master Installer—Change Destination Folder Screen.

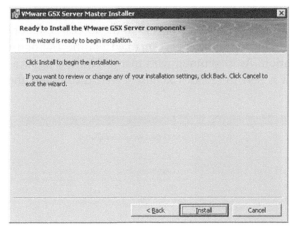

Figure 19.13 VMware GSX Server Master Installer Ready to Begin Installation Screen.

directory. Clicking the OK button accepts the installation path and returns to the previous Custom Setup screen. Clicking the Next button brings up the Ready to Install the VMware GSX Server components screen (see Figure 19.13).

This is the last screen of a custom installation before the actual install takes place. To make any final changes, the Back button is available. To continue the installation, click the Install button to begin copying files to the host server.

If the Master Installer detects that the host server has the CD-ROM autorun feature enabled, the screen shown in Figure 19.14 will prompt for input during the install.

Figure 19.14 VMware GSX Server Master Installer Disable CD-ROM Autorun Screen.

Disabling Autorun will prevent undesirable interactions between the host server and the virtual machines. If the autorun feature is left enabled, CD-ROMs intended for a guest operating system may start on the host operating system, or a CD-ROM may start simultaneously on both the host server and the virtual machine. It is recommended to allow the installer to disable this feature.

Two program shortcuts are then created on the desktop: VMware GSX Server Console and the VMware Virtual Machine Console. The VMware GSX Server Console will launch the virtual machine console for the local host while the VMware Virtual Machine Console will allow a virtual machine console connection to either the local host server or a remote host server. It is important to note, starting with GSX Server 3, these two console applications are identical in functionality unlike previous releases.

Assuming there are no errors, the Installation Wizard Completed page will appear (see Figure 19.15). It simply provides a report as to the success or failure of the install. There is a single button on this page marked Finish. The finish button concludes the installation. As is common with many Windows applications, after clicking Finish, it is best to reboot the host server to complete the installation process.

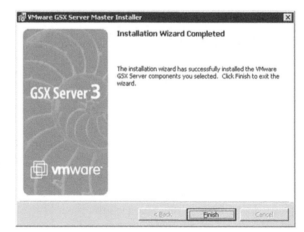

Figure 19.15 VMware GSX Server Master Installer—Installation Complete Screen.

GSX Server for Linux Requirements

Before executing the master installer, there are a few important things to keep in mind. VMware GSX Server and VMware Workstation cannot be installed on the same host server. If Workstation is already installed, it must be removed from the host server before installation of GSX Server begins. Otherwise, the Workstation application is automatically upgraded to GSX Server. Additionally, multiple versions of GSX Server cannot be installed on the same host server. If a previous version or build of the product already exists on the host server, then the upgrading GSX Server section in chapter 23 should be followed, otherwise, the previous installation should be removed before continuing. If GSX Server is allowed to continue the installation with a previous version already installed, the choices made during the earlier installation become the defaults for the new installation.

In order to install GSX Server, the root account must be logged on. This account restriction is only for installation of the product. Once installed, the product can be initiated and run by a user with normal user privileges.

 Before installing GSX Server, make sure the Linux distribution is for a server and not a workstation. If it is a workstation distribution, make sure to install the inetd process in order to connect to the VMware Virtual Machine Console and VMware Management Interface.

Preparing the Host Server

Preparing the host server is the first in a critical series of steps ensuring that the system will be stable and provide adequate performance. Because a virtualization host server will by its very nature be placed under a heavier load than a normal server, it is important to properly tune the server for the most optimal performance possible. There are many articles on the Internet that speak on the subject of performance tuning a server. However, this section will attempt to provide a number of steps that may be beneficial. Because all operating systems and servers are not identical, these options should be tested before using them in a production environment. Assuming the server has had its internal hardware components installed and the server has been racked:

- Ensure the server is properly cabled with the necessary power cables. Dual power supplies connected to separate power leads is preferred.
- Connect any KVM type solution to the host server for remote management.
- Connect all Ethernet ports that will be used (unused ports can also be connected if desired).
- Upgrade to Gigabit Ethernet if possible.
- Team multiple network adapters for best performance.
- Download and install the latest BIOS and then configure its settings appropriately.
- Download and upgrade any firmware that needs to be updated.
- Configure the RAID controller.
  1. Configure the RAID controller for optimized write operations.

2. A multi-channel controller card should be configured with one channel configured as a mirrored pair for the operating system and the other channel configured as RAID 5 with four or more drives in the RAID set if possible for the virtual machines.
3. The default stripe size is acceptable.
4. Assign physical hard drives.
5. Create logical volumes.

- Delete all existing partitions including any server manufacturer's support partition.
- Format using a high-performance file system such as EXT3 or XFS.
- Install and configure the host operating system.

Preparing the Host Operating System

The host operating system is the next critical step in building the proper platform for GSX Server. The detailed steps involved with installing the host operating system will not be covered in this book. It is assumed that a basic level of understanding and experience with installing the server operating system already exists. The proper configuration along with all required steps is covered below.

- Apache server must be installed, started, and operating without errors.
- Ensure that the kernel is compiled to use Intel's Physical Address Extension (PAE) feature if greater than 4GB of memory is being used.
- Confirm the correct amount of memory is being reported by the host operating system.
- Ensure that the swap partition is of adequate size.
- Stop any unnecessary processes or daemons.
- Install only the necessary packages and applications rather than loading down the base host operating system. It should only serve as the virtualization platform.
- Install the libdb.so.3 library from the Linux distribution media before installing the VMware Management Interface.
- Install an X server before installing the VMware Virtual Machine Console. If an X server is not installed, install libxpm.so.4 from the Linux distribution media.
- The real-time clock function must be compiled into the Linux kernel.
- GSX Server for Linux requires the parallel port PC-style hardware option (CONFIG_PARPORT_PC) be built and loaded as a kernel module.
- If a software firewall is installed with the operating system, ensure ports 902, 8222, and 8333 are open to allow connectivity to the management interface and the console.
- Optimize IDE hard disks with hdparm.

- Install any updates or patches available for the Linux host server.

Installing VMware GSX Server for Linux

The VMware GSX Server for Linux master installer is very similar to most Linux application installations. This section will include step-by-step instructions to identify the installation choices that are available and should be chosen, along with descriptions and reasons why each choice is being made as well as what other choices are available and what they do.

There are two ways to start the GSX Server installation, either by CD-ROM or by a downloaded file. The installation steps are the same except for the starting location. If the installation is being performed with a downloaded file, the installation steps will begin in the directory where the file was downloaded. The following steps start off with an installation from the CD-ROM.

 The steps below are described using a Red Hat Linux host. Be aware, some of the commands used below may be different for other versions of Linux. Also, VMware provides both RPM and tar file packages for installation. Choose the method that best supports your version of Linux.

To start the installation from the CD-ROM, mount the CD-ROM drive and change to the Linux directory on the CD by performing the following commands:

```
mount /dev/cdrom /mnt/cdrom
cd /mnt/cdrom/Linux
```

VMware GSX Server for Linux is distributed in two formats: an RPM file and a tar archive file. Once the CD is mounted and the directory location has been changed, one of these installation file formats must be executed. Choose from the following:

- The RPM installer—to use the RPM installer:
  - Run the RPM command against the .rpm installation file.

    ```
    rpm -Uhv VMware-gsx-<xxxx>.i386.rpm
    ```

    (where <xxxx> is the series of numbers representing the version and build number of the product)

 If the previous GSX Server version 2 is already installed on this host server, the pre-built module RPM package from the version 2 release must be removed. To remove it, the following command should be executed from a command prompt:

```
rpm -e VMwareGSXKernelModules
```

- The TAR installer—to unpack the tar archive:
  - Copy the tar archive to a directory on the host server's hard drive such as /tmp.

    ```
    cp VMware-gsx-<xxxx>.tar.gz /tmp
    ```

    (where <xxxx> is the series of numbers representing the version and build number of the product)
  - Change to the directory where the file was copied by issuing the following command:

    ```
    cd /tmp
    ```
  - Unpack the archive with the following command:

    ```
    tar zxf VMware-gsx-<xxxx>.tar.gz
    ```

    (where <xxxx> is the series of numbers representing the version and build number of the product)

 This command extracts all of the VMware GSX Server installation files into a new directory called vmware-gsx-distrib.

- Change to the installation directory with the following command:

  ```
  cd vmware-gsx-distrib
  ```
- Run the installer program with the following command:

  ```
  ./vmware-install.pl
  ```

 The vmware-install.pl is a Perl script. If running the above command either does not execute the script or causes an error, then either Perl is not installed or it is not in the /usr/bin directory. Install or locate the Perl executable on the host server. If the executable is not in the /usr/bin directory, create a symbolic link to the correct location.

- VMware recommends accepting the defaults to all of the installer's questions. The installer will prompt for the install directories for the binary files, daemon files, library files, manual files, documentation files, init directories, and init scripts.

After completing the initial VMware GSX Server installation, it is important to configure the program before using it for the first time. There are several steps that must be completed to properly configure GSX Server.

Execute the following Perl script to begin the configuration process:

```
./vmware-config.pl
```

If the GSX Server application is being installed on a Mandrake Linux host server, the configuration script will prompt for the location of lspci. The following path should be entered in response to the question: /usr/bin/lspcidrake.

When using the RPM package to install the product, this script will need to be run separately from the command line. When using the tar file archive, the installer offers to launch the configuration program.

 The vmware-config.pl script can be used to reconfigure the GSX Server whenever the kernel is upgraded. Reinstalling GSX Server is not necessary. The script can also be used to reconfigure networking options for the GSX Server. For example, if during the initial installation you chose to not install host-only networking but later realized that you need it, you can run the script again at a later time to add it.

Pressing the <ENTER> key will bring up the end user license agreement (EULA) page. The license agreement contained here should be read very carefully. The license agreement can be paged through by pressing the SPACEBAR. Accepting the license agreement is a legally binding agreement. To accept the agreement and continue on with the install, answer yes to the Do you accept? prompt. If it does not appear, press the Q key to get to the next prompt. Not agreeing to the license agreement will cancel the installation.

The system then prompts for networking configuration of the virtual machines:

```
Do you want networking for your virtual ma-
chines?
```

Answer the question "yes." For now, it is enough to know that by allowing networking, the script configures and enables bridged networking on VMnet0. This section will not go into detail about the various forms of virtual networking; however, this topic will be covered in detail in chapter 22.

Next, the system prompts whether or not NAT should be enabled.

```
Do you want to be able to use NAT networking
in your virtual machines?
```

Typically, the answer to this question should be "yes." If the host server is using the only IP network address on the physical network, this option will allow the virtual machines on that host server to connect to an external network. When answering "yes," the script then responds with the following question:

```
Do you want this script to probe for an unused
private subnet?
```

Again, the typical answer should be "yes." In order for the virtual machines to have networking functions as expected, the virtual network will need a range of valid IP addresses. The script will then probe for an unused private subnet. The alternative is to answer "no" and then enter the information in manually.

 If the host server is on a private subnet, there is a possibility that the script could choose a subnet that will cause a conflict. Check the IP configuration of the host server and verify that the subnet chosen by the script does not match.

The system then prompts whether or not host-only networking should be enabled. The following question is asked:

```
Do you want to be able to use host-only net-
working in your virtual machines?
```

Host-only networking provides a networking connection between the virtual machines and their host server. Because of the limiting nature of host-only networking, the suggested answer here is "no." If the plan is to setup an isolated virtual network where network traffic is confined between the virtual machines and their host server, then the answer to this question is "yes." If answering in the affirmative, the script will then prompt whether or not it should probe for unused private subnets, just as it did in the previous section discussing NAT. The same issues and concerns addressed with NAT and probing should be considered here.

Once networking has been addressed, the install needs to be told which port the VMware Virtual Machine Console should use when connecting to the GSX Server host remotely. The default port is port 902. If this port is already being used by another application or the network administrator deems it a security risk to assign a default value, a different port can be chosen and entered here.

 If the default port of 902 is not selected, it is important to make note of the selected port number. This new port number will be needed later when trying to connect to the host server via the console.

If the host server is being upgraded from a previous version of GSX Server, the following prompt will appear:

```
Do you want the installer to set up permis-
sions for your registered virtual machines?
This will be done by setting new permissions
on all files found in /etc/vmware/vm-list.
```

This should be answered Yes by entering Y. The registered virtual machines will be upgraded with the following new permissions:

- Read, write and execute—set for the user (the owner) who created the virtual machine
- Read and execute—set for the primary group to which the owner belongs
- Read—set for users other than the owner or a member of the owner's group

The system will then prompt for the directory where the virtual machine files will be located. By default, this directory is located in the `/var/lib/vmware/Virtual Machines` directory on the host server.

 It is important to make sure that this directory is located on a large enough file system to accommodate the large file space that virtual machine files need. Remember, virtual machine disk files are gigabytes in size and can accumulate very rapidly if they are not kept under control. It is very easy to lose track of disk space when creating multiple virtual machines. The more people with access to the host server and with the ability to create virtual machines makes keeping track of disk space that much more difficult.

Finally, the installation will prompt for the GSX Server serial number. It should be entered into the system exactly as it appears with the hyphens. The serial number is then saved into the host server's license file. Assuming there are no problems, the installation will then display a message stating the configuration has completed successfully, otherwise, the configuration program will need to be executed again.

Installing the VMware Management Interface for Linux

There are two ways to start the VMware Management Interface installation, either by CD-ROM or a downloaded file. The installation steps are the same except for the starting location. If the installation is being performed with a downloaded file, the installation steps will begin in the directory where the file was downloaded. The following steps start off with an installation from the CD-ROM.

 The steps below are described using a Red Hat Linux host. Be aware that some of the commands used below may be different for other versions of Linux.

In a terminal window, log in as the root user or become root so that the installation process can begin. To start the installation from the CD-ROM, mount the CD-ROM drive and change to the Linux directory on the CD by performing the following commands:

```
mount /dev/cdrom /mnt/cdrom
cd /mnt/cdrom/Linux
```

The tar archive should be copied to a directory on the hard drive. A typical directory location is the /tmp directory. The following command should be executed:

```
cp VMware-mui-<xxxx>.tar.gz /tmp
```

(where <xxxx> is the series of numbers representing the version and build number of the product)

Change to the directory location where the file was copied as in the above example, the /tmp directory by entering the following command:

```
cd /tmp
```

Next, unpack the tar archive by executing the following command:

```
tar zxf VMware-mui-<xxxx>.tar.gz
```

(where <xxxx> is the series of numbers representing the version and build number of the product)

Change to the installation directory and run the installation program.

```
cd VMware-mui-distrib
./vmware-install.pl
```

Press <ENTER> to continue and then read the EULA. If it is found agreeable, then accept the EULA to continue, otherwise the installation ends.

It is recommended to accept the default directories for the management components, the binary files, the management interface files, the init directories, and the init scripts. Doing so will make using and administering the product much easier later on.

The configuration program, vmware-config-mui.pl, should then be allowed to run. After which, the default session timeout for the management interface should be entered. The default value is 60 minutes, which should be appropriate for most installations. If a 60 minute timeout value is deemed too long or too short, a new value should be entered here before continuing.

Once completed, log out of the root account and exit, or continue on to the installation of the VMware Virtual Machine Console.

Installing the VMware Virtual Machine Console for Linux Hosts

There are two ways to start the Virtual Machine Console installation, either by CD-ROM or a downloaded file. The installation steps are the same except for the starting location. If the installation is being performed with a downloaded file, the installation steps will begin in the directory where the file was downloaded. The following steps start off with an installation from the CD-ROM.

 The steps below are described using a Red Hat Linux host. Be aware that some of the commands used below may be different for other versions of Linux.

Again, it is important to be logged in as root. Either log in as root or change to root before starting the installation. To start the installation from the GSX Server CD-ROM, mount the CD-ROM drive and change to the client directory on the CD by performing the following commands:

```
mount /dev/cdrom /mnt/cdrom

cd /mnt/cdrom/Client
```

The VMware Virtual Machine Console for Linux is distributed in two formats: an RPM file and a tar archive file. Once the CD is mounted, unzip the client installer archive to a directory on the local machine, for example, the /tmp directory.

```
unzip VMware-gsx-server-linux-client-<xxxx>.
zip -d /tmp
```

(where <xxxx> is the series of numbers representing the version and build number of the product)

 When using the tar package, make sure the directory where the untar will take place does not contain any files from a previous console tar installation.

Then change to the /tmp directory where one of these installation file formats must be executed. Choose from the following:

- The RPM installer—to use the RPM installer:
  - Run the RPM command against the .rpm installation file.
    ```
    rpm -Uhv VMware-console-<xxxx>.i386.rpm
    ```
    where <xxxx> is the series of numbers representing the version and build number of the product)
- The TAR installer—to unpack the tar archive:
  - Unpack the archive with the following command:
    ```
    tar zxf VMware-console-<xxxx>.tar.gz
    ```

(where <xxxx> is the series of numbers representing the version and build number of the product)

 This command extracts all of the VMware Virtual Machine Console installation files into a new directory called vmware-console-distrib.

- Change to the installation directory with the following command:
    ```
    cd vmware-console-distrib
    ```
- Run the installer program with the following command:
    ```
    ./vmware-install.pl
    ```
- The EULA will have to be accepted in order to continue.
- It is recommended to accept the default directories for the binary files, library files, manual files and documentation files.
- If the `Do you accept?` prompt does not appear, press the Q key to continue.
    Execute the following Perl script to begin the configuration process:
    ```
    ./vmware-config-console.pl (EBL)
    ```

 When using the RPM package to install the console, this script will need to be run separately from the command line. When using the tar file archive, the installer offers to launch the configuration program. Answer Yes when this prompt appears.

The system will then prompt: `What port do you want the remote console to use to connect to server`—where port 902 is the default. However, if a different port was selected during the GSX Server software installation, that port number should be entered here.

This is the last stage of the VMware Remote Console installation. Once completed, log out of the root account and exit, or continue on to the installation of the VmPerl Scripting API.

Installing the VmPerl Scripting API on a Linux Host

There are two ways to start the VmPerl Scripting API installation, either by CD-ROM or a downloaded file. The installation steps are the same except for the starting location. If the installation is being performed with a downloaded file, the installation steps will begin in the directory where the file was downloaded. The following steps start off with an installation from the CD-ROM.

The steps below are described using a Red Hat Linux host. Be aware, some of the commands used below may be different for other versions of Linux.

Again, it is important to be logged in as root. Either log in as root or change to root before starting the installation. To start the installation from the GSX Server CD-ROM, mount the CD-ROM drive and change to the client directory on the CD by performing the following commands:

```
mount /dev/cdrom /mnt/cdrom
cd /mnt/cdrom/Client
```

The VmPerl Scripting API for Linux is distributed as a tar archive file. Once the CD is mounted, unzip the client installer archive to a directory on the local machine, for example, the /tmp directory.

```
unzip VMware-gsx-server-linux-client-<xxxx>.
zip -d /tmp
```

(where <xxxx> is the series of numbers representing the version and build number of the product)

Then change to the /tmp directory to unpack the tar archive:

- cd /tmp
- Unpack the archive with the following command:

```
tar zxf VMware-VmPerlAPI-<xxxx>.tar.gz
```

(where <xxxx> is the series of numbers representing the version and build number of the product)

The command extracts all of the VMware VmPerl API installation files into a new directory called vmware-api-distrib.

- Change to the installation directory with the following command:

```
cd vmware-api-distrib
```

- Run the installer program with the following command:

```
./vmware-install.pl
```

- Press <ENTER> to read the EULA. The SPACEBAR will page through the text. If the Do you accept? Prompt does not appear, press the Q key to get to the next prompt. The EULA will need to be accepted in order to continue.
- The recommended directory for the VmPerl API executable files is the default location where Perl is usually installed on the host: /usr/bin.
- The recommended directory for the VmPerl API library files is the default location /usr/lib/vmware-api. This directory also includes a SampleScripts directory that contains example code to demonstrate the uses of the VmPerl API.

- ■ The recommended directory for the VmPerl API documentation is the default location /usr/share/doc/vmware-api.

This is the last stage of the VMware VmPerl Scripting API installation. Log out of the root account and exit the system.

Summary

VMware GSX Server can either be installed on a Microsoft Windows host server or on a Linux host server. Neither installation should be any more complicated than installing many other application types on either of the operating systems. Just because the application may be more complicated than say a word processor, the installation process should not be considered as something difficult. On the other hand, because of the nature of the product, the requirements and preparations needed before installation can begin are probably more involved than most applications. Additionally, because virtualization hosts by their very nature are more demanding on the server load, performance tuning and optimizations should be performed on the host and the host operating system to ensure the best results possible. Following along with the procedures and step-by-step instructions provided in this chapter, the setup and installation of the virtualization product becomes somewhat simplified.

Chapter 20

Configuring VMware GSX Server

Once the installation of VMware GSX Server is complete, it is ready to be configured for daily use. This chapter covers the tools and techniques to properly configure, manage, and secure VMware GSX Server once it has been installed. It is critical that VMware GSX Server be properly configured to garner all of the performance benefits and security settings that are made available. By using the VMware supplied management tools, managing your virtual machines and physical host servers become less of an obstacle when trying to create a virtualized environment. Once the virtualization environment is installed, it is important to become familiar with the VMware management tools in order to create, modify, and maintain the virtual machines and the environment.

VMware Management and Configuration Tools

Once VMware GSX Server is installed, how is it managed and configured? One of the primary strengths of GSX Server is its ability to manage the environment remotely. Unlike some virtualization products, it does not restrict control and interaction with the virtual machines to the host server. VMware offers various tools to help manage and configure the GSX Server host and its virtual machines. There are three tools supplied with the GSX Server product: VMware Virtual Machine Console, VMware Management Interface, and VMware Scripting APIs. The VMware Virtual Machine Console enables control over GSX Server and its virtual machines from a remote client or directly on the host server. The console is provided as a client installation package that can be downloaded from the host server. The VMware Management Interface is a Web-based tool that provides a high-level view of the GSX Server host. It provides local and remote management and configuration of the host server as well as the virtual machines. For a more customized and automated way of managing the virtual machines and the host server, VMware provides a set of scripting APIs. And finally, there are a number of third-party tools designed to manage GSX Server environments. VMware itself has even released an add-on tool to help better manage a larger deployment environment—VMware VirtualCenter. The following section will provide more detail around the VMware Virtual Machine Console and the VMware Management Interface.

VMware Virtual Machine Console

The VMware Virtual Machine Console is a client-based management tool designed to ease the management of GSX Server virtual machines. By combining the best abilities from the previous version's local and remote consoles into a single console, it is possible to manage virtual machines either directly from the host server or remotely from a client machine or another host in the exact same manner. When GSX Server is installed on the host, the VMware Virtual Machine Console is installed by default. Remote management and connecting to virtual machines from a client workstation require a separate installation of the console. For convenience, the VMware Management Interface provides a download option of the console for a remote client installation or it can be installed from the GSX Server installation media. Using the console, the following options can be performed:

- Control and alter the power state of the virtual machines on the host server.
- Create, remove, and delete virtual machines.
- Create a screenshot of a virtual machine.
- Create hot key combinations to interact with virtual machines.
- Connect to a virtual machine or GSX Server host.
- Control the virtual machine display—either normal or full screen mode.
- Take or revert to a snapshot of a virtual machine.
- Enable and disable SSL-encryption for console sessions (administrator and root users only).
- Configure the default location for virtual machines.
- Configure the host server's memory allocation and process priority for virtual machines.
- View and modify virtual machine behavior during system startup and shutdown.
- View and modify the configuration of virtual networks on the host server.
- Add, configure, and remove devices in a virtual machine.

Requirements

Before launching the VMware Virtual Machine Console, there are certain requirements and restrictions that should be taken into account.

- The host name or IP address of the host server must be known in order to connect to it remotely.
- The proper port must be opened when using a firewall (by default, port 902). If the port number was changed on the GSX Server host, the port number used by the console will need to match.
- A valid user account and password for the host server is needed in order to authenticate. The account must also have the proper permissions needed in order to connect to the server and its virtual machines.
- Consoles launched from the VMware Management Interface using either a Netscape or Mozilla browser must configure the MIME type for the console. Internet Explorer is automatically configured during installation of the console.
- When connecting to an older version of GSX Server or ESX Server, some of the controls and functionality of the interface change to accommodate the differences between the platforms.

To get started, launch the VMware Virtual Machine Console from either a GSX Server host machine or a client workstation that has the console application installed. When the console is launched from a client workstation, a log-in screen appears (see Figure 20.1) requesting the host name to connect to, along with a valid user name and password combination for authentication into the remote host server. The Host name can either be the host name of the server or its IP address.

When the console is launched from a local GSX Server host machine, a log-in screen appears offering a connection to either the local host or a remote host (see Figure 20.2). Selecting Local host automatically authenticates into the console with the current user credentials. Selecting Remote host prompts for the same

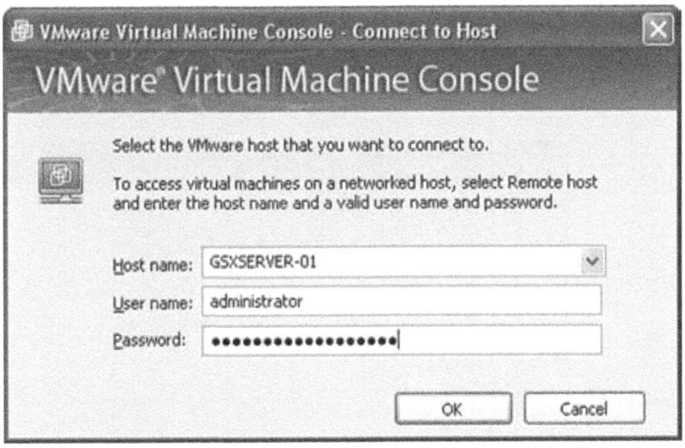

Figure 20.1 VMware Virtual Machine Console—Remote Log In.

Figure 20.2 VMware Virtual Machine Console— Local Host Log In.

information requested when the console is launched from a remote client workstation—it requests the host name to connect to, along with a valid user name and password combination for authentication into the remote host server. The Host name can either be the host name of the server or its IP address.

If this is the first time you have launched the console and you did not enter the serial or license number during the GSX Server installation (only an option on a Windows host), now is the time to enter it. If the system does not prompt for the information, you should enter it by choosing Help > Enter Serial Number. The system will then prompt for your Serial Number, Name, and Company Name (see Figure 20.3). The serial number is located on the registration card that came with the VMware GSX Server media or in the e-mail message that came with the electronic distribution.

On a newly installed GSX Server host, the console offers very few options other than host server configurations. Since there are no virtual machines configured on the host server, the console will be fairly sparse in detail and many options will be grayed out. For discussion purposes, the console screen will be divided into five functional areas: the Application Menu Bar, the Toolbar Menu,

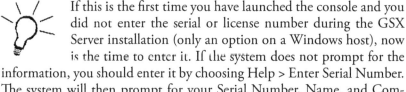

Figure 20.3 Enter Serial Number.

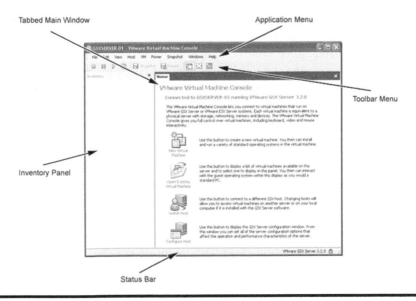

Figure 20.4 VMware Virtual Machine Console—Five Functional Areas.

the Inventory Panel, the Tabbed Main Window, and the Status Bar (see Figure 20.4). Each of these areas along with their options will be described in detail.

Once virtual machines have been created and registered on the host server, the console window begins to populate with more information, detail, and options (see Figure 20.5). Chapter 21 will walk through the preparation, creation, and

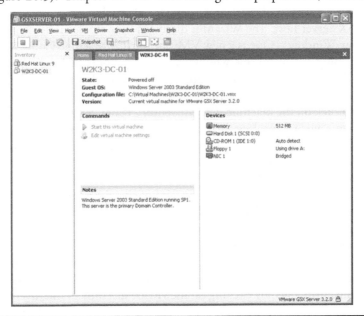

Figure 20.5 VMware Virtual Machine Console—Populated.

installation stages of building a new virtual machine. For discussion purposes, virtual machines have been added to the GSX Server host to show and explain all options available. Keep in mind that before creating a virtual machine, there may be important configuration changes that need to be made to the host server. These configuration changes will be discussed throughout the remainder of this chapter.

Application Menu Bar

Much like many other applications, the VMware Virtual Machine Console offers an application menu bar across the top of its window. The menu bar offers a row of high-level command options from which all operations can be initiated. There are nine pull-down menu options available on the menu bar: File, Edit, View, Host, VM, Power, Snapshot, Windows, and Help (see Figure 20.6). Each pull-down menu option along with its sub-menu choices will be detailed below.

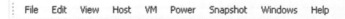

Figure 20.6   Application Menu Bar.

File Menu

- New Virtual Machine—Launches the New Virtual Machine Wizard, a convenient way of creating a new virtual machine configuration on the GSX Server host. The Wizard is discussed in more detail in chapter 22.
- New Window—Opens a new VMware Virtual Machine Console window. Opening a new console window is one way to manage and interact with multiple GSX Server hosts simultaneously from the same client machine.
- Open Virtual Machine—The easiest method to attach to a virtual machine is to click on the machine in the Inventory Panel. However, there are times when a virtual machine may not appear in the Inventory Panel, such as when the virtual machine is removed from inventory (VM > Remove from Inventory) or copied over from another host server. To open the virtual machine, choose File > Open Virtual Machine and click Browse to browse to the configuration file (.vmx or .cfg) of the virtual machine. The virtual machine will be added to the Inventory Panel and attached to the Tabbed Main Window.
- Close—Choosing File > Close while a virtual machine is selected in either the Inventory Panel or the Tabbed Main Window will remove the virtual machine connection in the Tabbed Main Window. The virtual machine can be reattached by clicking on the virtual machine in the Inventory Panel. Choosing Close will not change the power state of the virtual machine

or permanently remove it, it simply detaches the virtual machine from its tab view.

- Capture Screen—Creates a screen shot of a virtual machine in the Tabbed Main Window. The screen shot image is then saved as a bitmap (.bmp) file on a Windows host server or as a portable network graphics (.png) file on a Linux host server. This is a convenient method of capturing a screen shot of the virtual machine window without the surrounding console window. When using a remote console connection, the file is stored on the client machine rather than the GSX Server host.
- Exit—Ends the current console session and closes the console window.

Edit Menu

- Cut, Copy, and Paste—While VMware Tools is running and the option is enabled, the system will allow cut, copy, and paste between applications in the virtual machine and the host server or between two virtual machines.
- Preferences—The Preferences dialog box allows users to specify or change settings that apply to all virtual machines running in the console. The settings changes are user specific, which means settings changes made by one user do not affect the settings for another user. The Preference dialog box offers the following tab options: Workspace, Input, and Hot Keys.

Setting Workspace Preferences

On the Workspace tab (see Figure 20.7), the following options are configurable:

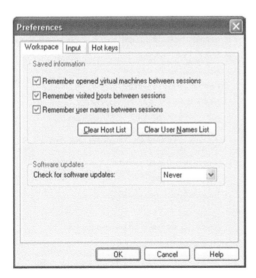

Figure 20.7   Setting Workspace Preferences.

- Remember opened virtual machines between sessions—A tab for each opened virtual machine is displayed each time the console is opened.
- Remember visited hosts between sessions—The name of any GSX Server host previously connected to in a console session will appear in the console's log-in dialog box. The list can be cleared by clicking Clear Host List.
- Remember user names between sessions—Any user names used in previous console connections appear in the console's Log-in dialog box. The list can be cleared by clicking Clear User Names List.
- Check for software updates—GSX Server can be configured to automatically check for product updates that are available. The interval can be changed from never, daily, weekly, or monthly.

Input Settings

The Input tab (see Figure 20.8) allows for settings changes to adjust how the virtual machines grab control of the keyboard and mouse. The virtual machine is also said to have gained focus when the keyboard and mouse input have been grabbed. The following preferences can be configured:

- Keyboard and Mouse—When VMware Tools is either not running or not installed, VMware needs to provide a way for the virtual machine to gain control of the keyboard and mouse from the host server. By allowing either grab on mouse click or grab on key press, GSX Server takes control of the keyboard and mouse after the first primary mouse click in the virtual machine console window or after the first keystroke is sent to the virtual machine. The virtual machine is then said to have focus as it has taken

Figure 20.8   Input Settings.

control of the keyboard and mouse away from the host server. To release control back to the host server, a key combination is pressed (the default is CTRL+ALT). To regain control or focus back within the virtual machine, a mouse click or keystroke must be performed again.

- Cursor—These options are effective only while VMware Tools is running inside of the guest operating system. Selecting Ungrab when cursor leaves window and Grab when cursor enters window allows the mouse pointer to freely move between the virtual machine and the host server in a seamless fashion. Selecting Hide cursor on ungrab makes the mouse pointer disappear in the guest operating system once focus is returned back to the host operating system. This is especially useful in eliminating any confusion when the guest and host operating systems use identical mouse pointers.

- Copy and Paste—In order for copy and paste functionality to work, VMware Tools must be running in the guest operating system. This option is particularly useful when needing to copy and paste text between the host and the virtual machine or between virtual machines. Selecting Enable copy and paste to and from virtual machines turns this feature on. For example, CTRL-C can be used to copy a sample of text to a Windows host server clipboard, and then the mouse can be moved into a Linux guest operating system where the middle mouse button can be used to paste the sample of text into a terminal window. Chapter 22 further explores the cut and paste option and also provides information on how it may be considered a security risk as well as how to disable the function from end users.

 VMware GSX Server uses the CTRL+ALT key combination to release the mouse and keyboard focus or grab from a virtual machine. If the console is being used on a laptop computer, there may be a problem when grabbing and ungrabbing input. Some laptop computers use the same key combination to suspend the laptop. VMware GSX Server can use either the left or right CTRL+ALT keys, while most laptops use the left-hand keys to perform the suspend function. In this case, try using the right-hand keys on the keyboard to perform the ungrabbing feature in GSX Server.

Hot-Key Preferences

Hot-key sequences (see Figure 20.9) are used to interact with virtual machines. By default, the CTRL+ALT key combination is used to start a hot-key, but if this key combination interferes with another application on the host server that uses the same hot-key combination, the default can be changed to CTRL+Shift+ALT or some other custom combination using CTRL, Shift, and ALT keys. Figure 20.10 shows other hot-key sequences that can be used.

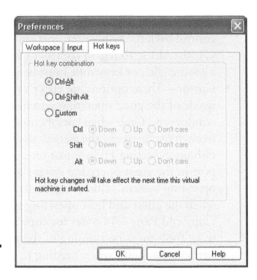

Figure 20.9   Hot-Key Preferences.

Hot-Key	Description
ALT+TAB	Changes between applications within the guest operating system
ALT+ESC	Shifts between application windows within the guest operating system
CTRL+ALT+Delete	The command is received by both the host and guest operating system. Used to shut down or log off the operating system.
CTRL+ALT+Insert	The command is used to shut down or log off the guest operating system.
CTRL+ALT	Releases mouse and keyboard grab or focus from the guest operating system to the host. If the virtual machine is in full screen mode, it returns the virtual machine to window mode.
CTRL+ALT+<Enter>	Expands the current virtual machine into full screen mode. Repeating the command switches the next virtual machine into full screen mode when running multiple virtual machines.
CTRL+ALT+<Space>	Sends any command into the guest operating system so that GSX Server does not process it. Hold down CTRL+ALT and press and release the spacebar and then press the next key in the sequence. For example, to send CTRL+ALT+ESC to the guest rather than having the host intercept, enter the following: 1. Press and hold CTRL+ALT 2. Press and release <SPACE> 3. Press and release ESC 4. Release CTRL+ALT

Figure 20.10   Hot-Key Sequences.

View Menu

Using the View menu, there are a variety of ways to manipulate the display of both the console window and the virtual machines.

- Full Screen—Using full screen mode, the virtual machine's display fills the screen so that borders from the console window are no longer viewable. Full screen mode not only makes the virtual machine's display appear as if it was the local computer, it also provides the virtual machine with a performance increase. Using the CTRL+ALT key combination will exit full screen mode and return the virtual machine to window mode.
- Quick Switch—Quick switch mode is similar to full screen mode except that it keeps the tabs at the top of the screen for easy switching between active virtual machine tabs or the Home tab. To activate quick switch mode, either select View > Quick Switch or press the F11 function key. To exit from quick switch mode, either press the F11 function key again or move the mouse pointer to the top of the screen to activate the hidden menu and then select View > Quick Switch.
- Autofit—Autofit is an item that can be toggled on and off. When toggled on, the console window automatically adjusts when the guest operating system resizes its display. When toggled off, the console window can be adjusted and resized manually.
- Fit—If Autofit is toggled off, Fit can be selected to resize the console window to accommodate the virtual machine's display.
- Fit Guest to Window—When Fit Guest to Window is selected, GSX Server automatically adjusts the Windows guest operating system display settings so the virtual machine will fill as much of the screen as possible. The Fit Guest to Window option only works if the guest operating system is running the current version of VMware Tools and Autofit is toggled off.
- Go to Home Tab—Selecting Go to Home Tab will automatically shift focus to the Home tab. If the Home tab is closed, selecting this option will open it and then shift focus to the tab.
- Inventory, Toolbar, Status Bar, and Virtual Machine Tabs—Each of these items can be toggled off to simplify the display screen and reclaim real estate or toggled on to provide navigational control and display information.

Host Menu

The Host menu provides options that affect the host server directly whether it is opening a new connection, configuring the virtual network settings, or modifying host settings such as memory, process priority, or secure connections.

- Switch Host—Each console can connect to one GSX Server host at a time. To switch hosts from within the console, choose Host > Switch Host and the console connection dialog box appears. Switching host connections will disconnect the console connection to the current host server.
- Virtual Network Settings—Selecting this option opens the Virtual Network Editor dialog window. The editor provides a feature rich environment to modify and configure the GSX Server virtual network and its adapters. It also provides a convenient method of controlling and configuring the DHCP and NAT service settings.
- Settings—The Host Settings dialog offers a number of configurable settings that apply to the GSX Server host. To set these global preferences, either the root or Administrator user must change these settings.

The General tab is used to specify the default directory path that GSX Server uses when a new virtual machine is created. This will be the parent directory for the virtual machine folder that is created and will contains such files as the configuration file, virtual disk files, log files, etc. The default path can either be typed in manually or the Browse button can be used to navigate to the directory.

GSX Server allows setting memory limits, set on the Memory tab, for all virtual machines and gives greater control over the host system memory dedicated to GSX Server. This includes controlling the extent to which the host operating system's memory manager is allowed to swap virtual machines out of physical RAM. Changing VMware's default values may have a negative affect on host or virtual machine performance. This topic is covered in more detail under Resource Management in chapter 22.

The Priority tab on a Windows host server can be configured to allow the Windows process scheduler to give more priority to the virtual machine processes. This will affect the performance of both the virtual machines and the host server. Priority can be set when the virtual machine has keyboard and mouse control (Input grabbed or focus) or when it releases control (Input ungrabbed) back to the host server. There are three priority levels:

1. Low allows other processes more processor time than VMware.
2. Normal allows for the same level as other running processes.
3. High allows the VMware process to be the preferred process.

There are four possible process priorities: high-normal, high-low, normal-normal, and normal-low. When the virtual machine process needs preferred priority, it can be set to high. When the virtual machine is idle, it might be set to low to allow other needed processes to take priority. Because changing process priority could cause complications, only an administrator is allowed to make these changes.

The Priority tab is for Windows host servers only. However, there are commands found within the Linux operating system that can perform this same task. The VMware process, along with any other process, can be altered to run with a specified process priority by using the nice or renice utility. The priority can be set to any value in the range of –20 to 20, with 0 being the base scheduling priority, 20 being the slowest, and –20 being the fastest priority.

The Connections tab will enable or disable the Secure Socket Layer (SSL) protocol for console connections across the network. SSL is enabled by default to ensure secure communications between the console and the host server. Only an administrator can change these settings.

VM Menu

The VM menu offers more direct control and configuration options that relate to the virtual machine rather than the host.

- Removable Devices is used to connect and disconnect removable devices that are configured for a running virtual machine. These devices can include floppy and CD/DVD-ROM drives, USB devices, and Ethernet adapters. It is also possible to edit the device settings. For example, a CD-ROM drive can be edited to mount a different ISO image or a virtual Ethernet adapter can be edited to use a different network connection type.
- Install VMware Tools prepares a virtual machine for the installation of VMware Tools. GSX Server temporarily connects the virtual machine's first CD-ROM drive to the ISO image that contains the VMware Tools installer for that guest operating system and begins the installation process. When it is finished, GSX Server restores the CD-ROM drive to its original configuration.
- Upgrade Virtual Hardware is employed when moving virtual machines created with GSX Server 2.x to a 3.x platform. The virtual hardware can be upgraded to provide full compatibility with the newer options found in GSX Server 3. Once the hardware is upgraded, the image can no longer be powered on under GSX Server 2.
- Connected Users shows a list of users that are connected to the virtual machine with a console or by using VMware Scripting API. The list shows each user name along with their corresponding IP address.
- Remove from Inventory removes the selected virtual machine from the Inventory Panel. It does *not* delete the virtual machine, it removes its listing only.

- Send Ctrl+Alt+Del sends the CTRL+ALT+DEL key sequence to the guest operating system of the selected virtual machine. By default, GSX Server also uses the hot-key combination CTRL+ALT+Insert to perform the same operation.
- Grab Input gives the selected virtual machine mouse and keyboard focus. This option is only available to a virtual machine if it is powered on. The option is probably most useful if there is no mouse control; the keyboard can be used to gain focus in the virtual machine.
- Delete from Disk is used to permanently delete the virtual machine. Unlike Remove from Inventory, which simply removes the listing of the virtual machine from the inventory, Delete from Disk will delete all of the files and folders associated with the virtual machine as well as removing it from the inventory listing. Because the deletion is permanent, the system will prompt for final confirmation.

Settings are established, when creating a new virtual machine, via the New Virtual Machine Wizard. However, there are other settings and options that can be configured on a virtual machine outside of what is offered by the Wizard. The virtual machine settings editor offers additional hardware choices, additional configuration selections, and new virtual machine options to both new and previously configured virtual machines. These options are offered on a per virtual machine basis, these are not global preference settings.

The Hardware tab of the Virtual Machine Settings Editor (see Figure 20.11) is considered the control center where devices can be added to a virtual machine, device settings can be changed, or devices can be removed from a virtual machine. It displays the virtual machine's current device list on the left, while displaying the device configuration settings on the right. Highlighting the device in the left-hand side will change the device settings available on the right-side. Each device type has its own settings that can be changed.

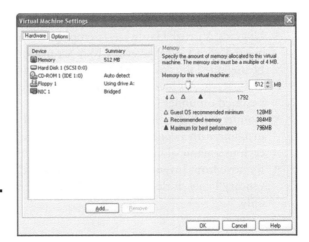

Figure 20.11 Virtual Machine Settings—Hardware Tab.

- Memory allocations to the virtual machine can be changed while the virtual machine is powered off. The minimum and recommended memory values are often found to be too low. A virtual machine's memory requirements are very similar to a physical machine. The old adage, the more memory the better, holds true even in a virtual machine.
- Virtual Hard Disk settings can be changed while the virtual machine is powered off. The disk file that the virtual hard disk is currently attached to can be changed by either typing in the full path and file name or using the Browse button to navigate to the new disk file. Clicking the Advanced button can also change the disk mode of the virtual hard disk. A virtual hard disk can be changed to an independent disk mode that is unaffected by the snapshot feature. It can then be classified as either a Persistent or Nonpersistent disk mode. A Persistent disk acts like a physical disk, all data is permanently written to the disk file. On the other hand, a Nonpersistent disk does not write changes to the disk file, instead, when the virtual machine is powered off or reset, the changes are discarded. Clicking the Defragment button will defragment the virtual hard disk. The data on the virtual hard disk is rearranged so that the individual blocks that make up the specific files become contiguous. This process is extremely time consuming and unless the correct defragmentation order is followed, it may not be time well spent.

Disk modes and disk defragmentation are covered in complete detail in chapter 22, including the proper steps used to defragment a virtual disk. The chapter also explains the various disk modes and how they each interact with the snapshot feature.

CD-ROM drive configuration settings can be changed while the virtual machine is running or powered off. The CD-ROM can access physical media either in the host server's CD-ROM drive or the client's CD-ROM drive. It can also access virtual media, known as ISO images.

Device status—For performance reasons, the connection status of a CD-ROM drive is a useful setting. A CD-ROM drive's connection status can be changed while the virtual machine is powered on or off. The virtual CD-ROM drive takes away processor performance when connected yet idle. When the CD-ROM drive is not in use, it can be disconnected by removing the checkmark and then later connected when needed. When connecting media to the virtual CD-ROM drive, an ISO image is the preferred method for administrative and performance reasons. However, when physical media is needed, GSX Server allows something most other platforms do not—it allows the physical media to be mounted and read from the client machine that is running the console rather than only using the host server.

Floppy drive can either access physical media mounted on the host server or virtual media known as floppy image files. Unlike the CD-ROM drive, a floppy drive can only be accessed by one machine at a time, either the physical host server or one virtual machine.

For performance reasons, the connection status of a floppy drive is a useful setting. A floppy drive's connection status can be changed while the virtual machine is powered on or off. The virtual floppy drive takes away processor performance when connected yet idle. When the floppy drive is not in use, it can be disconnected by removing the checkmark and then later connected when needed.

When connecting media to the virtual floppy drive, a floppy disk image is the preferred method for administrative and performance reasons. To create a new floppy image file, type in a path and file name and then click Create. To use an existing file, click Browse and locate the floppy image file.

- NIC changes the settings of the virtual network adapter.
  A virtual network adapter can be connected or disconnected while the virtual machine is running. Disconnecting the virtual network adapter would be an easy way to simulate a loss of network.

  By default, when creating a new virtual machine with the New Virtual Machine Wizard, the virtual machine is given a vlance network adapter. The vlance driver is installed automatically and works with almost every guest operating system available. If the host server is using Gigabit network adapters, it is recommended to change the adapter type to vmxnet as long as the guest operating system supports it. The vmxnet adapter is a higher performing network adapter but is also proprietary to VMware, which means that support for it is specific to the drivers found on VMware Tools.

  During the creation of a new virtual machine, one of the options is to setup a network adapter. The network type is requested: Bridged, NAT, or Host-only. Once a network type is selected, it does not mean that it cannot be changed. The network connection can be changed to any one of these types or it can be changed to a custom type and then assigned to a virtual switch.

In addition to modifying the settings of existing virtual hardware found in the virtual machine, the Hardware tab also provides the means to add or remove devices from the virtual machine's configuration. Clicking on Add opens the Add Hardware Wizard, which offers a number of additional hardware devices as shown in Figure 20.12.

Figure 20.12 What Type of Hardware Can Be Added.

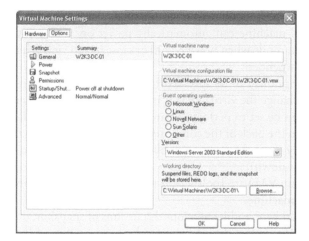

Figure 20.13 Virtual Machine Settings—Option Tab.

When an existing hardware device is selected, it can be removed from the virtual machine's configuration by clicking on Remove. For whatever reason, there is no warning or confirmation window. When remove is selected, the virtual hardware device is immediately removed along with any settings for that device.

The Options tab of the Virtual Machine Settings Editor (see Figure 20.13) is the control center for additional options other than those related to hardware. The available options are listed on the left-hand side, while the settings editor for the selected option is on the right-hand side.

- General tab options are used to change basic information about the virtual machine. Changing the virtual machine name will change its display name, the name that appears in the inventory and on the tab for that virtual machine. If this field is left blank, GSX Server uses the path to the configuration file.

  When the Guest operating system setting is changed, it changes the setting for the type of guest operating system in the virtual machine's configuration file. It does not actually change the guest operating system that is installed in the virtual machine. It does however use this setting to determine which VMware Tools should be installed inside of the guest machine, and which hardware parameters and features should be used or bypassed to offer the best performance.

  The Working directory is where the suspended state files, the REDO log files, and the snapshot files are stored. By default, this location is the same directory that stores the virtual machine's configuration file. For sizing or performance reasons, the directory can be changed to another location.

- The Power options determine how GSX Server handles a specific virtual machine when the application is started.

The virtual machine can be configured to automatically respond to certain events. The virtual machine can automatically power on after being opened, enter full screen mode when powered on, or close its tab view after being powered off or suspended.

The Toolbar power options can be specified to perform certain actions when they are used to change the virtual machine's power state. The power off and reset buttons can be set to perform a hard stop (analogous to pulling the power cord from the back of the computer) or a graceful shut down and reset (which cleanly stops the running applications and guest operating system prior to shut down).

The options in the Run VMware Tools scripts panel control when scripts are run for this virtual machine.

■ Snapshot settings located here, unlike previous discussions of snapshot, do not perform the snapshot, rather they determine the functionality of the snapshot feature itself.

Snapshots can be disabled for a virtual machine. If snapshots are not desired, this would keep a user from creating a snapshot on this particular virtual machine. Snapshots may not be desired because of the performance hit or the extra disk space it may use. If a virtual machine currently has a snapshot, the snapshot can be locked to help prevent accidentally overwriting it with a new snapshot.

This setting can specify the way GSX Server handles the snapshot when the virtual machine is powered off. The snapshot can be kept, discarded, or replaced.

■ Permissions. By default, only the user that created the virtual machine has access to it. The virtual machine is marked as private. This is especially useful if the virtual machine is still in the process of being finalized. To change the permission on this virtual machine to allow others to see it in the inventory, uncheck the Make this virtual machine private checkbox.

■ Startup/Shutdown. A virtual machine can be configured to alter its power state when the GSX Server host changes its power state. This becomes more important when multiple virtual machines owned by different users reside on a single host server. When one user reboots or shuts down the host server, all virtual machines can be cleanly shut down rather than just having the power pulled from them.

On a Windows host server, select the user account the virtual machine uses when it runs. This account is used to access network resources from within the virtual machine and access virtual machine resources that are on the network. In order make use of the startup/shutdown options, the virtual machine must be run as either the local system account or a specified user.

Select the startup and shutdown power options for this virtual machine. When the host server is powered on, the virtual machine can be configured to either remain powered off or power on as well. When the host server is powered off, the virtual machine can be configured to either perform a hard power off or a graceful shut down of the guest operating system before being powered off. This option can become critical over time. If a host server is rebooted accidentally but the virtual machine is not powered back on manually, a critical machine may not be online for a period of time. On the other hand, if a host server is powered off on a regular basis, and the virtual machines are repeatedly hard powered off, the guest operating system may become corrupted over time and eventually cease to function.

In order for these options to have any affect, the host server must be configured to determine if virtual machines should start up or shut down when the host operating system starts or shuts down. The host server is configured by using the VMware Management Interface.

▪ Advanced. There are two advanced virtual machine settings that normally do not get a lot of attention, because they are hardly used—and with good reason, they should only be used in an emergency type situation.

Run with debugging information. When this option is checked, the virtual machine is running in debug mode. This option is useful to enable if the virtual machine is exhibiting problems that are difficult to troubleshoot. By enabling debug mode, the virtual machine will collect additional debug information that may prove useful to VMware support to help troubleshoot the problem. The drawback to running the virtual machine in debug mode is the performance latency the virtual machine will suffer. Once the problem is identified or enough data is collected, it is recommended to immediately return the virtual machine to normal mode.

Disable acceleration. There may be occasions where a software application complains during installation inside of a virtual machine that it is running under a debugger causing the application to crash, lockup, or hang. If this happens, the disable acceleration setting may be a solution. This setting will slow down virtual machine performance, so it is only recommended to get beyond the installation problem. Once the installation problem is circumvented, the setting should be returned to normal to increase virtual machine performance. If the application will not run without acceleration being disabled, the application may not be a good candidate to run inside of a virtual machine.

Power Menu

The basic power operations for a virtual machine are analogous to the power operations on a physical computer: power on, power off, and reset. Perhaps somewhat less familiar are suspend and resume, which are similar to suspend or hibernation commonly found on notebook computers. These power operations are also found on the Toolbar Menu. The Power Menu also offers a graceful shut down or restart option. Choosing Power > Shutdown Guest or Power > Restart Guest cleanly stops the running applications on the virtual machine and then gracefully powers down the guest operating system, rather than just pulling the plug. Scripts in the guest operating system can also be run when a power state change is made but only if the virtual machine is running VMware Tools.

Snapshot Menu

A snapshot preserves the state of the virtual machine just as it was when the snapshot was taken. The Snapshot menu delivers three options: Save Snapshot, Revert to Snapshot, and Remove Snapshot. Save Snapshot provides the same functionality as the Snapshot button on the toolbar. Once the snapshot is taken, two choices are made available: the snapshot either needs to be committed or discarded. Choosing Snapshot > Revert to Snapshot will discard the changes made to the virtual machine since the last snapshot. Choosing Snapshot > Remove Snapshot will commit the accumulated changes by permanently writing them to the base disk. The snapshot can be removed any time while the virtual machine is powered off.

Windows Menu

The Windows menu offers navigational control between the active virtual machines much like selecting the virtual machine's tab with the mouse. One important distinction, the Windows menu supports keyboard control by cycling through the virtual machine tabs using CTRL+TAB to jump to the next tab window, or CTRL+Shift+TAB to jump to the previous tab window.

Help Menu

The Help menu provides numerous ways to receive help using VMware GSX Server. Help topics are available to explain the key steps needed to navigate and configure GSX Server. It also offers more detailed information in the form of a locally stored user's manual and guest operating system installation guide, along with specific links to the latest product documentation provided by VMware's Web site. Additionally, the Help menu provides access to online technical support, licensing information, and ways to manually check for product updates on the Web.

Toolbar Menu

The Toolbar menu (see Figure 20.14) provides an iconic way of viewing various options that are frequently used while working with virtual machines. The entire toolbar can be removed by selecting View > Toolbar. Each icon represented in

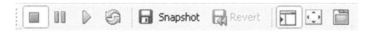

Figure 20.14 Toolbar - Access to Commonly Used Features.

the toolbar also has a corresponding action in the Application Menu Bar. The toolbar provides the following options:

- Power Off—Similar to pressing the power button on a physical computer, it powers off the virtual machine without cleanly stopping the running applications or gracefully shutting down the guest operating system. The button can, however, be configured to gracefully shut down the guest operating system before powering off the virtual machine by modifying VM > Settings > Options > Power and choosing the appropriate action in the drop-down list under Power Controls.

- Suspend—Similar to hibernate, the Suspend button will stop the virtual machine and save the entire state of the guest operating system to disk. The Power On button changes to a Resume button that then starts the virtual machine by using its saved state file and resuming where the virtual machine left off. This button is inactive and grayed out while the virtual machine is powered off.

- Power On—Powers on the virtual machine (much like pressing the power button on a physical computer while turned off). When the virtual machine is suspended, the button appears as Resume.

- Reset—Resets the virtual machine by hard cycling the power off and then on. Similar to resetting a physical computer by pressing its reset button. Like the Power Off button, the Reset button can be modified to stop the running applications, gracefully shut down the guest operating system, and then power the virtual machine back on. To configure the button, choose VM > Settings > Options > Power and then choose the appropriate action in the drop-down list under Power Controls. When a virtual machine is powered off, the button is inactive and grayed out.

- Snapshot—GSX Server allows a snapshot to be taken of the virtual machine while it is powered on, powered off, or suspended. Clicking the Snapshot button takes a snapshot of the virtual machine, i.e., it creates a file that preserves the state of the virtual machine just as it was when the snapshot was taken. Only one active snapshot can exist at a time. More information about the snapshot feature can be found in chapter 22.

- Revert—This icon is grayed out unless a snapshot for the virtual machine exists. If a snapshot does exist, clicking the Revert button will revert to the snapshot and discard all changes made to the virtual machine since the snapshot was taken.

- Show or Hide the Inventory—Clicking the button will either show or hide the Inventory Panel from the console. It provides the same functionality as View > Inventory or pressing the F9 function key.
- Enters Full Screen Mode—Allows the guest operating system to take up the entire screen. Running a virtual machine in full screen mode also improves performance. The option is not available while the virtual machine is powered off. To return to window mode, the CTRL+ALT key combination is used.
- Toggles Quick Switch Mode—Quick switch mode is similar to full screen mode but with tabs at the top of the screen to easily switch from one active virtual machine to another. Moving the mouse pointer to the top of the screen will reveal the hidden GSX Server menu.

Inventory Panel

The Inventory Panel is the panel on the left-hand side of the console that displays the names of virtual machines added to the list. When a virtual machine is created with GSX Server, it is automatically added to the inventory. To manually add a virtual machine to the inventory list, select File > Open Virtual Machine and browse to the virtual machine's configuration file. To remove a virtual machine from the inventory, select the virtual machine in the inventory and then choose VM > Remove from Inventory. This does *not* delete the virtual machine or its files. It simply removes the virtual machine from the listing. The virtual machine can be manually added back at any time. The inventory listing is used to interact with the virtual machines. By clicking on the virtual machine name, it appears in the Tabbed Main Window. By right-clicking the virtual machine name, a menu of options become available such as power state changes, snapshot features, removing from inventory, and altering its settings. Each of these options is covered in detail in the Application Menu Bar, where the same options exist.

Tabbed Main Window

The window contains the largest piece of console real estate. Depending on the tab and the power state of the virtual machine, the window can provide very different data and functionality. The window has three basic tab views: the Home tab, tabs for virtual machines that are powered on, and tabs for virtual machines that are powered off or suspended. The virtual machine's name is displayed in a tab at the top of the window and these tabs can be used to switch from one virtual machine to another.

- Home tab—The Home tab offers information about the host server that the console is connected to, the host name, and the GSX Server platform version. It also offers an iconic representation of four actions that can also be performed elsewhere in the product. The first is a link to the New Virtual Machine Wizard, used to create new virtual machines. The second is a button labeled Open Existing Virtual Machine, which is used to select a virtual machine that is available to the host server and then to display it inside the window. The third option, Switch Host, is used to connect to a different GSX Server. This option is the same as selecting Host > Switch Host. And finally, the forth option is the Configure Host button. It provides the same functionality as selecting Host > Settings. The GSX Server host configuration options can be changed to affect the operation and performance characteristics of the server.

- Powered Off or Suspended Virtual Machine—The tab displays information about the virtual machine such as its name, power state, guest operating system, location of its configuration file, and whether the virtual machine is configured for the current or older version of GSX Server. A free form notes field is available to make comments about the virtual machine, its configuration, etc. The devices can be doubled clicked to provide quick access and to change their configuration settings. In the commands window, the virtual machine can be powered on or resumed, or the virtual machine's settings can be changed in much the same way as was explained in detail when selecting VM > Settings.

- Powered On Virtual Machine—The console acts like a KVM solution when the virtual machines are powered on. Using the tabs at the top of the window, the virtual machines can easily be switched from one virtual machine to another. And, unlike a remote desktop connection, the console connection can watch the entire process of a virtual machine boot starting with POST (power on self test).

Status Bar

The Status Bar is at the bottom of the console window. As previously mentioned, displaying the Status Bar can be toggled on or off by choosing View > Status Bar. When toggled on, it provides valuable information. At a quick glance, the right-hand corner will specify the virtualization platform type (GSX Server or ESX Server) and version installed on the connected host server. It also displays whether the connected session is secure or not by displaying a lock icon, much like in a secured Web browser. Alert and informational messages can appear on the left-hand side of the Status Bar warning, for example, VMware Tools is not installed or the version is out of date. And when a virtual machine is powered on, the right-hand side of the bar also provides access to removable devices that are attached to the virtual machine. These icon representations of the devices can usually be right-clicked to connect, disconnect, or edit the devices. When there is activity, such as network traffic across the virtual network adapter, the icon will flash or light up green to represent the level of activity.

VMware Management Interface

The VMware Management Interface is a Web-based management tool designed to make managing GSX Server virtual machines less cumbersome by providing remote management of the entire host server. Because the tool is Web-based, as long as the user has the proper permissions to log in and is using a supported Web browser, the interface can usually be accessed remotely from almost anywhere. Using the tool, the following options can be performed:

- Monitor the state of the connected host server and its virtual machines.
- Control and alter the power state of the virtual machines on the host server.
- View detailed information about the virtual machines on the host server.
- Modify a virtual machine's configuration.
- Create and delete virtual machines.
- Attach to a virtual machine on the host server by using the VMware Virtual Machine Console.
- Enable and disable the SSL-encrypted management interface and virtual machine console sessions (administrator and root users only).
- View and modify virtual machine behavior during system startup and shutdown.
- View and modify the configuration of virtual networks on the host server.
- Download the VMware Virtual Machine Console for Windows or Linux.

Requirements

Before launching the VMware Management Interface Web tool, the following requirements and restrictions should be taken into account:

- A supported Web browser should be used. VMware recommends the use of Microsoft Internet Explorer 5.5 or 6.0, Netscape Navigator 7.0, Firefox 1.x, or Mozilla 1.x.
- Netscape Navigator and Mozilla-based browsers should have JavaScript and style sheets enabled in the advanced preferences (Edit > Preferences > Advanced).
- The host name or IP address of the remote host server must be known in order to connect to it.
- The proper ports must be opened when using a firewall (by default, 8222 and 8333 for the Web interface and 902 for the console).
- A valid user account and password on the host server is needed in order to authenticate. The account must also have the proper permissions needed in order to manage the server and its virtual machines.
- A maximum of eight simultaneous connections can be made to the management interface.

To connect to the management interface, a URL must be entered into the address bar of the Web browser. The URL used to connect to the server is https://<hostname>:8333 when connecting with SSL enabled. If SSL has been disabled, the URL used to connect to the server is http://<hostname>:8222. When connecting to the management interface from a Web browser on a remote machine or on the local host server, the host server's hostname or IP address can be used as the <hostname>. When connecting to the management interface from a Web browser on the local host server, localhost or the loopback address (127.0.0.1) can also be used as the <hostname>.

 The system will automatically redirect users to the appropriate URL based on whether or not SSL is enabled. For example, if SSL is enabled on the management interface session and the user enters http://<hostname>:8222, the session will be redirected to the secured site https://<hostname>:8333. The opposite is also true, if SSL is disabled on the management interface session and the user enters https://<hostname>:8333, the session will be automatically redirected to the nonsecure site, http://<hostname>:8222.

The Log-In Page

Once the URL is successfully entered, the VMware Management Interface Web application launches and the Log-in page appears (see Figure 20.15). The Log-in page prompts for a username and password for authentication into the system. The username and password combination entered should be for an account that has the appropriate privileges and access rights to the host server. The Log-in page also contains a drop-down menu allowing users to download installation packages of the VMware Virtual Machine Console. By default, the three packages that are offered include: VMware Virtual Machine Console for Windows,

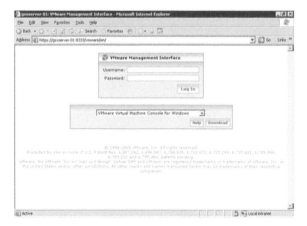

Figure 20.15 VMware Management Interface Log-In Screen.

VMware Virtual Machine Console for Linux (tar.gz), and VMware Virtual Machine Console for Linux (rpm). Which package downloaded is determined by the operating system on which the console is to be installed. One of these packages will need to be installed if a remote client is being used to access the host server and needs to connect to the virtual machine via the console.

On the Log-in page, enter the username and password with the correct privileges for the host server and then click Log In. The Status Monitor page will appear.

The Status Monitor Page

The Status Monitor page is divided up into five categories. The first area contains a high-level view of the GSX Server host by providing a host server system summary. The second area contains a high-level view that provides a list of all known virtual machines on the host server that the authenticated user has permissions to view. The third area provides a secondary link to download one of the three VMware Virtual Machine Console packages offered in the Log-in page. The fourth area allows for the creation of a new virtual machine by clicking on Add Virtual Machine. And finally, the fifth area provides for common controls, which are found on each main page, offering the ability to refresh the page, log out, close the page, or retrieve help. Each of these areas will be discussed in greater detail below.

Viewing System Summary

Under System Summary, the Status Monitor page (see Figure 20.16) provides useful information about the GSX Server host machine. The information is extremely helpful in keeping track of and monitoring the overall utilization of the host server. The summary is broken up into two categories: processor and memory.

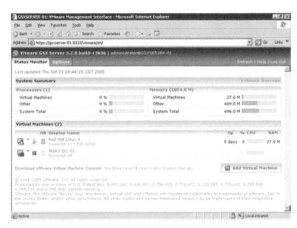

Figure 20.16 VMware Management Interface— Status Monitor Page.

- Processor—The System Summary shows the number of processors on the GSX Server host machine. In addition to the number of processors, it also gives a breakdown of the processor utilization by providing the average percentage of CPU being used by virtual machines, other running processes on the host server, and the total being used by the entire system for the previous minute.
- Memory—The System Summary shows the total amount of memory on the GSX Server host machine. Additionally, it gives a breakdown of the memory consumption by providing the average amount of memory being used by virtual machines, other running processes on the host server, and the total being used by the entire system for the previous minute.

Viewing Virtual Machines

Under Virtual Machines, the Status Monitor page (see Figure 20.17) provides useful information about the virtual machines on the host server in addition to providing a number of management features and controls. A list of all virtual

Microsoft Windows Guest Operating Systems

Linux Guest Operating Systems

FreeBSD Guest Operating Systems

Novell NetWare Guest Operating Systems

Other Guest Operating Systems

Figure 20.17 Terminal Icons Representing the Type of Guest Operating System.

machines registered on the host server that the authenticated user has permissions to view is displayed. The page offers several columns of information that are useful in providing quick-glance details about the virtual machines and information to help monitor their utilization.

- The terminal icon offers a quick graphical representation of most of the guest operating systems that can be selected at the time the virtual machine is created. If the virtual machine display name does not offer any indication of the guest operating system installed, the terminal icon may help identify the type of operating system.

    Clicking the pull down arrow next to the terminal icon displays a menu of options to help manage and configure that particular virtual machine. The following options are made available based on permissions and the current state of the virtual machine.
    1. Attach Console launches the VMware Virtual Machine Console and connects to this virtual machine. If the VMware Virtual Machine Console is not installed locally on the machine running the management interface, the browser will not know how to handle the .xvm file

extension, and prompts to either save or cancel the requested file. The console installation is provided on the log in page as well as the System Monitor page.

2. Properties launches a new browser window opening the Virtual Machine Overview page for this virtual machine. Clicking on Properties is the same as clicking on the Display Name link of the virtual machine.

3. Configure Hardware launches a new browser window opening the Hardware tab of the Virtual Machine Overview page for this virtual machine. The Hardware tab provides configuration changes such as adding, removing, or editing devices, as well as modifying the amount of memory installed on the virtual machine. Most options can only be executed when the virtual machine is powered off.

4. Configure Options launches a new browser window opening the Options tab of the Virtual Machine Overview page for this virtual machine. The Options tab provides a method of modifying the virtual machine's configuration settings, such as display name, suspend file location, system startup and shutdown options, as well as an option to modify the configuration file directly by clicking on Verbose Options. Most options can only be modified while the virtual machine is powered off.

5. Power State Options a number of power state changes for the virtual machine are offered: Shut Down Guest, Suspend after Running Script, Power On and Run Script, Restart Guest, Power Off, Suspend, Power On, and Reset.

6. Delete Virtual Machine can delete the virtual machine from the host server by removing the virtual machine from the listing and deleting its associated folders and files from the system (while the virtual machine's power state is off and permissions allow it).

■ The virtual machine's current power state is graphically represented by an icon to offer information at a quick glance. In addition to graphically representing the virtual machine's current power state, the button also acts as a control mechanism for the power state of the virtual machine. Depending on the user's permissions, the power state can be changed by selecting one of the following buttons in Figure 20.18.

Figure 20.18   Power State Buttons.

- Under the HB (heartbeat) column heading is a bar graph that represents the virtual machine's average percentage of heartbeats during the previous minute. If the guest operating system does not have VMware Tools installed, the heartbeat meter is disabled. Otherwise, the meter helps determine the virtual machine's overall health based on the heartbeats sent back from the VMware guest operating system service. The virtual machine is considered healthy when the meter is green and receiving 100 percent of its heartbeats, under heavy load when yellow and below 100 percent, and abnormal when the meter drops to 0 percent.
- The Display Name column provides quite a bit of information about a virtual machine. The display link indicates the display name for the virtual machine given at the time the virtual machine was created. If the display name is not specified, the path to the virtual machine's configuration file is displayed instead. The virtual machine's power state is displayed in text (Powered on, Powered off, Suspended, etc.) and matches the graphical representation in one of the previous columns. If the virtual machine is powered on, its Process ID or virtual machine ID is displayed. This information is useful when there is a problem with a virtual machine process. Using the Windows Task Manager or the Linux ps command to view the running processes, the virtual machine's PID can be identified to find the troubled process and killed if necessary. If VMware Tools is not installed in the guest operating system, it will also be noted here. And if the virtual machine is waiting for user input to answer a system message, a Waiting for input link will appear. Clicking this link provides more details about the virtual machine and opens a new window, the Virtual Machine Overview page. For more information, see the Virtual Machine Overview section later in this chapter.
- The Up column indicates the length of time the virtual machine has been powered on and running.
- The % CPU column indicates the average percentage of host processor capacity used by the virtual machine during the final minute before the Web page was last updated.
- The RAM column indicates the average amount of memory used by the virtual machine during the final minute before the Web page was last updated.

Download the VMware Virtual Machine Console

As in the Log-in page section, the Status Monitor page also provides a download link to the VMware Virtual Machine Console installation packages. By default, the three packages that are offered include: VMware Virtual Machine Console for Windows, VMware Virtual Machine Console for Linux (tar.gz), and VMware Virtual Machine Console for Linux (rpm). The package downloaded is determined by the operating system on which the console is to be installed. One of these packages will need to be installed if a remote client is being used to access the host server and needs to connect to the virtual machine via the console.

Add Virtual Machine

New virtual machines can be created by clicking Add Virtual Machine on the Status Monitor page. Creating a virtual machine and its configuration file in this manner is similar to creating a new virtual machine by using the New Virtual Machine Wizard in the management console and following the Typical path. The virtual machines created in the management interface are created on the host server that the management interface is currently logged into, just as if the virtual machine was created with the New Virtual Machine Wizard using the remote console. Once the virtual machine is created, its configuration settings can be updated and modified by using the settings editor in the console (VM > Settings) or most settings can also be changed by using the management interface. More information on creating a virtual machine with the console can be found in chapter 21.

Common Controls

The following controls appear on most of the Web pages in the management interface.

- Refresh—Clicking this link is similar to the refresh option found in most Web browsers. It will refresh or reload the current page to update the information found on that page. This option is useful to run just before making a power state change on a virtual machine to make sure the action doesn't conflict with a state change already made to the virtual machine by another user.
- Help—Clicking this link provides the online documentation for the active page in the management interface. This documentation is useful when there are options on the page that aren't clearly defined or explained.
- Log out—Clicking this link logs out of the management interface and returns to the Log-in page.
- Close—Clicking this link closes the active management interface window.

The Options Tab

To assist in the configuration process of the GSX Server host settings, the Options page provides for configuration of the security settings, network connections, and virtual machine startup and shutdown procedures.

- Security Settings—Administrator or root users have the option of enabling or disabling SSL session encryption. A checkbox selection can be made to enable or disable SSL encryption on either the VMware Management Interface or the VMware Virtual Machine Console session. This option is enabled by default, and as such, provides for secure, encrypted username, password, and network packets to be sent across the network to the GSX Server host.

■ Network Connections—Network Connections is used to configure and tune the network adapters used by the virtual machines. This configuration option is important if VMware VirtualCenter is being used to manage the virtual machines and the GSX Server host environments. Each adapter should be assigned a network label. Without a label, VirtualCenter cannot recognize the adapter.

■ Virtual Machine Startup and Shutdown—A system-wide startup and shutdown option, it can be configured to determine if virtual machines are powered on or powered off when the host server starts up or shuts down. The option to shut down the virtual machines when the host server is shut down is a powerful option. Without it enabled, if the host server is shut down while the virtual machines are still powered on, the virtual machines will be hard stopped as if they had their power cord pulled from the back of the machine. When enabled, the virtual machines can be signaled to cleanly shut down when the host server shuts down. The virtual machines can also have a specified startup order or they can be started in a random sequence. Specifying a startup sequence is an important option if a virtual machine has a dependency on another virtual machine starting first.

Virtual Machine Overview

Much like the Status Monitor page (see Figure 20.19), the Virtual Machine Overview page provides a display of useful summary information, only this time providing information related to the selected virtual machine, rather than an overview of the host. The following information is provided:

Figure 20.19 Virtual Machine Overview Page.

- The current power state of the virtual machine, whether it is powered on, off, or suspended.
- The virtual machine ID (VMID) and the process ID (PID). This number is useful when trying to locate the virtual machine in the running processes of the host server (either in the Windows Task Manager or the Linux Process Status).
- The number of virtual processors configured for the virtual machine.
- The average, minimum, and maximum percentage of the GSX Server host processor that the virtual machine used in the previous minute.
- The average, minimum, and maximum percentage of the GSX Server host memory that the virtual machine used in the previous minute.
- The up time or how long the virtual machine has been powered on and running.
- The status of VMware Tools on the virtual machine - whether it is running or not available.
- The average number of heartbeats received by a virtual machine.
- The IP address of the virtual machine.
- Links to modify the virtual machine's hardware and configuration file.
- The guest operating system installed inside of the virtual machine. This information is gathered from the virtual machine's configuration file.
- The amount of memory allocated to the virtual machine.
- The path to the virtual machine's configuration file (.vmx).

The Hardware Tab

Clicking on the Hardware tab (see Figure 20.20) lists the virtual hardware for the selected virtual machine. The virtual hardware is broken out into two categories: Removable Devices and Other Hardware. Removable devices include such

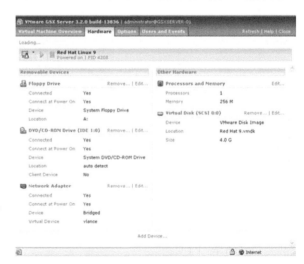

Figure 20.20 Virtual Machine Overview—Hardware.

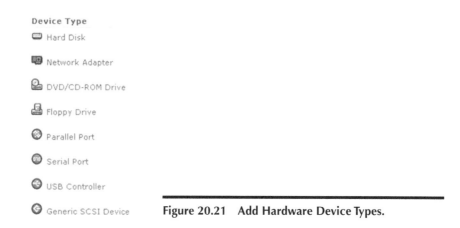

Device Type

Hard Disk

Network Adapter

DVD/CD-ROM Drive

Floppy Drive

Parallel Port

Serial Port

USB Controller

Generic SCSI Device

Figure 20.21   Add Hardware Device Types.

virtual hardware as the floppy drive, DVD/CD-ROM drive, and the network adapter. Other hardware may include such components as the virtual processor and memory, and the virtual disk. This page allows the virtual hardware for the selected virtual machine to be configured by either adding new devices, removing existing devices, or editing existing devices. Figure 20.21 provides a list of additional devices that may be added to a virtual machine.

When configuring the virtual hardware, different options or choices may be available based on the current power state of the virtual machine or the type of component being configured. For example, when configuring a removable device such as a floppy drive or a DVD/CD-ROM drive, if the virtual machine is powered off, then the device's connection status can be toggled on and off. Otherwise, the option is grayed out. Likewise, while a virtual machine is powered on, other options such as adding a new device, removing a device, or editing a device may become grayed out as well. When a virtual machine is powered off, the virtual device may also be modified to change the way it functions. For example, the virtual network adapter allows its network connection to be changed from Bridged to NAT or its virtual device to be modified from vlance to vmxnet. Additionally, a virtual disk may have its disk mode configuration changed from Persistent to Nonpersistent. Network adapter connection types and virtual disk modes are covered in detail in chapter 22. It is safe to say however, that most virtual hardware can only be configured while the virtual machine is powered off.

The Options Tab

The Options page (see Figure 20.22) allows for review and modification of basic information about the selected virtual machine. It also offers direct access to the selected virtual machine's configuration file. These configuration options include the following:

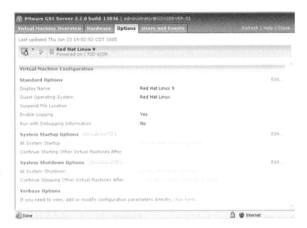

Figure 20.22 Virtual Machine Overview— Options.

- Display Name—descriptive name used to identify the virtual machine in the management interface or the console virtual machine listing. As a best practice, the display name should be an informative name to provide some level of detail about the virtual machine, such as its operating system, department, or functional role. The display name can be changed while the virtual machine is either powered on or off.
- Guest Operating System—indicates the guest operating system selected during the creation of the virtual machine. While it should match the guest operating system that is installed on the virtual disk, it does not have to match for the virtual machine to power on and function. Therefore, do not assume that what is populated here is in fact the operating system that is installed.
- Suspend File Location—specifies the location of the suspended state file. By default, the suspended state file is stored in the directory where the virtual machine's configuration file resides. Suspend files can become very large in size, therefore it is recommended that the suspend file location is stored on a physical disk with enough space to accommodate it.
- Enable Logging—indicates whether logging for the virtual machine is enabled. Logging of a virtual machine may accumulate large amounts of data that in turn may take away precious disk space from a host server, which is one reason to disable logging. However, if a virtual machine crashes or VMware support is needed to troubleshoot a problem with the virtual machine, these log files may be required to diagnose the problem.
- Run with Debugging Information—indicates whether the virtual machine is running with debugging information. By default, this option is disabled. Enabling this setting will affect the performance of the virtual machine; however, if the virtual machine is exhibiting problems, enabling this feature may help troubleshoot the issue.

- Startup and Shutdown Options—indicates whether the virtual machine should start when the host server starts or shut down when the host server is shut down. The virtual machines can also be set to stagger starting up or shutting down so that multiple virtual machines do not all start or stop at the same time, which could cause a performance problem for the host server or the virtual machines on that host server.
- Verbose Options—allows the virtual machine's configuration file to be modified directly. VMware recommends only an experienced and advanced user modify the file directly. Modifying the configuration file with an incorrect setting can cause the virtual machine to no longer boot.

Users and Events Tab

The Users and Events page (see Figure 20.23) contains information that relates to the virtual machine such as currently connected users, permissions of the current user, and events that have taken place in relation to the virtual machine.

- Virtual Machine Console Connections—identifies a list of users that are connected to the virtual machine either with a console connection or by using a VMware Scripting API. The list provides the date and time stamp along with the IP address of the user connected to the virtual machine. This feature provides important information when trying to determine security issues related to access of a virtual machine.
- Permissions—indicates what abilities the currently logged in user has on the virtual machine. The following options are either allowed or denied.

Figure 20.23 Virtual Machine Overview—Users and Events.

1. View virtual machine status
2. Modify virtual machine configuration
3. Control virtual machine (powering it on, off, or suspending it)

■ Events—displays a log of the 15 most recent actions or events recorded for the virtual machine. The log shows date and time stamps for the event along with an explanation. Information can include a power state change on the virtual machine (powered on, off, or suspended), errors produced, or GSX Server question and answer information. The event log retrieves its data from the log file for the virtual machine's configuration file. By default, this log file is stored in the virtual machine's directory. On a Windows host, the default directory is <installdrive>:\Virtual Machines\ <guestOS>. On a Linux host, the default directory is /var/lib/vmware/ Virtual Machines/<guestOS>. Many of these events are also tracked on a Windows host server in the Windows Event Viewer under the Application log using VMware GSX Server as the source and Virtual machines as the category.

Security

In the past, the computer industry has been focused on security, primarily being concerned with defending against external threats. Perimeters were created to help ward off these threats by introducing various tools such as antivirus software, firewalls and intrusion detection and prevention systems. However, as the human factor (namely end users) grew within the industry, security problems were faced on two fronts: servers still needed protection from external threats more than ever, but now they also needed protection against threats from within. Add virtualization into the server mix and security concerns become that much more exasperated. Why? With the addition of the GSX Server environment into the physical environment, both the guest operating system and the host operating system must deal with security concerns and issues.

In order to properly secure a host and guest operating system in a GSX Server environment, it is important to undergo proper planning when creating virtual machines. In other words, it is important to fully understand the role and function of all virtual machines that are created. For example, a virtual machine or group of virtual machines created to test an application may be configured in an isolated network environment. This configuration may not cause as much security alarm as a virtual machine that is created to act as the production network domain controller. Additionally, a virtual machine acting as a Web server may raise even more alarm since it is being directly accessed by unknown users from the Internet. This section will outline the various methods to help deal with the security concerns and issues brought about with the introduction of virtualization.

Securing the Host Server

This section describes a number of methods to properly secure the GSX Server host. Keep in mind, the GSX Server host is still a physical server. Any normal best practices used to secure other physical servers in the environment should also be followed, unless it negatively impacts something required for VMware GSX Server to operate properly.

Antivirus Software

A Windows host operating system exposed to the outside world needs to have virus protection installed. It is important to monitor the performance of the host server, to make sure that real-time virus scanning does not interfere with the virtualization processes or the virtual machines. If performance is running too high, it might make sense to change the real-time virus scanning to only scan modified files. It is also important to disable scanning any of the following by using an exclusion rule: the installation path of GSX Server and any virtualization files such as virtual disk files, suspend files, configuration files, floppy images and ISO images.

Prevent Virtual Machines from Running in Full Screen Mode

On a Linux host server, the vmware-remotemks binary (the program that allows the VMware Virtual Machine Console to connect to a GSX Server host remotely) runs as root with the setuid bit set. This allows a virtual machine to enter full screen mode. To disable the setuid bit and keep the program from running as root, switch to the root user and change to the directory where vmware-remotemks was installed. The default location is /usr/bin. Type the following command at a terminal:

```
chmod -Xs vmware-remotemks
```

Doing so will increase host security, but the down side to disabling the setuid bit is that virtual machines on the host server will no longer be able to enter full screen mode.

Network Segmentation

Depending on the role of the virtual machines, it may be a good idea to segment the physical servers from the virtual machines by creating multiple networks at the physical switch. If the virtual machines are being created for some other purpose other than production environment resources, segmenting the two networks (physical and virtual) will help to secure the production environment from loosely controlled virtual machines that may not be up to production security standards.

Securing IIS for GSX Server for Windows Hosts

GSX Server for Windows uses Microsoft's Internet Information Server (IIS) to host the VMware Management Interface. In order to maintain security, commonly used best practices to secure IIS should be followed. In addition to these best practices, the following suggestions can also be used to help secure the environment.

- Do not host other Web sites on the GSX Server host machine. Web sites should be hosted on nonvirtualization-based physical servers or within virtual machines.
- With the exception of the VMware Management Interface Web site, all other Web, FTP and SMTP services listed in the IIS Manager should be removed.
- IP address restrictions can be used to limit access to the management interface.
  1. In IIS Manager, in the Web Sites directory, right click the management interface Web site and then select Properties.
  2. Click the Directory Security tab.
  3. Click Edit in the IP address and domain name restrictions section.
  4. Click either Granted access or Denied access. When selecting Denied access, access to all computers and domains are denied. When selecting Granted access, access to all computers and domains are granted, except to those specifically denied access.
  5. Click Add and then select either Single computer or Group of computers.
  6. Enter either the IP address or the Network ID and Subnet mask and then click OK.
- Increase the VMware Management Interface application protection option from Low (IIS Process) to High (Isolated). This setting helps reduce the risk of compromise by any unforeseen vulnerability within the management scripts.
  1. In IIS Manager, in the Web Sites directory, right click the management interface Web site and then select Properties.
  2. Click the Home Directory tab.
  3. Set the value for Application Protection to High.
  4. Click OK to confirm the settings change.
  5. Stop and start the IIS service to allow the change to take effect.
- The configured IIS file extensions used by the VMware Management Interface scripts do not perform a check to see if the script file exists before attempting to execute it. There could be a security risk allowing a remote user to invoke the script interpreter without needing to pass it a legitimate file that exists. To circumvent this potential security problem, the Check that file exists option should be enabled in the file extension mappings for .pl and .xvm.

1. In IIS Manager, in the Web Sites directory, right click the management interface Web site and then select Properties.
2. Click the Home Directory tab and then click Configuration.
3. Under Application Extensions, select .pl and then click Edit. Select the Check that file exists option and then click OK.
4. Under Application Extensions, select .xvm and then click Edit. Select the Check that file exists option and then click OK.
5. Click OK to confirm the settings changes.
6. Stop and start the IIS service to allow the change to take effect.

Securing Connections with SSL

By default, GSX Server 3 has SSL enabled for secure connections using both the VMware Virtual Machine Console and the VMware Management Interface. Using SSL for the console and the management interface connection keeps the network traffic secure by encrypting the username, password and network packets sent to the GSX Server host. With SSL enabled, GSX Server creates its own security certificates and stores them on the host server. Unfortunately, these certificates are not signed by a trusted certificate authority, and therefore do not provide authentication. If encryption is needed across remote connections externally, a certificate from a trusted certificate authority should be purchased. To use a purchased security certificate, use the information below.

- On a Windows host, run the Microsoft Management Console (MMC) and select the purchased certificate. If the VMware Management Interface is ever upgraded, the certificate will need to be reassigned to the management interface.
- On a Linux host, copy the purchased certificate for the VMware Management Interface to /etc/vmware-mui/ssl. The management interface certificate consists of two files: the certificate is the mui.crt file and the private key is the mui.key file. The private key file should be assigned permissions so that only the root user can read it. If the management interface is upgraded or removed on a Linux host, the certificate and directory remain in place.

Restricting Virtual Machine and Virtual Disk Creation

Any user with access to the GSX Server host, by default, has the ability to create a virtual machine or a virtual disk file on the host server. While many users may be allowed to access the host server, as a security precaution for the host server and all running virtual machines, the number of users allowed to create virtual machines or disk files should be limited. Without any controls in place, a user may accidentally consume too much disk space on the host server or add an unpatched virtual machine that could cause security problems for the other virtual machines or physical machines on the same network. To restrict the ability to create a virtual machine or virtual disk on the host server, the following steps should be performed:

1. On the GSX Server host, create a file and assign it a name (referred to as <name> going forward).
2. Assign write permissions to <name>, only to the users and/or groups that are allowed to create a virtual machine or virtual disk on that host server.
3. Use a text editor to modify the GSX Server configuration file. If the host server is a Windows server, the file is C:\Documents and Settings\All Users\Application Data\VMware\VMware GSX Server\config.ini. If the host server is a Linux server, the file is /etc/vmware/config.
4. The following lines should be added to the configuration file:

   ```
   Serverd.doCreateCheck = "TRUE"
   Serverd.createCheckFile = "<name>"
   ```

   Where <name> is the name of the file created in Step 1.
5. Save the file and then close and exit the text editor.
6. On a Windows host, restart the VMware Registration Service by opening the Services console, right click the service and select Restart. On a Linux host, restart the vmware-serverd process with the following command:

   ```
   kill -TERM `pidof vmware-serverd`
   ```

   If the vmware-serverd process does not restart automatically, reboot the GSX Server host.

Now, only users or members of the group with write access to the <name> file can create virtual machines or virtual disk files on the host server. If a change is made to the user or group list in the file permissions of <name>, then Step 6 will need to be executed again to update the GSX Server host with the permission changes.

Disabling Guest Operating System Logging

Virtual machines can log troubleshooting data into a log file stored on the host server's disk drive. These log files are not secured. Any user or process in the virtual machine can maliciously use this logging process to cause large amounts of data to be logged. The data may eventually grow large enough to fill up the host server's hard disk, thereby leading to a denial of service. To secure the host, this logging feature can be disabled on the host server by adding the following line to each virtual machine's configuration file:

```
isolation.tools.log.disable = TRUE
```

If you disable this logging feature, VMware Support may not be able to provide any help troubleshooting problems that might arise. Logging may need to be re-enabled and the problem may then need to be reproduced. Keep in mind, this option only disables logging from the guest operating system and does not disable logging generated by GSX Server.

Changing the Console Port Number

By default, the VMware Virtual Machine Console connects to the GSX Server host and its virtual machines on port 902. If this port is already used for another application, deemed a security risk because it is a default port, or if the port number needs to be different per host because different groups of users are accessing different host servers then the port number should be changed on the host and the remote console accessing it.

Changing the Port Number on a Windows Host or Client

In order to change the port number on a GSX Server for Windows host server, the following line must be added to the config.ini file located in C:\Documents and Settings\All Users\Application Data\VMware\VMware GSX Server:

```
authd.port = <NewPort>
```

Where <NewPort> is the modified port number that all consoles need to use to properly connect to the GSX Server host or its virtual machines.

In order to change the port number used by the console, whether on the Windows host server or client, a config.ini file must be created and placed in C:\ Documents and Settings\All Users\Application Data\VMware\VMware Virtual Machine Console. The following line should be added to the file:

```
authd.client.port = <NewPort>
```

Where <NewPort> is the modified port number that all consoles need to use to properly connect to the GSX Server host or its virtual machines. The authd. port on the GSX Server host must have this same port number assigned.

To assign the port number to a specific user that is using the console installed locally on the Windows host server, add the following line to the preferences. ini file located in C:\Documents and Settings\<user name>\Application Data\ VMware:

```
authd.client.port = <NewPort>
```

Where <NewPort> is the modified port number that only this specified user account will use to properly connect to the GSX Server host or its virtual machines. The authd.port on the GSX Server host must have this same port number assigned in the config.ini file.

Changing the Port Number on a Linux Host or Client

In order to change the port number on a GSX Server for Linux host server, the first step is to determine whether the host server is configured to use xinetd or inetd. If the host server is using xinetd, the following line located in /etc/xinetd/vmware-authd must be changed:

```
port = 902
```

Change the port number to the new port number that all consoles need to use to properly connect to the GSX Server host or its virtual machines.

If the host server is using inetd, the following line located in /etc/inetd.conf must be changed:

```
902 … vmware-authd
```

Change the port number to the new port number that all consoles need to use to properly connect to the GSX Server host or its virtual machines.

In order to change the port number used by the console, whether on the Linux host server or client, the following line should be added to either /etc/vmware-console/config or /usr/lib/vmware-console/config:

```
authd.client.port = <NewPort>
```

Where <NewPort> is the modified port number that all consoles need to use to properly connect to the GSX Server host or its virtual machines. The authd.port on the GSX Server host must have this same port number assigned.

To assign the port number to a specific user that is using the console installed locally on the Linux host server, add the following line to ~/.vmware/preferences:

```
authd.client.port = <NewPort>
```

Where <NewPort> is the modified port number that only this specified user account will use to properly connect to the GSX Server host or its virtual machines. The authd.port on the GSX Server host must have this same port number assigned in its vmware-authd file. When this user is logged in, the modified port number in the preferences supersedes the port number specified in the config file.

Securing the Virtual Machine

This section describes a number of methods to properly secure the virtual machines. Keep in mind that virtual machines still function as if they were physical servers. For the most part, any best practices that are normally followed to secure physical servers should also be followed for virtual machines.

Antivirus Software

A Windows guest operating system exposed to the outside world needs to have virus protection much like a physical server. It does not matter if antivirus software is installed on the host server. A virtual machine needs its own copy of antivirus installed. Unlike a physical server, there are a few things to consider when configuring an antivirus solution in a Windows guest operating system.

- Make sure you account for the extra overhead that an antivirus solution provides when creating a virtual machine configuration file. During the planning process, make sure enough disk space is available for virus definition downloads and enough memory and processor is available to run the software and the virus scanning.
- If there are a number of running virtual machines on the host server, be sure to stagger the virus scanning schedule. If all of the virtual machines on the host server start their virus scans at the same time, the host server performance may become starved for resources.
- If the antivirus software provides real-time scanning, monitor the processor utilization to make sure the process is not running higher than normal. In some cases, real-time virus scanning on the guest operating system may spike to a percentage of utilization beyond what is acceptable. If this is the case, modifying the real-time scan to only scan files that have been modified as opposed to all files should bring processor utilization back to a normal and acceptable amount.

Operating System and Application Security Patches

It is important to keep the guest operating system and all applications up to date with any security patches or service packs. Operating systems and applications installed on a virtual machine suffer from the same security concerns and problems as those faced in a physical server. If an application such as a Web server (IIS or Apache) becomes exploited, it should be patched immediately. However, if a guest operating system comes out with a new update, it is not always a good idea to quickly update the virtual machine. A new service pack in the guest operating system may cause problems for the host platform. Case in point, the Windows Server 2003 Service Pack 1 was not officially supported as a guest operating system until VMware GSX 3.2. While that does not mean that the service pack would not function correctly in the virtual machine, it does mean that it was not supported. And as such, VMware support would not be able to help troubleshoot any problems that may arise.

Network Isolation

A simple way to secure a virtual machine from the outside world is to create its configuration file without a virtual network adapter. In a workstation class virtualization environment, this option might be common. But in a server class virtualization environment, chances are the virtual machine is going to have to at least interact with other virtual machines. In this case, one possible solution is to segment the virtual machine into an isolated virtual network environment. By creating the virtual machine with a virtual network adapter configured for host-only networking, the virtual machine can remain isolated from all external networks, which in turn gives the virtual machine an added layer of security.

Marking the Virtual Machine as Private

By default, when a new virtual machine is created, it is created as private. When marked as private, only the user that created the virtual machine can see it in the inventory of the host server. Other users cannot browse to the virtual machine or add it to their inventory. Therefore, marking the virtual machine as private can add to the virtual machine's security. To mark a virtual machine as private after it has been created, complete the following steps:

1. Select the virtual machine in a console and then select VM > Settings to open the virtual machine settings editor.
2. Click the Options tab and then click Permissions.
3. To mark the virtual machine as private, activate the checkbox next to Make this virtual machine private.
4. Click OK to save the settings and close the settings editor window.

Virtual Machines and File Permissions

As explained in previous chapters, virtual machine components are simply made up of files that reside on the physical host server. Two common file types are the configuration file (.vmx) and the virtual hard disk (.vmdk), both of which reside on a physical disk. File permissions on these and other files or folders are very important for security reasons. Without the proper security permissions, the virtual machines become exposed. If the files are not secured, any one of the following scenarios could occur:

- Virtual machine files can be copied elsewhere with the intent of hacking into and exploiting the guest operating system at a later date.
- Virtual machine files can be copied elsewhere with the intent of stealing private data, software, or code.
- Virtual machine files can be accidentally or maliciously deleted causing the virtual machine to be rendered useless.
- A malicious user can alter the security settings on the files to lock out the real owner of the virtual machine.
- A user may connect to a virtual machine and alter the guest operating system or software in an unwanted manner.

Access to a virtual machine is based on the user permissions granted to the virtual machine's configuration file. On a Windows host server, when a user connects to the VMware Virtual Machine Console or the VMware Management Interface, the VMware Authorization Service requests a username and password for authentication. On a Linux host server, the VMware authentication daemon (vmware-authd) requests a username and password and then passes them to the Linux Pluggable Authentication Modules (PAM) for authentication. Different permissions allow for access to virtual machines in different ways. They include:

- Browsing a virtual machine allows the user to connect to the virtual machine with a console, however they can only see the virtual machine's power state. There is no interaction with virtual machine whatsoever. To browse a virtual machine, the user needs the following permission: on a Windows host server—Read; and on a Linux host server—read (r) permission.
- Interacting with a virtual machine allows the user to change the virtual machine's power state or connect and disconnect removable devices. To interact with a virtual machine, the user must have the following permissions: on a Windows host server—Read & Execute; and on a Linux host server—read and execute (r and x).
- Configuring a virtual machine allows the user to add and remove virtual hardware to and from a virtual machine. To configure a virtual machine, the user must have the following permissions: on a Windows host server—Read and Write permissions for the virtual machine's configuration file as well as the virtual machine resources; and on a Linux host server—read and write (r and w).
- An administrator or root user may configure the GSX Server host or any virtual machines on that host. On a Windows host server, the user must be a member of the host server's Administrators group. On a Linux host server, the user should have root access to the directories containing the virtual machine files. To have specific administration over a single virtual machine, the user should have Read & Execute and Write permissions on a Windows host server or read, write, and execute (r, w, and x) permissions on a Linux host server to the particular virtual machine.

Permissions for Removable Devices for Virtual Machines

Normal users and processes within virtual machines have the ability to connect or disconnect certain devices identified in a virtual machine's configuration file. For example, a virtual machine may have a CD-ROM drive attached, yet disconnected, that points to physical media in the host server's CD-ROM drive.

This CD-ROM may contain confidential data that should not be exposed to a normal user with access to a virtual machine. Once a user has access to the virtual machine in this state, they can gain access to the data on the CD-ROM by simply connecting the removable device. Another example, a normal user that has access to a virtual machine in the production network may accidentally or maliciously remove a virtual network adapter from the virtual machine, causing a denial of service. To prevent these things from happening, add the following option to the virtual machine's configuration file.

```
<device>.allowGuestConnectionControl = FALSE
```

Where <device> is a device name specified such as ethernet0.

Summary

After the installation of VMware GSX Server is complete, the host server is ready to be configured for daily use. To help with that process, VMware provides two solutions to help configure and manage both the virtual machines and the host environment. Both solutions provide similar management and configuration features but offer them in a different way. One solution is a Web-based management tool called the VMware Management Interface. It provides additional resource monitoring information that can prove useful during troubleshooting and to help balance out the placement of new virtual machines. The other solution is a client-based management tool called the VMware Virtual Machine Console. In addition to providing management and configuration options, it also provides a KVM-like remote control feature to connect to, view, and interact with the virtual machine's desktop. Host configuration does not stop there. With the addition of virtualization, an already high network security level just got multiplied. Security has become a big concern, and with the ease at which a virtual machine is created and added into a network, more security initiatives need to take place. While there are ways to lock down and secure GSX Server and its virtual machines, it is important to remember, the old faithful security efforts for a physical server and environment still hold true in a virtual machine and a virtual environment.

Chapter 21

Creating a VMware GSX Server Virtual Machine

Going beyond the basic installation and configuration of GSX Server, this chapter provides a step-by-step process for creating a virtual machine and installing its guest operating system on the GSX Server platform. The chapter stops short of going through an entire guest operating system install, instead focusing on the steps that lead up to and follow the operating system installation. Before a virtual machine is created, the virtual machine's configuration should undergo a process of proper preparation and a decision-making process to determine the use of the virtual machine. Once that is complete, the virtual machine is added through the creation of a configuration file. The configuration file is a collection of settings and resources that, when bound together, form the virtual execution environment. Once created, the final step is to power the virtual machine on and install the guest operating system.

Preparation

The first thing to do to prepare for the creation of a virtual machine is to determine the purpose or use of the virtual machine. It is important to properly size and scope the virtual machine before blindly creating its configuration. Additionally, proper planning is important when creating template images, rather than creating a department filled with time consuming one-off images that totally negate one of the time saving features of using virtualization. Below are sample questions that should be asked during the preparation stage; however, chapters 6 and 24 go into much further detail to help with this process.

- What operating system is needed?
- What applications need to be installed?
- How much memory does this configuration require to operate smoothly?
- How much disk space is needed?
- What type of networking, if any, is required?
- What other resources or devices are needed in this configuration?

Once the planning stage is complete, it is important to gather all of the software and hardware needed to create the virtual machine. A physical server with the proper hardware and enough resources available to run GSX Server and the virtual machine is needed. The operating system software (media and/or ISO images), application software, drivers (floppy disks, media or images) as well as any license keys all need to be accumulated for use during the creation process.

There are also many concerns that should be noted before attempting to start the virtual machine creation process.

- Screen savers should be disabled on the host server before the guest operating system is installed.
- Screen savers on the guest operating system may be too CPU intensive for the host server. In some cases, it may cause a Linux host server's X server to lock-up and freeze.
- Verify the operating system media or image is not an OEM copy that requires installation on specific hardware. If so, when the initialization process begins, the virtual hardware will not match the expected vendor hardware and the installation will fail.
- As with physical servers, a separate operating system or application license is usually required for each virtual machine that gets an installation. Verify the software license agreement to make sure to stay in license compliance.
- A guest operating system's hibernation feature is not supported and should not be used, instead, it should be disabled in favor of using the VMware suspend feature.
- Microsoft's Activation policy can cause havoc when creating a template image or when making configuration changes to a virtual machine. Certain configuration changes may require reactivating the guest operating system. It is therefore best to either create the virtual machine in its final form with little to no changes made after the fact or to use volume license key media where activation is not required.
- Migrating virtual machines from one host to the next that use a different type of processor may cause an issue. For example, Red Hat Linux 9.0 is sensitive to moving from AMD to Intel and vice versa because during installation a kernel is chosen that is optimized for that specific processor. The kernel may contain instruction sets that are only available for the original processor and may cause adverse effects when executed against a different processor type.

Once a process is in place, creating and provisioning virtual machines becomes a much easier operation.

Creating a Virtual Machine

GSX Server offers a number of ways to create a new virtual machine. They can be created by using the VMware Virtual Machine Console, the VMware Management Interface, VMware VirtualCenter, third-party management tools or even through the use of scripts. Each of these options basically accomplishes the same thing: they create a virtual machine configuration file, complete with the settings and resources needed to be a working virtual machine. This section will cover step-by-step instructions using the Virtual Machine Console method. To illustrate, the following steps can be used to create a new virtual machine using the New Virtual Machine Wizard option located in the console.

New Virtual Machine Wizard

To create a new virtual machine:

1. Launch the VMware Virtual Machine Console.
2. Select File > New Virtual Machine or from the Home tab click the New Virtual Machine icon and the New Virtual Machine Wizard will start (see Figure 21.1). To navigate through the Wizard, Next and Back buttons are located at the bottom of the screen. If at any point an incorrect selection is made, click the Back button to navigate to the previous screen. Click Next to begin.

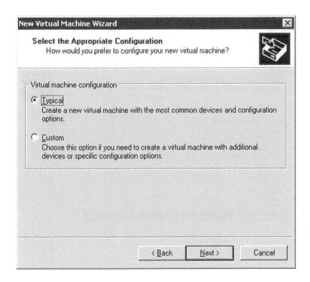

Figure 21.1 New Virtual Machine Configuration.

3. Select the appropriate configuration
   The Wizard then prompts for a virtual machine configuration method and offers two types: Typical and Custom. Selecting the Typical option will create a virtual machine with the most common devices and basic configuration options while selecting the Custom option will create a virtual machine with additional devices and offer several more configuration screens. To gain better control over the creation of the virtual machine, click the Custom option and then click Next.

 The custom option contains all of the screens found within the typical option in addition to more features and screens.

4. Select a guest operating system (see Figure 21.2).
   Select the desired guest operating system that will be installed in the virtual machine. By selecting a radio button for the guest operating system family, different operating system versions are offered in a drop-down list. The Wizard will make default configuration choices based on the operating system selected. If the operating system of choice is not listed, select Other. For this example, Windows Server 2003 Standard Edition will be selected. Click Next to continue.

5. Name the virtual machine (see Figure 21.3).
   The Wizard then prompts for the virtual machine name and the location to store the files that are associated with the virtual machine. By default, the virtual machine and its directory folder are named for the version of the operating system selected in the previous step. With proper planning, these names should be changed to something more appropriate to better identify the virtual machine or its function. For this example, a Windows Server 2003 domain controller will be created and appropriately named W2K3-DC-01. Click Next to continue.

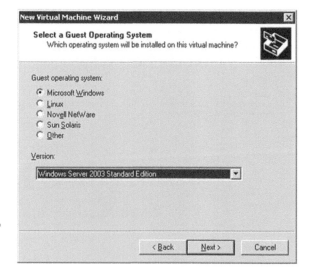

Figure 21.2   Select a Guest Operating System.

Figure 21.3. Create a Name for the Virtual Machine.

 Each virtual machine will have its own directory that stores all of its associated files such as the configuration file, the disk file(s) and the NVRAM file. By default, on a Windows host server, the virtual machine directory is located on Z:\Virtual Machines (where Z is the VMware install drive). On a Linux host server, the default virtual machine directory is /var/lib/vmware/Virtual Machines. For performance reasons, the default directory should be on a different local drive from the host operating system. To make that change in the console, select Host > Settings > General and select a new unique directory.

6. Set access rights (see Figure 21.4).
    By default, the access rights to a newly created virtual machine are marked as private. When a virtual machine is marked as private, only the user that

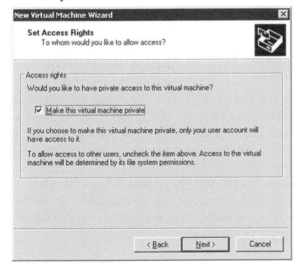

Figure 21.4 Setting Access Rights.

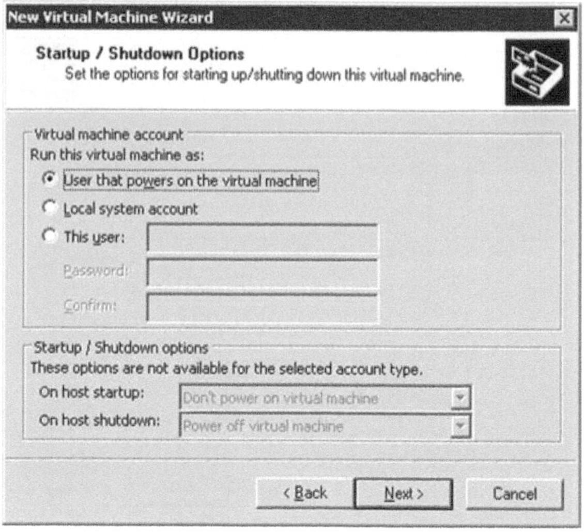

Figure 21.5 Modifying Startup/Shutdown Options.

created the virtual machine can see it listed in the inventory listing. As an example, this feature is useful when creating template images. Until the guest operating system is finished being configured, no other user should have access to the virtual machine. Once completed, the permission can be changed to allow the virtual machine to show up in inventory for other users to view. Access rights can be changed at any time by selecting VM > Settings > Options > Permissions. For more information about permissions and security, see chapter 20. For now, leave the virtual machine marked as private and click Next.

7. Startup/Shutdown options (see Figure 21.5).
   There are two choices to be made on this screen, choose the user account for running the virtual machine (Windows host only) and the host startup and shutdown options.

   Under Virtual machine account on a Windows host server, select a user account for the virtual machine to use when it is powered on. This determines the network permissions from within the virtual machine and access to virtual machine resources on the network. There are three possible choices:

   - User that powers on the virtual machine—The virtual machine runs as the user account that powered it on. When other users connect to the virtual machine, it still runs as the user that initially powered it on. The user account lock on this virtual machine goes away when the virtual machine is powered off. It is important to make sure the virtual machine and its files are in a location that is accessible to that user.
   - Local system account—This option can only be enabled by an administrator. The reason being, with this option activated, the virtual ma-

chine runs as the local system account (administrator). In general, it is not recommended to use the local system account; if compromised, it has unlimited access to the operating system resources. Additionally, it only has access to the local storage and cannot access files across the network.

■ This user—The virtual machine will run in the user context for the specified user account. A local user account or local administrator account can be used; however, it can also specify a fully qualified domain account that will allow access to virtual machine files spanning the network (as long as the proper security is assigned to the user account).

Under Startup / Shutdown options on either a Windows host or a Linux host, select how the virtual machine's power state should be handled when the host server's power state changes. This option can only be enabled while the virtual machine is powered off and the virtual machine is configured to run as an administrator user. It is important to understand, if this feature is not activated and the host server is powered off, the virtual machines will not be gracefully powered down. Instead, it will be as if the plug was pulled from the wall. This option is also useful when boot order of the virtual machines on a host server is important. For example, perhaps a virtual machine acting as a domain controller needs to boot first, followed by a DHCP server, then an application server, etc. Setting this option will help facilitate that function.

For now, accept the default values and leave the selection as User that powers on the virtual machine. These options can be changed later by selecting VM > Settings > Options > Startup/Shutdown from the console.

 After setting the virtual machines on a host server to automatically start up after the host boots and shut down when the host is shut down, you can also change the order in which it happens. In other words, you can stagger the power on and power down of virtual machines to control their boot order. Staggering the boot order can be important if the virtual machines have a dependency on one another (e.g., a database server may need to be powered on before an application server that has a dependency on a database being up and reachable). Once the configuration change has been made to shut down and start the virtual machines automatically, add the following option to the virtual machine's configuration file:

```
autostart.order = <n>
```

The value of <n> must be a multiple of 10, and it controls the order in which virtual machines start up and shut down. For example, the first virtual machine would have a value of 10, with the second virtual machine having a value of 20, the third a value of 30 and so on until the last virtual machine in the list is modified.

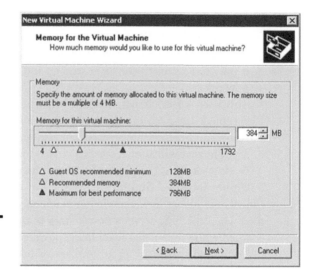

Figure 21.6 Allocating Memory for the Virtual Machine.

8. Memory for the Virtual Machine (see Figure 21.6).
    The Wizard provides a guide to help identify the amount of RAM that should be allocated to the virtual machine. Based on the guest operating system selected earlier in the configuration process, the Wizard provides the minimum amount of memory recommended by the operating system manufacturer and a GSX Server recommended range from normal to maximum performance along with the total amount of memory available to all running virtual machines.

    To change the amount of memory, the Wizard provides a sliding scale that can be moved left to right, a spin controller with selection arrows up and down, and an input field. Each of these can be used to allocate the appropriate amount of memory to the virtual machine. GSX Server requires that the memory configuration be entered in multiples of 4MB.

    For this example, leave the GSX Server recommended value of 384MB. This is sufficient to install the operating system. It can later be modified to increase the amount of memory based on the usage of the virtual machine.

 GSX Server currently has a maximum of 3.6GB of memory that can be allocated to any one virtual machine at a time. It also has a memory limit based on the file system storing the virtual machine disk files. If the virtual machine is stored on a FAT16 or FAT32 Windows file system, the 3.6GB maximum is lowered to 2000MB. Therefore, if your virtual machine will require more than 2000MB of memory, make sure the virtual machine is stored on a Windows NTFS file system.

Figure 21.7   Select a Virtual Machine's Network Type.

9. Network type (see Figure 21.7).
    Several networking options are offered: bridged, network address transla-
    tion (NAT), host-only networking, or no networking. Bridged network-
    ing uses a virtual Ethernet adapter. It is used when the host server is on
    a network that has the ability to give separate IP addresses to the virtual
    machines (either manually or via DHCP) and host network or Internet
    access is required. If the host network does not have enough IP addresses
    to be distributed to the virtual machines and host network and Internet
    connectivity is required, NAT networking can be selected. If the only
    network access that is required is the virtual network and access to the
    host server, host-only networking can be selected. If there is no need for
    network connectivity of any kind, selecting do not use a network connec-
    tion is appropriate although not as likely in a server virtualization plat-
    form such as GSX Server. For more details about VMware GSX Server
    networking configuration, see the Virtual Networking section in chapter
    22.
        For now, select Use bridged networking. This option can easily be
    changed once the virtual machine is created by selecting VM > Settings >
    Hardware, selecting the network adapter and then changing the network
    connection setting.
10. Select I/O Adapter Types (see Figure 21.8).
    Both an IDE and a SCSI adapter are by default added to the virtual
    machine. While the IDE adapter is always ATAPI, there are two SCSI
    adapter types to choose from: BusLogic and LSI Logic. Based on the guest
    operating system chosen in Step 4, GSX Server will select a default SCSI
    adapter. Most guest operating systems will default to BusLogic. However,

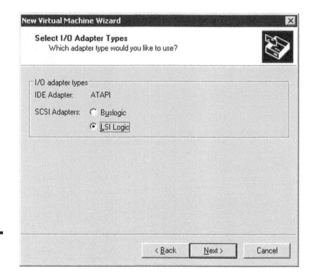

Figure 21.8 Select I/O Adapter Types.

newer operating systems such as Windows Server 2003 and Red Hat Enterprise Linux 3 default to the higher performing LSI Logic adapter. If the operating system does not have the appropriate driver for the adapter built-in, it must be downloaded. For more information on adapter types, read the section Virtual Hard Disk Drives in chapter 22.

Choosing a SCSI adapter in this step does not determine what type of hard disk will ultimately be attached to the virtual machine. The disk type will be determined in Step 12. Therefore in this example, take the default that matches the Windows Server 2003 guest operating system—LSI Logic.

11. Select a Disk (see Figure 21.9).

This step allows the hard disk of the virtual machine to be selected. There are three options to choose from: create a new virtual disk, use an existing virtual disk or use a physical disk.

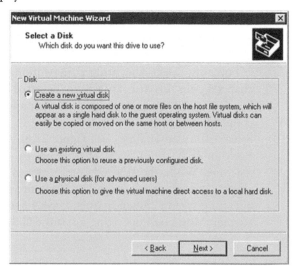

Figure 21.9 Select the Virtual Machine's Disk.

- Create a new virtual disk—Select this option to create a new, unformatted virtual disk. The virtual disk will appear as a file with a VMDK extension. The attributes assigned to the disk file will be answered in the remaining steps.
- Use an existing virtual disk—Select this option to attach a virtual disk file that was previously created. The virtual disk file may either be a previously used virtual hard disk or a template image. The Wizard will then ask for the location of the virtual disk. It can either be manually entered or the browse button can be used to navigate to the disk file.
- Use a physical disk (for advanced users)—Select this option to install the guest operating system on a physical or RAW disk. Currently, GSX Server only supports booting from an IDE disk, although a SCSI disk can be added later as a secondary drive. If this option is selected, the Wizard presents a list of available hard drives on the host server and a decision must be made to either use the entire disk or a partition on the disk. VMware strongly cautions against using this feature. By selecting a physical disk, the virtual machine misses out on so many of the features that virtual disks bring to virtualization.

For this example, select Create a new virtual disk and click Next to continue.

12. Select a Disk Type (see Figure 21.10).

Select the disk type for the new virtual disk to be created, either IDE or SCSI. Once again, the Wizard will make a recommendation based on the guest operating system chosen for the virtual machine in Step 4.

For this example, keep the recommended disk type of SCSI and click Next.

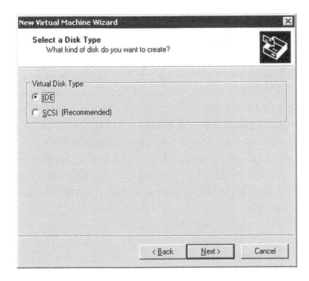

Figure 21.10   Select a Disk Type (IDE or SCSI).

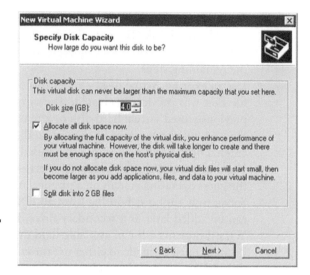

Figure 21.11 Specify Virtual Hard Disk Capacity.

13. Specify Disk Capacity (see Figure 21.11).

This step helps define the sizing of the virtual hard disk. There are three selections that need to be made: sizing of the disk, the allocation of disk space and whether or not the disk file should be split out into multiple files.

- Disk size (GB)—Enter the size of the virtual disk to be created. There are size limitations. The first limitation is the amount of free hard disk space on the physical disk where the virtual disk is being created. Virtual disk files themselves also have a size limitation. A virtual disk can be as small as 100MB and can be as large as 128GB when created as an IDE virtual disk and 256GB when created as a SCSI virtual disk. The default size is 4GB, which is an acceptable size for this example.
- Allocate all disk space now—Select this option by activating the check box. The default setting is to allocate the full size of the virtual disk file when the virtual disk is created. By pre-allocating the disk space, a fixed disk is created that offers better performance for the virtual machine. However, disk space can be a commodity, and if the file is going to be backed up or moved around a lot, it makes sense to uncheck this option and allow the file to start small and grow as needed, thereby creating a dynamically expanding disk. Fixed disks and dynamically expanding disks are covered in detail in chapter 22. For this example, uncheck the check box and allow the system to create the disk file as a dynamically expanding disk.
- Split disk into 2GB files—Selecting the checkbox will split the virtual disk into multiple 2GB files. By deselecting the checkbox (removing the checkmark), the virtual disk file will be created as one single

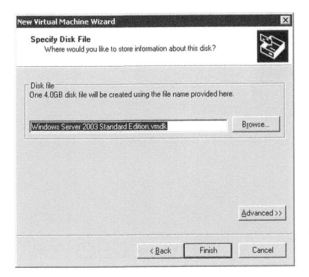

Figure 21.12 Specify Virtual Hard Disk File.

VMDK file. If the file system storing the virtual disk file is a file system that does not support files larger than 2GB in size (such as FAT16), the checkbox should be selected to split the files out into files 2GB or smaller in size. For this example, deselect the checkbox and create the virtual disk file as a single file.

14. Specify Disk File (see Figure 21.12).
    Specify the name and location of the virtual machine's disk files. By default, GSX Server will automatically locate the disk file in the same path as the configuration file described in Step 5. It also defaults the disk file name to the guest operating system version selected in Step 4. For good house keeping purposes, the disk file name should be changed to match the name of the registered virtual machine in Step 5. For this example, the virtual disk file should be named W2K3-DC-01.vmdk.

    To specify which virtual device node should be used by the virtual disk or to use independent disk mode, click the Advanced button.

15. Specify Advanced Options (see Figure 21.13).
    Specifying a disk mode adds another layer of complexity to a virtual disk but allows for certain special configurations to exist. One such example is to exclude one or more virtual disks from a virtual machine's snapshot. The following choices are available to an independent disk.

    - Persistent—Changes are immediately and permanently written to the disk.
    - Nonpersistent—Changes made to the virtual disk are discarded when the virtual machine is either powered off or reset.

    For this example, do not select independent disk mode.

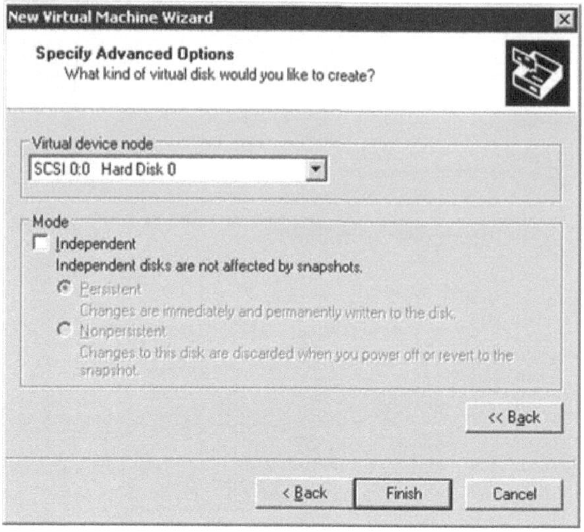

Figure 21.13   Specify Advanced Options.

After reviewing the selections made, click the Finish button to complete the New Virtual Machine Wizard. Finally, GSX Server creates the virtual machine configuration file and the virtual disk file. The virtual machine is in a similar state to a brand new computer with a fresh boot drive added. A new hard drive needs to be formatted with a file system and then have an operating system installed on it. If the virtual machine is powered on before that happens, a message similar to that in Figure 21.14 may be shown.

Before the virtual machine can be used, the blank virtual hard disk must be partitioned and formatted allowing a guest operating system to be installed. This is also the opportunity to make any modifications to the configuration file or add any additional virtual devices to the virtual machine. To do so, select VM > Settings and use either the Hardware or Options tab.

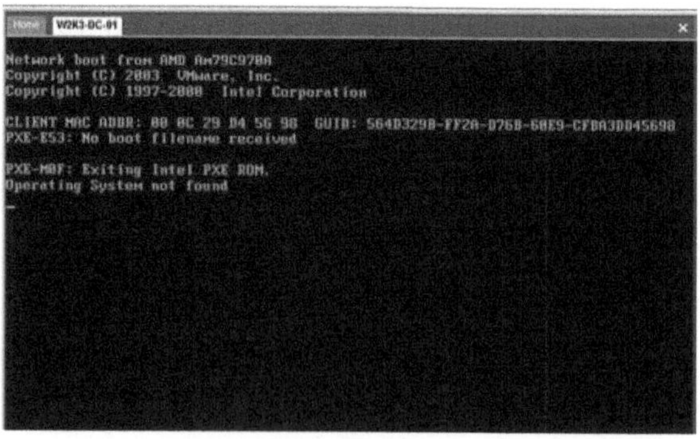

Figure 21.14. Virtual Hard Disk without an Operating System

If your host servers are configured with gigabit adapters and VMware Tools offers vmxnet driver support for your guest operating system, now is the perfect time to change the default vlance adapter to the higher performing vmxnet adapter. In a Windows virtual machine, once the guest operating system has completed its installation and added the vlance adapter through plug-and-play, it may become problematic to then change out the network adapter in favor of using vmxnet. Changing the adapter after the fact may cause an issue known as a ghosted network adapter, thereby causing TCP/IP problems for the virtual machine. When the configured vlance adapter is later replaced by the vmxnet adapter, the vlance adapter and its settings still reside in the Window's registry and it is hidden from the Device Manager; network troubleshooting can be difficult.

Once the virtual machine has been configured with the desired resources, it is time to power the virtual machine on and install the guest operating system.

Installing a Guest Operating System

Installing a guest operating system onto a virtual machine's hard drive is just like installing an operating system on a physical computer. The installer for the guest operating system has no knowledge that it is being installed onto a virtual machine. Any devices, peripherals, or resources assigned to the virtual machine will be recognized and configured as if they were assigned to a physical computer. The basic steps for a typical guest operating system installation include:

1. Launch the VMware Virtual Machine Console.
2. Verify all devices and resources are properly configured.
3. Attach the guest operating system media to the virtual machine.
4. Power on the virtual machine.
5. Follow the operating system installation instructions provided by the vendor.

GSX Server offers four convenient ways to attach or mount CD-ROM media to a virtual machine. It can be attached by inserting a physical CD/DVD-ROM into the physical host server's CD/DVD-ROM drive or into the client computer's CD/DVD-ROM drive or it can also be attached as an ISO image file located on the host server or remotely on a network server. To use the client's CD/DVD-ROM drive, the virtual machine must be connected via the VMware Virtual Machine Console on the client. This is a convenient way of remotely accessing CD/DVD-ROM material when access to the physical host server is impossible for security or logistic reasons. Using an ISO image rather than physical media is still probably going to be the preferred method of mounting CD/DVD-ROM media for a number of reasons:

- ISO images have a faster access time than physical disc media.
- They are quickly and more easily mounted to a virtual machine.
- Physical access is no longer needed to a physical CD/DVD-ROM drive.
- The information is on a DVD, but the host server and client machine only have a CD-ROM drive installed.
- Physical media can become scratched or smudged, causing installation problems.
- Acquiring physical media from those that control it in the organization can become bothersome.
- Physical media often mysteriously disappears and its whereabouts can remain unknown.

To attach the media, open the virtual machine's settings editor (select VM > Settings) and then select the Hardware tab followed by the CD-ROM drive (see Figure 21.15). To attach physical media, select the Use physical drive radio button and then choose either Host or Client. To attach an ISO image, select the Use ISO image radio button and either type the full path and file name of the ISO image or click Browse and navigate to the ISO image file. Make sure the Device status has Connect at power on activated with a checkmark.

The next section provides more detailed steps on installing a Windows Server 2003 and a Red Hat Linux 9.0 guest operating system.

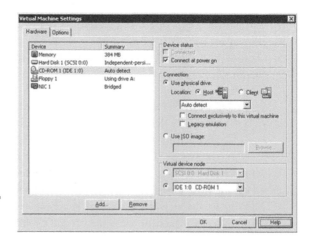

Figure 21.15 Attaching CD/ROM Media.

Installing a Windows Guest Operating System

GSX Server supports a wide array of Microsoft Windows operating systems. Continuing with the earlier example, a Windows Server 2003 Standard Edition guest operating system installation will be detailed.

1. Once the Windows Server 2003 media is mounted, power on the virtual machine by clicking the Power On button.
2. As long as the boot order in the BIOS has not been changed, the virtual machine will boot from the CD-ROM media and the Windows installation begins. If CD-ROM is not listed before hard disk, update the BIOS boot order to allow the virtual machine to boot off the CD-ROM media.
3. If the virtual disk drive was created as SCSI, a driver may need to be added to the operating system installation. Windows will prompt for any third-party SCSI or RAID drivers that need to be installed. If SCSI was chosen, a driver dependency exists based on the SCSI adapter type (BusLogic or LSI Logic) and the guest operating system chosen. If the operating system does not have a built-in driver for the adapter, a floppy disk or floppy image containing the driver must be created. When prompted, click F6 and attach the floppy media to the virtual machine. When prompted for drivers, click S to specify a driver and then press <ENTER> once the floppy media is mounted. The driver will then be installed during the SCSI and RAID driver installation section of the operating system. For this example, the virtual machine was created with a SCSI virtual disk and an LSI Logic SCSI adapter. Windows Server 2003 contains a built-in driver for the LSI Logic controller, and therefore, does not need a third-party driver diskette.
4. If the vlance network adapter was enabled, an AMD PC/NET Family Ethernet Adapter would be detected and set up automatically. In this example, the vmxnet network adapter was enabled. Since the operating system does not have a built-in driver for this network card, the device will not be configured until VMware Tools is installed and the vmxnet driver is added to the system.
5. Follow the installation steps according to the instructions on the screen just as if the operating system were being installed on a physical server.

 Until VMware Tools is installed on the virtual machine, the GSX Server console window does not use full mouse integration. Until the tools are installed, VMware uses a focus or mouse grab feature whereby selecting the virtual machine window by clicking the mouse pointer inside the window, the focus is shifted from the host operating system to the guest operating system. The mouse and keyboard are now active within the virtual machine window. To release focus, GSX Server uses a default key combination, CTRL+ALT. To regain focus within the virtual machine window, simply click the mouse pointer inside the window. The mouse grab will once again activate, and focus is retained inside of the virtual machine. Once VMware Tools is installed, full mouse integration is enabled and the mouse cursor can freely move outside of the virtual machine window by moving the mouse cursor to the host operating system without the need for the CTRL+ALT key combination.

 When the Windows installation finishes and reboots, to log on to the system, VMware remaps the CTRL+ALT+DELETE key combination to CTRL+ALT+INSERT. The key combination can also be passed to the virtual machine by using the menu system in the console, selecting VM > Send Ctrl+Alt+Del.

After the guest operating system installation is completed, VMware Tools should immediately be installed. To learn more about VMware Tools, see chapter 22.

VMware Tools for a Windows Installation

VMware Tools supports all Windows guest operating systems. The detailed steps for installing VMware Tools vary from one version of Windows to the next. The installation procedures listed below will follow along with the previous example of a Windows Server 2003 Standard Edition guest operating system. To install VMware Tools, follow these steps:

1. After the virtual machine is powered on, log on to the virtual machine as an administrator.
2. Once the guest operating system has settled down, click VM > Install VMware Tools. The system prompts with a warning message stating the guest operating system must be running to continue. Since the virtual machine is powered on and an administrator account is logged in, click Install to continue.
3. If autorun is not enabled in the guest operating system, the VMware Tools installer must be launched manually. Click Start > Run and enter D:\ setup\setup.exe (where D: is the drive letter of the first virtual CD-ROM drive). The InstallShield Wizard launches the application and the VMware Tools welcome page appears. Click Next to begin the tools installation.

You do not need a physical CD-ROM drive or physical media to install VMware Tools. The tools are supplied by VMware and are located on an ISO image that is copied to the host server during the GSX Server installation. When VMware Tools is installed, the ISO image is automatically mounted to the virtual machine. Once the tools installation is complete, the ISO image will unmount itself from the virtual CD-ROM drive that then returns to its previous state.

4. The Setup Type dialog box appears and offers three installation choices: Typical, Complete and Custom.
   - Typical—A typical installation only installs the features that are used by VMware GSX Server. Unless the virtual machine image is going to be shared with a Workstation environment, the typical installation method is an appropriate choice.
   - Complete—A complete installation installs all program features. The complete installation should be selected if the virtual machine is going to be shared with a Workstation environment. The install adds features that are supported in other platforms, but not GSX Server.
   - Custom—A custom installation gives control over which individual features are installed and where they are installed. The installer can always be run again at a later time to add or remove individual features. In this example, select the Typical installation and click Next to continue.
5. The Wizard is now ready to begin installation. This is the last opportunity to make any changes to the VMware Tools installation. To make changes, click Back until the dialog screen appears where changes are needed. If no changes are necessary, click Install to begin the installation.
6. The installer begins copying files. When the installer begins to install the virtual drivers, one or more Digital Signature Not Found dialog boxes may appear. The virtual drivers are safe to install, and the dialog can be safely allowed to continue.
7. After the installer finishes installing the drivers, a second dialog box appears warning hardware acceleration may not be enabled in the virtual machine. To increase mouse and video performance, hardware acceleration should be enabled. Click Yes. The installer will open the Display Properties window. From the Settings tab, select Advanced > Troubleshoot and slide the Hardware acceleration slider bar to Full and then apply the change.
8. Once the installation Wizard has completed the install, click Finish to exit the Wizard. To initialize any new drivers that have been installed, the virtual machine should be rebooted.

The installation of VMware Tools in a virtual machine is a one time event. After the installation, the enhanced drivers and features that were added will be used by the guest operating system just like any other driver updates performed on a physical server. VMware Tools should be installed in every individual virtual machine as well as any template images that may be created. It is possible for new, updated versions of VMware Tools to get released. If that happens, the tools can be removed, added or upgraded like many other Windows applications.

Installing a Linux Guest Operating System

GSX Server supports a wide array of Linux operating systems. For this example, a Red Hat Linux 9.0 guest operating system installation will be detailed.

1. Once the Red Hat Linux 9.0 media is mounted, power on the virtual machine by clicking the Power On button.
2. As long as the boot order in the BIOS has not been changed, the virtual machine will boot from the CD-ROM media and the Red Hat installation begins. If CD-ROM is not listed before hard disk, update the BIOS boot order to allow the virtual machine to boot off the CD-ROM media.
    Red Hat Linux 9.0 needs to be installed using the text mode installer. Figure 21.16 shows the installation choices that are available once the Red

Figure 21.16   Red Hat 9.0 Installation Choices.

Hat Linux 9.0 CD-ROM boots. Choose the text mode installer by typing linux text and then press <ENTER>.

3. Follow the installation steps according to the instructions on the screen just as if the operating system were being installed on a physical server. To ensure a successful installation, follow the choices outlined in the following steps.

4. Choose the language that should be used during the installation process. Then choose the model of keyboard that is attached to the host server. In this example, the English language was selected and US was chosen as the keyboard selection.

5. The next screen is the Mouse Selection screen. The two best selections here are Generic - 3 Button Mouse (PS/2) (select Emulate 3 Buttons for three button mouse support in the virtual machine) or Generic Wheel Mouse (PS/2) (if a wheel mouse is connected). In this example, a generic wheel mouse is selected.

6. For Installation Type, choose either Workstation or Server. This is a high-level detail as to what types of software will be installed on the virtual machine. A more fine grained packaging selection comes later in the install. For this example, Server is selected.

7. A warning message may appear stating the partition table is unreadable, as shown in Figure 21.17. It simply means that the virtual hard drive needs to be partitioned and formatted before the installation can take place. Select Yes to initialize and erase all the data on the virtual hard drive. It does not affect the physical hard disk on the host server.

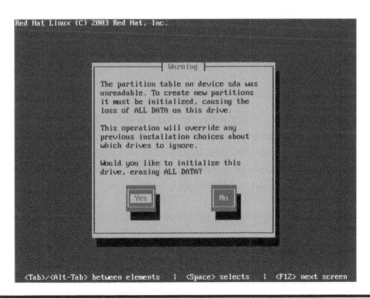

Figure 21.17   Warning to Partition and Format the Virtual Hard Disk.

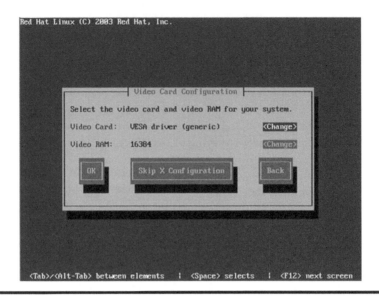

Figure 21.18 Video Card Configuration Option.

8. If the virtual machine was configured with a network configuration, LAN settings can be configured in the Network Configuration screen. Either bootp/dhcp can be selected to allow DHCP to automatically assign TCP/IP settings or the networking settings can be manually entered.
9. In the Video Card Configuration screen (see Figure 21.18), select the Skip X Configuration option.

After the guest operating system installation is completed, VMware Tools should immediately be installed. To learn more about VMware Tools, see chapter 22.

VMware Tools for a Linux Installation

VMware Tools supports many different flavors or versions of the Linux guest operating system. The detailed steps for installing VMware Tools can vary from one flavor of Linux to the next. The installation procedures listed below will follow along with the example of a Red Hat Linux 9.0 guest operating system. To install VMware Tools, follow these steps:

1. After the virtual machine is powered on, log in to the virtual machine as root.
2. Once the guest operating system has settled down, click VM > Install VMware Tools. The system prompts with a warning message stating the guest operating system must be running to continue. Since the virtual machine is powered on and the root account is logged in, click Install to continue.

VMware Tools for a Linux guest operating system must be executed while the system is running in text mode. You cannot install VMware Tools from a terminal in a GUI X session. If your virtual machine boots to an X server automatically, you can switch to a text workspace by using the default keys - CTRL+ALT+SPACEBAR, release the SPACEBAR and press the function key (for example F2) for the workspace you want to use.

3. As root, mount the VMware Tools ISO image, uncompress the installer while in the /tmp directory and then unmount the ISO image. In keeping with the example, the following steps are performed on a Red Hat Linux 9.0 installation (the commands should be modified to follow the conventions used for other Linux flavors):

```
mount /cdrom
cd /tmp
tar zxf /mnt/vmware-linux-tools.tar.gz
umount /mnt
```

You do not need a physical CD-ROM drive or physical media to install VMware Tools. The tools are supplied by VMware and are located on an ISO image that is copied to the host server during the GSX Server installation.

4. The VMware Tools installer is uncompressed to the vmware-tools-distrib folder. Change to that folder and run the installer.

```
cd vmware-tools-distrib
./vmware-install.pl
```

5. The installer then prompts about default directories. In this example, accept the default directories by responding Yes to each question.
6. Once the final directory is accepted, the VMware Tools configuration program should be executed. The system may ask about running the configuration program /usr/bin/vmware-config-tools.pl. It may prompt: Do you want this program to invoke the command for you now? If so, select Yes to allow the configuration program to execute. Otherwise, run the configuration program manually by entering:

```
./vmware-config-tools.pl.
```

7. To change the virtual machine's display resolution, select the number that corresponds to the desired resolution.
8. The configuration is complete. Log out of the root account.
9. Start X window to launch the graphical environment.
10. In a terminal session, launch the VMware Toolbox by executing the following command:

```
vmware-toolbox &
```

The installation of VMware Tools in a virtual machine is a one time event. After the installation, the enhanced drivers and features that were added will be used by the guest operating system just like any other driver updates performed on a physical server. VMware Tools should be installed in every individual virtual machine as well as any template images that may be created. It is possible for new, updated versions of VMware Tools to be released. If that happens, the tools can be removed and added like many other Linux applications. To remove VMware Tools from the Linux guest operating system, log in as root and execute the following command:

```
./vmware-uninstall-tools.pl.
```

Summary

One of the most important aspects about creating a virtual machine is to make sure that proper planning and preparations are in place. It is important to properly size and scope the virtual machine before blindly creating its configuration. Performing these tasks up front will ultimately save time on the back end. Through careful planning and design of the virtual machine, a template image can be created and replicated hundreds of times without the need to waste valuable manpower creating one-off images each time a new virtual machine is needed. GSX Server makes creating virtual images an extremely easy process by providing the New Virtual Machine Wizard. Creating a new Windows or Linux virtual machine is as simple as stepping through a number of easily answered questions, ultimately leading up to the creation of a new virtual machine configuration file. The configuration file is a collection of settings and resources that when bound together form the virtual execution environment. Once created, the final step is to power the virtual machine on and install the guest operating system. Installing the guest operating system is just as easy as installing the operating system on a physical server. Once the guest operating system has been installed, it's a good idea to immediately install VMware Tools on the virtual machine. Installing VMware Tools will enhance the performance and the experience of using a virtual machine.

Chapter 22

VMware GSX Server Advanced Topics

Virtual machines, disks, networks, and platform extensions for guest operating systems as they relate to VMware GSX Server are discussed in great detail in this chapter, rounding out the platform-specific knowledge required to successfully build and manage a GSX Server implementation.

VMware Tools

A very important component of VMware GSX Server is VMware Tools. VMware Tools is a suite of drivers and utilities that boosts the performance of GSX Server virtual machines and enables added features to improve the management of virtual machines by GSX Server. The installation of the tools can only be performed after installing a guest operating system into a virtual machine. And although VMware Tools is bundled with VMware, the installation of the tools is not done automatically nor is it required for the guest operating system to function.

Although VMware Tools does not require a lot of disk space on the virtual machine, it does require a supported guest operating system and access to a virtual CD-ROM drive since the tools come packaged in an ISO format. GSX Server provides ISO images for the following: Windows, Netware, Linux, and FreeBSD. When the tools are selected to be installed, the ISO image for the appropriate guest operating system is temporarily mounted to the virtual machine's first virtual CD-ROM drive and the installation process begins.

Think of a virtual machine as you would a physical computer. If you install an operating system on a physical computer, chances are the computer will operate fairly well with most devices functioning with an out of the box generic driver installed by the operating system. However, if you want the latest 3-D graphics card to perform with all of the bells and whistles that you expected when you purchased it, you will probably want to install an optimized driver for the video card. VMware Tools can be thought of as this "optimized driver."

Installing VMware Tools will install virtualization aware services along with device drivers that do a better job programming the virtual devices than the drivers installed by the guest operating systems. Each feature is covered in the following sections.

Time Synchronization

With VMware Tools installed, the date and time in the guest operating system can be synchronized with the date and time in the host operating system once every minute. It becomes important when responding to various system events such as: taking a snapshot, reverting to a snapshot, resuming a suspended machine and shrinking a virtual disk. For best accuracy, it is recommended to run a time synchronization tool on the host server and disable any time synchronization tools on the virtual machine except for the VMware Tools time synchronization. Using multiple time synchronization tools on the virtual machine can cause more harm than good.

There are also instances where time synchronization should be disabled. If the virtual machine is configured as a domain controller, it is recommended that the virtual machine use an external source for time synchronization rather than the host server. It is also recommended to disable the host time synchronization feature when the host operating system and the guest operating system are configured for different domains or different time zones. To completely disable time synchronization in a virtual machine with VMware Tools installed, edit the virtual machine's configuration file with a standard text editor and set the following options:

```
tools.syncTime = FALSE
tools.synchronize.restore = FALSE
time.synchronize.resume.disk = FALSE
time.synchronize.continue = FALSE
time.synchronize.shrink = FALSE
```

Clipboard Integration

With VMware Tools installed, a virtual machine can allow clipboard integration to occur between the virtual machine and its host or with other running virtual machines. It allows text or graphics from one virtual machine to be copied and pasted to its host machine or another virtual machine and vice versa. The feature is operating system specific and commands may vary from one operating system to the next. For example, in Microsoft Windows, pressing CTRL-C or selecting Edit > Copy is usually the method to copy the highlighted text selection to the clipboard and then pressing CTRL-V or selecting Edit > Paste is usually the method to paste the text from the clipboard.

 If you are copying text from a Windows host into a Linux guest operating system and you have a three button mouse, you can paste the text by using the middle mouse button. Otherwise, if you only have a two button mouse, you can paste the text by clicking both mouse buttons at the same time.

To completely disable clipboard integration in a virtual machine with VMware Tools installed, edit the virtual machine's configuration file with a standard text editor and set the following options:

```
isolation.tools.copy = FALSE
isolation.tools.paste = FALSE
```

Virtual Machine Heartbeat

When VMware Tools is installed in a guest operating system, the virtual machine sends a heartbeat to GSX Server so that it can monitor whether or not the guest operating system is running. A bar graph that represents the average percentage of heartbeats received by a virtual machine each minute can be located in the VMware Management Interface. The heartbeats represent the overall health of the guest operating system; however, a guest operating system that is being heavily utilized of its resources may not send 100 percent of the expected heartbeats but still be considered operating within normal parameters. If the heartbeat drops to zero on an actively running guest operating system, the virtual machine can be considered to be operating abnormally.

 When VMware Tools is either not installed or not running, the guest operating system will not send any heartbeats. Additionally, the bar meter in the VMware Management Interface will be disabled and any scripts or applications that require monitoring the heartbeat percentage will no longer function correctly.

Passing a String from Host to Guest

One of the features gained by installing VMware Tools in the guest operating system of the virtual machine is the ability to pass a string from the virtual machine's configuration file on the host server to the guest operating system. To pass the string to the guest operating system, edit the virtual machine's configuration file and add the following line:

```
machine.id = "Example String"
```

The most obvious use of the machine.id parameter is to pass items such as a machine name or an IP address. By combining a number of scripting methods, such as scripting the configuration files of the virtual machines, the guest operating system retrieval side and then the Microsoft SysPrep component, a single virtual configuration file and virtual disk file can be batch replicated a number of times, each booting as a unique virtual machine.

For example, the virtual machine's configuration file can be modified with the following string:

```
machine.id = "W2K3-VM1 192.168.0.2"
```

The virtual machine would then be scripted to retrieve the string information. In a Windows guest operating system, the command to retrieve the string is:

```
VMwareService --cmd machine.id.get
```

In a Linux guest operating system, the command to retrieve the string is:

```
/etc/vmware/vmware-guestd --cmd 'machine.
id.get'
```

(If the object is to customize the Linux guest operating system's hostname or IP address, the above command should be added to the Linux startup script before the network startup section.)

The string would then be used in any number of scripts to modify the guest operating system's information. As a simple example, in a Windows 2000 Server guest operating system, the NetShell utility can use the contents of the string and then set the new hostname and IP address for the virtual machine. The scripting can be as simple or complex as the contents of the string require.

 For security reasons, you probably want to disable this feature unless you specifically require passing in string information to the guest operating system. To prevent the host operating system and the guest operating system from communicating by passing a string to the virtual machine, set the following line in your virtual machine's configuration file:

```
isolation.tools.machine.id.get.disable = TRUE
```

Passing Information between Guest and a VMware Scripting API

With VMware Tools installed on a guest operating system, the VMware guest operating system service allows information to be passed between a guest operating system and a VMware Scripting API script as well as from the script to the guest operating system. More information on the VMware Scripting API will be covered in chapter 25.

Run Script When Power State Changes

Scripts can be executed in the guest operating system when the virtual machine's power state changes: the virtual machine is powered off, powered on, suspended, or resumed. However, scripts can only be executed if VMware Tools is running on the guest operating system.

By default, VMware Tools installs a set of scripts that will be executed during a virtual machine power state change. For example, on a Windows host, the default script releases the virtual machine's IP address when a virtual machine is suspended and then renews the IP address when the virtual machine is resumed. On a Linux host, the default script stops networking on the virtual machine when it is suspended and then starts networking when the virtual machine is resumed.

In addition to the default scripts provided by VMware, custom scripts can be written to help automate guest operating system operations when the virtual machine's power state is changed. These scripts must be batch file scripts for Windows hosts and any executable format such as shell or Perl scripts for Linux hosts. These scripts will need to be associated with their respective power states. For more information on script association, see the VMware Tools Properties and VMware Toolbox sections below.

 In order for your customized scripts to work, the following conditions must apply:

1. VMware Tools and its guest operating system service must be running in the virtual machine.
2. The version of VMware Tools running in the guest operating system must be updated to the current version.
3. Depending on the operation of your script, the virtual machine must have a virtual network adapter connected; otherwise the power operation will fail.

Scripts cannot be executed in NetWare, FreeBSD, or Windows 95 guest operating systems.

Execute Commands after Power off or Reset of a Virtual Machine

With VMware Tools installed in a Linux guest operating system, it is possible to execute specific commands when the virtual machine is shut down or restarted. This is in addition to any script that may have been specified when the virtual machine was shut down as in the previous example.

In order to execute commands, the following file needs to be modified:

```
/etc/vmware-tools/tools.conf
```

The above file can be modified with the following commands:

```
halt-command = <command>
```

Or

```
reboot-command = <command>
```

(where <command> is the command to execute when you shut down or restart the guest operating system respectively)

Mouse Integration

After installing VMware Tools, full mouse integration is enabled. It allows the mouse to freely move between the host operating system's desktop and the virtual machine window, as well as from one virtual machine window to another. Without the tools installed, the mouse grabbing and movement is limited—to move the mouse cursor from the virtual machine window to the host server's desktop, a keyboard combination key (CTRL+ALT) must be pressed to release the mouse control from the active window.

When you install a guest operating system without VMware Tools, VMware uses PS/2 port emulation for the mouse and transmits information with relative packets. This means that when moving the physical mouse around the desktop, what is being sent over the PS/2 port is 2 to the left, 1 down, 3 to the right, or in other words, positional changes and how far the mouse has moved in any direction. With VMware Tools installed, VMware uses an Absolute Pointing Device. VMware can then send absolute packets over the PS/2 port to VMware's own special driver. It tells the guest operating system the exact position of the mouse on the screen.

The Absolute Pointing Device provides certain benefits to the host server and its virtual machines:

1. Better Terminal Services Support—When using the relative mouse mode that is provided when the tools are not installed, Microsoft Terminal Services is rendered almost useless. Mouse control is practically nonexistent until the VMware Tools are installed and the mouse mode changes to using relative packets.
2. Seamless Host/Guest Mouse Responsiveness—The same physical behavior of the mouse on a Windows host will result in different behavior on a Linux virtual machine. The Absolute Pointing Device can tell the guest operating system exactly where the cursor is and can compute that as a function of what the host thinks. This makes the cursor and mouse behave more like any other application as opposed to a separate machine.
3. Enables Host Cursor—By changing the shape of the cursor on the host to the same shape of the cursor on the virtual machine, the time to redraw the cursor is removed and therefore the user perceptible lag goes away.

Enhanced Virtual Display

VMware Tools contains a device driver for VMware's SVGA display adapter that is optimized for the virtual machine based on the guest operating system that is installed. The SVGA display adapter implements VGA, VESA BIOS, and VMware's own proprietary SVGA interface. VMware's driver provides the guest operating system access to VRAM for the video draws where the VRAM is actually just system memory that is mapped to the host server's RAM. The enhanced virtual display driver also provides the virtual machine with significantly faster overall performance, support for up to 32-bit color quality and higher display resolutions. The video enhancements also allow the virtual machine to be viewed in full screen mode, where the entire screen can be used to view the guest operating system rather than just being able to view it in a window on the host server. Without VMware Tools, the virtual machine's display environment is limited to the VGA graphics mode of 16 colors and a maximum resolution of 640×480. Without the VMware driver, virtual machine performance will suffer and many applications may fail to function or install because of the low color quality and poor resolution.

Enhanced Network Adapter

VMware Tools contains a networking device driver that supports some guest operating systems. This driver can replace the out of the box vlance driver (an emulated AMD PC/Net 32 NIC) with the vmxnet driver (a VMware PCI Ethernet Adapter), which provides better network performance. The increase in network performance is most noticeable if the virtual machine is connected to a Gigabit Ethernet card on the host server.

 The AMD PC/NET 32 NIC is an older card that runs at 10 Mb/sec. You might be wondering, if your host server has a 10/100 network adapter and you are using the vlance driver in your virtual machine, does this mean that your guest operating system will be limited to 10 Mb/sec? Typically, the answer will be no. The guest operating system will still try to push data packets through the card as fast as it can based on the host CPU load and the physical Ethernet bandwidth on the host. One exception might be if the guest operating system tries to set the TCP window size smaller so that it can throttle down the transmission speed to a level where congestion and data loss does not occur.

 Switching between the AMD PC/NET 32 and the vmxnet network adapter in a Microsoft Windows operating system can cause a problem with IP conflicts. The term ghost NIC describes the problem. If the initial AMD PC/NET 32 NIC was assigned an IP address, and then you swapped it out with the vmxnet NIC and assigned it the previous NIC's IP address, you have in essence created a ghost NIC. While the AMD PC/NET 32 card no longer shows up in the Windows Device Manager, it is still there as a hidden device and is still populated throughout the guest operating system's registry. The best way to swap network adapters is to first uninstall and remove the AMD PC/NET 32 device, power off the virtual machine and change the network adapter from vlance to vmxnet, power the virtual machine back on and allow the system to find the new hardware.

BusLogic SCSI Controller

VMware Tools contains a special VMware virtual SCSI driver that supports some guest operating systems and it can also be downloaded from the VMware Web site. The virtual SCSI driver is compatible with the BusLogic BT-958 SCSI host adapter. When creating a virtual machine, the BusLogic SCSI controller is the default controller for older guest operating systems. And although some guest operating systems may include a driver for the BusLogic virtual SCSI adapter, the VMware supplied driver can be used to achieve enhanced SCSI device performance. Excluding this feature prevents this driver from being used within the virtual machine. If the virtual machine is either configured to use IDE or the LSI Logic driver or if it has no need to access any SCSI devices, then the BusLogic driver may not be needed and can be excluded from the VMware Tools installation.

Some recent guest operating systems, such as Microsoft Windows Server 2003, contain LSI Logic drivers that can take advantage of the virtual LSI Logic adapter for better device performance. And the LSI Logic SCSI controller is the default for some newer guest operating systems such as Microsoft Windows Server 2003 and Red Hat Enterprise Linux 3.

VMware Tools Control Panel—Properties (Toolbox)

After VMware Tools is installed inside of the guest operating system, an application called the VMware Tools Control Panel is installed. While the guest operating system is running, the application provides an added feature set and more flexibility and control to the virtual machine.

The Control Panel is configured and accessed differently, depending on the guest operating system version installed. In a Windows guest operating system, the Control Panel is called VMware Tools Properties. In a Linux guest operating system, the Control Panel is called VMware Toolbox. While the options presented in each version of the Control Panel are similar, the method of configuring and accessing them are different enough to discuss each separately.

VMware Tools Properties (Windows Guest Operating System)

There are several tab options available in the main window of the VMware Tools Properties application. For example, in a Windows Server 2003 guest operating system, the application has five tabs that include: Options, Devices, Scripts, Shrink and About. To launch the application, either double-click the VMware Tools icon in the system tray of the guest operating system or go to Start > Control Panel > VMware Tools. A general overview of each tab follows.

Selecting the Options Tab

Selecting the Options tab displays two miscellaneous options (see Figure 22.1). The first is a checkbox to either enable or disable time synchronization between the guest operating system and the host server. The second is a checkbox to either display or not display the VMware Tools icon in the guest operating system's system tray.

Time synchronization between the virtual machine and the host operating system allows the clock in the guest operating system to synchronize to the time of the host operating system's clock. For more detail on when it is or is not appropriate to use time synchronization along with other command-line entries that are available, see the Time Synchronization section at the beginning of this

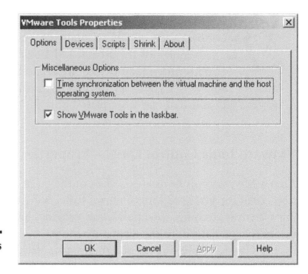

Figure 22.1 VMware Tools Properties—Options Tab.

chapter. To turn the feature on or off, select or deselect the checkbox accordingly.

 You can only synchronize the clock in the guest operating system to the time in the host operating system when you set the clock in the guest operating system to an earlier time than the time set in the host.

The Show VMware Tools in the taskbar checkbox is only found on the VMware Tools Properties for Windows. By deselecting the checkbox, the VMware Tools icon will no longer be displayed in the guest operating system's system tray. The application however will still be available by launching it from within the guest operating system's control panel.

Selecting the Devices Tab

When the Devices tab is selected, a list of removable devices is shown in the window (see Figure 22.2). Removable devices can include floppy and CD-ROM drives, virtual network adapters, audio devices, and serial or parallel ports. Each of these devices has a checkbox, which when checked connects the device to the virtual machine and when unchecked disconnects the device from the virtual machine. For example, if the virtual machine has been compromised and a Denial of Service attack ensues, the virtual network adapter can be quickly unchecked and the network card becomes disconnected from the guest operating system. While these options are also conveniently located in the VM > Removable Devices menu in the virtual machine window, the Devices tab becomes more convenient when the virtual machine is running in full screen mode.

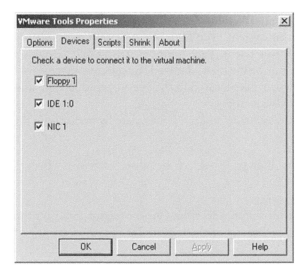

Figure 22.2 VMware Tools
Properties—Devices Tab.

 Only the devices found in the virtual machine's configuration file prior to being powered on can be connected or disconnected in the Devices tab. And for some devices, such as the floppy drive, that cannot be shared because they are already in use by the host server or another virtual machine, you may encounter an error while trying to connect the device. If you receive an error message, make sure the device is not mounted by the host operating system or connected to any other virtual machine running on the host server.

Selecting the Scripts Tab

The Scripts tab (see Figure 22.3) controls a set of default and custom scripts that help automate guest operating system operations when the virtual machine's

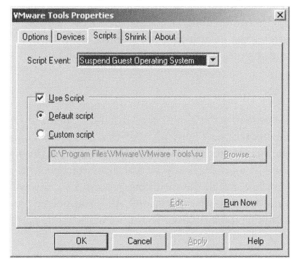

Figure 22.3 VMware
Tools Properties—Scripts
Tab.

power state is changed with one of the following: Suspend, Resume, Power On and Shut down guest operating system. The four power states are listed in a drop-down list box labeled Script Event. Each script that is associated with a different power state change can be enabled, disabled, or selected to run now. The default scripts are .bat files that are located in the guest operating system in C:\Program Files\VMware\VMware Tools.

Changes to the scripting can be made for each power state by performing the following steps:

1. From the Script Event pull down list, select the power state with which to associate the script.
2. Perform one of the following:
   a. To change to a custom script, select the Custom Script radio button and then click Browse. Browse to the location of the saved script and select it.
   b. To modify or customize a script, select either the Custom Script or Default Script radio button and point to the script to be modified. Click the Edit button to open the script into the default editor so that changes can be made to the script.
   c. To test and verify the script, click the Run Now button once the script has been identified.
   d. To disable the script from running, select the Script Event and then uncheck the Use Script check box.
3. Click Apply to save the settings.

 A custom script can also be created and used to help automate the virtual machine during a power state change. You can use the default scripts as a starting point, but it is best to always create a new file rather than just modifying the existing default .bat files. If you choose to simply modify the default scripts, be warned, if you or someone else comes along and reinstalls VMware Tools on that guest operating system, the default scripts will once again be installed and will overwrite the changes you have made.

Selecting the Shrink Tab

Shrinking a virtual disk means reducing the size of the virtual disk file that resides on the host server. The Shrink tab (see Figure 22.4) gives access to the components needed to compact the virtual disk files on the host server by reclaiming the unused space found in the virtual disk. If any virtual disk attached to the virtual machine is capable of going through the shrinking process, two tabs will appear: Supported partitions and Unsupported partitions. An unsupported partition is a partition that is not eligible for shrinking. Examples of ineligible parti-

Figure 22.4 VMware Tools Properties—Shrink Tab.

tions include partitions on removable devices, partitions on remote devices and partitions that are read-only. The Supported partitions tab displays the partitions in the virtual disk that VMware Tools is able to prepare for shrinking.

Shrinking a virtual disk using VMware Tools Properties is a two-step process. The first step is the shrinking preparation stage that occurs inside the virtual machine. The second step is the shrinking stage that occurs outside the virtual machine. To shrink a partition, follow these steps:

1. Select the Supported partitions tab. All of the partitions that are capable of undergoing the shrinking process should be displayed here proceeded by a checkbox. Check the partitions to shrink and then click the Prepare to shrink button. VMware Tools will prepare each selected partition for shrinking, one after the other. A progress bar will appear for each partition to show the preparation completion rate of each selected partition and is followed by a dialog box with the prompt "Do you want to shrink your disk(s) now?"

2. Clicking No can delay the shrinking of the virtual disk for a later time. Clicking Yes will freeze the virtual machine and begin the second stage where the actual shrinking process takes place. Depending on the shape and size of the file, this stage may take some time. A progress bar will appear to help show the time it will take to complete this stage. Upon completion, the virtual machine will resume normal operation after the shrink process is complete and the disk file on the host server should now be smaller than when the process was started. For more detail on shrinking disk files, see the section titled Shrinking Virtual Hard Disk Drives in this chapter.

In some cases, you cannot shrink one or more disks. If this is the case, a message indicates why the shrink is not possible. This can happen if:

- One or more of your disks are physical (raw) disks.
- One or more of your disks had their disk space fully allocated when the disk was created.
- Your virtual machine contains a snapshot.
- One or more of your disks is not used in independent-persistent mode or is an older virtual disk that is not in persistent mode.
- One or more of your virtual disks are stored on a CD-ROM.

Selecting the About Tab

Selecting the About tab (see Figure 22.5) provides useful information about the VMware Tools installed in the guest operating system. Along with VMware's copyright information, the tab displays the build version of the VMware Tools and a line item indicator whether or not the guest operating system service is running. At a quick glance, both of these items can help during troubleshooting.

VMware Toolbox (Linux Guest Operating System)

There are several tab options available in the main window of the VMware Tools for Linux application. For example, in a Red Hat Linux 9.0 guest operating system, the application has four tabs that include: Devices, Scripts, Options, and Shrink. To launch the VMware Tools control panel, at a command prompt, type: "vmware-toolbox &". A general overview of each tab follows.

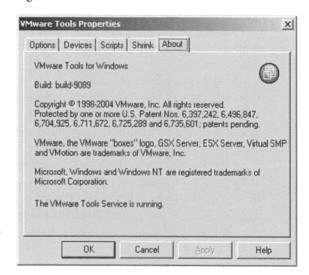

Figure 22.5 VMware Tools Properties—About Tab.

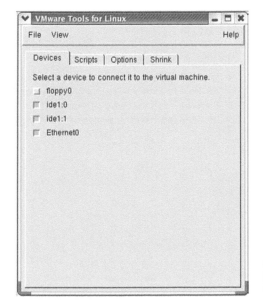

**Figure 22.6   VMware Toolbox—
Devices Tab.**

Selecting the Devices Tab

When the Devices tab is selected (see Figure 22.6), a list of removable devices is shown in the window. Removable devices can include floppy and CD-ROM drives, virtual network adapters, audio devices, and serial or parallel ports. Each of these devices has a checkbox, which when checked connects the device to the virtual machine and when unchecked disconnects the device from the virtual machine. For example, if the virtual machine has been compromised and a Denial of Service attack ensues, the virtual network adapter can be quickly unchecked and the network card becomes disconnected from the guest operating system. While these options are also conveniently located in the VM > Removable Devices menu in the virtual machine window, the Devices tab becomes more convenient when the virtual machine is running in full screen mode.

Only those devices found in the virtual machine's configuration file prior to being powered on can be connected or disconnected in the Devices tab. And for some devices, such as the floppy drive, that cannot be shared because they are already in use by the host server or another virtual machine, you may encounter an error while trying to connect the device. If you receive an error message, make sure the device is not mounted by the host operating system or connected to any other virtual machine running on the host server.

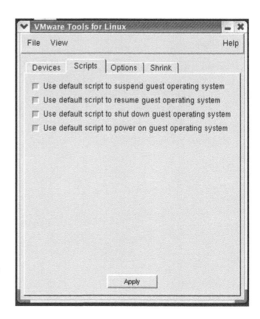

Figure 22.7   VMware Toolbox—
Scripts Tab.

Selecting the Scripts Tab

The Scripts tab (see Figure 22.7) controls a set of default and custom scripts that help automate guest operating system operations when the virtual machine's power state is changed with one of the following· Suspend, Resume, Shut down, and Power On guest operating system. A default script for each of the four power operations is listed in the Script Tab window proceeded by a checkbox. These default scripts are located in the guest operating system in /etc/vmware-tools.

While logged in as the root user, changes to the scripts can be made for each power state by performing the following steps:

1. Select the appropriate power state.
2. Perform one of the following:
   a. To change to a custom script, click Browse and browse to the location of the script and select it.
   b. To modify or customize a script, click Edit to open the script in vi so that changes can be made to the script.
   c. To test and verify the script, click Test.
   d. To disable the script from running, select the path to the script and delete it.
3. Click Apply to save the settings.

 A custom script can also be created and used to help automate the virtual machine during a power state change. You can use the default scripts as a starting point, but it is best to always create a new file rather than just modifying the exist-

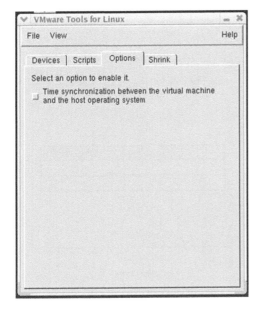

**Figure 22.8   VMware Toolbox—
Options Tab.**

ing default scripts. If you choose to simply modify the default scripts, be warned, if you or someone else comes along and reinstalls the VMware Tools on that guest operating system, the default scripts will once again be installed and will overwrite the changes you have made.

Selecting the Options Tab

Selecting the Options tab (see Figure 22.8) displays a single miscellaneous option. The only option available is to enable or disable time synchronization.

Time synchronization between the virtual machine and the host operating system allows the clock in the guest operating system to synchronize to the time of the host operating system's clock. For more detail on when it is or is not appropriate to use time synchronization along with other command-line entries that are available, see the Time Synchronization section at the beginning of this chapter. To turn the feature on, make sure the checkbox is selected.

 You can only synchronize the clock in the guest operating system to the time in the host operating system when you set the clock in the guest operating system to an earlier time than the time set in the host.

Selecting the Shrink Tab

Shrinking a virtual disk means reducing the size of the virtual disk file that resides on the host server. The Shrink tab (see Figure 22.9) gives access to the com-

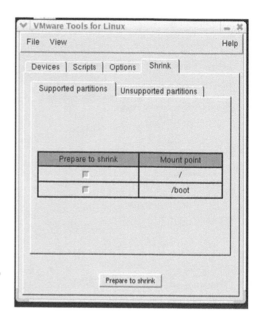

Figure 22.9 VMware Toolbox—Shrink Tab.

ponents needed to compact the virtual disk files on the host server by reclaiming the unused space found in the virtual disk. If any virtual disk attached to the virtual machine is capable of going through the shrinking process, two tabs will appear: Supported partitions and Unsupported partitions. An unsupported partition is a partition that is not eligible for shrinking. Examples of ineligible partitions include partitions on removable devices, partitions on remote devices and partitions that are read-only. The column to the right of the partition name displays the exact reason a partition cannot be prepared for shrinking. The Supported partitions tab displays the partitions in the virtual disk that VMware Tools is able to prepare for shrinking.

 To ensure that the entire virtual disk is shrunk, it is important to run VMware Tools as the root user (su -). If shrinking is attempted on a virtual disk as a nonroot user, prepare to shrink will not work on the parts of the virtual disk that require root-level permissions.

Shrinking a virtual disk using the VMware Toolbox is a two step process. The first step is the shrinking preparation stage that occurs inside the virtual machine. The second step is the shrinking stage that occurs outside the virtual machine. To shrink a partition, follow these steps:

1. Select the Supported partitions tab. All of the partitions that are capable of undergoing the shrinking process should be displayed here proceeded by a push button. Select the partitions to shrink and then click the Pre-

pare to shrink button. VMware Tools will prepare each selected partition for shrinking, one after the other. A progress bar will appear for each partition to show the preparation completion rate of each selected partition and is followed by a dialog box that prompts "Do you want to shrink your virtual hard disk(s) now?"

2. Clicking No can delay the shrinking of the virtual disk for a later time. Clicking Yes will freeze the virtual machine and begin the second stage where the actual shrinking process takes place. Depending on the shape and size of the file, this stage may take some time. A progress bar will appear to help show the time it will take to complete this stage. Upon completion, the virtual machine will resume normal operation after the shrink process is complete and the disk file on the host server should now be smaller than when the process was started. For more details on shrinking disk files, see the section titled Shrinking Virtual Hard Disk Drives in this chapter.

 In some cases, you cannot shrink one or more disks. If this is the case, a message indicates why the shrink is not possible. This can happen if:

- One or more of your disks are physical (raw) disks.
- One or more of your disks had their disk space fully allocated when the disk was created.
- Your virtual machine contains a snapshot.
- One or more of your disks is not used in independent-persistent mode or is an older virtual disk that is not in persistent mode.
- One or more of your virtual disks are stored on a CD-ROM.

Virtual Machines

Deleting a Virtual Machine

There comes a time when a virtual machine will need to be removed or deleted from the GSX Server host. The virtual machine may become problematic and unusable, it may no longer be needed or may no longer serve a purpose, or disk space on the host server may need to be reclaimed for virtual machines that are more important. Whatever the reason, GSX Server offers three ways to delete a virtual machine from the host server: by using the virtual machine console, the management interface, or the scripting APIs. As a security measure, virtual machines can only be deleted by the Administrator or root user. As a secondary precaution, when deleting a virtual machine manually by using either the console or the management interface, the system will prompt for confirmation before actually deleting anything. The reason for such concern, when deleting a virtual machine from the host server, all files associated with the virtual machine are deleted (virtual disk files, configuration files, log files, the NVRAM file, and any suspended state or snapshot files).

1. Deleting a virtual machine using the VMware Virtual Machine Console
   a. Make sure the virtual machine is powered off.
   b. Select the virtual machine's tab in the virtual machine display or select it in the inventory.
   c. Choose VM > Delete from Disk
   d. Click Yes at the prompt to confirm deletion of the virtual machine.
2. Deleting a virtual machine using the VMware Management Interface
   a. Locate the virtual machine in the VMware Management Interface.
   b. Make sure the virtual machine is powered off. If the virtual machine is suspended, resume it and then power it off.
   c. Access the virtual machine menu and click the arrow to the right of the terminal icon.
   d. Select Delete Virtual Machine and a dialog box will appear that states it will delete all virtual machines files. Click Ok to delete the virtual machine and all of its associated files, otherwise, click Cancel.
3. Deleting a virtual machine using the VMware scripting APIs.

```
'***************************************************
*****************
'*
'* VMware GSX Server Delete VM VBScript
'*
'* gsxdelvm.vbs
'*
'* This script can be executed using Microsoft Win-
dows Script Host
'*
'* cscript.exe gsxdelvm.vbs [VmConfigFilePathAnd-
Filename]
'*
'* or
'*
'* wscript.exe gsxdelvm.vbs [VmConfigFilePathAnd-
Filename]
'*
'***************************************************
*****************


Dim connectParams        ' As VmCOM.VmConnectParams
Dim server               ' As VmCOM.VmServerCtl
```

```
Dim vm                  ' As VmCOM.VmCtl
Dim vmConfigFilePath    ' As String
Dim vmDisplayName       ' As String
Dim statusMessage       ' As String

' Constant Values Obtained From VmCOM.dll
Dim vmExecutionState_Off ' As Long
Dim vmErr_VMBUSY         ' As Long

vmExecutionState_Off = 2
vmErr_VMBUSY = -2147220971

On Error Resume Next

vmConfigFilePath = WScript.Arguments(0)

Set connectParams = CreateObject("VmCOM.VmConnect-
Params")
Set server      = CreateObject("VmCOM.VmServerCtl")
Set vm          = CreateObject("VmCOM.VmCtl")

server.Connect connectParams
vm.Connect connectParams, vmConfigFilePath

If Not Err.Number = 0 Then
   If Err.Number = vmErr_VMBUSY Then
      statusMessage = "The specified virtual machine
is currently "
      statusMessage = statusMessage & "in use by
the GSX Console."
   Else
      statusMessage = "An unexpected error oc-
curred. Error Number="
      statusMessage = statusMessage & Err.Number &
", Description="
      statusMessage = statusMessage & Err.Descrip-
tion
   End If
Else
   vmDisplayName = vm.Config("displayname")
   If vm.ExecutionState = vmExecutionState_Off Then
     server.UnregisterVm vmConfigFilePath
```

```
        statusMessage = vmDisplayName & " deleted
successfully."
    Else
        statusMessage = "The virtual machine, " & vm-
DisplayName
        statusMessage = statusMessage & ", must be
powered off and"
        statusMessage = statusMessage & " must not be
waiting for "
        statusMessage = statusMessage & "user input
before it can "
        statusMessage = statusMessage & "be deleted."
    End If
End If


' Display status messages, if needed
If Len(statusMessage) > 0 Then
    WScript.Echo statusMessage
End If


' Cleanup
Set connectParams = Nothing
Set server = Nothing
Set vm = Nothing


' End of script
```

Suspending and Resuming Virtual Machines

One especially useful feature of VMware GSX Server is the option to suspend and resume a virtual machine. Suspend literally allows a guest operating system image to be suspended. What does that really translate to? VMware freezes all of the guest operating system's running processes and saves its memory image to a file. In other words, any applications, open documents, or open windows that are running at the time the virtual machine is suspended will still be running when the virtual machine is resumed because the content and state of the virtual machine is the same as it was when it was suspended. Once the virtual machine is suspended, it can be resumed at a later time even if the VMware GSX Server application is restarted or the host server is rebooted.

When a virtual machine is suspended, VMware creates a file with a .vmss extension on the host server's disk that contains the entire state of the virtual machine. By default, the file is stored in the same directory as the virtual machine's configuration file (.vmx). When performing a resume of a suspended virtual machine, GSX Server looks for the .vmss file in the same directory, and then uses the file to restore the virtual machine's state.

 Another way to think of suspending a virtual machine is to put it into the context of a physical computer. For example, placing a notebook computer into a Suspend-to-Disk or Hibernate mode shuts down most of the notebook computer electronics, reducing the drain on the battery and leaving the notebook computer ready to resume operations in a matter of seconds. When the mode is activated, the state of the notebook computer is written to a reserved area on its hard disk allowing it to resume where it left off even if the battery drains completely. If you have ever used a notebook computer, chances are you probably have used this feature.

There are a few considerations that should be taken into account before using the Suspend and Resume feature. First, changing a configuration file after suspending is a bad thing! VMware advises that changes should not be made to a configuration file after suspending the virtual machine because the virtual machine will not properly resume if the configuration file is inconsistent with the suspended virtual machine. Second, using Suspend and Resume can consume a lot of disk space on the host server. Depending on the amount of RAM that was allocated to the virtual machine, the .vmss suspend file can become extremely large in size. A suspend file will be at least as large as the amount of RAM given to the virtual machine. Therefore, it is important to make sure that enough free space is allocated on the host server to accommodate these large files. Finally, it is important to note that the suspend location does not have to be the default location of the configuration file. In fact, for performance reasons discussed below, it might make more sense to change the storage location to something more appropriate. The default storage location can either be changed by using the Management Interface or the VMware Console.

The speed at which GSX Server can suspend or resume a virtual machine depends on a number of factors. One factor is how much data has changed while the guest operating system has been running. The more disk operations that VMware has cached, the more it must write to disk during a suspension. In general, the first suspend operation takes longer than subsequent suspend requests. A second factor is the speed of the host server's disk and file system. First and foremost, a SCSI controller and SCSI disk drive will perform better than an IDE controller and ATA disk and is therefore the recommended choice for the host server. A performance boost can also be gained by separating the system disk and the VMware disks on to different controllers and drives. Doing so should help control the disk I/O bottleneck when suspending or resuming a virtual machine. As previously stated, performance is affected by the amount of RAM allocated to the virtual machine. The more RAM allocated to the virtual machine translates to a larger memory state that needs to be copied to the suspend file which in turn means a larger file and more time to write to the file.

So why use Suspend and Resume? One reason is that it allows the user to stop working on a server at any given point in time and then to restart working on that server in the same state it was when originally stopped. All too often while working on a project, interruptions occur and sidetracks happen. Rather than closing down all open items and shutting down the server for a period of time, it may make more sense to simply suspend the guest operating system and then later resume exactly where the system left off prior to suspension. If nothing else, it helps avoid the lengthy shutdown and boot process of a Windows guest operating system.

Another reason to use the Suspend feature is to help diagnose and analyze a compromised system. For example, a virtual server in a network environment becomes compromised and hacked by an outside individual. Suspending the virtual machine freezes all running processes and saves the memory image to a file. By isolating the network environment for that virtual machine and then resuming it exactly as it was before, the machine is then capable of being analyzed while still in its running state.

A less glamorous use of the Suspend feature is to save system resources on the host server. If a guest operating system is not in use but still powered on, the virtual machine is still consuming both processor and memory cycles from the host server. Even if the virtual machine is completely idle, it still has a lock on the amount of RAM that was allocated to it when it was powered on. It may be impossible to power on new virtual machines if the host server's entire RAM is already allocated to machines that are powered on and idle. Thus, if a virtual machine is going to sit idle and not be used for any other function or process, it makes sense to suspend it and resume it later when needed.

Virtual Hard Disk Drives

Virtual machines, like a physical computer, contain their own set of hard drives. In a virtual machine these hard drives are known as virtual disks. They store the operating system, applications, and data files on one or more of these virtual disks. Unlike their physical counterparts, GSX Server gives the option of undoing changes that are written to the virtual machine's hard drive. Another key feature of virtual disks is their portability. Because virtual disks are stored as files, they can be easily moved to a new location on the same host server or to a different host server. Virtual disks can also be created on a Windows host server running GSX Server for Windows and then moved to a Linux host server where they can be used with GSX Server for Linux and vice versa. Virtual disks also have a distinct advantage over physical disks because they offer disk resizing—shrinking and expanding their disk capacity.

This section explores virtual disks in greater depth and explains in detail the different interfaces used and the various types and modes of virtual disks along with how to interact with them. In chapter 3, virtual hard disk concepts were covered in a broad and generic sense, discussing virtual disks across a virtualization vendor neutral platform. This chapter will go into more detail and reintroduce those concepts as they pertain to VMware GSX Server.

It is important to reinforce the concept and understanding of exactly what a virtual disk file is and how it functions. An easy way to think about virtual disk files is to compare them to a Zip archive file. If you had a number of photographs on your computer that you wanted to store on your hard drive, but you did not want the clutter of all those files, you could archive it by zipping those files into a single Zip file, say photos.zip. If you copied that single file elsewhere, you would need a program such as WinZip to open and read that file. Otherwise, it is just a large file taking up space. This is very similar to the way a virtual disk works. It is a single file (or group of files) with a .vmdk extension that contains many files within it. These files just so happen to be operating system files, applications, documents, and sure maybe even photos. The program needed to open these files and interact with them is VMware GSX Server.

Virtual Hard Disk Drive Controllers

Chapter 21 introduced how a virtual machine is created in GSX Server with the New Virtual Machine Wizard. In the Wizard, one of the steps is to select an I/O adapter type to control the virtual machine's hard drive. The two types of I/O adapters (or virtual hard disk drive controllers) that can be installed in the virtual machine are IDE and SCSI. The IDE adapter is always ATAPI, while the SCSI adapter can be one of two types: BusLogic or LSI Logic.

An IDE adapter on a GSX Server virtual machine follows many of the same characteristics as a physical IDE adapter and it's also the easiest adapter to add to a virtual machine. All guest operating systems are able to add an IDE controller without having to download a special driver, which is the primary reason why it's so much easier to add than a SCSI adapter that usually requires adding an external driver. As far as connectivity is concerned, it is possible to install up to four IDE devices on a virtual machine. These devices can be hard disks, CD-ROM or DVD-ROM drives. The adapter has two channels (primary and secondary), each of which support up to two devices (master and slave). A virtual disk attached to an IDE adapter can be as small as 100MB in size or as large as 128GB.

A SCSI adapter in a GSX Server virtual machine also follows many of the same characteristics as a physical SCSI adapter. Unlike the IDE adapter, the SCSI adapter is not available in all guest operating systems and is more difficult to add to a virtual machine. In many cases, a special driver will need to be downloaded for a guest operating system to recognize the SCSI adapter. Connectivity on virtual SCSI allows for up to 21 devices to be connected across three virtual SCSI controllers. Generic SCSI support allows scanners, CD-ROM and DVD-ROM drives, tape backup drives and other SCSI devices to be used without the need for drivers in the host operating system. A virtual disk attached to a SCSI adapter can be as small as 100MB in size or as large as 256GB (twice as large in capacity as the largest available virtual disk using an IDE adapter).

To make matters more confusing, GSX Server supports two types of SCSI adapter: BusLogic and LSI Logic. The BusLogic adapter is compatible to a Mylex BT-958 host bus adapter while the LSI Logic adapter is compatible to a LSI Logic Ultra160 LSI53C10xx SCSI controller.

When creating a new virtual machine, most guest operating systems (except for newer operating systems such as Microsoft Windows Server 2003 or Red Hat Enterprise Linux 3) default to the BusLogic adapter. However, setting up BusLogic on some guest operating systems such as Windows XP Professional and Windows Server 2003 requires a special SCSI driver that can be downloaded from the download section on VMware's Web site. The driver is needed so the guest operating system can recognize the BusLogic adapter and the attached SCSI device.

One of the new features introduced with the VMware GSX Server 3.0 platform was a new SCSI adapter. The new LSI Logic adapter has improved performance and has been found to work better with generic SCSI devices. Its driver is included with newer operating systems, such as Windows Server 2003, however most operating systems do not come with the driver natively. This does not mean that the LSI Logic adapter cannot be used in guest operating systems that do not natively supply the driver. The driver can be downloaded from the Downloads section of the LSI Logic Web site (www.lsilogic.com).

 If you configured and completed the operating system installation for your virtual machine and originally created it with one type of SCSI adapter, for example, BusLogic but later determined that you really needed the LSI Logic adapter, there is a way to reconfigure the virtual machine without it blue screening or failing to boot properly. The problem comes into play when the virtual machine does not have the proper driver support for the SCSI adapter installed on the guest operating system. To add driver support for a Windows guest operating system, follow these steps:

1. Boot the virtual machine.

2. Download the appropriate SCSI adapter, either the BusLogic driver from the download area on VMware's Web site, or the LSI Logic driver from LSI Logic's Web site (the driver needed is for the LSI20320-R product).

3. Shutdown the virtual machine.

4. Add a new SCSI adapter to the virtual machine's configuration file, either by using the management interface, the console or by directly editing the configuration file. For example, to add a new LSI Logic adapter, add the following:

```
scsi1.present = "TRUE"
scsi1.virtualDev = "lsilogic"
```

5. Add a new placeholder SCSI hard disk of any size and attach it to the new SCSI adapter, for example, SCSI1:0.

6. Boot the virtual machine. On a Microsoft Windows guest operating system that supports PNP, the new hardware Wizard should detect the new SCSI adapter. Install the driver downloaded in Step 2 and then shutdown the virtual machine.

7. Modify the virtual machine's configuration by removing the newly added SCSI adapter and the SCSI placeholder hard disk (in this example, the SCSI1 devices).

8. Modify the original SCSI adapter by changing it to the new SCSI adapter type. To follow the above example, change the following:

```
scsi0.virtualDev = "buslogic"
```

Change to

```
scsi0.virtualDev = "lsilogic"
```

Your virtual machine should then boot up properly with the new SCSI adapter type. If you are changing the driver for a Linux virtual machine, you will need to install the driver module in the initrd image or compile the driver in the kernel.

 Linux distributions with kernels in the 2.4.18 series or later include a driver that supports the LSI Logic adapter. If the guest operating system has an older kernel, VMware recommends upgrading the kernel package to the latest version available for the distribution. There is no need to download the driver from the LSI Logic Web site.

 There is a common misconception about the use of IDE and SCSI disk drives in virtualization. Some people automatically assume that because their host server contains IDE drives, they must use virtual IDE disks. And vice versa, if their host server contains SCSI drives, they believe they must use virtual SCSI disks. This is not true. A virtual disk of either type can be used on either type of physical disk. In other words, the files that make up a virtual IDE disk can be used on either a physical IDE disk or a physical SCSI disk and the same can be said for a virtual SCSI disk. In fact, as long as the guest operating system contains or can install a driver for the SCSI adapter, it is the preferred adapter as far as performance is concerned. Even on a physical IDE drive, the virtual SCSI disk is able to outperform its IDE counterpart because the SCSI adapter in the guest allows the guest operating system to queue up more I/O requests. The SCSI adapter then passes those requests asynchronously to the host, which does a better job scheduling the requests than the guest.

Disk Types: Virtual and Physical

The most commonly found drive type in a GSX Server environment is the virtual hard disk. The virtual hard disk is created as a single file or a group of files that are usually located on the host server's hard drive. A virtual disk can be created in three different formats: fixed, dynamically expanding or the less commonly found experimental and legacy plain disk. There are also cases where a virtual machine may need access to a physical hard drive on the host server. This type of disk format is referred to as a physical or raw disk. VMware stresses that this type of disk configuration should be left to those individuals who consider themselves advanced users of virtualization. As expected, each format has their advantages and disadvantages, each of which will be covered in this section.

Virtual Disks

As explained, a virtual disk is composed of a single file or a group of files that are located on the host server's hard drive or on a remote server. When attached to a virtual machine, the guest operating system identifies it as if it were a physical hard drive. To a guest, there is no discernable difference. When a new virtual disk is created, it can be partitioned, formatted in a variety of file systems (such as NTFS or ext3) and then have an operating system installed, none of which affects the physical disk on which the file resides (other than taking up disk space of course).

 In addition to creating a virtual disk as one large file, GSX Server also offers the option of splitting the virtual disk into a set of 2GB files. This comes in handy if the virtual disk is stored on a FAT32 file system or a file system that has a 2GB file size limit such as FAT16.

Plain Disks

Plain disks are an experimental virtual disk type created under earlier versions of GSX Server. It was originally introduced as a feature in GSX Server 1 to overcome the 2GB limit applied to virtual disks. To get around the 2GB limit, plain disks create multiple files that together make up the plain disk. It is similar to a fixed disk in that the file is sized immediately to its maximum size, or in other words, the disk size is pre-allocated all of its space on the host server's hard disk when the disk is created. It is composed of at least two files, a .pln file and one or more .dat files, depending on the disk size. Since the .dat file is limited to 2GB in size, any disk file created that is larger than 2GB is broken out into multiple files. For example, if a 6GB plain disk is created named mydisk, four files will be created: mydisk.pln, mydisk.dat, mydisk-02.dat, and mydisk-03.dat. While the .dat files contain the data, the .pln file contains a small amount of text that maps the .dat files to the corresponding sectors of the plain disk. Plain disks have since become obsolete; however virtual machines created with plain disks in earlier versions of GSX Server will still run under newer versions of GSX Server.

 Earlier versions of GSX Server for Windows shipped with a command-line utility aptly called plainmaker.exe. A plain disk was created by entering the following information at the command prompt:

```
plainmaker.exe <path>\<diskname.pln> <disksize>
```

Where <path> is the path to the plain disk file, <diskname.pln> is the name given to the newly created plain disk and <disksize> is the size in MB with which the plain disk should be created.

The utility, like the files it creates, has become obsolete and has since been replaced with a more modern version of the command-line utility, the VMware Virtual Disk Manager utility.

Fixed Disks

A fixed disk is a virtual hard disk drive that most closely resembles a physical hard disk drive. When created, the file is sized immediately to its maximum size, consuming an equal amount of storage from the host server. Like all virtual hard disk drives, the fixed disk is empty upon creation. For example, when a 10GB fixed virtual hard disk drive is created, a static 10GB file is created on the host server that represents the fixed disk and will contain all of its data. The file on the host server will always remain 10GB in size. It will not change, even when data is written to the fixed disk or when data is deleted from the fixed disk. Fixed disks will typically provide better performance than dynamic disks because there is no overhead due to file growth. By pre-allocating the disk space, it also ensures that the host server does not run out of disk space.

So, what is the downside to using a fixed disk? The most obvious answer is a fixed virtual disk immediately consumes a lot of disk space on the host server. To create a large virtual disk with a pre-allocated amount of disk space means the cost is paid up front rather than as needed as with a dynamically expanding disk. And since the virtual disk is pre-allocated to the entire amount of disk space needed, it also takes a longer time to initially create the disk. And once the disk is created and used, it takes that much longer to backup the disk file, move it to a different host server, or make a copy of it. And finally, a fixed disk cannot be resized or defragmented by using the GSX Server tools.

Dynamic Disks

A dynamic disk is a virtual hard disk drive that begins as a sparse file, consuming only the amount of storage from the host server that is needed, and grows as new data is written to the virtual hard disk drive. When created, the maximum size of the disk is specified, but the file representing the disk is sized only to the size needed to store its data at that point in time. The dynamic disk cannot grow in excess of its maximum size. For example, when a 10GB dynamic virtual hard disk drive is created, the maximum size of 10GB is stored within the dynamic disk's internal data structure. The file on the host server that represents the dynamic disk at first may only be a few kilobytes in size. Once the process of installing a guest operating system begins, the dynamic disk will grow as new data is written to fill the disk. When files are deleted from a dynamic disk, the file on the host server that represents the dynamic disk will not change (it will not shrink). Instead, the deleted sectors are marked and then reused as necessary.

The main advantage of this type of virtual disk is that a minimal amount of hard disk space on the host server is used from the outset and it automatically expands as needed. Since the virtual disk size is smaller, it requires less storage on the host server, can be backed up to a file server for archiving more quickly than a fixed disk, can be cloned faster and can be moved to another host server more easily. Dynamically expanding disks can also be resized or defragmented by using the GSX Server tools.

So why not always use dynamically expanding disks? The biggest drawback to using this type of disk is that its performance is slower than a fixed disk due to the overhead of keeping track of file growth. Another contributing factor to the slow performance problem is disk fragmentation. Dynamic disks are more prone to quickly becoming fragmented because of the way it handles growing the file while disk writes and deletions are taking place. As the file grows, sectors in the virtual disk are not being written in order as the virtual machine's operating system touches the virtual disk. Unfortunately, only a physical or raw disk can guarantee to have sectors in order. A less common problem is the possibility of losing track of how much disk space on the host server has been allocated to existing dynamic virtual disks. It is possible to over allocate disk space by creating too many dynamic disks only to have them all grow at a rate that encompasses the entire free disk space of a host server.

Physical Disks (Raw)

A physical or raw disk allows a virtual machine direct access to an existing local disk or partition. The primary scenario for this type of disk is a dual boot environment where GSX Server can run multiple guest operating systems from existing disks and/or partitions. Using physical disks is an advanced feature of the GSX Server platform that is not intended for inexperienced users. Setting up a physical disk configuration is more complicated than using a virtual disk in a virtual machine. Unless there is a specific need to use physical disks, VMware strongly recommends using virtual disks.

 If you must use a physical disk, it is important to note that GSX Server does *not* support booting a guest operating system from a physical SCSI drive. In order to boot a guest operating system from a physical disk or partition, you must be using physical IDE drives. Although you cannot boot from it, a physical SCSI disk can be added as a secondary disk on the virtual machine.

When deciding to use physical or raw disks in the virtual environment, there are a few considerations that should be taken into account. Some of these considerations may be a deal breaker while others may simply be a hindrance.

- Dual booting the same operating system in a virtual machine and on the host server will usually cause problems because of the different hardware recognized by the operating system. One method to resolve the problem is to create different profiles for each environment and choose the appropriate profile during boot up.
- There are numerous operating systems that are not supported to be run as guests in a virtual machine using a physical disk.
- Microsoft dynamic disks are not supported for use in physical disk configurations under GSX Server. If this disk type is used, the drive can be converted back to basic, which is supported. However, doing so will destroy all data currently on the disk.
- A physical disk cannot be resized. The shrink and expand function that can be performed against a virtual disk cannot be performed against a physical disk.

Although the physical disk is intended for a more experienced group of users, VMware has attempted to create safety features for physical disk use. GSX Server uses description files to control access to the physical disks on the system. The description files contain access privilege information that controls a virtual machine's access to the partitions on the disk such as the ability to mark certain partitions as read-only or unreadable. It helps to protect from accidentally deleting or corrupting something on the physical disk partitions.

Virtual Disk Access Modes

VMware GSX Server is extremely flexible when it comes to the wide range of disk modes that it offers. Disk modes determine how changes are saved to the disk. And it is these disk modes and their advanced disk options that provide virtualization with the ability to perform many of the additional capabilities that have been discussed throughout the book. GSX Server provides a wide range of support: it offers backward compatibility for legacy disk modes, support for independent mode, as well as its snapshot feature. This section covers each of these advanced disk modes.

Legacy Disk Modes

In versions of GSX Server prior to version 3, the product supported three disk modes that had to be individually assigned to each virtual disk that was attached to the virtual machine: persistent, nonpersistent and undoable. Some features that were introduced in GSX Server 3, such as snapshots, are not available to virtual machines that were created with prior versions of the product and running old versions of the virtual hardware. However, a virtual machine created in one of these earlier versions of GSX Server can be booted in a GSX Server 3.x installation and if the virtual machine does not get its hardware upgraded, it will be identified by the system as a legacy virtual machine. The disk mode on these legacy machines can be changed by manually editing the virtual machine's configuration file and altering its mode to one of the legacy modes. For example, to change a virtual machine's primary SCSI drive to a nonpersistent disk mode, the following configuration change can be made: SCSI0:0.mode = "nonpersistent".

Persistent Mode

Virtual disks configured in a persistent mode require the least amount of administrative effort. Disks with this configuration behave just like conventional disk drives on a physical server. Therefore, any changes made to the file system of a virtual disk in persistent mode are immediately and permanently written to the disk. This mode is the most straightforward and provides the best overall performance.

Nonpersistent Mode

Virtual disks configured in a nonpersistent mode do not save the changes made to the disk; instead they are discarded when the virtual machine is powered off. The virtual disk then returns to its original state prior to the mode being changed to nonpersistent. How does this happen? When the virtual machine is powered on for the first time after the mode change, the virtual disk file gets placed into a "locked" state and from that point forward the virtual disk is only read by the virtual machine. Any writes to the virtual disk are then written to another file called a redo log file. While the virtual machine is powered on, any changes being made are written to and subsequently read from the redo log file rather than the disk file. The redo log file is deleted (along with all of the changes made while powered on) when the virtual machine is powered off and a new redo log file is created if the virtual machine is powered back on.

Nonpersistent mode is a convenient way to always return a virtual machine to a pristine condition. It is a handy feature for a software testing group. Iterations of testing can be completed and in between each test the virtual machine can be returned back to its original state by simply being powered off.

Undoable Mode

Virtual disks configured in an undoable mode are very similar to virtual disks configured in a nonpersistent mode. When the virtual machine is powered on for the first time after the mode change, the virtual disk file gets placed into a "locked" state and from that point forward the virtual disk is only read by the virtual machine. Any writes to the virtual disk are then written to another file that is created called a redo log file. While the virtual machine is powered on, any changes being made are written to and subsequently read from the redo log file rather than the disk file. Unlike the nonpersistent mode that discards any changes that have been made, when a virtual machine is powered off and its virtual disks are configured in undoable mode, a dialog box prompts with three options: commit, discard and keep.

- **Commit Changes**
  When committing the redo log file, all changes made in the redo file are permanently merged with the virtual disk file. After the commit has completed successfully, the redo log file is deleted. Depending on the amount of data added and the number of changes made in the guest operating system, the commit command may take quite some time to complete. The fewer amount of changes made, the less time it will take to commit.
- **Discard Changes**
  Discarding the changes made to the redo log file will reset the virtual disk back to the state it was in before changes began writing to the redo log file. Because changes in the redo log file are not merged into the virtual disk, it becomes an easy way to back out of a problem state. Even if the virtual machine blue screens or kernel panics, it can be fixed by discarding the changes and returning to the previous state where the guest operating system was functioning correctly.

- **Keep Changes**
  Keeping the redo log file helps to postpone deciding whether or not the redo log file should be committed or discarded at power down. On the next power on, the redo log file is detected and can either be committed or discarded at that time or it can continue to allow changes to be appended to the redo log file. All previous changes prior to the virtual machine being powered off still exist, and all new changes will continue to write to the same redo log file.

Independent Disk Mode

Independent disk mode adds another layer of complexity to a virtual disk but allows for certain special configurations to exist. One such example is the option of creating and running a virtual disk on a CD-ROM or DVD-ROM rather than using a host server's hard disk. Another reason to choose independent disk mode is to exclude one or more virtual disks from a virtual machine's snapshot. Rather than using the snapshot feature, independent disks are offered the following disk mode options:

- **Persistent**
  Any changes made to the file system are immediately and permanently written to the disk. All changes to an independent disk in persistent mode remain even if the virtual machine's other disks revert to the snapshot.
- **Nonpersistent**
  Changes are not written to the disk file but to a separate redo log file on the host server. These changes are then discarded when the virtual machine is powered off or reverted to the snapshot. The option is selected when running a virtual machine from either a CD-ROM or DVD-ROM.

To configure a virtual disk as an independent disk, choose VM > Settings from the virtual machine console, select the virtual disk to be modified, and then click the Advanced button. On the Advanced Virtual Disk Settings page, select the Independent check box and then choose one of the disk modes for the disk.

Disk Snapshots

A new feature released in GSX Server 3 is the ability to take a snapshot of a virtual machine at any time and then revert to that snapshot at any time. A snapshot of a virtual machine can be taken while it is powered on, powered off, or suspended (unless the virtual machine is on a Linux host server, then, a snapshot should not be taken while the virtual machine is being suspended). The snapshot preserves the entire state of the virtual machine (the state of all its virtual disks, the contents of its memory, its power state, and its configuration settings) as it was when the snapshot was taken. By reverting to the snapshot, all changes made to the virtual machine since the snapshot was taken will be discarded.

Once snapshot is selected, the virtual machine begins saving and reading any changes made to the virtual machine to one or more redo log files. These files have .REDO as part of the filename and they are located in the virtual machine's working directory. Depending on the amount of time, writes, and changes that take place, these redo log files can grow quite large until some action takes place that affects the virtual machine's snapshot.

- **Remove the snapshot**
  When the snapshot is removed, the accumulated changes that have taken place and stored in the redo log files are permanently merged into the original or parent disk file. The process is similar to the commit command used in GSX Server 2.x.
- **Revert to the snapshot**
  When reverting back to the snapshot, the changes stored in the redo log files are discarded or thrown away. The process is similar to the discard command used in GSX Server 2.x.
- **Take a snapshot**
  Taking a snapshot of a virtual machine that already has an attached redo log file will merge the current redo log file into the parent disk and then create a new redo log file to accumulate any subsequent changes made.

You can take as many snapshots as you like, but keep in mind you are only allowed one active snapshot at any given point in time. This means, when you click on snapshot again, the previous snapshot will be replaced. The good news is, unless you requested the application to stop warning you, the system will prompt you with a "Do you want to replace it?" warning.

You may be wondering how a snapshot differs from the older disk modes you might be used to from previous versions of GSX Server or one of VMware's other virtualization platforms. Some of the more common differences are explained here.

1. Using snapshot affects all disks that are attached to the virtual machine (except for independent and raw disks) as a group rather than having to modify each virtual disk individually in the configuration file.
2. Snapshots, unlike legacy disk modes, also affect changes made to the configuration file. In other words, if you take a snapshot and then make a configuration change, you need to take another snapshot if you want to

keep that configuration change active. Otherwise, if you revert the snapshot, you lose the configuration changes along with the disk changes.

3. The snapshot feature is easier to use and manage than using the legacy disk modes. Snapshot options (snapshot, revert and remove) are available throughout the GUI interface either through buttons, menu drop downs or through settings.

Snapshot Settings

There are several snapshot settings that can be changed at any time while the virtual machine is powered off. In the console, select the virtual machine and then go to VM > Settings > Options > Snapshot to make a snapshot settings change.

- **Disable snapshots**
  Allows the snapshot feature to be disabled. The option can only be checked off if the virtual machine does not currently have a snapshot or a redo log file associated with the virtual machine. If it does, the snapshot must first be removed and then the feature can be activated.
- **Lock this snapshot**
  By checking the box, the current snapshot will be prevented from being updated. In other words, once activated, the system will no longer allow a new snapshot from being taken.
- **Power options**
  There are four available options that can be selected to specify how GSX Server should handle the snapshot when the virtual machine is powered off.
  1. Just power off—leaves the snapshot as is.
  2. Revert to the snapshot—discards the changes so the virtual machine always starts in the same state.
  3. Update the snapshot—replaces the previous snapshot by taking a new snapshot of the virtual machine just before it is powered off.
  4. Ask me—prompts for a response on what to do with the snapshot when the virtual machine is powered off.

Snapshots and Legacy Virtual Machines

If the virtual machine was created in GSX Server 2 and the virtual hardware has not been upgraded to the new virtual hardware found in GSX Server 3, the virtual machine is considered to be running in legacy mode. As explained in Legacy Disk Modes, its virtual disks are configured with one of three options: persistent, undoable, and nonpersistent. So how do these legacy modes interact with the newer snapshot feature?

- **Persistent mode**
  There is no snapshot. Changes to the file system are immediately and permanently written to disk. While the virtual machine is powered off, a snapshot can be taken at any time.
- **Undoable mode**
  A virtual disk configured in an undoable mode has a snapshot. A snapshot can either be updated or removed at any time while the virtual machine is powered off.
- **Nonpersistent mode**
  A virtual disk configured in a nonpersistent mode also has a snapshot. A snapshot can either be updated or removed at any time while the virtual machine is powered off. To keep things consistent with the legacy disk mode, the virtual machine is set to revert to the snapshot every time it is powered off. However, the behavior can be changed in the virtual machine settings editor any time the virtual machine is powered off.

Snapshot Considerations

The new snapshot feature in GSX Server offers a lot of new possibilities and options to using virtual servers. However, as always, there are a few considerations that should be taken into account before jumping in. When taking a snapshot, it is important to be aware of other activity that is going on inside of the virtual machine and what the impact might be of reverting to a snapshot. To minimize the impact, it is best to snapshot a virtual machine when there are no applications actively communicating with other servers. If an application is in the midst of communicating with another server, the snapshot process may cause confusion on the virtual machine, the application, or the other server it is communicating with. Another consideration to keep in mind is the level of impact that a snapshot can have on a host server. Depending on the amount of time and number of changes that have taken place in the guest operating system since the last snapshot, the size of the redo log file can become quite large before the next snapshot is taken. The larger the file, the longer it takes to remove or commit the previous snapshot. During this time, performance of the host server may suffer, keeping other consoles from connecting to the host server or cause users trying to connect to the system to see an error that the VMware Registration Service is not running. And finally, as these redo log files grow, it is important to be aware how much disk space they have accumulated. If not carefully monitored, these disk files can start to fill up the host server's disk storage rather quickly.

VMware Virtual Disk Manager

VMware Virtual Disk Manager is an offline disk manipulation utility that allows the creation, modification, and manipulation of virtual disk files. The tool can be executed from a command line, where parameters, switches, and arguments are passed. It can also be leveraged and called from within a script. It provides a number of features and multiple ways of automating management of virtual disks that were not possible in earlier versions of GSX Server. The virtual disk manager can be used to:

- Create a stand-alone virtual disk file without creating a new virtual machine.
- Convert a virtual disk type from fixed to dynamic or vice versa. Or convert a virtual disk from a single file to a 2GB split file or vice versa.
- Expand the size of a virtual disk so that it is larger than the size it was originally created with.
- Defragment a dynamically expanding virtual disk.
- Prepare and shrink a dynamically expanding disk on a Windows host server while the virtual machine is powered off.
- Rename and/or relocate a virtual disk.

The VMware Virtual Disk Manager tool is executed from either a command prompt or a terminal on the GSX Server host. On a Windows host server, the program is located in the following directory by default: C:\Program Files\VMware\VMware GSX Server. To run the program, execute the following command: vmware-vdiskmanager. There are a number of parameters and switches than can be passed. A list of these options and examples can be displayed by executing the tool without passing in any parameters. Some of the key features are described in detail below.

Enlarge a Virtual Disk

One key feature is the ability to enlarge a virtual disk so its maximum capacity is larger than when it was originally created. All too often, a virtual disk is created without any size planning involved or found to be improperly sized after the fact. Once the operating system and applications are installed, the disk size starts to quickly fill up and may approach its maximum size. The virtual disk manager tool provides a way to expand the disk file to a more appropriate size. It is important to note that the size specified is the new size of the disk, not how much it should increase. The following example illustrates how to expand an existing disk, origDisk, to a new maximum capacity of 25GB.

```
vmware-vdiskmanager -x 25GB origDisk.vmdk
```

 When you enlarge or expand the virtual disk's capacity, VMware immediately recognizes the new disk and file size. However, the partitions on the guest operating system remain unchanged. On a Windows guest operating system, if you look at Disk Management, the system should now have an unallocated amount of disk space equal to the difference between the new maximum capacity size and the original amount of allocated partition space. If you wish to resize the original partition, you will need a third-party tool such as Partition Magic, QtParted for Linux or for a Window's guest operating system, Microsoft's DiskPart tool that comes with Windows XP Professional and Windows Server 2003 and is available in the Resource Kit for Windows 2000 Server.

Prepare and Shrink a Virtual Disk

Another key feature is the ability to shrink a dynamically expanding virtual disk file located on a Windows host server. Shrinking a virtual disk should not be confused with decreasing an existing disk's maximum capacity. Instead, it should be understood that shrinking a virtual disk simply means that it is reclaiming unused space on the disk. When a file is deleted, most operating systems do not immediately overwrite the actual data. Rather, they update the file system table to reflect that the file is no longer there. To reclaim the space, the old data needs to be zeroed out on the virtual disk. This is a two step process.

The first step is to prepare each volume on the disk for shrinking. The volume can be mounted by using a third-party tool such as the VMware DiskMount Utility. Once the volume is mounted, the virtual disk manager can prepare the disk for shrinking. For example, if the volume is mounted on the M: drive, the following command should be executed:

```
vmware-vdiskmanager -p M:
```

Once the preparation is complete, unmount the volume. This is repeated for each volume on the virtual disk that needs to go through the shrinking process.

After preparing all the volumes on the virtual disk, the next step is to actually shrink the disk. As an example, the following command will shrink the virtual disk named origDisk:

```
vmware-vdiskmanager -k origDisk.vmdk
```

Converting a Virtual Disk

A final key feature discussed is the ability to convert a fixed disk to a dynamically expanding disk and vice versa. Sometimes, it is difficult to decide whether or not a pre-allocated disk or a growable disk is needed in any given circumstance. In the past, if the wrong choice was made, it was painful to fix and had to be done with using third-party tools. The virtual disk manager now allows an easy way to convert from one type to the other. The following example converts a fixed disk to a dynamically expanding disk:

```
vmware-vdiskmanager -r -t 0 sourceDisk.vmdk
targetDisk.vmdk
```

Virtual Networking

Virtual networking is an important component of GSX Server and it allows a wide range of configurations to take place. However, it is possible to create a virtual machine that has no communication with any other server, physical or virtual. While that scenario may be likely in a workstation class virtualization environment, it is probably less true in a server class virtualization environment such as GSX Server. It is more likely the virtual machine will need to interact with other servers to share files, applications, Web pages, printers or to act as a proxy server or firewall. A virtual machine may also need access to the internet or the ability to host services for other machines outside of its LAN. This section will outline the concepts behind networking in GSX Server and cover the various components needed to get a basic network up and running.

Virtual Network Components

Before configuring a virtual network, it is important to gain an understanding of the various networking components that GSX Server has to offer. As mentioned in previous chapters, VMware offers three types of network configuration: bridged, NAT and host-only networking. In order to facilitate these configurations, VMware makes use of the virtual switch, the virtual network adapter and in some cases a virtual DHCP server.

Bridged Networking

A bridge allows a virtual machine to access a network being used by the host server. The easiest way to think of a bridge is to consider the virtual network adapter in the virtual machine as being connected to the physical Ethernet adapter in the host server.

Host-Only Networking

The host virtual adapter creates a virtual Ethernet LAN on the host server that allows communication between the host server and the virtual machines on that host server. By default, the host virtual adapter is not connected to any external network.

NAT Networking

A NAT (network address translation) device enables communication between virtual machines and the external network. Using a NAT device becomes extremely advantageous when there is a limited amount of IP addresses available on the physical network and those IP addresses are being used by the physical servers.

Virtual Switch

A virtual switch is similar to a physical switch in that it connects networking components together. A virtual switch can be connected to the physical network or it can be completely virtual and therefore isolated from the outside network. GSX Server allows a total of 10 switches on a Windows host server and up to 100 switches on a Linux host server. And each switch can have one or more virtual machines connected to it at any given time. Since each virtual machine has its own virtual network adapter that is connected to the virtual switch, the GSX Server network basically becomes an extension of the physical network it is connected into. The virtual network can therefore become as simplistic or complex as needed.

Virtual switches are identified or labeled as VMnet[N], where [N] is a numeric value between 0 and 9 on a Windows host server and 0 to 99 on a Linux host server. By default, a few of the switches are assigned specifically named configurations. Out of the box, the bridged network normally uses VMnet0, the host-only network uses VMnet1, and the NAT network uses VMnet8. These defaults can be changed if necessary.

DCHP server

The DHCP (dynamic host configuration protocol) server is useful when virtual machines are configured to use host-only or NAT configurations. The DHCP server provided by VMware works very much like a DHCP service configured in a Windows or Linux operating system. It provides a range of IP addresses to virtual machines that are not bridged to an external network.

Network adapter

A single virtual network adapter is added to each virtual machine that is created. In fact, up to three virtual network adapters can be configured in each virtual machine. Generally, a single virtual adapter per virtual machine is all that is necessary.

 So if a virtual machine only needs a single adapter, why would VMware allow for up to three adapters on a single virtual machine? The most common answer is for routing or security purposes. If you need to multi-home your virtual machine (allow it to access more than one subnet), it will need to be configured with multiple adapters assigned to different virtual switches. And for security reasons, you may want to create a more complex virtual network that uses a virtual machine to act as a firewall to isolate segments and control the traffic that can pass through. Just like a physical network, you have a number of options available to configure your virtual network.

As previously explained, there are two types of network adapters: the AMD PC/NET 32 compatible NIC that uses the vlance driver and the VMware PCI Ethernet Adapter that uses the vmxnet driver. When a new virtual machine is created, the default network adapter is the AMD PC/NET 32 device. Of the two adapters, it offers more compatibility with a wider support of guest operating systems. The VMware PCI Ethernet Adapter does not offer native support in any guest operating system. It requires a VMware specific driver that must be installed, either manually or by installing the VMware Tools. For the trouble and effort of installing the vmxnet driver, it offers better performance, most noticeably if the host adapter is Gigabit Ethernet.

GSX Server Network Configurations

The three types of networking configurations found in GSX Server have already been identified and described in the previous section. The following will attempt to go into more detail and illustrate the configurations that are automatically created when the standard networking options are selected in the New Virtual Machine Wizard or when making a change in the virtual machine settings editor. In each of these configurations, a Windows host can connect an unlimited number of virtual devices to a virtual switch, while a Linux host can only connect up to 32 devices.

Bridged Networking

If the host server is on an Ethernet network, bridged networking is probably the easiest way to connect the virtual machine to the local area network and to the internet. It is as easy as installing an Ethernet adapter into a physical server and joining it into the LAN. A Linux host server can use bridged networking to connect to a wired network while a Windows host server can connect to either a wired or a wireless network. Keep in mind, when using bridged networking, the virtual machine has two-way communication on the LAN. That means, it can access other equipment on the network and it can be contacted by other equipment on the network. Figure 22.10 depicts a host server and three virtual machines using bridged networking.

 It is important to note, if you choose bridged networking, your virtual machines need to have their own unique network identity. This typically means that the virtual machines need their own IP address. You cannot share an IP address with the host server or another machine on the network. Always consult with the network administrator for an available IP range or make use of a DHCP server in the network. Selecting an IP address that is assigned to another

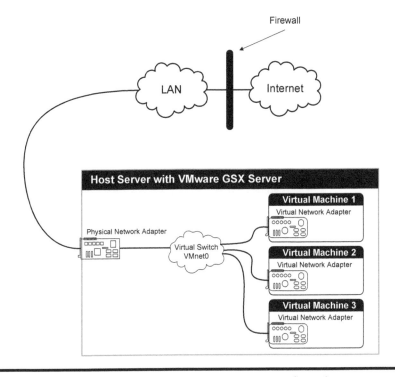

Figure 22.10   VMware GSX Server Bridged Networking Configuration.

device on the network will lead to IP conflicts and cause intermittent network problems that may be troublesome to diagnose.

When should bridged networking be used?

- When the LAN is Ethernet
- When the LAN has enough free IP addresses to use
- When virtual machines need Internet and LAN access
- When virtual machines are hosting applications

Network Address Translation (NAT) Networking

NAT networking is similar to host-only networking but with the added feature of network address translation, which allows the virtual machine to transcend the private network and communicate with the external LAN as well as the Internet. When unable to assign virtual machines an IP address on the external network, NAT is a good alternative to bridged networking.

When using this type of networking, the guest operating system does not have its own IP address on the external network. Instead, a private network is set

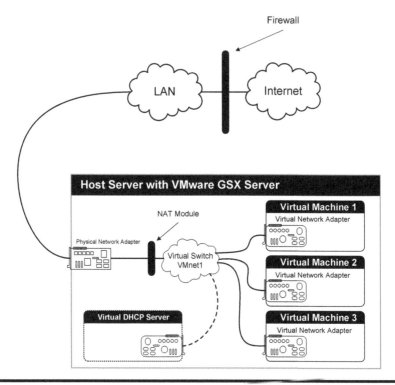

Figure 22.11 VMware GSX Server Network Address Translation (NAT) Networking Configuration.

up on the host server, much like the host-only network, and the guest operating system receives an internal IP address from the VMware virtual DHCP server. The virtual machines then communicate with a router node, the VMware NAT device, which passes network data between one or more virtual machines and the external network. Communication across the NAT device is recorded in a translation table and the traffic is then funneled back to the correct destination. Figure 22.11 shows a typical NAT networking configuration. Notice the extra NAT node and its placement.

NAT will allow virtual machines to use many standard TCP/IP protocols to communicate with other machines on the external network. For example, it can open a Telnet or FTP session on another computer. Unfortunately, a problem with NAT networking is the default configuration does not allow computers on the external network to initiate connections to the virtual machines. That means, the default configuration does not allow a virtual machine to act as a Web server or an FTP server because it only allows the opening of an initial connection from a client behind the NAT node and not from a computer on the external network or the Internet.

When should NAT networking be used?

- When connecting to Token Ring adapters—Bridged only works with Ethernet
- When external network IP addresses are not available
- When virtual machines need Internet and LAN access
- When a Linux host uses a wireless networking adapter
- When securing virtual machines from network attacks is an issue

Host-only Networking

Unlike bridged networking, host-only networking provides a network connection between the host server and the virtual machines located on that server. It uses a virtual Ethernet adapter that is visible to the host operating system. The entire network infrastructure is virtual and isolated from everything outside of the host server. Only the virtual machines on the host and the host virtual adapter are connected to a private TCP/IP network. Communication is not only allowed between the host server and the virtual machines, but also between virtual machines located on the same host. Addresses on this private network are provided by the VMware DHCP server. Figure 22.12 shows a host-only network and depicts how the network is completely contained within the host server and isolated from the LAN.

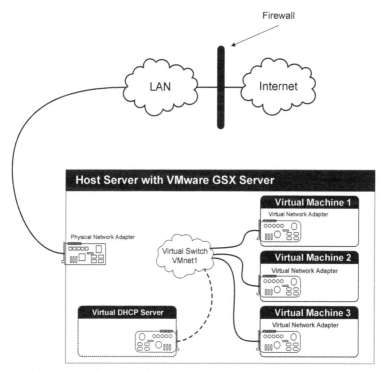

Figure 22.12   VMware GSX Server Host-Only Networking Configuration.

When should host-only networking be used?

- When isolating virtual machines from systems outside the host computer
- When the host itself is already isolated

Host-only and NAT DHCP Server

One of the most tedious tasks for a network administrator to perform is to manually enter the IP address, subnet mask and other networking information on an operating system so that the new server can communicate with the network when it comes online. The answer is the Dynamic Host Configuration Protocol (DHCP). In order to ease this process, a virtual DHCP server is automatically installed with GSX Server. Since host-only and NAT networking use a private virtual network, each virtual machine and the host must be assigned addresses on the private network. This is usually accomplished with the VMware DHCP server, although addresses can also be assigned statically from a pool of addresses that are not used by the DHCP server. For a list of address assignments on a private VMware class C network, see Figure 22.13.

 The VMware DHCP server does not service DHCP requests from virtual or physical servers residing on a bridged network.

Host-Only Network		
IP Range	**Address Use**	**Example**
x.x.x.1	Host server	192.168.0.1
x.x.x.2 - x.x.x.127	Static addresses	192.168.0.2 - 192.168.0.127
x.x.x.128 - x.x.x.253	DHCP addresses	192.168.0.128 - 192.168.0.253
x.x.x.254	DHCP server	192.168.0.254
x.x.x.255	Broadcast	192.168.0.255
NAT Network		
IP Range	**Address Use**	**Example**
x.x.x.1	Host server	192.168.0.1
x.x.x.2	NAT node	192.168.0.2
x.x.x.3 - x.x.x.127	Static addresses	192.168.0.3 - 192.168.0.127
x.x.x.128 - x.x.x.253	DHCP addresses	192.168.0.128 - 192.168.0.253
x.x.x.254	DHCP server	192.168.0.254
x.x.x.255	Broadcast	192.168.0.255

Figure 22.13   Address Assignments for Host-Only and NAT Networking.

Generally speaking, a randomly assigned DHCP address is the norm for virtual machines that are used infrequently or for a short period of time. A good example of a dynamic virtual machine is a test server. Typically, the virtual machine is configured and powered on to run a specific test. And when that test is successful, the virtual machine is usually powered off and recycled. If however a virtual machine is static and used for extended periods of time, it is probably a better idea to statically assign it an IP address or to configure the DHCP server to always assign the same IP address to each of these virtual machines. This can be accomplished by assigning each virtual machine a static MAC address and then configuring the DHCP server to always assign an IP based on that MAC address. As an example, to assign IP address 192.168.0.128 to a virtual machine named "StaticVM" with a MAC address of 00:50:56:01:02:03, the following can be added to the VMware DHCP configuration:

```
host StaticVM {
   hardware Ethernet 00:50:56:01:02:03;
   fixed-address 192.168.0.128;
   }
```

Configuring the DHCP server

VMware's DHCP server can be configured by manually editing its configuration files or on a Windows host server by using the GUI. See Figure 22.14.

On a Linux host server, the DHCP configuration file and lease file can be modified by editing them directly with a standard text editor. The default configuration and lease files are located at:

```
/etc/vmware/vmnet[N]/dhcp/dhcp.conf
```

```
/etc/vmware/vmnet[N]/dhcp/dhcp.leases
```

Where [N] is the vmnet network, i.e., host-only is vmnet1 and NAT is vmnet8

On a Windows host server, the DHCP configuration file and lease file can be modified by editing them directly with a standard text editor. The default configuration and lease files are located at:

```
C:\Documents and Settings\All Users\Application
Data\VMware
```

The two files are respectively named vmnetdhcp.conf and vmnetdhcp.leases

On a Windows host server (see Figure 22.14), the DHCP server can also be configured by using the Virtual Network Editor by selecting Host > Virtual Network Settings > DHCP.

DHCP and NAT Networking

One additional difference between host-only and NAT networking is the additional configuration information supplied by the DHCP server for NAT

	GSX Server for Windows	GSX Server for Linux
DHCP Config File	C:\Documents and Settings\A l Users\Application Data\Vmware\vmnetdhcp.conf	/etc/vmware/vmnet[N]/dhcp/dhcp.conf
DHCP Lease File	C:\Documents and Settings\All Users\Application Data\Vmware\vmnetdhcp.leases	/etc/vmware/vmnet[N]/dhcp/dhcp.leases
	Where [N] is the vmnet network, i.e. host-only is vmnet1 and NAT is vmnet8 Consult the DHCP server documentation for specific configuration information	

Figure 22.14 DHCP Configuration File Locations.

networking. This information includes the default gateway and the DNS server. The DHCP server sets the virtual machine's default gateway and DNS server to the IP address of the NAT node (x.x.x.2). This causes all outbound IP packets and DNS requests to be forwarded to the NAT node.

The NAT node then acts as a DNS server for the virtual machines on the NAT network. The NAT node is more like a DNS proxy that forwards DNS requests on to the host server's DNS server. Any responses come back to the NAT node and are then forwarded back to the virtual machines.

 While there are numerous packet sniffing utilities readily available for download on the Internet, VMware GSX Server makes troubleshooting the network easier by providing two simple tools packaged with the platform product. The first is a command-line packet sniffer utility. The Windows version is named vnetsniffer.exe and is located in the VMware GSX Server folder while the Linux version is named vmnet-sniffer and is located in your VMware binary directory. To run the utility, from a command-line, enter in the program name (either vmnetsniffer or vmnet-sniffer) and pass in the argument for the VMnet you want to troubleshoot. For example, on a Windows host enter: `vmnetsniffer VMnet0`. On a Linux host enter: `vmnet-sniffer /dev/vmnet0`.

To gather utilization statistics on the different VMnet interfaces, a Windows host server also has a utility named vnetstats.exe located in the same directory as the sniffer utility. Running vnetstats from a command-line will return information such as packets received, transmitted, and dropped along with errors for that specific VMnet interface. You can also pass in the interval argument to get a real-time look at utilization.

Dynamic Versus Static MAC Addresses

Every Ethernet network interface card, whether physical or virtual, has a unique identifier assigned to it known as the media access control or MAC address. Ethernet MAC addresses are typically shown as a string of 12 hexadecimal digits. The first six digits identify the vendor ID or the manufacturer of the network card and are known as the Organizational Unique Identifier (OUI). The OUI prefixes are assigned to organizations by the IEEE. The last six digits are assigned by the manufacturer of the network card and are known as the burned-in addresses (BIA). VMware's organizationally unique identifier has been assigned as 00:50:56. So, for example, a VMware MAC address may be identified as 00:50:56:01:23:45.

VMware GSX Server automatically assigns each of its virtual network adapters a MAC address dynamically when the virtual machine is powered on. While it may at first appear easier on the administrator to allow the software to dynamically assign MAC addresses to the virtual network adapters, there are a few concerns that should be identified that are associated with that choice.

VMware guarantees that virtual machines will be assigned unique MAC addresses as long as the virtual machines are contained within the same physical host server. While the software does attempt to automatically assign unique MAC addresses to virtual machines spanning across multiple physical host servers, it does not guarantee that it will be successful doing so. Unfortunately, if it fails to assign a unique MAC address, it becomes very difficult to troubleshoot the intermittent networking issues associated with a duplicate MAC address on the network. Since GSX Server is an enterprise virtualization platform, the likelihood that the environment consists solely of one physical host server is probably extremely rare. The larger the virtualized network environment, the more likely it is that a duplicate MAC address will be given out.

The other problem associated with dynamically assigned MAC addresses is the rigidity with which the virtualized environment must be maintained. In other words, in order to remain somewhat confident that the MAC addresses of the virtual machines will remain unchanged by the software, the virtual machine, its configuration file and the network adapter must remain static. Thus, if any of the following scenarios take place, VMware cannot guarantee that a virtual network adapter will retain the same MAC address.

1. The virtual machine's configuration file should not be moved. The MAC address will more than likely be reassigned if the configuration file is either moved to a different file location on its current physical host server or moved to an entirely different physical host server.

2. Certain settings found within the virtual machine's configuration file should not be altered. When editing the configuration file directly through a text editor, the following options should not be removed or changed else the MAC address will more than likely be reassigned.

    ```
    Ethernet[n].generatedAddress
    Ethernet[n].addressType
    Ethernet[n].generatedAddressOffset
    uuid.location
    uuid.bios
    Ethernet[n].present
    ```

    In the above example, [n] represents the number of the virtual network adapter such as Ethernet0.

3. A virtual network adapter should not be removed from the virtual machine or changed to a different type of adapter (such as switching between vlance and vmxnet). In either case, the virtual network adapter will more than likely be assigned a new MAC address.

Assigning a Static MAC Address

In order to guarantee that the same MAC address gets assigned to a virtual machine, even if that virtual machine is moved from one physical host server to another, or to guarantee a unique MAC address is assigned to each virtual machine in any size network environment, the MAC address can be statically assigned rather than having the GSX Server software dynamically assign it.

To assign a unique MAC address to any virtual machine, the configuration file (either .cfg or .vmx) will need to be manually updated with any standard text file editor. As an example, if the first virtual Ethernet adapter is being modified, the following lines in the configuration file will need to be removed:

```
Ethernet0.generatedAddress
Ethernet0.addressType
Ethernet0.generatedAddressOffset
```

The following line will then need to be added to the configuration file:

```
Ethernet0.address = 00:50:56:AB:CD:EF
```

VMware GSX Server does not support arbitrary MAC addresses, therefore, the above format must be used when statically assigning a MAC address to a virtual machine in order for it to boot.

In the above example, CD and EF can be any valid hexadecimal number between 00 and FF; however, AB can only be assigned a valid hexadecimal number between 00 and 3F. It is important because the hexadecimal value above 3F in the fourth octet or AB position is where VMware starts its dynamic assignment of MAC addresses. Choosing a hexadecimal value above 3F may cause conflicts between the dynamically assigned MAC addresses and the statically created MAC addresses. It is equally important to keep a single point of control or a master list on all statically assigned MAC addresses. If a statically assigned MAC address is duplicated between two or more virtual machines, a conflict will occur and problems will arise.

Resource Management

While GSX Server does enable the allocation of memory resources, it falls short of the amount of resource management that the VMware ESX Server product provides. To enable more control over the allocation of resources, including processor resources, there are a number of third-party tools to consider. Microsoft has developed the Windows System Resources Manager (WSRM) for use with Windows Server 2003, both the Enterprise and Datacenter editions. Another third-party tool to help optimize work load management is ARMTech for VMware developed by Aurema.

GSX Server allows the setting of memory size of each virtual machine and the amount of the host server's memory that can be used for those virtual machines.

It can also control the extent to which the host operating system's memory manager is allowed to swap virtual machines out of physical RAM. It is important to keep in mind that changing these settings can affect both virtual machine and overall system performance.

Host operating systems do not perform well when they are starved for memory. When a Windows or Linux host server does not have enough memory to use, it starts to thrash. Performance suffers as it starts swapping between RAM and its paging file on disk. GSX Server attempts to keep the problem from happening by enforcing a limit on the amount of memory that a virtual machine can consume. To ensure that the host operating system can function while virtual machines are consuming its RAM, the system reserves an amount of memory available for the host server.

The reserved amount of memory for virtual machine consumption is an adjustable number by an administrator user. The setting can be changed in the console by selecting Host > Settings > Memory. This window allows the modification of two memory settings, the amount of RAM reserved for all running virtual machines and how the system should allocate the RAM to the virtual machines.

The reserved memory setting specifies the maximum amount of host RAM that GSX Server is allowed to use. The value is set via a sliding scale. It is important to remember, setting the value too high will take away RAM from the host server and any applications running on the host server. It can lead to thrashing since the host server has no choice but to page to disk, which then causes the host server's performance to suffer. Setting the value too low will cause the virtual machine performance to degrade and it lowers the count of virtual machines that are able to power on simultaneously.

 Virtual machines can consume a large amount of memory in order to function properly. You may have created a number of virtual machines on your host server and wondered why all of your virtual machines did not power on. You took into account the amount of RAM reserved for the host server and the amount of RAM assigned to each virtual machine and it was equal to the amount of physical RAM installed in the host server. So what's the problem? The virtual machine also consumes some amount of memory overhead. The actual amount depends on the size of its virtual disk, its behavior and the amount of memory assigned to the virtual machine. Figure 22.15 shows the typical amount of overhead that a virtual machine consumes, based on the amount of memory assigned to it.

GSX Server also attempts to keep virtual machine performance high by limiting the number of virtual machines that can be run simultaneously based on the amount of RAM specified in the application settings. The machine will fail

Assigned Amount of Memory to the Virtual Machine	Additional Amount of Overhead Needed
Up to 512MB	Up to 54MB
Up to 1GB	Up to 62MB
Up to 2GB	Up to 79MB
Up to 3.6GB	Up to 105MB

Figure 22.15   Virtual Machine Memory Overhead.

to power on if there is not enough memory available to do so. To increase the number of virtual machines that can be powered on and run, adjust the amount of memory allocated to each virtual machine. Another option is to adjust the amount of virtual memory the host server can swap to disk. While it may allow more virtual machines to power on and run, it will affect virtual machine and host server performance because the system is now swapping more memory to disk, a much slower process. To make the change, adjust the setting in Host > Settings > Memory and choose one of these options under Additional memory:

- Fit all virtual machine memory into reserved host RAM
- Allow some virtual machine memory to be swapped
- Allow most virtual machine memory to be swapped

By fitting all virtual machine memory into the reserved host RAM, the virtual machines will operate with the best level of performance. The restrictions are set to the amount of memory available in the reserved memory section. The next two options will allow an increase in the number or memory size of virtual machines that can run on the host server at a given time. Unfortunately, the performance of the virtual machines and the host server will suffer as the paging from RAM to disk increases.

GSX Server for Windows also allows the changing of the priority that the Windows process scheduler gives to the virtual machines. It affects the performance of both, the virtual machines and the Windows host server. An administrator can change the priority settings by selecting Host > Settings > Priority and using the drop-down lists.

- Change Input grabbed from either normal to high for virtual machines when they have keyboard and mouse input.
- Change Input ungrabbed from either normal to low for virtual machines when they do not have keyboard and mouse input grabbed.

Performance Optimization

Many software applications offer ways to optimize their performance in various environments. VMware GSX Server is no exception. The information presented below may prove valuable in enhancing GSX Server's performance. It does not however specifically address performance optimizations for the guest operating system or the host operating system.

Guest Operating System Selection

When creating a virtual machine for the first time, one of the steps is to identify the guest operating system. It is important to make sure that the correct guest operating system is selected for each virtual machine created. Based on the selection, GSX Server optimizes certain internal configurations. Making the wrong selection probably won't cause a virtual machine to run incorrectly, but it may degrade the virtual machine's performance. For example, when creating a new Windows Server 2003 virtual machine in the New Virtual Machine Wizard and selecting Microsoft Windows as the guest operating system, make sure to select the proper version in the drop-down list rather than just taking the default.

File System Selection

When using a Windows operating system, there are different choices of file system available: FAT16, FAT32, and NTFS. NTFS is a higher performing and more secure file system than the older FAT file systems. It is faster at reads and writes and can handle larger file sizes—important when dealing with large virtual disk files. At the same time, using the FAT file system will cause performance degradation on virtual machines that require larger sums of memory. How can that happen? If a virtual machine is stored on a FAT file system, GSX Server cannot allocate more than 2GB of memory to that virtual machine. Doing so will cause the virtual machine to not power on.

Memory

Virtual machines and physical servers both have a desire to consume memory. Increasing the amount of memory is one of the best ways to enhance performance. Running low on memory can negatively impact both host and guest performance. When starved for memory, operating systems are forced to swap to disk, which is much slower than RAM. Adding more memory to the physical server and allocating more memory to the virtual machine is a key component for optimization.

CPU

Like memory, a virtual server environment consumes a lot of CPU cycles. On a normal physical server, a machine having 20–30 percent CPU utilization is probably standard. On a GSX Server, 70–80 percent is probably more likely. To gain a significant amount of performance, a multiprocessor server is welcomed and likewise, the faster the processor(s) the better. To make the best use of the processors on a GSX Server host, it is best to not share the server with any other running applications. In other words, dedicate the server host to being a virtualization platform host rather than also using it as a Web server, a database server, or a file server for other applications.

Debugging Mode

A virtual machine hosted in GSX can be configured to run in one of two modes: normal mode and debugging mode. While the debugging mode is great for troubleshooting (it adds more detail to the log file), it causes the virtual machine to run slower than in normal mode. If performance is slower than expected, verify the configuration is not set to run in debug mode.

Disk File Location

A simple technique to help GSX Server performance is to not use virtual disks that are on remote servers and accessed across a network. GSX Server involves a lot of intensive disk access, so unless the network is extremely fast and comparable to local disk I/O, running virtual disks over a network can hurt performance. If the virtual disks must reside remotely, consider taking a snapshot so the changes are stored locally in the working directory. Another performance technique is to separate the host operating system from the virtual disk files. Placing the operating system on drive C: and the virtual disk files on drive D: can help prevent disk I/O bottlenecks and thus improve performance.

Virtual Disk Types

Selecting the right virtual disk type for the job is important. There are many scenarios where a dynamically expanding or sparse disk is the best choice because of the capabilities that it offers. But when looking to optimize virtual disk speed, the fixed disk or preallocated disk is the faster performing disk type. However, if a dynamically expanding virtual disk is needed, there are ways to increase its performance. One way, albeit risky, is if the virtual disk has a Windows operating system installed on it and it is using an NTFS file system, consider turning on write caching for NTFS. If data integrity is important, do not try this method as problems may arise if the system is improperly turned off or a host server failure occurs. Another option is to create a fixed disk to start the installation of the guest operating system and then complete any application installs that are needed. Once the virtual machine setup is completed, use VMware Virtual Disk Manager to convert the fixed disk into a dynamically expanding disk. And finally, to optimize a virtual disk it should be defragmented often.

Disk Fragmentation

Without going into what disk fragmentation is, suffice it to say virtual disks, like physical disks, suffer the same fate of not handling the disk space freed up by deleted files very well. All disks, physical, fixed, and dynamic can become fragmented over time. However, fragmentation is usually worse for dynamic disks. To optimize a disk the right way, it needs to go through a defragmentation process in the proper order; otherwise, the work done in previous steps may be undone (see Figure 22.16). The first step is to defragment the file system of the guest operating system with the guest powered on. The next step is to defragment the dynamically expanding virtual disk file with the guest powered off. Select either the VMware Virtual Disk Manager utility or choose defragment from the virtual machine settings editor (VM > Settings) and then click on Defragment. Finally, defragment the file system on the host server while the virtual machines are powered off using the same defragmenting tool normally used to defragment a physical disk.

Virtual Disk File System of a Virtual Machine

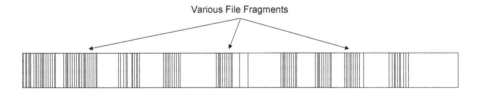

Physical Disk File System of a Host Server

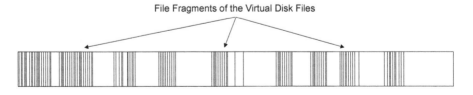

Figure 22.16   Disk Fragmentation.

CD-ROM and Floppy Drive

Some operating systems poll the CD-ROM drive every second or so to see if there is a disc present in the drive. Polling can cause GSX Server to connect to the host CD-ROM drive, which in turn can make the CD-ROM drive spin up, resulting in the virtual machine appearing to pause. A good approach is to configure the virtual machine's CD-ROM drive to be disconnected during startup. If the virtual machine needs access to the CD-ROM, it can be connected manually at that time. The same approach can be used for the floppy drive. During boot, the virtual machine slows down while it checks for the existence of a floppy disk making the post screen that much slower. Additionally, leaving the floppy drive and the CD-ROM drive connected but idle takes away a small amount of processing power from the host as well as the virtual machine. Disconnecting the drives until needed therefore offers a two-for-one optimization.

Full Screen Mode

For the best performance, if the virtual machine and the host do not need to share a screen, the virtual machine should be run in full screen mode as opposed to window mode. The most noticeable improvement comes from using full screen mode while the guest is in VGA mode. On a Linux host, full screen VGA mode uses the underlying video card directly causing the graphics performance to be close to that of the host. On the other hand, window VGA mode requires considerably more resources for emulation. So during a graphical installation of the operating system, using full screen mode will result in quite a performance boost.

Linux Swap Space Configuration

On a Linux host server, proper configuration of the swap space and the /tmp directory can affect system performance. The swap partition on the host server should be at least two times the amount of the physical memory on the host. For example, if the host server has 1GB of memory, the swap partition should be at least 2GB in size. It is important to make sure that the /tmp partition on the host server is large enough and has ample free space available. Since Linux distributions only reserve about 10 percent of /tmp for use by root processes, if the /tmp partition reaches 90 percent capacity, nonroot applications will no longer be able to write to it. It is important to make sure these values are configured correctly because the default settings may be incorrect.

Automated Installation

Starting with the GSX Server 3.0 release, VMware delivered an unattended automated installation package for high volume server deployments. In order to take advantage of the feature, the server on which GSX Server is going to be installed must be a supported Microsoft Windows host operating system. In addition, the server must have the Microsoft Windows Installer runtime engine version 2.0 installed. The 2.0 version was released with Microsoft Windows 2000 Server SP3 and is included with Microsoft Windows Server 2003. If the host operating system is Windows 2000 Server, it is important to check the version of the file located in the following path:

```
%windir%\system32\msiexec.exe
```

If the proper version of the runtime engine is not installed, the engine will need to be upgraded by executing instmsiw.exe. For specific instructions on how to do so, visit the Microsoft Web site.

To install the GSX Server application on a Windows host using the unattended automated install, complete the following steps:

1. Open a command prompt on the host.
2. Extract the individual installation package files by typing the following on one line:

   ```
   VMware-gsx-server-installer-<xxxx>.exe /a /s
   /x /d C:\temp\gsx
   ```

   (where <xxxx> represents the version and build number and C:\temp\gsx represents the temporary location of the extracted files)
3. Using the extracted .MSI files, run the automated installation by typing the following on one line:

   ```
   msiexec -i "C:\temp\gsx\VMware GSX Server.msi"
   ADDLOCAL=ALL /qn
   ```

   (Where the ADDLOCAL option defaults to install all GSX Server components)

The automated installation can be customized by passing in optional parameters (see Figure 22.17). At the same time, different MSI packages can be executed to install different components of the product.

The installation can be customized further by using a combination of the ADDLOCAL and REMOVE options. The following components can either be added or removed:

- All, the default, includes all of the options listed.
- Network, includes the following network adapters: bridged (VMnet0), host-only (VMnet1), and the NAT (VMnet8). It can also include the VMware DHCP and NAT service.
- The VMware DHCP service
- The VMware NAT service

Property Name	Description	Default Value
DESKTOP_SHORTCUT	By default, GSX Server shortcuts are added to the desktop of the host server. To prevent the shortcuts from being added to the desktop, add the following option to step3: DESKTOP_SHORTCUT=0	1
DISABLE_AUTORUN	Disables the CD autorun functionality on the host server. This option is disabled by default. To enable CD autorun, add the following option to step3: DISABLE_AUTORUN=0	1
REMOVE_LICENSE	When uninstalling GSX Server, this option will remove all stored licenses on the host server. The default setting keeps the licenses in case of a reinstall or an upgrade. To have the installer remove licenses, add the following option to step3: REMOVE_LICENSE=1	0 0
SERIALNUMBER	This option automatically enters the serial number during the automated install. To supply the product's serial number, add the following option to step3: SERIALNUMBER=<enter product serial number>	N/A

Figure 22.17 Automated Installation Optional Parameters.

To include a component, use it with the ADDLOCAL option. To exclude a component, use it with the REMOVE option. For example, to install everything except the VMware DHCP service, specify the following:

```
msiexec -i "C:\temp\gsx\VMware GSX Server.msi"
ADDLOCAL=ALL REMOVE=DHCP /qn
```

When executing the command in step 2 above, the individual installation packages are extracted to C:\temp\gsx. A separate MSI package will be created for the VMware GSX Server and the VMware Management Interface. Therefore, if the VMware Management Interface is not needed, it does not have to be installed with the automated installer; simply install the VMware GSX Server. msi. To install the VMware Management Interface, use the VMware Management Interface.msi file.

To specify a different install directory, the following option can be added to the automated installation:

```
msiexec -i "C:\temp\gsx\VMware GSX Server.msi"
INSTALLDIR=C:\Mypath ADDLOCAL=ALL /qn
```

Installing Patches and Updates

A new feature added in GSX Server 3.0 is the ability to allow GSX Server to automatically check to see if there are any updates available for the product. By default, the product checks for updates once a week and if an update exists a message is displayed when a console is launched. Unfortunately, it only automatically checks for software updates when the product is started, not while the product is simply up and running. The interval for the automatic update check can be changed to something other than the weekly default. Changes can be made by choosing Edit > Preferences > Workspace and then selecting the interval in the drop-down list next to Check for software updates. The choices are:

- Never—Choose this setting to not allow the product to check for updates.
- Daily—Automatically check for updates when the product is started and at least one day has elapsed since the last time the product was started.
- Weekly—Automatically check for updates when the product is started and at least one week has elapsed since the last time the product was started. (The default setting.)
- Monthly—Automatically check for updates when the product is started and at least one month has elapsed since the last time the product was started.

Updates for the product can be checked for manually by choosing Help > Check for Updates on the Web at any time.

 If you are running GSX Server behind a proxy server, make sure to configure it correctly. If GSX Server is running on a Windows host, make sure your browser is configured to connect to the internet through your proxy server. If GSX Server is running on a Linux host, make sure to configure http_proxy with the name and port number of the proxy server.

When the GSX Server product is registered with VMware Support, emails with information on security updates, version updates and patches will get sent to the contact email address. VMware also has a download section and a security updates page on their Web site. For example, when a security vulnerability was found in the version of OpenSSL that shipped with the GSX Server product, VMware notified customers and supplied an updated patch to fix the security hole. As of this writing, the GSX Server Security Updates Web page can be found at www.vmware.com/download/gsx_security.html.

Summary

Rounding out the platform-specific knowledge required to successfully build and manage a GSX Server implementation, this chapter went into great detail to discuss virtual machines, disks, networks, and platform extensions for guest operating systems in a GSX Server environment. VMware Tools are an important component of VMware GSX Server. By installing the tools, a suite of drivers and utilities are added to the virtual machine that greatly boosts its performance and also enables added features that help improve the management of virtual machines by GSX Server. Two important components of virtualization are also covered in great detail: virtual hard disks and virtual networking. Both components are explained at great lengths. The various disk types, controllers, and disk modes are covered along with a discussion on GSX Server's snapshot function. Virtual networking in GSX Server offers a number of methods of connecting virtual machines to a private network, a corporate LAN and to the Internet. By adding multiple virtual network adapters and configuring virtual switches, a highly complex virtual network can be created to meet almost any configuration need. The chapter ties the advanced concepts together and appropriately ends with a number of ways to optimize the host server and effectively manage its resources.

Part VI

Advanced Concepts

Chapter 23

Upgrading VMware GSX Server and ESX Server

VMware GSX Server and ESX Server are two of the most widely distributed and deployed server virtualization platforms in the industry. To retain this status, VMware is continuously releasing new features with each minor and major release, making the virtualization platforms more robust, secure, and easier to use while at the same time extending its capabilities. This chapter describes the benefits of upgrading to the latest release, useful considerations during the upgrade planning stage, and a step-by-step upgrade process not only for the physical host server, but for the virtual machines as well.

VMware GSX Server 3.2

The following sections describe the benefits, planning considerations, and upgrade steps for VMware GSX Server 3.2 on a Linux or Windows host system. Many of the feature benefits have been realized with the release of GSX Server 3.0 and 3.1.

Benefits of Upgrading

In addition to numerous bug fixes, VMware has released a number of new beneficial features to the platform since the release of GSX Server 3.0. There is little reason not to upgrade a GSX Server 2.x environment to 3.2. The bug fixes alone make the upgrade process worth the effort. However, it is the additional operating system support and added features that make the decision to upgrade to the latest release a no-brainer. With bug fixes and expanded operating system support, it even makes sense to upgrade from an earlier version of GSX Server 3.0 to the latest release of 3.2. The list of these added host and guest operating systems along with some of the more important new features added since the release of GSX Server 3.0 is detailed below.

New Operating System Support

VMware GSX Server has one of the most impressive lists of supported host and guest operating systems on the market. With the release of GSX Server 3.2, VMware not only expanded the 32-bit host and guest operating systems further, they also added full support and experimental support for 64-bit host operating systems on the AMD64 and Intel EM64T processors. With such a large list of supported operating systems, GSX Server continues to offer customers the freedom to choose the operating system that works best for each scenario.

VMware GSX Server 3.2 has full support for the following 64-bit host operating system:

- Microsoft Windows Server 2003 x64 Edition on AMD64 and Intel EM64T processors.

Experimental support for the following 64-bit host operating systems has also been added:

- Red Hat Enterprise Linux 4
- Red Hat Enterprise Linux 3 Update 4
- SUSE LINUX 9.2
- SUSE LINUX 9.3
- SUSE LINUX Enterprise Server 9 Service Pack 1

Support has been added for the following 32-bit host and guest operating systems:

- FreeBSD 4.6.2, 4.8, 5.0, and 5.1 (pre-release version)
- Microsoft Windows Server 2003 Service Pack 1
- Microsoft Windows code-named Longhorn (experimental support)
- Mandrake Linux 10 and 10.1
- NetWare 6.5 Server
- Red Hat Enterprise Linux 2.1 Update 6, 3.0 Update 4 and 4.0
- Solaris 9 and 10 Operating System x86 Platform Edition (experimental support)
- SUSE LINUX Enterprise Server 9 Service Pack 1
- SUSE LINUX 9.2
- SUSE LINUX 9.3 (experimental support)
- Turbolinux Server 7.0, 8.0 and Workstation 8.0

iSCSI Clustering Support

VMware GSX Server 3.2 has added support for clustering using the iSCSI protocol. Clustering with iSCSI is the only way to use GSX Server to cluster across multiple hosts. It is also an easier clustering method to configure when compared to previous methods. To learn more about clustering with a virtual machine, see the Clustering section of chapter 26.

Manage Virtual Disks Using VMware Virtual Disk Manager

VMware GSX Server 3.1 added a utility that can be executed from command-line or within scripts that can create, manage, and modify virtual disk files. This command-line tool is far superior to the previously packaged utility, Plainmaker, which simply created virtual disk files. For more information, see VMware Virtual Disk Manager in chapter 22.

VirtualCenter Enabled

As of GSX Server 3.1, VirtualCenter is fully capable of managing and provisioning virtual machines across multiple GSX Server hosts, and these virtual machines can also be migrated between other GSX Server hosts and ESX Server hosts that are managed by VirtualCenter.

Secure Connections Updated

SSL is now enabled by default for remote connections using the VMware Virtual Machine Console and the VMware Management Interface. The 3.1 release incorporates the latest version of OpenSSL, 0.9.7d, to correct various vulnerabilities.

Snapshots

GSX Server 3.0 removed the need to configure each virtual hard disk of a virtual machine with its own disk mode, i.e., Persistent, Nonpersistent, and Undoable. Instead, a new feature called Snapshot was introduced where a point-in-time copy of a virtual machine's state can be saved to disk. In functionality, it is similar to using multiple disk modes. A snapshot copy of a virtual machine can be taken, which then causes all new disk writes to save to a REDO log file rather than changing the parent or the original disk file. Later, the snapshot copy can either be reverted (discarded) or committed back into the original disk file. To learn more about this new feature, see the Snapshot section of chapter 22.

Improved Virtual Disk and Network Performance

Migrating from a GSX Server 1.x or 2.x platform to a GSX Server 3.x can improve both virtual disk and networking performance by 10–20 percent.

Increased Memory Support for Virtual Machines

In order to handle larger applications and validate server consolidation on the GSX Server platform, VMware had to increase the amount of memory that could be allocated to a single virtual machine. This memory allocation amount was increased to 3.6GB.

Added New Linux Kernel Support

As newer Linux kernels continue to get developed at a record pace, VMware must keep on track to remain up to date with the latest kernels. VMware has added support for the Linux 2.6 kernel in a Linux guest operating system.

Added New Support Scripts

To help troubleshoot and diagnose problems with GSX Server, a new set of support scripts were added to help collect the appropriate log files and system information needed by VMware technical support. To gather a large subset of data, a simple script can be run rather than manually accumulating all of the appropriate log files. This helps VMware's technical support group to get exactly the right data needed to help troubleshoot customer problems.

Remote Client CD/DVD-ROM Support

CD/DVD-ROM physical media can now be mounted on the client workstation's CD/DVD-ROM drive and accessed inside of the virtual machine rather than needing to mount the media on the host server itself. This is important for a number of reasons, including logistics and security when it comes to accessing a host server.

New LSI Logic SCSI Adapter for Virtual Machines

A new virtual SCSI adapter, the LSI Logic virtual SCSI adapter, was added as an alternative to the BusLogic SCSI adapter used in earlier versions. Newer operating systems such as Microsoft Windows Server 2003 and Red Hat Enterprise Linux 3.0 provide native support for this adapter. Other operating systems will need to download and install the driver in order to support the new adapter.

Virtual Machine Compatibility

Virtual machines created with GSX Server 3 are compatible with VMware Workstation 4 and ESX Server 2. This provides for easier virtual machine migration between the three platforms.

Planning the Upgrade

The following sections describe best practices and how to plan for the upgrade of a GSX Server environment. Before removing or upgrading the existing environment, there are a few steps that should be taken into account to ensure a successful upgrade experience.

How to Handle Virtual Machine Disk Modes

Before upgrading the current GSX Server installation, it is important to prepare the virtual machines for upgrade by using the current release that was used to create them. The most straightforward upgrade would probably be a virtual machine with a single virtual disk in persistent mode. Unfortunately, that isn't always the case. An existing virtual machine may have multiple virtual disks, or its virtual disk may be using undoable or nonpersistent disk mode. In fact, an existing virtual machine may have multiple virtual disks where each disk is using a different disk mode.

The simplest approach to upgrading is to convert all virtual disks to persistent mode. Before doing so, it is important to handle the virtual machine in its current disk mode. Resume or power on the virtual machine as configured in the current GSX Server installation. Next, shut down the guest operating system and power off the virtual machine. Once completed, either discard or commit the changes as appropriate for each virtual disk. While powered off, use the Configuration Editor to change all disk modes to persistent. After the platform is upgraded, the virtual machine can either use the Snapshot feature or one of the independent disk modes found within GSX Server 3.2.

Shut Down and Power off all Virtual Machines

Before upgrading GSX Server, it is important to verify that all virtual machines on the host server are powered off. If any virtual machine is suspended, use the current GSX Server installation to resume and power it back on, then shut down the guest operating system, and finally power off the virtual machine. It is important to perform this action while the current version is still installed. If the virtual machine is left in a suspended state and the host server is upgraded, the virtual machine can only be powered on by discarding or losing the saved state session or by resuming the virtual machine with the correct version of the GSX Server product.

Make a Backup of the Virtual Machine Disk Files

As a precaution, it is advised that a backup copy of all virtual machine files be made for any existing virtual machine being migrated to the new version of GSX Server. The backup should include the virtual disk files, the configuration file, and the nvram file. There are two basic reasons for this. The first reason, depending on the upgrade path, if a virtual machine has its hardware upgraded for full compatibility with the latest GSX Server version it can no longer be used in the previous version. This is important if there is a need to keep older template images, or if the environment is running in mixed mode, where some servers are going to remain using the older version for backward compatibility, testing, etc. If the virtual machine is not going to be upgraded, it can run in legacy mode; however, it runs without the new hardware or many of the new features provided by GSX Server 3.2. And second, Murphy's Law applies: Anything that can go wrong will go wrong. It is better to be safe than sorry, so any virtual machine that cannot be replaced should be backed up.

Make Note of Custom Network Settings on a Windows Host

If any network settings were customized or if a custom network was created, make note of these settings before the current version of GSX Server is uninstalled. Custom network settings can be any configuration changes made to DHCP, NAT, and bridged virtual devices, as well as any devices added besides the default VMnet0, VMnet1, and VMnet8. Unlike virtual machines and licensing, custom network settings cannot be preserved during a product upgrade and must again be configured once the new version is installed. Keep in mind, this only affects Windows hosts, therefore Linux hosts do not have this problem. To view and configure most custom network settings on Windows hosts, use the host virtual network settings editor. A standard text editor can be used to view the settings changes made to the NAT and DHCP configuration files.

Upgrading the Windows Host Server

Upgrading to a newer version of GSX Server for Windows is a relatively easy task. Whether upgrading from an older version, such as a 1.x or 2.x release, or simply upgrading from an earlier build of version 3, the steps are basically the same when it comes to the host server.

1. Before upgrading the host server, make sure the planning process has been performed (i.e., backups, disk mode changes, and all virtual machines should be powered off).

2. Uninstall the current installation. As explained in chapter 19, GSX Server will not install on a host server that already contains VMware components. This includes other versions of GSX Server, Workstation, VMware ACE, or the ESX Server remote console. Because GSX Server for Windows does not perform an upgrade over a previous installation, the previous install must first be removed. Depending on the version of GSX Server already installed, the uninstall methods may be slightly different. See Uninstalling GSX Server Version 1 or Uninstalling GSX Server Version 2 or 3 below for additional information.

3. The uninstaller may offer to remove VMware licenses from the registry, do not allow it. VMware recommends that licenses in the registry be maintained.

4. The uninstaller may offer to remove log-in information for the virtual machines, do not allow it. Removing the log-in information will change the virtual machine's configuration to run as the user that powers on the virtual machine rather than a specific user.

5. Once the current product has been removed, the host server should be rebooted to start clean.

6. Install the latest version of VMware GSX Server for Windows by following along with the proper steps in chapter 19.

7. After the installation has completed, the host server should be rebooted.

Uninstalling GSX Server Version 1

Prior to the upgrade, GSX Server 1.x should be safely removed from the system by following the instructions below. Uninstalling the server software and components does not affect the virtual machines.

1. To uninstall the server software, go to Start > Programs > VMware > VMware GSX Server Uninstallation and follow the onscreen instructions.

2. To remove the VMware Management Interface, use Add/Remove Programs in the Windows Control Panel, select VMware Management Interface, click Change/Remove, and follow the onscreen instructions to remove the application.

3. To remove the VMware Remote Console, use Add/Remove Programs in the Windows Control Panel, select VMware Remote Console, click Change/Remove, and follow the onscreen instructions to remove the application.

4. During the uninstallation of the product, the system may prompt to remove the VMware licenses from the registry. It is recommended to keep the licenses in the registry in case of the necessity of reinstallation, or in this case, an upgrade.

5. The host server should then be rebooted to complete the uninstallation process.

Uninstalling GSX Server Version 2 or 3

Prior to the upgrade, GSX Server 2.x or 3.x should be safely removed from the system by following the instructions below. The steps provided will remove all installed components from the host server, which may include the server software, the console, the management interface, and the scripting APIs. Uninstalling the server software and components does not delete the virtual machines.

1. To begin the uninstall process, choose Add/Remove Programs in the Windows Control Panel, select the VMware GSX Server Installer, and then click Change.
2. After the master installer launches, click Next.
3. Select Remove and then click Next.
4. To begin, click Remove.
5. During the uninstallation process, the system may prompt to remove the VMware licenses from the registry. It is recommended to keep the licenses in the registry in case of reinstallation of the product, or in this case, an upgrade.
6. The system may then prompt whether to keep any log-in information for the virtual machines configured to run as a specific user account. If this information is deleted, after the upgrade, the virtual machines will be configured to run as the user that powers on the virtual machine rather than a specific user.
7. To complete the uninstallation process, click Finish once all components are removed.
8. The host server should then be rebooted to complete the uninstallation process.

Upgrading the Linux Host Server

VMware GSX Server for Linux provides two installation packages, the tar installer and the RPM installer. Upgrading from either GSX Server 1.x or 2.x to version 3 requires the full version of VMware GSX Server 3 for Linux Systems. Depending on the installer package used to originally install the 1.x or 2.x version of the product on the host server, one of the following packages will be used to upgrade the existing host server. Each of the two packages provides a different upgrade path. These procedures can also be followed if upgrading to a newer version of the 3.x platform. Before upgrading GSX Server versions, make sure to follow all options in the planning stage and make sure that all virtual machines on the host server are powered off.

Upgrading from the tar Install

If the tar installer was originally used to install the current version of the product, and the tar installer will be used to install the new version, the only extra step needed is to make sure the directory where the new tar package will be extracted does not already contain files from the previous GSX Server build. The old version of the product does not need to be uninstalled. Instead, simply follow the installation steps for a new install on a Linux host server in chapter 19.

 The installation steps found in chapter 19 may show different options from those displayed during an upgrade from a previous version. During an upgrade, the selections made in the previous installation become the defaults in the upgrade process.

Upgrading from the RPM Install

Unlike the tar installer, if the current GSX Server installation was installed using the RPM installer then the current product needs to be uninstalled before upgrading to the new version.

Uninstall the RPM Package

To uninstall the current GSX Server installation created with the RPM package, open a terminal and log in as root. Remove the software by running the following command (used to uninstall both the server software and the VmPerl API if installed):

```
rpm -e VMware-gsx
```

To uninstall the Linux console that was installed with the RPM package, enter the following:

```
rpm -e VMware-console
```

To uninstall the VMware Management Interface, run one of the following:

       `/usr/bin/vmware-uninstall-mui.pl` (GSX Server 2.x or 3.x)

Or

       `/home/vmware/mui/bin/vmware-uninstall-mui.pl` (GSX Server 1.x)

Once the current GSX Server product and its components have been removed, the upgrade to the new version can continue. The installation steps for GSX Server for Linux in chapter 19 should be followed.

Unlike GSX Server for Windows, the Linux version does require any special action on the user's part in response to whether or not you want to keep the old license. When upgrading the Linux version, the license remains in place.

Upgrading the Guest Operating System

The following sections describe how to use older virtual machines created in GSX Server 1, 2, or even earlier versions of 3 within a newer version of VMware GSX Server 3. There are a few changes that need to be made to the virtual machine; specifically, upgrading its virtual hardware and its VMware Tools. Older virtual machines do not need to have their virtual hardware upgraded in order to be used in the newer environment, but failing to upgrade its virtual hardware will identify it as a legacy virtual machine. This statement is generally true; however, it is not without caveats. A virtual machine created in GSX Server 1 must have its virtual hardware upgraded before it can be used in a GSX Server 3 environment. When a virtual machine of this type is powered on, it is presented with two options: upgrade the virtual hardware or shut down. Powering on the virtual machine without upgrading its virtual hardware is not an option. On the other hand, a virtual machine created in an earlier GSX Server 3 release does not need its virtual hardware upgraded—it is already at the latest version. To upgrade one of these virtual machines, the latest VMware Tools needs only to be installed.

Using an Older Virtual Machine Without Upgrading Its Virtual Hardware

A virtual machine created with GSX Server 2 and then used in an upgraded GSX Server 3 environment should function properly without upgrading its virtual hardware. However, it will not have the benefits of certain new features, such as better performance, improved networking, improved virtual disk formats, and the ability to take live snapshots while the virtual machine is powered on. Additionally, the management interface and the console will identify it as a legacy virtual machine and disable many of the features available to a new or upgraded virtual machine. The console will also warn that the virtual machine's VMware Tools is out of date. Without upgrading the virtual machine hardware, the latest VMware Tools can still be installed in the guest operating system. The old tools should not be removed before installing the new version.

While this certainly is not the optimal solution, it does have one benefit. By not upgrading the virtual machine's virtual hardware, the virtual machine can be started in both, the original GSX Server 2 environment as well as the GSX Server 3 environment. However, each time the virtual machine is moved from one environment to the other, GSX Server will update the CMOS resulting in the guest operating system detecting hardware changes even without upgrading virtual hardware. If the guest operating system is one that requires activation, such as Windows XP Professional or Windows Server 2003, this may cause a problem. The benefit of being able to move the virtual machine from one environment to another does not outweigh the negatives. If there is a need to use this image in both environments, a backup copy should be made leaving the original setup for a GSX Server 2 environment and its copy upgraded to make full use of GSX Server 3 and the features that it has to offer.

Using an Older Virtual Machine and Upgrading Its Virtual Hardware

Upgrading an older virtual machine that is migrated from either GSX Server 1 or 2 allows the upgraded virtual machine to have access to a whole list of new features. Upgrading the virtual hardware allows for better overall performance of the virtual machine, improved networking, improved virtual disk support, and the ability to take live snapshots while the virtual machine is powered on. The downside to upgrading is that it is a one-way process. The actual upgrade is irreversible and makes the disks attached to the virtual machine incompatible with the earlier platforms.

The upgrade process can be somewhat lengthy and confusing, but it is important to consider each step along the way to understand the details of what is happening behind the scenes in order to ensure a successful upgrade.

Upgrading a Windows Guest Operating System

In keeping with the examples throughout the book, a Microsoft Windows Server 2003 guest operating system will be described as it undergoes an upgrade of its virtual hardware. The following steps provide an example of a virtual hardware upgrade; however specific steps may vary based on configuration of the virtual machine.

1. Before beginning the upgrade process, make sure to create a backup copy of the virtual hard disk file.
2. Power on the virtual machine and allow GSX Server to update the CMOS. As a result, the guest operating system should detect new hardware and automatically install drivers for any new devices it detects.
3. Once the virtual machine settles, the console should identify the virtual machine as legacy. Do not upgrade virtual hardware at this time.
4. The Status Bar should have identified that VMware Tools is out of date. Select VM > Install VMware Tools to begin the VMware Tools installation process. Do not remove the old version of VMware Tools before the new version is installed. The new version of the tools provides drivers that will be needed when the virtual hardware is upgraded.

5. Shut down the guest operating system and power off the virtual machine.
6. Select VM > Upgrade Virtual Hardware. This should only be performed after VMware Tools is installed.
7. A message warns that the operation is irreversible and recommends that the virtual disks be backed up before proceeding. Since the files were backed up in Step 1, click Yes to continue.
8. A second message describes what is about to happen. Click OK to continue.
9. A progress bar displays the upgrade progress and relays how much longer until completion.
10. Once the process has ended, the virtual machine should be powered back on.
11. If Windows identifies any new hardware, click Yes to install it and navigate to `c:\Program Files\VMware\drivers` to install the drivers.
12. Restart the virtual machine.
13. Check Device Manager to make sure there are no missing drivers and to make sure that all hardware is correctly installed.

Even after a successful upgrade, there is still a potential for problems.

- Wrong video drivers—Sometimes when upgrading, the video drivers do not get upgraded from the Standard SVGA to VMware SVGA II. When this happens, mouse control becomes somewhat flakey. Check the VMware Tools installation, and try to reinstall the video adapter.
- Mouse problems—The mouse may not be responsive after the upgrade. Check Device Manager to make sure the mouse driver was updated. If there is a problem, the mouse may be showing up as PS/2 rather than VMware Pointing Device.
- Wrong SCSI adapter type—GSX Server 3 introduces the LSI Logic SCSI adapter. If the old virtual machine was originally built with a BusLogic SCSI adapter, changing the configuration settings to point to the wrong adapter will blue screen the virtual machine.
- TCP/IP problems—This can happen if during the upgrade process the virtual network adapter is upgraded. This can cause a ghost NIC problem, where the original TCP/IP settings are still in the registry for the original network adapter and now the new network adapter is trying to use the same IP address. To remove a ghost NIC from the registry, follow these steps:
  1. Select Start > Run
  2. Enter cmd.exe and press <ENTER>
  3. At the command prompt, enter set devmgr show nonpersistent devices=1

4. Enter Start DEVMGMT.MSC and press <ENTER>
5. Select View > Show Hidden Devices
6. Expand the Network Adapters tree. Right click the dimmed network adapter and select Uninstall
7. Close Device Manager

Upgrading a Linux Guest Operating System

In keeping with the examples throughout the book, a Red Hat Linux 9.0 guest operating system will be described as it undergoes an upgrade of its virtual hardware. The following steps provide an example of a virtual hardware upgrade; however specific steps may vary based on configuration of the virtual machine.

1. Before beginning the upgrade process, make sure to create a backup copy of the virtual machine's files.
2. Power on the virtual machine and allow GSX Server to update the CMOS.
3. When Kudzu appears, follow the instructions to detect any new hardware and install the proper drivers.
4. Once the virtual machine settles, the console should identify the virtual machine as legacy. Do not upgrade virtual hardware at this time.
5. The Status Bar should have identified that VMware Tools is out of date. Select VM > Install VMware Tools to begin the VMware Tools installation process. Mount the tools and follow the normal installation method. The new version of the tools provides drivers that will be needed when the virtual hardware is upgraded.
6. Shut down the guest operating system and power off the virtual machine.
7. Select VM > Upgrade Virtual Hardware. This should only be performed after VMware Tools is installed.
8. A message warns that the operation is irreversible and recommends the virtual disks be backed up before proceeding. Since the files were backed up in Step 1, click Yes to continue.
9. A second message describes what is about to happen. Click OK to continue.
10. A progress bar displays the upgrade progress and relays how much longer until completion.
11. Once the upgrade is complete, power on the virtual machine.
12. When Kudzu runs, it may detect an Ensoniq:ES1371 [AudioPCI-97] sound device.
13. Click Configure.
14. When finished, reboot the virtual machine.

VMware ESX Server 2.5

The following sections describe the benefits, planning considerations, and upgrade steps for VMware ESX Server 2.5.

Benefits of Upgrading

VMware continuously strives to keep ESX Server in the forefront of the virtualization platform race. With each release, VMware continues to not only resolve issues and create bug fixes, it also increases platform support for new guest operating systems, applications, and hardware devices. The benefit of upgrading from an ESX Server 1.x platform to an ESX Server 2.x platform is like night and day. With each major and minor dot revision of the ESX Server 2.x platform, VMware has improved the security, stability, and performance of the product. But it is the continually growing added feature list that makes upgrading to the latest release of ESX Server worth the minimal amount of upgrade effort. A list of some of the more important new features added with the release of ESX Server 2.5 is detailed below.

New Guest Operating System Support

Adding to its already impressive listing of supported guest operating systems, ESX Server 2.5.x adds support for these operating systems in virtual machines:

- FreeBSD 4.10
- Microsoft Windows Server 2003 Service Pack 1
- Novell NetWare 5.1 Service Pack 7
- Novell NetWare 6.0 Service Pack 5
- Novell NetWare 6.5 Service Pack 2
- Novell OES Service Pack 1
- Red Hat Enterprise Linux 2.1 Update 6, Update 7
- Red Hat Enterprise Linux 3.0 Update 4, Update 5
- SUSE LINUX Enterprise Server 9 Service Pack 1, Service Pack 2
- SUSE LINUX Professional 9.1, 9.2, 9.3

The VMware Systems Compatibility Guide for ESX Server 2.x contains the complete list of fully qualified and supported guest operating systems. It is available on the Web at http://www.vmware.com/pdf/esx_systems_guide.pdf (an Adobe Acrobat document).

Boot from SAN

ESX Server version 2.5 allows the installation of ESX Server in a diskless operation mode where the ESX Server boot partition is hosted on a SAN. Adding this feature greatly enhances support for common blade and rack mount configurations.

Improved Raw SCSI Disk Access

ESX Server 2.5 includes support for raw LUNs as virtual disks using Raw Disk Mappings (RDMs) and pass-through RDMs. Raw Disk Mappings are special files on VFMS-2 volumes that allow access and management of raw SCSI disks or LUNs as VMFS files. New features for using RDMs include:

- REDO logs are now allowed to be added to raw disks.
- Raw disks can now be managed as easily as virtual disk files.
- Virtual compatibility RDMs enable backup offloading solutions to allow ESX Servers to be backed up faster without any load being placed on the virtual machines or the Service Console.
- Physical compatibility RDMs enable SAN replication software to run inside the virtual machines.
- VirtualCenter support for clustered virtual machines is improved.
- VMotion can be used to migrate virtual machines using raw LUNs.

Improved SSH Security

ESX Server version 2.5 now uses SSH Protocol Version 2 as the default secure log-in client. The newer protocol offers both security and feature improvements over its predecessor. With an increase in tools used to conduct person-in-the-middle attacks against SSH-1, it is wise to move to the more secure protocol version.

Improved Support for Clustered Virtual Machines

Microsoft Cluster Server (MSCS) clustering of virtual machines that use shared disk access is now more reliable. To learn more about clustering, see chapter 26.

Added Support for Scripted ESX Server Installations

The previous ESX Server installer required user interaction to make choices while being prompted during the installation process for each server. The installation procedure has been greatly improved with the 2.5 release by allowing unattended installations of ESX Server on physical hosts by pointing the installer to the installation CD or to a network share hosting the installation files, and to a script that contains the configuration choices to be made during the installation. This process greatly reduces the time required for multi-server installations common to blade servers.

Additional Support for Disaster-Recovery Backups of Virtual Machines

Virtual disk snapshot scripts have been added to the ESX Server 2.5 Service Console to allow administrators and management routines to create crash consistent backups of entire virtual machines.

Expanded Server Hardware Support

ESX Server 2.5.x expands its list of fully supported industry leading rack and blade servers from companies such as Dell, HP, and IBM. Some of the new supported server hardware include: Dell PowerEdge 1855 MC Blade Server, HP BL20p G3 and BL25p Blade Servers, HP ProLiant DL380 G4, IBM eServer BladeCenter HS20-8832 and 8843, IBM eServer xSeries 346, and IBM eServer 326 with AMD Opteron processors.

More importantly, VMware ESX Server 2.5.2 also adds support for dual-core processors from AMD and Intel. A complete list of supported hardware is available at http://www.vmware.com/pdf/esx_systems_guide.pdf (an Adobe Acrobat document).

Planning the Upgrade

The following sections describe best practices and how to plan for the upgrade of an ESX Server 2.5 environment. Before upgrading the existing environment, there are a few simple steps that should be taken to ensure a successful upgrade experience.

Commit or Discard Changes to Disks Prior to Upgrade

Before upgrading the current ESX Server installation, it is important to prepare any existing virtual machine that will be used in the new environment by first modifying it in the current version. While the most straightforward virtual machine upgrade would be a virtual machine with a single virtual hard disk in persistent mode, this is not always going to be the case. An existing virtual machine may contain a virtual hard disk that is configured in a different mode such as undoable or append mode. It is also quite possible to have a virtual machine configured with multiple virtual hard disks where each disk is configured to use a different disk mode.

Resume or power on the virtual machine as configured in the current ESX Server installation. Next, shut down the guest operating system and power off the virtual machine. Once completed, either discard or commit the changes to the disk when prompted for each virtual disk.

Shut down and Power off Virtual Machines

Before upgrading ESX Server, it is important to verify that all virtual machines on the host server are powered off. If any virtual machine is suspended, use the current ESX Server installation to resume it, shut down the guest operating system, and finally power off the virtual machine. It is important to perform this action while the current version is still installed. If the virtual machine is left in a suspended state, it can only be resumed by the original version of ESX Server. If the host server is upgraded, the virtual machine can only be powered on by discarding the saved state session and the suspended state is lost.

Backup Virtual Machine Disk Files

As a precaution, it is advised that a backup copy of all virtual machine files is made for any existing virtual machine being migrated to the new version of ESX Server. The backup should include the virtual disk files (.vmdk), the configuration file (.vmx), and the nvram file. There are two basic reasons for this. First, depending on the upgrade path, if a virtual machine has its hardware upgraded for full compatibility with the latest ESX Server version it can no longer be used in the previous version. This is important if there is a need to keep older template images, or if the environment is running in mixed mode, where some servers are going to remain using the older version for backward compatibility, testing, etc. If the virtual machine is not going to be upgraded, it can run in legacy mode; however, it runs without the new hardware or many of the new features provided by ESX Server 2.5. And second, why take a chance of losing the virtual machine? It is better to be safe than sorry, so any virtual machine that cannot be replaced should be backed up.

 While backing up files, it is probably a safe bet to backup the vm-list file. It resides as /etc/vmware/vm-list. Once the upgrade is complete, restore or copy the file back to its original location in /etc/vmware. Backing up the file can keep you from potentially having to register each virtual machine again.

Upgrading a Previous ESX Server Release to ESX Server 2.5

Upgrading to the latest version of ESX Server is a relatively simple task. However, support for directly upgrading from a previous version will vary depending on the upgrade version selected. The latest release, ESX Server 2.5.2, supports direct upgrades from the following releases:

- ESX Server 2.5.0 (with or without patches)
- ESX Server 2.5.1 (with or without patches)

- ESX Server 2.1.2 (with or without patches)
- ESX Server 2.1.1
- ESX Server 2.1.0
- ESX Server 2.0.1 (with or without patches)
- ESX Server 2.0.1 Security Update
- ESX Server 2.0.0 Security Update

Although upgrading from ESX Server 1.5.x to ESX Server 2.5 is not supported, ESX Server 1.5.2 Patch 5 (with or without the Security Update) can be upgraded to ESX Server 2.1.2, which can then be upgraded to an ESX 2.5.2 system.

Upgrading with a CD-ROM

To perform an upgrade from one of the supported ESX Server versions listed above to ESX Server 2.5.x (2.5.2 recommended), the steps are basically the same. The installation CD-ROM (either the media received from VMware or the ISO file downloaded from the VMware Web site) can be used to upgrade the previous release by following these steps:

1. Before upgrading the host server, make sure the planning process has been performed (i.e., backups, disk mode changes, and all virtual machines should be powered off).
2. When using the ISO image to create physical CD ROM media, make sure to MD5SUM the image to ensure a noncorrupt package.
3. Insert the installation media into the host server's CD-ROM drive.
4. Boot the server from the CD-ROM. If the server does not boot from the CD-ROM, ensure that the BIOS is set to allow the server to boot from CD-ROM. If the BIOS change was necessary, reboot the server with the CD-ROM still inserted.
5. At the first installer screen, select Upgrade Existing System.
6. An End User License Agreement (EULA) screen is displayed. In order to continue with the upgrade, the terms of the license agreement must be accepted.
7. The installer then verifies if enough swap space exists for the new service console. If the swap space is found insufficient, the installer prompts for the location to place a new swap file. The default location should be adequate.
8. The installer begins the upgrade process of the ESX Server.
9. Once the final screen is displayed signaling the completion of the upgrade process, the ESX Server should be rebooted.
10. When upgrading from an ESX Server 1.5.2 installation, ESX Server 2.x licenses will need to be entered, along with a VMware Virtual SMP for ESX Server license if one exists.

11. With the increased focus on security, the upgraded ESX Server will disable the FTP and Telnet services on the host server even if these options were allowed in the previous configuration.

12. Once the ESX Server is rebooted, a final upgrade of the VMFS volume can take place. If deemed appropriate, the VMFS volume can be upgraded from VFMS-1 to VMFS-2 to gain improvements in the performance of the virtual machines located on the volume.

 During the upgrade process, the ESX Server installer renames the `/etc/vmware/vmware-device.map.local` file to `/etc/vmware/vmware-device.map.local.orig`. Once the upgrade is complete, it is important to compare the original file against the newly created `vmware-device.map.local` file. Because some driver locations may have changed, it may be necessary to make changes and customizations to the file.

Upgrading with a Tar Archive

If physical access to the host server is unavailable (and therefore the host server's CD-ROM drive), an alternative upgrade method is to use a downloaded tar archive file. However, when using the tar archive file method, upgrading directly from releases prior to ESX 2.0 is not supported. The following steps should be performed.

1. Before upgrading the host server, make sure the planning process has been performed (i.e., backups, disk mode changes, and all virtual machines should be powered off).

2. Reboot into Linux using `/sbin/lilo -R linux` and `/sbin/reboot` (check the /etc/lilo.conf file for different entries).

3. Log in with the root account or log in with another account and change to superuser.

4. Verify enough free disk space exists on the server before performing the upgrade.

5. Create a directory (mkdir) named `upgrade` or some other descriptive name. The directory must be accessible to the service console on the server being upgraded.

6. Copy the tar archive file to this directory. The file name should be similar to `esx-version-build-upgrade.tar.gz`. As an example, `esx-2.5.2-16390-upgrade.tar.gz`.

7. Change (cd) to the directory above, in this example, `upgrade`.

8. Make sure to MD5SUM the tar file to make sure the package is not corrupt.

9. Extract the contents of the tar file by entering the following command: `tar zxf esx-2.5.2-16390-upgrade.`

10. A new directory is created. Change to the directory, in this example, `esx-2.5.2-16390-upgrade`.
11. Execute the following script: `./upgrade.pl`
12. Follow along with the upgrade process.
13. When prompted, reboot the server to complete the upgrade process.
14. With the increased focus on security, the upgraded ESX Server will disable the FTP and Telnet services on the host server even if these options were allowed in the previous configuration.
15. Once the ESX Server is rebooted, a final upgrade of the VMFS volume can take place. If deemed appropriate, the VMFS volume can be upgraded from VFMS-1 to VMFS-2 to gain improvements in the performance of the virtual machines located on the volume.

During the upgrade process, the ESX Server installer renames the `/etc/vmware/vmware-device.map.local` file to `/etc/vmware/vmware-device.map.local.orig`. Once the upgrade is complete, it is important to compare the original file against the newly created `vmware-device.map.local` file. Because some driver locations may have changed, it may be necessary to make changes and customizations to the file.

Migrating Older ESX Server Virtual Machines

The following section describes how to use older virtual machines created with previous versions of ESX Server prior to the ESX Server 2.5 release. Older virtual machines created with ESX Server 1.5 can work as is; however, to take advantage of the newer features offered in the current release, there are steps that should be taken to upgrade the virtual machine. Specifically, these steps include upgrading the virtual machine's virtual hardware and its VMware Tools. While older virtual machines do not necessarily need to have their virtual hardware upgraded in order to function properly, failing to do so will identify it as a legacy virtual machine. While virtual hardware and newer VMware Tools can be added to a legacy virtual machine, multiprocessor support cannot. To achieve virtual SMP support, a virtual machine must be created under ESX Server 2.x and the platform must have a VMware Virtual SMP license installed.

 Virtual machines created with ESX Server 1.0 or 1.1 can be migrated to ESX Server 2.5.2, but they must undergo a multiple stage upgrade path. These virtual machines must first be upgraded from ESX Server 1.0 or 1.1 to ESX Server 1.5. Once the virtual machine is upgraded and running under ESX Server 1.5, it can then be upgraded to work with ESX Server 2.5.2.

If the guest operating system on the virtual machine is one that requires activation such as Microsoft Windows XP Professional or Microsoft Windows Server 2003, upgrading the virtual hardware and VMware Tools will likely require the virtual machine to go through the activation process again due to significant changes to the hardware.

Upgrading a Virtual Machine

Upgrading an older virtual machine that was created under ESX Server 1.0, 1.1, or 1.5 allows the upgraded virtual machine to have access to a whole list of new features. Upgrading the virtual hardware also allows for better overall performance of the virtual machine. The downside to upgrading the virtual hardware is that the upgrade is a one-way process. The actual upgrade is irreversible and makes the disks attached to the virtual machine incompatible with the earlier platforms.

The upgrade process can be somewhat lengthy and confusing, but it is important to consider each step along the way to understand the details of what is happening behind the scenes in order to ensure a successful upgrade. The following steps provide an example of a virtual hardware upgrade; however, specific steps may vary based on virtual machine configuration.

1. Before beginning the upgrade process, make sure to create a backup copy of the virtual hard disk file.
2. Verify the value of the guestOS parameter in the virtual machine's configuration file. Because these values have changed between releases of ESX Server 1.x and 2.x, this value may likely need to be modified and updated.
3. Power on the virtual machine under the new platform and allow ESX Server to update the CMOS.
4. Once the virtual machine settles, the console should identify the virtual machine as legacy. Do *not* upgrade virtual hardware at this time.
5. The Status Bar should have identified that VMware Tools is out of date. Update VMware Tools in the virtual machine by removing the old tools and then installing the latest tools. The new version of the tools provides drivers that will be needed when the virtual hardware is upgraded.
6. Shut down the guest operating system and power off the virtual machine.
7. On the Status Monitor page in the Management Interface, click the arrow to the right of the terminal icon and select Configure Hardware. On the Hardware tab, click Upgrade Virtual Hardware. This should only be performed after VMware Tools is installed.

8. Since the files were backed up in Step 1, it is safe to click OK to upgrade the hardware.
9. Once the upgrade process has completed, the virtual machine can be powered on.
10. If any new hardware is identified and installed, the virtual machine should be rebooted and then properly configured.

Summary

VMware GSX Server and ESX Server have been widely distributed and deployed over the past few years. To keep current customer satisfaction high and to enter new markets, VMware has continuously updated and released new platform versions to offer a more robust, secure, and feature rich product. To keep up with the growing demand of a constantly changing IT market, both products have had their capabilities extended in order to meet these challenging requests. In order to properly upgrade the platform from one version to another, it is important to create and follow an upgrade strategy that takes into account both the physical host server and the virtual machines as well. There are numerous upgrade options available to accomplish the same end result, but no matter which upgrade method is chosen, it is safe to say that upgrading the VMware GSX Server or ESX Server platform is a wise decision.

Chapter 24

Guest Operating System Techniques

When planning, implementing, and administering virtualized systems, much of the focus is placed upon the optimization of the host server, the host server's operating system, and the virtualization platform. It is often easy to overlook the importance of having a thorough guest operating system and disk image management strategy.

Based upon many years of practical image building, this chapter goes beyond the basics of installing a guest operating system into virtual machines, focusing on creating robust, clean, and clonable guest operating system images. It discusses the challenges of cloning images and provides valuable information on post-cloning steps. Building and managing an effective image library is also presented along with the challenges of patch management and image sizing. A discussion of alternate guest operating systems concludes this chapter. The best practices and techniques presented here will lead to high quality virtualized systems.

Images

Within the context of server virtualization, the term image is defined as a file containing the representation and data of a virtual hard disk drive that resides on a virtualization host server. Images can be empty, unformatted, without partitions, just as a real hard disk drive may be blank. Images can have one or more partitions and file systems just like a physical hard disk drive. Images usually contain the guest operating system of a virtual machine as well as other applications and data. Images do not necessarily have to contain a guest operating system and may contain application files or just data. A virtual machine will commonly have just one virtual hard disk drive attached that will point to an image on the host server. Just like a physical hard disk drive, the virtual hard disk drive may have more than one partition, each of which may be mounted to the virtual machine's guest operating system and may be displayed as more than one hard disk drive, such as the C: and D: drives in Windows or more than one mount point in Linux, such as / and /boot (root and boot). Virtual machines can have more than one virtual hard disk drive attached. Each virtual hard disk drive is represented by an image residing on the host server. Virtual hard disk drive images that contain an installed guest operating system may also be referred to as a guest operating system image. Virtual hard disk drive images created by a particular virtualization platform may differ greatly in format from those of other virtualization platforms and they will generally not be directly compatible. Virtual hard disk drive images are very different from images used to create virtual floppy disk drives and virtual CD/DVD-ROM drives. Throughout this chapter, the unqualified term, image, refers to a single virtual hard disk drive file. ISO images used as virtual CD/DVD-ROM drives will be referred to as CD/DVD images and images of floppy diskettes used as virtual floppy disk drives will be referred to as floppy images.

Template Guest Operating System Image Concepts

Effective deployment of virtual machines is one of the keys to success for implementing and managing a scalable virtualized system. Template guest operating system images, referred to as templates, allow easier deployment of virtual machines. There are many other phrases used throughout the industry to refer to templates including base images, gold images, golden masters, master images, and reference images. A template is a reference set of one or more virtual hard disk drive files (also called images) that represent a single virtual machine and its guest operating system used to deploy new instances of the virtual machine through a process called cloning. Additionally, a template may or may not also include a copy of the virtual machine's configuration file. If a template includes a copy of the virtual machine's configuration file, it is called a configured template. If the template does not include a configuration file, it is called an unconfigured template. The basic term, template, may refer to either a configured or an unconfigured template. All templates must include one or more image files.

A fundamental set of templates includes one template for each operating system used within an organization. Typically, a set of templates may include more than one template using the same version of an operating system configured differently, such as having different virtual disk sizes and partition layouts or having a different set of base operating system services in each template to support different use cases. The guest operating systems within templates often contain the most recent revisions of system files, patches, virus definitions, and other updates and are usually clean, not having entries in system logs, histories, most

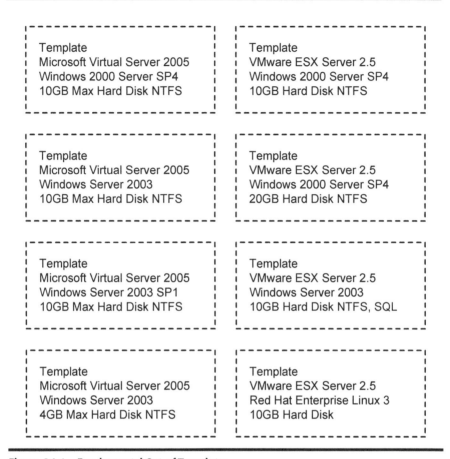

Figure 24.1 **Fundamental Set of Templates.**

recently used lists, and the like. Figure 24.1 displays a logical view of an example set of templates for an organization using Microsoft Virtual Server and VMware ESX Server virtualization platforms.

The Figure 24.2 and Figure 24.3 show an examples of what the template files may look like based on the templates described in Figure 24.1.

Figure 24.2 **Example Template Files for VMware ESX Server.**

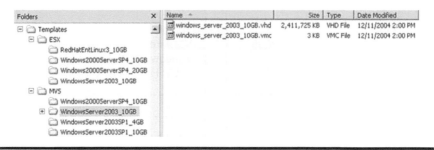

Figure 24.3   Example Template Files for Microsoft Virtual Server.

What makes templates so powerful is that they simplify the deployment of new virtual machines by reducing most of the work of image creation to a simple file copy operation. The idea is to make a copy of an existing template, either manually or by an automated process, which provides a bootable, usable virtual machine that only needs minimal configuration changes and possibly have specialized applications installed.

A traditional physical server deployment may take an average of four work-hours to provision, including time to unpack, assemble, rack, cable, and install a base, unconfigured operating system that does not have any applications or any recent updates installed. If another four hours is factored in to include the installation of applications, patches, and other updates, the total provisioning time easily reaches eight hours. Compare this to a typical virtual machine deployment using a planned template-based process. The copy process may take thirty minutes and manually creating the virtual machine may take another five minutes. At this point, the virtual machine is bootable, has some or all of the necessary applications installed, and has recent patches and updates applied. Another ten minutes may be spent on post-deployment configuration tasks. The traditional physical server deployment may take eight hours, but the virtual machine deployment leveraging templates takes only a fraction of that time, forty-five minutes. That's more than a 1000 percent reduction in deployment time! It is a valid argument that a traditional deployment may take less than eight hours, possibly as little as three hours. It is also possible to enhance the provisioning of virtual machines using templates and automated processes, reducing the deployment time even further.

It is common for virtual machines deployed using templates to require a minimal amount of post-deployment configuration tasks. These tasks vary depending on the operating system used and how the virtual machine is intended to be used. The most common post-deployment configuration tasks are machine identity-based, including assigning a unique hostname and network address (if the virtual machine has virtual network devices installed as most do). If the virtual machine has a Microsoft Windows NT-based operating system installed (Windows NT, Windows 2000, Windows XP, Windows Server 2003, or Windows Vista), these tasks include assigning the machine a new SID, a special Windows-specific security identifier. Other post-deployment tasks include joining the machine to a domain and installing application software.

There are tools that assist in the provisioning of new computers that can help with the post-deployment configuration tasks, especially concerning the SID in Windows operating systems. Microsoft offers Sysprep, a utility originally created for OEM computer manufacturers that ship preinstalled Microsoft Windows operating systems with their computers. Sysprep cleans the operating system's histories and logs and prepares the system as if it were a freshly installed copy of Windows not yet configured. Sysprep is typically run as the last configuration step, just before the completion of the creation of the template image. When a virtual machine that was created from a template containing a prepared Windows operating system is first booted, the user is prompted for the Administrator password, hostname, regional settings, TCP/IP configuration and the machine then has a new SID assigned. The Sysprep process can also be fully automated, although some mechanism must be used to gather the new hostname and IP address from an external source (such as DHCP for IP addresses).

Sysiternals offers a free tool named NewSID, written by Mark Russinovich and Bryce Cogswell, which can also generate and set a new random SID value, set the system's SID to a known SID value, and change the hostname. This tool has a Windows Wizard-style GUI interface or can be used from command-line, which makes it automation-friendly. The source code is also provided freely for download.

Some virtualization use cases, such as on-demand or utility computing, often require isolated environments that are short-lived. These isolated environments, consisting of one or more virtual machines, can be deployed in such a manner that does not require the traditional post-deployment configuration tasks. Duplicate hostnames, IP addresses, and SIDs are only issues that plague traditional networked systems. Through the use of network isolation, such as private VLANs or Layer-3 routing techniques, it is possible to create perfectly clonable templates that require zero post-deployment configuration tasks, further reducing deployment times.

Another important aspect that must be considered when creating a new template is if the design will leverage differencing disk technology. At the current time, Microsoft Virtual Server is the only server virtualization product that fully supports this feature. When using differencing disks, the new template is either a base disk image to which differencing disks will be attached or it will be a differencing disk attached to an existing base disk image (another template). Differencing disks (diff disks) are virtual disk images used to modify an exiting base disk image, its parent disk. They contain only the changes and additions to the parent disk. The usefulness of diff disks is apparent when a set of images have the exact same foundation, mainly consisting of the operating system, configuration, and other common software and the deltas between the different images is relatively small.

Consider this example where it is required that there are three virtual servers: a Web server, a small database server, and a proxy server. Each of these servers will use Microsoft Windows Server 2003 Standard Edition as their operating system. First, a base image template is created by installing the operating system, all patches and security updates, virus protection software, and some software agents for the corporate management and monitoring servers. Next, three diff disks are created, each attached to the base image template. The combination of each diff disk along with its parent disk creates a unique virtual disk image (or template). The first diff disk is then booted and has Microsoft IIS World Wide Web services installed and configured. The second diff disk has Microsoft SQL Server Standard Edition installed and configured. The third diff disk has Microsoft Internet Security and Acceleration (ISA) Server installed and configured. Each diff disk is also prepared by Sysprep so that upon deployment it will receive a unique Administrator password, hostname, IP address, and regional settings. At this point, four templates have been created. The base disk image is a template by itself. The base disk image plus the first diff disk together create the second template. The base disk image plus the second diff disk together create the third template and the base disk image plus the third diff disk together create the fourth template. Using diff disks, four templates were created without the need to recreate or copy the base disk image, saving time. Additionally, the base disk image or any of the diff disk themselves can further be extended by attaching a new diff disk.

Differencing disk technology as implemented in Microsoft Virtual Server allows diff disks to be attached to another Microsoft Virtual Server virtual disk file. That virtual disk file can be a standalone, base image or another diff disk. When a diff disk is attached to another diff disk, this is called diff disk chaining. At this time, Microsoft Virtual Server allows up to sixteen disks to exist in a diff disk chain. Although diff disks can be used to effectively save time, there is a penalty to using them. Using diff disks has a small impact on I/O performance, which grows with each diff disk that is added to the diff disk chain. Using one or two diff disks in a diff disk chain has a minimal, mostly unnoticeable impact on server I/O performance, but as this chain grows, the performance impact is more prevalent.

Another benefit of using diff disks can be leveraged by on-demand or utility computing systems. If a system has many virtual machines using diff disks in which all share a common base disk image, the images used by any of the virtual machines can be easily and quickly changed to another image by simply changing out the diff disk image. Diff disk images are typically smaller than their parent disks because they only contain the differences, not the complete system installation. Therefore a typical dynamically expanding parent disk may have a maximum size of 20GB and an actual size of 2.5GB, but diff disks based on this disk may be between 300MB and 600MB each. Of course, it is possible for diff disks to grow larger than their parent disk.

Differencing disks do have a drawback when used with traditional, non-transient virtual machines. Updates to the base disk image cannot be applied to the base disk image without breaking the diff disk chains bound to the disk. Updates must be duplicated, both in terms of effort and storage across all leaf-node diff disks.

When creating template images, the size of the disk files can cause problems. Generally, the template disk files should be sized using an average disk size commonly used in an organization. This may be 4GB, 8GB, 10GB, 20GB, or more. When using templates having dynamic disks, there is less of an issue since the disks only consume the amount of storage required by the data stored within the disk. When working with fixed disks, the template disk image size is much more of a concern because storage is usually limited for most organizations. One method used to save massive amounts of storage space when working with fixed disks is to create the template disks at the bare minimum size required to install the components which will be cloned, such as 3GB or 4GB. The disadvantage of this method is that the disks must undergo an expansion process after cloning in order to bring them up to their proper production size, such as 10GB or 20GB. When expanding a disk, not only must the virtual disk have its size extended, but one or more partitions residing within the virtual disk may also have to be resized using specialized partition tools so that data corruption or loss does not occur.

Effectively Creating and Optimizing Template Guest OS Images

A major component of virtualized computing systems is template image management. It is important to have a well-defined methodology which documents how templates are created, managed, and deployed. This methodology should be a living document that is updated anytime a new lesson is learned during the template creation process, due to new technologies, overlooked features, features that have never been used before, or new applications. The following steps provide a good start on that methodology by providing the specific steps and considerations learned through years of image creation experience.

The most important step in effective template image creation is creating a solid plan. The plan is different from the methodology in that the methodology defines the overall process that governs template image creation, management, and deployment, whereas the plan governs the creation of a single template image. Before beginning to install operating systems and software applications, you must have a plan in place to define all of the attributes that make up the template image. This includes specifying the operating system and the software to be installed, the virtualization platform the template is compatible with, required resources (CPU, memory, disk storage, networking, etc.), and how the template image is expected to be used.

During the planning stage, define or obtain the following information:

- Determine if the template will be created from scratch or from an existing template.
- Determine if the template will consist of one or multiple virtual machines.
- The virtualization platform and version that will host the template.
- The operating system and version to be installed.
- The licenses for the operating system and all software applications.
- The initial Administrator or root password of the operating system.
- The initial hostname of the operating system.
- The amount of memory or minimum memory required by the template.
- The number of virtual disks of which the template will consist.
- The size or maximum size of each virtual disk.
- The partition layout of each disk including volume names and mount points.
- The file system to be installed on each partition.
- Determine if each disk will be fixed or dynamically expanding.
- Determine if the template is a base disk image or a differencing disk.
- If the template is a base disk image, determine if differencing disks are expected to be used and what their uses may be.
- Determine the virtual disk controller type, if applicable.
- Determine the virtual disk controller interface type, such as IDE or SCSI.
- Determine the device ID of each virtual disk.
- Determine the disk persistence mode of each virtual disk.
- The number of virtual IDE CD/DVD-ROM devices.
- Determine the device ID of each virtual IDE CD/DVD-ROM devices.
- The number of virtual network adapters required by the virtual machine.
- The type of each virtual network adapter, if applicable.
- The initial TCP/IP settings for each network adapter.
- Determine which operating system components need to be installed.
- Determine which operating system components need to be removed.
- The configuration of the operating system and its components.
- Determine the list of software applications that need to be installed.
- Determine which software applications are cloning-friendly and may be installed as part of the template image.
- The order of operations for the build of the template.
- Identify the development virtualization host server in which the template image will be created.

This list of information will not only be a guide during the creation of the template but can (and should) be used to document the template for future use.

It is very important to determine if the template can be created from an existing template. Obviously, the first template in a system will likely be created manually as will the first template image for each supported virtualization platform and guest operating system combination. It is highly recommended to create a library of fundamental templates. This is simply a set of templates in which each template defines a single virtual machine with a single disk containing the default installation of each supported guest operating system for each supported virtualization platform. The fundamental template library provides a shortcut in the creation of all future templates, in most cases. The ability to create a template using an existing template, either as a copy of the existing template or as a differencing disk attached to the existing template, is a very powerful concept that saves valuable time.

Templates, which are used to refer to a disk image that is intended to be cloned to enable fast virtual machine deployment, may actually consist of one or more disk images for a single virtual machine. Templates can also consist of one or more disk images for multiple virtual machines. This can occur if there is a group of virtual servers that have interdependencies and must be deployed as a whole unit. Before a new template can be created, the number of virtual machines that the template represents must be defined.

Template disk images are generally not compatible across different virtualization platforms by default. Because of this fact, it must be known ahead of time for which virtualization platform the new template will be created. When defining this requirement, it is also important to note the exact version of the virtualization platform as well. This is because there is no guarantee that virtual disk images created for a particular version of a virtualization platform will be compatible with future versions of that same platform. Documenting the version of the virtualization platform now will likely save many headaches later.

The guest operating system and the exact version that will be installed into the template image must be defined. This is one of the more critical pieces of information that is needed. It is also very useful to note each operating system hotfix, patch, service pack, or any other updates planned on being installed into the operating system. This information may be needed when determining compatibility with application software as well as when managing a library of template images.

If the operating system chosen requires licensing, acquire all license keys for the operating system and its components as necessary. Be sure to understand the types of licensing required and any activation requirements that also may exist. Some software licensing and activation schemes are not very friendly to cloning. When dealing with Microsoft licenses, volume license keys and installation media are preferred because they almost always have activation features disabled and are enterprise deployment friendly and friendly to cloning. Obtain the license keys of all software planned to be installed into the template. Be sure that no software is missing its license registration and that no software is installed into the template using a trial license, which will likely expire after a period of time (such as 30 days). It is never fun to discover that a critical piece of software installed into a template has an expired license 30 days after the template has been created.

The initial system password must be documented. This is the default password of the Administrator account in Windows operating systems or the root account password in Unix/Linux-based operating systems. Some template management schemes may use one password for all template images. This is probably not a good idea and may not be allowed by corporate security policies. This password should ideally follow the same requirements as any production system and should be a strong password. The primary reason for this is if the template is deployed to a virtual machine and the password is accidentally not changed to a new unique password, it will still be relatively safe.

The initial hostname used in the guest operating system should be unique among all other templates that are created as well as production systems. Ideally, this would be a short, descriptive name describing the use of the template image. It could also begin with a code used to define the computer as a template image just in case the template is deployed to a virtual machine and the hostname is not properly changed to a new, unique hostname. In this case, the code would allow a system administrator to quickly identify the problem and address the issue accordingly.

Define the minimum or recommended amount of memory that the template image requires. Although memory is the easiest resource to modify in a virtual machine, it is useful to document at least the minimum amount of memory required to run the virtual machine effectively.

For each virtual machine defined by the template, define the number of virtual disks that will be created and attached to each virtual machine. In most simple cases, this will be a single virtual machine with a single virtual disk (or virtual hard drive). Depending on the layout and usage of the virtual machine, it is possible to have more than one disk. For each virtual disk defined in the template, define the maximum storage size of each disk and how the virtual disk is to be partitioned. For example, a simple Windows disk layout may have a 10GB virtual disk with a single primary partition of 10GB, while another classic example is a Windows system consisting of a single 10GB virtual disk that has a 4GB system primary partition and a 6GB data partition. A typical Linux system may have a 10GB virtual disk with a 50MB boot partition, a 1024MB swap partition, a 4GB root partition, and the remainder of the disk is free space that may be allocated as needed at a later date. Once the size of each virtual disk and the number and size of each disk partition is determined, define the volume names, mount point, and file system type of each partition. In a Windows system the volume name may be the default volume name assigned by the operating system (usually Local Disk), the mount point is usually C: for the first partition, and the file system may be NTFS or FAT32. In a typical Linux system volume names are ignored, the mount point for the boot partition is /boot, the mount point for the root partition is /, and the swap partition does not have a mount point. The root partition may have the ext2 or ext3 file system installed.

Depending on the supported features of the virtualization platform, it may be necessary to determine if each virtual disk will be fixed or dynamic. Fixed disks are created as a file in the host server that is the same size as the virtual disk's maximum storage capacity. Dynamic disks are created as a file in the host server that only uses as much disk space as is needed at a point in time and will grow as needed until it reaches the virtual disk's maximum storage capacity. Some virtualization platforms, such as VMware ESX Server only support fixed disks, which is good for performance. Microsoft Virtual Server supports both fixed and dynamically expanding disk models.

Another important consideration that must be recognized in the planning stage is if the template will be a base disk image or a differencing disk image. A base disk image is a stand-alone virtual disk that has no dependencies on any other disk. A differencing disk has a direct dependency on its parent disk, which may be a base disk image or another differencing disk. If the template image is a differencing disk, special considerations must be taken into account during the actual construction of the image to avoid unnecessary bloating the differencing disk image file. The parent disk (and the parent disk's parent disk, recursively) must be documented as this information is critical during deployment of the template. If the template is a base disk image, it is also useful to note whether the template is planned to have differencing disks attached and what their uses may be.

Depending on the virtualization platform being used to create the template, it may be necessary to document the type of virtual disk controller being used. For instance, VMware ESX Server 2.x supports two virtual disk controller types, vmxbuslogic (BusLogic) and vmxlsilogic (LSI Logic). Disks created for one controller type may not be directly compatible with the other, so it is very important to note the virtual disk controller type to help save time during deployments of the template. It is also important to know which virtual disk controller type will be used for backwards-compatibility determination of the template between different versions of the same virtualization platform and to know ahead of time what additional device drivers may be needed based upon the virtual disk controller type and guest operating system combination.

Most virtualization platforms support the concept of virtual IDE or virtual SCSI disk controller interfaces. Just as in the physical hardware world, the virtual disk controller interface counterparts are not compatible with one another. Virtual disks created to use an IDE interface cannot be used with a virtual SCSI controller and vice versa. In most cases, virtual disks should be created to use the virtual SCSI interface when available.

Aside from the disk controller type and disk controller interface type, it is equally important to determine the virtual disk ID during the planning stage for each virtual disk attached to the virtual machine. Almost all server virtualization platforms allow the selection of the disk ID, which is represented by the IDE channel and device number when using an IDE disk interface and by the SCSI controller ID and the SCSI channel on which the disk is attached when using a SCSI disk interface. The virtual disks should always be attached to the same virtual disk controllers using the same disk ID so that the guest operating system always recognizes the same disk configuration each time it is booted. When using an IDE disk interface, the bootable disk traditionally has an ID of 0:0 or Primary channel, device 0. The most common SCSI disk ID is 0:0, meaning that the disk is attached to SCSI controller 0 on channel 0.

Although almost all virtual servers are used in a manner that is very similar to their physical counterparts, it is not necessarily true that all virtual disks will use the standard disk persistence mode after deployment. Standard disk persistence mode refers to a virtual disk that acts in the same manner as a physical disk device in regards to the permanency of new data. When new data is written to the disk the changes are effective immediately on that disk. In VMware, this disk mode is named persistent and in Microsoft Virtual Server this is referred to as a disk that has undoable disks disabled. Another common persistence mode that is commonly used is what VMware names append mode and Microsoft Virtual Server refers to as undoable disks that are enabled. When a virtual disk is in append mode (or undoable disks are enabled), a new virtual disk file, called either a redo disk in VMware or an undo disk in Microsoft Virtual Server, is created that is linked to the original virtual disk. The original virtual disk, or parent disk, is placed in a read-only state. All modifications to the disk are written sequentially into the redo disk. The redo disk acts much like a transaction log. Together, the parent disk and the redo disk comprise a single virtual disk. When a read occurs on the disk, the virtualization platform must determine if each readable block of data on the disk that is to be read has been modified. Each readable block of data that has been modified is read from the latest entry for that block in the redo disk while unmodified data blocks are read from the original, parent disk file. Using alternate persistence modes incurs some I/O overhead, but offers some very powerful features. In on-demand or utility computing scenarios, the virtual machine's disks are usually placed in append or undoable mode so that changes can be quickly discarded. During the planning stage, it is recommended to note each virtual disk's post-deployment persistence mode and the usage type of the template.

Depending on the intended usage type of the template, virtual CD/DVD-ROM devices may or may not be needed. Most server virtualization platforms allow up to four IDE-based virtual CD/DVD-ROM devices to be attached to a virtual machine, each of which may be mapped directly to a physical CD/DVD-ROM device on the virtualization host server or may have ISO images mounted acting as virtual CD/DVD-ROM drives. In most cases, especially in traditional data center scenarios, it is useful to have one virtual CD/DVD-ROM device attached to the template just in case it is needed in the future. It is very easy to mount and change ISO images or map the virtual CD/DVD-ROM drive to a physical CD/DVD-ROM drive while virtual machines are powered on and running, but if the original template did not have any virtual CD/DVD-ROM devices attached, virtual machines deployed using that template would have to be powered off in order to add new hardware, in this case the CD/DVD-ROM device. Just as with IDE-based virtual disks, virtual CD/DVD-ROM drives are IDE-based and each device will have a unique IDE-style device ID, such as 1:0 for the secondary master device. In the planning stage, the number of virtual CD/DVD-ROM devices required, their intended usage, and each IDE device ID should be documented.

A very important part of planning a new template is to determine the number of virtual network adapters that will be used. Most templates will have at least one virtual network adapter, although it is not absolutely required and some use cases may not need virtual network adapters. For those templates that do need virtual network adapters, the virtual network bindings and configuration settings of each virtual network adapter in the virtualization platform must be documented.

Some virtualization platforms support more than one virtual network adapter type and this usually affects which network adapter driver is used within the template's guest operating system. It is very important to document the network adapter type setting of each adapter. Changing this at a later time is possible, and if it is not documented could be changed inadvertently, possibly causing binding issues or creating ghost network adapters in the template's guest operating system, which should be avoided. Although in most cases ghost network adapters (also called ghost NICs) may not cause any real issues, in some cases, especially when working with sensitive networking configurations and applications, they may cause some very subtle issues that are difficult to track and debug.

As a best practice, the initial TCP/IP settings of each virtual network adapter must be documented and should be set to use safe settings. Safe settings include the use of DHCP or the use of a non-publicly routable static IP address that has been reserved for development or testing usage on the network. The idea is to avoid IP address conflicts when new instances of the template are deployed (or at least to minimize the chances thereof). Although there are some deployment techniques that can help minimize this issue as well (discussed later), it is generally recommended to use all available techniques that avert networking issues such as IP address and MAC address conflicts, which can potentially cause major issues on a network. The initial TCP/IP settings, including the initial IP address if using a static IP address, must always be documented so that the deployers of the template know what to expect when instances of the template are brought online.

A list of specific guest operating system components needed in the template should be documented. For each component, it should be noted whether the component is automatically installed with the operating system or if it has to be installed as a separate task. The configuration of each component should also be determined ahead of time. A list of operating system components installed by default that are not needed and must be removed should also be included in the planning documentation for the template. Common operating system components in Windows environments include IIS, Terminal Services, Internet Explorer, and Message Queuing.

The main focus of documenting the configuration of the guest operating system includes its security settings and groups, user accounts, permissions, and the configuration settings of all of its installed components. Another important consideration is remote access for administration of the deployed instances of the template. It is very useful to use built-in technologies like Microsoft Windows Terminal Services and Remote Desktop to manage Windows-based templates.

A list of all applications that will be installed into the template is needed along with all relevant licensing information for each application. It must be determined in the planning phase if a particular software application is cloning-friendly or not.

Cleanup

The last set of steps in the process of creating optimized template image is the cleanup phase. Cleaning up the image creates a pristine environment that is free of the contamination of use that occurs while building the image. Cleaning up the image mostly involves emptying or deleting specific log files and temporary files. The exact steps used to clean an image vary between guest operating systems and applications installed into the image.

The basic guidelines for cleaning most Windows guest operating systems are provided here. These guidelines may be adapted to other operating systems as needed.

- Disable System Restore and remove restore points (Windows XP only).
- Remove any unneeded applications and system components.
- Run a registry cleaner (optional, then uninstall registry cleaner).
- Optimize malware, spyware, and antivirus scan filters and schedules.
- Perform a final malware, spyware, and virus scan.
- Remove all unneeded malware, spyware, and antivirus applications, if necessary.
- Delete or empty application logs as necessary.
  - IIS logs: %windir%\system32\logs
  - SQL Server logs
- Clean up all user profiles.

- Clear AutoComplete Forms and Passwords
- Clear Cookies
- Clear History
- Clear Temp directory
- Clear Temporary Internet Files / Browser Cache
- Clear Recently Used Files
- Delete all Windows and application Most Recently Used (MRU) lists
- Remove unneeded system temporary files.
  - %WINDIR%\TEMP
  - %WINDIR%\SYSTEM32\URTTEMP
  - Lost cluster chain data from the CHKDSK utility
- Empty the Recycle Bin.
- Event Logs
  - Application
  - Security
  - System
  - Other
- Defragment all virtual hard disks.
  - Commit any redo disk and then place the disk in persistent mode
  - Erasing (then uninstall eraser)
  - Make sure there is at least 20 percent free space on the disks to be defragged
  - Remove the paging file
  - Reboot
  - Defrag
  - Replace the paging file
  - Reboot

If the guest operating system is Windows XP, it is wise to disable System Restore and remove all restore points. This will not only free up disk space, but can also improve performance of Windows XP because extra processor and disk resources will not be required to monitor the operating system and create restore points. It is likely that restore points created before the finalization of a template image will never be used, so their value is greatly diminished in this context. Since most virtualization platforms have an undoable disk mode (or Append mode), the Windows XP System Restore feature should be completely disabled during the beginning of the template image creation process and the undoable disk can be used to roll back to previous states as required.

The following steps are used to disable System Restore in Windows XP:

- Click the Start button on the Windows Taskbar.
- Open Control Panel.
- In Control Panel, open the System applet.

- On the System Properties dialog box, click the System Restore tab.
- Check the checkbox labeled, "Turn off System Restore on all drives."
- Click the OK button at the bottom of the System Properties dialog box. A popup dialog box titled, "System Restore," will appear with the following message, "You have chosen to turn off System Restore. If you continue, all existing restore points will be deleted, and you will not be able to track or undo changes to your computer. Do you want to turn off System Restore?"
- Click the Yes button.

For more information regarding System Restore in Windows XP, see the Microsoft Knowledge Base article 302796, "How to troubleshoot the System Restore tool in Windows XP," available at http://support.microsoft.com/kb/302796/en-us.

The next step in cleaning a template image is to remove any and all unneeded applications and operating system components. Often, the default installation scripts for an operating system may install many unnecessary operating system component modules and applications. Any of these components and applications that will never be used should be explicitly and cleanly removed, preferably by an uninstallation process or script. For instance, when creating a purely base Windows 2000 Server SP4 stand-alone server template image that should consist of the base operating system, Service Pack 4, and all up-to-date security patches, system components such as IIS (including FTP, NNTP, SMTP, and WWW servers) and Message Queuing should be uninstalled. There may also be a requirement for a Windows 2000 Server SP4 stand-alone Web server template image that can later be created by using the previous template image and adding in IIS with only the WWW server operating system component.

An optional step during cleanup if the template image is using one of the many Windows operating system is to run a Windows registry cleaner. These applications crawl through the Windows registry looking for inconsistent registry entries and are especially good at finding and removing unneeded registry entries left over from uninstalled applications and components.

If the template image has malware, spyware, or antivirus applications, it is recommended to optimize their scanning parameters and schedules. Often, it is a good idea to disable any real-time scanning in order to improve the performance of virtual machines created from the template. This recommendation may conflict with corporate policies. Instead of using real-time scanning, the template should be configured to use scheduled scans. It is recommended that automatic updates for malware, spyware, and antivirus applications also be enabled and scheduled, if possible. Once the malware, spyware, and antivirus applications are configured, perform one last full system scan.

Locate all application log files and either remove them or empty them. This will create a very clean starting point for virtual machines created from the template. They will not be contaminated with old, useless log entries that were created when the image itself was created. Inevitably, these just serve to impede the diagnosing of and future problems.

In order to clean up all user profiles in a template with Windows installed, it is easier to log on as an individual user and perform the proper cleanup steps.

- Clear AutoCompleteForms and Passwords.
  - Click the Start button on the Windows Taskbar.
  - Open Control Panel.
  - In Control Panel, open the Internet Options applet.
  - In the Internet Properties dialog box, click the Content tab.
  - In the Personal Information section of the Content tab, click the Auto-Complete button.
  - In the AutoComplete Settings dialog box, in the Clear AutoComplete History section, click the Clear Forms button, then click the OK button on the confirmation dialog box.
  - In the AutoComplete Settings dialog box, in the Clear AutoComplete History section, click the Clear Passwords button, then click the OK button in the confirmation dialog box.
  - In the AutoComplete Settings dialog box, click the OK button at the bottom.
  - In the Internet Properties dialog box, click the OK button.
- Clear Cookies.
  - Click the Start button on the Windows Taskbar.
  - Open Control Panel.
  - In Control Panel, open the Internet Options applet.
  - In the Internet Properties dialog box, click the General tab.
  - In the Temporary Internet files section of the General tab, click the Clear Cookies button, and then click the OK button in the confirmation dialog box.
  - In the Internet Properties dialog box, click the OK button.
- Clear History.
  - Click the Start button on the Windows Taskbar.
  - Open Control Panel.
  - In Control Panel, open the Internet Options applet.
  - In the Internet Properties dialog box, click the General tab.
  - In the History section of the General tab, click the Clear History button, then click the Yes button in the confirmation dialog box.
  - In the Internet Properties dialog box, click the OK button.
- Clear Temp directory.
  - Right-click the Start button on the Windows Taskbar and then click the Explore menu option on the popup context menu.
  - A Windows Explorer window will open.

- Browse to the path of the current user's profile, usually located in C:\
  Documents and Settings\[Username].
- Locate a subdirectory named Local Settings and then another subdirectory named Temp.
- Delete all directories and files from this Temp directory.
- Close the Windows Explorer window.
  - Clear Temporary Internet Files/Browser Cache.
    - Click the Start button on the Windows Taskbar.
    - Open Control Panel.
    - In Control Panel, open the Internet Options applet.
    - In the Internet Properties dialog box, click the General tab.
    - In the Temporary Internet files section of the General tab, click the Delete Files button.
    - In the Delete Files confirmation dialog box, check the Delete all offline content checkbox and then click the OK button.
    - In the Internet Properties dialog box, click the OK button.
  - Clear Recently Used Files.
    - Right-click the Start button on the Windows Taskbar and then click the Explore menu option on the popup context menu.
    - A Windows Explorer window will open.
    - Browse to the path of the current user's profile, usually located in C:\
      Documents and Settings\[Username].
    - Locate a subdirectory named either Recent or My Recently Used files.
    - Delete all files except for the Desktop.ini file.
    - Close the Windows Explorer window.

Cloning Template Images

The concept of cloning existing images is a very powerful benefit of utilizing server virtualization that allows new virtual machines to be deployed very quickly. The basic idea of cloning an image is to simply make a copy of the virtual hard disk drive file (or files) on the host server, rename the copy of the file, and attach it to another virtual machine, either on the same or another host server. In and of itself, the copying of the virtual hard disk drive file is easy, but it is not the complete process. There are many caveats and considerations regarding the cloning of images, especially guest operating system images.

The advantage of cloning images is that it greatly simplifies and accelerates the deployment process for virtual machines by reducing most of the tasks required in building new images. Cloning does not necessarily remove all tasks from the deployment process, but it does reduce the most repetitive and time-consuming tasks. Typically, cloning reduces the number of steps in the deployment process by at least 100 percent over a completely manual process in which the image is completely built from scratch.

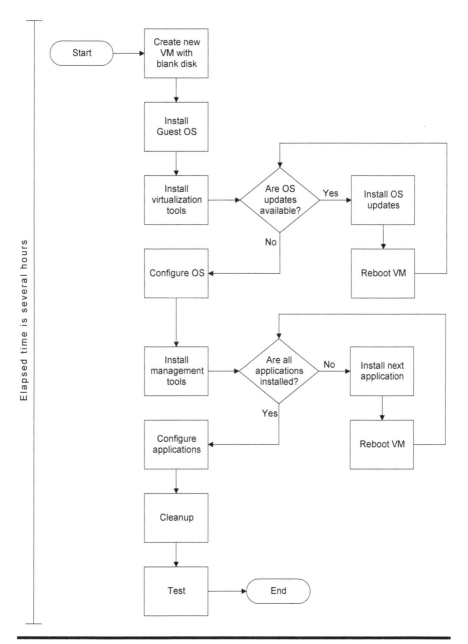

Figure 24.4   Image Creation Workflow Using a Manual Process.

Consider the differences between Figure 24.4 and Figure 24.5. If the image being created has a total of five updates, including a service pack, anti-virus updates, and three critical security updates, and each update represents two steps and the image has a total of three applications that need to be installed, each counting as two steps, the manual process described in Figure 24.4 would consist

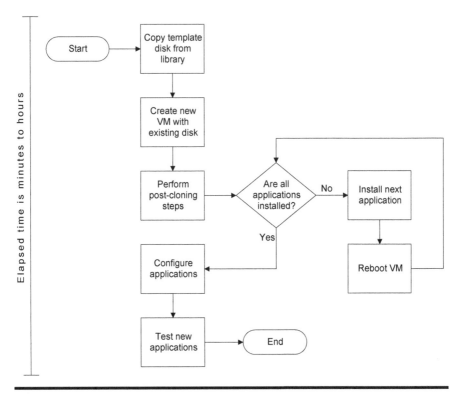

Figure 24.5   Image Creation Workflow Using a Cloning Process.

of twenty-four steps. One of the three applications is not cloning-friendly; therefore it cannot be included in the template image used in Figure 24.5. The cloned process would consist of seven steps, five base steps plus the two steps required to install the non cloning-friendly application. The reduction in the number of steps is more then 342 percent and the most repetitive, time-consuming steps have been removed from the process.

The following list will assign time values to the steps shown in Figure 24.4 using a process that does not use cloning:

- Create New VM with Blank Disk = 5 minutes
- Install Guest OS = 90 minutes
- Install Virtualization Tools = 5 minutes
- Each OS update will take 15 minutes including the time it takes to reboot the virtual machine (5 updates) = 75 minutes
- Configure OS = 30 minutes
- Install Management Tools = 30 minutes
- Each application installation will take 45 minutes including the time it takes to reboot the virtual machine (3 applications) = 135 minutes

- Configure Applications = 60 minutes
- Cleanup = 15 minutes
- Test = 60 minutes
- Total = 8 hours and 20 minutes

The following list will assign time values to the steps shown in Figure 24.5 using a cloning process:

- Copy Template Disk From Library = 20 minutes
- Create New VM with Existing Disk = 5 minutes
- Perform Post-Cloning Steps = 20 minutes
- Each application installation will take 45 minutes including the time it takes to reboot the virtual machine (1 application) = 45 minutes
- Configure Application = 20 minutes
- Test New Applications = 15 minutes
- Total = 2 hours

The reduction in time caused by the application of cloning can be significant, as shown in the total time differences between the examples presented in the lists above. The examples show realistic times taken between a process that does not use cloning and a process that does use cloning to deploy a virtual machine. The examples display a more then 400 percent improvement in time when using cloning versus building the image from scratch. If the application in the not cloning-friendly example was cloning friendly, it could have been installed into the template and would have resulted in a time reduction of 1,250 percent by eliminating the last three steps of the cloning process. Both processes are completely manual and can be further optimized through the use of automation.

Cloning template images is not without its own set of unique issues. Although almost any image can be cloned, it is wise to have a cloning strategy that is an integral part of the overall template system. Instead of just ad-hoc cloning other existing, production images, a set of templates should be created and these templates should be cloned when deploying virtual machines. A system of tightly controlled, optimized templates from which all deployments derive will greatly reduce common errors and issues that can arise during deployments, making deployments more efficient. For example, a common beginner's mistake is to quickly clone a production image of a virtual machine. A maintenance window is granted to shut down the production virtual machine and during that window its image is copied. The production virtual machine is started and brought back online. A new virtual machine is created and configured using the copy of the production virtual machine's image. The new virtual machine is booted. Because of lack of forethought into the cloning process, the beginner has now allowed 2 computers with conflicting host names, IP addresses, possibly even MAC addresses or even Windows SIDs to exist on the same network. This kind of situation can wreak havoc on the network and repairing the damage may cause, at minimum, a disconnection of a network connection until the switch or router has its translation table cleared to fix the duplicate MAC or IP address-to-MAC address resolution. The problems described in the example above can easily be avoided by having a solid cloning and template image strategy as well as following some good best practices regarding creating and configuring new virtual machines.

An essential part of the cloning strategy is knowing which software packages and applications are cloning-friendly and which are not. A cloning-friendly software package is one that can be cloned freely without causing operational issues. Cloning-friendly software packages are those that do not bind themselves to the guest operating system's or the virtual hardware's unique identifiers such as the hostname, the Windows' SID, IP addresses, MAC addresses, and so on. Applications and software packages that bind themselves to unique identifiers are not considered to be cloning-friendly. They will often break upon the cloning of the template since the template's post-deployment configuration process will almost always change these values within the guest operating system and the MAC address assigned to each virtual network adapter must be unique across all virtual machines on the network.

Another type of application that is not cloning-friendly is an application that generates its own unique identifier during installation. Upon cloning the template, the application will work properly until it communicates with another cloned copy of itself in which case it breaks because the two "unique" instances of the application have identical unique identifiers. The Microsoft Distributed Transaction Coordinator (MSDTC) is notorious for this problem, which often manifests itself when two instances of Microsoft SQL Server cloned from the same template attempt to perform a distributed query within the bounds of a transaction.

It is often difficult to know how an application binds itself to various properties, but sometimes it is possible to determine the bindings and perform custom operations to fix the broken application, such as modifying configuration files, database entries, or registry values. These fix-up steps must then become part of the post-deployment configuration process for templates containing these types of applications. Applications that can be cloned and then fixed during post-deployment configuration can be considered cloning-friendly as long as the required fix-up steps are documented and implemented each time the template is cloned.

In some cases though, the necessary values that need to be fixed or updated may be stored in an encrypted format or location that may make it impossible to clone the application. In this case, the application is considered to not be cloning-friendly.

Cloning-friendly applications can be installed and configured normally during the template build process. Applications that are not cloning-friendly must be installed after each instance of the template is deployed, either manually or using an automated installation process. Applications that are not cloning friendly introduce more complexity, deployment time, and risk into a cloning strategy.

Once a template has been created and placed into its storage location, it is ready to be cloned. Cloning the template involves making a copy of the template's files, transferring them to the proper host server and creating a virtual machine on the host server using the copied files. File transfer methods commonly used in this process include FTP, SMB (shared folders or UNC paths), or the Linux scp command. When working with template files larger than 2GB, it is important to use a file transfer tool capable of handling large files. Not all FTP clients, for example, can handle files larger than 2GB.

When working with configured templates, templates that include disk files as well as virtual machine configuration files, the cloning process is more simplified. All of the template files should be copied and transferred from the template's storage location to the host server using either FTP, shared folders, the scp command, or any other valid file transfer method. The configuration and disk files should be renamed as necessary following any prescribed naming conventions used by the organization. The configuration file should then be editing using a text editor such as Notepad in Windows or vi in Linux or ESX. The key values that must be changed include the name or label of the virtual machine and the file path or name of the disk files. This is a key step in producing a unique virtual machine. The virtual machine can then be created by registering the configuration file using the management tools for the particular virtualization platform (see chapters 12, 17, and 22 for more information). Once the virtual machine has been registered, the cloning process is complete. If necessary, any post-cloning configuration steps should be performed.

Unconfigured templates, templates that only contain disk file(s), use a slightly different approach in the cloning process because they do not include a virtual machine configuration file. The same process is used to copy and transfer the template file(s) from their storage location onto the host server. After the file transfer is complete, the file(s) should be renamed, following any prescribed naming conventions used by the organization. Because there are no configuration files, a new virtual machine must be created using the management facilities of the virtualization platform. During the virtual machine creation process, an existing disk option should be chosen and the new virtual machine should point to the cloned disk file(s). Once the new virtual machine has been created, post-cloning steps can be performed, if necessary.

Creating and Managing a Template Image Library

A template image library is a centralized storage location for all of an organization's templates. It can be as simple as a file server or NAS device or as complex as several LUNs of a SAN mounted to various file servers and accessed through a centralized Microsoft Windows Server Distributed File System (DFS) root. The main concept to keep in mind is that templates should be organized, accessed, and maintained in a central location.

Summary

There are several issues that must be addressed when implementing a template image strategy but the two biggest issues are template image storage and optimizing the image creation process. Although the basic concepts of template images are fairly simple, effectively using templates and creating a strategy for template images is an involved process that can dramatically reduce deployment costs of new servers if implemented properly.

Chapter 25

Scripting with Microsoft Virtual Server, VMware GSX Server and ESX Server

Where the consumer versions of Microsoft Virtual PC and VMware Workstation come with command line control, no such simplicity is available with the virtualization server products. Virtualization server control is achieved through the graphical user-interfaces or programming. There is a lot of sample source code that either comes bundled with the products or is downloadable from the vendor support site; however this does not mean that all critical information is covered in detail. VMware provides their sample scripting examples installed with their products and Microsoft has a support site dedicated to scripting Virtual Server. Rather than reiterating what is bundled with the products, this chapter is taking a real-world need like performing backups of virtual machines and presents a walk-through on how to accomplish that task with each of the scripting application programming interfaces (APIs).

Getting Started with Application Programming Interfaces (APIs)

The starting point in writing a script or "scripting" any application is to find out what language bindings are provided to drive the product's automation facilities. Sometimes it is a built-in scripting language, other times it is a static or dynamically loaded native library or a managed programming assembly or interop library like for a Microsoft .NET service. In the case of Microsoft Virtual Server and VMware GSX Server on Windows their scripting interfaces are driven by a Component Object Model (COM) library that is registered with Windows upon product installation. For VMware ESX Server its scripting interface is driven by Perl version 5.6 integration modules. Since both vendors' virtualization product APIs on Windows are written in COM, they are easily accessible through Visual Basic scripting, VBScript. For complex automation and complex data structure manipulation it is necessary to use an integrated development environment (IDE) and either the Visual Basic or C++ programming language, however for simplicity and ease of use the examples used in this chapter will be based on VBScript.

The VMware Application Programming Interface

VMware refers to their APIs as VmCOM and VmPerl named after the bindings they are implemented with respectively. The programmable objects in VmCOM are registered under the ProgId VMComLib.*. For ESX Server or GSX Server on Linux, the underlying API bindings are written in Perl version 5.6 modules. VMware provides both VmCOM and VmPerl access on Windows and only VmPerl on Linux since COM is not available. Figure 25.1 contains the high-level interfaces used to access specific VMware functionality.

The definitive reference guide for these interfaces is provided in a document entitled VMware Scripting API Guide (Adobe PDF format). The latest Scripting API guide is available on VMware's Web site at http://www.vmware.com/support/developer/scripting-API.

VMware VirtualCenter Infrastructure Software Development Kit (SDK)

In addition to the host-level scripting APIs, VMware also publishes a set of high-level Web Services interfaces to manage an entire data center installation of GSX Server and ESX Server called the VMware Virtual Center Infrastructure SDK. The Virtual Center Infrastructure SDK is not as easily scriptable and uses a Common Information Model (CIM)-based object and data model for each host, virtual machine, and guest it manages. It is possible to script the Virtual Center Infrastructure SDK using any client that can interpret a Web Services Definition Language (WSDL) specification. WSDL automation is available

Interface Name	Manages
VmConnectParams	Connecting to virtual machines
Vm ServerCtl	Operations for all virtual machines
VmCollection	General collections of VMware objects
VmCtl	Operations for a specific virtual mahine
VmQuestion	Virtual server status and interactive management prompts

Figure 25.1   High-Level VMware Interfaces.

through a WS-* compatible Perl library but is usually done from a Java2 or .NET integrated development environment. The Virtual Center Infrastructure SDK is beyond the scope of this chapter but the offering demands additional investigation if systems management of virtual machines on a site-wide deployment scale is important.

The Microsoft Virtual Server 2005 Application Programming Interface

The Microsoft Virtual Server API is called the Microsoft Virtual Server 2005 COM API and is registered in the COM registry under its ProgId "VirtualServer.Application." The Virtual Server COM API is a rich set of interfaces that handles host and guest OS device and power state management, monitoring, and control. In fact the entire Web-based Virtual Server Administrative Console is a natively built Web server CGI component that uses the COM API exclusively to manage Virtual Server. Anything that is possible via the Web interface is scriptable by programming. The API contains a few options that are not exposed through the Web interface and that makes it a bit more powerful than the user interface such as creating virtual machines and virtual networks in arbitrary path locations.

For reference, the complete set of interfaces in the Virtual Server API are listed in Figure 25.2, Figure 25.3, and Figure 25.4.

Microsoft Virtual Server 2005 COM Interfaces

The starting point to managing all of the Virtual Server 2005 interfaces is the IVMVirtualServer interface. IVMVirtualServer has many methods that return

Interface Name	Manages
IVMAccessRights IVMAccessRightsCollection	User and Group Access Rights: accounts and permissions for accessing Virtual Server
IVMAccountant	CPU scheduling, disk and network i/o counters and VM uptime
IVMDHCPVirtualNetworkServer	DHCP parameters for virtual networks
IVMDisplay	Dimensions, video mode and thumbnail of guest OS displays.
IVMDVDDrive IVMDVDDriveCollection IVMDVDDriveEvents	Collection of and specific CD/DVD device media connected to a host drive or captured virtual media and insertion/removal of media event notification.
IVMFloppyDrive IVMFloppyDriveCollection IVMFloppyDriveEvents	Floppy device media connected to a host drive or captured virtual media and insertion/removal of media event notification.

Figure 25.2 Virtual Server General Security and Removable Media Interfaces.

IVMGuestOS	Guest OS services: Heartbeat, time synchronization, VM Additions and orderly OS shutdown.
IVMHardDisk IVMHardDiskConnection IVMHardDiskConnectionCollection	Collection of and specific virtual Hard Disk files of IDE and SCSI disks, including Undo disks.
IVMHostInfo	Detailed CPU, memory, OS, networking, serial and parallel ports and removable devices of the host system.
IVMKeyboard	Simulation of typing keys in a Guest OS.
IVMMouse	Guest OS mouse status and simulation of button and mouse clicks.
IVMNetworkAdapter IVMNetworkAdapterCollection	Collection of and characteristics of virtual network adapter cards.
IVMParallelPort IVMParallelPortCollection	Collection of and characteristics of the virtual parallel port (LPT).
IVMRCAuthenticator IVMRCAuthenticatorCollection	Collection of and enumeration of supported Authentication methods over the VMRC remote console interface.
IVMSCSIController IVMSCSIControllerCollection	Collection and parameters of the virtual SCSI controller cards including bus sharing.
IVMSecurity	Applies fine-grain security controls over Virtual Server objects.
IVMSerialPort IVMSerialPortCollection	Collection of and characteristics of the virtual serial ports.
IVMSupportDriver IVMSupportDriverCollection	Collection of and enumeration of support drivers installed on the host system.
IVMTask IVMTaskCollection	Collection of and enumeration of task status for long running operations like merging undo disks or starting up a virtual machine.

Figure 25.3   Virtual Server Guest OS Interfaces.

IVMVirtualMachine IVMVirtualMachineCollection IVMVirtualMachineEvents	Collection of and top-level managing objects and events for a Virtual Machine.
IVMVirtualNetwork IVMVirtualNetworkCollection	Collection of and enumeration of physical and virtual networks that virtual network adapters are connected to.
IVMVirtualServer IVMVirtualServerEvents	Collection of and top-level managing objects and events for Virtual Server 2005.

Figure 25.4   Virtual Server Host, Virtual Machine Events, and Network Interfaces.

concrete instances of all other interface types. Next to IVMVirtualServer, the object accessed the most frequently is IVMVirtualMachine and in turn the IVMGuestOS object is used to manage such operations as graceful guest OS shutdowns.

Controlling a Virtual Server Through Scripting

The preceding sections described the APIs and their access interfaces, this section will apply the APIs in a useful exercise. Each of the APIs organizes the controls over virtual servers into a set of interfaces and objects representing the virtual server application, a virtual machine, and many of its attached virtual devices. As virtual machines are created, each virtualization platform builds collections of objects that compose a complete state of the host installation. In addition to the basic objects, the control of the virtual machine breaks down further into a family of related operations like power state management (e.g., turning the virtual machine on, off, or suspending it) and virtual device management—changing the state of the attached virtual hard disks, CD/DVD-ROM media and virtual networking (e.g., connecting and disconnecting media or networking access). As calls are made into API methods or to update the state of virtual server objects, the calls are actually updating either the underlying virtual machine configuration or the internal running states of the virtualization platform. In many cases scripting API invocations are manipulating the same control methods that the graphical user-interfaces of Microsoft Virtual Server and VMware are.

 Because scripting is another aspect of controlling a virtualized server, conflict is avoided by controlling the server through the graphical user-interface or through scripting, these are mutually exclusively. This means that only one control method can be used at a time, not both simultaneously. What happens if the exclusivity rule is not followed? A change in one control method affects the internal state of other controlling environments. In other words there is no proper arbitration or brokering.

While the graphical user-interfaces are generally status reflecting point-and-click tools, scripts are usually not and are not expecting their basic assumptions to be disrupted by changes by the virtualization platform GUIs. It is safest to run a script on a virtual machine when the graphical user interface is not running. Where this is unavoidable, do not have virtualization management screens active for the same machines accessed through scripting automation. Even if the GUI is running an "observation mode" and not changing a virtual machine's configuration, the GUI and script sometimes have to have locking access to the underlying object resources, which are not designed to be shared. The locking prevents either control method from obtaining the write-exclusivity required to change makes. These types of locking errors are difficult to debug and diagnose or worse resolve themselves, which just leads to user frustration and testing problems.

Programming References Are a Key to Success

There is a saying, "Sometime you don't know, what you don't know." This most certainly applies to scripting. There are a lot of possible dead ends and roadblocks than can be run into, this is why it is critical to have technical references available. With this in mind, it is important to become familiar with the programming references for the virtual server product(s) that are going to be scripted against. For Microsoft Virtual Server the main source of reference is the "Virtual Server Programming Guide" in the Virtual Server Start menu group and available code examples in Microsoft's Script Center Repository at http://www.microsoft.com/technet/scriptcenter/scripts/default.mspx. The Programming Guide is the ultimate reference for every object, method, property, constants, and enumerations. The Script Center Repository is a collection chocked full of sample code and best practices that provide just enough information to cobble together a solution or to get familiar with subtle details on a particular operation like shutting down a virtual machine.

For VMware GSX Server and ESX Server the choice is installing the Scripting API and downloading the latest documentation from VMware at http://www.vmware.com/support/developer/scripting_download.html. If the API is installed, the sample scripts are in \Program Files\VMware\VMware VmCOM Scripting API\SampleScripts. As with most references it is unnecessary to read them cover-to-cover. It is only necessary to index and search through the references as needed.

Real-World Scripting: Backing up Virtual Machines

Now armed with all the information and references needed, the best way to learn is by writing a script that is not only useful, but used on a regular basis to solve a problem. One of the most common problems with running virtualization is that the difficulty of backing up the environment is multiplied by an order of magnitude, because now instead of just backing up the host, the backup must include all of the virtual machines. These virtual machines represent running machines themselves, so to just backup the host is not enough to have the virtual machines covered. Backing up running virtual machines is a challenge because the virtual machine hard disk files are large and open or "in use." This is further compounded by the fact that the content state of the virtual machine is changing while you are backing up. Assuming there is a maintenance window for each virtual machine, it is better to take that machine temporarily out of service, back it up, and then finally start it again. That sounds easy but virtual machines can be in various power states of operation like turned off, suspended, or running. Backups should not be disruptive, so the expectation is to backup a single virtual machine at a time and leave it in the same state as it was before the backup took place. If a virtual machine were on, it is expected to be able to safely shutdown the guest operating system and back up the virtual machine files, then restart the machine. Finally, to minimize downtime the scripting APIs have special access to features of virtualization like undoable disks or redo logs that allow capturing changes to a snapshot of the virtual hard disk while it is running. In other words, virtual machine backups can minimize downtime if a backup creates a runtime redo log or undoable drive that allows the base disk to be backed up with a consistent disk state (meaning no writes are occurring to the base disk during backup, because it is in a read only mode). After the backup, the virtualization platforms can merge any changes made briefly during the backup and continue. The advantage of this flexibility is that downtime is minimized to that virtual machine's backup time. It does not always require a restart to enable a layer of differencing disk or merge the differences once a backup is complete, assuming the write changes during the backup are reasonably small (a few hundred MBs at most).

Security and Microsoft Virtual Server

As part of Microsoft's Trustworthy Computing Initiative, Microsoft performed a comprehensive security audit of Virtual Server API and the access methods needed to invoke it. To simplify the scripting code, if Distributed COM (DCOM) allows remote scripting of Virtual Server it is easiest to set the authentication and impersonation defaults in the dcomcnfg MMC snap-in to "Connect" and "Impersonate" respectively. Without these changes, additional programmatic COM security initialization using COM's CoInitialize and CoInitializeSecurity with principal identity (log-in) information is required to run these scripts. Those additional security modes are not covered in this chapter.

Backing Up Microsoft Virtual Server

The backup strategy here is to access Virtual Server and get a list of registered virtual machines, for each virtual machine, obtain its pre-backup power state, shutdown the machine if is running, then defer the backup of the virtual machine files themselves to the preferred backup method and resume the operation of the virtual machine in the same power state as before the backup. The main takeaway here is to not simply shutdown all virtual machines, back them up and power on without regard to their initial state. This would be problematic if you do not have the host capacity to run all registered machines simultaneously. Below is the code to do this:

```
'Enable error handling
On Error Resume Next
'Instantiate a Virtual Server COM API object
Set objVS = CreateObject("VirtualServer.Application")
'Get a collection of all virtual machines
Set colVMs = objVS.VirtualMachines
'Iterate through the collection of virtual machines
For Each objVM in colVMS
        'objVM is the currently selected VM from the
        collection
        'Get the current VM's power state and save for
        later
        Set objPowerState = objVM.State
        If (Not objPowerState = vmstate_Off Then
            'The VM is ON, request a shutdown
            'if VM Additions are installed
            Set objGuestOS = objVM.GuestOS
            If (Not objGuestOS is Nothing) Then
                'We have VM Additions, request a graceful
                shutdown
                Set ShutdownTask = objGuestOS.Shutdown()
                'Wait for the Guest to shutdown
                    ShutdownTask.WaitForCompletion()
            Else
                'One choice is to powerdown the VM to
                'prevent virtual disks from changing
                objVM.TurnOff()
                'Another possibility is to Save the VM
                State
                Set SaveTask = objVM.Save()
                SaveTask.WaitForCompletion()
            End If
    End If
    '''''''''''''''''''''''''''''''''''''''''''''''''''''''
'''
    'Backup the files using your preferred backup method '
    '''''''''''''''''''''''''''''''''''''''''''''''''''''''
'''
    'Recall the original power state and restore it
    If (Not objPowerState = vmstate_Off Then
```

```
        ' The machine was running before the backup,
        resume operations
        If (objPowerState = vmstate_Running) Then
            'This will startup or unsave a virtualm
            machine
            Set StartupTask = objVM.Startup()
            'This is optional. Comment out to speed up
            backups
            StartupTask.WaitForCompletion()
        End If
    End If
Next
```

Backing Up VMware GSX Server

To backup GSX Server, first the VMware inventory of virtual machines must be accessed and a list of registered virtual machines must be gotten. Then for each virtual machine, obtain its pre-backup power state and shutdown the machine if it is running. Next, defer the backup of the virtual machine files themselves to the preferred backup method and resume the operation of the virtual machine in the same power state as before the backup. The main takeaway here is to preserve the initial state all virtual machines. If this was not done and all machines were powered on simultaneously, then the host could run out of capacity when trying to run all registered machines simultaneously.

```
'Instantiate GSX Server vmCOM API objects
Set cp = CreateObject("VmCOM.VmConnectParams")
Set server = CreateObject("VmCOM.VmServerCtl")
'Connect to GSX Server
server.Connect cp
'Get a collection of all virtual machines
Set vmCollection = server.RegisteredVmNames
'Iterate through the collection of virtual machines
For each vmName in vmCollection
    'Instantiate a vmCOM Control object
    Set vm = CreateObject("VmCOM.VmCtl")
    s = "path=" & vmName
    On Error Resume Next ' Clear error object
    'Connect to this virtual machine by path
    vm.Connect cp,vmName
    If err.Number = vmErr_VMBUSY Then
        'Include warning
        s = s & " UNAVAILABLE (controlled by local
        console)"
```

```
ElseIf err.Number <> 0 Then
   'If not busy get error
   s = s & " ERROR CONNECTING desc='" & err.
   Description & "'"
Else
   'Reset error control, making errors fatal past
   this point
   On Error Goto 0
   s = s & " state=" & State2Str(vm) & " os=" & _
      vm.Config("guestos")
   'Check to see if a vmQuestion is pending against
   'the virtual machine
   If vm.ExecutionState = vmExecutionState_Stuck
   Then
       'Retrieve the question and answer choices
       Set q = vm.PendingQuestion
       Set choices = q.choices
       s = s & " question= '" & q.text & "'
       choices="
       For each choice in choices
          s = s & "[" & choice & "] "
       Next
       'Check for redo log questions
       Set r = new RegExp
       r.pattern = "undoable disk"
       r.ignorecase = True
       Set matches = r.Execute(q.text)
       If matches.count > 0 Then
          'Check for OK or redo log answers in
          choices
          For i = 1 to choices.count
             If choices(i) = "Append" Or _
                choices(i) = "Keep" Or _
                choices(i) = "OK" Then
                WScript.Echo(s)
                s = "      --> Automatically " _
                & "selecting '" & q.choices(i)
                vm.AnswerQuestion q,i
                Exit For
             End If
          Next
       End If
   End If
End If
```

```
    'Get the current VM's power state and save for later
    Set objPowerState = vm.ExecutionState
    If (objPowerState <> vmExecutionState_Off Then
        'The VM is ON, request a shutdown
        Vm.Stop cp, vmName
    End If
    '''''''''''''''''''''''''''''''''''''''''''''''''''
'''

    'Backup the files using your preferred backup method '
    '''''''''''''''''''''''''''''''''''''''''''''''''''
'''

    'Recall the original power state and
    'restore it
    If (objPowerState <> vmExecutionState_Off) Then
        ' The machine was running before the backup,
        ' resume operations
        If (objPowerState = vmExecutionState_On) Then
            vm.Start cp, vmName
        End If
        End If
    End If
Next

'Utility function: Convert virtual machine state to a
printable string
Function State2Str(vm)
  Select Case vm.ExecutionState
    Case vmExecutionState_On
      State2Str = "ON"
    Case vmExecutionState_Off
      State2Str = "OFF"
    Case vmExecutionState_Suspended
      State2Str = "SUSPENDED"
    Case vmExecutionState_Stuck
      State2Str = "STUCK"
    Case Else
      State2Str = "UNKNOWN"
  End Select
End Function
```

Backing Up VMware ESX Server

The backup strategy in this case is similar to VMware GSX Server, which is to the VMware inventory of virtual machines must be accessed and a list of registered virtual machines must be gotten. Then for each virtual machine, obtain its pre-backup power state and shutdown the machine if it is running. Next defer the backup of the virtual machine files themselves to the preferred backup method and resume the operation of the virtual machine in the same power state as before the backup. The point here is to preserve the initial state all virtual machines, just as it was for GSX Server. If this was not done and all machines were powered on simultaneously, then the host could run out of capacity when trying to run all registered machines simultaneously.

```perl
# Import vmPerl API Packages
use VMware::VmPerl;
use VMware::VmPerl::VM;
use VMware::VmPerl::Server;
use VMware::VmPerl::ConnectParams;
# Use Perl strict checking
use strict;
# Get Server authentication information from the com-
mand-line arguments
my ($server_name, $user, $passwd) = @ARGV;
# Change this to your Administration port if it is
different.
my $port = 902;
# Create a ConnectParams object using authentication
credentials
my $connect_params =
    VMware::VmPerl::ConnectParams::new($server_name,
    $port,$user,$passwd);
# Create a Server object
my $server = VMware::VmPerl::Server::new();
# Establish a persistent connection with server
if (!$server->connect($connect_params)) {
    my ($error_number, $error_string) = $server->get_
    last_error();
    die "Could not connect to server: Error $error_number:
        $error_string\n";
}
# Get a list of all virtual machine configurations
registered
# with the server.
my @list = $server->registered_vm_names();

# Check the list of virtual machines for errors
if(!defined($list[0])) {
```

```perl
    my ($error_number, $error_string) = $server->get_
    last_error();
    die "Could not get list of VMs: Error $error_
    number: $error_string\n";
}
# Declare a local configuration for a virtual machine
instance
my $config;

# Iterate through the collection of virtual machines
foreach $config (@list) {
    # Declare a VM placeholder object
    my $vm = VMware::VmPerl::VM::new();
    # Connect to the VM, using the ConnectParams object.
    if (!$vm->connect($connect_params, $config)) {
        # Couldn't connect, report the error message
        my ($error_number, $error_string) = $server-
        >get_last_error();
        print STDERR "Could not connect to VM $config:
        Error " .
            " $error_number: $error_string\n";
    } else {
        # Get the current VM's power state and save for
        later
        my $power_state = $vm->get_execution_state();
        if (!defined($power_state)) {
            # Couldn't get a VM's power state,
            # report the error messsage
            my ($error_number, $error_string) =
                $server->get_last_error();
            print STDERR "Could not get execution state
            of VM " .
            "$config: Error $error_number: " .
            "$error_string\n";
        } else {
            if ($power_state == VM_EXECUTION_STATE_STUCK) {
                # If stuck, try to answer the
                # pending question and continue
                my $question = $vm->get_pending_question();
                my @choicesText = $question->get_choices();
                my $choicesCount = scalar(@choicesText);
                if ($choicesCount <= 1) {
                  $vm->answer_question($question, 0);
```

```
            }
        }
        $power_state = $vm->get_execution_state();
        if ($power_state == VM_EXECUTION_STATE_ON) {

            # The VM is ON, request a shutdown
            $vm->stop(VM_POWEROP_MODE_TRYSOFT)
        }
        #############################################
##########
        # Backup the files using your preferred backup
method #
        #############################################
##########
        # Recall the original power state and restore it
        if ($power_state != VM_EXECUTION_STATE_OFF) {
            print "Re-powering $config...\n";
            if (!$vm->start()) {
                # If an error occurs, report it
                # and continue
            my ($error_number, $error_string) =
                $server->get_last_error();
            print STDERR "Could not re-power VM " .
            "$config: Error " .
            "$error_number: $error_string\n";
            }
        }
    }

    # Destroy the virtual machine object and
    # disconnect from the virtual machine instance.
        undef $vm;
    }
}
# Destroy the server object and disconnect from the
host server.
undef $server;
```

Summary

Scripting is important in automating many of the daily operations when leveraging virtualization. To prepare to write scripts involving virtualization, a familiarity with programming or at least prior scripting experience with VBScript or Perl is valuable. In addition to scripting experience, making sure that all of the proper reference material is at hand makes the scripting process a far easier task. When using both VMware's and Microsoft's virtualization technologies, scripting can provide many customizable and advanced capabilities over that of the GUI-based interfaces. Utilizing scripting is a necessity when using virtualization in any large scale deployments.

Chapter 26

Other Advanced Topics

Building upon the information presented up to this point, this chapter introduces advanced topics including backing up and restoring virtualization host servers and virtual machines, server clustering in a virtualized environment, working with ISO images, and physical server to virtual server (P2V) image conversions. Each topic is discussed from the proper planning stages through practical implementations.

Back Up and Restore

This section describes best practices for IT administrators and backup administrators to use when backing up and restoring virtualization host servers or virtual machines. Host servers and virtual machines have the same requirements as physical servers when it comes to back up and restore functionality. As company or customer data is a top priority, administrators require a backup and restore solution be easy to setup and manage, cost-effective, and, above all else, dependable.

Planning Stage

As a backup administrator in charge of validating and ensuring data integrity, it is important to create and maintain a backup plan for a new virtualization environment. While planning and preparing the backup solution, it is important to consider the following questions.

- What needs to be backed up and how often?
- What solution is needed to recover individual files on the virtual machine?
- What solution is needed to recover the entire virtual machine?

- Is there a backup solution already in place for physical servers?
- Is backup software and licensing already owned?
- Will backup agents be needed on the virtual machines? On the host server? Or both?
- What is the ultimate target destination for backed up data? Local storage? Tape media? Network storage?

There are several possible approaches for backing up data. The answer could be any one of these options or a combination of these options.

Backing Up the Host Server

Backing up a host server can be accomplished in a number of ways. To completely back up the entire host server environment for a given point in time, two of the more simple and traditional methods may be employed. By utilizing either a server/agent backup software package such as VERITAS Backup Exec or an imaging solution such as Symantec Ghost or Altiris Deployment Solution, the entire host server can be backed up. These solutions are fairly simple to implement and are well documented. The only exception to this is that these packages have to be slightly adjusted in their use because there is now a virtualization layer added to the mix. If the host server contains any registered and powered on virtual machines, they must be powered off before the host server and its virtual machine directories can be backed up.

Advantages
- Everything on the host server is backed up at one time providing ease of back up operation.
- Back up processes and methodologies are similar to backing up a normal physical server.
- If a catastrophic system loss occurred, the entire host server can be quickly restored.

Disadvantages
- Any restores are to a single point in time where the data is already considered stale.
- Individual files in a virtual machine cannot be restored.
- Backups and restores using this method can be extremely time consuming as well as taxing on a server's processor and network.
- Backups require large amounts of space (either disk, tape, or DVD media).
- If not performed properly, it may result in data loss.
- The backup is not considered live, which means all virtual machines residing on the host server that are also being backed up must be either powered off or suspended prior to the backup taking place.

The virtualization host server should not have many changes other than periodic upgrades from the platform vendor. Backing up the entire host server to simply back up the virtualization platform is not recommended. Rather than backing up the platform and restoring it, most platforms are either simple enough to reinstall or they offer an automated installation path that is usually faster than doing a full system restore. If the backup route is chosen, it will become quite clear rather quickly that a full host server backup will not be needed as frequently as a backup of the virtual machines and their associated data files.

Backing Up Individual Files from within the Virtual Machines

The best way to backup individual virtual machine files on virtual machines that require constant uptime (such as a typical 99.9% service level agreement or SLA, providing 24/7 uptime) is by using traditional backup and restore processes by installing a backup agent in each virtual machine's guest operating system. By connecting directly through the network to a backup server, the backup agent on the guest operating system can completely backup and restore individual files on the virtual machine. Through either a manual or automated fashion, the agent can be instructed to transfer the selected data from inside of the guest operating system to a local or remote destination, such as tape, a disk array, or writeable CD/DVD media.

This follows the same standard procedures that would be followed when installing a backup agent onto a physical server. There are many backup solutions currently on the market with one of the more popular being VERITAS Backup Exec, which also happens to be supported by all three major virtualization platforms. Most backup products today are wizard driven and provide some type of automated scheduling method in which to archive the data. Backup archives can be complete backups, incremental backups, or differential backups. Each of these archiving schemas has advantages and disadvantages associated with them, but selecting the right solution is dependant on the situation and the type of data being backed up.

The primary disadvantage to using traditional backup and restore technologies inside of a virtual machine is the time it takes to backup the data as well as the performance hit taken in network traffic and processor load. It is important to realize that when the backup agent begins reading the data from the virtual machine and transfers it across the network, the host server will be taxed quite a bit. The virtual machine's guest operating system will be under a great deal of stress and so will the virtualization layer. The problem can be multiplied if a large number of virtual machines residing on the same host are all scheduled to perform their backups around the same time. The reverse is also true, if a restore of data is attempted using this type of method, it can be a slow and strenuous exercise on all of the systems involved.

Advantages
- Can restore individual data files.
- Can restore database data via the normal database-specific method.
- Backups can be performed live on running virtual machines.
- A company's normal backup and restore procedures and methodologies can be followed.
- Most backup server or backup agent software solutions can be used as long as it runs on the guest operating system on the virtual machine.
- It simplifies the backup process when all machines (physical and virtual) use the same backup strategies.

Disadvantages
- This approach does not take advantage of the file encapsulation of a virtual machine.
- A backup agent/software license must be purchased for each virtual machine, which can grow quickly and become quite costly.
- If a disaster strikes, it may take longer to first restore the entire virtual machine, load it with recovery software, and then restore the data from each of the different backups, rather than just backing up and restoring the entire virtual machine.
- Can cause a network and processor performance hit depending on the amount and type of data being backed up or restored, or the number of virtual machines simultaneously backing up or restoring files.

Backing Up Virtual Machines with a Host Operating System Backup Agent

Another backup method often used is one that makes use of a backup agent running on the host server. This backup solution closely follows a standard network backup solution and should fit into most methodologies quite well.

Before going out to purchase a backup software package, there are a few considerations to take into account when using this backup strategy. It is important to make sure that the selected backup agent software is compatible with the virtualization host platform and its file system. For example, not all backup software is compatible with VMware ESX Server's VMFS file system. Equally important, virtual machines should be powered off or suspended before a backup agent is allowed to backup the virtual machine disk files, saved state files, configuration files, and any other files that may reside in the virtual machine directory. Otherwise, the effect on the virtual machine will be similar to pulling the power cord from the back of the server. When the virtual machine is powered on, it may or may not boot. If the virtual machine does boot, there is still some chance that the data may be corrupted in some form. If a virtual machine is going to be moved from one host server to another, it is safer to power down the virtual machine rather than suspending it as there can be problems with resuming a suspended machine on a different hardware platform than it was originally suspended on. And finally, while some backup software packages claim to have open file agents, they do not always work reliably when backing up open virtual disks that are gigabytes in size. The best implementation is still to power down the virtual machine prior to backup.

The processes discussed above can be automated in a number of different ways to provide a successful backup solution. Most backup software sold today provides some mechanism to execute batch jobs or scripts. Using one of these methods, virtual machines can be powered off or suspended as needed before the backup agent begins copying its files. For example, VMware offers a set of command-lines that are useful in creating simple batch files to perform these functions (powering off, starting, suspending, and resuming virtual machines).

To power off the virtual machine, the suspend batch file should include the following line:

```
vmware-cmd <path_to_config_file>\<config_file>.vmx stop
```

Once the virtual machine is powered off, the backup agent can safely begin backing up the virtual machine's directory and files. Once the backup is complete, the agent can launch the post-backup batch file containing the following line to power on the virtual machine:

```
vmware-cmd <path_to_config_file>\<config_file>.vmx start
```

Advantages
- The entire virtual machine directory can be backed up at one time providing ease of backup operation.
- Backup processes and methodologies are similar to backing up files on a normal physical server.
- Combining backup agents with scripting and batch files allows complete automation in the backup strategy, and keeps the virtual machines error free.

Disadvantages
- Any restores are to a single point in time where the data is already considered stale.
- Individual files in a virtual machine cannot be restored.
- Backups and restores using this method can be extremely time consuming as well as taxing on a server's processor and network.

- Backups require large amounts of space (either disk, tape, or DVD media)
- If not performed properly, it may result in data loss.
- The backup is not considered live, which means all virtual machines residing on the host server that are being backed up must be either powered off or suspended prior to the backup taking place.

Backing up Individual Virtual Machine Files without Backup Agents

By far, one of the simplest methods of backing up a virtual machine is to make use of the virtualization feature known as encapsulation. This feature allows the host server to view each virtual machine as a file with a .dsk, .vmdk, or .vhd extension. By taking advantage of this feature, an entire virtual hard disk can be effectively backed up with a simple copy command. Along with base virtual disk files, backup copies of REDO or undo disks, suspended state files, and virtual machine configuration files can also be made. Backing up an individual virtual machine can be a manual process that is started at any given point in time or it can be automated through some type of scripting method. Using this simple approach, it is very easy to restore a virtual machine's file to a different host server with the assurance that it will register and function just as it did on the host server on which it was backed up.

 Keep in mind that virtual disk files should not (typically) be backed up while the virtual machine is powered on. When the virtual machine is powered on, the base disk file is open and being written to by the virtual machine. In most cases, powering off or suspending the virtual machine before making a copy is the best solution as it closes the virtual disk file from actively being written to and therefore makes it safe to backup. Alternatively, there are other solutions out there that attempt "live" backups, where the virtual machine can remain powered on. Using VMware's snapshot feature, a virtual machine can be placed into REDO mode, where all new writes are captured by a REDO log file rather than writing to the base disk. This method allows the base disk to be copied off, and the REDO log file can later be committed back into the base disk. Other methods include "near live" backups, where downtime may be as short as 1 minute. By using a combination of scripting, the virtualization suspend feature and shadow copy (using vshadow. exe from the Volume Shadow Copy Service SDK), a virtual machine can be backed up with minimal downtime. Scripting backup solutions is also explained in more detail in chapter 25.

If the virtual machine disk images are stored on a storage area network (SAN), use the SAN features supplied by the SAN vendor to make backup copies of the disk images. The SAN management software can be used to schedule checkpoints on the disk back end to guarantee a backup from a specific time frame.

VMware ESX Server 2.5 provides an easy to use tool that supports live backups of running virtual machines. The tool is named vmsnap.pl. It can list all virtual machines that are available for backup, and it supports local or remote backup destinations. To backup a running virtual machine registered as W2K3-DC-01, the following command can be executed:

```
./vmsnap.pl -c /root/vmware/W2K3-DC-01/W2K3-DC-
01.vmx -d /virtualmachines/localbackup -l
```

By executing this command, a live virtual machine registered as W2K3-DC-01 with its configuration file located at /root/vmware/W2K3-DC-01 is backed up to a local directory named /virtualmachines/localbackup.

```
Running ./vmsnap.pl -h provides the following in-
formation.

vmsnap [-a server_name] [-c config_file] [-d local_
dir] [-R remote_dir] | [-g] | [-h] | [-V] [-l] |
[-m] [-r]
-a server_name Specify an archive server
-c config_file Specify a VM configuration file to use
for vmsnap
-d local_dir Specify a local directory for vmsnap
-R remote_dir Specify a remote directory for backup
-g List all available VM's for backup
-h Help
-V Version
-l Perform local backup only
-m Generate the man page for this program
-r Commit the redo logs in case they are already
present
```

Advantages
- Backups and restores are extremely easy to perform and can be as simple as using a file copy command.
- Expensive third-party software to perform backup and restore procedures are not needed.

- Existing hardware can be used to house and restore virtual machine disk files.
- If using a SAN, file consistency is guaranteed by SAN checkpointing.

Disadvantages
- Adds another layer of complexity to the environment since it does not make use of current backup and restore procedures and methodologies.
- Individual files in a virtual machine cannot be restored. A potentially large multi-gigabyte file must be restores to simply restore a single file, which increases restore time.
- Need to checksum verify the files to make sure there is no file corruption during the copy process.
- Difficult to perform live backups without scripting knowledge.
- Not all SAN solutions are supported by the different virtualization platforms.
- A SAN solution is extremely expensive.

Clustering

Clustering is used today for providing redundancy and performance over that of a single server machine. On physical clusters the redundancy is not only in having at least two copies of an operating system cooperatively running, but two physical machines hosting these operating systems. By running on multiple host machines, if there is a failure on one of the host machines, the other machine can take over all of the activities of the failed machine. Clusters can also be multi-node clusters. Multi-node clusters are those comprised of three or more clustered systems. Multi-node clusters provide even greater performance and resiliency than that of a two node cluster.

It is important to realize that the performance gained in a cluster is only achieved when the cluster has more than one node that is active. An active cluster node is one that participates in providing services to clients actively. A passive cluster node is one that waits for the failure of another node, then upon recognizing the failure replaces the failed node and becomes and active node. Clusters with more than one active node at a time are called Active-Active Clusters. Clusters with only one active node at a time are called Active-Passive Clusters. Performance is only enhanced on Active-Active Clusters as they can service a larger number of requests, due to more compute power being available. The danger in Active-Active Clusters is that is if all of the nodes are highly utilized and one fails, then the people requesting services from the cluster will notice a loss of performance. The flip side of this is that it is better to see slow performance than to see a failure in service all together.

Clustering Disk Technologies

There are several clustering disk technologies that are fundamental to clustered environments. These clustering disk technologies include:

- Shared SCSI
- iSCSI
- SAN

Shared SCSI is the oldest disk clustering technology available. Shared SCSI simply ties a SCSI disk array to a pair of SCSI disk controllers. The SCSI controllers are said to "share the SCSI disk array across a shared bus." This sharing allows for the quorum to be created and data to be simultaneously read by all clustered nodes. There can only be one cluster node that can be designated to write at a time. The reason for only a single node being able to do a write is because if multiple nodes wrote data at the same time in the same place, data loss would occur. Shared SCSI is commonly used for two node packaged cluster solutions.

The newest and least expensive of the three disk technologies is iSCI. It is based on encapsulating SCSI commands inside of IP packets. iSCSI runs across standard Ethernet and can use standard 100Mb or 1000Mb network cards (when 10Gb Ethernet becomes available, iSCSI will support this as well). iSCSI is based on two components, an initiator and a target. The target is the shared storage location (this is analogous to the shared disk array). The initiator is the equivalent to the controller. The target can be driven by software running on Linux or Windows, or by an appliance such as a Network Appliance Filer. The initiator is run as a driver on a server and appears as a SCSI hard disk to the operating system. The initiator can also be a special iSCSI controller card. This card is a hybrid between an Ethernet network card and a SCSI controller. It appears to the server's operating system as a SCSI controller with a SCSI hard disk connected to it; however it is actually running a special embedded software program that allows it to communicate over the network independently of the server's operating system.

SAN is the most expensive solution of the three storage technologies, however it does provide the best performance. A SAN is comprised of several components including an HBA (Host Bus Adapter), a Fiber Channel Switch, and a disk array. Each of these components requires special configuration to work properly. The HBA acts as a SCSI hard disk controller by providing access through the Fiber Channel switch to the disk array. The Fiber Channel switch connects many servers to the disk array. The disk array stores all of the appropriate data just like a standard SCSI array (in fact, some SAN arrays are comprised of SCSI-based disks, while others are Fiber Channel-based disks.) SANs also require specialized SAN management and configuration software. SANs must have security and configuration information setup and maintained. SANs are complex and usually require some type of training for technical staff or a consultant to provide expertise in properly installing and configuring a SAN solution.

Clustering in Virtualization

Virtualization provides a host of new avenues for clustering. Clustering has always been an expensive proposition because of the requirement of so much additional hardware. Each additional machine that needed to be clustered, as mentioned before, requires a new host server. Virtualization can eliminate the need to buy a new physical host each time redundancy is desired. This is because virtualization can allow multiple cluster nodes from different clusters to reside on the same physical server. This solution is an incredibly cost effective alternative to that of an Active-Passive Cluster. This solution will not work well when applied to an Active-Active Cluster solution. Active-Active Cluster solutions are more likely to have continuously high demands, so sharing physical hardware between multiple high demand cluster nodes would not be a good practice. Virtualization can provide an excellent platform for conducting tests and learning more about how to cluster active-active-based systems.

Virtual to Virtual Clustering on a Single Host

Clustering two or more virtual machines that reside on the same physical host can provide several benefits. If there is a fear that an application has stability problems and may crash the operating system that it is running on and greater reliability is needed, then an Active-Active Cluster or an Active-Passive Cluster can be configured. Earlier, it is mentioned that Active-Active clusters are not recommended on virtualization platforms, however if the nodes are not being highly utilized and only nodes servicing the same cluster are operating on a single host server, then this configuration should work acceptably. Active-Passive Clusters can be setup on the same single physical host and depending on utilization; multiple different Active-Passive Cluster nodes can be simultaneously operating on a single physical host. Multiple different Active-Passive Cluster nodes are shown in Figure 26.1.

Virtual to virtual clustering also provides a method of testing how an application would need to be configured and how it would behave on a physical cluster without having to purchase and configure a physical cluster. This can prove to be very valuable when trying to qualify an application and justify a physical cluster configuration for a production system.

Virtual to virtual clustering involves two nonstandard hardware configuration components. They are a second SCSI controller with a shared disk and a second network card with a network that is connected only to other clustered nodes. The shared disk is where all the critical information that must be stored and read

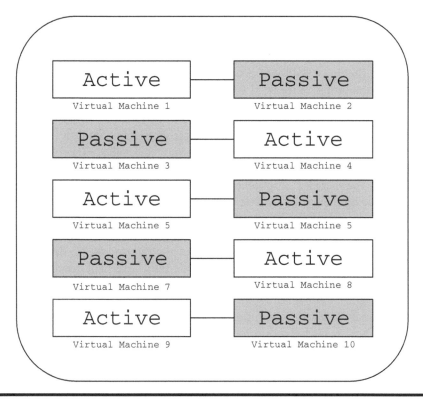

Figure 26.1 Clustered Virtual Machines on a Single Physical Server.

by the clustered nodes is held. The second network card provides a heartbeat and sometimes replication services between other cluster nodes.

VMware GSX Server Virtual to Virtual Clustering

Clustering is supported on VMware GSX Server and is fairly straight forward. To setup a cluster on GSX Server, two virtual hard disks must be created for each cluster node. The first virtual hard disk can be either IDE or SCSI, where as the second virtual hard disk must be a pre-allocated SCSI disk. All other SCSI disk types including expandable SCSI-based disks are not supported, but may still work. A separate virtual SCSI controller is recommended if both the boot and shared disks are SCSI. To share the SCSI disk, support SCSI reservations in GSX Server must also be activated.

To activate SCSI reservations:

- Edit the virtual machine's configuration file (after the virtual machine is turned off).

- Add a line in the SCSI portion where the separate virtual SCSI controller is, this line should have the SCSI number of the SCSI controller and a declaration that the bus is shared. If the SCSI controller is scsi2 for example, then the line would read `scsi2.sharedBus = "virtual"`. This line shares the entire SCSI 0 bus.
- Save the new virtual machine configuration file and exit.

The first virtual hard disk will act as the operating system boot disk and will provide the location for the base operating system to be installed. The second virtual hard disk will be the clustered disk, which is where the quorum is created. The quorum is the shared disk space in a cluster that is made available to all cluster nodes allowing them to share data between each other. The operating system being installed on the first virtual hard disk must provide clustering services, such as Microsoft Cluster Service or VERITAS Cluster Service, and those services must be active for clustering to work. Once the quorum is set, depending on what application is being installed or used on the cluster will decide what next steps are necessary to activate or use any cluster aware applications.

 VMware's terminology for a disk that can be used simultaneously by multiple virtual machines is called a shared disk. This shared disk must be a SCSI-based disk and is where the quorum resides.

There are several important caveats to be aware of when setting up the shared virtual disk and reservations. These caveats include:

- The SCSI-2 disk is the only bus sharing protocol supported.
- SCSI disks can only be shared between virtual machines that reside on the same physical host server.
- Ensure that all virtual machines sharing a virtual hard disk have SCSI bus sharing enabled.

The only other step necessary to configure a GSX Server virtual machine is a second network card. The second network card is tied to a network that only other cluster nodes should be tied to. This network supplies replication information and a heartbeat between all of the other clustered nodes.

VMware ESX Server Virtual to Virtual Clustering

Much like GSX Server, clustering is supported on ESX Server natively. There are some differences between the two however. One difference is that ESX Server does not support IDE-based virtual hard disks, even for booting. Another difference is in the configuration of virtual hard disks for clustering. This is due primarily to several factors including the change over from the Bus Logic controller in previous versions of ESX Server to the LSI Logic controller. This virtual SCSI controller is one of the many components that must be configured for clustering to work on ESX Server. A minimum of two virtual hard disks is required to set-up an ESX Server-based virtual cluster. Each of the two virtual SCSI hard disks must be attached to a separate SCSI controller. The first controller will hold the booting operating system, while the second controller will connect to the shared virtual hard disk. The shared virtual hard disk will contain the clustered information, whether that is a database, Web site, or other type of application. Only data stored on the shared virtual hard disk is available to all of the clustered nodes (virtual machines).

 At present, only two nodes are supported currently under ESX Server 2.5. This limitation may be removed in a future release.

To create clustered nodes under ESX Server, follow these steps:

- Create a virtual machine with a SCSI disk residing on a VMFS partition.
- Create a new virtual hard disk (in persistent mode) tied to the virtual machine that was just created and connect the virtual hard disk to a second SCSI controller.
- Change the second SCSI controller's configuration for bus sharing from none to virtual.
- Ensure that the virtual machine has two virtual network adapters, if it does not, add an additional network adapter.

Microsoft Virtual Server Virtual to Virtual Clustering

Microsoft Virtual Server is configured identically to VMware's GSX Server. However, Virtual Server will support clustering only when the host is running Microsoft Windows Server 2003 Enterprise Edition.

The virtual machine cluster nodes require at least two virtual hard disks. The first hard disk, which will be the boot disk, should be attached to a virtual IDE controller interface. The second virtual hard disk should be attached to a virtual SCSI controller with shared bus enabled. The first virtual hard disk can be dynamically expanding or fixed in size, however the second virtual hard disk should only be a fixed disk. This is because the second disk is going to be the quorum disk and therefore there should be no changes in the disk since it is shared between all of the cluster nodes. Virtual Server is only designed to support a two node cluster. The shared virtual hard disk must be formatted with NTFS—no other format is supported for clustering under Virtual Server.

There should also be two virtual network interface cards attached to each virtual machine. One of the virtual network cards will be for access from the outside, whereas the other virtual network card will be for the private cluster network. The private network will support a heartbeat for failover monitoring and data replication services. This is the network that Microsoft Cluster Services will be using to keep the clustered nodes in synch.

 SCSI controllers in shared bus mode support only one virtual hard disk attached to the controller. For normal uses a single SCSI controller is preferred. It is possible to have up to four SCSI controllers with shared buses, each with one virtual hard disk attached for a total of four shared virtual hard disks.

To create clustered nodes under Virtual Server, follow these steps:

- Create a virtual machine with an IDE virtual hard disk and two virtual network cards.
- Edit the virtual machine to add a SCSI controller in shared bus mode.
- Create a fixed virtual hard disk and attach it to the SCSI controller.
- Connect one network adapter up to a private virtual switch and connect the other to the public virtual switch.

 The shared virtual hard disk that Virtual Server uses cannot have undo disks enabled. This can not only cause problems with cluster integrity, but is not supported by Microsoft.

Virtual to Virtual Clustering Across Multiple Hosts

Clustering virtual machines across two or more physical hosts provides a highly optimized and redundant system. The primary use for virtual to virtual clustering across multiple hosts is in production environments where mission critical applications are running. Many small applications that in the past would have had to be put on a separate clustered physical server to ensure redundancy without impacting other applications can now be consolidated onto one physical server. Instead of having to by three or even four servers (one for each application) and then having to buy another a second machine for each application to cluster them. Figure 26.2 shows an example of the virtual to virtual clustering configuration described above.

Virtual to Virtual Clustering Across Multiple GSX Hosts

Virtual to Virtual clustering across multiple hosts is supported in GSX Server, however only by leveraging iSCSI-based technology. GSX Server does not support clustering across remote storage due to the potential of data loss or corruption. VMware does provide support for two node clusters across physical hosts using iSCSI. iSCSI is a fairly new technology that uses the IP protocol to send

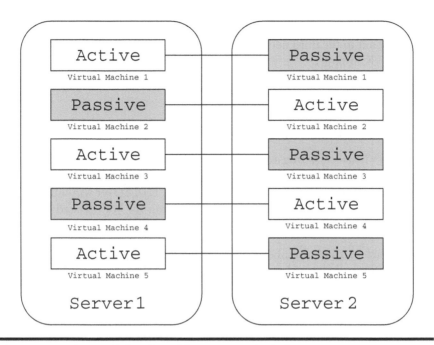

Figure 26.2 Clustered Virtual Machines on Two Physical Servers.

SCSI commands from one machine to another. This provides the least expensive remote disk-based solution available today. iSCSI is supported by most major storage vendors in at least one of their product lines, including HP, IBM, EMC, and Network Appliance. Only the Microsoft iSCSI initiator is supported. The iSCSI initiator should be run across a virtual network interface operating on the vmxnet-based driver.

To configure GSX Server for virtual to virtual clustering across multiple GSX Server hosts, follow these steps:

- Create a virtual machine as the first cluster node.
- Add two additional virtual network cards; there should be three total network cards counting the default and the two additional.
- Configure one network card for outside access or to provide services on the network.
- Configure the second network card on a private network that will communicate with the other clustered node as the heartbeat.
- Configure the third network card as the remote disk network (this network should point to the iSCSI target that will house the quorum and any shared data disks).
- Install Windows Server 2003 Enterprise or Windows 2000 Advanced Server on the virtual machine.

- Install the Microsoft iSCSI initiator software onto the virtual machine and attach it to the third network card. It also must be pointed and attached to the iSCSI target.
- Create the cluster and point the clustering service to the iSCSI disk for the quorum.

Virtual to Virtual Clustering Across Multiple ESX Hosts

Virtual to Virtual clustering across multiple ESX hosts can be accomplished with either Shared SCSI or with a SAN solution. ESX Server is the only platform that supports both Shared SCSI and a SAN solution. ESX Server will only support clustering across two ESX hosts. The configuration for both Shared SCSI and SAN solutions will be covered below:

- Create a virtual machine as the first clustered node.
- Configure the virtual machine with a second network card (for the cluster communications / heartbeat).
- Set the second network card to be on a network that only communicates with the other clustered node.
- Create a separate VMFS partition for the quorum disk to reside.
- Set the shared VMFS partition access to shared
- Create a second virtual SCSI controller with a virtual hard disk in Persistent mode.
- Change the second virtual SCSI controller's properties so that bus sharing is enabled and set to physical.

 Only put a single virtual hard disk file inside of a shared VMFS partition. This will solve many file locking issues that can be associated with storing multiple shared disks on the shared VMFS partition.

Virtual to Virtual Clustering Across Multiple Virtual Server Hosts

Virtual to Virtual clustering across Virtual Server hosts is done through the use of iSCSI. This is the only way to achieve clustering of virtual machines across hosts under Virtual Server. Clustering up to 8 nodes is possible under virtual server, using Microsoft Cluster Services. To do this, the iSCSI target is created on a machine on a network accessible by all of the virtual machines (spread across two or more physical hosts.) Each virtual machine would have the Microsoft iSCSI initiator installed and pointing to the target. The target is where the quorum would reside.

The Microsoft iSCSI Initiator 2.0 is the minimum version that can be used to achieve this configuration. This configuration also requires that Microsoft Virtual Server 2005 R2 as the minimum release of Virtual Server.

The following are the steps necessary to create each cluster node for configuring Virtual Server for clustering across physical hosts:

- Create a virtual machine with an IDE virtual hard disk and three virtual network cards.
- Connect one virtual network adapter up to a switch that is accessible by the clustered virtual machines across all of the hosts, this is for the heartbeat.
- Connect the second virtual network adapter to the public virtual switch to provide external services
- Connect the third virtual network adapter to a network dedicated to iSCSI.
- Once the virtual machine is brought up and the iSCSI Initiator is installed, point the initiator at the target and setup the quorum.

Virtual to Physical Clustering using GSX Server

Virtual to Physical clustering using GSX Server is configured using iSCSI in the same fashion that Virtual to Virtual clustering is setup and installed. The only exception to this is the use of a physical machine in place of a second virtual machine for the other cluster node. The quorum should be located on a different machine than where either the physical cluster node or the virtual cluster node resides.

Virtual to Physical Clustering Using ESX Server

Virtual to Physical clustering using ESX Server is nearly the same setup as that of a Virtual to Virtual cluster across multiple physical hosts, with one exception. To achieve a Virtual to Physical cluster, RAW disk mode should be used. This will allow an ESX Server virtual machine to be a node on a cluster comprised of virtual or physical servers. The necessary additional steps to utilize RAW disk mode over the configuration in Virtual to Virtual across multiple physical hosts is outlined below:

- Map the physical disk to a virtual disk by selecting the LUN and making sure that the partition is 0 to identify the entire physical disk and not an actual partition.
- Select the secondary controller and attach it to the RAW disk.

- Set the secondary controller to physical shared bus mode.
- Complete the configuration and install as it would normally be done.

Virtual to Physical Clustering Using Virtual Server

Virtual to Physical clustering using Virtual Server is done just as it was in Virtual to Virtual clustering across multiple physical hosts, with iSCSI. The steps are the same as that of configuring Virtual Server clustering across physical hosts. The only exception to this is the use of a physical machine in place of a second virtual machine for the other cluster node. The quorum should be located on a different machine than where either the physical cluster node or the virtual cluster node resides.

Other Virtual Disk Images

When talking about server virtualization, it is impossible to have a discussion about virtual machines without mentioning virtual hard disk files. Throughout the book, virtual hard disk files are mentioned in almost every chapter. They have been defined, their various types explained, their modes of operation discussed, their various formats identified, their controller interfaces have been listed, they have even had best practice solutions detailed. However, there are other types of virtual disk images that are almost as important when discussing and using server virtualization. And although they have been mentioned in other sections of the book, they have not been given their proper due. Most, if not all of the virtualization platforms currently on the market have some type of support for the virtual floppy disk and the virtual CD-ROM image. Each of these will be discussed throughout the remainder of this section.

What is a Virtual Floppy Disk Image?

Simply stated, a virtual floppy disk image file is an exact and complete image or copy of all the data that a physical floppy disk would contain. The image contains information on the disk format, file system data structure, boot sector, directories, and files. The method of accessing a virtual floppy disk image will vary depending on the host system or the virtualization platform. To retain compatibility with its physical counterpart, a virtual floppy disk image has the same size limitations as the physical disk it has virtualized. The virtual floppy disk has a 1.44MB maximum capacity. Since virtual floppy disk files do not have large storage capacities, they are typically used to move around small amounts of data, especially if virtual networking is unavailable. Like the physical floppy disk, a virtual floppy disk is mostly used to provide software drivers for devices during guest operating system installations.

Creating Floppy Disk Images on Linux and Windows

Virtualization supports virtual floppy disk files. So where do these files come from? And how are they used? While there are vendors that offer virtual floppy disk images for download, it is just as easy to create one from a physical floppy disk or to create a new blank image. This process can take place on either a Linux or Windows server.

When using a distribution of the Linux operating system or the VMware ESX Server console operating system, the kernel typically provides an extraordinary amount of support and built-in utilities to assist with creating and working with floppy disk image files. On the other hand, when working with a Windows operating system, third-party tools will typically need to be downloaded and installed in order to perform similar functionality.

Linux Operating Systems

How to Extract a Floppy Disk Image

When creating a virtual floppy disk image by extracting data from a physical floppy disk, the entire contents from the physical floppy disk can be copied directly to an image file. For example, to make an image file named `drivers.flp` from a diskette that is already in the floppy drive, use the following dd command on the block device:

```
# dd if=/dev/fd0 of=drivers.flp bs=512
```

The above assumes the floppy disk is in the A: drive (`/dev/fd0`), `if=` and `of=` are the input and output files respectively, and `bs` represents the block size in bytes to be read and written.

How to Create a New Floppy Disk Image

To create a new, blank floppy disk image (rather than creating a floppy disk image from an existing physical floppy disk as above), most of today's Linux versions offer the mkdosfs command. The command can be used to create the floppy image and create a file system on it (such as MS-DOS), while avoiding having to use the dd command to create the file. The file created is a sparse file, which actually only contains the meta-data areas (such as the boot sector, root directory, and FAT). Once the file is created, it can be copied to a floppy disk, another device, or mounted through a loop device.

```
# mkdosfs -C drivers.flp 1440
```

The device given on the command line should be a filename (for example, `drivers.flp`), and the number of blocks must also be specified, in this case, 1440 for the size of a floppy disk.

How to Mount a Floppy Disk Image

Using a Linux distribution, one of the most convenient ways to access a floppy disk file system on the host server is to use the loopback mount feature. Once the floppy image is mounted using this method, the files contained within said file system are then accessible on some specified mount point. After doing so, the mounted image and its files can be accessed with normal tools and manipulated much like a physical floppy disk. As an example of using the loopback mount feature, the root user (or a user with superuser privileges) may enter the following commands to mount the previously created `drivers.flp` (the virtual floppy disk image file).

```
# mkdir /mnt/image

# mount -t msdos -o loop=/dev/loop0 drivers.flp
/mnt/image
```

In the example, a directory is first created to serve as a mount point for the loopback device. Since there are currently no other loopback devices already mounted, it is safe to proceed with using loop0. The mount command then mounts an image named `drivers.flp` that uses a MS-DOS file system. The files located on the drivers.flp image should be accessible at `/mnt/image`.

Unmount

As soon as you are finished using the floppy disk image, it is important to unmount the image from the host operating system and then free the loopback device. While there are multiple loopback devices available (/dev/loop0, /dev/loop1 … /dev/loopn), they should be cleaned up when no longer in use for other users. To help, the following commands can be executed:

- cat /proc/mounts—To find out which loopback devices are in use
- umount—The command used to unmount the file system (in this example, `# umount /mnt/image`). Notice, the unmount command is umount and not unmount. Do not be confused by this.
- losetup—To free the loopback device, execute the losetup command with the –d option (in this example, `# losetup -d /dev/loop0`).

Windows Operating Systems

Creating a Floppy Disk Image

To create a virtual floppy disk image file on a Windows server, third-party tools will need to be downloaded and installed. There are quite a few tools available that can perform this task. There is a mixture of these utilities scattered across the Internet—some are freely distributed as open source projects, some are distributed as shareware with different licensing mechanisms, while others are commercially written and available for pay.

When going down the free or open source route, there are plenty of products to choose from, in fact, way too many to list here. One of the projects released under the terms of the GNU General Public License (GPL) is RawWrite Studio. It offers a collection of tools such as RawWrite for Windows, a free, open source Win32 port of the older DOS rawrite program. It also offers DD, a command line tool similar to the UNIX/Linux command line tool of the same name. This suite of tools offers a free solution for reading and writing disk images on Windows.

Keeping with the free and open source theme, another suite of tools released under the GNU GPL is the Cygwin package. The package provides a port of many of the popular GNU development tools to be used in a Microsoft Windows environment. Many of these UNIX/Linux utilities can be called from a Windows command shell, and provide similar functionality as the commands covered in the Linux section of this topic.

However, one of the more popular Windows tools used to create floppy disk images from either a physical floppy diskette or from ad-hoc files and directories is a shareware utility called WinImage. WinImage is a powerful disk utility that can also inject files into and extract files from a disk image. It can also create empty floppy disk images that can be used at a later time. Figure 26.3 shows a floppy disk image being created by WinImage. The program is simple and easy to use, making use of menu options and drag and drop functionality, as well as batch operations for automation purposes. More information on the product can be found on its Web site at http://www.winimage.com.

 WinImage offers two floppy disk image formats: IMA and IMZ (see Figure 26.3). When using WinImage to create the image file, it is important to save the file format as IMA. The IMA format is an uncompressed file format, while the IMZ format is a compressed file format that may not be acceptable to your virtualization platform.

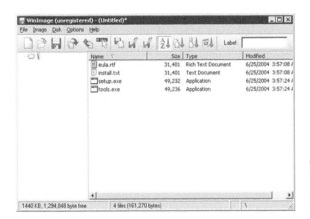

Figure 26.3   Creating a Floppy Image with WinImage.

If there is one thing about floppy disk images that should be discussed because it sometimes causes confusion with people who are new to using disk images, it is to understand that the file extension on a floppy image is not necessarily set in stone. In other words, most applications including virtualization each have their own file extension for a virtual floppy disk image—some are even free form. As an example, VMware uses .FLP, Microsoft uses .VFD, Raw-Write uses .IMG, and WinImage uses .IMA or .IMZ. Whatever program is used to create the image, chances are its file extension will be acceptable to the virtualization platform. Most platforms will mount any floppy image file, no matter what the extension. A problem may come into play when searching for floppy images with an unexpected file extension using the browse button; the images may have to be manually entered using the fully qualified path and file name or the existing extension can simply be changed to match the extension requested by the platform.

How to Mount a Floppy Disk Image

Once the virtual floppy disk image is created, how is it accessed on a Windows server? Just as with the image creation process, there are a number of different applications available to mount floppy images to a Windows server. There are too many to list here, however, one freely distributed and open source application that many people in the virtualization community are well aware of is a program named Virtual Floppy Drive written by Ken Kato and hosted on the VMware's back Web site located at http://chitchat.at.infoseek.co.jp/vmware. Using this application, a virtual floppy image can be mounted to a Windows server as a virtual floppy drive, and the contents of the image file can be directly accessed much like a physical floppy diskette—viewed, edited, renamed, deleted, or new files can even be created.

Since this book discusses server virtualization, chances are you are making a virtual floppy disk to mount inside of a guest operating system and not necessarily on the host. Rather than relying on downloaded tools or seemingly complicated commands inside of the host operating system, most virtualization platforms offer a simple method of mounting these floppy disk images. From within the virtualization platform, edit the virtual machine's configuration file (usually with some sort of client or GUI interface) and modify the floppy disk configuration to point to a floppy disk image file rather than a physical drive.

What Is an ISO Image?

The simplest definition, an ISO image is a single file that contains the complete image of a physical CD-ROM. Going by the more restrictive definition, an ISO image is a file that contains an image of an ISO 9660 file system, which is a standard CD-ROM file system that allows a PC, MAC, or any other major computer platform that has a CD-ROM drive to read from the same CD-ROM. The standard, issued in 1988, was created by an industry group known as High Sierra. Established was the concept that an ISO image is created by copying an entire disc, from sector 0 to the end, into a file and naming it with an .iso extension. As a result of using this filename extension (.iso), any file that contained a sector-by-sector CD-ROM image was hereto referred as an "ISO Image".

ISO images are mostly used as installation media for operating systems and application software. Using an ISO image has distinct advantages over using a physical CD-ROM. The first advantage noticed is the increased speed. As a read-only media, the ISO image is read at speeds up to 10 times faster than the best physical CD-ROM drives, because it is a file that is leveraging the speed and performance of a hard disk. Another advantage of using an ISO image, it never smears, scratches, or breaks – things that are all too common with physical media. Additionally, an ISO image is far less likely to disappear, because borrowed CD-ROMs are always returned to their rightful place, right? And finally, it is much easier to mount or attach an ISO image to a physical server or a virtual machine than it is to gain physical access to the server in order to use physical media. Access to a physical server can be difficult to achieve due to separation by distance, security clearance, company policy or any other number of reasons.

Creating ISO Images on Linux and Windows

Much like the virtual floppy disk file, a virtual CD-ROM file or ISO image can be offered as a download or just as easily created from physical CD-ROM media. For instance, Microsoft offers most of their operating systems and applications for download in ISO image format for their MSDN subscribers. VMware also offers their products for download in ISO image format on their Web site for registered customers. Downloadable ISO images are also the most popular method of distribution for most Linux operating systems.

 Not to confuse anyone, ISO images do not have to be images of operating systems or applications. They can also be images that simply contain large amounts of data that can be used as the modern day sneaker net—a way to transfer this data from one machine to the next without the need for a physical or virtual network.

Linux operating system distributions and the VMware ESX Server console provide an extraordinary amount of support with built-in utilities to assist in creating and working with ISO image files. The Windows operating system typically requires third-party tools to be downloaded and installed in order to perform similar functionality.

Linux Operating System

Creating ISO Images

ISO images can be created in multiple ways, such as extracting the contents of physical CD-ROM media and exporting it into an ISO image file, or by creating a temporary directory and then populating it with files and directories arranged in a file structure that are then made into an ISO image file.

When creating an ISO image file by extracting the data from a physical CD-ROM drive, the entire contents from the CD-ROM media can be copied directly to an image file. For example, to make an ISO image file named RedHat9.iso from media that is already loaded in the CD-ROM drive, use the following dd command:

```
# dd if=/dev/cdrom of=/isoimages/RedHat9.iso
```

The above assumes the CD-ROM drive is mounted with the physical media loaded and that the /isoimages directory exists. In the command, if= represents the input device, and of= represents the output directory and the ISO image file name that is created.

An ISO image file can also be created without the need for existing physical CD-ROM media. By using the free, native Linux utility mkisofs, an ISO image can be generated from a prearranged group of files and directories. For example, to create an ISO image file named MyUtilities.iso of the entire directory structure from /local/image, use the following command:

```
# mkisofs -o /isoimages/MyUtilities.iso /local/image
```

In the above command, an ISO image named MyUtilities.iso is created in /isoimages and is comprised of all the files and directories located in /local/image. The mkisofs man page should be referenced for more details.

How to Mount an ISO Image

On either a Linux distribution or the ESX Server console, an ISO image can be mounted and then accessed as if it were a physical CD-ROM. One of the most convenient ways to mount the ISO image is to use the native loopback mount feature found in most Linux distributions. As an example of using the mount command to access an ISO image, the root user (or a user with superuser privileges) may enter the following commands to successfully mount the previously created image, `MyUtilities.iso`.

```
# mkdir -p /mnt/iso
# mount -t iso9660 -o loop=/dev/loop0 /isoimages/
MyUtilities.iso /mnt/iso
```

In the example, a directory is first created to server as the mount point for the loopback device. If there are currently no other loopback devices mounted, it is safe to proceed with using loop0. The mount command then mounts the ISO image named `MyUtilities.iso`, which uses the ISO9660 CD-ROM format. The "o –loop" switch means to mount the file as a block device. The files located on the ISO image should then be accessible at `/mnt/iso`.

Unmount

As soon as you are finished using the ISO image, it is important to unmount the image from the host operating system and then free the loopback device. While there are multiple loopback devices available (/dev/loop0, /dev/loop1 … /dev/loopn), they should be cleaned up when no longer in use for other users. To help, the following commands can be executed:

- cat /proc/mounts—will note , loopback devices are in use.
- umount—The command used to unmount the file system (in this example, `# umount /mnt/iso`). Notice, the unmount command is umount and not unmount. Do not be confused by this.
- losetup—To free the loopback device, execute the losetup command with the –d option (in this example, `# losetup -d /dev/loop0`).

Windows Operating Systems

Creating an ISO Image

To create an ISO image file on a Windows server, third-party tools will once again be needed. There are numerous tools available for download on the Internet, in fact, too many to list in this chapter. Some are freely distributed as open source projects, some are distributed as shareware, and others are commercially available.

The Cygwin package (discussed earlier when describing tools to create the floppy disk image) offers a free tool suite that was released under the GNU GPL. The package provides a port of many of the popular GNU development tools to be used in a Microsoft Windows environment. Many of these UNIX/Linux utilities can be called from a Windows command shell, and provide similar functionality as the commands covered in the Linux section of this topic.

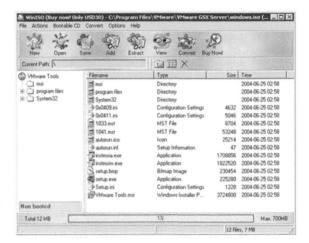

Figure 26.4   Creating an ISO Image with WinISO.

There are many commercially available utilities that can be used to create ISO image files in a Windows environment. Most of these utilities operate in a similar fashion, making use of a Windows Explorer type interface that leverages drag and drop functionality to add or remove files and folders into a creation window and then followed up with some sort of create button. Two of the more popular commercial applications are WinISO (available at www.winiso.com) and CDE-veryWhere (available at www.cdeverywhere.com). Creating an ISO Image with WinISO is shown in Figure 26.4.

How to Mount an ISO Image

Once the ISO image is created, there must be a way to mount the image on a Windows server so that the data on the image can be accessed. There is a way, and as usual, there are many utilities available to perform this function. Two commercially available products are CDSpace 5 (http://en.cdspace.com/main/main.asp) and Virtual CD (http://www.virtualcd-online.com). However, one tool in particular stands out, and seems to be one of the most widely used tools of its kind—and it's free! Daemon Tools (http://www.daemon-tools.cc), like the other two applications, is a tool used to mount one or more ISO images as virtual CD/DVD-ROM devices within a Windows operating system.

Because we are talking about server virtualization, you are probably more interested in how to mount your ISO images inside of the guest operating system, rather than the host operating system. Rather than downloading applications inside of the guest operating system, the virtualization platform can be used to mount the ISO images so that the virtual machine can access them. Using the virtualization platform, the virtual machine's configuration file can be modified, either through a client or management interface, to add a virtual CD-ROM drive to its list of virtual hardware. Once the virtual CD-ROM drive is added, it should be configured to point to an ISO image rather than the host's physical CD-ROM drive. When this is accomplished, the guest operating system is then able to access the ISO image just as if it were physical media.

Building an ISO Image Library

The benefits of using an ISO image have already been explained. However, to recap, ISO images offer faster read access times, they can be used when access to the physical server is unavailable, and they do not scratch, smudge, break, or walk away. Sure, ISO images have benefits over physical media, but once the images are created, where should they be stored? After all, CD-ROMs are comprised of quite a bit of data that when converted to ISO images translates into a lot of needed disk space. For this reason alone, the creation of an ISO image library should be carefully thought out and well planned.

ISO images should be stored in a central storage location, a library that is accessible by the host servers and the virtual machines. Host servers should then have a separate partition created on its local storage to temporarily house ISO images as needed. These images should be rotated in and out locally, only when creating a new image or installing a new application. As explained throughout the book, to take full advantage of the economies of scale that virtualization provides, template images, rather than one-off image creations, should be the normal best practice followed. Once a template image is created, and a base platform is available for any particular guest operating system, there is no longer a need to have the ISO image stored locally. If for some reason a new installation is needed, the ISO image can then be copied back down from the remote storage or library server to the ISO partition created on the local storage of the host server.

It is important to create a clear and understandable layout on the ISO image library. If an image cannot be identified and located, then the consolidated image library has not done its job. It is therefore important to create directories and subdirectories to properly categorize ISO images, and it is equally important to come up with an easily identifiable naming convention for both the image files and the directories. These names should be short and concise, yet descriptive and easily discernable. The ISO images themselves should be named in a way that is quick to identify yet still easy to type (such as entering the name during a file transfer or when mounting the image inside of the virtualization platform). Names similar to w2k3std.iso (Microsoft Windows Server 2003), mssql2000sp4.iso (Microsoft SQL Server 2000 SP4), or rhlinux9_1.iso (Red Hat Linux 9 CD 1) can be used. When naming files, it is also important to keep case in mind. If using a Linux-based operating system (including VMware ESX

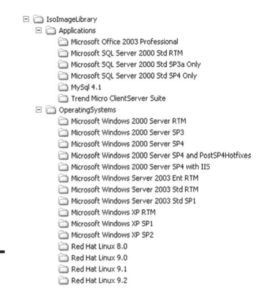

Figure 26.5   Example ISO Image Library Server Folder Structure.

Server), it can prove to be quite difficult to copy and mount ISO images that alter case in the naming convention. Directories should also be broken out into different categories such as operating systems and applications, and then further broken down into subdirectories such as Microsoft Windows and Linux. The directory structure should be defined by the types of ISO images in each organization. However keep in mind, organizations can change, so plan for the future. A quick example of an ISO image library structure is provided in Figure 26.5.

Depending on the infrastructure of the library server and the virtualization environment (such as operating system, file system, and security), these ISO images will need a method of transfer from storage to host server. Whether file copy, secure copy (SCP), or FTP is being used to transfer the file, it is important to make sure that the file is transferred in binary and in its entirety. All too often, there have been cases where a bad copy of an ISO image has caused a problem, whether it is with a guest operating system installation or an application installation, and has resulted in hours of wasted time trying to troubleshoot the issue. Because ISO images can be fairly sizeable, it is important to verify the file integrity when transferring or copying these files. This is evident as more Internet Web sites that offer ISO images as downloads are also offering the MD5SUM for that image. After the download, an MD5SUM can be checked on the downloaded file and compared to the MD5SUM from the original (a 32 character key).

MD5 Sums are 32 character strings that are the direct result of running the MD5 Sum program against a particular file. Since any difference between the two ISO image files will result in two different string values, MD5 Sums can be used to determine that the ISO image is a bit-for-bit copy of the remote image. Without going into further detail about MD5SUM itself, it is important to discuss how to make this comparison. Once again, the Linux operating system natively supports a command to perform the task at hand. In order to check the MD5SUM of an existing ISO image file, the following command can be executed against the file:

```
# md5sum filename.iso
```

A Windows operating system will need third-party software downloaded and installed in order to perform this same verification process. There are several MD5SUM applications available for the Windows operating system. Two free, open source applications that provide the same information as the Linux md-5sum command are: winMd5Sum—a GUI tool that offers additional features (http://www.nullriver.com/index/products/winmd5sum) and MD5Summer— also feature rich (http://www.md5summer.org/).

Running the MD5 Sum check against these large files may take some time. However, it's better to waste a little bit of time up front performing the verification process than it is wasting time and energy trying to troubleshoot why an installation does not work.

Physical to Virtual Conversions (P2V)

The conversion of a physical machine to a virtual machine is a complex process. There are rewards to this process in that if a machine cannot be rebuilt and configured in the same way on a virtual machine. There are several reasons that this problem can occur including; an operating system that is no longer supported or a legacy application that is no longer supported and the media cannot be located or does not exist any longer. These problems and others have created the need for the P2V process.

There are several ways to achieve a successful P2V outcome:

- Imaging-based conversions, i.e., Altiris, Symantec Ghost, Acronis True Image
- P2V tools, i.e., VMware P2V Assistant, Microsoft VMTS, Platespin Power P2V
- Manual conversions and custom solutions

Each of the above solutions will be explored further in this section.

Imaging-Based Conversions

Successful conversions from physical to virtual machines can be achieved through the use of imaging tools. The process for these conversions includes capturing an image of the bootdisk, operating system, and all associated software. Once the image is created, it must be transferred to an empty virtual hard disk. This can be achieved by loading an imaging boot disk inside of a virtual machine and imaging a connected virtual hard disk or mounting a virtual hard disk as another physical drive with a tool such as the VMware DiskMount utility. Once the image is transferred, the virtual machine can be booted. The operating system inside the virtual machine will boot up and automatically detect and adjust to the new virtual hardware that it has been moved to. This will complete the P2V process using the imaging approach.

P2V Tools

P2V tools provide a more streamlined approach than that of the Sysprep and Image process. P2V tools essentially wrap up the capabilities of an imaging tool and Sysprep into a single automated package. The process for these tools is very similar, but far more automatic. An example of this is VMware's P2V Assistant Tool. P2V Assistant involves a boot disk that does a binary dump of all of the data from the physical machine's boot and operating system disk(s) directly to a virtual hard disk. During this process it also modifies the proper configuration settings and drivers necessary for the operating system to boot up properly at the conclusion of the conversion process. The transfer completes and once the virtual machine is started, the operating system boots and is ready for use. This process is not without fault as with any complex automated processes, there can be problems and glitches with conversions. These can normally be fixed through manually editing and tweaking the converted image.

Manual and Custom Conversions

Manual and custom conversions should only be done by someone very experienced with both virtualization technology and the specific operating system that is being converted. There are several consulting firms that provide these types of services as it is such a difficult process. These types of conversions are commonly done on systems with highly customized operating systems or application stacks that do not lend themselves to being converted easily with either of the other two methods described previously.

Manual conversions on the Microsoft Windows platform are probably the most complex conversions. This is due to the windows registry changes that are necessary to support a conversion in addition to services and drivers that must be altered. In some cases there can even be conflicts between other services and drivers that are already preexisting on the system.

Manual conversions on Linux-based platforms can have their own problems depending on how customized the version of Linux that is being used is. One thing that will offer an ease of conversion is the support of Linux inside of Microsoft Virtual Server 2005-based virtual machines.

Please note, it is important to remember that even after a successful conversion that the virtualization guest operating system tools should be loaded inside of the guest operating system. A word of caution however, before installing the virtualization tools, a backup should always be made of the successfully converted image.

Summary

When working with server virtualization in an enterprise environment, there are certain advanced topics that are sought after. These topics include backing up and restoring virtualization host servers and virtual machines, server clustering in a virtualized environment, working with ISO images, and physical server to virtual server (P2V) image conversions. Backing up and restoring virtual machines can be handled in a number of ways, including many of the methods and practices that are currently being used throughout physical environments. However, it is important to remember that virtual machines offer encapsulation and portability, and these features can be taken advantage of while undergoing a back up and restore process in ways that physical machines cannot. Likewise, server virtualization features also open up new avenues when it comes to server clustering. In the past, clustering has always been an expensive proposition because of the costs associated with the additional hardware required. Virtualization greatly reduces these cost barriers, and at the same time, offers numerous methods of performing this valuable datacenter function.

Imaging plays a major role in a virtualized environment. This chapter discusses two very important imaging technologies: ISO images (virtual CD-ROM media) and physical server images. ISO images become an important part of creating and maintaining virtual machines. Because physical access to a host server is not always available, a method of delivering and installing operating systems and applications to the virtual machines becomes important and equally challenging. Through the process of creating a virtual image of the CD-ROM media and then mounting and accessing it remotely, this obstacle is easily overcome. The challenge then becomes how to manage these ISO images. It becomes important to create a central repository or library of these images where the files and directories are clearly labeled to identify its contents. Another type of imaging, server imaging, may sound somewhat familiar. Unlike server imaging in a physical environment, the imaging process in a virtual environment breaks the physical barrier. Through a transferring process known as P2V (physical to virtual), an image of a physical server can be created and then migrated to an entirely different compute environment, in this case, a virtual machine that is composed of completely different hardware. There are numerous tools on the market along with various methods available that attempt to perform the same function—migrate the contents of a physical server (operating system, applications, files, users, etc.) into a virtual machine and then have that virtual machine power on and function in the same manner as the original physical server.

Part VII

Resources

Chapter 27

Tools and Utilities

Whilst working with server virtualization, there are various software tools and utilities that are used to solve the many small problems frequently encountered and to simplify tasks. The tools covered in this chapter are mostly third-party tools and utilities not included with the virtualization platforms. Although some of the tools discussed are commercial and require that licenses are purchased, others are free or even open source. Some of the tools are included with the various Linux and Windows operating systems. The tools have been organized into major functional categories, but some tools are used for multiple functions and may be covered in more than one category.

Communications Tools

The most fundamental tools often employed are those used to remotely connect to the host server and virtual machines. The communications tools covered here are broken down into two major groups: command-line interface and graphical user interface (GUI).

When working with Linux hosts or guest operating systems or the VMware ESX Server Service Console, telnet or the more preferred SSH tools are most commonly used. Telnet is not as preferred because of security reasons. All of the data transmitted using the telnet protocol is sent over the wire in clear text, including passwords. SSH (secure shell) uses encryption to protect the data (and your credentials). When using a Windows workstation, Putty is one of the most commonly used SSH clients, mainly because it is small, fast, and free. Microsoft does not ship an SSH client with Windows, therefore a third-party SSH client, like Putty, has to be used. Windows does ship with a command-line telnet client, but it is highly recommended to never use telnet and to always use SSH for remote command-line access to servers.

In the graphical user interface group, there are a number of different technologies. One of the most predominant GUI remote control technologies is Microsoft Remote Desktop, also referred to as Microsoft Terminal Services. Remote Desktop is one of the most performant and robust remote desktop GUI technologies available. Since Windows 2000 Server, Microsoft has allowed a total of two concurrent Remote Desktop client licenses per instance of Windows to be used for remote administration purposes without the need for additional licenses. In order to use Remote Desktop, the target computer, that is, the computer to which one connects must support either Microsoft Terminal Server in Remote Administration mode (Windows 2000 Server) or Remote Desktop (Windows XP, Windows Server 2003, Windows Vista). Either the older Microsoft Terminal Services Client (MSTSC) or the newer Microsoft Remote Desktop Connection client (often preferred) must reside on the workstation. Microsoft has also released a Mac-compatible version of the Remote Desktop client application. Alternatively, there is a free application named rdesktop for Linux that allows Linux clients to connect to Windows hosts using Remote Desktop as well as a free, open source, Java-based Remote Desktop client named properJavaRDP that can be used with any operating system supporting a compatible Java runtime environment.

Aside from Microsoft's Remote Desktop technologies, there are other GUI remote control technologies available, such as Symantec's pcAnywhere and Remotely Anywhere, two commercial applications that use proprietary technologies to deliver an interactive remote desktop. Another very popular choice is the freely available, open source VNC (Virtual Network Computing)—available for both Linux and Windows. VNC clients and servers are cross-platform compatible and therefore makes it easy to manage Linux and Windows servers, but the performance leaves much to be desired. Aside from the original VNC available as RealVNC, there are other variants that have additional capabilities including file transfer features such as TightVNC and UltraVNC.

See Figure 27.1 for additional information on the communications tools presented here.

Disk Tools

Disk tools are utilities that operate on a virtual hard disk image file in some significant fashion. The specific tools covered in this section include defrag.exe, Eraser, Virtual Disk Driver (VDK), and the VMware DiskMount Utilities.

When using Windows guest operating systems, the Windows defrag.exe utility is used to help compact files in the virtual hard disk image file so that the free space will be moved toward the end of the physical file. This is usually done prior to a shrink operation on an image or to remove extents containing only free space from a sparse virtual hard disk image file. The defrag.exe tool in Win-

Communication Tools				
Tool Name	**Type**	**License Type**	**Free**	**Hosted on SourceForge.net?**
PuTTY	CLI	Open Source	Yes	No
http://www.chiark.greenend.org.uk/~sgtatham/putty/				
ssh	CLI	N/A	Yes	No
The ssh command is included in most Linux and Unix operating systems.				
telnet	CLI	N/A	Yes	No
The telnet command is included in most Linux, Unix, and Windows operating systems.				
Microsoft Remote Desktop Client for Macintosh	GUI	Commercial	Yes	No
http://www.microsoft.com/downloads/details.aspx?FamilyID=6573f9f1-8ae1-4da9-ab5c-f8457ecdaf2d&displaylang=en				
Microsoft Remote Desktop Client for Windows	GUI	Commercial	Yes	No
http://www.microsoft.com/downloads/details.aspx?FamilyID=80111F21-D48D-426E-96C2-08AA2BD23A49&displaylang=en				
properJavaRDP	GUI	Open Source	Yes	Yes
http://properjavardp.sourceforge.net/				
rdesktop	GUI	Open Source	Yes	Yes
http://www.rdesktop.org/				
Symantec pcAnywhere	GUI	Commercial	No	No
http://www.symantec.com/pcanywhere/				
Remotely Anywhere	GUI	Commercial	No	No
http://www.remotelyanywhere.com/template.asp?page=products				
RealVNC	GUI	Open Source	Yes	No
http://www.realvnc.com/				
TightVNC	GUI	Open Source	Yes	Yes
http://www.tightvnc.com/				
UltraVNC	GUI	Open Source	Yes	Yes
http://ultravnc.sourceforge.net/				

Figure 27.1 Communications Tools.

dows will not only defragment the files within the image, but it will attempt to move them to the beginning of the disk. Sometimes the defrag operation may have to be run more than once on a single image to achieve the desired amount of compaction of the file system.

In order for extents within a virtual hard disk image file that contain only free space to be recognized as being empty, they must contain all zeros. Unfortunately, when files are deleted, the data still remains intact; it is just flagged in the file system as having been deleted. Eraser is a free tool used to overwrite all of the free space on a hard disk with user-defined patterns, including patterns containing only zeros. Eraser can be used to zero-out the free space so that the extents containing only free space within the virtual hard disk image can be recognized as being completely empty by virtualization platform-specific tools. It is very useful to zero-out the free space in an image just before compacting a sparse virtual hard disk image in order to remove the free space from the image file and reduce its overall size.

For large disk image file copies are successful, the md5sum tool in Linux or VMware ESX Server's Service Console can be used to generate a checksum of the source and destination files. If the checksums match, the file transfer was successful. Windows does not ship with an md5sum command as do most Linux and Unix operating systems, but a compatible, free version is included with Cygwin, a free, open-source, Linux-like environment for Windows. Another free, open-source md5 checksum utility for Windows operating systems is md5summer, which sports a graphical user interface. Md5summer produces checksums compatible with those generated by the Linux and Cygwin md5sum commands.

Virtual Disk Driver, called VDK, is a very powerful, free, open source utility that allows many different formats and versions of VMware virtual hard disk images to be mounted within a Windows operating system as if it were a physical hard disk drive. Once mounted, the virtual disk drive can be accessed in read-only or read-write modes just as if it were a normal disk. This is a very useful tool for manipulating an image when performing advanced tasks such as Virtual-to-Virtual image conversions or IDE-to-SCSI disk conversions. This tool is similar to the VMware DiskMount Utility, but mounts disks using a different technique.

The VMware DiskMount utilities are a set of tools similar to VDK that allow a VMware virtual hard disk image to be mounted within a Windows operating system, assigning it a drive letter. The mounted disk can be accessed in read-write mode mostly as if it were a physical disk attached to the system. Currently, there are 3 different VMware DiskMount Utilities:

- **VMware DiskMount Utility**
  Also referred to as the VMware GSX Server DiskMount utility, it can mount disk files created with the following VMware platforms:
  - VMware ACE (Non-encrypted disks only)
  - VMware ESX Server 2
  - VMware GSX Server 2.5.1
  - VMware GSX Server 3
  - VMware Workstation 4
  - VMware Workstation 5
- **VMware ACE DiskMount Utility**
  Mounts disk files created with the VMware ACE Manager application. There are currently two versions of this utility:
  - Version 1.0.0 Build 11627, released on 12/21/2004
  - Version 1.01 Build 14573, released on 08/04/2005
- **VMware Workstation DiskMount Utility**
  There are versions of the utility each supporting a different version of VMware Workstation disks:
  - Version 4.5.2 Build 8848, released on 06/11/2004

Disk Tools				
Tool Name	**Type**	**License Type**	**Free**	**Hosted on SourceForge.net?**
Microsoft Disk Defragmenter	GUI	Commercial	No	No
Included in Microsoft Windows operating systems				
Executive Software Diskeeper	GUI	Commercial	No	No
http://www.executive.com/defrag/defrag.asp				
Eraser	GUI	Open Source	Yes	Yes
http://www.tolvanen.com/eraser				
md5sum	CLI	N/A	Yes	No
The md5sum command is included in most Linux and Unix operating systems as well as Cygwin.				
md5summer	GUI	Open Source	Yes	No
http://www.md5summer.org				
Virtual Disk Driver, VDK	CLI	Open Source	Yes	No
http://chitchat.at.infoseek.co.jp/vmware/vdk.html				
VMware DiskMount Utility	CLI	Commercial	Yes	No
http://www.vmware.com/download/diskmount.html				
VMware ACE DiskMount Utility	CLI	Commercial	Yes	No
http://www.vmware.com/download/diskmount.html				
VMware Workstation 5 DiskMount Utility	CLI	Commercial	Yes	No
http://www.vmware.com/download/diskmount.html				

Figure 27.2   Disk Tools.

- Version 5.0 Build 13124, released on 04/07/2005
- Version 5.5 Build 18463, released on 11/29/2005

See Figure 27.2 for additional information on the disk tools presented here.

Disk Imaging Tools

Disk imaging tools have been in use for a long time and they can be just as helpful when working with virtual machines as they are when used with physical computers. Disk imaging tools allow entire hard disks or partitions to be copied at a low level in their entirety in an image file that can then later be restored to the same or another computer, usually of the same type. The images that these tools produce are very different from virtual hard disk images and each tool has its own image file format. The different images produced by these tools are generally incompatible with each other. Disk imaging technology allows much faster deployment of physical computers and can be used to help convert physical computers to virtual machines. They can also be used to help convert virtual machines of one virtualization platform to an image of another virtualization platform.

Disk Imaging Tools				
Tool Name	**Type**	**License Type**	**Free**	**Hosted on SourceForge.net?**
Acronis TrueImage	GUI	Commercial	No	No
http://www.acronis.com				
Altiris	GUI	Commercial	No	No
http://www.altiris.com				
dd	CLI	N/A	Yes	No
The dd command is included in most Linux and Unix operating systems as well as Cygwin.				
Microsoft ADS	CLI	Commercial	Yes	No
http://www.microsoft.com/windowsserver2003/technologies/management/ads/default.mspx				
Symantec Ghost	GUI	Commercial	No	No
http://www.symantec.com				

Figure 27.3   Disk Imaging Tools.

The Linux/Unix dd command is a very powerful utility that is used to es-sentially copy data from a device or file into another device or file, optionally converting the data. It can be used to create images of disks, including hard disk drives, floppy disks, and CD/DVD-ROM discs or to copy raw data in whole or in part from one device into another device. The dd command can also be used to move data residing in virtual hard disk images during IDE-to-SCSI conver-sions, virtual-to-virtual conversions, or physical to virtual conversions. In Win-dows, the dd command is included with Cygwin, a free, open-source, Linux-like environment for Windows. There is another freely available, open source version of dd for Windows operating systems called dd for Windows.

In the commercial disk imaging tool space, the most popular tool is by far Symantec's Ghost. Competing with Ghost are Acronis' TrueImage and the Alti-ris solution. These tools allow physical as well as virtual hard disks to be imaged either locally on a machine or to a remote disk accessible over a network. Images produced by these tools can be restored either locally from a CD/DVD-ROM disc, from another hard disk, or from a remote, networked disk or file share.

Microsoft has a proprietary solution for simplifying the deployment of Win-dows-based systems called Microsoft Automated Deployment Services, or Mi-crosoft ADS. Microsoft ADS can perform basic volume imaging but also adds additional enterprise capabilities such as centralized management and image storage and dynamic PXE booting and remote deployment of images.

See Figure 27.3 for additional information on the disk imaging tools pre-sented here.

Floppy Disk Image Tools

Most server virtualization platforms support having the virtual floppy disk drive of a virtual machine map to a floppy disk image file that resides on the host

Floppy Disk Image Tools				
Tool Name	Type	License Type	Free	Hosted on SourceForge.net?
RawWriteWin	CLI	Open Source	Yes	No
http://uranus.it.swin.edu.au/~jn/linux/rawwrite.htm				
WinImage	GUI	Shareware	No	No
http://www.winimage.com/winimage.htm				
Virtual Floppy Drive	CLI	Open Source	Yes	No
http://chitchat.at.infoseek.co.jp/vmware/vfd.html				

Figure 27.4 Floppy Image Tools.

server. Before a floppy disk image can be mounted to a virtual machine, it must be created. A few good tools can perform this task.

RawWriteWin is a free, open source Win32 port of the older DOS rawrite program. It is used to capture an image of a physical floppy diskette into a floppy image file.

WinImage is an easy-to-use, shareware Windows application that creates floppy disk images from physical floppy diskettes or from ad-hoc files and directories. It can also edit and view the contents of existing floppy images. WinImage also works with ISO images and other nonstandard disk image formats.

There are too many other floppy imaging tools to mention here, but Jeremy Davis has an article hosted on fdos.org outlining many of them (http://www.fdos.org/ripcord/rewrite).

There is a free, open source program named Virtual Floppy Driver available on Ken Kato's Web site that can mount floppy images to a Windows operating system as a virtual floppy drive. It allows the contents of the floppy image to be accessed much like a physical floppy diskette including viewing files, editing files, creating new files, deleting files, etc.

See Figure 27.4 for additional information on the floppy image tools presented here.

ISO Image Tools

ISO images are used with most virtualization platforms as virtual CD-ROM or DVD-ROM drives mounted to a virtual machine. They can be used as bootable media, if the virtual BIOS supports bootable CD/DVD-ROM media, and as standard CD/DVD-ROMs, allowing data to be directly accessed by the guest operating system of virtual machines. There are several tools used to work with ISO images.

CDmage is a free, closed source tool for Windows platforms. It is especially useful when working with CD images of multiple types, including ISO images as well as the many CD image types created by other CD recording software.

Another handy free tool is Daemon Tools, a tool used to mount one or more ISO images as virtual CD/DVD-ROM devices within a Windows operating system. Daemon Tools can be used on any Windows installation, although it is generally not needed within a virtual machine, since most virtualization platforms can already mount ISO images to a virtual machine. Daemon Tools is more useful when used on workstation computers to quickly access data from ISO images in a read-only mode, and is treated as if the actual CD/DVD-ROM media were actually present.

IsoBuster is a commercial CD/DVD-ROM data recovery tool that can be used to extract very specific portions of data from a CD/DVD-ROM or an ISO image. It is very useful when used to extract the boot image from an existing bootable CD/DVD-ROM media for use in other ISO images.

ISO Recorder is a free, third-party Power Toy add-on for Microsoft Windows XP. It adds integrated CD-to-ISO image and CD-to-CD data transfer. This is a very quick tool used to make ISO images from existing CD/DVD-ROM media in Microsoft Windows XP only.

The Microsoft Virtual CD-ROM Control Panel for Windows XP is a free, unsupported tool from Microsoft. It adds the ability to mount ISO image files as virtual CD/DVD-ROM devices to Microsoft Windows XP only. This tool is similar to Daemon Tools.

The Linux command, mkisofs, is used to create ISO images in the Linux operating system. It is basically used to create an ISO image from a pre-built

ISO Image Tools				
Tool Name	**Type**	**License Type**	**Free**	**Hosted on SourceForge.net?**
CDmage	CLI	Commercial	No	No
http://cdmage.orcon.net.nz/frames.html				
Daemon Tools	CLI	N/A	Yes	No
http://www.daemon-tools.cc/dtcc/portal/portal.php				
IsoBuster	CLI	Commercial	No	No
http://www.smart-projects.net/isobuster/				
ISO Recorder	GUI	N/A	Yes	No
http://isorecorder.alexfeinman.com/isorecorder.htm				
Microsoft Virtual CD-ROM Control Panel	GUI	Commercial	Yes	No
http://download.microsoft.com/download/7/b/6/7b6abd84-7841-4978-96f5-bd58df02efa2/winxpvirtualcdcontrolpanel_21.exe				
mkisofs	CLI	N/A	Yes	No
The mkisofs command is included in most Linux and Unix operating systems.				
WinISO	GUI	Commercial	No	No
http://www.winiso.com				
WinImage	GUI	Shareware	No	No
http://www.winimage.com/winimage.htm				

Figure 27.5   ISO Image Tools.

directory of files. The Linux dd command can be used to create an ISO image from an existing CD/DVD-ROM media in a mounted device.

WinISO is a commercial Windows application designed to work with ISO images. It can create ISO images from files and directories using drag-and-drop from Windows Explorer, create ISO images from CD/DVD-ROM media, edit existing ISO images, extract or remove files from existing ISO images, and can perform BIN to ISO image conversions.

WinImage is a shareware Windows application that is similar to WinISO in functionality and features and it also adds the ability to work with floppy disk images. WinImage also supports many nonstandard disk image formats.

See Figure 27.5 for additional information on the ISO image tools presented here.

Image Cloning Tools

When cloning hard disk images, there are some tools that can be used to help give the cloned images a unique identity. Microsoft Sysprep is a free deployment tool from Microsoft used to prepare an OEM distribution of the Windows operating system for initial configuration and use by an end-user. In server virtualization, it can be used to change the SID and other unique values as well as help cleanup the operating system for initial use after cloning an image.

NewSID is a free, open source tool from Sysinternals, written by Mark Russinovich and Bryce Cogswell. It is used, either interactively or through command-line, to change the Windows SID and hostname values. It can generate a new, random SID or use a specified SID value.

See Figure 27.6 for more information on the image cloning tools presented here

Image Migration / P2V Tools

When working with server virtualization, it is often useful to be able to convert images from one virtualization platform to another (V2V) or even convert a physical server into a virtual machine without having to manually rebuild

Image Cloning Tools				
Tool Name	**Type**	**License Type**	**Free**	**Hosted on SourceForge.net?**
Microsoft Sysprep	GUI	Commercial	No	No
http://www.microsoft.com/downloads/details.aspx?familyid=A34EDCF2-EBFD-4F99-BBC4-E93154C332D6&displaylang=en				
Sysinternals NewSID	GUI/CLI	Open Source	Yes	No
http://www.sysinternals.com/ntw2k/source/newsid.shtml				

Figure 27.6   Image Cloning Tools.

the server (P2V). There are several commercial tools designed to perform these tasks.

The HP ProLiant Essentials Server Migration Pack available from Hewlett Packard is designed to help simply P2V and V2V conversions supporting VMware ESX Server, VMware GSX Server, and Microsoft Virtual Server. It is a commercial product and has been designed to be used in conjunction with HP ProLiant servers and HP Systems Insight Manager.

Leostream provides a commercial P2V conversion product named Leostream P>V Direct that can convert a running Microsoft Windows-based server into a virtual server without the need to reboot the system. The Leostream P>V Direct product supports VMware ESX Server, GSX Server, and Workstation as well as Microsoft Virtual Server platforms.

Microsoft offers a free P2V tool named Virtual Server 2005 Migration Toolkit designed to convert a physical server running supported Microsoft guest operating systems into a Microsoft Virtual Server–compatible virtual machine.

Platespin offers a commercial product, Platespin PowerConvert. This application is designed to fully automate anywhere-to-anywhere conversions between physical servers, virtual machines, and disk image archives. The product, previously known as Platespin PowerP2V, has evolved into a suite of three products:

- PowerConvert Universal
- PowerConvert for Consolidation
- PowerConvert for Recovery

PowerConvert handles conversions from heterogeneous physical hardware environments and most major virtualization platforms.

Image Migration / P2V Tools				
Tool Name	Type	License Type	Free	Hosted on SourceForge.net?
HP ProLiant Essentials Server Migration Pack	GUI	Commercial	No	No
http://h18004.www1.hp.com/products/servers/proliantessentials/valuepack/smp/				
Leostream P>V Direct	GUI	Commercial	No	No
http://www.leostream.com				
Microsoft Virtual Server 2005 Migration Toolkit	GUI	Commercial	Yes	No
http://www.microsoft.com/windowsserversystem/virtualserver/evaluation/vsmt.mspx				
Platespin PowerConvert	GUI	Commercial	No	No
http://www.platespin.com/products/PowerConvertMain.aspx				
VMware P2V Assistant	GUI	Commercial	No	No
http://www.vmware.com/products/p2v/				
VMware Virtual Machine Importer	GUI	Commercial	Yes	No
http://www.vmware.com/download/ws/				

Figure 27.7 Image Migration / P2V Tools.

VMware offers a commercial tool named VMware P2V Assistant. It is designed to perform P2V conversions of servers running supported Microsoft Windows operating system into VMware ESX Server, VMware GSX Server, or VMware Workstation virtual machine images. VMware also offers specialized training and services offerings along with the P2V Assistant product.

VMware also offers a free tool, VMware Virtual Machine Importer. This tool simplifies V2V conversions of Microsoft Virtual Server or Microsoft Virtual PC images into VMware-compatible virtual machine images.

See Figure 27.7 for more information on the image migration and P2V tools presented here.

Management and Monitoring Tools

Server virtualization platforms generally include at least one management interface that is used to view system status and create and edit host and virtual machine settings. These management interfaces are designed for use on a single host server and a single server virtualization platform, giving a limited view of the overall server virtualization deployment. There are many commercial software products available that provide a centralized management or automation platform for a multi-host, enterprise server virtualization deployment (see Figure 27.8).

Leostream VirtualController, Platespin Operations Management Center, and VMware VirtualCenter are three very similar server virtualization management products. They all perform very similar roles and are, for the most part, competing products in the market. Generally, these products all perform similar centralized monitoring and management of virtual machines across many host servers, virtualization host servers, template images, and provisioning. Similarly,

Management and Monitoring Tools				
Tool Name	**Type**	**License Type**	**Free**	**Hosted on SourceForge.net?**
Leostream VirtualController	GUI	Commercial	No	No
http://www.leostream.com				
MOM 2005 Management Pack for Virtual Server	GUI	Commercial	No	No
http://www.microsoft.com/downloads/details.aspx?FamilyId=B8BBF08F-134A-46CE-9D63-FB7EF5258059&displaylang=en				
Platespin Operations Management Center	GUI	Commercial	No	No
http://www.platespin.com/products/POMC.aspx				
Platespin PowerRecon	GUI	Commercial	No	No
http://www.platespin.com/Products/PowerRecon.aspx				
VMware VirtualCenter	GUI	Commercial	No	No
http://www.vmware.com/products/vmanage/vc_features.html				

Figure 27.8   Management and Monitoring Tools.

they all have one or more centralized dashboard-type views of the overall system. The biggest differentiators between these products are that while Leostream and Platespin are considered third-party products, they do provide multi-server virtualization platform support including support for Microsoft Virtual Server, VMware ESX Server, and VMware GSX Server. VMware VirtualCenter on the other hand is a highly-integrated offering made available directly from the virtualization platform vendor, but it only supports VMware server virtualization products. All of these products use a centralized server and distributed management agents within the host servers and/or virtual machines.

The Microsoft Operations Manager 2005 Management Pack for Virtual Server is an add-on for Microsoft's MOM server monitoring solution. This add-on updates MOM with capabilities of monitoring the performance and availability of Microsoft Virtual Server virtual machines. Although this product does not offer any management capabilities and only works with Microsoft's Virtual Server platform, it is a supported product offering directly from the Virtual Server platform vendor that extends the existing investment in MOM.

Another product offering from Platespin, Platespin PowerRecon, offers a consolidated vault of performance data that can be collected from any Windows-based server, including physical servers, host servers, and virtual machines. It is used in the long-term analysis of overall system performance and compliments the other products described in this section. One of its primary uses is to monitor the performance of physical servers to discover good candidates for migration from physical servers to virtual machines in server consolidation projects.

Single User Virtualization Platforms

Single user, workstation-class virtualization product offerings from Microsoft and VMware are great tools that can be used in conjunction with server virtualization (see Figure 27.9). Microsoft's Virtual PC and VMware's VMware Workstation are designed for use on a single desktop or laptop computer, generally supporting one or two virtual machines powered on at a time. They can be used by authors of server images for those organizations on a budget or can be used to quickly and independently test ideas for use in server images. Images cre-

Single User Virtualization Platforms				
Tool Name	Type	License Type	Free	Hosted on SourceForge.net?
Microsoft VirtualPC 2004	GUI	Commercial	No	No
http://www.microsoft.com/windows/virtualpc/default.mspx				
VMware Workstation 5	GUI	Commercial	No	No
http://www.vmware.com/products/desktop/ws_features.html				

Figure 27.9   Single User Virtualization Platforms.

ated with Microsoft's Virtual PC can be converted into Microsoft Virtual Server images and VMware Workstation images can be converted into VMware ESX Server or VMware GSX Server images with minimal effort.

VMware Player

During VMware's VMworld 2005 conference held in Las Vegas, Nevada, VMware released a new, free tool named VMware Player. VMware Player is a desktop application that can run virtual machines created with the following platforms:

- VMware ESX Server
- VMware GSX Server
- VMware Workstation
- Microsoft Virtual PC
- Microsoft Virtual Server
- Symantec LiveState Recovery disk

VMware Player can run 32-bit and 64-bit virtual machines simultaneously, allows full access to host PC devices, has configurable networking support, and other integrated features including copy and paste as well as Google search capabilities. Although it does not allow users to create new virtual machines, it does allow users to use existing virtual machines without requiring a full virtualization platform. This allows virtual machines to be shared freely. VMware Player is available as a free download for both Windows and Linux host PC platforms at http://www.vmware.com/products/player.

Other Tools

This section covers some other useful miscellaneous products and tools available for working with server virtualization projects and related tasks (see Figure 27.10).

Cygwin is a Linux-like environment for Windows-based operating systems. It provides Windows ports of many generally available Linux commands and tools that can be accessed through the Cygwin command-line shell. Although Cygwin does not run Linux programs under Windows, it can be effectively used to work with Linux files such as rpm and tar files or when a similar capability is needed, such as the dd command.

Sysinternals is a freeware site sponsored by Winternals that provides many very useful free tools and utilities not available elsewhere. Many of these free tools are available along with source code. NewSID, covered in the Image Cloning Tools section above, is available from this site. Another very useful tool available from the Sysinternals site is WinObj. The WinObj tool allows a visual view of the Windows Object Manager namespace. It can be used in conjunction with

Other Tools				
Tool Name	**Type**	**License Type**	**Free**	**Hosted on SourceForge.net?**
Cygwin	CLI	Open Source	Yes	No
http://www.cygwin.com				
Sysinternals WinObj	GUI	N/A	Yes	No
http://www.sysinternals.com/ntw2k/freeware/winobj.shtml				
vmktree	GUI	N/A	Yes	No
http://tihlde.org/~larstr/vmktree				
VMware VMotion	CLI	Commercial	No	No
http://www.vmware.com/products/vmanage/vc_features.html#vmotion				
VMware Virtual Infrastructure SDK Package	GUI	Commercial	Yes	No
http://www.vmware.com/support/developer				
VMware Virtual SMP	GUI	Commercial	No	No
http://www.vmware.com/products/server/vsmp_features.html				

Figure 27.10 Other Tools.

tools such as the Linux dd command (also available under Cygwin for Windows) and the VDK tool (see Disk Tools above) in order to perform advanced image conversions such as converting an virtual machine disk image from IDE to SCSI or when performing V2V tasks, converting a virtual machine image from one virtualization platform to another.

Vmktree is a free Web-based tool for use with VMware ESX Server 2.0 and higher. It works in conjunction with VMware ESX Server's vmkusage performance monitoring package to provide useful, Web-based graphs of performance data.

VMware offers a technology named VMotion™ that works with VMware ESX Server and SAN storage technologies. VMotion allows live virtual machines to be moved from one ESX host server to another without any downtime, allowing enhanced support for maintenance and fail-over scenarios.

The VMware Virtual Infrastructure SDK package is a free offering that allows developers to easily automate VMware's virtual infrastructure through the VMware VirtualCenter Web Service interface. This SDK is dependent upon VMware VirtualCenter and can be used to control and manage data from VMware ESX and GSX host servers and virtual machines.

VMware also offers an add-on for VMware ESX Server named Virtual SMP. Virtual SMP allows virtual machines hosted on the VMware ESX Server platform to be configured with up to two virtual processors. When used on VMware ESX host servers that have two or more processors, virtual machines with two enabled virtual processors are able to function with real symmetric multiprocessing (SMP), enabling a performance boost for multi-threaded, resource intensive applications. In the future, it is likely that VMware will extend Virtual SMP to handle more than two virtual processors, such as adding support for either two-way or four-way virtual machines.

Summary

Although most server virtualization platforms provide many features, tools, and utilities to work with the platform's technologies, there are many other useful tools available that provide alternate and/or extended capabilities to those working with server virtualization technologies. The tools covered in this chapter in no way represent all useful commercial, shareware or free tools, utilities, or products. As the landscape of server virtualization evolves, many more tools will likely be created that will extend the capabilities available today. For an updated list of available tools and links, please visit http://www.vmbook.info.

Chapter 28

Related Products and Open Source Projects

There are several other virtualization technologies to be aware of. These products and projects touch on the new wave of virtualization technologies that could be taking hold over the next two or three years. This chapter looks at the other commercial products available in the virtualization platform space and the open source efforts to provide virtualization platforms. Each product or project has its own unique combination of strengths and weaknesses. This chapter will explain what each product does and what capabilities it provides.

Commercial

The commercial products available today take many unique views as to how virtualization will change the enterprise data center of tomorrow. Each of these solutions was created to solve a specific need originally and has evolved to attempt to address many other needs as well. Some of these have begun to win broader market space and adoption, whereas others have been unable to achieve much traction in the marketplace.

Cassat

Cassat's (http://www.cassatt.com) Collage product provides an automation mechanism for delivering operating system images, applications (e.g., Oracle, Java Virtual Machines, and Web servers) out to bare metal servers (see Figure 28.1). This is accomplished through a separate management networking scheme that also allows for the second path to act as a backup pathway for access. Collage

**Figure 28.1
Cassat.**

requires separate switches with VLAN support and storage available to the network (such as NAS-based solutions).

At the heart of the Collage system are controller nodes. These nodes provide the interfaces and coordination of all services that Collage initiates. Collage leverages several "out-of-band" monitoring methods to get service level capabilities including SNMP, JMX, and MJ4. This allows for agentless monitoring of systems. This system provides a great deal of flexibility and management by leveraging the concept of pools of resources for management, "Golden Images" for provisioning, and basic, low-level monitoring mechanisms.

The Collage solution provides virtualization through abstraction by removing hardware dependencies from the management aspect. This can be considered both a strength and a weakness. The strength of "abstraction through removal" is that there are no additional agent components introduced to the hardware of software stacks. This eliminates customer fears that instabilities in the system may have been introduced by the solution. The weakness of this solution is that the expectation is that a unique operating system image be created for each hardware profile (unique hardware configuration) that exists on the network. This solution is similar to a more powerful Symantec Ghost-based solution.

Parallels

In December of 2005, another commercially available virtualization platform entered the market. Parallels, Inc. (http://www.parallels.com) introduced Parallels Workstation 2.0, a hypervisor-powered desktop virtualization solution. Developed by a privately held software company in Herndon, Virginia, the team has been focused on virtualization technologies since 1999. Parallels Workstation 2.0 is the company's desktop virtualization platform, which directly competes with VMware Workstation and Microsoft Virtual PC.

Since the product was released at the end of 2005, it has an uphill battle to compete with products that have been out for over six years. However, the platform does offer some interesting and significant benefits to try and break into the desktop virtualization market. A key positioning strength is the product's pricing point. When the platform was announced, the company introduced it with an industry-leading price of $49. But more to the point is the company's technology and their broad guest operating system support. The product's lightweight hypervisor inserts a thin layer of software between the physical hardware of the machine and the primary operating system that directly controls some hardware profiles and resources. Their technology also leverages the virtualization instructions set provided by Intel's Virtualization Technology (VT) architecture. With the lightweight hypervisor and by leveraging Intel VT, Parallels is able to improve virtual machine stability, reliability, and performance.

Parallels supports a broad range of guest operating systems including a wide range of Microsoft desktop operating systems (Microsoft DOS 6.22, Microsoft Windows 3.1 through Windows XP), Microsoft server operating systems (Microsoft Windows NT Server 4.0 SP6 through Microsoft Windows 2003 Server), multiple Linux operating systems (including distributions from Debian, Fedora, FreeBSD, Mandriva, Red Hat, and SUSE), as well as multiple operating systems from the OS/2 and eComStation family.

Like VMware, Parallels supports multiple host operating systems from Microsoft and various Linux distributions, giving it a wider distribution channel. The company is currently working on a server-class virtualization product and plans to have it ready in 2006.

Serenity Virtual Station (SVISTA)

The Serenity Virtual Station (http://www.serenityvirtual.com) solution was originally developed to enhance Serenity's flagship product known as eComStation (see Figure 28.2). This solution provided a type of cross platform API instead of

Figure 28.2 Serenity Virtual Station.

virtualization, for IBM OS/2-based operating systems, allowing them to provide compatibility with more current Microsoft Windows-based applications while still providing IBM OS/2 application support. IBM OS/2 is still in use in some financial institutions and in large concentrations in Europe. For this reason, Serenity continued to build upon eComStation and later out of the need to future proof eComStation, created Virtual Station.

Virtual Station provides many of the features found in VMware Workstation and Microsoft Virtual PC. The virtualization layer of Virtual Station is unique and does provide the ability to run on several host operating systems including Linux, FreeBSD, Microsoft Windows, and IBM OS/2 eComStation. This is powerful in that a virtual machine created on any one of these supported host platforms can be used by Virtual Station running on any of the other supported host platforms. The weakness of Virtual Station virtual machines are that they are not quite as performant as its competitors' virtualization solutions, such as VMware Workstation.

Virtual Iron (VFe)

Virtual Iron (http://www.virtualiron.com) is a newcomer to the virtualization space having only recently appeared on the market (see Figure 28.3) . The Virtual Iron solution appears to provide a unique and powerful solution leveraging a Linux layer and several virtualization techniques. This allows VFe (the present product name) to present hardware resources from many separate machines as a single machine to the applications that run on top of the platform. This approach allows for simplification of management and the ability to alter the resources of a virtual machine without the need to reboot.

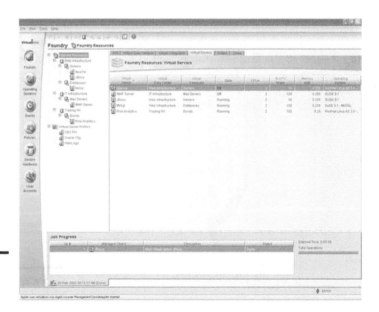

**Figure 28.3
Virtual Iron
(VFe).**

VFe provides a great deal of flexibility in being able to present up to a virtual machine comprising of up to 16 processors with vast amounts of memory and disk resources. VFe also provides fine-grained control over network and I/O resources. The first of two limitations is that VFe can only run Linux applications and those applications must be built to run on either Red Hat or Novell/SUSE. The second limitation is that a very high-speed interconnect between all the standard x86 servers must be used. The interconnect used is Infiniband, which is not a ubiquitous technology at present and, until 10Gbit Ethernet becomes mainstream, the actual price to implement this solution in a average data center is up for grabs. VFe appears to have the same current limitations as the Xen project in that it is only capable of running Linux-based guest operating systems.

Win4Lin

Win4Lin Pro (http://www.win4lin.com) was originally developed by NeTraverse and was later acquired by a company named Win4Lin, which hired all of the NeTraverse staff. The Win4Lin Pro product (see Figure 28.4) is based on several proprietary efforts originally by NeTraverse and the QEMU open source project. Win4Lin Pro provides a thin sharing layer between the underlying Linux-based operating system and the Microsoft Windows-based operating system that runs on top of it. Win4Lin Pro is effectively translating the hardware that Linux sees and is presenting it in a user process as available hardware to the Microsoft Windows instance. Each user on the Linux system is allocated a complete installation of the Microsoft Windows operating system.

There are several performance advantages to this type of implementation in that it is very thin, while still providing some degree of isolation between Windows and the host operating system and each individual user. Because there is no real hypervisor operating in this implementation, it performs well. On the

Figure 28.4 Win4Lin.

other hand, it is far more prone to stability and compatibility problems than other forms of virtualization.

Open Source Efforts

There are several open source community projects that implement abstraction, emulation, isolation, and virtualization technologies. Some of the more popular of these projects are presented here.

BOCHS

BOCHS (http://bochs.sourceforge.net) is a virtual machine technology that is open source and has been around for a long time. BOCHS provides an entire virtual hardware layer and can be run on Linux, BSD, Windows, Mac, BeOS, and other operating systems (see Figure 28.5). The BOCHS hardware layer is unique in that it allows for the selection of the type and quantity (up to 16) of processors to emulate, regardless of the host machine's physical processor type or quantity. This is unlike any of the other hardware virtualization solutions that do not perform full processor emulation, but rely on pass-through techniques to the physical hardware layer. This feature does impose a serious lack of production-quality performance, a price to pay for the added flexibility.

BOCHS provides support for the following emulated processors: 80386, 80486, Pentium, Pentium Pro, and AMD64 CPU. It also Includes optional support of MMX, SSE, SSE2, and 3DNow! extended processor instructions. This is done through a binary translation engine; the ability to add support for other virtual processors is already in place. This flexibility leads the way to running virtually any x86-based operating system as a guest.

Figure 28.5
BOCHS.

The core strength of the way that BOCHS has been developed is that it has been written in C++. By doing this, Kevin Lawton, the original author of BOCHS, laid down a great deal of portability. There is usually a price for portability and this case is no exception. BOCHS does not provide a high-performance platform, which does not make it a good candidate for the enterprise. BOCHS delivers poor performance from nearly all aspects; however the fact that it can run almost any x86 operating system may outweigh the poor performance in certain situations.

Applications where BOCHS may be an excellent solution include support of very old operating systems that require outdated legacy hardware or development environments that are used for things such as hardware device driver debugging, simulation of hardware or operating system development. The ability to add custom virtual hardware monitoring hooks into the source code is something that may be incredibly valuable. Another incredible feature is the ability to simulate certain events, such as hardware faults occurring through custom code. This will provide information that would be very difficult and time consuming if it was attempted with physical hardware.

All in all, BOCHS is a project to watch as it is being advanced daily and is making considerable strides in adding additional functionality and options.

QEMU

The QEMU (http://fabrice.bellard.free.fr/qemu) project is an open source emulator providing the ability to run on a wide variety of platforms by doing dynamic translation of native CPU instructions (see Figure 28.6). The dynamic translation enables QEMU to provide a fast and efficient emulation by breaking down the processor instructions into small blocks of atomic instructions. These instructions are then processed, cached in a buffer, and then the responses returned as if the native processor had acted upon them. This project may not

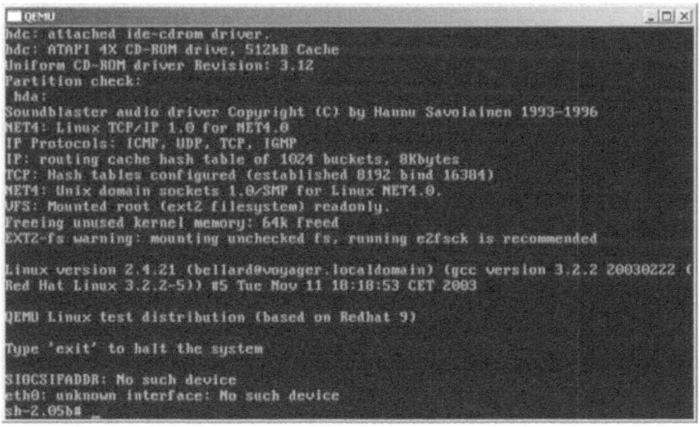

Figure 28.6
QEMU.

seem to fall into the virtualization camp; however there are two outside factors that have been taken into consideration.

The first factor is that additional work has been done to speed up the performance of QEMU in an attempt to match the speed and performance of several of the commercial products available. The heart of this project is called the QEMU Accelerator Module and it is an additional virtualization layer. This virtualization layer provides a significant performance increases and brings QEMU into the fold as a player in the virtualization space. This also shows that the combination of technologies from several of these sources can provide complementary benefits if implemented properly.

The second factor, which builds on the first, is the fact that Win4Lin Pro also leverages the same QEMU Accelerator Module that the QEMU project uses. This shows that even a thin virtualization layer can have multiple uses in the commercial space. It is important to note that the QEMU Accelerator Module is given away free to individuals, but is actually proprietary or closed source. Developed by Fabrice Bellard in France, the author of QEMU, Bellard licensed the QEMU Accelerator to Win4Lin and is at present willing to license the technology to other commercial entities based on negotiated terms.

The QEMU Accelerator Module actually passes through many of the commands that are normally dynamically translated. This provides the same strength and similar technical implementations to that of the VMware and Microsoft virtualization solutions. The weakness of this solution is the lack of support by the commercial vendors and the mixed compatibility depending on what host and guest operating system is used.

User-Mode Linux and VServer

User-Mode Linux (http://user-mode-linux.sourceforge.net) and VServer (http://linux-vserver.org) are more of isolation mechanisms than complete computer isolation style virtualization. They simply offer a way to install and protect several different distribution instances of Linux from each other. Both provide equivalent functionality and performance. The advantage is packing on a great deal of Linux installations onto a single server, which is incredibly advantageous for entities such as hosting providers. The disadvantages are primarily the inability to run Microsoft Windows-based operating systems or other operating systems not Linux-based. Another disadvantage is the requirement that all versions of Linux must support the native hardware configuration and processor to run and operate properly.

Xen

The Xen (http://www.cl.cam.ac.uk/Research/SRG/netos/xen) project started out at Cambridge University in the UK (see Figure 28.7). Xen is a hypervisor-

```
root@oss-0:~                                           _ □ ✕
Starting sshd.
sysctl: top level name 'hw' in 'hw.disknames' is invalid
Starting inetd.
Tue Nov  2 16:36:01 UTC 2004

NetBSD/i386 (demo-nb) (console)

login: root
Password:
Login incorrect
login:
login: root
Password:
Last login: Tue Oct 19 09:49:21 2004 on console
Nov  2 16:48:37 demo-nb login: ROOT LOGIN (root) ON console
Copyright (c) 1996, 1997, 1998, 1999, 2000, 2001, 2002, 2003, 2004
    The NetBSD Foundation, Inc.  All rights reserved.
Copyright (c) 1982, 1986, 1989, 1991, 1993
    The Regents of the University of California.  All rights reserved.

Nov  2 16:48:37 demo-nb login: ROOT LOGIN (root) ON console
NetBSD ?.? (UNKNOWN)

Welcome to NetBSD!
```

Figure 28.7   Xen.

based technology, otherwise known as a Virtual Machine Monitor (VMM). Like VMware's ESX Server, Xen runs on the bare metal hardware with no supporting operating system beneath it. Unlike VMware's ESX Server however, Xen uses a solution called paravirtualization.

Paravirtualization differentiates itself from standard virtualization in that instead of adjusting the virtualization platform to support different guest operating systems and their behaviors (specifically the processor instructions they invoke), the guest operating systems themselves are altered to support the virtualization platform beneath them. There are several advantages to this approach; the first is the ability to get at or near physical hardware performance inside of the virtual machines themselves. The second is the rapid portability that this provides—there are no special circumstances to deal with, all guests operate the same. The downside is also pretty significant. Because of its need for changes to the guest operating system, it can only support Linux and BSD variants at this time. There are other ports taking place, however the major guest operating system, Microsoft Windows, cannot be altered in this fashion because it is closed source.

Xen is planning to offer many new capabilities in their new release including full SMP support, live virtual machine migrations, scalability to 8TB of memory, performance improvements, and support for more QoS (Quality of Service) functions. Xen is poised to become a major player in the virtualization space. To date Xen has been able to also leverage the work of several other projects including BOCHS and QEMU. By leveraging these technologies, Xen has been able to implement many performance optimizations already created by these two projects.

Summary

There are many virtualization solutions available in both the commercial and open source areas, however each has limitations. If consideration is being given to one of these solutions over the two standards, VMware and Microsoft's virtualization solutions, then it is important to learn as much as possible through thorough investigation, research, and testing, before making any decisions. The most promising solutions on the commercial side are Win4Lin and Virtual Iron, however as of today, Virtual Iron VFe appears to be getting the most press although it has not been released. Win4Lin Pro is released and has been around for a while and is generally not well known. The most promising solutions on the open source side are BOCHS, QEMU, and Xen. Xen has a commercial aspect through a newly funded company named Xen Source that appears to have a chance at doing for Xen what Red Hat has done for Linux.

All of these solutions are unsupported by Microsoft as of this time. Therefore it is not recommended that any of these virtualization solutions listed above be used for a production data center to run Microsoft Windows-based guest operating systems. Microsoft will generally not provide any support for its operating systems running in these virtual machines unless the problem can be reproduced on a physical server.

Chapter 29

Other Virtualization Resources

In addition to the products and projects described in chapter 28 and throughout the book, there are also some third-party products and services, both large and small, available to address niche areas of server virtualization. This chapter provides a brief look at the resources provided by the major virtualization vendors along with other resources being made available through the Internet that deal with virtualization in one form or another.

Product Vendor Resources

Microsoft

http://www.microsoft.com/windowsserversystem/virtualserver/default.mspx
The Microsoft Virtual Server 2005 R2 Web page provides some of the most up-to-date information on the product (see Figure 29.1). It offers a number of relevant technical links along with links to numerous resource files. Microsoft provides many different ways to research and find answers to Microsoft Virtual Server 2005 R2 technical questions. Newsgroup support, a listing of the most frequently asked questions (FAQs), a number of product and technical white papers on the product, Web casts, online documentation and downloads that include product updates and add-on software are also provided.

There are also several other valuable links created from Microsoft insiders on their own personal blogs. These blogs represent a rich source of technical information around Virtual Server. It should be noted that this resource is not officially sanctioned by Microsoft. Many of these blog links can be found at http://www.vmbook.info/links.

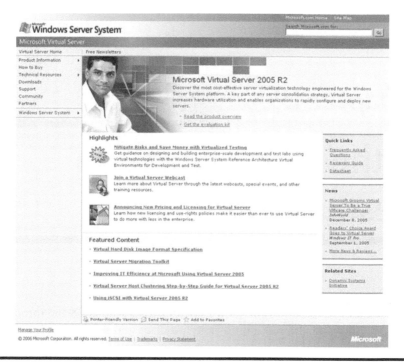

Figure 29.1   Microsoft.

VMware

http://www.vmware.com/

The VMware Web site provides a tremendous amount of resources relating to the various product offerings made by VMware (see Figure 29.2). They offer news and events that customers of their products will more than likely be interested in hearing about. They also offer the latest updates and security patches for all of their products in a download section. But perhaps the most important area on VMware's Web site is the VMware Technology Network (VMTN) page. This technical and community resource page provides links to documentation, FAQs, technical resources in the form of news and white papers, and developer resources in the form of code and SDK packages. VMware is also a big proponent for information sharing. The VMTN page provides for a searchable knowledge base as well as a discussion forum where users are able to post questions and receive answers from other users as well as from VMware employees. This resource is probably the most likely place to find answers to VMware product questions. Unfortunately, there can also be erroneous information posted by end users that must be waded through in order to find the correct answer to the question.

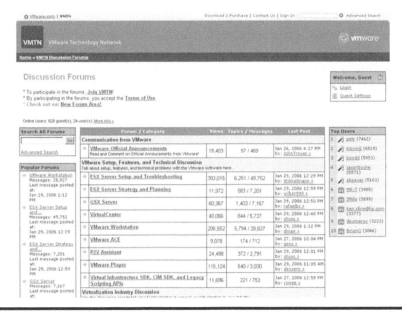

Figure 29.2   VMware.

Xen

http://www.cl.cam.ac.uk/Research/SRG/netos/xen/
Xen is an open-source virtualization project that was created at the University of Cambridge. The Cambridge Web site makes a number of resources available for the product (see Figure 29.3). It offers the standard documentation and FAQ's for the product, along with source code, and papers and presentations describing Xen's design and architecture. Because the project is open-source, there are already numerous user-owned Web sites covering the product and the support

Figure 29.3   Xen.

community is quickly growing with the incorporation of Xen's paravirtualization technology into Red Hat Linux, SUSE, and other operating system vendors' technology stacks. A simple Google of "Xen virtualization" will unveil a plethora of information and resources covering the product. For an in-depth listing of links and resources related to Xen, visit http://www.vmbook.info/links.

Computer Associates

http://www.ca.com/
Computer Associates offers virtualization integration into their Unicenter Network and Systems Management (Unicenter NSM) package (see Figure 29.4). Unicenter NSM can now monitor the health and availability of virtual machines running on VMware and Microsoft Virtual Server 2005. The product also provides such features as policy-based automation, root-cause analysis, reporting, and role-specific visualization. This software tool would appeal to current users of the Unicenter operations management software that are currently looking to implement server virtualization into their organization.

Figure 29.4   Computer Associates.

Dunes

http://www.dunes.ch/
Dunes enables IT personnel to perform what they do best by capturing and automating repetitive, tedious, and error-prone tasks. The software solution they provide offers a graphical interface used to program various operations into a virtual infrastructure (see Figure 29.5). Dunes Virtual Service Orchestrator (Dunes VS-O) is a virtual server software solution for VMware VirtualCenter and Microsoft Virtual Server 2005. Dunes VS-O is about capturing best practices and business policies to help make the data center more efficient and adaptive to changing business practices. By utilizing one of their other products, Dunes VS-M, a Microsoft Virtual Server environment can be centrally managed from a single console. Dunes VS-M gives a logical representation of the entire

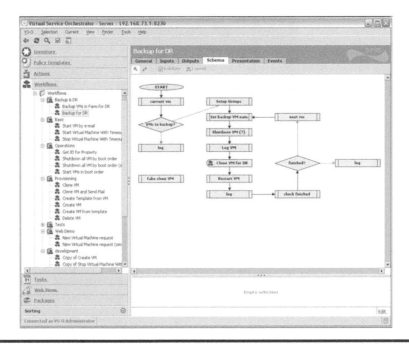

Figure 29.5   Dunes.

Microsoft Virtual Server infrastructure. The product is easily deployed without the need for agents being required on the host servers. Both products are available for installation on a Windows operating system.

IBM

http://www.ibm.com/

IBM is offering several solutions around virtualization including the IBM Virtual Machine Manager and the IBM Virtualization Engine Suite (see Figure 29.6). The IBM Virtual Machine Manager (VMM) is an extension to IBM Director that provides management of both physical and virtual machines all from a single console. VMM allows for the management of both VMware ESX Server and Microsoft Virtual Server 2005 environments using IBM Director. To create an even more advanced virtual machine management environment, VMM can also integrate VMware VirtualCenter with IBM Director. Another product offering, the IBM Virtualization Engine, enables individual distributed resources across the enterprise to function cohesively as a single pool or entity. The product allows for greater efficiency when accessing and managing resources across the organization. IBM is clearly hedging its bets by diversifying and spreading their risk across multiple technologies. They have strategically aligned themselves with most of the major virtualization platform vendors, including:

Figure 29.6   IBM.

Microsoft, VMware, and Xen. IBM is still one of the few companies around that offers a complete virtualization solution including hardware (server and storage), software, and services.

Leostream

http://www.leostream.com/
Leostream is a vendor agnostic virtualization management software company (see Figure 29.7). Leostream's Virtual Host Desktop Controller is a management product that attempts to solve a wide range of problems facing today's data centers: quality assurance, support, server consolidation, and disaster recovery. It contains features such as: performance monitoring and reporting, policy-based access control, fail-over for virtual and physical machines, and disaster recovery. The product manages virtual servers running under VMware ESX Server, VMware GSX Server for Windows, and Microsoft Virtual Server 2005 and is also compatible with VMware VirtualCenter. Additionally, Leostream offers its own version of P2V aptly named P>V Direct 2.0. Its claim to fame is the ability to perform a conversion directly from a running Windows server to a virtual server without the need for a CD, floppy disk, or a reboot. Its biggest drawback—it

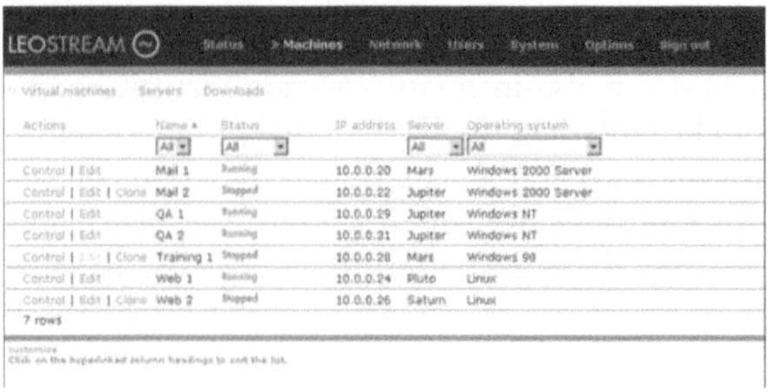

Figure 29.7   Leostream.

Figure 29.8   Platespin.

can only convert Microsoft Windows operating systems so there is no support for Linux.

Platespin

http://www.platespin.com/
Platespin currently has several virtualization products on the market that attempt to bring optimization to the IT industry and help to bring automation to the data center (see Figure 29.8). PowerConvert is a utility that attempts to provide 100 percent automated conversions between physical and virtual machines running either a Windows or Linux operating system. They also offer the Platespin Operations Management Center, a comprehensive physical and virtual server management solution. The product offers automated discovery, provisioning, management, and monitoring all from a single console. To help round out their product offering, they present the PowerRecon product, a resource measurement, data collection, and analysis tool designed to help a data center plan for server consolidation projects. According to Platespin, there have already been over 600 companies that have used their PowerConvert product. This is significant in that it not only shows that the product has gained traction in the marketplace and has matured rapidly, but that the marketplace is also quickly adopting virtualization as a platform.

Surgient

http://www.surgient.com/
As an early adopter of server virtualization, Surgient was a pioneering company becoming one of, if not, the first companies to leverage virtualization as an API

Figure 29.9   Surgient.

platform for a software solution (see Figure 29.9). Surgient provides on-demand applications that enable companies to increase the effectiveness of their direct sales, online marketing, technical training, and QA/Verification processes. Surgient has created its own virtualization vendor agnostic management interface that not only provides a comprehensive management solution, but when packaged with its application offerings, it enables the use of distributed enterprise application environments by any user, on-demand, from anywhere at anytime. It eliminates the complexities of hardware configuration and software environment provisioning. Surgient is able to offer its products to its customers in the form of a hosted solution as well as a licensed package.

Resources and Web Links

About Virtualization

http://www.about-virtualization.com/
Similar to Virtualization.info, this Web site attempts to cover all the latest news and information about virtualization (see Figure 29.10). The Web site provides an easy to read layout covering its news articles, and it also provides a number of links to items such as: white papers, interviews, product updates and patches, slide shows, and tools and utilities. A user forum is also provided using the popular phpBB software. Bloggers with virtualization knowledge and experience are welcomed to apply to provide content to the site.

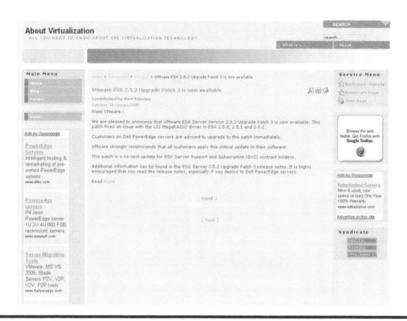

Figure 29.10   About Virtualization.

ExtremeVM.com

http://www.extremevm.com/
Founded in 2004 and officially launched in 2006, ExtremeVM.com is a community-oriented virtualization magazine created by virtualization enthusiasts for virtualization enthusiasts (see Figure 29.11). It sports a clean, easy-to-read design and offers articles, aggregated virtualization industry news, and community resources. It is an online-only magazine focused on fostering community involvement in the development of new ideas, uses, and applications for all virtualization technologies, including application virtualization, desktop virtualization, network virtualization, server virtualization, storage virtualization.

The MiniMe Project

http://www.vmts.net/minime.htm
This ambitious project is currently downloadable as a Beta release (see Figure 29.12). The project's goal is to provide a windows GUI management console that allows the management of VMware ESX, GSX and Microsoft Virtual Server through a single unified interface. The project is attempting to provide more sophistication than just a simple management interface. A current list of features includes: hot backup and restore, standby clustering, dynamic REDO creation,

Figure 29.11   ExtremeVM.com.

detailed guest configuration, and support for various authentication services such as LDAP, Active Directory, and SMB. The author is currently accepting feature requests and comments about the project.

Virtualization.info

http://www.virtualization.info/
This blog site is a great place to obtain aggregated news on virtualization (see Figure 29.13). It offers a very nice design that is easy-to-read and has a pleasant look-and-feel that is more unique than typical blog sites. To its credit, the site also offers numerous links to other Web sites, blogs and wikis that also offer news and information that pertains to virtualization. The Web site is presently operated by its creator, Alessandro Perilli.

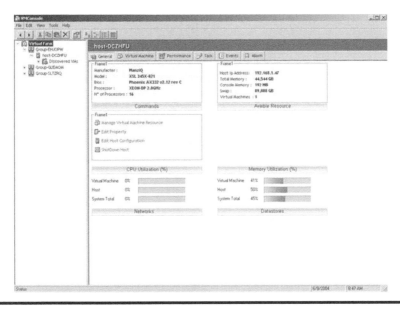

Figure 29.12 The MiniMe Project.

Figure 29.13 Virtualization.info.

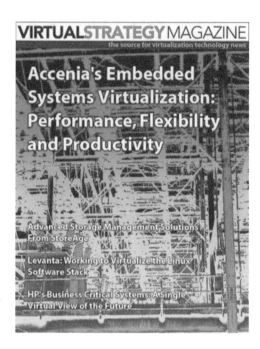

Figure 29.14 Virtual Strategy Magazine.

Virtual Strategy Magazine

http://www.virtual-strategy.com/

This is an online-only technical and news magazine that provides its readers with news and technical information that focuses solely on virtualization (see Figure 29.14). In addition to providing news, the magazine also provides technical tips, real-world experiences from virtualization users, and interviews with many key individuals in the virtualization field. For members of the Web site, free teleconferences and Web seminars are occasionally offered.

VMbook.info

http://www.vmbook.info/

VMbook.info is the official Web site supporting this book, Advanced Server Virtualization, VMware and Microsoft Platforms in the Virtual Data Center. Any errata, additional supporting materials, and resources for this book will be posted on the Web site. The Web site can also be used to contact the authors, if necessary, and provide any direct feedback.

VMware's Back

http://chitchat.at.infoseek.co.jp/vmware/

This Web site is operated by Ken Kato and provides a set of tools that Kato himself has written (see Figure 29.15). Two of the more popular downloads include

Figure 29.15   VMware's Back.

the Virtual Disk Driver and the Virtual Floppy Driver. The Virtual Disk Driver allows many versions of VMware's virtual disk files to be mounted to a Windows host machine and then used as a read-only or read-write disk drive. The Virtual Floppy Driver is a similar product, allowing a virtual floppy image to be mounted to a Windows host machine and used as a virtual floppy drive. The contents of which can be accessed directly by either viewing, editing, renaming, deleting, or creating files on a virtual floppy disk much like a real physical floppy disk. The site is available in both English and Japanese, and now offers a user forum powered by phpBB.

Summary

Server virtualization as a platform is starting to take hold and spread throughout the IT community. Its popularity and usefulness is evidenced by the numerous third-party software packages that are being developed, sold, and downloaded in addition to all of the news and information Web sites that are starting to appear across the Internet. The resources discussed in this chapter are but a brief look at the many informational Web sites, and commercial and public projects and products being offered to help fully utilize and understand server virtualization. These are only a select few of the server virtualization resources that are currently available and the list is continuously growing. Please visit http://www.vmbook.info/ (see above) for a more complete and current list of available resources and links.

Part VIII

Appendices

Appendix I

Deployment Planning Checklist

Use Case(s)
- ☐ Planning and Technical Teams Identified
- ☐ Problem Outlined and Detailed
- ☐ Solution Outlined and Detailed
- ☐ Use Case Document Created Including:
- ☐ Change Cause and Outcome
    - ☐ Change Impact to Systems
    - ☐ Change Impact to Processes and Job Functions
    - ☐ Business Constraints
    - ☐ Technical Constraints

Requirements
- ☐ Defined Constraints
- ☐ Project Limitations
- ☐ Time Limitations
- ☐ Scope Changes
- ☐ Inclusion of Use Case(s)

Deployment Plan
- ☐ Server Virtualization Platform Selected
    - ☐ Hardware Compatibility
    - ☐ Host Operating System Support
    - ☐ Guest Operating System Support
    - ☐ Application Support
    - ☐ Capacity and Scalability
    - ☐ Features, Manageability

☐ Performance
☐ Support, Maintenance, Training
☐ Cost

Hardware
☐ CPU Capacity/Performance Limitations
☐ Memory Limitations
☐ Network Limitations
☐ Compatibility
☐ Cost

Software Licenses
☐ In Compliance

Solution
☐ Vendor Support
☐ Scalability
☐ Redundancy, Backup Time and Availability
☐ Disaster Recovery
☐ Monitoring
☐ Networking
☐ Performance
☐ Security

Appendix II

File Extensions by Virtualization Platform

Virtual machines are typically stored on a host server and are made up of a set of files that are typically located in a directory created for the virtual machine. This chapter provides a simple view of commonly used file extensions sorted by server virtualization platform and a short description of each (see Figure 31.1).

Microsoft Virtual Server

- VHD

  The .vhd file is the virtual machine's disk file, which stores the contents of the virtual machine's hard disk. There are a number of ways this file can be implemented.

  - Fixed size disk

    The .vhd file is pre-allocated when the virtual hard disk is created. The host server must have enough free disk space to accommodate the size of the file. A fixed size disk cannot be resized.

  - Dynamically expanding disk

    The virtual hard disk is created as a sparse file and the .vhd file grows as the virtual machine adds data to the virtual disk. Virtual Server will send a warning if the virtual disk grows too large for the host file system.

  - Differencing disk

    A differencing disk sets up a parent and child relationship between virtual hard disk files. The differencing disk acts as the child, while the associated virtual disk acts as the parent. While the differencing disks created on the host machine may contain multiple files, they will appear

Virtualization Platforms

File Types		ESX	GSX	MSVS
	Disk File	DSK, VMDK	PLN, DAT, DSK, VMDK	VHD
	Config File	CFG, VMX	CFG, VMX	VMC
	Undo Disk	REDO	REDO	VUD
	Suspended State	VMSS	VMSS, STD	VSV
	Log Files	LOG	LOG	TXT
	Floppy Disk	FLP	FLP	VFD
	CDROM Image	ISO	ISO	ISO
	Network Configuration	N/A	N/A	VNC
	CMOS/BIOS	NVRAM	NVRAM	-
	Snapshot	N/A	VMSN	N/A

* ESX = VMware ESX Server, GSX = VMware GSX Server, MSVS = Microsoft Virtual Server

Figure 31.1   File Extensions At-A-Glance.

to the guest server as a single hard disk. While the virtual machine is in use, it will read from both, the parent and the child disk files. However, any changes or writes that occur will be written against and updated into the child disk file only.

- **VMC**

  The .vmc file is an XML file that stores metadata describing the virtual machine's configuration information. The file is created when a new virtual machine is created, and it contains the settings that make up the virtual machine. The contents can be modified by using the virtual machine settings editor or by using any third-party text editor.

- **VUD**

  The undo disk file is created automatically when a virtual machine configured with Undo Disks is powered on. When this feature is enabled, it universally applies to all virtual hard disks that are attached to the virtual machine. While the virtual machine is running, any changes made to the virtual disk are written to the .vud file; reads occur from the original virtual hard disk.

- **VSV**

  The .vsv file is created automatically when a virtual machine is suspended. The file contains the entire state of the virtual machine. Once suspended, the virtual machine is in a hibernation state, similar to that of a laptop computer. The .vsv file is then used to resume the virtual machine from the suspended state.

- **VNC**

  The .vnc file is an XML file that stores metadata describing the virtual machine's network configuration information. When a virtual network is created, a virtual network configuration file is created and by default placed in the `C:\Documents and Settings\All Users\Documents\Shared Virtual Networks` directory.

- **TXT**

  Virtual Server log files are stored in .txt files. An important log file to remember is the VSCrashLog text file. It is created when a virtual machine stops responding. When calling for support, Microsoft may request this file to help troubleshoot the problem.

- **VFD**

  The .vfd file is used to store content in the form of a virtual floppy disk. Virtual Server can mount most flat-file representations of a floppy disk, including floppy disks that are 720 KB or 1.44 MB in size.

- **ISO**

  The .iso file is used to store content in the form of a virtual CD/DVD-ROM. An .iso file can be downloaded from the Internet or created with ISO imaging tools as described in chapter 27.

VMware ESX Server

- **DSK**

  The .dsk file is a legacy virtual machine disk file. Earlier versions of the VMware ESX product used the .dsk extension, however, to gain cross platform parity, VMware ESX has moved to the .vmdk format.

- **VMDK**

  The .vmdk file is the virtual machine's disk file, which stores the contents of the virtual machine's hard disk. VMware ESX disk files are fixed in size, meaning it is pre-allocated to the full specified disk size when the file is created.

- **CFG**

  The .cfg file is a legacy virtual machine configuration file created with versions of VMware ESX Server prior to the 2.0 release. Virtual machine configuration files with a .cfg extension can still be accessed by ESX versions 2.0 and later.

- **VMX**

  The .vmx file is used to store virtual machine configuration information. This file is created when a new virtual machine is created, and it contains the settings that make up the virtual machine. The contents can be modified by using the virtual machine settings editor or by using any third-party text editor.

- **REDO**

  The .redo file is created automatically when a virtual machine's hard disk is configured in either undoable or append mode. While the virtual machine is running, any changes made to the virtual disk are written to the .redo log file.

- **VMSS**

  The .vmss file is created automatically when a virtual machine is suspended. The file contains the entire state of the virtual machine. The file is typically a few megabytes larger than the maximum amount of memory allocated to the virtual machine. Once suspended, the virtual machine is in a hibernation state, similar to that of a laptop computer.

- **LOG**

  One such important .log file is the virtual machine log file, vmware.log. This file contains key information about the virtual machine's activity. When troubleshooting, this .log file may prove useful to help diagnose problems.

- **FLP**

  The .flp file is used to store content in the form of a virtual floppy disk. VMware will mount virtual floppy disks with other extensions; however, when browsing for virtual floppy disks, VMware looks for .flp files by default. It is also important to note, .flp images should be 1,474,560 bytes long.

- **ISO**

  The .iso file is used to store content in the form of a virtual CD/DVD-ROM. An .iso file can be downloaded from the Internet or created with ISO imaging tools as described in chapter 27.

- **NVRAM**

  The .nvram file stores information about the virtual machine's BIOS/CMOS settings. If the file is not found or becomes corrupted, it is easily recreated by cycling the power on the virtual machine.

VMware GSX Server

- **VMDK**

  The .vmdk file is the virtual machine's disk file, which stores the contents of the virtual machine's hard disk. Almost all of a .vmdk's file content is the virtual machine's data; however, a small portion of the file is allotted to virtual machine overhead. There are a number of ways this file can be implemented.

  - The .vmdk file can be pre-allocated when the hard disk is created. The host server must have enough free disk space to accommodate the size of the file.

- A .vmdk file can also be created as a dynamic file. In this case, the .vmdk file grows as the virtual machine adds data to the virtual disk.
- A virtual disk can also be made up of a number of .vmdk files. If the virtual disk is created with the hard disk split up into multiple 2GB files, the number of files will depend on the size specified for the virtual hard disk.

- **DSK**
  The .dsk file is a legacy virtual machine disk file. Earlier versions of the VMware product used the .dsk extension, however, to gain cross platform parity, VMware has moved to the .vmdk format.

- **RAW**
  When the virtual machine is connected directly to a physical disk rather than using a .vmdk file, a .raw file is created. This file type stores a pointer and information about the partitions that the virtual machine can access.

- **PLN/DAT**
  The .pln and .dat files are a legacy virtual machine disk file. In order to create a virtual disk file outside of the VMware GSX console, VMware supplied a legacy utility named "plainmaker.exe". The .pln file contains information about the virtual disk while the actual virtual machine data is found in a series of .dat files.

- **VMX**
  The .vmx file is used to store virtual machine configuration information. This file is created when a new virtual machine is created, and it contains the settings that make up the virtual machine. The contents can be modified by using the virtual machine settings editor or by using any third-party text editor.

- **VMX.BAK**
  The .vmx.bak file is a backup file for a virtual machine's configuration. If the .vmx file becomes corrupted or gets deleted, the .vmx.bak file can be used in its place.

- **CFG**
  The .cfg file is a legacy configuration file used by earlier versions of VMware GSX Server.

- **REDO**
  The .redo file is created automatically when a virtual machine either has a snapshot taken or is powered up in the independent-nonpersistent mode. While the virtual machine is running, any changes made to the virtual disk are written to the .redo log file. If there are multiple files, VMware GSX Server will add a unique suffix to avoid a duplicate filename problem. The new file will take on the form of .redo_xxxxxx.

- **VMSS**
  The .vmss file is created automatically when a virtual machine is suspended. The file contains the entire state of the virtual machine. The file is

typically a few megabytes larger than the maximum amount of memory allocated to the virtual machine. Once suspended, the virtual machine is in a hibernated type state, similar to a laptop computer.

- **STD**
  The .std file extension is the legacy extension for suspended state files.
- **VMSN**
  The .vmsn file is the snapshot state file. When a snapshot is taken of a running virtual machine, its state is stored in the .vmsn file.
- **VMX.SAV**
  The .vmx.sav file is the configuration snapshot file. When a snapshot of a virtual machine is taken, the .vmx.sav file stores the current configuration of the virtual machine.
- **LOG**
  Two important .log files are the virtual machine log files—vmname.log and vmware.log. These files contain key information about the virtual machine's activity. When troubleshooting, these .log files may prove useful to help diagnose problems.
- **FLP**
  The .flp file is used to store content in the form of a virtual floppy disk. VMware will mount virtual floppy disks with other extensions; however, when browsing for virtual floppy disks, VMware looks for .flp files by default. It is also important to note, .flp images should be 1,474,560 bytes long.
- **ISO**
  The .iso file is used to store content in the form of a virtual CD/DVD-ROM. An .iso file can be downloaded from the Internet or created with ISO imaging tools as described in chapter 27.
- **NVRAM**
  The .nvram file stores information about the virtual machine's BIOS/CMOS settings. If the file is not found or becomes corrupted, it is easily recreated by cycling the power on the virtual machine.

Appendix III

Useful Log Files

For the most part, trying to diagnose a problem with a virtual machine or a virtualization host server is not that different than trying to diagnose a problem with an application or a physical server. Just as physical servers and applications exhibit strange behavior that lead to problems needing to be researched, virtualization hosts and virtual machines also have problems that need to be identified as quickly as possible to correct some adverse situation. One of the best places to start looking for answers is the virtualization log files. This chapter provides a quick reference to commonly used log files as well as their locations sorted by server virtualization platform (see Figure 32.1).

VMware GSX Server

If problems are encountered while running GSX Server, VMware requests that they are reported to the VMware support team. In order to report the problem and have VMware support help diagnose the situation, VMware provides a support script to conveniently collect all the necessary log files and system information needed for troubleshooting. The support script can only be run on the GSX Server host machine. Therefore, when encountering a problem with a remote client, log files must be obtained manually. This section will describe how to run the support script as well as identify most of the important GSX Server log files. Additionally, for GSX Server for Windows, various event entries are captured and logged in the Windows Event Viewer that may prove useful in troubleshooting.

Platform*	Log	Location
ESX	Service Console Messages	/var/log/messages
ESX	Service Log	/var/log/vmware/vmware-serverd.log
ESX	Virtual Machine Log	Located in the same directory as the VM's configuration file; vmware.log
ESX	VMKernel Log	/proc/vmware/log
ESX	VMKernel Messages	/var/log/vmkernel
ESX	VMKernel Warnings	/var/log/vmkwarning
GSX for Linux	Authorization Service Log	/var/log/vmware/vmauthd.log
GSX for Windows		%WINDIR%\System32\vmauthd.log
GSX for Linux	Installation Logs	/etc/vmware/locations
GSX for Windows		C:\Documents and Settings\<username>\Local Settings\Temp\VMInst.log
GSX for Linux	Management Interface Log	/var/log/vmware-mui/error_log
GSX for Windows		C:\Program Files\VMware\VMware Management Interface\mui.log
GSX for Linux	Registration Service Log	/var/log/vmware/vmware-serverd.log
GSX for Windows		%WINDIR%\Temp\vmware-serverd.log
GSX for Linux	Virtual Machine Console Log	/tmp/vmware-<username>/ui-<PID>.log
GSX for Windows		C:\Documents and Settings\<username>\Local Settings\Temp\vmware-<username>-<PID>.log
GSX for Linux	Virtual Machine Event Log	/var/log/vmware/event-<path_to_configuration_file>.vmx.log
GSX for Windows		C:\Program Files\VMware\VMware GSX Server\vmserverd\Root\eventlog\event-<path_to_configuration_file>.vmx.log
GSX for Linux	Virtual Machine Log	Located in the same directory as the VM's configuration file; <vmname>.log
GSX for Windows		Located in the same directory as the VM's configuration file; vmware.log
GSX for Windows	Other Messages and Warnings	Windows Application Event Log; Use the Event Viewer application to view these logs.
MSVS	All Logs	Windows Application and System Event Logs; Use the Event Viewer application to view these logs.

* ESX = VMware ESX Server, GSX = VMware GSX Server, MSVS = Microsoft Virtual Server

Figure 32.1 Log Files At-A-Glance.

GSX Support Script

On a Windows host machine, use the following steps:

1. Open a command prompt (CMD.EXE).
2. Change to the GSX Server program directory by entering the drive letter and path that was used during installation. The default directory is `C:\Program Files\VMware\VMware GSX Server`.
3. Run the support script by executing the following: `cscript vm-support.vbs`.
4. Once the script completes, it displays the name of the directory where the output files have been stored. These are the support files that should be zipped and included with support requests. The files are also now conveniently located in one place to help internal troubleshooting.

On a Linux host machine, use the following steps:

1. Open a terminal screen.
2. Run the support script as either the root or the user who is running the virtual machine. Execute the following script: `vm-support`. Some of the information cannot be collected if the script is not executed by root. If this information is needed, VMware support may ask that the script be executed again as root.
3. A compressed .tgz file is created in the current directory. This file should be included with support requests. This file can also be uncompressed to help internal troubleshooting as the log files are now conveniently located in one place.

Log Files

The following log files are created by GSX Server and are the log files that get collected by the support scripts described above.

■ Virtual Machine Log File
If a virtual machine either crashes or ends abnormally, this file should be saved off immediately for the affected virtual machine. It is important to save off this file before the virtual machine is powered back on. The log file is located in the same directory as the affected virtual machine's configuration file. On a Windows host, this file is identified as `vmware.log`. On a Linux host, this file is identified as `<vmname>.log`.

■ Virtual Machine Event Log File
Another useful file in the event that a virtual machine crashes or ends abnormally is the virtual machine's event log. Each virtual machine on a

host includes an event log file that can be identified as `event-<path_to_configuration_file>.vmx.log`. On a Windows host, the default location of the file is `C:\Program Files\VMware\VMware GSX Server\vmserverdRoot\eventlog`. On a Linux host, the log file is located in `/var/log/vmware`.

- VMware Virtual Machine Console Log File
  The VMware virtual machine console also keeps a log file. If any problems are encountered on a remote client while using the virtual machine console, this log file should be helpful in diagnosing it. On a Windows host, the log file is identified as `vmware-<username>-<PID>.log` and is located in the user's TEMP folder. The default location of this folder is found at `C:\Documents and Settings\<username>\Local Settings\Temp`. On a Linux host, the log file is identified as `ui-<PID>.log` and is located in the user's TEMP folder. The default location of this folder is found at `/tmp/vmware-<username>`.

- VMware Management Interface Log File
  The VMware management interface keeps a log. If a problem is encountered while using the management interface, this log file can help diagnose the problem. On a Windows host, the log file is identified as `mui.log` and the default location is `C:\Program Files\VMware\VMware Management Interface`. On a Linux host, the log file is identified as `error_log` and the default location is `/var/log/vmware-mui`.

- VMware Authorization Service Log File
  The VMware authorization service can be setup to keep a log. By default, it does not. However, by performing the following manual steps, the service can be setup to keep a log file, which may prove helpful when diagnosing problems.
  - Using a text editor, open the following file:
    - On a Windows host, edit the `config.ini` file. The file is located by default in `C:\Documents and Settings\All Users\Application Data\VMware\VMware GSX Server`.
    - On a Linux host, edit `/etc/vmware/config`.
  - The following lines should be added to the file:
    ```
    vmauthd.logEnabled = TRUE
    log.vmauthdFileName = "vmauthd.log"
    ```
    This creates a file called `vmauthd.log`. On a Windows host, this file is located by default in the system directory, usually `%WINDIR%\System32`. On a Linux host, this file is located by default in `/var/log/vmware`.
  - Save and close the configuration file. On a Linux host, logging is enabled immediately. On a Windows host, the VMware Authorization Service must be restarted before logging can take place.

- VMware Registration Service Log File
  The VMware registration service keeps a log. If a problem is encountered while connecting to virtual machines or using the management interface, this log file may help in diagnosing the problem. On a Windows host, the log file is identified as `vmware-serverd.log` and is located in `%WIN-DIR%\Temp`. On a Linux host, the log file is also identified as `vmware-serverd.log` but is located in `/var/log/vmware`.
- VMware GSX Server and VMware Virtual Machine Console Installation Log Files
  On the host server, VMware creates an installation log file while installing GSX Server. On a remote client, VMware creates an installation log file while installing the VMware virtual machine console. If a problem is encountered while installing either application, this log file may help in diagnosing the problem. On a Windows host, the log file is identified as `VMInst.log` and is saved in the TEMP directory. By default, this directory is `C:\Documents and Settings\<username>\Local Settings\Temp`. On a Linux host, the log file is identified as `locations` and can be found in `/etc/vmware`.

VMware GSX Server Events on Windows

GSX Server also sends information to the Event Viewer on a Microsoft Windows host server. When troubleshooting, the Event Viewer may help provide insight by providing the following types of information:

1. Changes to a virtual machine's power state—was the virtual machine powered off or suspended?
2. The addition or removal of a virtual machine from the host's inventory list—was the machine removed?
3. The deletion of a virtual machine from the GSX Server system—was the virtual machine deleted along with its disk files?
4. Messages and warnings from the GSX Sever host along with responses to the messages and warnings—when the host server prompts with a warning or message to the user, it is logged in the Event Viewer along with the response given by the user.

To view event log entries relating to GSX Server, use the following steps:

1. Select Start.
2. Select Control Panel.
3. Choose Administrative Tools.
4. Select Event Viewer.

5. Select the Application log on the left side column.
6. The right side column contains the list of events identified with VMware as the source.

VMware ESX Server

If problems are encountered while running ESX Server, VMware requests that they are reported to the VMware support team. In order to report the problem and have VMware support help diagnose the situation, VMware provides a support script to conveniently collect and package all relevant ESX Server log files as well as system and configuration information needed for troubleshooting. The support script can only be run on the ESX Server host machine. This section will describe how to run the support script as well as identify most of the important ESX Server log files.

ESX Support Script

On an ESX Server host machine, use the following steps:

1. Open a service console window.
2. Log in as the root user.
3. For ESX Server versions 2.1.x and earlier, the latest vm-support script should be downloaded from VMware's Web site. Archive the original vm-support script and then replace it with the newer version. For ESX Server 2.1.x and 2.0.x, the script is located in /usr/bin. For ESX Server 1.5.x, the script is located in /usr/lib/vmware.
4. Execute the following script: /usr/bin/vm-support (For ESX 1.5.x, run /usr/lib/vmware/vm-support).
5. The resulting file will be saved as a compressed .tgz file called esx-<date>-<unique-xnumber>.tgz. The script will display the output filename and the file location.
6. The output file should be included with support requests made to VMware. It can also be uncompressed to help with internal troubleshooting as the log files are now conveniently located in one place.

Log Files

The following log files are created by ESX Server and are among the log files collected by the support scripts described above. Log files such as VMkernal Warnings, VMkernal Logs, and Service Console Logs can be viewed through the GUI VMware Management Interface by logging in as root and choosing Options followed by System Logs. These and other log files can also be viewed directly by accessing the service console. If the VMkernel fails, an error screen normally appears for a short period of time and then the virtual machine reboots. Additionally, when configuring the virtual machine, a VMware core dump partition should be specified. By doing so, the VMkernel may also generate a core dump file and an error log.

Virtual Machine Log File

If a virtual machine crashes or ends abnormally, this file should be saved off immediately for the affected virtual machine. It is important to save off this file before the virtual machine is powered back on. The log file is located in the same directory as the affected virtual machine's configuration file and is named `vmware.log`.

VMkernal Warnings

The VMkernel warnings log file is a good resource when experiencing problems with the ESX server or the virtual machines. From the console, the data is logged at `/var/log/vmkwarning`. The log should be checked periodically for any alerts that may get recorded.

VMkernel Messages

The VMkernel messages log file is a good resource when experiencing problems with the ESX server or the virtual machines. From the console, the data is logged at `/var/log/vmkernel`. The log should be checked periodically for any alerts that may get recorded.

Service Console Messages

The service console messages log file is a good resource when experiencing problems with the ESX server or the virtual machines. From the console, the data is logged at `/var/log/messages`. The log should be checked periodically for any alerts that may get recorded.

ESX Server Service Log

If a problem is encountered while connecting to virtual machines or using the management interface, this log file may help in diagnosing the problem. The log file is identified as `vmware-serverd.log` and is located in `/var/log/vmware`.

Microsoft Virtual Server

Problems while running Microsoft Virtual Server 2005 should be reported through normal Microsoft support channels. It is important to note that Microsoft Virtual Server does not create log files, but instead uses the Microsoft Windows Event Viewer for all system related communications. It is recommended that the host server's Event Viewer and the Microsoft Virtual Server Event Filter should be checked for reported errors or problems. This section will explain how to identify entries and problems in Event Viewer regarding Microsoft Virtual Server.

Event Viewer Steps

To view event log entries regarding Virtual Server, use the following steps:

1. Select Start.
2. Select Programs or All programs.
3. Select Microsoft Virtual Server.
4. Choose Virtual Server Administration Website.
5. On the left hand side under the Virtual Server heading select Event Viewer

Another way to view event log entries regarding Virtual Server is:

1. Select Start.
2. Select Control Panel.
3. Choose Administrative Tools.
4. Select Event Viewer.
5. Select "Virtual Server" on the left side column.
6. The right side column contains the list of events.

Interpret Log Entries

For in-depth troubleshooting, it is recommended that the Windows Event Viewer be used instead of the Virtual Server Administrative Website version. This is due to the flexibility provided by the rich GUI interface and the fact that the Web site version is limited to a fixed number of entries, by default, five on the main status page and twenty on the event viewer page. The Windows Event Viewer however, provides 16MB of entries, more than enough to see if there are any error trends or how long an error has been occurring. Entries for Virtual Server in Event Viewer can be broken up into several categories. Below is a list of event types and their descriptions.

Virtual Server

The Virtual Server events listing are comprised of interactions between the host server and the virtual machines. Examples include MAC address changes, virtual server configuration file changes, and Virtual Server service status changes.

Virtual Machine

Virtual Machine events provide status on user and virtual machine interactions and configuration/state changes. Examples include users connecting via remote console, virtual machine starts and stops, virtual disk creation, and volume space remaining.

Disk Operation

Disk Operation provides status on changes to virtual hard disks. Examples include creation and changes to disk types.

Setting Change

The Setting Change events are related to virtual machine hardware changes. Examples include video resolution changes, changes to the virtual network that a virtual machine is attached to, guest operating system changes, and the presence of VM additions.

Remote Control

Remote Control lists events relating to the VMRC (this is the virtual keyboard, video, and mouse console). Examples include NTLM authentication, VMRC connects, VMRC disconnects, and VMRC idle connection disconnects.

Appendix IV

Useful TCP/IP Ports

Server virtualization and its related technologies commonly use TCP/IP network protocols to provide specific features such as management of the virtualization host server or providing remote access to the virtual machine. This chapter consolidates the most commonly used TCP and UDP ports in use and provides information on what features use the port (see Figure 33.1). If the host server is behind a firewall, the firewall may need to be reconfigured to allow access to the appropriate ports.

VMware Ports

- 8222 (HTTP)
  Used to connect to the VMware GSX Server host machine by using the VMware Management Interface (if SSL is disabled). For backward compatibility, ESX Server handles this port as an HTTP redirect to TCP port 80.
- 8333 (HTTPS)
  Used to connect to the VMware GSX Server host machine by using the VMware Management Interface (uses SSL). For backward compatibility, ESX Server handles this port as an HTTPS redirect to TCP port 443.
- 80 (HTTP)
  Used to connect to the VMware ESX Server host machine by using the VMware Management Interface in a low security environment.
- 443 (HTTPS)
  Used to connect to the VMware ESX Server host machine by using the VMware Management Interface in a medium to high security environment.

Port	TCP/UDP	Protocol	Virtualization Platform*	Description	Security
21	TCP	FTP	ESX, GSX, MSVS	File transfers	Low to medium
22	TCP	SSH	ESX	Remote aceess	Medium to high
23	TCP	Telnet	ESX	Remote access	Low
80	TCP	HTTP	ESX	Web management interface	Low
111	TCP	-	ESX	Portmap - NFS	Low to medium
137	TCP/UDP	-	MSVS	Kerberos V5 ticket granting authority	Low to high
138	TCP/UDP	-	MSVS	Kerberos V5 ticket granting authority	Low to high
443	TCP	HTTPS	ESX	Web management interface	Medium to high
902	TCP	-	ESX	VMRC- VMware Remote Console	Low to high
1024	TCP	HTTP	MSVS	HTTP to MSVS Administration Website	Low to high
3389	TCP	RDP	GSX, MSVS	RDP to Windows Host OS	Low to high
5900	TCP	-	MSVS	VMRC - Virtual Machine Remote Control	Low to high
8222	TCP	HTTP	GSX	HTTP to GSX Management Interface	Low
8333	TCP	HTTPS	GSX	HTTPS to GSX Management Interface	Medium to high

* ESX = VMware ESX Server, GSX = VMware GSX Serve⁻, MSVS = Microsoft Virtual Server

Figure 33.1   TCP/IP Ports At-A-Glance.

- 902 (vmware-authd)
  Used when connecting to virtual machines by using the VMware Virtual Machine Console in both GSX and ESX.
- 21 (FTP)
  Used for transferring files between machines. Often used in a low to medium security environment.
- 22 (SSH)
  Used to establish a secure shell connection to the ESX service console, the GSX Server for Linux host server or a Linux virtual machine. Often used in a medium to high security environment because it is more secure than connecting with a simple Telnet connection.
- 23 (Telnet)
  Used to establish a non-secure shell connection to the ESX service console, the GSX Server for Linux host server or a Linux virtual machine in a low to medium security environment.
- 3389 (RDP)
  Used to connect to either the GSX Server host machine or a Microsoft Windows virtual machine.
- 111 (portmap)
  Used by the NFS client when mounting a drive on a remote machine in a low to medium security environment.

Microsoft Virtual Server Ports

- 5900 (VMRC)
  Used to connect to virtual machines by using the Microsoft Virtual Machine Remote Client. Note that this can be changed to another port from a range of 5900 – 5999.
- 1024 (Virtual Server)
  Used to connect to the Microsoft Virtual Server Administration Website.
- 137 and 138 (Windows)
  The TCP and UDP ports used for the Kerberos V5 ticket-granting authority.
- 88 (Virtual Server)
  The TCP and UDP port used for the Kerberos V5 ticket-granting authority.
- 21 (FTP)
  Used for transferring files between machines. Often used in a low to medium security environment.
- 3389 (RDP)
  Used to connect to either the Microsoft Virtual Server host machine or a Microsoft Windows virtual machine.

Appendix V

Useful Linux Commands for Windows Users

For a Microsoft Windows user first diving into either VMware GSX Server for Linux or VMware ESX Server, there may be a lot of new terminology or commands that do not look very familiar. Some of these commands, more than others, may be called upon numerous times to successfully navigate either product. This chapter will hopefully lessen some of the confusion a new GSX Server for Linux or VMware ESX Server user may face. It is not meant to provide an in-depth tutorial on Linux commands. The goal of this chapter is to attempt to provide a Windows user with a general explanation of some of the more commonly used commands. Figure 34.1 will attempt to draw a comparison between the DOS/Windows commands and their Linux counterparts. Other useful commands that can be used to help navigate VMware ESX Server can be found in Figure 34.2.

DOS Command	Linux Command	Action
..\	../	Parent directory
.\	./	Current directory
\	/	Directory path delimeter
CD	cd	Used to change directory
CHDIR	pwd	Displays current directory location
CLS	clear	Clears the screen
COPY	cp	Used to copy a file
DATE or TIME	date	Shows the server's date and time
DEL	rm	Used to delete or remove a file
DIR	ls or ls -l	Used to provide a directory listing
EDIT	vi	Editor program used to edit a file
EXIT	exit	Exits a shell
FDISK	fdisk	Used to partition a hard drive
FORMAT	mke2fs	Used to format a partition for ext2 or ext3 file system
HELP or /?	man	Provides an online manual or explanation of a command
HOSTNAME	hostname	Used to print the host name of the server
IPCONFIG	ifconfig	Used to display the network interface configuration
MEM	free	Shows the free memory on the server
MKDIR	mkdir	Used to create a new directory
MORE	more	Pipes the output of a file a single page at a time
PING	ping	Used to send ICMP packets to a server
PKZIP	tar, zip, gzip and gunzip	Used to compress and uncompress files and directories
RENAME or MOVE	mv	Used to rename or move a file
RMDIR	rmdir	Used to remove a directory
RMDIR /S or DELTREE	rm -R	Removes all directories and files recursively below a specified directory
ROUTE PRINT	route -n	Used to print the routing table
TRACERT	traceroute	Used to show routes and hops to a given network address
TYPE	cat	Dumps the contents of a file to the screen
VER	uname -a	List the operating system version
WIN	startx	Command to start the GUI window application
XCOPY	cp -R	Used to copy all files in directory recursively

Figure 34.1   DOS and Linux Equivalent Commands.

Command	Actions	Example Use
chgrp	Change ownership of each file to group	chgrp newgroup newDisk.vmx
chmod	Change permissions on files using numeric values to represent rwx	chmod 755 newFile.htm
chown	Change ownership of a file	chown newuser newDisk.vxm
dd	Can copy raw data and disk images to and from devices	dd if=/dev/cdrom of=/isoimages/linux.iso
fdformat	Does a floppy disk format	fdformat /dev/fd0
find	Finds files under a specified directory that match conditions you specify	find / -name myfile*
grep	Search for a specified text pattern in a specified directory or list of files and display the lines in which the text pattern is found	grep "file info" *
groupadd	Adds a new group	groupadd newgroup (Adds a new group named newgroup to the system)
halt	Performs a halt on the server - Does "force power off" for the VMs	
head	Displays the first 10 lines of a file unless otherwise stated	head -15 myfile.txt (would list the first 15 lines of myfile.txt)
kill	Kills a specified process	kill 194 (kills the process with PID 194) kill -9 is a sure way to kill a process -use as a last resort
kudzu	A tool used to detect and configure new hardware	When in doubt, select "do nothing" - kudzu may remove hardware dedicated soley to the VMs
ln	Creates a link from one file or directory to another file or directory	ln -s /root/vmware/program runme (creates a symbolic link between the program in /root/vmware and runme
lsmod	List all loaded modules	
lspci	List PCI devices available to the service console	lspci -v (list all in verbose mode)

Figure 34.2a   Other Useful VMware ESX Server Commands.

Command	Actions	Example Use
md5sum	Check the integrity of a file	md5sum /vmfs/vmhba0:0:0:1/newDisk.vmdk
mount and umount	The command manually mounts and unmounts CD-ROMs, floppies, local partitions and remote directories to a selected directory	mount /dev/cdrom umount /dev/cdrom mount /mnt/floppy
ntpdate	Takes an NTP server as a parameter and synchronises the clock once. It doesn't work when the local NTP daemon is running.	ntpdate faketimeserver.com
passwd	Changes a password	passwd username (changes the password for a user named username)
ps	Show names, process IDs (PID), and other information for running processes - Similar to Windows TaskManager.	ps -ef (shows full information about every running process)
reboot	Performs a reboot of the server - Does "force power off" for the VMs	
scp	Securely copy a file from one ESX server to another	scp cdromimage.iso root@mymachine.domain.tld:/isoimages/
shutdown	Generic command for shutting down or rebooting the server	shutdown -h 10 (halts the server in 10 minutes) shutdown -r now (shut down and restart the server immediately)
su	Switch to the root user	
tail	Like head but displays the last 10 lines of a file unless otherwise stated	tail -15 myfile.txt (would list the last 15 lines of myfile.txt)
useradd	Adds a new user to the system	useradd newuser (adds a new user named newuser)
usermod	Modifies the system account files to reflect the changes that are specified on the command line	usermod -d /home/newuser newuser (modifies the home directory for the newuser to /home/newuser)
vdf	vdf is an ESX Server customized version of the df command. Displays free space for all mounted file systems, including VMFS.	vdf -h
who	shows the user names of all users logged into the system	
whoami	shows the user name you are currently logged in with	

Figure 34.2b Other Useful VMware ESX Server Commands.

Glossary

Append Disk Mode

Configuring a VMware ESX Server virtual hard disk in Append Mode stores any changes made to the virtual hard disk in a redo log file. All changes are continuously added to the redo log file until it is either discarded (removed) or committed back into the parent disk file.

Bridged Networking

Bridged networking means a virtual machine runs on a virtual network that is connected to an existing physical network via the physical network adapter. While the VM shares the host's Ethernet connection, it appears as a full-fledged host on an existing physical network with its own MAC address and TCP/IP address.

BusLogic SCSI Controller

VMware virtual machines can use a virtual BusLogic SCSI adapter to control its virtual hard disks. Most virtual machines use the BusLogic adapter by default. It emulates a Mylex BusLogic BT-958 compatible host bus adapter.

Child Disk

A virtual hard disk file that is a derivative of another virtual hard disk. The child disk reads data from the other virtual hard disk (the parent) and combines the read data with its own to give the appearance that the child holds all of the data itself. See Parent Disk.

Clone Image

An exact replica of a previously created image (a copy).

Compact

The act of reducing the size of a dynamically expanding virtual hard disk by removing the unused or zeroed space from the disk file, typically used in a Virtual Server environment. Similar to VMware Shrink.

Console

See VMware Virtual Machine Console.

Commit

The act of modifying a virtual hard disk associated with a virtual machine on which an undo, rollback, or snapshot feature is enabled. This process modifies the parent virtual hard disk file by merging the changes made in the undo disk or redo log file into the virtual hard disk file.

Configuration

See Virtual Machine Configuration.

Configuration File

See Virtual Machine Configuration File.

DHCP

Dynamic Host Configuration Protocol server. See Virtual DHCP Server.

Differencing Disk

A binary overlay virtual hard disk file that records disk write requests to itself and responds to reads either by providing the information directly or requesting the data from the disk it is an overlay on top of.

Disk Chaining

The creation of a series of disks in which multiple parent child relationships occur. An example would be a primary virtual hard disk that has three children with each of those children having three children. This would mean that there are three primary disk chains and nine secondary (or sub) disk chains.

Dynamic Disk

See Dynamically Expanding Disk.

Dynamically Expanding Disk

A virtual hard disk drive that begins as a sparse file, consuming only the amount of storage from the host server that is needed, and grows as new data is written to the virtual hard disk drive. When created, the maximum size of the disk is specified, but the file that represents the disk is sized only to the size needed to store its data at that point in time. The dynamically expanding disk cannot grow in excess of its maximum size.

Emulation

This is the source of most or all of the functionality of the actual device that it is based on. Emulators are usually used for compatibility or debugging purposes. Emulators can also provide equivalent functionality to a hardware or software implementation at a lower cost (and probably lower performance) than the actual hardware or software.

EULA

The end user license agreement is a legal contract between the manufacturer and the end user of an application. The EULA details how the software can and cannot be used along with any restrictions that the manufacturer imposes.

External Networking

A virtual network that is configured to use a physical network adapter to connect virtual machines with external physical servers, virtual machines, or resources. See also Internal Networking.

Fibre Channel

A set of ANSI standards that comprise technologies used as an interface to mass storage devices and storage area networks implemented used copper or optical fiber mediums.

Fixed Disk

See Fixed Size Disk.

Fixed Size Disk

A virtual hard disk drive that most closely resembles a physical hard disk drive. When created, the file is sized immediately to its maximum size, consuming an equal amount of storage from the host server. Like all virtual hard disk drives, the fixed disk is empty upon creation.

Full Screen Mode

This is the display mode of a virtual machine where its display fills the entire screen rather than running in a resizable window.

Fragmentation

The condition where files on a disk are broken up and scattered across the disk, causing a decrease in disk speed as the drive is forced to search throughout the hard disk for different parts of a file and then put the pieces back together into a single file. Fragmentation is a frequent problem with dynamically expanding disks.

Guest Operating System

The operating system installed and running inside of a virtual machine.

Guest Server

See Virtual Machine.

HBA

See Host Bus Adapter

Heartbeat

A signal emitted at regular intervals that represents the overall health of the guest operating system.

Host Bus Adapter (HBA)

A hardware adapter card that connects the host to a device, e.g., a SCSI disk, an array of SCSI disks, or a storage area network using Fibre Channel or iSCSI technologies.

Host Only Networking

The host virtual adapter creates a virtual Ethernet LAN on the host server that allows communication between the host server and the virtual machines on that host server. By default, the host virtual adapter is not connected to any external network.

Host Operating System

The operating system installed on the physical server that is running the virtualization software.

Host Server

The physical server on which the virtualization platform is installed.

Inventory

A listing of the virtual machine names that have been added to the host server. A virtual machine in the inventory listing can be launched, configured, or removed.

Independent-Disk Mode

A virtual disk created using this mode is unaffected by the VMware GSX Server Snapshot feature. Independent disks can be identified

Internal Networking

A virtual network that is configured to not use a physical network adapter. All network traffic is confined to the host server allowing only virtual machines on the same host server to communicate with each other.

ISO Image

An ISO image is a single file that contains the complete image of a physical CD-ROM. The image is a file that contains an image of an ISO 9660 file system, which is the standard CD-ROM file system created by an industry group known as High Sierra.

Linked Disk

A virtual hard disk file that provides a thin layer of information and pass-through to a physical disk or partition.

Loopback Adapter

An adapter that points back to itself (forming a logical loop). Loopback network adapters allow virtual machines to communicate with their physical hosts. Loopback disk adapters allow file systems to be mounted locally (such as ISO images).

LSI Logic SCSI Controller

VMware virtual machines can use a virtual LSI Logic SCSI adapter to control its virtual hard disks. The LSI Logic adapter has improved performance and has been found to work better with generic SCSI devices. Its driver is included with newer operating systems, such as Windows Server 2003, however most operating systems do not come with the driver natively.

Logical Unit Number (LUN)

An address of a disk or storage device. The term is used to describe SCSI disk identifiers as well as logical volumes in storage area networks.

LUN

See Logical Unit Number

Merge

To combine the contents of a disk chain or a parent and child into a single virtual hard disk image.

Microsoft Virtual Server

A Virtualization Platform that runs as an application on top of Windows XP Professional and the Windows Server 2003 Family. Microsoft Virtual Server is very similar to VMware GSX Server in the way it leverages a host platform. See GSX Server.

Mouse Capture

See Mouse Grab.

Mouse Grab

The term is used to describe the virtual machine's capture control of the mouse and keyboard. When the mouse pointer is clicked inside the window of a virtual machine, the virtual machine takes control of the mouse and keyboard away from the host server. The mouse pointer is grabbed when the virtual machine has focus. Control can be released from the virtual machine by pressing a hot-key combination.

NAT Networking

A NAT (network address translation) device enables communication between virtual machines and the external network. Using a NAT device becomes extremely advantageous when there is a limited amount of IP addresses available on the physical network and those IP addresses are being used by the physical servers.

New Virtual Machine Wizard

VMware GSX Server's easy to use, point-and-click interface to create a new virtual machine configuration. The Wizard walks through the steps of creating the new virtual machine, and offers a typical and custom path to follow, as well as suggesting default values where appropriate.

Nonpersistent Disk Mode

Configuring a VMware virtual hard disk in Nonpersistent Mode stores any changes made to the virtual hard disk in a redo log file. All changes are continuously added to the redo log file, which is then discarded after the virtual machine is powered off.

P2V (Physical to Virtual)

The conversion process of taking a physical machine's contents (operating system, applications) and moving it inside of a virtual machine.

Parent Disk

The disk image that becomes read-only due to having other virtual hard disks having become dependent on it. The virtual hard disks that are dependent on it are using binary overlay technology to give the appearance of a single virtual hard disk. These dependent disks are child disks. See Child Disk.

Persistent Disk Mode

Configuring a VMware virtual hard disk in Persistent Mode writes all changes immediately and permanently to the virtual disk. Disks in this mode behave exactly like a conventional disk drive in a physical computer.

Physical Address Extension (PAE)

Enables an operating system to recognize greater than 4GB of physical memory on a server. 32-bit based machines have a standard limit of 4GB of RAM, however due to operating system and application needs, this limit was extended with PAE technology to a maximum of 128GB of memory, assuming the physical server can support it.

Physical Disk
See Raw Disk.

Pre-allocated Disk
See Fixed Size Disk.

Quick Switch Mode
A display mode offered in the VMware GSX Server remote console where a virtual machine's display fills most of the screen. Tabs at the top of the screen are used to quickly switch between virtual machine displays.

Quorum Disk
A shared disk in which a clustered server node reads and writes shared data between other clustered nodes. This is required for all shared storage cluster solutions.

Raw Disk
A hard disk that is attached to a virtual machine and is mapped to a physical disk drive or partition on the host server. It does not offer many of the benefits commonly found in a virtual hard disk.

REDO Log
The file that stores the changes made to a VMware virtual hard disk that is either configured in one of the following modes: Append, Undoable, Non-persistent, or when using the GSX Server snapshot feature.

Register
When a virtual machine configuration file is created, the virtual machine is added to the virtualization platform's inventory list and can then be accessed and managed by the platform's tools.

Resume
When a virtual machine is placed into a suspended or saved state, it can be returned to a live, operating state by being resumed. Once the virtual machine is resumed, the operating system and all applications and processes are returned to the same state as they were prior to suspending or saving state.

SAN
See Storage Area Network

Saved State
Similar to laptop hibernation, a virtual machine running on the Virtual Server platform can be placed into a state where the guest operating system's running processes are frozen and its memory is saved to an image file (.vsv). Restoring a virtual machine from a saved state returns it to the same condition it was in before the state was saved. See also Resume and Suspend.

Secure Socket Layer (SSL)
A protocol standard for establishing a secure communications channel to prevent the interception of critical and confidential information. It works by using a private key to encrypt data that is transferred over the SSL connection.

Server Consolidation
Takes many physically separate servers with unique applications and combines those applications (sometimes with and sometimes without the operating

system) onto a single physical host. The primary technology driving this trend is virtualization.

Service Level Agreement (SLA)

The requirements a customer (internal or external) has been given by the provider of services (commonly hosting) for uptime, response time, support, and other measurable metrics.

Shrink

The act of reducing the amount of file system space occupied on a dynamically expanding virtual hard disk. If there is any empty space in the virtual disk, shrinking reduces the amount of space occupied by the virtual disk file on the host drive. Fixed size or pre-allocated virtual disks, and physical disks cannot go through the shrinking process. Similar to the compact feature found in Virtual Server.

Simulation

Hardware and/or software that pretends to be a different hardware or software interface for testing, troubleshooting, and prototyping purposes. A simulator is usually far less complex and far faster to implement and use than the real thing.

Storage Area Network (SAN)

A network of storage devices that enable block-level data transfer between connected hosts. Storage area networks use technologies such as Fibre Channel and iSCSI to interconnect hosts to storage devices. Storage devices implemented in a SAN are usually abstracted or virtualized into logical volumes.

Snapshot

A new feature found in VMware GSX Server 3. The snapshot preserves the entire state of the virtual machine (the state of all its virtual disks, the contents of its memory, its power state, and its configuration settings) as it was when the snapshot was taken. By reverting to the snapshot, all changes made to the virtual machine since the snapshot was taken will be discarded. A snapshot can typically be taken while the virtual machine is powered on, off, or suspended.

Suspend

Similar to laptop hibernation, a virtual machine running on the VMware platform can be placed into a state where the guest operating system's running processes are frozen and its memory is saved to an image file (.vmss). To return a suspended virtual machine to operation, use the resume feature. Resuming a virtual machine from a suspended state returns it to the same condition it was in before it was suspended. See also Resume and Suspend.

Symmetric Multi Processing (SMP)

An architecture allowing several Central Processing Units (CPUs) to work collaboratively providing an increase in computational efficiencies. Essentially many CPUs can act like one very powerful CPU.

Template Image

An image created with the intention of being replicated and reused many times.

Template Library

An organization or collection of template images.

Undo Disk

A virtual hard disk that is a disposable child disk, created with the specific purpose of being frequently deleted and then recreated. See Child Disk.

Undoable Disk Mode

In VMware ESX Server, a virtual disk configured in undoable mode will write all changes to a REDO log file. When the virtual machine is powered off, the system presents a list of choices commit, discard, or keep the changes.

Unregister

The process of removing a virtual machine from a virtualization platform's inventory listing. Once unregistered, the virtual machine can no longer be accessed from the platform's administration interface. The virtual machine is not, however, deleted from the system. Its configuration file, disk files, and log files remain on the system. The virtual machine can be added back to the inventory by registering the configuration file. See Register.

V2V (Virtual to Virtual)

The process of converting a virtual hard disk image type and its contents to a different virtual hard disk image type with contents (e.g., converting a VMware ESX virtual hard disk image to a Microsoft Virtual Server virtual hard disk image).

Virtual DHCP Server

Offered in many of the virtualization platforms, it is an emulated Dynamic Host Configuration Protocol (DHCP) server used to provide dynamic IP addresses and related information to DHCP configured virtual machines.

Virtual Hard Disk

A virtual disk is composed of a single file or a group of files that are located on the host server's hard drive or on a remote server. When attached to a virtual machine, the guest operating system identifies it as if it were a physical hard drive.

Virtual Floppy Disk

A virtual floppy disk is a file that is an exact and complete image or copy of all the data that a physical floppy disk would contain. The image file contains information on the disk format, file system data structure, boot sector, directories, and files.

Virtual Hardware

The devices used during the configuration of a virtual machine. These devices include the virtual hard disk, Ethernet adapter, serial and parallel ports, video adapter, DVD/CD-ROM drives, and floppy drives.

Virtual Machine

It is a self-contained operating environment that behaves as if it is a separate computer. A virtual machine emulates a complete hardware system, including the processor, network adapter, removable drives, peripherals, and other devices. Multiple virtual machines configured with different guest operating systems are capable of operating on the same host server simultaneously.

Virtual Machine Additions

A collection of drivers, services, registry entries, and files that provide performance and interactivity optimizations between Microsoft Virtual Server virtual machines and the host on which they are operating.

Virtual Machine Configuration

The details and specifications of what virtual devices are found in a virtual machine and how they are mapped to host files and devices.

Virtual Machine Configuration File

A file that stores a virtual machine's configuration. It is created when the virtual machine is created for the first time.

Virtual Machine Remote Control (VMRC)

A client and server application provided by Microsoft Virtual Server that allows a running virtual machine to be managed remotely. An ActiveX control is downloaded to the local computer and the virtual machine is then accessed through a KVM type connection.

Virtual Network

An emulation of a physical network. It can be configured to provide access to an internal or external network resource for one or more virtual machines. It may include a virtual DHCP server that can provide IP addresses to virtual machines on the network, or in some cases even NAT.

Virtual Network Adapter

The virtualization platform emulates some type of physical network adapter or NIC. Like a physical network adapter, a virtual network adapter is assigned a unique MAC address, IP address, and can be configured in a number of different network configurations.

Virtual Server

An abbreviated name for the Microsoft Virtual Server 2005 product.

Virtual Switch

A logical switch inside of a virtualization platform providing an interconnection between a single physical network interface and one or more virtual machines or simply an interconnection between one or more virtual machines.

Virtualization

A technology providing a layer of abstraction from physical hardware and creating separate logical environments for operating systems or application instances to execute.

VLANCE

One of two types of virtual network adapter supported by VMware. The VLANCE virtual NIC is an AMD PCNET-32 compatible virtual adapter. It is supported by almost all guest operating systems and is installed by default. See also VMXNET.

VMRC

See Virtual Machine Remote Control.

VMware Authorization Service

The service used by VMware to authenticate users. This process is known as vmware-authd on Linux and ESX hosts.

VMware ESX Server

VMware's flagship virtualization product, ESX Server is datacenter-class server virtualization software used for consolidating and partitioning servers in high performance environments. Installed on top of bare metal rather than being installed on top of another operating system such as Windows or Linux, ESX gains performance increases through its highly efficient hypervisor/kernel. ESX Server is also capable of virtual SMP.

VMware GSX Server

VMware's GSX Server product is enterprise-class virtualization software used for server consolidation, disaster recovery and software development streamlining. GSX Server is the most flexible server virtualization platform available because of its wide support of x86-based platforms and its incredible list of supported host and guest operating systems.

VMware Management Interface

A Web browser-based utility used to control, configure, and monitor VMware virtual machines and its host server.

VMware Registration Service

The service used by VMware to manage connections to the virtual machines and the management interface. The process is known as vmware-serverd on Linux and ESX hosts.

VMware Virtual Machine Console

A client-based management tool designed to ease the management of GSX Server virtual machines. Using the interface, it is possible to manage virtual machines either directly from the host server or remotely from a client machine or another host in the exact same manner. The console provides a KVM style view into the virtual machine as well as a way to configure, control and operate the virtual machine and its host server.

VMware Tools

A suite of drivers and utilities that boosts the performance of a virtual machine and its guest operating system and enables added features to improve the management of virtual machines. Key features can include an enhanced video driver, mouse driver, and network driver, as well as time synchronization, clipboard integration, power state scripting, and the ability to shrink virtual disks.

VMware Tools Service

A component that is installed with VMware Tools that performs various functions in the guest operating system such as time synchronization, sending heartbeats to VMware, and passing strings between the host and guest operating system.

VMXNET

One of two types of virtual network adapter supported by VMware. The VMXNET virtual NIC is a VMware specific virtual adapter. No guest operating system has native support for this adapter, which means a VMware specific driver is required and support is not available for all guest operating systems. See also VLANCE.

X86

The Intel hardware Central Processing Unit (CPU) instruction set and platform on which the majority of servers in use today operate on.

Index

Page numbers in italics refer to figures and tables.